AN INTRODUCTION TO SOCIOLOGY

THE VAN NOSTRAND SERIES IN SOCIOLOGY

Edited by
WILBERT E. MOORE

Professor of Sociology, Princeton University

Additional titles will be listed and announced as published.

Society

WALFRED A. ANDERSON

Late of Cornell University

In collaboration with

FREDERICK B. PARKER

University of Delaware

Its Organization and Operation

D. VAN NOSTRAND COMPANY, INC.

Princeton, New Jersey

Toronto   New York   London

D. VAN NOSTRAND COMPANY, INC.
120 Alexander St., Princeton, New Jersey (*Principal office*)
24 West 40 Street, New York 18, New York

D. VAN NOSTRAND COMPANY, LTD.
358, Kensington High Street, London, W. 14, England

D. VAN NOSTRAND COMPANY (CANADA), LTD.
25 Hollinger Road, Toronto 16, Canada

PRINTED IN THE UNITED STATES OF AMERICA

TO

AGNES

AND

OUR FIVE GRANDCHILDREN

Penelope, Victoria, John, Christina and Patricia

FOREWORD

THE authors of this book have brought to its writing their long experience as teachers of sociology. In doing so, they have accepted the risks implicit in a "student-centered" exposition, rather than one that appeals primarily to the scholarly interests of professors. The risk is real, for as book-buyers students constitute a captive clientele. Of all classes of consumers, textbook purchasers normally have the least choice in the selection of merchandise. Their preferences are likely to be effective only at the extremes of enthusiasm or displeasure, and sometimes not then.

Nothing that I write here will change these fundamental facts, but I do commend this book first to teachers who will "role play" to the extent necessary to think of the students' approach to a subject that will be novel to most.

Nor by emphasizing the utility of this book as an educational tool do I mean to derogate its intellectual or scholarly qualities. These are displayed in organization and exposition, in emphasis on the basic propositions or laws that sociology has to offer, and by appropriate guides to the research studies and theoretical works that provide the foundations of contemporary sociological knowledge. By the same token, the authors have avoided the common temptation to provide a statistical compendium, an anthology of contemporary sociological writing in a variety of exotic tongues and styles, or a grab-bag of chapter headings and sequences, in the vain hope that teachers who prefer some other approach will provide their own organization.

The book is, above all, organized or systematic. And what it organizes are principles and generalizations. The standard sociological concepts and perspectives that the conscientious teacher wants the introductory student to learn are here. They are here in the form of meaningful propositions that show the utility of concepts rather than in the form of an empty dictionary of sociological language.

Finally, to the possibly rare student who wanders through the "front matter" of any book and happens to read this, I commend the book as an excellent and often exciting introduction to the study of the science of social action, relations, organization, and change. The authors have summarized chapters and have emphasized the main points of their exposition in boldface headings. This provides a quick overview, or aid to review. But they were not just filling up space in the actual exposition and elucidation. The student who reads every word will not then "know all about sociology." No one does, or could. But failure to read between the headings would miss the factual foundations of our knowledge, the real if regrettable complexity of social analysis, and, not least, the limits of our knowledge or the dimensions of our ignorance, which, in any science, is the most challenging reason for learning.

WILBERT E. MOORE

Princeton, New Jersey
February, 1964

PREFACE

THE publication of yet another introductory text in sociology would seem to be a gratuitous contribution to the field. Indeed, in some quarters, it has become a minor fashion to berate the textbook as a purveyor of "watered-down," predigested intellectual food. (Such critics frequently overestimate the student's capacity to assimilate undigested—indeed, sometimes undigestible—"original" materials.) Be that as it may, we believe we have produced a useful and effective text for the beginning student.

Withal, our claims are not immodest. We do not present a new system of sociology. But we do provide a schema for discussing sociology systematically. The framework which depicts our concept of the field appears in the first chapter. Centrally placed in Figure 1 are the five basic structures of society: *ecological entities, groups, institutions, organizations,* and *collectivities.* These are discussed in Chapters 7 through 17. The sides of the surrounding octagon represent the factors or processes which interact reciprocally with the structures and with each other: *natural* and *cultural environment* (Chapters 3 and 4), *socialization* (Chapter 5), *social integration* (Chapter 18), modes of *social interaction* (Chapter 19), *social differentiation* (Chapters 20 through 22), *social change* (Chapter 23), and *social control* (Chapter 24). This skeletal structure is designed to articulate the anatomy of sociology for the student, who often complains that he "can't see what it's all about" or "how it fits together." Of course, we recognize that the subject can be dissected and structured in many legitimate ways.

The text itself is divided into four parts. Part I—*Introduction*—contains a brief preview of the field; Part II—*Foundations of Organized Social Behavior*—deals with the essential bases of social order: environmental adjustment and culture, communication, socialized individuals, and the structuring process; Part III—*The Organization of Societies*—contains the analysis of the five major classes of human relationship structures; and Part IV—*The Operation of Societies*—is composed of the chapters dealing with the societal processes in their varied forms.

A brief statement of content precedes each chapter. Within the chapters, the significant concepts or topics are introduced with complete sentences. These serve as pegs on which the subsidiary points can be hung and, put together in a running summary, they provide a more detailed preview and review of content. To facilitate the continuous flow of the textual exposition, the longer illustrations, supplementary slants, and sidelights are set apart in boxes distributed throughout the book. Questions for discussion, suggested topics for reports, and supplementary readings are presented at the end of each chapter.

We have limited goals in respect to content. We have not, to be sure, produced a "streamlined" text. But, on the other hand, we have not tried to make one volume serve as a statement of principles, a compendium of data, and a source book of readings. We have found from experience that the beginning student, confronted with a vast array of diverse materials, often loses his way or fails to see the forest for the trees. We have thus been more generally constricted by the Websterian definition of a textbook as "a systematic presentation of the principles and vocabulary of a subject." The volume, therefore, contains no tables, graphs, or other representations of empirical material. The modest amount of statistical data is woven into the discussion itself. A few figures, however, are employed to clarify certain concepts. Experience and inquiry have indicated that the instructor will commonly prefer to present to his students empirical and other materials relevant to his own interests. This is as it should be. Consistent with our general approach, we have tried to maintain relative simplicity and clarity of analysis and style.

WALFRED A. ANDERSON
FREDERICK B. PARKER

ACKNOWLEDGMENTS

We owe many debts to many persons. We stand intellectually on the shoulders of others—especially our teachers and colleagues. These include, for the senior author, Dwight Sanderson, Pitirim Sorokin, Carl Taylor, L. L. Bernard, F. S. Chapin, Elsworth Faris, E. W. Burgess, Charles E. Ramsey, Olaf F. Larson, and Robin M. Williams, Jr., and for the junior author, Julian L. Woodward, Robert L. Sutherland, Meyer F. Nimkoff, Howard W. Odum, Rupert Vance, Guy B. Johnson, and Lee M. Brooks. (The junior author would like to pay special tribute to Walfred Anderson, who helped to introduce him to the study of sociology at Cornell University more than several years ago.)

We express our deep appreciation to all these men from the past. We wish to thank Wilbert E. Moore, former editor of The Van Nostrand Sociology Series, for his assistance in the preparation of the volume. We are also indebted to Professor Robert F. Eshleman, who read the entire manuscript and made many helpful criticisms.

Finally, we are very grateful to Mrs. Frances Ganous and Mrs. Fay Wertman, who always cheerfully performed the laborious tasks of typing and revising the final drafts of the manuscript.

The following have granted us permission to reproduce material for some illustrations in this book: D. Biebuyck, University of Delaware, pp. 29, 32, 33, 37, 39, 56, 57, 71, 72, 182, 210, 323; J. Sonnenfeld, University of Delaware, pp. 38, 65, 162 (top), 211; F. S. Chapin, *Cultural Change*, New York, Century Company, 1928 [p. 336], by permission of Appleton-Century-Crofts, Inc., p. 44; Department of Child Development and Family Life, Cornell University, p. 78 (bottom); Maryland Agricultural Experiment Station Miscellaneous Publication No. 358 [p. 13], p. 99 (top); Cornell University Agricultural Experiment Station Bulletin No. 786 [p. 41], p. 99 (bottom); Division of Urban Affairs, University of Delaware, p. 106; W. K. Kellogg Foundation, pp. 127 (bottom), 279 (top); *Agricultural Leaders Digest*, Corsicana, Texas, p. 220; Adding Machine Division, National Cash Register Company, Ithaca, New York, p. 220; Scintilla Division, Bendix Corporation, p. 220; and Cornell University News Bureau, p. 279 (center).

W. A. A.
F. B. P.

CONTENTS

PART FOUR   THE OPERATION OF SOCIETIES:
Social Action and Interaction, Social Differentiation, Social Stratification, Social Change, and Social Control

NOTE TO THE INSTRUCTOR

IN THE division of labor between textbook and teacher, the teacher has prior rights in the student. One of these, we believe, is the right of the instructor to prepare his students for the study of sociology in his own fashion. Therefore, instead of including the usual chapters on orientation, we limit our contribution to a few suggestions for the process. These grow out of our own experience and are offered for their possible helpfulness.

1. *Sociology as a "style of thinking."* Most students will have had little or no experience with sociology and therefore will be unfamiliar with its frame of reference. We suggest that they be "taken where they are" and immediately given some sense of the nature of its approach. On the initial contact, students can be drawn into a discussion of the proposition (adapted from the late Carl Becker): "Everyman his own sociologist." For example, the class may be given one simple datum: "Joe is a 16-year-old boy living in the slum section of a large city." The students will make generally accurate inferences about such aspects of Joe's pattern as probable size of family, nationality extraction, leisure-time interests, attitudes toward schooling, "manliness," and so on. At a more complex level, when presented with some of the variations in the incidence of suicide, students can usually reveal at least a faint grasp of Durkheimian thinking. Reflection on the discussions will demonstrate that most young people already have some capacity for making sociological observations. In this connection, it is advisable to offer a warning about the "common sense" fallacy and the deceptiveness of familiarity. Also, the student can be led to appreciate, perhaps for the first time, that human behavior—normal and deviant—is ordered, patterned, or socially structured and cannot be adequately explained by individual psychology (the reductionist fallacy).

These reflections, in turn, can suggest to the student that to "Know thyself" means also to "Know thy society." Moreover, this preliminary exercise offers an opportunity to indicate the wide ranging sources of sociological information. We would point out, for example, that the materials in the text and boxes of the present volume come from personal experience and observation, newspapers, magazines, literature, classic treatises in various fields, professional journals, and scholarly books of theory and research. To suggest, with due caution, that "Sociology is where you find it" is to encourage the student to develop a generalized habit of "thinking sociologically." (At some point, the instructor will undoubtedly wish to distinguish between sociology and the other social sciences and especially between sociology and social work.)

2. *The emergence and modern growth of sociology.* Although the origins of sociology in the thought of Comte and others may be noted, it seems generally more valuable to document its recent expansion and growth in academic and public stature.

3. *The question of sociology as science.* Instructors are commonly impelled at the outset of the introductory course to argue the cause of sociology as science—often with a vigor that betokens a defensive posture. We frankly believe that the effort at this time is not very fruitful and may, indeed, baffle and bore the beginning student. It is suggested, rather, that the basic issues and the methodological questions and techniques be dealt with later in the course and preferably in connection with the presentation of actual research studies relevant to the topic under discussion. We would also propose that the related problem of values be similarly deferred.

4. *Uses of sociology.* To complete the general orientation, and to appeal especially to the interest of potential members of the profession, we

urge the importance of giving students a few illustrations of some of the areas in which sociology is applied—for example, in research, consultation, and administration in industrial, military, hospital, educational, and other types of organizations; in city planning, housing, market research, advertising, public opinion and public relations; and in criminology, penology, and minority group agencies or commissions.

Without overstressing the vocational aspects of the subject, such a presentation will demonstrate the growing awareness and acceptance of sociology outside the academic world. It may also help the student to see more clearly the significance and relevance of the concepts and principles discussed in the text.

W. A. A.
F. B. P.

PART ONE

INTRODUCTION:
Preview

1

SOCIETIES AS SYSTEMS OF HUMAN RELATIONSHIPS

*A*LL NORMAL *human beings live in societies and develop their personalities within them. People, once conditioned by societies, can hardly exist outside of them for long and remain wholly normal.*

Human societies are over-all social systems in which people are united by shared or reciprocal relations into corporate entities defined by social, cultural, and geographical boundaries. They come into existence as the products of many forces: human needs, self-interests and desires, mutual agreements, mutual aid, and others. Despite distinctive differences, they all have common basic characteristics.

I. SOCIETY AND THE INDIVIDUAL

Personality Is a Product of Society

Every normal human being lives in a society. Nowhere does a person habitually live in isolation. Long ago Aristotle remarked that he who does not need society is either a beast or a god. He insisted that man is by nature a social animal.

The ordinary person, however, does not fully grasp the import of the statement that every human being *lives* in a society. Just what does it mean? The meaning can be brought into sharp focus by saying that virtually everything that we think, say, and do and *how* we think, say, and do it from the time of birth until the time of death are influenced by society's organization and operation. We learn, grow, and mature through our experiences in society: it provides our standards of behavior through its norms and indicates to us that we must make the acceptable adjustments to these standards. What we wear and how we wear it, who can wear it and when he can wear it, what we eat and how we eat it, and countless other simple acts of living are almost wholly socially determined. Since the reach of society extends from these elemental activities into every aspect of our living, our whole life is inseparable from it.

It conditions all our reactions, that is, our general attitudes and values come primarily from the social organization that surrounds us.

SOCIETY'S IMPACT Let us see what the impact of society is, for example, upon the native Samoan—as Margaret Mead describes it:

The Samoan background which makes growing up so easy, so simple a matter, is the general *casualness* of the *whole society*. For Samoa is a place where no one suffers for his convictions or fights to the death for special ends. Neither poverty nor great disasters threaten the people to make them hold their lives dearly and tremble for continued existence. No implacable gods, swift to anger and strong to punish, disturb the even tenor of their days. Wars and cannibalism are long since passed away and now the greatest cause for tears, short of death itself, is a journey of a relative to another island. No one is hurried along in life or punished harshly for slowness of development. And in personal relations, caring is as slight. Love and hate, jealousy and revenge, sorrow, and bereavement, are all matters of weeks.[1]

American society has quite a different impact upon us.

Dan Crawford, a missionary who had spent nearly a half century in a tribal society in central Africa, emphasizes the system of thought this society imposed upon its people.[2] His description of how difficult it was for him to think as these people thought except after years of association illustrates the force of a society's impact on an individual. It took years of contact for him to shed his Western conceptions and to become able to "think black." Cooley recognized the relationship when he said that "self and society are twinborn" and "self and society go together, as phases of a common whole." [3]

The Impact of Society Is Natural and Necessary

Society begins to mold us from the moment of birth. Under normal circumstances, we come into the world as members of a family. This is the first unit in society that communicates "the ways of the folk" to us, starting the process of changing a bit of biological flesh, endowed only with potential, into a human personality. Subsequently, the larger kinship unit, our play companions, school groups, church organizations, special interest associations, and many others, in an ever-widening circle instill their expectations and exert their pressures so that we are constantly in contact with other persons and can carry on through units developed by them. Life for each of us is a natural process of continuous activity in and through the forms of human association in our society. At every moment, we carry on activities through such forms of association or we are preparing to do so.

Success and happiness depend upon our effectiveness in these human relationships. A recent study has pointed out that two-thirds of the youth dismissed from their first jobs were discharged not because of lack of work efficiency but because of inability to adjust to other persons in their associational situations.[4] Even more serious, most cases of mental breakdown result, not from physiological deficiencies, but from sociological deficiencies—the inability to adjust to others in society.

Man, Once Conditioned by His Society, Can Hardly Live Outside of It and Remain Normal for Long

The story Admiral Richard Byrd told in *Alone* of the effects of his voluntary, Antarctic winter-night isolation of four and one-half months near the South Pole illustrates this principle. In the early part of his stay he thought he had

learned what the philosophers have long been harping on—that a man can live profoundly without masses of things. . . . [Then as time went on] . . . for all my realism and skepticism there came over me, too powerfully to be denied, that exalted sense of identification —or oneness—with the outer world which is partly mystical but also certainty. A man can isolate himself from habits and conveniences—deliberately, as I have done, or accidentally, as a shipwrecked sailor might—and force his mind to forget. But the body is not so easily sidetracked. . . . That is where the conflict arises. I don't think that a man can do without sounds and smells and voices and touch, any more than he can do without phosphorus and calcium.[5]

Many societies capitalize on this need for familiar human association when they use banishment as one of the severest forms of punishment. Men can hardly survive, they know, in complete exile from their groups.

Separation of Individuals from Human Association Is Almost Unknown

Few people ever live for any length of time apart from the influences of a society. Isolation even for brief periods is never experienced by the vast majority. Most people who want solitude must consciously withdraw and build barriers between themselves and their social organization to cut off communication.

COLLEGE-STUDENT EXPERIENCE   To demonstrate the fact that few of us ever experience any important separation from the influences of our society, we asked over 7500 students in university classes to indicate if they had ever spent a single 24-hour period in the approximately twenty years they had lived when they did not associate in some manner with one or more other persons. Ninety-seven of each 100 had never had such an experience.

Participation in Society Is Necessary for the Development of a Human Personality

What would happen if a child born with a normal body and provided with sufficient sustenance to assure living were deprived of human contacts and did not take part in the social organization about it? Most students question the authenticity of cases of feral—untamed, undomesticated, wild—children who have been reared by animals. But enough cases of extreme isolation in early childhood and of autistic children are known to substantiate the principle that normal participation in a human society is a necessity for the development of human personality.

CASES OF FERAL MEN AND ISOLATES Many cases and legends of "wild" children have been reported in history. One, briefly noted, concerns an Irish boy found living with sheep and bleating like them. His features were animal, his body covered with hair. He did not react to people and was fierce and untamable. His skin was thick and his sense of touch blunted so that stones and thorns were unnoticed.[8]

The Reverend J. A. L. Singh reports the story of Kamala and Amala, so-called wolf-children at Midnapore, India, in a fascinating book entitled *Wolf-Children and Feral Man*. Bettleheim

---

BOX 1 "CHICKEN BOY" FOUND IN IRISH HEN HOUSE GRUNTS LIKE ANIMAL AND SHUNS HUMAN FOOD

Belfast, Northern Ireland, Sept. 13.—Police discovered today a boy—apparently about seven—who they said has never bathed, cannot eat human food, who grunts like an animal and roosts like a chicken.

Sgt. Hugh Ross said the "pitiful little boy" was found in a hen house at Down Patrick, County Down, 15 miles from Belfast.

He has been taken to a home in Belfast, and turned over to a team of physicians for examination.

Sgt. Ross said a group of children playing "hide and seek" ran into the hen house which adjoins a cottage occupied by a widow and her two grown daughters.

The children found the boy perched on a roost with the hens and roosters.

"He cannot talk. He cannot walk, and he cannot eat human food," the police sergeant said. "He has been reared like a chicken."

The mat of hair on his head did not appear ever to have been cut or washed. He had clawlike fingernails which probably never had been trimmed.

Said William Hamilton, official of the National Society for Prevention of Cruelty to Children:

"He gets about by hopping like an ape, and he replies to voices with grunts in a half human fashion." [6]

MAN SEALED IN "TOMB" 10 YEARS BY MOTHER WANTS TO GO BACK

New York, April 27.—A shaggy-bearded man of 33, dug out after ten years of fantastic solitude in a dank cubbyhole, yearned today to return to the tomb-like cubicle in which his mother sealed him when war broke out in Europe.

Shoeless, filthy, his clothes in rags [. . . .] one-time college student, stood on wobbly legs and blinked into the unaccustomed glare of electric lights.

"I liked it in there," he said. "I'd like to go back. I don't care about the outside world."

Police took him to a hospital.

The man told a strange story of voluntary exile since 1939, when his mother sealed him off from the world with a wall of wood and plaster.

[. . . .] spent the ten years in a tiny walled-in cubicle built in the corner of a littered third floor bedroom in a brownstone house in the Greenpoint section of Brooklyn.

His father, who runs a tailor shop in the same building, said he never knew the man was imprisoned in the house.

The cubicle, about three feet wide and five feet long—scarcely big enough to hold [. . . .] when he stretched on the floor to sleep—had been devised, police said, because his mother presumably wanted him to escape being drafted.[7]

compares these girls with autistic children—children suffering from extreme emotional deprivation who were treated in the Orthogenic School of the University of Chicago.[9] His conclusion is that so-called feral children, when compared with autistic children, are suffering from extreme emotional isolation combined with experiences which they interpret as a threat to their lives.

Kingsley Davis reports the case of an illegitimate child kept in extreme isolation for nearly six years because of the disapproval of an angered grandfather.[10] Emaciated, undernourished, and apathetic, the child's physical and mental condition revealed how little development had taken place because normal contacts were absent. Her physical resources, operating alone, could contribute little to making her a person. She did learn simple activities and before her death, could repeat words, talk in phrases, walk well, and follow directions. Davis says of this that "socialization, even when started at the late age of six, could still do a great deal toward making her a person." It is doubtful, however, that she could have become a fully normal person.

These cases of extreme isolation illustrate the need for society as the foundation for adequate adjustment to life. There is no language without society for there is nothing for which language is needed. There would be no communication and so no facts, attitudes, or skills which we learn only through communication. Societies, then, are the essential milieus in which all persons *must* live. How then may we describe societies?

II. WHAT ARE SOCIETIES?

Societies, Arising from Reciprocal Human Relations, Are the Largest Over-All Organizational Systems that Unite Men in Corporate Syntheses Acting as Units in Given Geographic Areas

Nicholas J. Spykman has made the profound statement that "the processes of life create forms and embody themselves in structures. The forms of life, although the products of its processes, yet limit and define them. But life eternally transcends its self-created forms in order to find embodiment in new and better forms. These successive discrete forms direct and modify the ceaseless flow of life until, no longer capable of giving it adequate expression, they are superseded in turn by other forms." [11]

This is true of human as well as of all other forms of life. Men in spatial proximity and social contact with other men create social forms. They embody them in human relationship structures, which, in turn, "limit and define" the relationships that take place among us. They "direct and modify their ceaseless flow."

Societies are man's most generalized and inclusive relationship structures. They are the over-all organizational systems encompassing all the interrelated units that bind us together through interaction. They exist as realities apart from the particular individuals that compose them in that the shared actions that unite the parts and give them a continuity are independent of any particular persons.

We recognize our own complex society that includes a large territory and many millions of people of different races and nationalities. We note its division into innumerable groupings, cities, and towns, and its multitude of different pursuits, values, and customs. Yet, we know that it has an organization and a cultural content binding all into a single unit with regard to the major purposes of living. Also, we recognize simple societies consisting of groupings of people living almost completely on what nature directly provides. Their tools and elementary weapons are limited to bows and arrows and crude cutting blades; their places of abode are constantly shifting; their values are centered primarily on providing their day-to-day necessities for food, clothing, and shelter. Yet, they also have an organization binding them into a functional unit with regard to their interests and the aims of their living. Between these two extremes, there exists a variety of these over-all organizational forms which bind men in given areas together in an ordered way of living that supports their common interests and values.

Societies Are the Product of Many Forces

What is it that leads men to form societies? It is impossible to be sure of their origin, but we recognize in operating societies forces that are important in their creation.

THEORIES OF ORIGINS Rather than to note here all the forces important to the creation of societies, we will only indicate what appear to be the more significant influences. We shall review briefly some of the theories that have been advanced to explain their origin.

HUMAN NEEDS Societies pre- and postdate particular individuals. They were here before us; they will be here after we leave. Since they have a continuing existence independent of particular individuals, particular individuals could not be their creators. However, people coming into life with needs soon acquire characteristics that lead them to associate. This fact brings societies into being.

Plato's (427–347 B.C.) explanation of the origin of societies stressed the many needs of people and their own limitations in supplying them. He emphasized several factors—many different human needs; differences in individual abilities; mutual association; cooperation between people—in explaining why societies originate:

A State, I said, arises, as I conceive, out of the needs of mankind; no one is self-sufficing, but all of us have many wants. Can any other origin of a State be imagined?
There can be no other.
Then, as we have many wants, and many persons are needed to supply them, one takes a helper for one purpose and another for another; and when these partners and helpers are gathered together in one habitation the body of inhabitants is termed a State.[12]

MAN'S SOCIAL NATURE Aristotle (384–322 B.C.) saw the beginnings of society in the inherent social nature of man. It may be questioned if man is inherently social; however, he probably develops such a nature very soon.

SOFTENING HUMAN SENTIMENTS Lucretius (ca. 99–55 B.C.), the Roman philosopher, seeking to free men from the terror of the gods, used his poetic skill to describe "the Nature of Things." He felt that society's origin was primarily the consequence of softening of human sentiments and of obedience to the conventions—those social practices which have their sanction in common practice. (See Box 2.)

SELF-INTEREST Niccolò Machiavelli (1469–1527) emphasized man's self-interest and the insatiable character of his desires, particularly for prestige and material prosperity, as the chief forces in the creation of society.[14]

CONTRACT THEORY A number of thinkers, such as John Locke (1632–1704) and Jean-Jacques Rousseau (1712–1778), stressed that societies came into being when individuals "contracted" with each other to cooperate in the control of the forces of nature playing upon them. Their self-interests and the utility of working together to assure existence and human comfort led men to form societies by agreement. Through this seemingly deliberate action, men exchanged the vices and virtues of the state of nature for the advantages of human society.

SOCIABILITY AND SYMPATHY Auguste Comte (1798–1857), French philosopher and inventor of the term "sociology," believed that society originally rested on the sociability and sympathy of men. These were expressed in the family as the true original unit from which the larger units flowed.

SYSTEM OF MUTUAL RELATIONS Emile Durkheim (1858–1917) pointed out: "Society has for

---

BOX 2

Next, having gotten them huts and skins and fire; and when women
Mated with man shared a man's abode; and when families duties
Therein were learnt; and as soon as they saw their own offspring arising;
Then 'twas that mankind first began to lose power of endurance.
Fire made their gelid frames less able to bear the cold weather
Out 'neath the open sky; their virility Venus exhausted;
Children's caresses too easily sapped the proud spirit of parents.
Neighbors in those days, too, began to lose power of endurance.
Neither to inflict nor receive any hurt, and asked for indulgence
Towards their women and bairns, as with cries and gesticulations
And in their stammering speech they tried to explain to each other
That it is meet and right that all should pity the helpless.
And although harmony could not be won in every instance,
Yet did the greater part observe the conventions uprightly;
Else long since would the human race have been wholly abolished,
Nor could their seed till this present day have continued the species.[13]

---

its substratum the ensemble of the associated individuals. The system formed by their union, which varies according to their number, their disposition over the surface of the territory, the nature of and the number of ways of communication, constitutes the base upon which the social life arises." [15]

He reasoned that when men came together in interaction they formed a system from their mutual relations that was a specific reality with a character that was inexplicable in terms of its individual members. Thus, for him, society is created *sui generis*. It consists of these systems of realities that transcend the units of which they are composed.

MUTUAL AID Peter Kropotkin (1842–1921), Russian sociologist, stressed mutual aid as the principle giving rise to and maintaining societies: "Sociability and need of mutual aid and support are such inherent parts of human nature that at no time of history can we discover men living in small isolated families, fighting each other for the means of subsistence. On the contrary, modern research proves that since the very beginning of prehistoric life men used to agglomerate into clans or tribes, maintained by an idea of common descent and by worship of common ancestors. For thousands and thousands of years this organization has kept men together, even though there was no authority whatever to impose it." [16]

INTERESTS AND NEEDS Gustave Ratzenhofer (1842–1904) said that society exists only in the social process resulting from the total of mutual relationships existing among a number of individuals. He said that these relationships are based on human interests growing out of needs.

Albion Small (1854–1926) utilized Ratzenhofer's idea of interests and constructed a set of six primary concerns: health, wealth, sociability, knowledge, beauty, and rightness. Man struggles to achieve the satisfaction of these interests and develops society as a means for their satisfaction.[17]

CONSCIOUSNESS OF KIND R. M. MacIver, following F. H. Giddings, implied that human society arose when men recognized some sort of "belonging together" because of a sense of likeness and of something that is common to them. The family in some form was the first society, he suggested, and said that "the sense of likeness was focussed on kin-membership, closely uniting the ideas of likeness of body and of mind." [18]

These summary statements re-emphasize the fact that social thinkers through history have recognized many forces as being responsible for the creation of societies. A summary listing of these indicates their diversity: human needs, differences in individual abilities, man's friendliness, his attitudes of sympathy, his self-interest and unsatisfied desires, his mutual agreements to assure existence, improvements and comfort, mutual aid, and the satisfying of vital interests. All of these and others, no doubt, are forces that brought human societies into being.

Societies Have Some Common Foundational Characteristics

It becomes possible at this point to indicate some of the common characteristics of societies as over-all systems uniting men into operating entities. These set the general problems of our study. Societies range from small isolated units in a limited territory to complex entities that include large numbers of people covering a wide territory. Although societies vary considerably, we find that they have some similar basic characteristics.

Societies, then, are (1) relatively large numbers of people (2) living together in a definite geographical area and (3) having reciprocal relationships with each other. These relationships result in (4) systems of association where (5) acceptance of desirable mutual interests and goals has been reached so that (6) cooperating together is possible. This gives (7) unity to the whole which is fostered by (8) a developed sense of sharing in (9) an interdependent mode of life held together by (10) established norms and (11) interrelated statuses.

The Problem of This Volume Is to Study Societies as Wholes

The preceding paragraph sets the problem of our study. It is our purpose to describe the organization and operation of societies as wholes —this is the field of sociology. It is the science that has for its task the description of the structure and functioning of these over-all systems in which we live.

III. DIAGRAM OF THE FIELD OF SOCIOLOGY

A Brief Summary of the Relationship Between the Parts of the Diagram

At this point, we present our diagram of this field of study (Fig. 1) with a brief series of

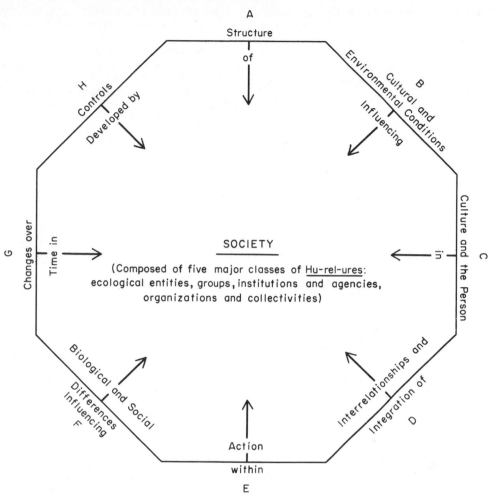

Fig. 1. The Field of Sociology

Components A through H interact upon each other.

statements about the relationship between the parts. The diagram charts the central phenomena upon which sociology focuses its attention. First, and most broadly, are (A) societies and the structural forms of which they are composed. It is through these that the social systems they create function and in which our behavior as human beings expresses itself. These structures, which we call "hurelures" (see Chapter 6), will be analyzed in detail.

These structural forms and societies themselves could not exist unless people were able to carry on meaningful contacts with each other. Communication through the use of symbols, especially spoken and written language, is the basis for the transference of ideas that makes possible social systems.

Further, there are related elements that must be considered if we are to obtain a comprehensive view of these phenomena in an operational sense. Each society has (B) a cultural heritage or historical background that influences its organization and operation at a given time. Each society is conditioned by the physical and biological environment in which it is set. Out of these, a people build their distinctive way of living—(C) their culture. Personalities, rooted in their genetic heritage, are produced by a socializing process. These form major areas of our study.

All the major forms of association in a society are (D) interrelated and integrated by their commonly accepted values. This permits a society to operate as an ordered system. But societies are never static. There is always (E) action within them (and between them). These actions take definite forms that must be considered, also. Societies also make some (F) biological and cultural differences among their people socially significant. As a consequence, accommodations to these variations are required to make social interaction possible. These accommodations lead to systems of hierarchical relations having different degrees of rigidity and range from open forms, where movement up and down the social scale by a society's members is relatively free, to closed forms where their social position is fixed for life.

Because societies are never static, (G) change in the structure and functioning of societal forms over time by modification or replacement is inevitable in spite of formidable obstacles. Stability within societies is maintained by (H) social controls, which seek to govern behavior through the internalization of social norms and values within individuals or through inducing conformity by other means.

Enough has now been said about the general nature of societies to provide the background for our more detailed study of their organization and operation as the essential subject matter of sociology.

Before we begin this detailed study, it will be profitable to consider the cultural antecedents of societies as they condition social structure and function. This is the task of our next chapter.

References

1. Mead, Margaret, *Coming of Age in Samoa* (New York, William Morrow and Company, January, 1930), pp. 198–199. Copyright, 1928, by William Morrow and Company, Inc.
2. Crawford, D., *Thinking Black* (London, Morgan and Scott, 1912).
3. Cooley, Charles H., *Social Organization* (New York, Charles Scribner's Sons, 1920), pp. 5 and 8.
4. Bristow, Gwen, "Why Were They Fired?" *This Week Magazine* (July 11, 1954), p. 6.
5. Byrd, Richard E., *Alone* (New York, G. P. Putnam's Sons, 1938), pp. 120, 128, and 129.
6. Associated Press dispatch, *Journal-Every Evening* (Wilmington, Del., September 13, 1956).
7. Associated Press dispatch, *Journal-Every Evening* (Wilmington, Del., April 27, 1949).
8. Park, Robert E., and Burgess, Ernest W., *Introduction to the Science of Sociology* (Chicago, University of Chicago Press, 1921), p. 241.
9. Singh, J. A. L., and Zingg, R. M., *Wolf-Children and Feral Man* (New York, Harper and Brothers, 1940); Bettleheim, B., "Feral Children and Autistic Children," *American Journal of Sociology*, 64 (March, 1959), pp. 455 ff.
10. Davis, Kingsley, "Extreme Isolation of a Child," *American Journal of Sociology*, 45 (January, 1940), pp. 554–564, and "Final Note on a Case of Extreme Isolation," *American Journal of Sociology*, 50 (March, 1947), pp. 432–437.
11. Spykman, Nicholas J., *The Social Theory of Georg Simmel* (Chicago, University of Chicago Press, 1925), p. 20. Copyright, 1925, by the University of Chicago.
12. Plato, *The Republic* (Oxford, England, The Clarendon Press, 1925), p. 49.
13. Lucretius, Titus, *On the Nature of Things* (New Brunswick, N.J., Rutgers University Press, 1950), pp. 200 and 201. Translated by W. Hannaford Brown.
14. Machiavelli, N., *The Prince*, in *Harvard Classics*, 36 (New York, P. F. Collier and Son, 1910).
15. Durkheim, Emile, *The Elementary Forms of Religious Life* (Glencoe, Ill.: The Free Press, 1947), pp. 16 ff.

16. Kropotkin, Peter A., *Mutual Aid* (New York, Alfred A. Knopf, 1914), pp. 118 ff.
17. Small, Albion, *General Sociology* (Chicago, University of Chicago Press, 1905), pp. 425 ff.
18. MacIver, R. M., *Society: Its Structure and Changes* (New York, Ray Long and Richard R. Smith, Inc., 1931), p. 7.

Questions for Study and Discussion

1. Compare the picture of sociology presented in the chapter with your earlier "image" or "expectations" of the field.
2. Have you ever spent as many as 24 hours in complete isolation from human contacts? If so, under what circumstances? 48 hours? Under what circumstances? What is the significance of this?
3. What are feral men? Look up and consider the cases given by Park and Burgess in their *Introduction to the Science of Sociology,* and in Singh and Zingg, *Wolf Children and Feral Man.* Do these cases seem reasonable to you? Why or why not?
4. How would you show that normal physical and mental equipment is not enough for normal personal development?
5. Study the statement quoted from Spykman. Show how it applies to human life.
6. What theory or theories of the origin of societies seem most reasonable to you? Why?
7. What is the focus of attention in this volume? How does the sociological approach to society differ from the psychological? the historical? the economic?
8. At this stage, what do you understand "social structure" to mean?
9. Can you see the pattern of thought in the diagram of the field of sociology?
10. Look through the volumes by Merton, Broom, and Cottrell and by Lipset and Smelser (listed below). What do they show you about the scope and methods of sociology?

Suggested Topics for Reports

1. Interview a number of senior majors in sociology and report on (a) their reasons for selecting this field, and (b) the kinds of employment they plan to enter after graduation.
2. Examine the first three issues of the *American Journal of Sociology* and the last three issues of the *American Sociological Review* and report on the differences you note in topics discussed, the kinds of data presented, and the research methods employed.
3. Trace the emergence of sociology in the thought of Auguste Comte, the "father" of sociology.

Supplementary Reading

Bierstedt, Robert, *The Social Order.* New York: McGraw-Hill Book Co., Inc., 1963.
Coser, Lewis A. (ed.), *Sociology Through Literature.* Englewood Cliffs, N.J.: Prentice-Hall, Inc., 1963.
Davis, Kingsley, *Human Society.* New York: The Macmillan Company, 1949.
Furfey, Paul H., *The Scope and Method of Sociology.* New York: Harper and Brothers, 1953.
Johnson, Harry M., *Sociology: A Systematic Introduction.* New York: Harcourt, Brace and Company, 1960.
Lipset, Seymour and Smelser, N. J. (eds.), *Sociology: The Progress of a Decade.* Englewood Cliffs, N.J.: Prentice-Hall, Inc., 1961.
Loomis, Charles, *Social Systems.* Princeton, N.J.: D. Van Nostrand Company, Inc., 1960.
MacIver, R. M., *Society: A Textbook of Sociology.* New York: Farrar and Rinehart, Inc., 1937.

Merton, R. K., Broom, L., and Cottrell, L. (eds.), *Sociology Today: Problems and Prospects*. New York: Basic Books, Inc., 1959.

Park, Robert E., and Burgess, Ernest W., *Introduction to the Science of Society*. Chicago: University of Chicago Press, 1921.

Parsons, Talcott, *The Social System*. Glencoe, Ill.: The Free Press, 1951.

Simmel, Georg, *The Sociology of Georg Simmel* (ed. by Kurt Wolf). Glencoe, Ill.: The Free Press, 1951.

Simpson, George, *Man in Society*. New York: Doubleday Company, Inc., 1954.

Von Weise, Leopold and Becker, Howard, *Systematic Sociology*. New York: John Wiley and Sons, Inc., 1932.

Zetterberg, Hans L., *Social Theory and Social Practice*. New York: Bedminster Press, 1962.

2

SOCIETIES AND THEIR CULTURAL ANTECEDENTS

*E*ACH *society has a cultural heritage that influences its organization and operation. American society, for example, is the product of its religious heritage; its European population and national heritages; the development of a distinct Euro-American culture; the Renaissance, Reformation, and French and American political revolutions that produced her emphasis on freedom; the emergence of modern science; and the Industrial Revolution that applied power machinery to the processes of economic production. and created her machine-marketing economy. Each society acquires its major themes or characteristics from its cultural heritage.*

I. THE LONG-TIME VIEW

We Can Understand Societies More Adequately in the Light of Their Cultural Backgrounds

All societies have an antecedent cultural background. Someone has said that "the present is the living sum-total of the past." While this is an overstatement, it is nevertheless true that the main pattern of any society is tied to its cultural heritage. The organization and operation of a particular society can therefore be better comprehended if we know at least the main outlines of its cultural antecedents. There is a continuousness in social organization just as there is in all nature. No social element is a product of the present alone but is interwoven with this continuity. For example, each society has a system of economic organization which has its roots in the past. We can hardly understand this organization unless we know the stages through which it has passed. Each society has a population stock. How many of our views about it be understood without some knowledge of its origin? What seem to be strange ideas and practices often appear not so strange, when we know how they relate to the times that produced them.

Over the entrance to the Archives Building

in Washington, D.C., is inscribed the following: "What's Past Is Prologue. Study the Past." A cultural heritage contributes the ideological conceptions and material substances with which a society operates. Knowledge of it will give us understanding.

Two General Concepts—of Time and of Accumulation—Give Us Perspective

PHYSICAL TRAITS Man's biological and social roots are sunk in the eons of time. Recounting the theories of man's biological origin and his slow physical development through the ages is unnecessary; we can accept the evidence of anthropologists that man appeared as a sub-human form one to two million years ago and reached his present form about 40,000 to 50,000 years ago.[1] Man developed those biological characteristics that made him more efficient in adapting to his environment and began the slow process of building his social organizations. The achievement of an upright physical position that freed his hands and made movement more rapid, the opposable thumb that made handling and using material objects more effective, the development of a complex brain that made reasoning possible, the heritage of eyes that allowed wide vision, and a vocal apparatus that has the capacity for a broad range of sounds took centuries to accomplish. But they are the chief physical traits of man leading to his creation of societies.

BIOLOGICAL URGES   Early man, just as does modern man, possessed basic biological urges (notably sex and hunger) that were essential to his survival. Because these urges brought him inevitably into association with his kind, they fostered the development of human groupings. What these earliest groupings were is a matter for conjecture, but they were probably units similar to the family. Time played its role and gradually made the family the basic group. It was based upon a relatively permanent arrangement of males and females in pairs. From this foundation, man evolved kinship units, clans, and tribes and, over the centuries, an increasing variety of structures of human relationships that make up his present-day societies. Today's societies are what they are because of the very long process of accumulation.

The Development of Tools Illustrates the Accumulation Process

We often refer to man as the "tool-using animal." No other animal uses instruments of his own manufacture to aid him in making goods. These tools—extensions of man's hands and arms—have accumulated by the thousands until almost every occupation in our industrial society has its own special tools made of whatever material best suits the purpose. In a parallel manner, the "tools" of social relations have accumulated from man's earliest efforts to adjust to his fellows.

F. Stuart Chapin has summarized this process which has occurred over the long stretch of cultural history. He shows how tools, fire, burial practices, and other elements important in the present social organizations of man reach back into the early days of man's beginnings and how they have piled up at an accelerating rate as time moved on. The following is exemplar:

> Stone implements increase in number and variety. Bone tools are added. Metals become utilized. The stream thickens. Gradually bone and metal replace stone, which in these later times is used only for building purposes. Language becomes articulate. Theological, philosophical, scientific and technical vocabularies elaborate and enlarge. The original human institution of the family continues, but its early functions and prerogatives are split off. These grow and elaborate into separate institutions of the state, industry, the church, edu-

cation, business and a host of others. And always, woven in and out, back and forth, throughout the whole growing fabric of culture traits, there is the sinuous thread of written language, externally stored mental patterns and ideas, reinforcing, strengthening, stiffening, and yet flexing the stream of culture.[2]

II. ANTECEDENTS OF AMERICAN SOCIETY

A Description of the Cultural Antecedents of a Particular Society Can Illustrate Their Importance in Understanding Societies

The thesis of this chapter is that our understanding of the organization and operation of any society at a particular time requires some knowledge of its cultural background, since societies are built upon these antecedents. We have shown that the societies of present-day man stretch back into his earliest efforts and are still influenced by these attempts of man to adjust to his environment.

Now our task is to take a particular society as an illustration and indicate how its present is related to its past. Any society could serve this purpose. If we were to choose India we would find, for example, that Hinduism influenced the basic character of its culture. We would see that the Hindu doctrine of inner concentration and contemplation, the belief in reincarnation, the striving to achieve release from "Karma," and the caste differences that rigidly stratify the population are all ancient cultural products that we must examine to understand the India of today.

American society provides the most appropriate illustration of our theme. We shall therefore review certain major cultural antecedents that have contributed to the formation of our society and that still influence its pattern of organization and operation.

The Christian Religion Has Contributed Two Basic Concepts to American Society: the Supreme Value of the Individual and the Possibility of a Just Social Order

American society is predominantly Christian in its religious origin and outlook. The system of socially transmitted moral and religious ideas that are its heritage comes chiefly from the life and teachings of Christ. Over half of this society's population claims affiliation with Christian churches. Additional millions are its constituents. Other forms of religion in this society are relatively small in both number and size. The most important of these, Judaism, is actually the forerunner of Christianity.

VALUE OF THE INDIVIDUAL   Two ideas from Christianity are of extreme importance in our understanding of American society, for they undergird its social organization. The first is the premise that every human being is of infinite value: every life has sanctity. Christianity's founder insisted from the beginning that every person is a child of God. God is each person's loving Father. Thus, every soul has unlimited worth, and life is to be lived as an expression of that worth. The ideal model is portrayed in the life of Jesus. Since all men are sons of God, all men are brothers. It would follow that, since all men are brothers, all men must aid each other.

THE KINGDOM OF GOD ON EARTH   According to this teaching, men are to live together to build the Kingdom of God on earth, a realm of justice and honesty. Man is to abide by the rules of justice in his relations with other men. Wrongdoing—sin—is the violation of these rules in human relationships. "What doth the Lord require of thee, but to do justly, and to love mercy, and to walk humbly with thy God" is its creed for living. These noble conceptions of the value of the person and the purposes of social living are now supporting ideals for the Western world.

For centuries following their inception, these teachings of Christ were submerged in a mass of dogma and rite from which they are not yet completely freed. But with the coming of freedom of thought and expression in religion, these two ideas have served as impelling goals.

Europe's Structure Contributed the Ideals of Nationalism to American Society

A second important cultural antecedent of American society was the formation of the European national pattern. The history of Europe from the third to the sixteenth centuries was largely one of the formation of modern nations: England, France, Germany, the Scandinavian countries, and so on. Beginning about the third century, the tribal peoples of the north and west areas of Europe began one invasion after another toward the south. Some were absorbed. Others settled down to form the basic population stocks of newly forming societies. The occupation of Britain by the Angles and the Saxons, and the settlement of the Lombards

north of Italy, gave these regions their people and their names—France, England, Lombardy. Down to the end of the sixteenth century and the destruction of the Spanish Armada, Europe was going through its nation-forming experiences.

CULTURE-BUILDING AND NATIONALISM   Each of these developing nations was building its own culture around common language, common territory, common government, economic interests, art, and literature. These became cherished possessions. The preservation of the nation rose to be of pre-eminent value to European societies, a value about which much of recent European history has centered.

NATIONALISM A MAJOR VALUE   This concern to establish and preserve a national character grew to be one of the mainsprings of the new American society too, as desirability of its own separate existence increased. Pride in nation, often to the point of chauvinism, has characterized the spirit of American society from its founding to the present. These sentiments are part of the European heritage.

Europe also Gave America Her Basic Population Stock

The inhabitants of Europe have belonged to the white race since prehistoric days. The inhabitants of American society also are predominantly of the white race, since most migrants came from these European nations. In 1960, of 180 million inhabitants in the United States, about 89 per cent were white.[3] The North American continent filled up rapidly with white people from the beginning of its settlement. Of over 38 million immigrants to this nation between 1820 and 1945, Asia contributed only 2 per cent, Africa and other areas no more than 1 per cent, and other sections of the North and South American continents, 11 per cent.[4] The society's original population stock consisted overwhelmingly of white people from northwestern Europe.

The Blockade of the Eastern End of the Mediterranean Sea in the Fifteenth and Sixteenth Centuries, Resulting in the Discovery of the American Continents, Led to the Development of an Euro-American Culture Around an Atlantic Ocean Setting and to a New Occidental World View

In 1453, Constantinople, at the juncture of the European and Asiatic continents in the southeast, was captured by the Ottoman Turks. The Ottoman Empire, in expanding across the whole of the eastern end of the Mediterranean Sea and the north of Africa, set up a blockade of the routes between the Mediterranean commercial cities and the oriental lands that had been their main sources of trade.

EASTWARD OUTLOOK The chief outlook of the European societies that centered around the Mediterranean was in an eastward direction until the end of the fifteenth and the middle of the sixteenth centuries. The Romans had invaded the north in the earlier centuries, conquered Gaul and other areas, and provided these tribal societies with much of the organizational foundation for their developing systems. Migrating tribes, moving southward across Europe and settling north of Italy to develop national units, had made contacts with the Mediterranean societies, which helped to shift the Mediterranean outlook toward the north and west.

CHANGE TO A WESTERN OUTLOOK But the blockade of the water and overland trade routes to the East severed almost completely the connections of these Mediterranean societies with the Orient. These societies then turned their eyes westward toward the Atlantic Ocean and northward to the newly developed nations of Europe. The newly developed nations sought contacts with the oriental world through overseas routes. In the process, they not only came upon the American continents, but they also set the stage for the creation of an Euro-American culture centered around the Atlantic Ocean. The Atlantic Ocean became the commercial pathway of European nations, and the North American continent became their direct goal. The routes across the Atlantic to this land developed rapidly, causing European economic expansion soon to center in large measure around this ocean.

WHAT MIGHT HAVE HAPPENED We might conjecture as to what could have happened to Europe, and as a consequence to American society, if the Turks had not blockaded the Mediterranean routes in the fifteenth and sixteenth centuries. Is it not conceivable that increased relationships between European and Asian societies might have developed? Europe might have become oriental in its cultural organization. However, the rather sharp separation between the West and the East as a result of the blockade, the common consensus of the developing societies in the north of Europe, and the discovery and use of the Atlantic Ocean and its

bordering land bodies directed Europe's attention to creating the Euro-American cultural organization that now characterizes our American society.

The Renaissance and the Reformation Stimulated Freedom of Intellect and Freedom of Religion

ASCETICISM AND OTHER WORLDLINESS The early centuries of Christian expansion in Europe saw the development at first of an asceticism that looked upon the world as evil. The way of salvation for Christians became one of withdrawal from the world. The dominant religious view stressed preparation for the hereafter rather than for life in this world as the primary motive of existence. These dogmas of the expanding Church became axiomatic truths. Heresy-hunting became the employment of Christian leaders.

REVIVAL OF LEARNING AND REFORMS IN RELIGION But beneath these developments there grew an energetic movement of thought against these other-worldly conceptions. The Renaissance, with its revival of learning, was the movement in Europe that recovered freedom of intellect from the bondage of ecclesiastical and political limitations. It promoted practical conceptions of the world and man, encouraged men to inquire and criticize, and evolved humanistic attitudes toward man's problems and his destiny on this planet. It made thinkers curious about nature and the life around them.

The Renaissance cannot be separated from the Reformation. The mass of the religious followers were conformists as a matter of course. The differences in views that arose might have been resolved had it not been for conditions within the Church itself. One source of difficulty was the behavior of the clergy. From the twelfth to the sixteenth century there was constant complaint within the Church as well as without about the immoral example set by the monks, friars, and nuns. Other abuses stirred opposition: the sale of indulgences, vice and rioting in connection with the rapidly increasing number of holy days, and misuse of Church masses and ceremonials. The emphasis of the Church on gaining material possessions also brought condemnation from the people, especially when the Church's action was joined with demands for tax exemption. Also, the new nations had become strongly self-conscious, and the growing spirit of nationalism also became a forceful rival to the power of the Church.

These circumstances made a cleavage within the Church inevitable, and it came in 1517 when a German monk, Martin Luther, nailed his 95 theses to the church door at Wittenberg as a challenge to the propriety of the indulgence system.

EMANCIPATION FROM ECCLESIASTICAL DOMINATION We must recognize that the Renaissance and the Reformation did not accomplish complete freedom of thought and religion in Europe. They did, however, emancipate Europe from the clutches of complete ecclesiastical domination and opened the doors to other forces that pushed the idea of freedom in the affairs of men further toward its goal. The idea that social institutions like the Church are instruments to be used by man to help him solve his problems and not as agencies to dominate his ways of thinking and acting began to be a part of European belief. Our American society absorbed these views.

The Emergence of Science Brought European and American Societies to the Modern Era

Nothing is so practical as a scientific principle. It is possible for man to solve some of his problems by trial and error or by accident, but the surest way for meeting practical situations is through knowledge of the principles by which phenomena operate.

The traditional explanation of the world of nature and of man in Europe before the middle centuries was the supernaturalistic one. Contacts with the Orient had brought Europe into touch with mathematics and astronomy, which led it to new conceptions of the universe. The Renaissance stressed the secular viewpoints of the Greeks. Students of the natural world fastened attention upon the laws by which the universe operates.

The consequence of these studies was the stimulation of other types of scientific curiosity that resulted in the scientific revolution of the seventeenth and eighteenth centuries. Principles about the conservation of energy, of dynamics, and of the nature of matter in physics were produced. Expanded knowledge of the chemical elements, the development of a chemical nomenclature, knowledge about the nature of compounds—all advanced man's understanding of his world. Man moved forward, then, in biology and geology until his explanation of life processes gave new perspective, not only upon the natural world but also upon man and man in his social relations as part of the natural world.

These scientific advances introduced the experimental method in study. They pointed to the possibilities residing in the application of the scientific point of view for improving the lot of man. They brought European and American societies to the threshold of their great technological advances.

The American and French Revolutions Spread the Idea of Freedom to the Political Structure of Western Societies

The American and French political revolutions were the inevitable consequences of the scientific and philosophical viewpoints of the seventeenth and eighteenth centuries. The underlying concepts of the scientific revolution were that man must always use his reasoning faculties; nature must be subjected to the disinterested scrutiny of man's mind; and nature "must be put on the rack" and compelled to bear witness so that she could be controlled to serve man's ends.

Such ideas were soon applied by the social philosophers to the day-by-day problems of man. Montesquieu, Voltaire, and Rousseau—among others—paved the way for the doctrine of natural rights and the equality of men. The Reformation with its emphasis on man's thinking through his own spiritual problems supported the views of the philosophers about man's social conditions. "Are these social conditions that man finds himself in reasonable?" they asked. To this, the philosopher's answer was "No." Such an answer was an expression of a growing belief that change was desirable. These beliefs spread among the people through pamphlets and books and in cafes and theaters. When he saw the books of Voltaire and Rousseau, Louis XVI, in his temple prison, said, "Those two men have destroyed France." Napoleon remarked, "The Bourbons might have preserved themselves if they had controlled written materials."

FREEDOM IN THE AFFAIRS OF LIFE The American colonists heeded this philosophy. Many had come to these new shores to escape the domination of the European order. The social class system that gave a man "a station to which God had called him" and made impossible any chance to change that station, or any right to question it, did not fit this changing world. The growing merchant, manufacturing, and professional classes insisted on change. The submerged peasantry was groaning under tyranny. It was only "Common Sense," in the phrase of Thomas Paine, that there should be a declaration of independence: it came in July, 1776.

Liberty and equality formed the basis for the governing of men, and these sentiments were specified in the declaration of the original thirteen states when it claimed: "We hold these truths to be self-evident: That all men are created equal, that they are endowed by their Creator with certain unalienable rights, that among these are life, liberty, and the pursuit of happiness, that to secure these rights, governments are instituted among men, deriving their just powers from the consent of the governed." This statement summed up a view widely held in eighteenth-century Europe.

The storming of the Bastille in Paris (July, 1789) showed that the French wanted these ideals promoted by the French philosophers to be applied at home. France was given her "Declaration of the Rights of Man and of the Citizen": "Men are born and remain free and equal in rights." "Law is the expression of the general will. Every citizen has a right to participate personally or through his representatives, in its formation. It must be the same for all." These ideas were the forces that ushered in French political democracy, after periods of internal turmoil.

England's "Magna Carta," France's "Declaration of the Rights of Man and of the Citizen," and America's "Declaration of Independence," and its borrowed Bill of Rights, gave the United States the liberty of government and the equality in social relations that are the support of this society.

III. THE INDUSTRIAL REVOLUTION AND AMERICAN SOCIETY

The Industrial Revolution Ushered in a New Era in American Society

The scientific advances of the seventeenth and eighteenth centuries brought European and American societies to the beginning of a new cultural era. The advances resulted in the application of power-driven machinery to the production and distribution of economic goods. Subsequently, we shall see how this was the most epoch-making change in the culture of the Western world and in the transformation of its way of life. We call it the Industrial Rev-

olution because it replaced the old methods in these societies.

Europe's economic life was changing swiftly as a consequence of oceanic commerce. New goods in increased quantity and quality were becoming a part of the people's daily living. The increased desire for material things was not limited to the upper class of nobility and clergy but was spreading speedily to the growing middle class of merchants, traders, master workmen, and others.

The accumulation and use of money for increased production led to the development of investment and modern capital programs. The invention of machines using power sources other than human or animal seemed inevitable at this stage. The close relation between Europe and the new American society meant that any changes occurring in Europe would be made in America at virtually the same time.

Changes in Technology Came First in England and Were Applied First in the Textile Industry

The revolution in the textile industry of England was a natural one since this industry was basic in her whole economy. Water power was available in various places, but not generally. The invention of the flying shuttle, the water wheel operating a roller spinning frame, the spinning jenny, and Crompton's mule for spinning thread made for rapid growth in this industry.

STEAM ENGINE In 1769, James Watt patented a separate steam condenser that led to the making of a practical steam engine. It was the most important invention of the eighteenth century for England. The use of steam power rapidly spread in the textile and other industries since England had an unlimited coal supply. Productive capacity increased tremendously.

COTTON GIN The invention of the cotton gin by Eli Whitney in 1793 made American raw cotton available. This too expanded the English textile industries and became the foundation for a rapidly growing textile industry in the United States.

Steam as the Chief Early Power Source, Soon Used in All Industries, Was Rapidly Applied to Transportation

The inventions by Cort and Darby in England that replaced charcoal in blast furnaces with coal led to modern methods of making steel. Since this gave more durable materials for machinery, the steam engine was then applied to locomotion. Railways and steam boats became chief instruments for transportation.

Man had arrived at a cultural threshold in technological accumulation in which newly invented machines could be piled one on another at an ever-increasing rate. These inventions and discoveries were, of course, responsible for man's creation of an industrial civilization.

The Application of Power-Driven Machinery Gave Europe and America the Factory System of Processing Economic Goods

GUILD PRODUCTION Before the application of machine techniques, the chief mode of making goods in the Western world was the handicraft system. A master workman would gather several apprentices around him, and each worker would learn the techniques required to produce the goods with hand tools and eventually become a master workman with a definite trade.

FACTORIES The transition from the handicraft to the factory system came with opposition. The use of power-driven machines could not be stopped, however. The engines furnishing power and the machines making the goods had to be close to each other so they could be fitted into the necessary system of shafts and belts. Concentration of power source and a number of interdependent machines in a single place created the factory. Since a number of workers were gathered in a single place, organization and control of workmen and work conditions made factory management essential. Workmen developed the labor union to represent their interests as the factory method became more universal.

The Concentration of Factories Led to the Industrial City

TYPES OF CITIES The concentration of factories in a central place is responsible for creating the industrial city, primarily devoted to the making of goods. Man had previously developed governmental and protective cities, as well as educational, religious, recreational, and commercial cities. Each was characterized by service to some major societal need.

INDUSTRIAL CITIES NOW DOMINATE The Industrial Revolution brought into existence the city devoted primarily to the making and distribution of goods. America is now dotted with these from east to west and north to south: Fall River, Worcester, Pittsburgh, Akron,

Birmingham, Flint, Tulsa, Chicago, St. Louis, New Orleans, Seattle, Houston—to name a few. Most of the cities that developed around the manufacture of specific products have taken on other functions, making them diversified in character. But it is still the processing and distributing of goods that characterize most of these concentrated population centers.

Increased Shifting of Population Became a Characteristic of Industrial Economy

The centralization of factories and the growth of cities meant increased population movement. Stability of population was a general characteristic in handicraft and agricultural economies. People in these economies were largely self-sustaining because they produced within their own areas most of their food, clothing, and shelter. Population was relatively fixed geographically, and movement took place between areas only as a consequence of strong pressures.

EBB AND FLOW OF ECONOMIC LIFE The Industrial Revolution gave an ebb and flow to economic life that set up strong currents of internal population shifting. Factories pulled people to the cities from the rural areas. Unemployment in one and the possibility of employment in another caused movement between production centers, while movement to new frontiers of industry and agriculture led to shifting from region to region.

MAJOR POPULATION MOVES American society has experienced three major types of population movement in the last 100 years, in addition to the flow of immigrants to its shores. There has been movement of people from rural areas to urban centers, movement from the East to the Midwest and on toward the far West, and movement from the South to the North. Each year there is considerable change in residence in this society, also. One in every five of the 171 million persons one year old or over in April, 1959, was living in a different house from the one in which he had lived a year earlier.

A new internal movement is now taking place as a consequence of the general use of the automobile and hard-surfaced roads and the availability of electricity and mechanical devices in rural areas. It is the suburban or fringe trend— the movement of families to the residential suburbs of cities and into the open country along paved highways. In 1920, the nonfarm population living in rural territory was only 19 per cent of the population. It had increased to 26 per cent of the total population by 1950.

The population in the urban fringe—the territory within the standard metropolitan statistical areas but outside the central cities—increased 48.5 per cent between 1950 and 1960.[5]

The Corporation Became the Major Form of Business Organization after the Industrial Revolution

The capital necessary to do business before the commercial era of the fifteenth and sixteenth centuries was furnished chiefly by rich individuals. The commercial era started the growth of the joint stock company in which capital was provided by a number of persons. It took more capital to provide ships and other trading facilities than one person could usually furnish. These companies helped to build the merchant empires of the Mediterranean region as well as those of Holland and England.[6]

CORPORATIONS PROVIDE CAPITAL The development of the factory system of production expanded the corporate business method. Machines, buildings, land, raw materials, and wages for large numbers of employees required capital investments generally beyond the ability of a single person. The capital was obtained by forming a corporation, wherein individuals purchase stock in the enterprise at a price per share. They are remunerated from the profits of the business in proportion to the number of shares owned. The operation of the business is entrusted to a board of directors who are responsible to the stockholders for the conduct of the enterprise.

Division of Labor and Specialization Accompanied Machine Production Systems

The general use of machines produced subdivision of jobs and the development of specialization throughout the economic system. Specialization of work characterized handicraft economy also, for it produced the carpenter, the blacksmith, the shoemaker, the tailor, and others. These specialists, however, usually made the whole item on which they were working. But when machines came, total jobs were broken down into many parts. Individuals attached to a machine repeated the same activity over and over; machines and workmen were synchronized. The production line became the symbol of machine organization.

MAN AND MACHINE Machine specialization has often been damned for its presumably demoralizing effect upon the worker. Many writers, with perhaps an overly romanticized view of human toil in the past, have indicted the machine on the ground that it destroys the mental zest of the human operator. It has been argued that the machine process reduces the workman to such a narrow mechanical routine that the impulse to creativity is destroyed. Beatrice Webb, commenting on such effects of the Industrial Revolution in England, said, "That same revolution had deprived the manual workers—that is, four-fifths of the people of England—of their opportunity for spontaneity and freedom of initiative in production. It has transformed such of them as had been independent producers into hirelings and servants of another social class." [7] There has long been lively discussion of the issue on this side of the Atlantic. In typical American fashion, it gave rise in modern times to the "human relations" movement in industry. The recognition of the adverse consequences of mechanized work on human personality has resulted in the development of the sciences of industrial psychology, industrial sociology, and personnel management. Many programs for making occupations more tolerable have resulted. The whole issue, however, may eventually be resolved by modern automation.

We must remember in retrospect that the lot of most workmen under handicraft and other economies was often far worse than the conditions of present-day workmen. Edwin Markham, standing spellbound before Millet's "Man with the Hoe," asked with passion:

Is this the Thing the Lord God made and gave
To have dominion over sea and land;
To trace the stars and search the heavens for
    power;
To feel the passion of Eternity? [8]

Specialization now Characterizes All Forms of Occupational Activity

Division of labor and specialization not only came to manufacturing. They became a part of all phases of production in Western society. The classified index of occupations and industries of the 1950 United States Census, for example, lists 153 double-column pages of occupations and 75 triple-column pages of industries. Many of the professions, such as law or medicine, and most other occupations have become further subdivided into many specializations. There are over 15,000 specific occupations and 12,000 industries classified in the

United States Census at the present time. The *Dictionary of Occupational Titles* lists 39,000 occupations and 35,000 job definitions. This specialization is one of the major factors in the increased complexity of today's societies.

The Revolution Increased Quantity Production Enormously

The rate of production of goods and services by workers in Western societies varied little over the centuries before the Industrial Revolution. Then came this speedy expansion of industry leading to fantastic increases in production. In American society, total production of goods increased nearly 200 times while the population increased approximately 40 times from the beginning of its national existence. Productivity per worker increased sixfold in spite of a work week that is now only one-half as long as in the early days. It would have taken about 300 million workers in 1850 to produce what fewer than 60 million produced in 1960.

SERVICE WORKERS EXCEED PRODUCTION WORKERS American society passed a significant milestone in 1956. The number of people employed in the production of goods was fewer than the number employed in other activities—government, trade, finance, utilities, and transportation. The output of production workers in manufacturing, mining, agriculture, and construction has risen so rapidly that many workers have been released for employment in service occupations. This shift has had significant effects upon the occupational and social structure.

SCIENCE AND POWER THE CAUSES These changes have occurred because of the use of science and power-driven machines, not because of an increase in man's own work capacity. Workers need to put forth much less physical effort today to accomplish much more than under previous conditions. Work has become less arduous, yet productivity has increased manyfold. Each person in American society has six times as much energy working for him today as in 1900 and no less than 2,000 times as much as at the beginning of the nineteenth century. This has unloosed a flood of production, the end of which is not in sight. When atomic energy is harnessed to productive activities, the increase in production can reach fantastic levels.

AGRICULTURAL PRODUCTION AS AN ILLUSTRATION Agriculture illustrates this development remarkably well. We know that in 1820 it took 80 per cent of the population of the United States to raise the food and fiber necessary for the whole population; only 20 per cent were engaged in other pursuits. In 1960, less than 20 per cent of the population raised the food and fiber for the whole population and even then there was a large surplus. Over 80 per cent were engaged in other pursuits.

The United States Department of Agriculture announced, for example, that in 1957 farmers in this country intended to plant the smallest acreage of corn since 1885—74.4 million acres. They planned to do this when the country had 170 million people to feed compared with less than 60 million people in 1885. The dramatic fact here is the tremendous increase in productive yield by which vastly greater output is obtained from less acreage. Commercial fertilizers, plant breeding, and power-farming have brought this about.

There were no tractors on American farms in 1820. In 1960, there were over 4.5 million—more than one tractor to each farm. Over 55 million acres of crop land which had gone into feed for horses and mules became available for food for people by 1960 because of the substitution of tractors. (Nor should we overlook the fact that this revolution in technology also resulted in a vast improvement in the quality of goods and services we enjoy.)

Increase in Quantity and Quality of Production Brought a Rising Level of Living

The application of power machinery to the processing of economic goods has made possible a level of living in which serious want and prolonged privation are characteristic of only a small segment of American society. The necessities—food, clothing, shelter—are created in abundance. In addition, there are automobiles, telephones, radios, television, running water, paved and improved streets, public schools, sanitary systems, and virtually every other thing to provide good living conditions.

This does not mean, of course, that every area and every family has these things. There are lags in meeting the needs of "disadvantaged" areas and of many unfortunate and incapacitated people. But it does mean that all areas and families can have these commodities if the nonmaterial aspects of our social organization can be brought into balance with the ever-increasing wealth of goods and services.

THE EMPHASIS ON GOODS There are many people who are skeptical about the value of this rise in the level of living. They feel that material *things* are overemphasized at the expense of morale and spirit. This view, however, really hides the true meaning of these changes. This enrichment liberates man from material want. It gives the creative, the avocational, and the spiritual faculties a chance to develop. The society can produce a richer culture motivated by high ideals. "It is difficult," the Chinese proverb says, "to tell the difference between right and wrong when there is not enough food." Greece brought forth one of the remarkably creative cultural eras in world history when she had slaves to do the routine producing. Inanimate machines are the slaves in industrial societies.

A New Class Structure Resulted from the Industrial Revolution

In historical societies, people have been distributed in more or less separate classes on the basis of possessions, achievements, power, and status. These hierarchical aggregations developed common attitudes, values, and forms of behavior.

STRATIFICATION IN EUROPE BEFORE THE INDUSTRIAL REVOLUTION   European societies had a rigid stratification that had existed for centuries before the Industrial Revolution. It was a twofold differentiation in that the upper class was but a small part of the total population but it had control because it owned the land. It was further strengthened by a monopoly of the high offices in Church, army, and state. The burdens of the lower class can hardly be exaggerated. They varied over time only in the degree to which the privileged were exploitive or oppressive.

THE RISING MIDDLE CLASS   Prior to the Industrial Revolution, however, commerce and handicraft industry were expanding rapidly. The production of manufactured articles of every sort to be sold in faraway places increased on a large scale and gave strength to a rising middle class. Wholesalers, merchants, bankers, and major store operators were the controllers of business. Lawyers, government officials, judges, and public servants came from these families. Desire for power and privilege increased as their wealth increased. These middle-class leaders or bourgeoisie began to push aside the nobility and clergy who now were often financially dependent on them. The development of manufacturing enterprises added numbers and strength to this class. Only the capable and rich could organize and finance these activities.

The capitalist owners from commerce and industry took over and gave Western societies a new controlling class.

NEW LOWER CLASSES   New lower classes also came into being. Serfdom that bound men to the place of their birth and obligated them to a manorial lord passed away as the new economic order emerged. Town workers were emancipated from their trades as factories and new occupational opportunities developed. The doctrine of freedom in economic affairs—*laissez faire*—slowly spread to the workers. Working men became separated by differences in the skills required for their jobs. These changes resulted in an emergent lower or working class.

EARLY AMERICAN CLASS STRUCTURE   Early American society reflected European class distinctions. Differences in social relations began to appear as the mercantile class in the North and the plantation owners in the South rose to dominance. The early colonists, however, in both New England and the South, included only a few members of European nobility—"dukes don't migrate." They were largely recruited from exceedingly humble origins. Five classes were pretty well defined in this period: a top class of clergy and "gentlemen"; a second class of artisans and freeholders—"goodman" and "goodwife," they were called; a third class of unskilled workers, addressed by their first names only; a fourth class of indentured servants; and a fifth class of Indian and Negro slaves. Class distinctions were carefully respected. Only "ladies and gentlemen" could wear lace, silver, and gold; "goodman and goodwife" could not. Seating in church was guarded particularly and emphasized "dignity, age, and estate." [9] All this went before the winds of nineteenth-century industrialism.

Impersonal Relationships Characterized Industrial Production and Led to New Devices to Overcome Injurious Consequences

In the handicraft system, manufacturing was carried on chiefly in the homes of the workmen. Intimate associations existed among the workers. Masters might occasionally abuse apprentices, but direct associations engendered a concern for their welfare. These personal relationships were broken when the factory supplanted the domestic system.

EARLY CONDITIONS   In its beginnings, the factory system caused much misery for the workers. Workingmen and their families crowded industrial towns. Labor was plentiful. The capitalist doctrine justified making as much profit and paying as low wages as possible. Absentee investors were concerned only with dividends. Women and children as well as men had to work in the mills to earn enough for family survival.

Workers were helpless before the industrial magnates. At first, efforts of workingmen to organize were forbidden by law as injurious to industry and dangerous to society. There was a great lag between the swift development of production technology and the social arrangements for the protection of workers.

These circumstances led to some efforts at amelioration. Governments found it necessary to pass laws limiting age, hours, and conditions of work, especially for women and children. Combinations of workingmen were legalized in Europe at the end of the first quarter of the nineteenth century.

COLLECTIVE BARGAINING Organization for the purpose of bargaining collectively was labor's most effective weapon to deliver it from insecurity. Because the individual worker was powerless in the system, he had to organize. The labor union movement evolved in Europe and the United States between 1825 and the present time. In the United States, the struggle culminated in the Wagner Labor Disputes Act of July, 1935, which established the full legality of collective bargaining. The powerful labor union is thus one of the chief results of the Industrial Revolution.

NEW ECONOMIC PHILOSOPHIES Many questions arose concerning the ultimate implications of this new system. These issues have found expression in the clash of ideologies of the nineteenth and twentieth centuries. Just as capitalism challenged its forerunners, it is now under attack by other systems, especially that of communism. (These new systems will be discussed in later chapters.) As industrialism spreads over the world, the conflict becomes global.

References

1. Kroeber, A. L., *et al.*, *Anthropology Today* (Chicago, University of Chicago Press, 1953), pp. 77–193.
2. Chapin, F. Stuart, *Cultural Change* (New York, The Century Company, 1928), pp. 51 and 52. By permission of Appleton-Century-Croft, Inc.
3. United States Department of Commerce, Bureau of the Census, *Statistical Abstract of the United States, 1962*, Table 15, p. 24.
4. Bernard, William S., *American Immigration Policy—A Reappraisal* (New York, Harper and Brothers, 1950), and Bruce, J. C., *The Golden Door* (New York, Random House, 1954).
5. United States Department of Commerce, Bureau of the Census, *Statistical Abstract of the United States, 1961*, Table 25, p. 33. Also *Characteristics of the Population*, Vol. I, Part A (1960), Table P, p. xxv.
6. Berle, A. A., and Means, G. C., *The Modern Corporation and Private Property* (New York, The Macmillan Company, 1933), Chaps. 1 and 2, pp. 1–18.
7. Webb, Beatrice, *My Apprenticeship* (New York, Longmans, Green, & Co., 1926), p. 335.
8. Markham, Edwin, *The Man with the Hoe* (New York, Doubleday, and McClure Co., 1899), p. 16.
9. Wecter, Dixon, *The Saga of American Society* (New York, Charles Scribner's Sons, 1935), pp. 41 ff.

Questions for Study and Discussion

1. Give some illustrations of how the organization of our present-day society is rooted in the past.
2. Discuss the accumulation of tools in terms of its present-day social significance. Show how accumulation is significant in other areas of societal life.
3. Select a society and list briefly the cultural antecedents that influence its present-day organization and operation.

4. Select some antecedents from American society other than those presented in this chapter and show their significance in its organization and operation.
5. Show how the application of power-producing machinery ushered in a new era for the societies of the Western world.
6. Discuss the consequences of factory manufacturing on social relations and economic activity.
7. Consider the beneficial and detrimental consequences of division of labor and specialization in the functioning of societies.
8. What is the relationship of the industrial system to quantity and quality production of goods? To levels of living?
9. How was social class structure influenced in Western nations by the Industrial Revolution?
10. How is the development of modern cities related to the factory system and to division of labor?
11. How has the mechanization of agriculture in American society influenced its social organization?

Suggested Topics for Reports

1. Write a brief imaginative report on what might have been our experience and present status if the thirteen colonies had not gained their independence from England.
2. Using a census or other sources, chart the flow of immigrants from some one European nation to America and map the distribution of this population in the United States over the years.
3. Make a study of a new African nation showing how its cultural antecedents have affected its current development.

Supplementary Reading

Ashley, Roscoe L., *Our Contemporary Civilization*. New York: Henry Holt and Company, Inc., 1935.

Barnes, Harry Elmer, *An Economic History of the Western World*. New York: Harcourt, Brace and Company, 1937.

———, *History and Social Intelligence*. New York: Alfred A. Knopf, 1926.

Brunner, Edmund de S., and Hallenbeck, Wilbur C., *American Society: Urban and Rural Patterns*. New York: Harper and Brothers, 1955.

Chapin, F. Stuart, *Cultural Change*. New York: The Century Company, 1928.

Cheyney, E. P., *The European Background of American History*. New York: Harper and Brothers, 1904.

Gras, N. S. B., *An Introduction to Economic History*. New York: Harper and Brothers, 1922.

Hallenbeck, Wilbur C., *American Urban Communities*. New York: Harper and Brothers, 1951.

Odum, Howard, *Understanding Society*. New York: The Macmillan Company, 1947.

Robinson, James H., *Mind in the Making*. New York: Harper and Brothers, 1922.

Rose, Arnold M. (ed.), *The Institutions of Advanced Societies*. Minneapolis: University of Minnesota Press, 1958.

Russell, Bertrand, *Proposed Roads to Freedom*. New York: Henry Holt and Company, Inc., 1919.

Toynbee, Arnold J., *A Study of History*. Abridgment of Vols. 1–6 by D. C. Somervell. New York: Oxford Press, 1947.

PART TWO

THE FOUNDATIONS OF ORGANIZED SOCIAL BEHAVIOR:

Culture, Communication, Persons, and Structural Patterns

3

ENVIRONMENTAL ADJUSTMENT
AND CULTURE CREATION

P EOPLE *living together must make adaptations to the natural environment that surrounds them as well as to each other. The adjustments of men in groups to the natural environment result in their creation of physicosocial, biosocial, psychosocial, and institutional environments. Men are creating or adding to their culture, that is, their distinctive way of living, when, in adaptation to each other and the natural environments, they build these social environments.*

Culture, as the distinctive way of living in a society, is built by invention and discovery, accumulation, selection, and diffusion. Cultures vary from society to society because of differences in their environments, their isolation, their culture base and technological position, their dominant themes, and ethnocentrism.

Adaptation to Environment Is a Universal Phenomenon

We know that man everywhere, like all other animals, is dependent upon his natural environment. The earth is his dwelling place. He must adjust to it and the forces of the limitless space that influence it. The earth varies so greatly in what it offers for man's survival that adjustments vary widely. Consequently, his societies differ considerably. In one area, the climate is frigid or the soil is thin, and nature supplies few plants and animals: working together to get sufficient food and clothing must be continuous. In another region, the climate is torrid and enervating, but the soil is productive in abundance: man's life here is static. Climate is invigorating in another, but soil must be worked: man's labor here is stimulating, and his efforts to produce are successful. The environment may thus play varied roles in man's life. It sets an infinite range of possibilities that can become a part of his social organization if he avails himself of them. The social organizations man creates in these diverse circumstances reflect his adjustment to them.

I. THE NATURAL ENVIRONMENT

The Natural Environment Has Two Major Divisions: the Physical and the Biological [1]

We also know that man is everywhere surrounded by a world of nonliving materials and forces and a world of living forms—that of plants and animals. They make up the stage on which man plays out his drama. They are not active determinants of the way he plays but they set conditions and possibilities. Man is the actor. How well he performs depends upon how well he uses his capacities to transform these surroundings and makes them serve his own ends.

The physical environment includes soil, topography, climate, and natural resources, such as minerals and oil; natural physical agencies, such as winds, tides, and moving water; and natural physical forces, such as gravity, radiation, and combustion.

THE EARTH SPHERES An interesting way to view man's physical environment is in terms of its spheres. There is first the lithosphere. The earth itself is a rock sphere, and man lives *on* it. He is a creature of its surface because he does not spend much time within or above it. Some of his comrades bore within it to get certain of the materials of which it is composed—coal, oil, and iron, some fly above it when they want to travel at high speed, but the habitat of all is its surface. Man's adjustments are chiefly to that surface, and his adjustments to other men are related chiefly to parts of that surface.

Second, there is the hydrosphere. Three-fourths of the surface of this lithosphere is covered with water, found in varying forms—from brooks to oceans. Man's contacts with other men are conditioned by them. Useful materials are obtained from them in some places. The depth of the water level that courses beneath the rock surface conditions his production of plants. Water rights become important aspects of social organization.

Third is the atmosphere, the layer of air that surrounds the lithosphere. Man survives because it is abundant and essentially clean. One of his problems is to prevent its contamination with gases from industrial plants and other sources that make it injurious to him and other useful living forms. Smog, so called, is a real problem in some areas.

A few years ago, the atmosphere was used only as the source of this invisible, odorless, and tasteless mixture of gases that supports man's breathing. Today, one of his chief mediums of transportation utilizes it: the airplane, the air lane, and the airport are now elements of man's social organization. He must regulate the way the atmosphere is used.

Fourth, there is the stratosphere, that upper portion of the atmosphere in which temperature changes but little and clouds never form. Man is now invading this realm, using it to fly from one place to another more swiftly and easily. Our stratoliners already ply this zone.

The Physical Environment Influences Man and His Societies in Direct and Indirect Ways

SOIL Our adjustment to the earth's surface is probably our most important adaptation for we live primarily on and from it. There is the varied character of the soil itself that determines what crops, if any, we can produce. The sandy desert stretching from the west coast of Africa across its north and through the middle of Asia is thinly populated because it produces only enough plant life to sustain a few people and animals. The mountains of the Tibetan and

other regions likewise support only small populations.

There are soils that produce crop after crop in large areas, however. These crops influence the development of man's agricultural regions and his way of living. Rupert Vance, who has presented an excellent portrayal of these interrelationships for the cotton areas of the American South, makes a statement that has application to many societies: "There exists a kind of natural harmony about the cotton system. Its parts fit together so perfectly as to suggest the fatalism of design. Nature's harmony of the soil, the rainfall, the frostless seasons, the beaming sun, and a transplanted tropic plant fit well with a transplanted tropic race, landless white farmers, and the slow but all surviving mule to supply the world's steady demand for a cheap fabric. The spinner, the cotton buyer, the landlord, the supply merchant, and the cotton farmer form an economic harmony that often benefits all except the producer, a complex whole that is so closely interconnected that no one can suggest any place at which it may be attacked except the grower; and the grower is to change the system himself, cold comfort for advice." [2] A major concern in any society is our conservation of this soil, for not only do we and the animals get our basic sustenance from it, but also the pattern of our social organization is conditioned by its use.

TOPOGRAPHY The contour aspects of this lithosphere condition the number and spatial arrangements of persons able to live in an area. Mountains do not permit large population concentrations. A city built on a hill cannot be hidden, but very few cities are built on hills. Our cities and towns locate on the plains where access is easiest. The neighborhoods that develop in the mountain valleys suffer from isolation and are often clannish. The development of the individualistic family form in Norway was, in part, a product of the narrow valley topography of the land. The psychology of the people too is affected by this condition. Isolation is reduced with the coming of the automobile but topography is important still in limiting group organization.

Topography also influences the unity of whole populations. It is only our conjecture, but a reasonable one, that the Allegheny Mountains running down the east side of the American continent had much to do with the early development of the United States. The common interests which the early American colonists developed might never have come about if these mountains had not been there and the pioneers had spread out into the fertile Mississippi Valley. The United States could conceivably still be a part of the British Empire.

The presence of mountains has also kept people apart. As William Cowper puts it:

Mountains interposed make enemies of nations,
Who had else like kindred drops
Been mingled like one.[3]

CLIMATE   Climate is the condition brought about by the temperature, rainfall, and prevailing winds that create area conditions ranging from extreme cold to extreme heat. They subdivide our earth into frigid, temperate, and torrid zones. The rhythm of the seasons gives some climatic variability to each area, but the temperate zones offer the most advantages for man to make effective adjustments.

Because climate is difficult to modify, our greatest successes have been in adapting to it. Everywhere man has constructed buildings in one form or another to provide a comfortable mode of living and working. The Arctic region, where only ice and snow are available for construction, has seen ingenious uses of these materials in the construction of abodes insulated with mosses and skins. On the Scandinavian Peninsula, we find wooden homes insulated against cold by mosses and seaweed.

The pioneers on the American prairie, as in all other places, faced the problem of shelter. The sod hut was a first adaptation. Rose Lee Wilder says of it: "Nothing could have been more cozy for wintertime, cooler in the summers." [4] Eventually came the modern structures whose central heating, insulation, and air conditioning give man living and working environments that let him forget the weather.

Adaptations are made too in extremely hot areas. Light clothing, open houses, adjustment of working hours, and siesta periods to overcome the debilitating effect of the heat are all aspects of the adaptations man has learned to make. Such plays as "White Cargo" and "Rain" have portrayed the influence of the heat and the humidity upon the bodies of men and also upon their mental outlooks.

RAINFALL   Rainfall, the basic provider of the lithosphere's water, is also an important conditioner of our adjustments. One of the critical needs in wide areas is for water of the right kind, at the right time, in the right place, and in the right amounts, while elsewhere most of

Modification of the natural environment: a fish trapping dam in a Congo forest and a power dam in western America.

the earth is covered with it. We sail for days across the Pacific Ocean and see on all sides water stretching to the horizons or watch the endless flow day after day of a mighty river like the Mississippi. We wonder why there needs to be a shortage of this commonplace substance. The rain falls on the just and the unjust alike, but it does not fall in all places alike. Egypt has less than one-half inch of rain per year. Were it not for the Nile, fed by the rains of central Africa, it would be as uninhabitable as the deserts to its east and west. The regular rainfall of the Mississippi Valley, on the other hand, supports an extensive agriculture that is the foundation of the way of life for a vast population.

Results are often disastrous when the rains do not come in areas that depend on them. Pearl Buck describes their significance in an area of China where famine stalked the land. When the rains of early summer did not come and the sun shone brilliantly each day, the earth dried up and cracked. The grain, which had sprouted and began to head out in the early season, stopped developing in spite of careful cultivation and finally gave only an insignificant harvest.[5]

Modern living places heavy demands on the natural water supply and is a major reason for many difficulties. The daily requirements of water for household and lawn purposes is 60 or more gallons per person per day in a society like the American, compared to five or six gallons among primitive people. Industry and agriculture make additional demands. The annual water supply bill for this society is estimated at 3 billion dollars per year. Maintaining a proper water supply is a major concern even in those areas where rainfall is considerable.[6]

WIND   The winds too are climatic features to which we must adjust. The gentle breezes bring our quiet rain and our growing grain, but the hot or cold blasts may burn or freeze it all. When the winds become violent and develop into cyclones or hurricanes, seemingly little stands against them. Their results are catastrophes.

The Presence or Absence of Such Resources as Coal, Iron, Oil, and Other Metals also Condition Man's Adjustments to the Physical Environment

Our adjustment to natural resources is an excellent illustration of the role the physical environment plays in our life. They cannot condition us directly if they are absent in the environment, but they may have no influence upon us even if they are present. Generation after generation of people have lived where many of these natural resources were plentiful, but they did not affect their way of living. Coal and iron have been around men for centuries in many places, but they play no part in their environments because they are not found and used.

OIL IN AMERICA   The first oil well in America was drilled at Titusville, Pennsylvania, in 1859. Before this time, white men had made the "dis-covery" when they came upon Indians who were soaking blankets with oil that came to the surface of a spring, then wringing the oil from the blankets and using it for lighting purposes. The Indians had not moved beyond this elemental step in its use. No one knows how long they had been following this practice, but its discovery by a people who knew how to exploit its potentialities made oil a chief element in our American industrial society. So it is with other components of the physical environment. We cannot yet change or control some of these, but our adaptations and uses are extensive where we have knowledge and ingenuity.

The Biological Environment of Plants and Animals also Requires Adjustments by Man

We are not only surrounded by physical materials and forces to which we adjust; there is also a world of natural living forms that also influence us—plants and animals. They appear in nature in visible and invisible forms. They include animals which we domesticate for food and clothing and others that are dangerous or destructive; plants that supply fuel, building materials, and food products as well as those that are poisonous or useless to us; insects and parasites that are directly harmful and innumerable microscopic forms, some of which produce diseases in man, animals, and plants while others are active in breaking down physical matter into usable forms for plants or aid in bodily processes.

The Natural Biological Environments Have Many Effects on the Societies of Men, Just as Do the Physical Environments

Usually we give attention to the influence of the larger living forms upon us. But the smaller, invisible forms are also significant in their effects. Man would probably not survive if it were not for the beneficent activities of soil bacteria. These aerate the soil, break down organic matter into plant foods, and fix atmospheric nitrogen in the soils, thus permitting the survival of plants and animals that we depend upon for our food supply. This account does not include all the essential factors for our survival, but it does indicate the role a part of this invisible world plays for us.

GERM THEORY OF DISEASE   Perhaps no discovery has had more important consequences for our survival than the discovery of the germ theory of disease. The spread of this knowledge to millions of people who think diseases result from the acts of demons or from other fallacious causes is one of our most important social tasks. Adequate information about the role of these invisible forms in disease production contributes to the reduction of illness and deaths from malaria, bilharzia, tuberculosis, and other diseases due to bacterial invasions of the body. It also aids in introducing the scientific viewpoint toward life.

The Larger Animals in Their Natural State also Condition Man's Societies

We adapt to the many types of animals on the earth by domesticating and breeding some as food and clothing resources and by avoiding or destroying others that are injurious to us.

DESTRUCTIVE ANIMALS One of our struggles is against destructive animals. The activities of small and large animals continue to hinder the efforts of American farmers to maintain an efficient agriculture. Such animals as deer, rabbits, and rats destroy quantities of grain. The pioneers encountered even greater difficulties from these sources.[7] Grasshoppers, locusts, and other insects too are man's formidable enemies, coming as certain as the seasons to devour grain, vegetables, and leaves.

FOOD AND CLOTHING SOURCES We have used some animals in their natural state to supply food and clothing. The direct use of these animal and plant products supplements organized production. Again, pioneers usually made use of these available natural materials. In the *Autobiography of a Farm Boy*, Dean I. P. Roberts listed some of those that were used in his New York community: "On our homestead, for instance, there were ten varieties of apples, peaches to eat, to dry and to drink in the form of brandy; plums, pears, quinces, cherries and grapes; wild strawberries, blackberries, huckleberries, red and black raspberries, elderberries and cranberries three miles away in the marsh; and currants and gooseberries by the bushel. . . . Plenty of game, too, especially squirrels, black, red and gray; pigeons in their season, wild ducks and geese at the foot of the lake six miles away. . . . There was an abundance of fish to be had by line or seine, to fry or salt down as you liked." [8]

RECREATION Adaptation to animals in their natural state has developed into major recreational activities in most societies. Hunting animals and birds as well as fishing are popular sports. New York State, for example, sold nearly 4 million dollars worth of licenses for hunting and fishing in the state for the year April 1, 1953, to March 31, 1954.[9] When this amount is extended proportionately to all the other states of this society, it would indicate that this type of adaptation is widespread.

The Larger Plants also Require Adaptations

Trees and plants provide us with material for fuel, clothing, and shelter, and their seeds yield fruits, nuts, and grains. Some provide materials for medicines, weapons, and tools.

PLANTS AS OBSTACLES Trees and plants are formidable obstacles when their growth is uncontrolled. Some are poisonous and call for special care in handling. Many contain chemical substances that man has learned to use in medicines and as coloring materials. In the Ozark region of Missouri, for example, cloth is still given a brown color by putting it in a solution made from walnut hulls, maple, or butternut bark.

II. THE SOCIAL ENVIRONMENT

Man Creates a Social Environment Which Is Derived from His Adaptations to the Natural Environment and to Other Men

We have so far considered environmental adjustment to the physical and biological divisions of the natural environment in their unchanged and unmodified form. Some of our illustrations indicated, however, that man modifies these elements as he adapts to them. He changes their form and character to better serve his needs and purposes. He thus fashions a new environment, the social. It consists, in part, of all the nonliving and living forms that man develops by invention and domestication. These processes transform the original qualities of inanimate and animate substances in ways that bear the imprint of his creativeness. The objects he creates from nonliving materials are the *physicosocial* division; those he creates from living materials constitute the *biosocial* division of his *social* environment.

The Physicosocial Environment of a Society Includes Both Simple and Complex Physical Objects

SOCIALLY CREATED OBJECTS Regard the paper clip. The man who invented it made a sizable fortune. We recognize it as a physical object for it is made of metal, an inorganic substance. But this clip is more than a physical object; it is a social object as well. The metal was mined, processed to remove impurities, shaped into wire, and coated and pressed into its final form by human labor. It is not a part of the environment of societies which have no need for clipping paper together. But it is a vital, perhaps indispensable, device in modern society. It is not, therefore, simply a physical object but a physicosocial object.

Such artifacts are produced for almost all aspects of our life. In a sense, many of them are extensions of our physiological equipment—arms, hands, legs. Flying overhead is a large intricate machine—an airplane. It too is both a physical and social object, an interrelated unit of humanly formed physical parts built into a single system powered by man for flying. A vast collection of such socially created material objects that make up the physicosocial environment of societies lies between these two extremes—the paper clip and airplane—and, indeed, extends far beyond them. Physicosocial objects are so much a part of American culture that people from other societies sometimes criticize us as being too materialistic. Almost every human service among us—from baking bread to teaching school—employs great quantities of physicosocial objects.

MASTERY GIVEN This physicosocial environment results from our efforts to master our surroundings. The objects in and of themselves are nonmoral. The sheer use of such things in any area of life is not a moral question. *How* we use them may involve moral principles. We

Traditional tools used by the native Congolese blacksmith.

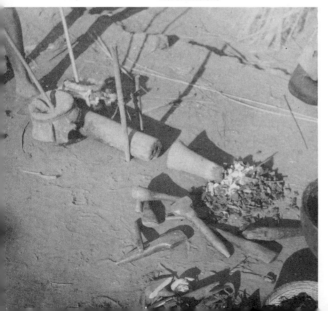

might even ask if it is not immoral for us to fail to use our ingenuity to develop physicosocial objects as completely as possible for better adjustment to our environment. There is no necessary truth in the statement Prime Minister Nehru is reported to have made to Bishop Oxnam: "As the machine becomes more human, the human becomes more machine-like."

PHYSICOSOCIAL TOOLS The primary function of the components of the physicosocial environment is, of course, to serve as tools. Everywhere men are tool-makers and tool-users. We differ from other animals in that we alone make and use tools. Societies do vary greatly in the extent to which they have developed these physicosocial materials, but as Carlyle put it, a long time ago: "Man is a Tool-using Animal. . . . Nowhere do you find him without Tools; without Tools he is nothing, with Tools he is all." [10]

AVOCATIONS But man creates physicosocial objects other than tractors and ball-point pens to serve his ends. He makes ice skates, baseballs, football stadia, artists' stands, cameras, clarinets, and a host of other things that serve his avocational and recreational purposes. Some he creates just for the sheer pleasure of aesthetic experience. Jewelry, pottery,. statues, monuments, paintings—to indicate a few—are a physicosocial world that add the beautiful to the useful and necessary. All these make worlds of physical objects which we enjoy and to which we adjust.

The Biosocial Environment Includes the Animals and Plants Man Has Adapted for His Uses

We also change some of the natural animals and plants to fashion biosocial environments in which we function.

Cultivated corn or rice, domesticated cows or water buffaloes, are not just biological forms; each is also as much a social form as an automobile is. The original characteristics of these living things are changed so that they differ from their wild states. These domesticated plants and animals provide us with food, clothing, shelter, tools, ornaments, pets, and power sources. Agriculture, as the industry for producing domesticated plants and animals, is the chief part of this biosocial environment.

DOMESTICATION OF PLANTS AND ANIMALS How man domesticates living forms is a fascinating story. The breeding of maize, or Indian corn, is an historic illustration. Originally, it grew in wild bushy form in the tropical countries of Central America. The Indians taught the white settlers along the James River in Virginia to use and produce it. By 1800, over 2 million bushels were exported from the American colonies, which indicates the rapid growth in its production. A century and a half later, the corn crop for the United States was just under 3.5 billion bushels. While the tremendous expansion of acreage accounts for much of this production, the breeding of highly productive varieties and the development of hybrids have played an important role. The Midwest corn belt is a dominant region in American society which determines the activities of millions of people and shapes the social system in which they play their roles. Similar illustrations could be given for all the chief plants and animals we now include in our biosocial world.

Here then is a derived social world of biological forms that is a basic part of the drama of human societies and in which our activities as individuals are involved from birth. Edna Ferber expresses this in her *American Beauty* wherein one of her child characters is constantly being impressed by the importance of the tobacco crops. If the crops were good and abundant, then the father could add farm tools and animals, the mother could buy better clothes, and the rest of the family would also enjoy things they wanted.[11]

The Psychosocial Environment Is the Result of Man's Adjustments to Other Men as They Together Adapt to the Natural Environment

Men adjust to the natural environments and fashion parts of their social environment composed of physical and biological objects. But because men practically always operate in interrelationship with other men in these adaptations, and because they also adapt directly to other men, they create an environment based on the interactions among them. The repeated, uniform, and approved ways of thinking that come from the interrelationships are mirrored in repeated, uniform, and approved ways of acting. So man establishes his "idea worlds" that are the thought patterns of his societies, which express themselves in societal action patterns just as individuals develop habits of thought that guide individual habits of action.

ORDER AND STABILITY Societies would be impossible if there were no uniform ways of thinking expressed in sanctioned ways of per-

Pygmy of Ituri forests playing a musical bow and Congolese-Bapende musicians performing on a xylophone.

forming because instability would disrupt the daily operations of a society. We see millions of people conduct business, exchange messages, do jobs, and associate peacefully with remarkably little confusion or delay and repeat their performance daily because their relationships are systematized through these patterned ways of thinking and acting that become the norms or standards for the behavior of the individual.

TRADITIONS AND CUSTOMS The uniform sanctioned habits of thought we follow in a society are its *traditions*, transmitted from generation to generation as the society's meanings, norms, and values. The uniform approved ways of acting we follow are its *customs*, transmitted from generation to generation by tradition and usually made effective by social approval. Each custom has behind it a tradition; they must be bound together for the sanctioned act is an expression of a socially sanctioned idea. The American custom of observing the Fourth of July as a holiday expresses the idea of patriotism, specifically through recognizing the anniversary of the signing of the Declaration of Independence. Bowing more gracefully, more deeply, and more often than the person to whom one is bowing is a Japanese custom that rests on the idea of proper deference to others. Customs supported by traditions develop with respect to virtually all areas of social life: eating, dressing, mourning, rejoicing, attending school, religious observances, greeting others, burial of the dead, and treating strangers. No aspect of life that involves others escapes this formalizing process since it establishes acceptable adjustments among people. Bacon said: "Since custom is the principal magistrate of man's life, let men by all means endeavor to obtain good customs." [12]

These customary ways of thinking and acting that serve as the "magistrates" of our lives arise as slow, unpremeditated accumulations of social experience under changing environmental circumstances. They are based in most instances on their successful use by individuals in satisfying personal purposes. For example, it is said that the custom of shaking hands in greeting was a way of being sure that neither person held a deadly weapon. Over a period of time, it became a customary act of greeting, and its origin was lost in the dim past.

The Total Body of a Society's Traditions and Customs Constitute Its Folkways

William Graham Sumner coined the term "folkways" to describe these uniform ways of thinking and acting which we follow in a society.[13] They prescribe the rules of conduct that are deemed the right ways and are usually followed in the same manner without reflection or thought. Often we do not know why we conform to these social usages. They originated as effective means to some societal ends, became standardized, and have been automatically transferred from generation to generation. They make up the important *norms* or rules we absorb and follow, although their origins may not be known to us.

Conformity to the folkways is expected of each member of society, so that order is maintained and the values of the society preserved. Driving or walking on the side of the road, eating at given periods and in definite ways with prescribed instruments, marrying and raising a family in the prescribed manner—all dictated by the folkways—are examples of ways that maintain the smooth operation of our social system.

CONFORMITY A KEY OBJECTIVE Thus conformity to the patterned ways is a key objective in every society. Societies begin to assure this conformity through the early education of children. Here the attitudes of others who already follow these norms are made a part of the child's attitudes and habits. He is given approval on the basis of the way he acts. The child learns to rise automatically with others when the flag of the nation passes in review, to wear his clothing just as others in his society do, or to show respect for elders in the manner his society prescribes. Our automatic performance of acts supported by social approval is exceedingly useful to us as individuals also, for we do not then have to solve a problem every time the same situation arises.

Some of these customary ways are not rigidly prescribed, though we are expected to follow them. In our society we do not *have* to shake hands or bow when greeting a friend or tip our hat to women or elderly persons when we meet them. We may be considered ill-mannered if we do not follow the customs, but there is no compulsion to do so.

CONFORMITY NOT AUTOMATIC Most people will usually follow the folkways. Others, however, do not do so closely, and a few may largely ignore them. The same people may observe some folkways closely while not observing others. A business man may be scrupulously honest in his business activities, yet drive his automobile at a speed and in a manner not in conformity with the norms or rules of the road. Our behavior in conformity with the social norms is not automatic; instead, it depends finally upon the extent and type of our conditioning. Societies continually remind their members of those customary ways that maintain the welfare of the whole community and use many methods to assure observance. (See Chapter 24, on social control, for further discussion.)

Some of the Folkways Become Compulsive and Are Called the Mores

Some of our uniform ways of thinking and acting that establish the norms for our behavior become not only proper ways of thinking and acting but the *only* right ways of thinking and acting. They then move up to the plane of compulsion. Their "rightness" is associated with our view of the welfare of the society. They are not only judged useful but necessary to our society's well-being and survival and so are ethically supported principles and practices that we must follow. They are called the "mores" when they reach this stage.

William Graham Sumner introduced this term. It is the plural of the Latin noun *mos*, meaning manner or custom. He added the idea of right, truth, and welfare by saying: "The Latin word 'mores' seems to be, on the whole, more practically convenient and available than any other for our purpose, as a name for the folkways with the connotations of right and truth in respect to welfare embodied in them." [14]

INVIOLATENESS OF THE MORES Societies endeavor to obtain conformity to the mores to facilitate their smooth operation. Of equal importance, they also seek to *conserve* themselves through them. A society makes them inviolate and exerts coercion to obtain observance if the norms have utility for the whole group and are considered vital to its existence.

A class of university students once visited a state prison. One of the students asked why a certain inmate was in prison. He was told that the man had two wives at the same time—a serious violation of our mores for American society allows only one wife at a time. Our society enforces this obligatory norm because it feels that deviation threatens a basic institution—the family—as well as society at large. Such enforced rules apply not only to family, but to property, education, decency practices, treatment of persons and animals, and many other situations involving the supreme values of society.

The Mores Usually Become Written Laws in Constitutional Societies

Usually, people abide by these rules not only because they are part of the approved social heritage, but also because disobedience incurs the extreme disfavor of associates. But when some persons invariably disobey certain rules, societies stipulate what is to be done in such cases. The definitions of these obligatory rules and the stipulation of consequences of their violation may not be in written form. They may be nonetheless effective, as social control in preliterate societies demonstrates.

WRITTEN LAWS The mores usually express themselves in written laws which define the acts and prescribe the penalties when the society operates through established governmental institutions. Not all of the mores are expressed as legal norms. On the other hand, there are many laws that express other controls of social organization than those contained in the mores. Laws are the rules made by an authorized government to define specific acts for the purpose of promoting orderly societal operation. The mores or obligatory norms are uniform, sanctioned ways of acting that have the force of law and are expressed as laws in most societies. Certain practices had the force of law in pioneer societies and often were laws, although enforcement was difficult because of the lack of officers. There "the law" was often executed by the injured persons who took "the law" into their own hands. Horse and cattle thieves were summarily hanged by the citizens in the pioneer West in America. The development of the organization of the society is important in new areas if the orderly enforcement of the mores is to supplant the disorderly.

The Mores Change but Only as a Consequence of Strong Pressures

The mores change only under the strongest pressures and over a long period of time since they express important values, set the basic standards, are considered indispensable to survival, and often become fixed in the law. It was considered right to own human beings and use them as chattels (slavery) in early American society. This practice had been a part of the organization of societies for many centuries, but it had been challenged on moral grounds as early as Augustine (354–430 A.D.). It was challenged in the same manner in early American society, especially in the North, on the grounds that it reduced human beings to things with no personal dignity. But in the South, where it provided necessary labor, it was fixed in the mores. It took years of agitation and finally a war between the states to achieve its abolition.

INDIA'S PROBLEM Change in the customary sanctioned ways may result from changes in the mode of life in a society brought about by social forces, such as industrialization, or through contact with other societies. India is experiencing many problems from these two circumstances. The use of automobile buses for human transportation makes it impossible for different castes to avoid associating with each other. The development of factories is compelling the breakdown of occupational separation on a caste basis. The dilemmas arising from such change may be illustrated in the following episode.

A few years ago a young "untouchable" in India heard cries for help from a well, jumped in, and rescued a child from drowning. It became known that he was an "untouchable" after the first compliments had been offered. The attitude of the crowd underwent an immediate change. Praise was turned to abuse: the "untouchable" had trespassed into a high caste compound and polluted the well by jumping into it. Today, this reaction would have occurred only among very conservative Hindus. The mores of any society are challenged by significant changes in the way of living in spite of opposition from those determined to uphold them

Fads, Fashions, and Crazes Are Imitative Phenomena

The folkways and mores are the significant aspects of the psychosocial environment because they express the chief norms of a society. But the relationships between people and their adaptations to the natural environments result in other psychosocial forms of interaction. We refer here to fashions, fads, crazes, beliefs, superstitions, taboos, rites, rituals, ceremonials, and science—and to the symbols through which we express them, such as books, magazines, pictures, statuary, musical compositions, and other forms with symbolic meaning.

FASHION A few years ago large numbers of male students at universities and colleges in America wore short leather jackets as topcoats. A year later a wool topcoat of various colors was the style. Then the rain-repellent coat with an inner lining followed. These students were following *fashion*.

Most people follow fashion as far as economic ability and social situation allow. In this respect, we try to be like others in groups with which we identify. We may here, for example, be expressing our desire for recognition from those in our social class and our desire to be different from those of other levels.

FADS AND CRAZES Such imitation followed with exaggerated enthusiasm and for a short time is a *fad* or a *craze*. Playing miniature golf swept across the United States some time ago. Elaborate equipment was built into many of these golf courses, and people of all ages were putting golf balls through pipes, tunnels, and over little bridges. The fad lasted only a year or so. Now, years after, we see a resurgence of this pastime.

Fashions and fads are not limited to dress or recreation alone for they occur in most areas of our activity. However, when particular ones —women's dresses, for example—are followed too generally, they are abandoned. Few women in American society dress identically except by accident.

Perhaps the important characteristic of fashions and fads in the psychosocial environment is that they "place no dependence on really vital motives of human action."[15] Our fashions in dress, for example, do not violate the demand of the mores that persons be acceptably dressed. Ridicule and other social pressures will usually force the abandonment of extreme variations in dress or other fashions.

Beliefs, Superstitions, and Taboos Express the Adoption of Ideas About Parts of Life as True

We develop *beliefs* in our adaptation to the natural environment and to each other. Beliefs are the acceptance of propositions about some part of life as true. They may be true or they may be false, but once we make them a part of our social system we do not easily or willingly relinquish them. Often impervious to reason or truth, they can hardly be extracted when once built into the thought patterns of youth. They are like frescoing. In this process, color is mixed through soft plaster then spread before it dries. The original color may be painted over, but it still remains in the plaster. Beliefs instilled early have the same persistent character. This would imply that our chief hope for making the most advantageous adjustments to our environments is in the development of beliefs based on validated knowledge.

SUPERSTITIONS Beliefs that are not founded on fact are *superstitions* that usually arise out of ignorance and fear of the unknown. One writer reports an illustrative experience: "The operator of a small boat on a river in central China passed from one passenger to another whispering something in each person's ear. My companion turned to me after the operator passed and said, 'Do not talk as long as we are passing under the bridge just ahead.' I kept silent. After the other passengers, all Chinese, began to talk, I asked why it was necessary to be silent when passing under the bridge. 'There is the belief among these river boatmen that if one talks while passing under the bridge, the river gods are offended.' The persons who talked are held responsible if anything happens to the boat on the journey." Such superstitions exist in many areas of life. We all seem to have some, even the man, who, when asked if he was superstitious, said, "Oh, no, but I better knock on wood."

TABOOS Many of our beliefs result in *taboos*, which is the setting aside of things or practices as forbidden by tradition and social authority. The Mormons erected a monument in Temple Square, Salt Lake City, to the gulls because these birds appeared at a critical time in early Mormon history and devoured the locusts which were destroying the crops. They also established a rule against killing these birds. Its origin illustrates the way such taboos may come about. A crisis—the destruction by locusts of food crops on which survival depended—was not controlled by the techniques available so the people turned to God to aid them. Fortunately, the gulls appeared and destroyed the insects, and this was interpreted as an answer to prayer. The people credited God with sending the gulls and gave the gulls a venerable place in their religious system by forbidding their destruction and by erecting a monument to remind the people of the occurrence. Now a taboo prevails.

SOCIAL VALUE OF BELIEF Beliefs, whether true or not, may serve socially valuable ends. They can support respect for law and the rights of others and establish firm attitudes toward social institutions, thus aiding their effective operation. Belief in the rightness of a governmental form, such as democracy, or the sacredness of a social relationship, such as marriage, contributes to acceptable behavior. The belief of the Tibetans that God sends down an incarnation of Himself into every generation results in great veneration for the person so designated and in genuine obedience to him. The danger in many beliefs is that they do not allow reason to work and may become so fixed that they stand in the way of new ideas.

Rituals, Rites, and Ceremonies Are Used to Emphasize the Importance of Certain Social Situations

Rituals, *rites*, and *ceremonies* are types of social actions used in societies to impress the significance of particular occasions, events, persons, or conditions upon all or some part of their members. Serving to move people by their appeal to the emotions through solemnity, gaiety, or beauty, they help to reinforce the values of segments of the society and to fix loyalty to them. They also point up the reality of the group to the members who are participating. For example, because the Sacrament of the Lord's supper is a definite part of the Christian Church organization, it emphasizes its reality.

Following a definite order in the conduct of religious services or lodge sessions illustrates

African pygmoids perform rites in preparation for the hunt.

Eskimo blanket-tossing ceremony celebrating a successful whale hunt.

our use of ritual and ceremony to celebrate particular practices. As these repeated actions condition all the persons involved to enter into the performance, they become a part of it rather than remain mere onlookers. Granting awards that have significance to a group for winning an athletic contest, completing a doctor's degree in an educational field, or obtaining a Nobel prize for literature are accompanied by ceremonies that illustrate their use in respect to particular achievements. Births, deaths, marriages, baptisms, and the signing of treaties and laws are ceremonialized as special occasions worthy of particular note. Initiations into offices represent ceremonies that recognize important changes in social status. The holidays —Christmas, Thanksgiving, the Fourth of July —all mark past events that are ceremonialized to epitomize an important phase of the life of the society. Each society develops rituals, rites, and ceremonies about practices and events that have significance to it. Such psychosocial forms aid social control by inducing loyalty.

SYMBOLISM IN RITES Our rituals, rites, and ceremonies use symbolism to promote their purposes. The symbolism usually stands for practices that will advance the welfare of the group. Without having direct efficacy in achieving the goal, it does call forth behavior that will express the group norms. However, in the course of time, some of these symbolic forms are credited with having direct power. The birth and purification rites of some primitive people who fear pregnancies and births, because they do not understand them, are thought to have cleansing power or the capacity to ward off evil spirits. Such forms, therefore, often stand in the way of the acceptance of practices that are more scientific and effective.

This problem also arises in modern societies. A familiar rite expresses the dedication of a child or adult to the practice of Christian principles as enjoined in the Christian baptismal ceremony. But many adherents believe the rite itself to have some kind of transforming power and that it must be performed in a distinctive manner to be effective. When rites or ceremonies are invested with direct powers, they may aid in controlling action just as any other superstition, but they make it difficult for reasoned action to take place. Once given the support of religious systems, many adherents accept rituals on authority and do little thinking about them.

Science Seeks the Principles by Which Phenomena Operate

Science is a most important aspect of our psychosocial environment. We define it as the measurement of related facts, relative to a specific order of phenomena, that is used to discover the principles by which these phenomena operate. Science tries to describe the universal aspects of the components of the environment to arrive at the permanent in the changing. It accomplishes this through (1) the careful observation and (2) classification of facts so as to make possible (3) descriptive generalizations that can be subjected to (4) verification. Since the generalizations of science are impersonal and verifiable, it is the most reliable method of discriminating between truth and error in man's effort to know. It subjects itself to constant self-criticism by dealing with phenomena as they are and recognizing no authority but the facts. No generalization is recognized as final in the face of new facts. The problem of control in societies will be greatly advanced when the content of our psychosocial environment can be described in scientific generalizations.

The Symbols We Devise to Transfer These Psychosocial Materials Are the Reservoirs for Our Psychosocial Environment

In the following chapter on communication, we shall show more specifically how language becomes written and materials are produced that can be handed from person to person and generation to generation. Thus, man has developed the symbols of books, magazines, and periodicals to be storage reservoirs for beliefs, traditions, customs, and scientific findings. Those who know the symbols can use the material. Other symbolic forms, such as paintings, pictures, sculptures, and art objects, that carry meaning to those who use them are also parts of this psychosocial environment. All of it constitutes a storage house of standardized symbols for conveying the content and meaning of this environment.

A Social Control Environment Is Developed to Provide the Mechanisms Through Which Controls May Operate

We have discussed the physicosocial, the biosocial, and the psychosocial levels of the total social environment that man creates about him. We have indicated that these features of the social environment include physical objects, do-

Two forms of cultural symbolism: the Oriental makes obeisant gesture to the tortoise; the head gear of a Bapende territorial chief is a symbol of his office.

mesticated plants and animals, modes of thought, beliefs, customs, mores, books, pamphlets, and other symbolic materials. The fourth important layer remains to be described.

Men in their relations to other men must have structures through which the various social elements can operate. Modes of thought, beliefs, customs, and mores require mechanisms to order and control their expression. Men develop this part of their social environment by the process of institutionalization leading to the formation of institutions and organizations and other less permanent social structures which channel behavior.

INSTITUTIONS AND ORGANIZATIONS *Institutions* are established normative patterns operating through institutional agencies which men develop to achieve the basic needs or objectives of a society. *Organizations* are systematically arranged units of people developed to achieve some specific objective or interest. We establish schools, churches, governments, and other institutional agencies through which the socially required forms of behavior can be expressed. We create lodges, clubs, scientific societies, and hosts of other organizations through which some common interest of a part of society may be realized. These constitute the chief structures in a society's control process. We will consider them more completely in later chapters since they are distinctive types of human relationship structures and play important roles in the operation of society. Institutional agencies and organizations are, however, specific parts of the social environment. As such, they condition the actions of individuals and groups in a society and serve as procedural means through which our adjustments can be made.

III. CULTURE AND CULTURE CREATION

The Adjustment of Men to the Environments and Their Production of the Social Environment Is Culture-Building

Man alone of all the animals creates and transmits a social environment; it is his unique characteristic. Other animals can acquire behavior patterns by imitating other animals or by resorting to trial and error. But they can do this only to a limited extent. They do not transmit their learned activities to future generations through language and other symbolic systems. Neither can they make physical objects to use as tools in their efforts to get food, shelter, and other goods, except within the narrow limits of their biological heredity, nor can they pass them on to succeeding generations. Man in adjusting to the natural environment —and to his fellows—fashions vast quantities of physical and biological materials and large bodies of thought and action patterns. All of these he uses to fulfill his desires and needs, which makes it possible for him to satisfy present and expanding wants, to satisfy new values and express creative desires, to store products

for future use, and to transmit them to succeeding generations through the symbol systems he evolves.

Culture Defined

The total content of this produced social environment of a society is its culture. It is the integrated, interdependent whole of these socially produced and socially inherited action patterns built around a body of socially created physical and biological materials. The *culture* of a society is, therefore, the total content of the physicosocial, biosocial, and psychosocial universes man has produced and the socially created mechanisms through which these social products operate. We build our society's cultural system as we recreate our natural environment and pattern our relations to each other. This is a society's way of living—the culture and the total social environment are synonymous.[16]

STRESS OF OTHER DEFINITIONS ON TOTALITY OF CREATED ENVIRONMENTS There are many definitions of culture in the sociological and anthropological literature. Most authors include all the major social components that bind men together in a society. Goldenweiser, an anthropologist, considers the culture of a society to include "our attitudes, beliefs and ideas, our judgments and values; our institutions, political and legal, religious and economic; our ethical code and code of etiquette; our books and machines; our science, philosophies and philosophers—all these things and many other things and beings, both in themselves and in their multiform inter-relations."[17] Cooley, Angell, and Carr say: "Culture is the entire accumulation of artificial objects, conditions, tools, techniques, ideas, symbols, and behavior-patterns peculiar to a group of people, possessing a certain consistency of its own, and capable of transmission from one generation to another. Culture, in other words, is the sum total of the transmittable results of living together."[18]

Others give briefer definitions. Sumner and Keller say: "The sum of men's adjustments to their life-conditions is their culture."[19] Sapir says it is technically defined by the culture-historian "to embody any socially inherited element in the life of man, material and spiritual." He uses the concept to "embrace in a single term those general attitudes, views of life, and specific manifestations of civilization that give a particular people its distinctive place in the world."[20] Bierstedt says: "Culture is the complex whole that consists of everything we think and do and have as members of society." [21]

These definitions and many others emphasize for us the important features of a culture: (1) it is a product created by the interactions between men in adaptation to their environments; (2) it includes all material and nonmaterial creations of man; (3) it is transmittable from generation to generation; and (4) it constitutes the social heritage of a society. Every child born in a society has his pattern of living determined by his social heritage. It is this heritage that binds us to and makes us part of our society.

The Parts of a Culture Are Conceptualized as Traits, Complexes, and Patterns

All societies have a culture, that is, a patterned whole consisting of the material and nonmaterial substances that give them designs for operating. All cultures have the same general basic organization although the cultures developed by societies vary one from another. The parts of these cultures have been conceptualized as culture traits, culture complexes, and culture patterns.

TRAITS *Culture traits* are the single elements or smallest units of a culture system we recognize for purposes of analysis. They may be folkways, such as the Chinese shaking their own hands and bowing slightly when greeting a friend, or a fork used for eating food in American society. Each of these elements of two different cultures can be described as unit acts or things distinctive to the culture. Any culture can be seen to include thousands of such unit acts and objects when we analyze the whole into its particular parts. The electric refrigerator is viewed as a culture trait of American society when we use it to illustrate a material component of this society. The high regard for the aged is a culture trait of the Japanese when seen as a nonmaterial component of their society.

This recognition of traits as the elemental units in any culture is important because it is from these specific acts and objects that the more complex culture forms are put together. Cultures are differentiated from each other by the variations in these observable traits and the complexes they form. Each trait and complex derives its significance from the way it functions in the society in which it has been developed. The natives of tropical areas have

no notion of the use of a pair of ice skates nor do the natives of a north temperate zone have much notion of the functions served by the bamboo rattles used by rice-growing people to drive away birds.

TRAIT COMPLEXES Culture traits do not usually appear singly or independently. They are customarily associated with other related traits to form unified clusters of traits and are called *trait-complexes*. The importance of the single trait is indicated when it fits into a cluster of traits, each one of which performs a significant role in the total complex. We can think of a baseball as a distinctive culture trait of American society, but the baseball itself is simply one trait in a whole series of related traits that form the baseball complex of this society. The alert student recognizes that the baseball; the bat; the bases; the pitcher's mound; the catcher's mitt, mask, and chest protector; the playing field, and the rules of the game are only a few of the many traits which combine into a total unity to form the baseball complex. Each of these traits is a single irreducible material or nonmaterial element shared by the society, but each gains meaning because it operates as part of the trait-complex. The baseball complex is built primarily about three traits—the ball, the bat, and the base. They are the *core* traits around which the whole complex is organized. Additional material and nonmaterial traits come into existence about them to form the total trait-complex. This is more than a mere additive operation; the associated traits operate in the total relationship to create a functional whole.

This also illustrates the interrelationship between structure and function in cultural phenomena, for the structure of these elements conditions the functioning of the whole in the playing of this game. The shape, size, and material composition of the baseball; the shape, size, and material composition of the bat; and the structural pattern of the playing field are a few of the structural characteristics of traits in this complex that influence its operation.

The functioning, that is, the playing of the game, we quickly recognize, would be vastly different than it now is if the baseball were larger (thus much more difficult to throw), if the field were larger or smaller, or if there were no foul territory. On the other hand, the structure of the complex would be different if the pitcher had to throw the baseball to the batter in only one way, if the batter, after striking the ball, had to run only to one base and back to the home base—in other words, if the functions to be carried out in the game were different. Any trait-complex has a form and a function. The interrelated traits carry out their specific roles to achieve the purposes or meanings of the complex. They are inextricably interwoven.

The operation of trait-complexes in a society implies that there are normative aspects that define the proper behavior related to them. Baseball, we know, is played by rules. The baseball is of a certain size, weight, and material. The bat is likewise of a definite material and length. This whole complex operates by standards that define the proper ways of playing. This is true for the functionng of all trait-complexes of a society and of the society as a whole. Because all the members of a society are expected to act in specific ways under certain conditions, or according to the societal norms, and because each complex implies a particular set of standards defining the expected behavior with respect to it, order in a society is guaranteed.

CULTURE PATTERNS A *culture pattern* is formed in a society as these different parts—traits and complexes—become related to each other in functional wholes or configurations. Each society has culture patterns that are distinctive to it, although they may vary in geographical scope. The rice-water buffalo pattern of south China and the cotton-tobacco pattern of the southeast section of the United States are two of a number of distinctive culture patterns *within* these societies, whereas the machine-marketing system may be regarded as a culture pattern of American society as a whole.

Culture patterns influence us as wholes. The cotton-tobacco pattern of the American southeast operating as a unit does not influence the person just in some of its parts; all of them affect his behavior. The youth among American Plains Indians reacted to their whole horse culture pattern and the expectations it imposed upon them by its forms, rituals, and obligations. It is in this way that standardization of our behavior in a society is accomplished. We absorb the elements of these patterns almost unconsciously and apply them in a similar manner so that we are often unaware of their importance as controls over us. This is what the society seeks to achieve: the common patterning of our behavior.

CULTURE BASE We have now seen that culture includes the sum total of all of man's cre-

ated environments. We have indicated that it is constituted of traits, trait-complexes, and patterns. It is clear to us that the content of these environments or the sum total of all the separate traits that make up the complexes and patterns is, for any society, enormous. This totality of all the cultural parts of a given society at a given time is its *culture base.*

A most significant concern about this culture base is that its size and character are important in the determination of the further development of the culture of a society. This brings us to the question of how culture is produced.

IV. CULTURE FORMATION

The Foundation upon Which Man Builds His Culture Is the Variety of Natural Environments the Universe Presents and His Own Capacity to Innovate

One of the important and interesting parts of our study is the consideration of how we produce culture. What are the processes by which we bring culture into existence? The answer to this question will tell us how we change our way of living in societies, add ideas and things to them, and slough off things and ideas that are no longer useful.

VARIATIONS IN NATURAL ENVIRONMENTS First of all, we know from our study of environmental adaptation that we must build our culture in differing natural environments. We have studied the way environmental differences condition the processes of adjustment. Now we emphasize again that their dissimilarity sets conditions upon which culture-building must necessarily rest. The cold extreme north and southern regions, the hot equatorial areas—some dry, others moist—the flat stretches of sand and the flat stretches of deep rich soil, the steep mountains and the rolling plains, and a thousand other variable characteristics of nonliving and living forms make up one vital dimension of culture building. Their variations make cultural variation certain.

PROPERTIES OF MEN The distinctive character of man himself is the second foundation of culture production. A compound of capacities, temperaments, and drives possessed in different amounts by individuals, he is himself the other basic element of the culture-building process. We shall not discuss these properties of man in detail here, since that is the business of another fascinating science—psychology. We accept for our purposes the psychologist's conclusion that men everywhere—white, yellow, black, Irish, German, Chinese, tall, short, heavy, or light—possess these characteristics in sufficient form and quantity to respond significantly and differently to stimuli found in their environment. We also accept their conclusion that no individuals have a monopoly on the capacity to innovate, that is, to produce ideas or things that are qualitatively new, because of any unique inherited characteristics. Any biologically normal person may introduce something new since he may react differently to the stimuli of his environment. These may appear to be different to him rather than to others.

This was the case of Michael Pupin, the Serbian peasant boy who became the American inventor of long-distance telephoning and multiplex telegraphy. He tells of a conversation with some peasants of his native village. He had returned to visit his native home after some of his inventions had been purchased by the Marconi company. He received a telegram from America while in the village informing him that the contracts for the purchase of some inventions had been completed. The local bearer of the telegram bragged to the natives of the delivery and of the ten florin tip he had received. The peasants would not believe that the telegram had come all the way from America in less than a day. Pupin explained that it could come in less than a minute.

Then a peasant with whom Pupin had gone to school as a boy asked, "Who invented all this?" Pupin answered that an American did, not revealing his own part in the inventions. "These Americans must be very clever," replied the peasant. "Yes, indeed, they are very clever people," was Pupin's reply. "Much more clever than anybody in this village?" the man asked. Pupin jokingly assured him that Americans were more clever than anybody in his native village, whereupon the man asked, "Then how in the name of St. Michael do you manage to make a living there?" [22]

Discovery and Invention Are the Foundational Activities that Underlie Culture Creation

Ages ago a primitive man grasped a log floating down a stream, found that it would hold his weight, and climbed on it. The discovery gave him an idea. He invented the boat. The two things that happened in this situation—discovery and invention—account basically for all the social equipment, material, and nonmaterial that we possess.

DISCOVERY   When we make a *discovery*, we find a principle or substance that always has existed. It was always true in the world of matter that some substances with certain properties would float on water while others with different properties would sink. We learned this in early childhood. Primitive man did not know why because he did not understand the physical law. Rather, he used trial and error to test these materials. He experimented with the materials in the situation he was facing. Experiment means, in Latin, to "try out," and is still a basic process in testing the principles and materials that make up today's cultures. We can expand applications when we discover principles. Primitive man's hollow log boat is now the great ocean liner because man discovered principles.

INVENTION   *Inventions* are adaptations or modifications of principles and things previously known to new situations, which result in new ways of using known forces and substances. Primitive man could not make a boat until he knew that wood floated in water and held up added weight. This knowledge made possible the creation of the boat, perhaps after much trial and error. The boat was inevitable once he had this knowledge. The Greeks, with all their knowledge, could not invent the automobile because they did not have the gasoline engine and other necessary devices and materials and did not know about them nor how to make or to get them. An invention often develops out of another or is a combination of other inventions and discoveries derived from previous experience.

Discoveries and Inventions May Be Accidentally Made

We now know that vitamins have always existed. They are contained in hundreds of living plants and animals, but they were only recently discovered (1897) by accident. Today, they are recognized as a necessity in proper diet but actually, they always have been a necessity. The story is told of a young doctor in the Dutch East Indian Islands, who left a flock of chickens in the care of a servant while he was away on a trip. The servant ran out of the polished rice he was told to feed the chickens and gave them unpolished rice instead. The chickens were so lively on the physician's return that he asked the servant what he had done to them. After the servant explained, the doctor reasoned that there must be something in unpolished rice that had caused the change. He substantiated this reasoning by experiment and called the substance he found "vitamin," or life-giving element.

Some items are invented by chance, too. The stethoscope, an instrument for examining the chest, was invented as a result of an accidental observation. A doctor saw a boy tapping the end of a long plank while his companions listened to the sounds coming through clearly by pressing their ears to the other end. He returned to his hospital, rolled a paper-backed book into a tube, and went from patient to patient listening to the variety of sounds coming from their chests. When Dr. Laeunac found that paper tubes were not substantial, he turned out a wooden cylinder on a lathe and called it his "stethoscope."

Cotton was little more than a pretty garden plant in the American South until Eli Whitney invented the cotton gin to separate the fibers from the seed. One night he saw a fox clawing at a chicken coop. All the fox's claws could pull between the slats was a bunch of feathers.

Whitney got his idea. He made a claw-like rake, the teeth of which reached between the slats of a grid filled with cotton balls. When rotated, the claws tore the fibers from the seed. This left the seed behind. The cotton gin, born from an accidental observation, made cotton cloth common the world over.

Accidental inventions are also made in the field of social relations. In 1878 and 1879, Memphis, Tennessee, was ravaged by epidemics of yellow fever. Thousands of people died and other thousands fled the city. The state's legislature repealed the city charter to control the situation, abolished the mayor-alderman form of government, and appointed a "legislative council" to control "the taxing district." The work of the council was so effective Memphis did not return to its mayor-alderman government but continued commission control. This was the accidentally invented form of the first commission-type of city government in the United States.

Man Now Depends More on Purposive than Accidental Discovery and Invention

Men, in most present-day societies, set out purposefully to attain a better mastery of their environments and enlarge their cultures through making planned inventions and discoveries. The accumulated milieu of new material, theory, and products is usually suggestive of other inventions and discoveries that would be helpful to different areas of life. New ideas are stimulated by favorable conditions and by specific inducements. More than 1000 suggestions are made per month to automobile makers for the improvement of cars. Only one of each 30,000 ideas is apt to be new and useful.[23] However, new inventions and discoveries pile up rapidly in every area of life.

The purposive achievement of discoveries and inventions is based on accumulated data, theory, and experience. Thousands of scientists are purposely using their instruments to discover oil, ores, and fissionable materials. Thousands of technologists are seeking to perfect machines and social mechanisms by adding something new from their experience. The typewriter had a cumulative total of 7678 patents on it between 1872 and 1923. Many of these patents represented only small improvements, but they illustrate the fact that inventions are purposefully made.

Invention and discovery do not now limit themselves to the slow process of piling one

Creation of the automobile resulted from the accumulation and combination of inventions over many years.

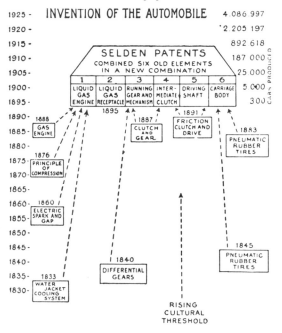

upon the other. They can be planned for and predicted. Of course, basic materials and principles must be available to make possible the projection of inventions through abstract inference. This is what happens in hundreds of instances. The atomic bomb is a recent illustration.

Doctor R. C. Gibbs of the Cornell University Physics Department pointed out, in a newspaper report on the invention of the first atomic bomb, that "in chunks too small to explode, pure U-235 or Pu-239 (plutonium) was gradually furnished to the Los Alamos laboratory. But long before any material was available to make a bomb, and even long before it was known whether the manufacturing plants would be able to furnish an adequate supply to make a single bomb, the complete design of the bomb construction was mapped out and determined in full detail. They had to be sure on every detail of the theory involved, for *theory alone* had to be their guide." [24] Actually, the bomb was first invented in the minds of men who possessed the mathematical, physical, and other principles, then transferred to blue prints, and finally constructed as the physical bomb.

Discoveries and Inventions Are Basic Activities in Social Relations as Well as in the Physical Universe

We are apt to limit our consideration to the material universe when we think of discoveries and inventions. Such discoveries and inventions as oil, pottery, the printing press, and the electric motor are so obvious in their influence that we often fail to recognize the importance of such *social inventions* and discoveries as language systems, commission government, planned parenthood, and folkways. But the material and nonmaterial, the physical and social, are so intricately interwoven that change due to inventions and discoveries in one almost inevitably sets the stage for inventions and discoveries in the other. We are constantly inventing new ideas to control aspects of our social organization changed by other inventions.

COOPERATIVE AS AN ILLUSTRATION   We may use the invention of the cooperative way of doing business to illustrate this process. This significant social invention grew out of the economic troubles of a community of weavers. Cooperative ideas were born in the textile town of Rochdale, England, in the early 1840's. The poverty of these textile weavers was appalling.

Because a strike for better wages was lost, and many were out of their jobs, they met to consider ways of organizing their economic life. A society—the Equitable Society of Rochdale Pioneers—of 28 members was formed. They invented the Rochdale principles by which to operate their economic affairs and began to do business in a small retail store. The principles they established were seven:

1. Membership open to everyone.
2. One member, one vote; no proxy voting.
3. Capital invested in shares was to be paid a moderate, fixed return.
4. The surplus to be returned to members to the degree to which they used the business—the patronage dividend.
5. Neutrality on the part of the cooperative in religion and politics.
6. Trading on a cash basis.
7. Education of members and nonmembers with references to these principles.

The new ideas the Rochdale weavers introduced were one vote per member regardless of the amount of capital invested; payment of a fixed interest on capital invested just as it pays fixed rents and wages; and the distribution of profits to the users of the enterprise as a patronage dividend in proportion to the amount of business each patron contributed.

This form of business operation has expanded from retailing to wholesale buying, manufacturing, transportation, and housing. It has introduced the only significantly different way of conducting business in our societies since the invention of the corporation. Its creation by plain, intelligent workers supports the idea that ordinary people can discover and invent.

The Role of the Innovator Is Important in Culture-Building

Neither invention nor discovery is self-generating. People must discover materials and principles; individuals must combine ideas and things to produce new ideas and new things and make them operative in societies. These facts emphasize that the innovator—the person with the searching mind—is important to culture-building. He is the individual who joins parts or ideas together into new syntheses and produces something new that, when applied, often changes the course of cultural development.

Many of us have the idea that the inventor or the discoverer is solely responsible for what has been produced and is the only essential factor in culture-building. Actually, two other factors are also necessary for invention and discovery: accumulations from the past and favorable circumstances in the present. Robert Fulton's "Clermont" appeared on the Hudson River in 1807 and made her successful journey to Albany. We think of Fulton as the inventor of the steamboat, but many persons had dreamed of ships that would travel the waters without oars or sails as far back as the time of Homer. None could build them because they did not have any power sources other than sails or oars to propel them; it is only that these had not been invented. But Watt's steam engine, which appeared in 1782, centuries after these first dreams, was successful when Fulton used it in his boat on the Hudson River. Others had built steamboats, but not until after the steam engine was available. The final development of an adequate engine furnished a power source which made possible the steamboat and eventually the steamship. This was something the centuries had been wanting. It had to wait both for the time, the accumulated inventions, and the men. There had to be men as well as conditions.

There are limitations in both the position of a Carlyle, who stressed the role of the great man as the true source of social development, and the position of those who see social developments as mainly the consequences of social forces in which individuals operate only incidentally. It is more accurate to say that in any social situation, the cultural base in a society at a given time, the particular social conditions at that time, and the presence of individuals who have the ingenuity to put together new things and new principles from this base are all essentials of culture formation.

Whether the process requires a particular man or men is not an answerable proposition. Whether it had to be Fulton, Einstein, Luther, or Lincoln can never be determined for their time and their conditions are never duplicated. Their time and their conditions did call them forth. Others may have answered had they not been there. The fact is that they were there. They were essentials in the situation. Their particular uniqueness, no doubt, influenced the results.

Man's Culture or Social Environment Accumulates

Our culture-building is also brought about by addition or accretion. Inventions and discoveries pile up, ever enlarging the total content of a society's material and social base. But inventions and discoveries seldom stand alone. The new has the germ of the additionally new within it. Man has invented the automobile, radio, television, the split atom, to give only four illustrations out of thousands since the beginning of the century. What additions to our environment these four are! But these are only a part of what has been added to societies as a result of their introduction. We are amazed at the number and variety of new tools the automobile mechanic now has that did not exist when automobiles were first brought to the shop for repairs 30-odd years ago, to say nothing about the additions to the car itself, such as the automatic clutch and power steering. These are also only a small part of the total changes that result from using the automobile. Thousands of miles of hard surfaced roads and hundreds of social regulations to control the use of the roads by car operators are also a part of a whole new automobile complex that has come because of this addition of "the horseless carriage." Almost every new invention or discovery gathers around itself elements that were previously nonexistent or separate from it and so grows into a whole that is made up of many new physical and nonphysical parts. It is not just a process of accumulating discrete items but of accumulating whole patterns that center about core items. This process is basic to the accelerating rate at which cultures are built. We are deliberately creating at a rate unknown to societies in any previous time because of the accumulated size of the culture base in our societies today and this process of social accretion. The last 50 years has seen more addition to the culture of the Western world than the previous 500 years. The next 50 years will probably see more addition throughout the world than the last 2000 years.

Selection Is Important in Culture-Building

A society does not add every new item or idea that is invented or discovered. There are thousands of material and nonmaterial inventions that get no further than their originators. A process of selection goes on discarding things and ideas that are not useful or acceptable to us at the time and adding those that have utility for us. A few years ago, when divorces skyrocketed in American society, Judge Ben Lindsay of Denver, Colorado, suggested the idea of companionate marriage to solve the problem. He suggested a trial marriage period after which the marriage would become permanent if the temporarily wedded man and woman desired it; otherwise, the marriage could be dissolved by common consent. This innovation was so contrary to the marriage mores of the society that most persons condemned it strongly.[25]

Some of our inventions are made a part of the culture almost immediately. The consolidated or central school is one, in that it caught on rapidly and spread throughout American society. On the other hand, some inventions must overcome many forms of opposition and are not used until situations compel their adoption. There has been as much need for the consolidation of churches in the rural areas of America to provide effective religious education programs as for the consolidation of schools. Acceptance is slow although various forms for unifying churches, such as federation and the larger parish, have been devised. Denominationally different individuals will join together to promote a common central school for their children. But these same persons oppose unifying their churches for common religious purposes. Fear of the loss of some unique belief or practice, fear of changes in particular practices or beliefs, fear of property loss or control, and opposition by church administrators who fear loss of membership and revenues constitute just a few of the obstacles in the pathway.

The selective process in culture-building occurs because the varying cultural forms striving to serve the same functions compete with each other for acceptance, much as variable biological forms compete with each other for survival. A large proportion of the population in Western societies have adopted the wrist watch. It was not a part of these cultures before World War I, when most watches were worn in pockets and fastened on chains or with pins. The greater utility of the wrist watch has practically eliminated these other forms in the competitive struggle. (We will deal further with these matters in our discussion of social change.)

Some Elements May Remain in a Culture as Survivals after They Have Lost Their Original Function, Meaning, or Value

A man purchasing a suit of clothing in American society today will commonly find that the lapels are notched and the left one has a buttonhole in it. Why does the bottom of each coat sleeve have three or four buttons on it? Neither the lapel, buttonhole, nor the buttons on the sleeves serve any purpose, yet they are on most men's suits. They are survivals, but once they had a function. Men used to wear only one coat. He turned the collar up, crossed the lapel, and fastened it to a button that was under the right lapel to protect his throat and neck. The notches made it fit properly. The sleeves were turned up and buttoned near the elbow to protect the coat sleeve when he was driving or riding horseback. Hence, the buttons and the false cut on the side of each sleeve. The original utility of the buttonhole is gone since men now wear a topcoat as well as a suitcoat in inclement weather. Many men never notice that it is there.

More important for us is the fact that modes of thought and action show similar "holdover" tendencies; few societies are without them. (We shall examine later the dysfunctional or injurious effects which survivals may have.)

The Culture Is also Built by Borrowing

The basic creative processes in culture-building are invention and discovery. It should be clear to us, however, that cultures are also built by borrowing. In fact, analysis of the cultural content of almost any society at a particular time shows that much of this content did not originate in the society but was brought in by diffusion from other societies. This would be particularly true of a young society like America. We pointed out in the chapter on cultural antecedents that our basic moral and religious ideas and practices, our concepts of nationalism and governmental organization, our forms of business organization and operation, and our methods of production and distribution, as well as many others, came from or by way of European societies. The early colonists brought them or imported them after arrival.

This spreading of culture content from one society to another and between areas of a particular society is *culture diffusion*. It occurs with respect to both material and nonmaterial elements. Persons moving into a society bring their old culture with them, and elements from it are added to the new culture.

There is a series of rural reconstruction centers at various places in the Nile Valley doing work in agriculture, handicrafts, and social welfare. They are promoted by the Ministry of Social Welfare of the Egyptian government,

Cultural diffusion: Western dress in the Near and Far East.

of Western missionaries. Since the peasants were much attracted to them, the monks decided to enter the same fields and add these activities to their own programs.

Cultural Diffusion Takes Place Today with Incredible Speed Within and Between Societies

The importance of diffusion in culture-building today is greatly enhanced by the speed with which both material and nonmaterial traits can be transmitted. Culture traits are now spread world-wide in months or years where formerly they required centuries. Three major conditions are related to this speed of diffusion: (1) the type of agents available to carry the traits, (2) the methods used to diffuse them, and (3) the conditions for acceptance in the culture contacted.

Hybrid corn, in the incredibly short period of a dozen years, almost completely replaced open pollinated varieties in our American corn belt. How could this happen, we ask? When hybrid seed became available by 1928 or 1929, farmers began trying it on a small scale to avoid serious risk. This practice went on for several years with a rapid increase in the number of operators planting it for the first time each year and a rapid increase in the extent of acreage planted by those who had adopted it. Three-fourths of all corn acreage in the Middle West was in hybrid varieties while 98 per cent of Iowa's corn acreage was planted to hybrid varieties by 1948.[26] Now, practically all corn acreage in America is in hybrid varieties.

Commercial salesmen gave the farmers their first knowledge of the seed. Neighbors who had used the seed successfully were most important in getting the farmer's first acceptance. Trial without great risk helped, while means of communication kept the public informed constantly of its success. All essential conditions for rapid adoption therefore were operative.

Our adoption of polio vaccine is another illustration of the incredible speed with which a new cultural material can now be diffused on a world-wide basis. The consequence of paralytic poliomyelitis had made people around the globe highly conscious of this disease. The fact that President Franklin D. Roosevelt was one of its victims was a strong sentimental factor in calling the disease to the attention of the public. Polio outbreaks in various societies made the conditions for the acceptance of a vaccine favorable.

but it is pointed out to us that their chief Egyptian promoter had gone to South India where a reconstruction program in Indian villages was under way. Here he gained a philosophy and a method for this work that he was now using in Egypt. The leaders of the Indian project were two Americans who had been trained in reconstruction programs in their homeland. "What I know of rural reconstruction methods," said the Egyptian director, "I learned in India from my American friends." Both material and nonmaterial elements were carried from America to India then to Egypt.

Another illustration will point out how an aspect of a culture is adopted when no conscious effort is being made to introduce it. A famous Buddhist monk in an Oriental country was training neophytes in the methods of doing social and educational work among peasants. This is contrary to the basic Buddhist doctrine that the world is evil and that we build our spiritual life by withdrawing from it. This Buddhist monk explained, when asked about it, that his organization had been watching the medical, educational, and agricultural programs

It was impossible for culture forms to spread rapidly when the chief agents of diffusion were direct contacts and means of travel were slow and communication cumbersome. The means are now available whereby culture traits are spread throughout a culture and between different cultures with considerable rapidity since many transportation devices, such as railroads and airplanes, and communication media, such as books and radio, have become a part of the cultural equipment of most societies.

V. CULTURE VARIATION

The Cultures of Societies Vary Widely in Form and Content

We have stressed the fact that all societies have similar needs to satisfy. This leads each to develop cultural traits and patterns to meet them. The *Outline of Cultural Materials,* published by the Human Relations Area Files, is a fascinating document.[27] It includes 88 divisions of major culture materials which are generally found in a culture system. Though each aspect is not present in every culture system, the outline, to say nothing of its detailed subdivisions and the actual materials that are components of the 150 different systems analyzed, shows that these features are present in most societies. They are all related to these needs and wants that appear in societies and with which man must deal.

The previous discussions in this volume, the work of many sociologists and anthropologists, and the vast content of the Human Relations Area Files show that, while the elements of culture systems are universally based on the common needs of men, the modes of satisfying them vary widely between societies. Getting food to the mouth, to use one simple cultural practice, ranges in perfectly acceptable forms, from eating with the fingers to eating with polished sticks to eating with cutting and lifting tools of metal, each of which must be held in the proper way in the proper hand. All people have need for ways to get food to their mouths. They do not necessarily need to use, nor do they use, the same ways or the same tools to perform this act. The same principle applies to the most complex aspects of cultural organization so that there is wide diversity among societies in their solutions to almost every one of their common problems. Language, food processing, clothing, houses, property

Cultural diffusion: marriages following Western styles are creeping into the oriental world; Japanese boys play the American national game.

rules, stratification systems, kinship roles, crime, religious beliefs and practices, to name some, may all develop differently in different societies.

There Are Six Major Factors in Cultural Variation

NATURAL PHYSICAL AND BIOLOGICAL ENVIRONMENTS The environments, we know, set the stage for adaptations. Hot or cold climates, fertile or sandy soils, dense or sparse vegetation, many or few animals, and other environmental situations set conditions in which cultural forms arise. Houses must be made of materials other than wood where there are few trees, as in the frigid north. Houses are usually made of wood where it is plentiful. In Sweden, however, where there is a great abundance of lumber, signs were once posted which, with other mass media, urged the people to use lumber in home construction. The reason behind this was that many persons were using brick, stucco, and stone, which cut the consumption of lumber. Variety usually occurs where there is choice of materials, but what is in the environment sets limits to what can be done and the forms it may take. Variation in culture content occurs because environments vary from area to area.

GEOGRAPHIC ISOLATION Societies that are geographically isolated evolve culture patterns that are distinctly their own, and they show little inclination to change them. American Indian tribes have absorbed some of the physical elements from the surrounding white culture but have retained, in their isolated positions, the nonmaterial patterns of their fathers. Lack of contacts emphasizes cultural rigidity. These societies have had little intercourse over the long stretch with each other so that they have built in the past without much outside influence. Cultural antecedents, the origins of which are lost in antiquity, not only give them uniqueness but also serve as barriers to keep them separated.

CULTURE BASE AND INTERNAL ELABORATION Our ways of living are built out of antecedent accumulations. What has been accumulated sets some limits to what can be developed. Some cultures have a small accumulation; others, large. The addition of new ideas and things is thus influenced variously. Differences may not be minimized. They may even be increased under such circumstances, for in the one instance the traits and complexes that can be elaborated are, by comparison, few, while in the other they are many. New traits and complexes that are developed vary as a consequence. The form and speed of the internal elaborations that take place thus influence the similarity or dissimilarity of the ways of living.

TECHNOLOGICAL POSITION The differences in the technological levels that societies have reached also account, in part, for their differences. Handicraft societies differ from machine societies, not only in their economic activities but also in almost all other aspects, since the dominant cultural traits and complexes of societies are interwoven. The equipment used, such as tools, and the operational methods employed in each economy, express the adaptability and inventiveness of those using them so that each culture evolves a uniqueness of its own that contributes to variation. This means that societies that are in a similar stage of technological development may vary widely from each other in the cultural forms they produce. Some cultures of the direct appropriation type do their hunting with bows and arrows, others with spears, or nets, or traps. Their nonmaterial forms show similar variation, with some using elaborate ceremonials in preparation for the hunt. Others have little or none, but some have such ceremonials following their hunting activities while others have none.

DOMINANT CULTURAL THEMES Another factor that causes cultures to differ from each other in content and organization is the central "focus of interest" or *dominant themes* they develop. Maurice Opler presents this point of view in his article on themes as dynamic forces in culture. He reports, for example, that the superiority of men over women is a main theme around which Apache Indian society is organized.[28] We recognize that Russian society is united around the major concepts of Marxian socialism; China was integrated about the family system with filial piety and the five relationships as major themes or focal points of interest; and ancient Egypt was organized about "netherworld" themes.[29] The themes in modern American society are fairly accurately stated as equality, individual opportunity, free enterprise, and large-scale mechanical production.

The major elements of a culture express these dominant themes. They give a culture a distinctive character and direction and also create, in part, a closed system. New traits or complexes are usually accepted only when they "fit" into the existing culture configuration or represent some values that can be absorbed without too greatly distorting the pattern.

ETHNOCENTRISM Understandably, people generally regard most highly the culture in which they have been reared. This attitude, called "ethnocentrism," is an almost automatic response when people compare their ways of living with others. From the beginning of socialization, the values and norms of our society have been impressed on us as the best values and the most proper norms. Devotion to them is taught and expected. The ways of our own society are the right ways: those of other societies are not only peculiar but are often wrong. It is thus often exceedingly difficult for the members of any society to be objective about ways of acting and of thinking that are different from their own. This is a strong barrier even to considering new conceptions, because it emphasizes retaining the *status quo* in spite of the fact that many of the forms have been borrowed. Such devotion to a society's cultural forms increases in-group attitudes and strengthens the force of "the cake of custom" and so makes change difficult. Our socially inherited religion, for example, is the only true religion. Consideration of the viewpoints of other religions is not usually tolerated.

Is a World-Wide Common Culture an Eventual Possibility?

The foregoing comments stress the variability in cultures and indicate conditions for the continuance of such variability. However, the possibilities for the rapid communication of culture traits under present conditions often lead us to wonder whether societies will develop a common cultural system in time. The way is open for increased similarity because of the increased diffusion of cultural elements already extant and the more favorable situation for further acceptance of traits due to these speedy means of transfer and the increased ability to recognize the uses to which new traits can be put. Our world is no longer made up of societies that remain isolated from each other.

Two things stand in the way of a world-wide common culture, however. One we have already stressed by indicating that, although societies have the same basic needs, these needs do not have to be satisfied in the same way and by the same techniques. All societies have need for knowledge, but we do not infer that they need the same knowledge.

All societies have need for practices related to property ownership, use, and transfer, yet it does not follow that these must be handled in the same way. Our needs must be satisfied under different natural environmental conditions. We invent different ways under these different conditions. Complete uniformity is hardly to be expected on this account alone, although this factor is only conditioning and not deter-

minative. We determine the adaptations we will make to the environment.

Furthermore, societies can select from the elements of other cultures those that can be fitted into their own system and reject those that do not. A society's culture is its way of life. This way of life, we repeat, is regarded as superior to others in its chief components. It is hardly to be expected that this attitude will be discarded easily. Societies do adopt significant elements from other cultures because they recognize their usefulness. But they integrate them into their own cultures by modifying the borrowed elements or by readjusting their own systems to make them fit without seriously changing their own patterns or values. The Japanese, for example, adopted the Western machine production system in a relatively short time. They fitted it into the pattern of their life without changing their social relationships or social values in any seriously disturbing ways. Societies will undergo significant cultural changes with increased diffusion, but the process will probably be one of integrating the new in such a way as to retain the essential character of the old. A common world-wide culture would seem a long way off.

Variations Within a Society Give Rise to Subcultures

As a society develops it becomes differentiated into subsystems or subsocieties. Each of these will tend to develop its own norms, values, argot, and other distinctive patterns—usually including some ethnocentrism. In this manner, occupational groups, social classes, religious sects, and deviant groups develop *subcultures*. One sociologist proposes that the term "contra-culture" be applied to those groups whose values conflict with those of the larger society.[30]

Such subcultures probably are indispensable to the continuity and development of a large, complex society and certainly perform valuable social functions for it. On the other hand, however, they may sometimes impede or impair the maintenance of social cohesion or integration.

References

1. The best comprehensive classification of the environments is that of L. L. Bernard. We follow it with slight modifications and abbreviations: Bernard, L. L., "A Classification of Environments," *The American Journal of Sociology*, 31 (November, 1925), pp. 318–332.
2. Vance, Rupert B., *Human Factors in Cotton Culture* (Chapel Hill, N.C., University of North Carolina Press, 1929), p. 295.

3. Cowper, William, "The Timepiece," *The Task,* Book II, line 17, in *Poems of Established Reputation* (Baltimore, Md., Warner & Hanna, 1804), p. 179.

4. Lane, Rose Wilder, *Let the Hurricanes Roar* (New York, Longmans, Green & Co., 1933), p. 15.

5. Buck, Pearl S., *The Good Earth* (New York, The John Day Company, 1931), pp. 69 and 70.

6. The United States Department of Agriculture, *The Yearbook of Agriculture, 1955,* Water (Washington, D.C., United States Printing Office, 1955), pp. 4, 5, and 7.

7. See Quick, Herbert, *The Hawkeye* (Indianapolis, Ind., Bobbs-Merrill Company, Inc., 1923), p. 18.

8. Roberts, Isaac P., *Autobiography of a Farm Boy* (Ithaca, N.Y., Cornell University Press, 1946), pp. 20 and 21.

9. State of New York Conservation Department, *Forty-Fourth Annual Report, 1954* (Albany, N.Y., Williams Press, Inc., 1955).

10. Carlyle, Thomas, *Sartor Resartus* (Chicago, W. B. Conkey Company), pp. 48–50.

11. Ferber, Edna, *American Beauty* (Garden City, N.Y., Doubleday, Doran, and Company, Inc., 1931), pp. 235–236.

12. Bacon, Francis, "Of Custom and Education," *Essays* (New York, John B. Alden, 1887), p. 146.

13. Sumner, William Graham, *Folkways* (Boston, Ginn and Company, 1906).

14. *Ibid.,* p. 38.

15. Simmel, George, "Fashion," *American Journal of Sociology,* 62 (May, 1957), p. 544.

16. Bernard, L. L., *Social Control* (New York, The Macmillan Company, 1939), pp. 7–9. Here Bernard uses the terms "cultural environment," "physico-cultural," "bio-cultural," and "psycho-cultural environments" instead of "social," "physico-social," and so on.

17. Goldenweiser, A. A., *Early Civilization* (New York, Alfred A. Knopf, 1922), p. 15.

18. Cooley, C. H., Angell, R. C., and Carr, L. J., *Introductory Sociology* (New York, Charles Scribner's Sons, 1933), p. 81.

19. Sumner, W. G., and Keller, A. G., *The Science of Society,* I (New Haven, Conn., Yale University Press, 1927), p. 46.

20. Sapir, Edward, "Culture, Genuine and Spurious," *American Journal of Sociology,* 29 (January, 1924), pp. 402 and 405.

21. Bierstedt, Robert, *The Social Order* (New York, McGraw-Hill Book Co., Inc., 1957), p. 106.

22. Pupin, Michael, *From Immigrant to Inventor* (New York, Charles Scribner's Sons, 1923), pp. 347 and 348.

23. *Automobile Facts* (Detroit, Mich., January, 1955), p. 6.

24. *The Ithaca Journal* (September 24, 1945), p. 1.

25. Lindsey, Ben B., and Evans, Wainwright, *The Companionate Marriage* (New York, Boni and Liveright, 1927).

26. Ryan, Bryce, and Gross, Neal, "The Diffusion of Hybrid Seed Corn in Two Iowa Communities," *Rural Sociology,* 8 (March, 1943), pp. 15 ff, and Ryan, Bryce, "A Study of Technological Diffusion," *Rural Sociology,* 13 (September, 1948), pp. 273 ff.

27. Murdock, G. P., *Outline of Cultural Materials* (New Haven, Conn., Human Relations Area Files, Inc., 1950).

28. Opler, M. E., "Themes as Dynamic Forces in Culture," *American Journal of Sociology,* 51 (November, 1945), pp. 198–206.

29. Sorokin, P. A., *Society, Culture, and Personality* (New York, Harper and Brothers, 1947), p. 319.

30. Yinger, J. Milton, "Contraculture and Subculture," *American Sociological Review*, 25 (October, 1960), pp. 625–635.

Questions for Study and Discussion

1. Give some illustrations of the interrelationships of the material and nonmaterial aspects of our culture.
2. Describe a culture complex of our society and show how each element functions within it.
3. Discuss the variations in environments and the characteristics of people as factors in culture creation.
4. Distinguish between invention and discovery. Show how an invention and a discovery helped to produce a significant change in the form and function of a social structure.
5. What is serendipity? Can you give an illustration of it that has had an important consequence in our society?
6. Discuss accumulation as a factor in culture creation.
7. Illustrate how cultural survivals undergo a change in function.
8. Discuss cultural diffusion as it is influenced by communication today.
9. Do you think mankind will develop a common culture? Discuss factors promoting or hindering it.
10. How do institutions and organizations constitute control environments in a society?
11. Would you use the concept "culture" and the concept "social environment" as synonymous terms?
12. Give some other definitions of culture used by anthropologists and sociologists. Compare them with our definition.

Suggested Topics for Reports

1. Make a catalogue of the traditions of your college or university. Have these grown weaker or stronger in recent years? Why?
2. Select a random sample of statutes in the legal code of your state and indicate which mores in American culture they express.
3. Select two or three pages of this book at random and look up each major word in a standard dictionary to determine its nationality-linguistic origin. Show what your findings reveal about language as a *product* and *agent* of cultural diffusion.
4. Consult a recent report on patents issued by the United States Patent Office and make a list of those new things which are likely to be selected for permanent incorporation in our culture.

Supplementary Reading

Barzun, Jacques, *God's Country and Mine*. Boston: Little, Brown and Company, 1954.

Beals, Ralph L., and Hoijer, Harry, *An Introduction to Anthropology*. New York: The Macmillan Company, 1953.

Benedict, Ruth, *Patterns of Culture*. New York: Penguin Books, 1946.

Bernard, L. L., *Introduction to Social Psychology*. New York: Henry Holt and Company, Inc., 1926.

Brunhes, Jean, *Human Geography*. New York: Rand McNally Company, 1920.

Chapin, F. S., *Cultural Change*. New York: The Century Company, 1928.

Foster, George M., *Traditional Culture: And the Impact of Technological Change*. New York: Harper and Brothers, 1962.

Goldschmidt, Walter (ed.), *The Ways of Mankind*. Boston: Beacon Press, 1954.

Huntington, Ellsworth, *Civilization and Climate*. New Haven, Conn.: Yale University Press, 1915.

———, *Principles of Human Geography*. Rev. by Earl B. Shaw. New York: John Wiley and Sons, Inc., 1951.

Kroeber, Alfred L., *The Nature of Culture*. Chicago: University of Chicago Press, 1952.

Linton, Ralph, *The Study of Man*. New York: D. Appleton-Century Company, 1936.

——— (ed.), *The Science of Man in the World Crisis*. New York: Columbia University Press, 1948.

Malinowski, Bronislaw, *A Scientific Theory of Culture*. Chapel Hill, N.C.: University of North Carolina Press, 1944.

Montagu, M. F. Ashley (ed.), *Culture and the Evolution of Man*. New York: Oxford University Press, 1962.

Mukerjee, Radhakamal, *Regional Sociology*. New York: The Century Company, 1926.

Murdock, George P., *Our Primitive Contemporaries*. New York: The Macmillan Company, 1934.

Ogburn, W. F., *Social Change*. New York: B. W. Heubach, Inc., 1922.

Sanders, Irwin T., Schwendaman, Joseph R., Woodbury, Richard B., *et al.*, *Societies Around the World*. 2 vols. New York: Dryden Press, 1943.

Slotkin, J. S., *Social Anthropology*. New York: The Macmillan Company, 1950.

Sorokin, Pitirim, *Contemporary Sociological Theories*. New York: Harper and Brothers, 1928.

Sumner, William G., *Folkways*. Boston: Ginn and Company, 1906.

Thomas, William I., *Primitive Behavior*. New York: McGraw-Hill Book Co., Inc., 1937.

Thomas, William L., Jr., *Man's Role in Changing the Face of the Earth*. Chicago: University of Chicago Press, 1956.

Vance, Rupert, *Human Factors in Cotton Culture*. Chapel Hill, N.C.: University of North Carolina Press, 1929.

White, Leslie A., *The Science of Culture*. New York: Farrar, Strauss and Cudahy, Inc., 1949.

Williams, James M., *Our Rural Heritage*. New York: Alfred A. Knopf, 1925.

4

COMMUNICATION IN HUMAN SOCIETY

*S*OCIETIES *could not exist without meaningful contacts between people. Communication is therefore a basic requisite to their existence. Man uses symbols to transfer ideas from person to person and within and between the representatives of his structural forms. Spoken and written language are his chief symbolic systems, but he develops many others. Man is the true symbol-user among all animals.*

Communication Is the Basis of the Existence of Societies and Their Structures

There could be no human relationship structures or hurelures, and so no societies, were it not for the mechanisms men develop for transmitting meaningful stimuli among them. Social life begins when people influence each other mutually and meaningfully by some means. People can only share common experiences, express wants and desires, create like ideas and feelings, and participate in a common social life when they can convey messages to each other through space and retain them in time.

DIFFERENCE BETWEEN MAN AND OTHER ANIMALS We note that one of the great differences between men and other animals is that men develop communication systems that go beyond the mere expression of individual physiological reactions. These systems convey meaningful messages. No other animal is able intentionally to develop methods for transmitting messages to others of its kind.

Man is able to bring into being, hold together, and give continuity to societies because he creates symbols that have meaning to others. Thoughts, beliefs, hopes, and aims can thus be directly and indirectly interchanged in the present and over a period of time. Ideas, the meaningful aspect of symbols transferred in the social act, are the essence of human society, as George Mead puts it.[1] Thus "significant symbols and reflective intelligence belong only to man." Symbolic behavior permits man to use foresight and to avoid to some degree the losses from trial and error since he can make his errors with symbols before they are made in overt behavior. His reflective behavior, based on meaningful symbols, allows him to reason from the present to the future and to anticipate and to predict the responses of others. These are acts no other animal can perform. We have referred to man as the tool-using animal—communication devices are among his indispensable tools. We may also refer to him as the symbol-using animal. Societies and societal structures are the results when man communicates symbolically with others. John Dewey expressed this connection when he said: "Society not only continues to exist by transmission, by communication, but it may fairly be said to exist in transmission, in communication. . . . Men live in a community in virtue of the things they have in common; and communication is the way in which they come to possess things in common."[2]

Communication Is the Transference of Thought Between Persons Through the Use of Symbols

A symbol is a sound, sign, or object that men develop to create in the minds of men uniform meanings that are representatives of the objects or ideas with which they are associated. The mere utterance of sounds or the making of bodily movements has no significance for men until they bring forth similar reactions in the person making the sounds or movements and in other persons. Thus if you say "Yes" or

shake your head up and down, it can have no meaning until those who hear or see these signs interpret them uniformly, that is, recognize your sounds and movements as meaning affirmation. Such action in a non-Western society may have a different meaning. These symbols are social products that are not dependent on specific individuals but are created by and exist in the collective organization of a society.

Almost anything can be used as a symbol so long as we can experience it in our senses and understand it to signify particular objects or ideas. The planting of a tall pole in the ground signified ownership of land to the natives in a South African society. The natives thought it meant a claim to their land when the British erected poles with flags on them, and a war resulted from this misunderstanding. Men traditionalize particular forms to convey ideas. These forms become the accepted symbols and are the conventional means of communicating. The common bases for symbol creation include motions, colors, objects, sounds, and marks.

Gestures Are Important Parts of the Communication Systems of Societies

Motions of some part of our body or gestures, as we call them when the motions are intended to express ideas or feelings, could well have been the elemental condition for the formation of man's first symbols. The infant involuntarily moves its head to avoid unwanted food. This automatic response, when satisfaction is achieved and made to express its own feeling, accomplishes its end—no more food. The movement is fixed in the child's behavior, and it is understood as a sign of refusal not only with respect to unwanted food, but to other things as well. Contacts had to be direct when men depended solely, if they ever did, on gestures. Only a minimal society could be developed based on them for only over long periods of time could gestures develop meaning over wide areas.

LIMITATIONS OF GESTURES It is estimated that we can make over a half million gestures by movements of the arms, hands, fingers, head, eyes, and other parts of the body, by changes in facial expressions and by assuming different postures.[3] Although gestures may communicate much, they could not easily develop into lan-

Communication by gesture: Mongo funeral "orator" and a member of a Bwami secret society.

guage systems because they limit the use of body parts, especially the arms and hands. The body parts are not left free for other activities, as is true in the use of spoken language. Also, persons using them must be in the same place and be able to see the movements. Gesturing, it is obvious, cannot be used over long distances.

VALUE OF GESTURING Gestures, however, are important communication techniques in most societies. Systems of gestures often supplement spoken language when people assemble for specific purposes and when distance limits the effectiveness of sounds. The signals of football and baseball umpires, the motions of traffic policemen, the movements of airfield landing crews are all aids to communication in important areas of life. The winking of our eyes, the shaking of our heads, the waving of our hands in specific ways effectively supplement other forms of communication in small groups. The deaf and dumb communicate through complete gesture systems.

EXPRESSION OF SAME THOUGHT BY A DIFFERENT GESTURE In American society, we wave our hand and arm, turning the palm of the hand upward at the wrist so that our hand moves toward us when we wish to call a person to us. In China, the hand is turned downward in waving and moves toward the one called. In a number of societies, nodding the head up and down means "No," while moving it sidewise means "Yes." In American society, these movements have the opposite meanings.

Colors Are Used as Symbols, Also

We use black as the symbol of mourning in Western societies. White is the symbol for mourning in many Asian countries, but white gowns express purity in Western societies. In Japan if you wish to present gifts in the most appreciated manner, you wrap them in red and white paper and tie them with red ribbon or white paper tied with gold and silver ribbon.

An almost universally used color scheme with specific meaning is the green, yellow, and red traffic signal. These color signals with red meaning "stop," green "go," and yellow "caution" control the responses of automobile drivers throughout our society.

Objects Too Are Used for Carrying Messages

Material objects, such as the badge and the uniform of the policeman, the button of the delegate to a convention, the pin of the fraternity or sorority member, and the gold ring

"Talking drum" of a Mongo community used for communication between villages of the tribe.

of the married person, are all symbols carrying a particular message to those who understand.

COLLECTIVE REPRESENTATIONS Such objects as the seal of our lodge, the flag of our nation, the cross or crescent of a religion are examples of *collective representations*, symbolic objects that pull people together and solidify them around the ideas for which the objects stand. Notice the behavior of a crowd when a national flag is ceremoniously raised. All are at attention; none talk or walk until the raising is completed.

UNIFYING QUALITY Successful leaders know the necessity for having such symbols to unify the thought and feeling of their constituents. Hitler, for example, was well aware of this. He wrote in Mein Kampf that at the time the first great mass meetings were called in 1920 the National Socialist Party had no party emblem: "The lack of such symbols had not only disadvantages for the moment, but it was unbearable for the future. . . . Meanwhile, I myself, after innumerable attempts, had put down a final form: a flag with a background of red, with a white circle, and in its center, a black swastika." [4]

Laughter Is a Universal Form of Sound Communication that Expresses Favorable or Unfavorable Reactions

Laughter is a human sound that shows mirth by facial expressions and movements of the vocal chords. It is commonly provoked by incongruous behavior or situations. William Hazlitt has said that "man is the only animal who laughs and weeps, for man is the only animal who is struck by the difference between things as they are and things as they ought to be." It does not appear to serve any specific physiological need in human beings, but it does permit the expression of emotion and release of feelings.

Laughter may serve as an effective communicating device among people by unifying a group in good humor and conveying either approval or disapproval. We like to have our companions laugh *with* us but not *at* us.

Sound Is the Basis of Spoken Language, the Major Communication Device of Societies

Man created his most valuable communication system when he developed spoken language.

SOCIAL CONDITIONING   We come into a society bound together by a spoken language; this is part of our social heritage. We begin to acquire this spoken language through learning in earliest childhood. Repeated sounds are associated with objects, persons, and places until the sound itself creates a "picture in our minds" —the idea or meaning. We thus acquire a "word" that is associated by common agreement with a definite thing or thought. It is not necessary for the sound to indicate any characteristic of the object or idea or to be directly associated with it in any definite way. All that is required is that the sound call up the same thing or idea in all of us who use it. If by common consent and conventional use, "cats" were called "dogs" and all of us understood "dogs" to be "cats" and we were conditioned to this, then "cats" would be "dogs" to us. Under those circumstances, when the sound "dog" was made to us, the picture of the animal we now get when we say "cat" would come to our minds.

The first words man used usually referred to concrete objects. In time, the number increased to include actions and attributes, expanded further to include qualifying words, and finally encompassed abstract words.

Our ability to express and to understand ideas reaches a high level when we are able to use abstract words. We then have the capacity to generalize our experience since we can discriminate between essentials and irrelevants and put our experience into conceptual terms. Now "blue" does not refer only to our "blue"

ball, for example, but to "blueness" wherever we see or hear the word. Our speech becomes a storehouse of terms referring to concrete objects and general concepts that allow for ever-widening expansion of thought. A large measure of our education is the acquiring of competence in the understanding, proper use, and application of concepts.

WORD COINING   Men coin words almost without limit since they are able to make a wide range of sounds. We have just used a word that illustrates the invention, the borrowing, and the expansion beyond its original meaning. "Coin" is from the Latin *cuneus*, meaning wedge or cornerstone. It was borrowed from Latin and made by persons now unknown to mean a piece of marked metal issued by a government to be used as a medium of exchange. It has been expanded to take on the meaning of fabricating since all coins are fabricated things. Thus man gets his words by creating them deliberately, by borrowing them from other languages, and by adding new meanings to existing ones to meet new needs.

WORD MEANING   Here we must re-emphasize that the chief requirement of a legitimate word is that its meaning be understood in the same sense by both speakers and listeners. Many words are created but die because they are not accepted generally. We have already pointed out that in sociology the word "mores" was introduced by William Graham Sumner and made to mean those sanctioned ways of thinking and acting that are compulsive in a society. Today, sociologists use it in the English language in this sense. It is defined in the dictionary as those "customs or conventions which have the force of law." Whether the word "hurelures" that we have coined and used in this volume has similar success remains to be seen.[5]

Man Has Created Many Languages: They Both Unify and Divide Societies

Our ability to make an unlimited range of sounds is the basis not only for single words but also for complete systems of words or languages. Nearly 2800 languages have grown from the few words first used by primitive man.[6] Each language constitutes the means whereby a society or a group of societies expresses its ideas. Thus it is the chief bond of societies for it makes possible a collective mental life. Beyond this, it is the preserver of societies for it makes possible oral tradition. The experiences of man are handed on from generation to generation so that societies exist not only for the present but for the future as well. Language is not only a powerful unifier of a society, it is also a strong force creating barriers between and within societies. Many thinkers have emphasized our need for a universal language to aid common understanding that would overcome some of the antagonisms between peoples. (See Box 3.)

Every Society Wants Its Own Language

Common traditions, common ideals, common territory, and common religion are important factors in a society's unity. But common language is probably the major factor in maintaining this unity. Therefore, societies press for its development.

INDIA AS AN ILLUSTRATION India is an interesting illustration of this. Here about 370 million people speak 33 major tongues and approximately 225 dialects. A major reform in the society since 1947 stresses a common language. Hindi has been adopted by the government as the national language. Its general use is vigorously promoted.

As in all such situations, there are difficulties. There is the feeling that if a subdivision gives up its language, it will lose its identity. This is in part the purpose of the common language.

Because each segment idealizes its language by extolling its virtues, consequently there is opposition to a national tongue. A philosopher from the south of India said that the opposition to Hindi was so strong in the area where Tamil and Telegu are the common languages that revolt was threatened if compromises were not offered.

So India works out a series of compromises. Hindi is the national language. But each of the fourteen states keeps its own local language. India is trying to bring unity out of a series of states most of which have different languages.

American Society Has the Continuous Problem of Assimilating Large Numbers of Persons with Languages Other than English

One of the fascinating stories in cultural development is the building of a unified American society from the linguistically heterogeneous migrants who made up its population stock. Over 40 million persons crossed the seas from many lands to make their homes in the United States between the time of the American Revolution and the present.

ASSIMILATION AND LANGUAGE One in every 20 white persons in the United States in 1960 was born in another country. There were an additional 24 million residents who were native

---

BOX 3

[Words are often just a jumble of noises to us when we do not understand the spoken language. Mark Twain describes this problem humorously in a conversation between Huckleberry Finn and his Negro companion, Jim:]

"Why Huck, doan' de French people talk de same way we does?" [asks Jim.]

"No, Jim; you couldn't understand a word they said—not a single word."

"Well, now, I be ding-busted! How do dat come?"

"I don't know; but its so. I got some of their jabber out of a book. S'pose a man was to come to you and say Polly-voo-franzy—what would you think?"

"I wouldn't think nuffn; I'd take en bust him over de head—dat is, if he warn't white. I wouldn't low no nigger to call me dat."

"Shucks, it ain't calling you anything. Its only saying, do you know how to talk French?"

"Well, den, why couldn't he say it?"

"Why, he is a-saying it. That's a Frenchman's *way* of saying it."

"Well, its a blame ridicklous way, en I don't want to hear no mo' bout it. Dey ain't no sense in it." [7]

[This inability to understand and appreciate other languages would be humorous to us, as in this instance, if it did not result in serious consequences.]

whites of foreign or mixed parentage so that of the 159 million white residents, one in each five was either born or had immediate ancestors from another society.[8] A 1940 Census report (there is none for 1960) shows that nearly 20 per cent of the white population spoke a mother tongue other than English or in addition to English.

ENGLISH AS THE MOTHER TONGUE America has never legally adopted a mother tongue. That English is the mother tongue is simply accepted by custom. The English took over the territory in precolonial times, and persons speaking English greatly outnumbered persons speaking other languages—about four using English to each one using other tongues at the beginning of the nineteenth century.

Other factors also contributed to the elimination of other languages. Great Britain has continuously contributed large numbers of her citizens to the annual immigrant population. Under present laws, the normal number of persons allowed to enter the country from England and Northern Ireland is 42 per cent of the total annual immigrant quota.

The foreign settlers scattered throughout the undeveloped land and settled in neighborhoods and communities of similar-speaking people. But they soon found it necessary to know English in order to engage in the expanding economic and social life. Most were willing, though often reluctantly, to add the new language to their working tools, and particularly to learn it to aid their children.

PERSISTENCE OF FOREIGN LANGUAGES There are forces, however, that support the persistence of other languages. Pride in the cultural accomplishments of their homelands upholds the desire of people to retain ties with them. Common language is a strong force in maintaining closely knit national units within an adopted land. A different language can often give support to unique religious viewpoints that some sectarian or denominational groups promote. The concentration of the non-English speaking immigrants in the northeast section of the United States, and especially in her large cities, promotes the persistence of foreign languages. New York City, for example, includes nearly 350,000 foreign-born Italians, largely concentrated in specific areas. (This is comparable to the number of Italians living in the city of Bologna, Italy.) The problem of language assimilation is difficult in these circumstances.

American society is still a multilingual land, especially in certain sections of the country and in many urban areas. But the foreign-speaking have always been a source of strength when they shared duties and rights with the native citizens. Edward Bok was led to ask in his autobiography: "I wonder whether, after all, the foreign born does not make in some sense a better American—whether he is not able to get a truer perspective; whether his is not the deeper desire to see America greater."[9]

Communication Took a Further Great Step Forward When Men Developed Marks on Materials to Stand for Things and Ideas, from Which Evolved Written Language

Man began the use of written symbols to carry messages when he started to make pictures on the ground, on stones, or on the walls of caves to inform his companions that animals or men were nearby. "Write" meant originally to scratch, and primitive pictographs actually were made by scratching on surfaces. Primitive man recorded his experience for others when he scratched the shape of a fish or an animal or scored the shape of a tree on some substance.

ORAL TRADITION AND PICTOGRAPHIC FORMS Man's retention of valuable experience depended upon his unaided memory until he learned to make meaningful marks. Oral traditions handed on the ideas and facts that were beneficial or desired. Legends, proverbs, and maxims were important in societies. Many facts and ideas were lost, however, since all of them could not be fixed in oral tradition.

The pictographic form of communication was definitely limited, too. The number of objects that could be pictured was few, and it was difficult to express thoughts and actions in this manner. Because pictures were poor devices to create ideas in the minds of those who do not already know the meaning, ideographs, which are combinations of pictures connoting ideas, were developed. Chinese written language is an illustration of an almost complete ideographic system.

The advantage of this system is that the ideograph, being fixed, always gives the same meaning, no matter how different the spoken languages. The natives of Canton in South China cannot understand what the natives of Peiping in North China say, but they can read their written messages since both use the same ideograms. The disadvantage of the system is that a knowledge of a large number of ideograms is required to read even simple material. In trying to overcome the illiteracy of China, a 1000-character system was thought necessary to read even simple materials.

MARKS AS REPRESENTATIVE OF SOUNDS Man's next forward step in written language was to let marks stand for the sounds he made. Here a few marks—26 in the Roman alphabet used almost wholly throughout Western societies— can be combined into many words in which spoken and written language are directly associated. This change to a system whereby combinations of alphabetic symbols stand for sounds —the phonetic system—meant great progress for man and his societies.

So man has evolved basic communication systems, especially spoken and written languages, that make possible the development, exchange, conservation, and perpetuation of his thoughts and actions. No useful knowledge need now be lost. What a limited world we would live in if our ancestors had not developed symbols to substitute for complete acts; what a boundless world it is for us because they did.

Written Languages Have Made the Expansion of Communication Techniques Almost Unlimited

Written materials were produced slowly since the first writing had to be done by hand methods that allowed for little duplication. The volume of written materials therefore was small. Written materials were at first limited to the small educated class, particularly the clergy who almost alone had the ability to write.

PRINTING The invention of printing from movable type ended this limitation. The first printed book was produced no more than 500 years ago although block printing was known in China in 50 B.C. Gutenberg's revolutionary invention stimulated reading and writing among all the people. No longer would small segments of the societies have a monopoly on knowledge. The information could be correct or corrected. No previous invention of man made the education of all the people so possible. Books are its most important product. As Milton says in his defense of a free press: "They do preserve as in a vial, the purest efficacie and extraction of that living intellect that bred them." [10] About 1000 new books are now produced in the United States every month of the year.

Newspapers—there were nearly 2000 English language dailies with a circulation of nearly 60 million copies in the United States alone in 1958 [11]—and magazines—hundreds of them ranging from general consumers magazines to special professional and trade journals—give the public possible contact with all avenues of experience and aid in personality enlargement and social control.

Letter-Writing and the Sending of Written Messages Became a Chief Way of Communication

The sending of messages between persons and places developed rapidly when writing became a common tool, the letter being one of the most important. National and international postal systems have evolved around their distribution. Today, these systems hold the world together in a vast network of closely interrelated communication services that operate under every circumstance. Post offices now literally cover the earth, bringing the remotest places and persons within reach. The United States has 42,000 post offices tied together by over 2 million miles of mail routes. They dispense the astronomical number of 22 billion ordinary postage stamps in a year.

PERSONAL LETTERS Personal letters have particular sociological importance. Sealed under the cover of a directed envelope and available only to the individual addressed, they become an especially intimate bond between people. They are, next to direct conversation, the best medium for expressions of a private nature. We can "let go" if we are sure of our correspondent, releasing our own thoughts and inspiring the thoughts of others. Yet, they can be most deadly poisons or sweetest perfumes, for their contents do not disappear, since they are usually put on durable materials.

Thomas and Znaniecki took advantage of this characteristic of the personal letter to analyze major motivations, and the result was one of the important early studies of social attitudes. They confirmed a classification of the chief wishes from their analysis of personal letters collected in Poland and the United States which relatives and friends had written to each other. The classification still has wide application.[12]

Few desires are stronger than the desire to receive mail. It has a mystery about it that intrigues. It is a tie with the outside world that spells new experience. We await the mail with expectation; we open letters with anticipation.

People give first attention to it. Advertisers know this and exploit this interest as a selling stratagem. Indeed, probably a great proportion of one's daily mail consists of letters with something being offered for sale.

The Expansion of Knowledge Has Led to Special Systems for Particular Areas of Experience

The rapid accumulation of stored knowledge in these symbol systems makes it impossible for any one of us to encompass even a small part of it. Educational systems now endeavor to give some knowledge of the basic arts and sciences so that we have an appreciation of their social significance. Then they specialize in training us to be competent in at least one major subject area. Societies depend increasingly upon the specialist, and the specialist depends upon the careful observation of a particular order of phenomena in order to discover their characteristics and apply the principles by which these phenomena operate.

SPECIAL VOCABULARIES   The specialist in each field is aided in transferring his materials meaningfully and economically to those within his own and related fields, for language systems make possible the creation of communication symbols necessary to his operation. Each subject matter area develops its own vocabulary, and there are usually particular symbols within each vocabulary that abbreviate it. Thus the chemist, the musician, the mathematician—to indicate a few—evolve symbolic systems that express the qualitative and quantitative characteristics of their phenomena.

Mass Communication Techniques Now Make Instantaneous Communication Possible on a World-Wide Basis

In spoken and written form man became able to transfer effectively his ideas through both the present and the future. Printing allowed material to be stored for the future and to be eventually distributed over wide areas. However, man still had the problem of communicating rapidly across long distances.

SPEED IN COMMUNICATING   Early man solved the problem of speed of communication by the use of drums carrying sound signals, by flaming arrows shot into the air, by rising smoke carrying sight signals, or by runners bringing the news on foot or on animals. Such methods, though, could not be universally used because they usually gave specific information about rather local matters. Although faster than direct contact, they were slow by modern standards. Even as late as 1825, when the Erie Canal in New York State was opened, the news was sent to New York City from upstate by a series of cannon shots.

TELEGRAPH   Then came inventions that solved the problem of speed. Samuel B. Morse had designed the magnetic telegraph in 1832. Twelve years later the first message—"What hath God wrought"—was sent over a telegraph line between Baltimore, Maryland, and Washington, D.C. Now the telegraph spans the world with almost instantaneous speed.

TELEPHONE   The telephone came in 1876. Today, only 87 years later, there are at least 100 million telephones in the world, over one-half of them in the United States. From the first marvel of a conversation from New York to Chicago in 1892, it is now possible for us to talk around the globe in a few short minutes.

RADIO   Radio transmission from an established station did not start until 1920 when the Westinghouse Electric Company built the first broadcasting station in Pittsburgh, Pennsylvania. Marconi had received a patent on wireless communication in England in 1896, and the first radio message was sent in December, 1902. In 1961, just 41 years after the establishment of the Westinghouse station, there were nearly 5000 stations broadcasting in the United States alone. Practically all homes in the nation—over 52 million—have one or more radios, while at least 170 million sets are now in use in the land. Radio, like the telephone and the telegraph, has circled the globe, too, with nearly 200 million more sets in use in other societies of the world.[13] Radio now supplements the other communication media in giving instantaneously news and entertainment to the whole world. It is said that the tolling of Big Ben in Westminster Abbey can be heard by radio in Sydney, Australia, halfway round the world, as soon as it is heard by the people of London on the streets below.

TELEVISION   Now there is television, where we not only hear but also see the action as it takes place. Invented only 30 years ago and with only 10,000 sets in use before the Pearl Harbor attack, television has expanded so rapidly that now there are over 50 million sets in use in the United States and over 30 million sets in other countries.[14]

The Results of These Developments Constitute New Epochs for Societies

This globe-circling revolution in communication with its rapid accumulation and spread of mass media results in profound effects upon societies and their relations. It means the universal linkage of experiences for us. Almost instantaneously far-flung societies are made aware of world events. This linking together of societies in common experiences enlarges the scope of social vision beyond local confines and makes all men more aware of the wider world.

The effects of mass communication within societies are no less dramatic and significant— however one may evaluate them. The varied regions of large sprawling countries become more closely linked and the differences among them progressively reduced. Through the services of network television, millions of Americans from Maine to California may, at the same moment, be responding uniformly to the courtroom forensics of a Perry Mason or a David Brinkley's wry wit. We sometimes speak critically of this effect as the "homogenization" of culture. This may mean, however, that many pepole are lifted to a level of culture, information, and social awareness never before enjoyed.

On the other hand, the totalitarian state has demonstrated the tremendous political potential of mass communication.[15] Typically, the closely organized power structure monopolizes all communication channels and is in a position to saturate the masses with political propaganda. The "official line" can be incessantly drilled into the populace to the exclusion of all competing ideas. Such complete control of communication is, of course, the basis of complete control of the society.

The Practical Necessities of Life Require Care in the Use of Communication Techniques

Each of us uses different forms of communication daily. The operations of society and individual living are influenced by the way in which we use these symbols. Wrong traffic and railroad signals, the failure of fog horns, misused words in documents, and many similar errors have serious consequences. Such difficulty is revealed in the following experience of a family which had changed its residence.

The family was storing its household goods with a warehouse company. The husband said to the warehouse representative that he would send a note to the company to inform them of the address to which the storage receipt should be sent after the moving vans had taken the goods from the home. The husband wrote the company about two weeks later the following note: "Please send the list of goods stored with you on (date given) to me at (and the address followed)." Nothing was heard from the company for a month. Then, to his amazement, the husband received a bill of lading for a carload of his household goods that had been packed and shipped by rail to him at the address he had given in the letter!

Had he asked the company to pack and ship his goods or had he simply asked for *a list* of his goods? His intention was to ask only for the list the company had made of the goods when they stored them. Any possibility of this error could have been avoided by him, however, by saying: "Please send me the storage receipt for the goods stored with you, and so on." The warehouse company interpreted the phrase "the list of goods" as meaning "the goods." Our lawyers say that a large proportion of the civil cases that come to our courts today relate to misinterpretation of the words we use.

This incident illustrates a second practical point about communication. One is obligated to answer business correspondence within a reasonable length of time. The warehouse company did not reply to the request for "the list of goods" for about 30 days after they received it. Had they replied within a reasonable time, saying they had received the request and would ship the goods shortly, the error in interpretation could have been corrected.

Confucius said: "When words are misused, affairs go wrong. When affairs go wrong, courtesy and music droop. When courtesy and music droop, law and justice fail—people can move neither hand nor foot. So a gentleman must be ready to put words into deeds. A gentleman is in no wise careless of words."[16]

Transportation May Be Considered an Aspect of Communication

The carrying of people and products from place to place is not communication in the strict sense, but it enhances social contacts through overcoming distance, quickening population movement, and promoting the distribution of people, things, and ideas. The means of bringing people and products to one another can therefore be considered instruments of communication. We could trace the development of the techniques of transportation and their ac-

Two modes of traveling in oriental society.

Mayflower, which brought the 125 Pilgrim Fathers over 300 years ago in 66 days. Today, majestic ocean liners cover this same distance in less than one-tenth of this time. The total waterborne commerce of the United States, including foreign imports and exports and domestic hauling on lakes and rivers, was close to one billion tons in 1956.

SOCIETIES TIED CLOSER BY RAILROADS Rolvaag expresses the feeling of midwestern American settlers when the railroads first came in the middle of the nineteenth century: "People felt that day a joy that almost frightened them; for it seemed now that all their troubles were over, that there could be no more hardships to contend with. . . . For now that the railway had come as far as this, it wouldn't take long before they would see it winding its way into Sioux Falls." [17]

Today, railroads cross all lands. The American network is a quarter of a million miles long, carries 500 million passengers, and pulls 3 billion tons of freight in a single year. We take them for granted.

A MORE EFFICIENT SYSTEM THROUGH THE AUTOMOBILE No present-day college student can remember back to the time when the automobile was not common in his society. But about 50 years ago there were fewer than 500,-000 of them in the United States; today there are over 60 million.

The automobile truck is changing transportation and transportation costs around the world. The famous camel caravans that carried the licorice, spices, cotton, and other goods from across the Euphrates and Tigris rivers in the Middle East to Aleppo and the port cities of the Mediterranean have all but disappeared. The truck is displacing them. In this Middle East area, it costs about one dollar per ton-mile to transport goods by human, donkey, or camel portage. In contrast, it costs less than three cents per ton-mile for truck hauls in the United States. In the Middle East, the cart driver gets $1.25 per day for wages; in the United States, the truck driver gets over sixteen dollars per day for a ten-hour haul. Yet, the cost of trucking is only one-half a penny per ton mile for wages in the United States contrasted with one dollar per ton-mile for wages in the Middle East. Primitive transportation destroys wealth almost faster than men can produce it.[18] Modern transportation is an important creator of wealth as well as a unifier of societies.

cumulation in much the same manner as we have the strictly communication techniques. Both are essential to the development and unification of societies.

SHIPS AS FIRST IMPORTANT VEHICLES The development of early societies came with the progress made in water transportation. The great civilizations of the Middle East were produced in the valleys of the Euphrates, Tigris, and Nile rivers. Their life depended upon these historic waterways. As ships grew larger, the cultures of Greece and Rome came into being, with the Mediterranean Sea providing the routes of trade and travel later. Later, sailing vessels and the steamships brought societies to interoceanic travel.

An Illustration of America's Transportation Development The crossing of the Atlantic Ocean has been re-enacted in 55 days in a sailing vessel that was a replica of the original

Native transportation in Alaska.

HIGHWAYS AS BASIS OF NEW PATTERNS We are aware that roads develop along with our modes of transporting. They probably multiplied when man settled down to cultivate his land. They lie silent on the earth like ribbons, binding villages, towns, cities, and rural areas together into unified wholes. Overland road systems declined in importance when railroads first came, but the automobile has restored them to prominence. They are now changing the shape of societies. Today, village communities extend far beyond their original boundaries. City workers spill over into the surrounding rural territory, and rural residents have their daily employment in city shops and factories. Farmers listen to prices quoted for hogs, cattle, corn, cotton, or wheat at the breakfast table, load their trucks—if the prices are favorable—and soon their products are at the market of choice because surfaced highways run by their farms or are only a short distance away.

Possibilities from Highways This new patterning means new possibilities. New school systems based on bus transportation, the enlargement and relocation of retail stores, new distributing centers, elaborate systems of traffic control, and the construction and maintenance of the roads themselves are all parts of our new pattern of life. The road systems outside of cities and towns in the United States total over 3 million miles and require tremendous outlays for upkeep and repair. Superhighways now make it possible to travel from New York City to Chicago—800 miles—without having to stop for a single traffic signal, cross a road or street intersection, or a railway line. The vast sixteen-year program for constructing 48,000 miles of interstate superhighways now underway dwarfs any public works program ever attempted by man.

Social Reorganization Is a Consequence New social problems are part of this development. Communities spring up where geographic conditions and social and economic circumstances operate to make settlement advantageous. New social control problems are created by the wider dispersal of people and by the highway pattern resulting from motels, trailer parks, and the mushrooming tourist business. The control of crime, for example, becomes more difficult as superhighways make it possible to travel speedily in high-powered cars. All police agencies assume expanded roles. This new pattern is responsible for interdependent social organization in which contrasts between urban and rural are no longer meaningful and where all segments of the population share in the life of the whole society to an extent never previously possible.

CLOSER BONDS THROUGH AIR TRANSPORTATION
The aviation industry has grown from a small
concern of a few men to one of the largest in
the entire world. International lines linking all
the major cities of the world have developed
in the brief period since Charles Lindbergh
soloed across the Atlantic in May, 1927. They
carry people and cargo at tremendous speeds so
that it is literally possible to board a plane at
7 A.M. in Rochester, New York, be in New
York City (350 miles away) by 9:30 A.M.,
carry out a day's work, leave New York at 5
P.M., and be in Rochester again by 7:30 P.M.
Jet-propelled planes are now carrying passengers at far greater speeds. For example, the first
jet-liner flight from London, England, to Johan-
nesburg, South Africa, covered 6724 miles in
less than 24 hours.

Communication and Transportation Make Us One World

What does this vast accumulation of communication and transportation techniques—
spoken and written languages, printed materials, telephone, telegraph, radio, television,
ships, trains, automobiles, airplanes—mean in
the organization and operation of our societies?
In answer to this, we would immediately say
that without communication and transportation
there would be no human relationship structures and no societies in the modern sense. They
upset old ways and stimulate the development
of the new. They make possible greater unification within societies. And today, they dramatically create the need and opportunity for the
unification of world society.

References

1. Mead, George H., *Mind, Self, and Society,* ed. by Charles W. Morris (Chicago, University of Chicago Press, 1934), pp. 75 ff.
2. Dewey, John, *Democracy and Education* (New York, The Macmillan Company,
   1916), p. 5.
3. Pei, Mario, *The Story of Language* (Philadelphia, J. B. Lippincott Company, 1949),
   p. 13.
4. Hitler, Adolph, *Mein Kampf* (Ralph Manheim ed.; Boston, Houghton Mifflin Company, 1940), pp. 730 and 735.
5. See Chap. 6.
6. *The World Book Encyclopedia,* 10 (Chicago, Field Enterprises, Inc., 1953), p. 4254.
7. Clemens, Samuel L., "The Adventures of Huckleberry Finn," *The Family Mark Twain*
   (New York, Harper and Brothers), p. 497.
8. United States Department of Commerce, Bureau of the Census, *Statistical Abstract
   of the United States, 1962,* Table 22, p. 29.
9. Bok, Edward, *The Americanization of Edward Bok* (New York, Charles Scribner's
   Sons, 1921), p. 451.
10. Milton, John, *Areopagitica* (London, Charles Wood, 1819), p. 17.
11. United States Department of Commerce, Bureau of the Census, *Statistical Abstract
    of the United States, 1961,* Table 696, p. 517.
12. Thomas, William I., and Znaniecki, Florian, *The Polish Peasant in Europe and
    America* (Boston, The Gorham Press, 1918).
13. United States Department of Commerce, Bureau of the Census, *Statistical Abstract
    of the United States, 1961,* Table 690, p. 514, and Table 1220, p. 940.
14. *Ibid.,* Table 1250, pp. 940–941.
15. Schram, Wilbur, and Riley, John W., Jr., "Communication in the Sovietized State,
    as Demonstrated in Korea," *American Sociological Review,* 16 (December, 1951),
    pp. 757–766.
16. *The Harvard Classics,* 44; Sacred Writings, 1, "The Sayings of Confucius" (New
    York, P. F. Collier, 1910), p. 41, Chap. 13, line 3.
17. Rolvaag, O. C., *Giants in the Earth* (New York, Harper and Brothers, 1938), p. 398.
18. *Automobile Facts* (Detroit, Mich., May, 1949).

Questions for Study and Discussion

1. Show the importance of symbols in communication.
2. How important are gestures to you in your social relations?
3. Discuss a national flag as a collective representation.
4. How do languages unify societies? Divide them?
5. Why does each people seem to insist on its own spoken language?
6. Discuss assimilation and language differences.
7. How has written language influenced the relationships between societies?
8. Show how the use of both spoken and written language often create problems within and between societies.
9. How would you defend the idea that transportation is an aspect of communication?
10. What are automobiles and roads doing to the community where you live?
11. Discuss the relationship of communication and transportation to the "one world" idea.

Suggested Topics for Reports

1. Observe closely and record for one full day the non-verbal gestures you and your associates use. Insofar as possible, in each instance, indicate what the gesture communicated.
2. Examine the flags of several countries and explain the symbolism of each of the component elements.
3. Examine and evaluate "Esperanto," "Basic English" or some other simplified system of linguistic communication.

Supplementary Reading

Allport, G. W., and Postman, L., *The Psychology of Rumor*. New York: Henry Holt and Company, Inc., 1947.

Berelson, Bernard, and Janowitz, Morris (eds.), *Public Opinion and Communication*. Glencoe, Ill.: The Free Press, 1930.

Carroll, John B., *The Study of Language*. Cambridge, Mass.: Harvard University Press, 1953.

Chase, Stuart, *The Power of Words*. New York: Harcourt, Brace and Company, 1954.

———, *The Tyranny of Words*. New York: Harcourt, Brace and Company, 1938.

Lindesmith, A. R., and Strauss, A. L., *Social Psychology*. New York: Dryden Press, 1949.

Pei, Mario, *The Story of Language*. Philadelphia: J. B. Lippincott Company, 1949.

Smith, Bruce L., Lasswell, Harold D., and Casey, Ralph D., *Propaganda, Communication, and Public Opinion*. Princeton, N.J.: Princeton University Press, 1946.

5

THE PERSON IN SOCIETY: SOCIALIZATION

PERSONALITY, *rooted in the genetic heritage, is produced by the socialization process. Each human being acquires a pattern of habits, attitudes, and traits that characterize him and make him a unique person. Individuals develop an awareness of themselves as persons chiefly through the role-taking process as they develop their personality. Persons may become mentally disorganized because of mental conflicts they are unable to resolve. Some, unfortunately, are never able to develop a normal personality.*

How Societies Influence the Individual and Make Personalities Is Now Our Concern

Societies, of course, are made up of human beings, and it is equally clear that it is the interrelationships among human beings that make societies. How they do so is the central part of our study. One of the aspects of our understanding of societies is how they, in turn, shape persons, for persons are the essential carriers of the culture of any society. This leads us to one of the paradoxes of life: persons produce societies and societies produce persons. This is to say, as Cooley put it, that "society and individuals do not denote separable phenomena, but are simply collective and distributive aspects of the same thing, the relation between them being like that between other expressions one of which denotes a group as a whole and the other the members of the group, such as the army and the soldiers, the class and the students, and so on." [1]

We want to give attention now to the person in society so we may see more clearly why the person is the primary carrier of the culture and how the society influences the person. This will also indicate to us how the society operates in personal relationships.

The Individual Is Born into an Operating Society

Any particular individual comes into an already organized society. It has operated before the individual exists both in time and in function. We use the term "individual" with definite intent because each child is born into a society a helpless human individual. He possesses a biological equipment that will operate to make life possible, if properly stimulated. He possesses no habits, no attitudes, no wishes, no sense of the world about him. In fact, he has few if any characteristics that distinguish him from other animals except his human form. He is not a person; this he must become. He does this in the society into which he is born and as a consequence of the influences it has upon his biologically inherited equipment. His existence is bound to the society of which he is a part. The biological equipment individuals inherit from the stock that produces them is the foundation upon which individuals are made persons by their participation in their societies. It is of importance for the qualities it possesses set limits to the developmental processes that are possible.

The Biological Basis of Personality Lies in the Genetic Heritage

Not only is each individual born into an operating society, he is also the product of a given biological stock. This biological stock passes on its qualities to the individual through the genes by an interchange of characters that gives each individual a biological structure and a set of tendencies and dispositions. Each parent transmits 24 chromosomes (or 48 in total) to the offspring at conception. These chromosomes carry the gene potentials for physical and mental growth to their offspring, which makes each individual a biological expression of this crossing. However, the genes can combine in many ways, so that any individual is never a simple addition of the characters passed on from the parents but a unique combination of the potentialities the combinations possess. The way in which the gene potentials express themselves is influenced to some extent by environmental conditions. For example, the average height of many populations in the United States, Europe, and Japan has increased steadily in the last 50 years. These changes are due primarily to environmental influences, especially nutritional advantages which these populations have increasingly enjoyed.[2] Environment begins to play a role in determining what we will be from the beginning, although the individual's development is founded on his biologically inherited potentials.

Many Biological Factors Contribute to Personality Development

It is obviously impossible for us, because of the multitude of biologically inherited factors in man, to describe all of those that contribute to his development. However, these have been grouped so that it is possible to indicate by categories those that appear important in changing the biological individual to a social person.

BODILY STRUCTURE We inherit bodily structures that influence our functioning. Our upright posture makes it possible for us to see considerable distances and to have our hands free; our head set on a swivel makes it almost possible for us to see in all directions around us; our apposable thumb makes it easy to hold objects for inspection and use; our complex voice mechanism makes vocal language and a wide range of tones possible; and our complex brain with an infinite number of possible neural connections all relate significantly to our personality development.

Of course, we vary in the possession of these characteristics so that their influences on our personality vary. The physically attractive person is influenced by his own appearance and influences others by it. Benjamin Franklin made an attractive physical impression by his looks and size. An English bobby, watching him walk down a London street, commented to his partner: "There goes a king." The phrase "the hypnotism of beef" was used to indicate the influence that the size of William Howard Taft, who was a large man, had on people. Persons who are limited physically can often overcome this to some extent by training and care of personal appearance.

The nerve and glandular systems are the chief inherited mechanisms in our emotional development. The ability of our nervous system to respond to stimuli is the base on which our learning rests. Some individuals inherit a nervous system that has little ability to respond. But the great majority have an average or better than average nervous equipment so that learning can progress in almost unlimited ways. Much of learning, assuming a normal nervous system, is related to what we already know and the efforts we put forth to learn. Our intelligence, founded in biology, is a social consequence.

The glandular system also stimulates our behavior. The internal glands pour chemical secretions (hormones) into the blood stream that stimulate action. Cretinism, for example, a congenital morbid condition associated with deformity, results from malfunctioning of the thyroid gland.

REFLEXES Reflexes are simple automatic responses of parts of our body to stimulation. These include the eye wink, salivation of the mouth glands at the sight of attractive food, knee jerk, and muscular contraction when pinched or pricked. Breathing, the beating of our heart, digestion, and other bodily activities are reflexes. Survival depends upon the automatic operation of some of these. The body dies if they cease. They are not learned, nor can they be modified much by learning. They are important limiting forces in our functioning. One of our most serious health problems is related to the automatic reflex operation of the heart. Although these reflex actions enter into the problem of personality development, their influence is limited since they are automatic and not modifiable to any great extent.

PHYSIOLOGICAL URGES Appearing at birth or shortly thereafter are the infant's inherited impulses to act. They are related to its organic needs and appear in the form of tensions. It must have food, oxygen, water, proper bodily temperature, rest, and sleep, and it must eliminate waste materials from the body. The child becomes restless and tense where these are not satisfied and seeks to satisfy the needs by such bodily reactions as squirming, kicking, crying, and moving about. These reactions are not tied to the means for satisfying the needs but are apparently used in efforts to find a solution. The sex and hunger urges are of major importance as far as our personality and its relation to society is concerned, although all the urges are significant in providing a condition for socialization. Societies have evolved elaborate systems about these for our conditioning so that we will operate as acceptable persons in their satisfaction.

We may use hunger to illustrate the importance of these physiological urges. The body must have energy-creating fuel obtained from the chemical composition of foods. Blood composition changes, the nervous system is stimulated, stomach muscles contract and cause pain, and general irritation increases when it is not present over periods of time. We feel uncomfortable. This irritation can increase to the point where we are sensitive only to food and objects so that in our deprived condition we may talk and dream about food continuously. The body reacts by loss of weight, and a state of complete insensitivity is reached if we are actually starving.[3]

To satisfy the big problem of hunger urge we use a large proportion of our time and energy. Most work is related to the food-solving problem. We may ask for aid if we have no work, and we may steal if we can get no aid. Much of crime is related to this problem, especially when weather is unfavorable and work is scarce. Winter usually sees an increase in crime that is related to providing food and basic sustenance.

TEMPERAMENT Temperament is the next pattern of behavior above the level of the reflexes that is founded on the biological heritage that influences personality. It is the prevailing mood characteristic of an individual. Usually, these moods are described as excitable, happy, sad, or dull. These emotional differences, which show up in young children and can continue through life, may be modified by social experience so that the moods are not unchangeable.

The physiological basis of temperament seems to be the condition of the endocrine or ductless glands. These units of the glandular system, discharging their hormones into the blood or lymph, influence the functions of the body and the emotional expressions that accompany them so that differences in energy, vigor, lethargy, and feebleness show up.

These consequences can be modified by mod-

ifying the functioning of the glands. Cretinism with its limited mental development and morbid mood is overcome to some degree by properly stimulating the thyroid gland with thyroxine. Other consequences of glandular malfunctioning may likewise be corrected.

Social experiences are also conditioning factors in glandular functioning and consequent temperamental expressions. Individuals may be generally aggressive in some societies while in others they may be passive and meek due to the influences of the culture, as shown by Margaret Mead in her studies of New Guinea societies.[4]

CAPACITIES The innate ability to learn is the most important heredity capacity upon which experience can build personality. It is based upon the inherited state of our nervous system. Some people are intellectually bright while others are mentally dull. Students of this inherited capacity point out that, in a general population, it follows a normal probability curve in distribution with a small percentage of a population inheriting an abnormally high, and a small percentage an abnormally low, capacity. The bulk of the population inherits a capacity centering around the average. This capacity to learn has limits for each of us due to the inability to influence the character of the inherited nervous system to any significant degree. Most people, however, have average intelligence so that ability to solve the problems they will meet in their societies is part of their inherited equipment. Furthermore, this capacity is never used to its fullest degree. Both our own efforts and those of societies are such as to limit the knowledge we acquire and the opportunities we enjoy to use it. One of the tragedies of mankind is the vast amount of intellectual power that goes undeveloped. William James, the famous psychologist, is reported to have said that the average man develops only about 10 per cent of his latent mental ability.[5]

These biologically inherited characteristics vary with each person so that developed personalities differ one from another. However, bodily structure, reflexes, physiological urges, temperament, and mental capacity constitute the organic foundations on which the personality is built. They provide the materials out of which the person is made. These materials have a wide range of potentiality in the average individual. The interactions that take place between us and the society of which we are a part produce our personality because we are plastic and teachable. The newborn human being, therefore, is a "candidate for personality," to borrow the phrase of Koenig, Hopper, and Gross.[6]

Maturation Must Occur Before the Society Can Produce the Person

These biological potentials possessed at birth cannot express themselves fully at that time because many of them have not matured. They must ripen, which is a slow process in the human being. We have little control over this growing process and can influence it only to a limited extent. We proceed through the irreversible cycle of childhood, adolescence, maturity, and old age. The changes in the organs and tissues of our body come primarily without influence from the outside and in the absence of learning. They must take place before the "candidate for personality" can be conditioned by the world of people. The nervous system, consisting of some 12 billion nerve cells and countless nerve fibres that penetrate into the muscular system and bring about coordinate movement, must continue to grow until it has developed a vast network that pervades every part of the organism. This produces patterned changes in the nerve cells and corresponding changes in our pattern of behavior. The infant notices a moving ring by four weeks of age and picks up an object by 24 weeks. At first, he is unaware of space and does not begin to sense it and distance until he is nine months old. He develops command of parts of the world about him by slow degrees. He masters form and concepts of cause by the same slow processes so that he can ask where, what, why, who, and how and be able to understand them when his mental maturity and experience give them meaning.[7] This developmental process must take place to make personalities possible. When it never occurs in some infants, their incomplete growth makes it impossible for them to meet the expectations of their society. Idiots, for example, are so lacking in mental growth that they cannot learn the simplest acts of personal care.

Personality, the Product of Socialization, Chiefly Distinguishes One Human Being from Another

Individuals usually possess, we have been saying, the inherited potentials that can make them persons under conditions of proper maturation and conditioning. This does not mean that the new human organism is a passive entity simply to be played upon. It is an active unit driven by the biological traits that react to the environment. Organisms become persons through the influence of environmental forces and through their own ability to respond and weave their responses into a unified body of habits, attitudes, and traits. These, in turn, control their thought and action and direct their reactions to the world about them as a consequence of interpersonal relationships. Becoming a person, therefore, means absorbing the symbol systems of a society in order to communicate with fellow men and develop those traits that express the norms and values of the society. The process by which this is accomplished is called *socialization*.

Personality is, then, the totality of habits, attitudes, and traits that result from socialization and characterizes us in our relationships with others. It is the set of unifying principles that controls our behavior and coordinates our impulses and actions in their response to the world about us. The person, consequently, is the socialized human individual. He is one who has acquired the behavior patterns society transmits to him and to which he reacts in his specific ways. No person is ever identical to another because the growth and expression of the varying biological potentials and the external environments that influence him are always different. Mankind is consequently a collection of unique persons. Each individual is distinguishable from every other individual because of his unique personality—his own organization of traits, attitudes, and habits. Societies condition the uniqueness so that a person's conduct

Ritual conferral of personality: during his first few days of life, an infant in this African tribe has no social personality. Here, a group of women are engaged in the "coming out" ceremony which bestows a name and personality upon the child.

conforms with cultural requirements that are conducive to societal welfare.

Socialization Is Based on the Learning Process

The development of a set of habits, attitudes, and traits that differentiates us as persons from every other person and that directs our response to others is founded on the learning process. This includes the acquisition of coordinated physical responses to stimuli, the fixing of experiences in the memory, and the development of ability to respond adequately to situations in our environment. It thus involves the development of understanding of situations that expresses itself in our actions.

We learn primarily through conditioning, that is, by response to situations as a consequence of acquired associations. Learning is a process we can direct while maturation is a condition over which we have little control. Learning may be accomplished in four ways: (1) The methods of trial and error or trial and success fix the response by repeated efforts that lead finally to a solution. (2) Conditioned response associates our unconditioned stimulus-response with our conditioned stimulus-response so as to bring forth the unconditioned response.

Mongo mother carries child in the typical way. Contrast with the "front carry" of American mothers. Could it have implications for socialization?

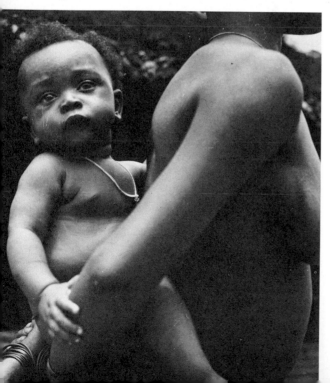

(3) Insight produces a solution suddenly without prior conditioning or trial and error. (4) Reasoning uses logic based on foresight that leads to the solution.

Our most important method of learning or becoming socialized is by acquiring from our fellow men, through communication, a knowledge of the contents of the culture of our society. We learn from other men and the symbol systems they create; we teach other men through communication and symbol systems that contain our past and present knowledge. Socialization occurs as a consequence of the internalization of learning. Personality is the expression among our fellows of this internalized learning.

Several Conditions of the Human Organism Prompt It to Become Socialized

We have pointed out that there are characteristics in our inherited biological organism that express themselves in various ways in response to the internal tensions our organism undergoes, as it is stimulated by its external environment. The child squirms, kicks, and cries as it responds to conditions within itself, such as the irritation from muscular contractions in the stomach that we call hunger pains. It responds to external stimuli, such as a too strong light or the pricking of a pin. There are persons in the external environment who also respond to the expressions the child makes to his frustrations. They also stimulate the child. The child reacts to these, attending to them as they do or do not satisfy his frustrations. These experiences lead the child to learn from them so that he becomes predisposed to certain responses when a similar situation again arises.

This means, in social situations, that the child learns to modify its reactions toward those who stimulate him so that their responses give him satisfaction. He learns that these satisfactions depend to a considerable extent upon the attitudes of others toward him. He learns to avoid reactions to them that bring him dissatisfaction. This capacity to adapt to others fixes in the mind social experiences that are remembered. These experiences in the form of stored ideas and mental images set the stage for the development of dominant habits and attitudes. These become the mental sets (attitudes) that predispose us to perceive, think, feel, desire, and act toward individuals and groups in definite manners. Acquiring attitudes toward the whole and not just to particulars makes the complete personality. It is social experience, then, that shapes the human organisms into personalities with specific habits and attitudes.

Unique Experience Is Important in This Socialization Process

THE DISTINCTIVENESS OF EXPERIENCE An important fact in the socialization process is that our experiences in interpersonal relationships are distinctive for each of us. It is easy to assume that individuals exposed to the same social stimuli in a common environment will react in the same manner. This is not necessarily true. Nor is it true that a common environment is the same for different persons. Elements in the common environment in almost all situations make our experiences unique for us because the integrating conditions are different for each of us. Each of us develops his own personal world in which norms and values have their distinctive meaning. It is in this sense that interpersonal relationships are unique and distinctive for each person.

THE RETROSPECTIVE ACT The retrospective act is what prompts our continuous adjustment to each unique experience.[8] We remember our experiences and recount them again and again. Our reactions to them modify their meaning and significance. There is a real truth in the admonition to "count your blessings, name them one by one" in its effect on socializing activities and their consequences in behavior. Wishes, habits, and attitudes are founded on the experiences that we recount continually. This reliving in the memory of our personally distinctive experiences makes them continuous factors in the socializing process. They lead us to normal, constructive personality organization or to its opposite.

Unique Experiences Are Not Always Crisis Experiences

It is easy for us to think of crisis experiences as those that are the distinctive ones. This is true in many instances. And they have profound consequences on our personality development and expression. When friends sought to console a soldier who lost a leg in the war, his response was, "Nuts, I didn't lose my leg; I gave it." Here was a constantly remembered experience that had all the possibilities for creating attitudes that could undermine a normal personality. Life includes many such crisis experiences: ill-health, a crippled condition, a child born mentally limited, or the death of a partner. Any such catastrophe can change the personality of the victim in proportion as he is able or unable to adjust to it as a result of his prior experience.

Any experience, however, is a unique one for each person. Being born a male and not a female, being the youngest and not the oldest child in the family, being saddled with a peculiar name, being compelled to take piano lessons, and a thousand other day-by-day occurrences are of extreme importance to the particular person, though they appear trivial to others. No experience can be considered unimportant in the development of personality. We develop habits, attitudes, and wishes that give our life its organization, primarily out of the everyday unpretentious occurrences that are unique *for us*.

Habits, Attitudes, and Wishes Play the Important Roles in Personality Development and Expression

HABITS We must consider the place of habits, attitudes, and other traits that characterize us as individuals in our relationships with others if we are to understand ourselves as societal products. We get mental impressions—notions, facts, ideas—from our relationships with others. These lead to ways of thinking and acting that become so natural as a consequence of repetition that they are expressed without premeditation. They become *habits*. The child not only learns to tie shoes almost automatically but also to think in response to repeated situations in routine ways. These almost automatic thought or action habits make it possible for us to react successfully without having to solve problems before responding. Most habits are exceedingly useful to us in adaptation to social situations in this sense.

ATTITUDES *Attitudes* are mental habits acquired from social experience that predispose us to react to specific objects, persons, or situations in a definite way. They are the crystallized habits of thought that we develop relative to social situations and that set us to respond in a certain manner. Our attitude is our psychological readiness to act; it is our fixed potential of behavior toward objects or conditions of some specific type. The behavior we carry out is, in the main, a response to our attitudes so that, if we know the attitudes of people, we can predict their behavior. The story goes that a woman in a Boston hotel called the hotel clerk complaining that the constant piano playing in an adjoining room made her nervous. She wished he would have it stopped. The clerk replied that he was sorry, that he wished he could help her, but the piano player was Paderewski practicing for his concert to be given that night in Symphony Hall. "Oh," came the quick response, "that's different." She immediately changed her demand and called in her friends to listen. A different attitude did its work. Her wish quickly changed. Attitudes are our prompters to behavior. Personality is in part the expression in action of the attitudes that dominate us.

A stoic proverb claims that men are tormented by the opinions they have of things rather than the things themselves. Such opinions of things—attitudes—come from learning in social situations so that such "memory spots" are social products. Some farmers hold that the only real economic producers are farmers. Such an attitude, right or wrong, develops only in a social situation where farming is an occupation and where it is related to other occupations. A society tries to internalize in individuals those attitudes that are in conformity with its norms so that our actions are in conformity with them and our personality expressions of them. Park and Miller pointed out a long time ago that "what distinguishes societies and individuals is the predominance of certain attitudes over others and this predominance depends . . . on the type of organization which the group has developed to regulate the expression of the wishes of its members." [9]

WISHES Personality is partly an expression of our attitudes in action. But our attitudes are related to our wishes. We are motivated to behave by our *wishes,* which can be as many as there are goals that have value for us. They extend from wanting to see a professional baseball game or a drink of water to becoming the most important person in a society. No matter what our specific wish—wishes are always specific and relate to some definite objective—it is based on our attitudes. We could hardly have a wish to see a professional baseball game unless we had some attitude toward the game that has been developed out of social experience. There is always some incentive to seek satisfaction based on our attitudes developed in the cultural milieu. The child desires some ice cream. The desire was not there at the start of life. Ice cream is a social product. Previous experiences with and attitudes developed toward it set the stage for the possible wish of the child to have ice cream. On the other hand, we may never

have heard of baseball. The suggestion that we watch a game may create the wish in us to find out more about this activity and so satisfy a partially completed experience.

Curiosity, the attitude of inquiry, is also the foundation for many of our wishes. Thus, when an automobile drove into a remote Chinese village, it brought forth practically every person in the village, all crowding insistently forward to see this thing that was vaguely known about through the channels of communication. Wishes based on attitudes, therefore, guide the continual round of activities in which we engage. They are the stimuli that set the course of action followed to achieve our goals. Usually, we must want before we can have. It is our desires that motivate our immediate actions based on the attitudes or mental sets we acquired from our social experience.

Wishes, we repeat, can be as many as there are goals that have value for us. Some have only slight importance and are often immediately dismissed. Others become the chief drives in our total behavior. Their importance to us may change as circumstances change. A famous author did not always want to be a writer. The birth of a defective child to whom this writer wished to give every care, yet whose care involved heavy expenditures, created the wish to write to be able to provide the care. Writing became his master motive. It still persisted after his financial problem was solved. His wish to continue writing took other forms, such as a desire to portray accurately the life of a people. His definitely personal experience and his intimate knowledge of a society's culture were motivators for carrying on a career that now has pre-eminence in his life.

Wishes may be many and varied. We satisfy them differently. The question is often asked whether there are universal wishes that are characteristic of most people in given societies, that is, whether people are in general motivated to achieve certain basic ends in the society of which they are a part. Several classifications of such wishes have been developed. One of the most commonly used is that of W. I. Thomas. Thomas, with Florian Znaniecki, first classified the basic wishes in their study of the Polish peasant. The classification was revised and explained in Child's *The Unconscious* as follows:

1. *New experiences* mean heightened states of stimulation, physiological expansion,

change, adventure, thrill. Interest in reports of the sensational, hunting game, pursuit in any of its various forms contain the pattern.

2. *Security* is the opposite of new experience. This contrast is often seen in work as against play, in utility as against pleasure, in saving as against spending. Youthfulness seeks new experience; old age, security.

3. *Desire for response* is found in love, in intimate privileges, in companionship.

4. *Desire for recognition* is satisfied in achievement of status, of fame, in approval in a large way.[10]

This classification of the wishes was not meant to include all of our wishes nor to imply that all of our wishes could be subsumed under these categories. The intention was to stress these as the significant areas of human behavior where we in our associations set up significant goals that constitute for us important aspects of living we almost universally desire to satisfy. For example, we universally, it appears, desire to be recognized, to count for something in our society. People may strive to satisfy this desire in different ways, some by holding office in an organization, others by being the strongest or most beautiful person in the community, and others by achieving some goal to which their fellow men give recognition.

Other classifications of wishes might be added, such as that of Cooley *et al.*: the need for self-expression; for appreciation; for a reasonable social security;[11] or of Ellsworth Faris, who in his course on social control reclassified the wishes of Thomas into the wishes of the appetites, such as hunger and sex; wishes for personal distinction; wishes for personal intimacy; wish for group superiority and loyalty.[12]

All such classifications (in which there is considerable overlapping) stress areas of social relationship and of personal behavior where our wishes serve as axes in our adjustment to situations. These classifications are general rather than specific, whereas our concrete wishes are related to a specific object or situation.

Habits, attitudes, and wishes, then, form the major socially acquired psychological components that orient our behavior in our interactions with others. They are an interlaced network of internal forces that prompt us to behavior. Habits make it possible for us to respond automatically to repeated situations; wishes motivate us toward objectives or goals; and

attitudes as mental sets dispose us to act in definite manners toward goals. All of these as expressed in societal relations bring into existence our personality.

The Chief Agencies of Socialization Are Our Families and Our Peer Groups

Every experience the individual has enters into his socialization. Thus, each influences the development of his personality. The habits, wishes, and attitudes that are characteristic of us as persons are built into us from the play upon us of all person-to-person experiences to which we have been subject. Consequently, the socializing agencies through which these experiences come are of major importance to us. If we operate in a situation where we are subject to a large and varied number of experiences, the problem of selection from among the values presented enters, and our socialization is complicated. Thus, those agencies that have a ready approach and to whom access is not denied have the better opportunity to influence us. Two social structures, our families and our peer groups, are the most important from this point of view.

THE FAMILY'S ROLE The *family* is our basic socializing agency. It is the unit that has direct, intimate, and almost exclusive contact in the earliest and most formative years of life. Its members interact with the child in satisfying its physical needs and, because it is of their own flesh and blood, their emotional responses are deep and meaningful. Physical care is accompanied by expressions of affection or rejection. As development takes place, feelings of approval or disapproval occur as the child learns to behave in the manner expected of him. Parental reactions to the child in terms of their hopes for it relative to looks, temperament, and intelligence become more pronounced and significant as these attributes are part of their own images of themselves.

The child reacts to all this and develops responses that become its attitudes, habits, and wishes. What they will be depends, in part, upon the nature of the attitudes expressed in the actions of his family. Where the child evokes love and affection from the family situation the resulting satisfaction and emotional calmness express themselves by his taking on the ideals and models of behavior set before him. If the family circumstances are otherwise, there may be abnormal socialization for the child always tends to take on the attitudes toward himself and his situations that others take toward him.

THE PEER GROUP'S ROLE The *peer group* of equals in age, experience, and status soon competes with the family as a socializing agency. Parents discover this abruptly when Johnny says or does something that they know was not a part of the family's mode of behaving. But it goes much further than this. As the peer group develops strong cohesion, it tends to take over the role of the family in socialization. Riesman and his colleagues go so far as to say that it is becoming our most important socializing agent since our societies now stress "other-directedness" as contrasted with "inner-directness" or "tradition-directedness." Nineteenth-century families, he says, inculcated their values and models of behavior by authority, and primitive societies depended on traditions. In modern societies, persons are "other-directed," taking their cues for their behavior from the approvals they get from their peers.[13]

The peer group like the pair exists for itself. It is a "we" group with strong solidarity and effective internal control. Therefore, it emphasizes conformity. When this solidarity supports family and societal norms, it then is a strong force for upholding these. When it does not support them, it presents the problem of risking the loss of peer group or of family and societal approval and support. Often, the peer group exerts its socializing power by achieving acceptance of its norms and values and replacing those of the family. Children in immigrant families are often confronted with this problem when they become members of peer groups that express cultural conceptions differing from those that prevail in their immigrant homes. Their parents may have little knowledge of the ways of their new society. The peer group is a more important avenue of instruction in the approved ways and so a more important socializing agency than the family. This is true in other situations also where the child, because of education and other experiences, grows away from his family and feels more acutely the need for peer group supports in achieving his goals.

The major consequence of all these socializing activities, from the viewpoint of society, is that the person is absorbing the standards of those influencing him so that the society's standards become chief motivators in his own behavior.

The Awareness of Self Is Created in Association with the Production of the Personality

Emerging concomitantly with the production of personalities, as collections of habits and attitudes built from experience in societies, is an awareness on the part of human beings that they are distinctive things with an existence apart from that of their environment. We develop a "self" while acquiring a personality. This rise of the sense of self, of "I," "me," "myself," does not refer simply to the awareness we develop with respect to our body but also to the awareness we develop relative to our ideas, desires, feelings and purposes as they express themselves in social situations. The self is a state of feeling we evolve about ourselves in our interactions with others. The newly born baby cannot perceive himself as an entity separate from his surroundings. He possesses no consciousness of himself. But he is expressing his sense of self when he says to his mother after she has referred to him as "the baby," "Don't you call me a baby; I am five years old." Here is feeling, opinion, and desire indicating that the child is thinking of himself as a distinct object in a definite social setting.

This development of the "self" as an idea about our self, a subject that it its own object supported by feelings that are held to in social situations, is another of the distinctive characteristics that we possess in contrast with other animals. Only man develops a self for only man communicates with other men in a cultural milieu in which he is aware of others and aware of himself as distinct from others. This development of *self*-consciousness as we are developing *social* consciousness is unique to the human species.

Self-Attitudes Are Developed Primarily Through the Process of Role-Taking

There could be no development of self if there were complete absence of social contacts. Such isolation, however, is almost impossible, as was pointed out in our first chapter. Therefore, each of us with a normal nervous system becomes a self as well as a person. How does this happen?

The child has social contacts from birth, especially with a mother who feeds and cares for him. Interactions with others also take place from the beginning. The others are playing roles in these contacts. The mother is performing the roles necessary to the care of the child. The father is doing his duties in providing for the child, loving it, talking to it. Brothers and sisters "baby-sit," watch over the child, and perform other services that are expected with respect to it. The child learns to adjust to these others in their role-performing situations. He wants things; some he gets and some he does not. There are prohibitions. Some things he learns to do automatically from these contacts. They establish themselves as his habits that are approved by others. The others talk to him. He learns to talk. He learns to talk in specific ways and at specific times. He learns that some things are his and some things belong to others. The child is gradually developing a recognition in these situations that there is a difference between himself and others as a consequence of his taking over into himself the attitudes, ac-

tions, and behavior patterns that the others express and he now expresses. He thus is an object to himself. He builds an image of himself as a distinctive thing from his taking "the role of the other which becomes sometimes 'sympathetic introspection' but, what is more important, leads the self to take the attitudes of the other to himself, thus becoming an object to himself, with all this implies." [14] (See Box 4.)

Playing at Roles Promotes the Process of Acquiring a Self

Sandra's father is a horseman who rides for exercise and plays polo for fun. He has riding horses at his suburban home. Sandra loves to sit in front of her father or mother as they ride around the pasture. She cannot ride by herself because she is only four years old. But she has a dozen or so stick horses, each with a name she

---

BOX 4

B (aged 14 months) was as curious about his environment as most children of his age. The knobs on the gas cookstove were particularly fascinating. The mother, though usually rather patient and indulgent toward his explorations, met these particular manipulative efforts with very firm "No! No's!," pulling him away and starting him off in other directions. After this interact had been repeated several times, B found the field clear for another try. He pulled up to the knobs and as he started to take hold he suddenly let loose a torrent of "No! No! No's!" with a vigorous shaking of his head; whereupon he backed off to survey the situation. He seemed a little surprised at hearing the parental admonition when no parent was present.

One late afternoon near the dinner hour B (now 26 months old) knotted his face into something of a scowl and pitched his normally low voice into something approaching an infant growl.

"I want some meat for my supper," he said to his mother. Then added, "I'm daddy and I've come home from work." The mother took the cue and addressed him as daddy, asked how his little boy B was, etc., etc.

At the table he insisted on taking his father's place at the head of the table, assigning the displaced parent to the high chair. He wished to serve but had to submit (after some protest) to being assisted in this part of his role. He admonished "B" not to spill his "brown milk" referring to the father's coffee. He referred to his milk as "white coffee" saying only big people could drink white coffee. After the meal B continued to act in his capacity as daddy and "read" a story to his "son" and finally undertook to put him to bed. The father finally balked at being put in the crib giving as his reason that the crib might break down. The two then agreed to "pretend" to put the father in the crib. It is interesting to note that if the father acted out of character B prompted him with very definite direction as to how "B" should act. Moreover if the mother or the maid did not treat B himself as father and the father as B, they were peremptorily put back into the proper relationship by B. [15]

has either made up herself or taken from the names of famous horses she has heard of, seen herself, or watched on television.

Sandra plays at riding horses when her grandparents come to visit. She puts on exhibitions of fancy riding, of cantering, of trotting. Her grandfather pretends he is announcing her at a horse show: "Miss Sandra Jane now

Moods and modes of socialization: spontaneous interaction in a children's play group and the serious business of taking on adult roles.

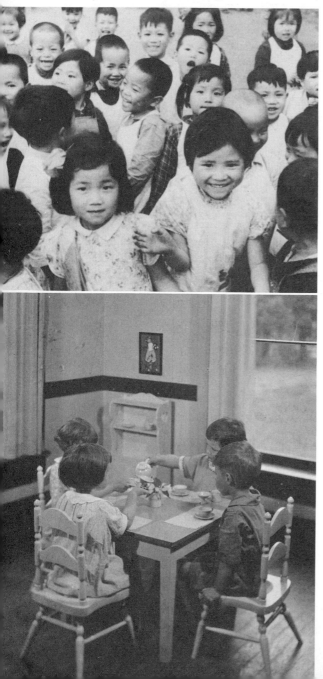

entering the ring riding her high-stepping beautiful pony." And Sandra comes into the living room, stepping high on her stick horse, Ginger, playing at the role of an exhibition horsewoman. She directs the horse, tells herself how to hold the reins, and gives instructions all around. All in all, she plays at the role of another while seeing herself in the light of these activities, thus defining herself by these situations. Children playing at housekeeping, wearing adult clothing, and doing innumerable things in imagination and imitation of the world about them become objects to themselves by assuming the roles of others and incorporating them into their personalities. The child recognizes himself as distinct from others, as a "self," by taking these roles of others and playing at them.

This Development of the Awareness of Self Is Illustrated by the Child's Acquisition and Use of Self-Words

Sandra calls Ginger, her stick horse, "my" pony. She tells her grandfather, "You" can sit over "there." She asks the other observers, "Will 'you' please sit on 'that' couch?" And she announces, "Now 'I' will show 'you' how Ginger can buck," when she puts on her riding exhibitions. She did not distinguish between "I," "you," "yours," and other indicators of her "self" feeling nor display understanding of the difference between herself and relevant others until after many conditioning experiences in which there was much confusion in the use of the self-other terms. But her conceptions of herself and what George H. Mead terms "the generalized other" became sharper as social experiences increased until Sandra now has a fairly unified self in which she is aware that she is a distinct personality in a world of persons.[16] (See Box 5.)

Self-Concepts Are Developed Chiefly in the Early Years of Life and in Primary Groups

Sandra's awareness of herself came in the early years of her life and in the intimate associations of the family of which she was a part. It was the intimate contacts with her mother and father that first gave orientation to her response to others and consequently her awareness of herself. So it is that all persons early in life become conscious of themselves as distinct social objects. The confidential, natural associations with family members, play companions,

BOX 5   Discovery of Self

"And then an event did occur, to Emily, of considerable importance. She suddenly realized who she was. There is little reason that one can see why it should not have happened to her five years earlier, or even five years later; and none, why it should have come that particular afternoon. She had been playing house in a nook right in the bows, behind the windlass (on which she hung a devil's-claw as a door knocker); and tiring of it was walking rather aimlessly aft, thinking vaguely about some bees and a fairy queen, when it suddenly flashed into her mind that she was she. She stopped dead, and began looking over all of her person which came within the range of her eyes. She could not see much, except a fore-shortened view of the front of her frock, and her hands when she lifted them for inspection; but it was enough for her to form a rough idea of the little body she suddenly realized to be hers.

"She began to laugh, rather mockingly. 'Well!' she thought, in effect: 'Fancy you, of all people, going and getting caught like this!—You can't get out of it now, not for a very long time: you'll have to go through with being a child, and growing up, and getting old, before you'll be quit of this mad prank!'

"Determined to avoid any interruption of this highly important occasion, she began to climb the ratlines, on her way to her favorite perch at the masthead. Each time she moved an arm or a leg in this simple action, however, it struck her with fresh amazement to find them obeying her so readily. Memory told her, of course, that they had always done so before: but before, she had never realized how surprising this was. Once settled on her perch, she began examining the skin of her hands with the utmost care: for it was hers. She slipped a shoulder out of the top of her frock; and having peeped in to make sure she really was continuous under her clothes, she shrugged it up to touch her cheek. The contact of her face and the warm bare hollow of her shoulder gave her a comfortable thrill, as if it was the caress of some kind friend. But whether her feeling came to her through her cheek or her shoulder, which was the caresser and which the caressed, that no analysis could tell her.

"Once fully convinced of this astonishing fact, that she was now Emily Bas-Thornton (why she inserted the 'now' she did not know, for she certainly imagined no transmigrational nonsense of having been anyone else before), she began seriously to reckon its implications." [17]

and neighborhood associates give us our basic conceptions of ourselves and of our relations to the world about us. Ideas about self are not fixed finally in these early years but the foundation stones are laid then in the primary group relationships. This period is without doubt the most important in the life of the individual in determining his ideas of himself and in molding his personality. Who others are and what they do are also exceedingly important in this developmental process because they are a part of the self.

Concepts of Self Dominate the Personality

The self is the controlling factor in personality after the individual has developed his sense of it. The awareness of "me" and of "you" gives the person his approach to the society about him. It is a major factor in determining the wishes that motivate his behavior. Recognizing the other in relation to self has introduced expectations from others and from self. Society is defined in terms of these expectations. Behavior and the character it gives to the person is an expression of reactions to these expectations. The desires are focused on ends that meet these expectations satisfactorily. We are, therefore, bundles of self-attitudes dominated by self wishes that express themselves in self-other relationships. We soon learn that our success is generally the consequence of the attitudes of others toward us. We can hardly be apathetic or stoical about this. Our own imagination of how others look at us leads us to judge ourselves, to evolve feelings about ourselves, and to react according to these feelings. This imagining of the way others think of us is the chief way we have of developing feelings and opinions of ourself. The organized person is one whose "I" and "me" feelings are those of satisfaction because he can judge that his appearance to others is one of satisfaction to them. This does not mean that approval is felt from all others. In fact, disapproval from some others in some situations is desired for their norms are not those that lead to approval from those with whom we wish to be identified. This domination of personality by our conceptions of self as built out of the imagining of how we appear to others means that there is usually continued striving in social relationships to achieve approval and to avoid disapproval. (See Box 6.)

Our Reference Groups Are Significant Factors in Personality Functioning

We see ourselves and the society about us from the viewpoints of the situations in which we operate. We define these situations in terms of the norms of the groupings that are significant to us. These definitions we make are thus limited to those segments of society we know and with which we can compare ourselves for the purpose of making self-judgment. For the most part, these are the groups in which we are members and operative and from which we get our perspectives and values. They are our chief *reference groups* from the point of view of both our perspectives and values. We compare ourselves with our reference groups and with our relevant others. We pattern our role performance according to the valuations that we see others have placed on our past role performance so that the behavior which expresses our personality is conditioned by them. This is but to say that the groups to which we belong and to which we orient ourselves are the primary determinants of our personality expression. We conform, in the main, to the norms of our membership groupings for it is they that give us approval and status.

But our orientation is often to persons and groups other than those to which we are specifically related. They may set forth norms that are different from or at odds with those of our own membership groups. They may also be mutually sustaining. Thus they can have an influence on our aspirations because they are also status-conferring. We do not wish to alienate ourselves from the groups with which we are identified, neither do we wish to alienate ourselves from those others to which orientation often seems desirable. This presents dilemmas for us. We are constantly confronted by these dilemmas and our necessity to react to them in our behavior situations. Our personality from this point of view reflects the manner in which we relate ourselves to both our membership and our nonmembership reference groupings and the role-conflicts these are likely to present to us. Newcomb points out that "most of us, most of the time, manage to take quite different roles, as prescribed by the same or different groups without undue conflict." [19]

Having stated the principle briefly, we now need to illustrate it so that its significance is made clear from our everyday activities. Each of us probably has a number of reference groups that influence our behavior. We may be a member of a fraternity, a church, a baseball or college team, and an Italian family and work at odd hours in a store with several others to help meet expenses. Each of these groups expects certain types of behavior from us for

---

BOX 6   Self and the Generalized Other

The Mead-Cooley interactionist framework provides a basis for the study of the genesis of self-conception. In using this framework to analyze the sources of differential self-evaluation in military groups, a direct relationship was found between self-conception, the perceived generalized other, and the actual responses of others. Further, a high degree of correspondence exists between self-conception and the perceived generalized other; this was not true for self-conception and the actual responses of others. . . . Persons whose self-evaluation disagrees with the evaluation rendered by the group are more likely to have a greater number of reference groups.[18]

---

each has its norms and values. Each may serve as a reference group for us. We may want to be president of our fraternity, so we react to its behavior requirements in order not to alienate our brothers and injure our chances of achieving our aspirations. Some may not be significant referents to us. Our work group may have little cohesion, and we ignore any influence it or its members may seem to have. Our Italian family has certain customs that are at variance with those of our college comrades. We adjust to these to retain the affection of our family by having some of our comrades visit in our home and enjoy our fine Italian food. We are constantly therefore expressing ourselves by adaptations to the groups of which we are members. These are our direct interaction reference groups.

But we want to be elected to Phi Beta Kappa or our engineering honorary fraternity, groups to which we do not belong. We use these as referents, too, by working at our academic responsibilities so as to maintain the type of scholastic record that merits our inclusion. Thus, we are continuously behaving in response to the norms of groups of which we are a part and of those of which we are not a part. These are the sources of the significant attitudes that mark our personalities.

Persons May Become Mentally Disorganized

We have achieved a major essential to a normal personality when we have organized the chief goals of our lives into an integrated whole so that there is unity of the self. It is true that all of us experience frustrations, that is, circumstances in which our desired goals are destroyed, made unattainable, or obstructed so that we experience disturbance and disappointment. They create crises for us since they introduce a break or a turning point in our relations to these goals. The seriousness of the crises depends upon the value of the particular goal. We meet most of these situations without great difficulty, and consequently their influence does not last. Most of them, indeed, are probably forgotten. Most of us function according to norms and conventions of our society in such a way that there are few serious conflicts with it. We exhibit the personal characteristics of sociable, contented persons.

On the other hand, relatively permanent consequences in personality disorganization result when frustrations are frequent or of such a nature that harmony between desired goals and possibilities of achievement are difficult to accomplish. It becomes difficult for us to maintain the organized self-expression that societies consider normal when we cannot forget disturbing experiences and similar ones occur or if we cannot reconcile them with our goals so that they remain inconsistent with our aims.[20] Our sense of security is disturbed. Our behavior is not dependable. Societies, however, are dependent upon the predictability of the overt behavior of its members. Personality difficulties arise when our behavior is in serious contrast to the standards of normality, and there is serious lack of social conformity. Societies do not usually concern themselves with our ideas or attitudes except where they portend damage to others or the society at large or lead to overt behavior that is harmful.

We invite serious mental disturbances that may destroy the unity of self if we cling to frustrating experiences or let mental conflicts persist. The effectiveness of outside assistance in overcoming personality disturbances is dependent upon our own desire to understand and deal with them constructively. This is the key to all efforts to give aid to mentally disturbed persons.

The Person Reacts to Mental Conflicts with Various Defenses

Psychologists and psychiatrists indicate a number of typical ways in which we adjust to mental conflicts arising from frustrating disturbances.

REPRESSION Repression is the exclusion from consciousness of unacceptable desires, impulses, and experiences, so that these frustrations are forced into the unconscious. We behave as if the frustrations were never there. The memory of our desire or act is removed. Forgetting an uncomfortable experience or banishing a desire is a common experience for all of us. This is part of being able to operate successfully in a society. Many natural desires are repressed for their direct expression is not approved by society. Societies hardly tolerate unlimited expressions of selfishness from us. Their transformation into constructive ambitions have, however, often been socially constructive. These individual desires that societies do not allow to be directly expressed can be socially beneficial when more socialized expressions are successfully substituted. Repression is, however, not completely possible so in unguarded moments or by peculiar acts, we exhibit the existence of the suppressed condition. The too great repression of normal desires, some psychiatrists point out, often leads us to serious mental conflicts.

AGGRESSION   Aggression is, in a way, the opposite of repression. Here we try to overcome the disturbance by some form of attack, which usually makes us aggressive. We do not wish to submit, especially when there is some indication that greater or different effort can overcome a frustration. The child says "I won't do it," and he may be persistent enough to overcome the determination of a weak parent. A candidate for political office tries again after one defeat on the theory that more aggressive campaigning will make up for the former deficit.

Sometimes, aggression expresses itself toward something or someone other than the real cause of the frustrating experience. The husband whose golf game has been frustrating "takes it out" on his wife or his children, or he may even "take it out" on himself by giving up the game. This decision is a way of making it impossible for this type of frustration to occur again. Usually, however, aggression finds other forms of expression than those directed against the self.

We often seek to overcome a frustration in one area by focusing renewed energy on a new objective. Thus we seek to compensate for one failure by going after something else. This substitution of goals has frequently led persons to achieve outstanding success in a field other than the one in which they originally hoped to succeed. Sometimes, exceedingly small persons try to compensate for their size by being overly assertive or by assuming an attitude of great importance. A case of delusory compensation is that of the mentally limited patient who insisted that he was a millionaire and owned the Empire State Building.

RATIONALIZATION   A common way of our adjusting to frustrating acts or desires and avoiding disturbing consequences is for us to think up justifying reasons that satisfy us. A writer who makes little progress because the ideas come hard and the work is tedious, will, instead of sticking it out, turn to something else, such as going out for a walk to get some exercise or going for a cup of coffee, on the theory that he needs the exercise or the break to clear his mind. Such reasoning and action often help for they may accomplish their end and, at the same time, avoid feelings of guilt caused by giving up the task.

Rationalization sometimes takes the form of refusing to admit to ourselves that the objec-

tive was ever wanted. The student who "busts" out of college justifies it to himself by denying that he ever wanted a college degree anyway and by reasoning that it is not necessary to success since so many succeed without college training. There are many ways for us to think up justifying reasons for inadequacies or failures that rid us of the guilt feelings that hurt our treasured self-esteem. For example, we decided to change our objective, or the conditions changed, or luck was against us, or more will be accomplished by doing something else—these and many other ways of thinking are common rationalizations among us. There is almost always available in each situation some explanation that can be used satisfactorily to remove or minimize our frustration. Almost everyone of us would have serious mental conflicts if this were not so.

PROJECTION   This is a form of rationalization where we put the responsibility for our problems on another person or an external condition. Other people and external conditions are important in practically everything we do. It is easy to reason that when things go wrong for us someone else or some condition is to blame. A candidate for political office says the reason he was defeated was not because the other person was a better candidate but because his supporters did not work hard enough to get out the vote or the rain kept the voters at home. He fails to recognize that those who voted for his opponent did not stay home because of the rain or the failure of the opponent's workers. Mothers often excuse their inability to manage their children by insisting that the father is too lenient. The father uses the same reason for the failure, only he asserts that the leniency is much worse in the wife than it is in him.

Persecution complexes develop when projections reach the point where we constantly find the responsibility for our limitations in others and we evolve the idea that they are doing this intentionally. The individual becomes paranoiac, that is, he suffers from chronic delusions of persecution that may also become associated with delusions of grandeur. This is an extreme form of projection.

IDENTIFICATION   This form of adjustment to frustration uses the achievements of others to give satisfaction when a person is limited or has had little success in accomplishing his own desires. (See Box 7.) The father who wanted to be an outstanding professional man succeeds vicariously when his son makes an outstanding

BOX 7   BALZAC IN BROOKLYN

The Most Devoted Balzac Scholar in the World
Models His Entire Life on His Famous Subject

Of the 450,000 people who have bought Stefan Zweig's posthumous biography of Balzac, nobody has read it with deeper emotions than William Hobart Royce, an obsessed man of 68 who frequently gives the impression that he *is* Balzac. A rare-book dealer by trade, Royce presents a fascinating case of personality transference. He has spent most of his life in a conspiracy with nature to duplicate in his own person the mind, body and spirit of the 19th Century French novelist. In some respects he has succeeded so well that Balzac fanciers meeting him for the first time often exclaim: "Honoré de Balzac in the flesh!"

In the flesh Royce like Balzac is round and plump, and he has cultivated to a hair the Balzacian mustache and chin tuft. A mighty eater, Balzac once demolished at a single sitting 100 oysters, 12 lamb chops, a duckling, a pair of partridges and a sole. Royce has never matched this record, but he is a multiple-course man himself and believes with Balzac that quantities of raw fruit are good for the health. To stimulate his brain cells Balzac-fashion, he occasionally takes snuff, drinks gallons of strong black coffee and smokes the great man's favorite pipe tobacco—Latakia.

Hewing to Balzac's working schedule, Royce sups and goes to bed as soon as he gets home from his bookshop, awakes at midnight and sits until dawn reading and writing about Balzac. During these sessions he wears, as Balzac did, a monk's robes. They are woven for him by Mrs. Royce, a patient woman who is inclined to humor these anachronistic fancies, and he has worn out two of them so far. He ignores the prosaic official address which the postal authorities have assigned to his three-story brick house—50 91 St., Brooklyn, New York, referring to it as *Les Jardies* (the gardens, in old French) after Balzac's villa outside Paris.[21]

reputation. A mother may get her satisfaction when her daughter has made a good marriage. Parents often identify their own wishes with those of their children. The parents may overcome some of their own disappointments when these work out together and are not in conflict.

A significant effect of motion pictures, television shows, plays, and stories, where individuals are pictured as achieving success, is that they give opportunity for people to put themselves in the position of the hero and so enjoy vicariously a psychological satisfaction that is otherwise impossible.

Anxiety and Insecurity that Cannot Be Successfully Resolved Lead to More Serious Forms of Personality Disorganization

Anxiety and insecurity are severe disturbances and lead to serious forms of personality disorganization if the usual defenses against frustrations do not remove the difficulties and if the mind cannot let go of the problem. We will simply mention these here and caution that the professional psychiatrist is best fitted to diagnose and prescribe for them.

NEUROSES   Neuroses are the milder forms of mental disorder. They express themselves in fixed ideas or obsessions, such as involuntary and repeated acts or compulsions or as unfounded fears or phobias. Their causes lie either in some physical condition or more probably in some functional disorder which, so far as is known, has no definite physical cause and is probably the result of inability to reconcile adequately our individual wishes with societal values. Freudians consider that neuroses are chiefly overcompensations for some organic inferiority, especially frustrated sex desire or sex indifference. Most psychiatrists give them wider explanation as flights from reality that is not tolerable to us. It is usually held that most of the neuroses are the consequence of functional disorder.

PSYCHOSES   These are the more serious forms of mental disorder. They are commonly associated with the legal term, "insanity." We are judged to be "insane" when, in the mind of a court, we are not legally responsible for our acts because we are thought to be unable to differentiate between right and wrong. Psychoses result from organic or functional causes. The psychotics cannot appraise reality in an adequate way because of distortions of memory and lack of proper orientation to time, place, and personal identity. They suffer from delusions, hallucinations, and other emotional disturbances. Recognition of the abnormal nature of their condition is usually lacking.

The most common forms of the psychoses are (1) schizophrenia, where the patient regresses to an infantile level and lives within himself in a world of self-love or narcissistic phantasy; (2) manic-depressive psychosis, where the patient is excessively excitable, generally optimistic but moves from elation to depression, changes rapidly from one topic to another, and is full of extravagant plans; (3) paresis, where there is general paralysis of the brain; and (4) paranoia, where the patient suffers from delusions of persecution or grandeur. This latter form or psychosis is particularly dangerous for the patient seeks revenge against fancied plots to harm him.

Societies Have Other Abnormal Personalities in Addition to the Mentally Disorganized

ABNORMAL NORMAL PERSONS Alcoholics, criminals, professional gamblers, prostitutes, and drug addicts are examples of other abnormal persons found in our societies. These persons may be completely normal so far as sheer mentality is concerned. What makes them abnormal is that the activities they pursue are in conflict with the acceptable behavior in their societies. They function contrary to the expectations and standards of their society. Criminals and professional gamblers, for example, are expressing antisocial attitudes they have acquired in their social experience. They may have no limitations so far as mentality is concerned, but there are serious limitations so far as personal goals are concerned. It may be that the social environment in which they were reared or into which they migrated contributed to their attitudes and behavior. But mental problems cannot be singled out as major factors in their deviant behavior in most cases. Their personality integration includes ends that their society does not regard as moral or as appropriate to the roles to be performed within it.

MENTALLY DEFICIENT A second class of abnormal personalities, other than the mentally disorganized, is the mentally deficient. These persons have always lacked the basic capacity for developing normal personalities. Idiots and imbeciles are so completely lacking in mental power and their behavior is so abnormal and conspicuous that they almost invariably require institutionalization, since there is no hope of improvement. Morons approach an adult level of intelligence. They, if properly guided, may be able to adjust to society acceptably though they can hardly be expected to develop a personality that allows complete performance of normal roles in society.

Societies Differ in the Extent to Which Maladjustment Exists

A number of comparative studies have led to the conclusion that societies differ in the extent to which mental disorders are prevalent within them. Malinowski observed in three separate cultures differences in the extent of neuroses, while Kardiner and Linton indicated that the Polynesians of the Marquesan Islands and Tanala of Madagascar differed decidedly in the extent to which these cultures produce personality problems.[22] Faris reported little mental disorder among the Congo Bantu, a fact he attributed to the absence of competition for social status in their integrated society because each person possessed a prescribed position and felt socially secure.[23]

Mental stress and strain can be common in a society like the United States where conflicts between the culture and the person are common. In such a society, the demand for success creates intense competition in all lines and leads to overaggressiveness, fear of failure, and loss of self-pride. Many of the goals the society stresses are exceedingly difficult for most of us to attain because of lack of means. Thus, a society itself may stimulate mental conflict by stressing goals which, if we fail to attain, may lead to self-attitudes that are demoralizing. Personality may be undermined by the insecurity developed from these societal demands if we have not developed a capacity to endure some frustration. The possibility is greater in a rapidly changing, complex society than in a slowly changing, simple society. This emphasizes our basic proposition that personality is, in the main, a societal product.

ALIENATION IN MODERN SOCIETY In the simple folk society, personality structure is coherently meshed with the social structure. Although this integration of the person and society may seem to impose a high degree of conformity and permit a low degree of freedom, the position of the individual is clear, stable, and meaningful to him. Objectively, the limits of his action may be narrowly circumscribed, but, subjectively, he is free of many of the uncertainties and insecurities which beset modern "civilized" man.

The tempo of social change and the pace and pervasiveness of industrialism and urbanism have strained or ruptured the traditional affinities and reciprocal commitments of the person and his society. The resulting malady has been diagnosed and labelled in a perplexing variety of ways. Two of its more conspicuous symptoms would seem to be existentialist philosophy and the "beatnik generation." Other expressions form a composite picture of the so-called "mass society." (See Box 8.) This condition today is commonly called *alienation*—a term which connotes detachment or estrangement.

Melvin Seeman offers an ordered statement of its varied meanings, which may be summarized as follows: [25]

1. *Powerlessness:* The individual feels that he cannot control the events which impinge upon him. (See Box 9.)

2. *Meaninglessness:* Faced with the many alternatives of a complex society, the individual is confused about what he ought to believe.

3. *Normlessness:* The rules governing the individual's behavior in attaining approved goals have weakened or broken down.

4. *Isolation:* The individual feels detached from or uncommitted to the goals or beliefs which are highly valued in his society.

5. *Self-estrangement:* The individual becomes disillusioned about his own identity and self-commitments. He turns upon himself the same attitude that he takes toward others.

Durkheim saw in this condition the major cause of suicide. Others would see it as the ominous prelude to the disintegration of the civilization.

It is not our intention to close this discussion with a preachment. We must recognize, however, that a normal person expressing himself in socially constructive acts—those that unify wishes, habits, and attitudes into a well-bal-

---

BOX 8

The conception of "Mass Society" can be summarized as follows: The revolutions in transport and communications have brought men into closer contact with each other and bound them in new ways; the division of labor has made them more interdependent; tremors in one part of society affect all others. Despite this greater interdependence, however, individuals have grown more estranged from one another. The old primary group ties of family and local community have been shattered; ancient parochial faiths are questioned; few unifying values have taken their place. Most important, the critical standards of an educated elite no longer shape opinion or taste. As a result, mores and morals are in constant flux, relations between individuals are tangential or compartmentalized rather than organic. At the same time greater mobility, spatial and social, intensifies concern over status. Instead of a fixed or known status symbolized by dress or title, each person assumes a multiplicity of roles and constantly has to prove himself in a succession of new situations. Because of all this, the individual loses a coherent sense of self. His anxieties increase. There ensues a search for new faiths. The stage is thus set for the charismatic leader, the secular messiah, who, by bestowing upon each person the semblance of necessary grace, and of fullness of personality, supplies a substitute for the older unifying belief that the mass society has destroyed.

In a world of lonely crowds seeking individual distinction, where values are constantly translated into economic calculabilities, where in extreme situations shame and conscience can no longer restrain the most dreadful excesses of terror, the theory of the mass society seems a forceful, realistic description of contemporary society, an accurate reflection of the quality and feeling of modern life.[24]

BOX 9

[Modern man] does not experience himself as the actual bearer of his own powers and richness, but as an impoverished "thing," dependent on powers outside of himself, unto whom he has projected his living substance.[26]

[The dilemma of "Organization Man" was presented by William H. Whyte, Jr.:] There are only a few times in organization life when he can wrench his destiny into his own hands—and if he does not fight then, he will make a surrender that will later mock him. But when is that time? Will he know the time when he sees it? By what standards is he to judge? [27]

[From an earlier day, John Steinbeck gave a poignant sense of the powerlessness of the Joads and their fellow "Oakies" as the owners try to explain why they must move from the land:]

Some of the owner men were kind because they hated what they had to do, and some were angry because they hated to be cruel—and all of them were caught in something larger than themselves. Some of them hated the mathematics that drove them . . . and some worshipped the mathematics because it provided a refuge from thought and feeling. . . . [They] would take no responsibility for the banks or the companies because they were men and slaves, while the banks were machines and masters all at the same time. . . .

"When the monster stops growing it dies. It can't stay one size."

"We know all that. It's not us, it's the bank. A bank isn't like a man. . . ."

"Yes, but the bank is only made of men."

"No, you're wrong there. . . . The bank is something else than men. It happens that every man in a bank hates what the bank does, and yet the bank does it. The bank is something more than men, I tell you. It's the monster. Men made it, but they can't control it." [28]

---

anced personality—is the person who will generally enjoy the greatest satisfactions in his relationships with others. The consequence is a satisfying attitude toward self and others and a gratifying sense of self-esteem and social worth.

References

1. Cooley, C. H., *Human Nature and the Social Order* (New York, Charles Scribner's Sons, 1902), pp. 1–2.
2. Stern, Curt, *Human Genetics* (San Francisco, W. H. Freeman and Co., 1955), p. 281.
3. Cannon, W. B., *Bodily Changes in Pain, Hunger, Fear and Rage* (New York, D. Appleton & Co., 1929), pp. 268–298.
4. Mead, Margaret, *Sex and Temperament in Three Primitive Societies* (New York, William Morrow and Company, 1935).
5. Carnegie, Dale, *How to Stop Worrying and Start Living* (New York, Simon and Schuster, Inc., 1951), p. 123.
6. Koenig, S., Hopper, R. D., and Gross, F., *Sociology—A Book of Readings* (Englewood Cliffs, N.J., Prentice-Hall, Inc., 1953), p. 72.
7. Gesell, A., and Ilg, F. L., *Child Development* (New York, Harper and Brothers, 1949), Part I, pp. 16–27.

8. Faris, E., "The Retrospective Act," *Journal of Educational Sociology,* 14 (1939), pp. 79–91.

9. Park, R. E., and Miller, H. A., *Old World Traits Transplanted* (New York, Harper and Brothers, 1921), p. 25.

10. Child, C. M., *et al., The Unconscious—A Symposium* (New York, Alfred A. Knopf, 1927), pp. 145–146.

11. Cooley, C. H., Angell, R. C., and Carr, L. J., *Introductory Sociology* (New York, Charles Scribner's Sons, 1933), p. 126.

12. From personal notes.

13. Riesman, David, *et al., The Lonely Crowd* (New Haven, Yale University Press, 1950).

14. Faris, E., "Mind, Self, and Society," *American Journal of Sociology,* 41 (May, 1936), p. 809. See also Mead, G. H., *Mind, Self and Society* (Chicago, University of Chicago Press, 1934).

15. Cottrell, L. S., "The Analysis of Situational Fields in Social Psychology," *American Sociological Review,* 7 (June, 1942), pp. 370–371.

16. Cooley, C. H., *Sociological Theory and Social Research* (New York, Holt and Company, Inc., 1930), pp. 229–247.

17. Hughes, R., *A High Wind in Jamaica* (London, Chatto and Windus, Ltd., 1929), pp. 134–136. Used with permission.

18. Reeder, Leo G., Donohue, G. A., and Biblarz, A., "Conceptions of Self and Others," *American Journal of Sociology,* 66 (September, 1960), p. 153. University of Chicago Press; copyright, 1960, by the University of Chicago.

19. Newcomb, Theodore, *Social Psychology* (New York, Dryden Press, 1950), p. 449.

20. For a study of the relation of self to personality disorganization, see Rosengren, William R., "The Self in the Emotionally Disturbed," *American Journal of Sociology,* 66 (March, 1961), pp. 454–462.

21. Kobler, John, "Balzac in Brooklyn," *Life,* 22 (February 24, 1947), p. 19.

22. Malinowski, B., *Sex and Repression in Savage Society* (London, Kegan Paul, 1927), pp. 85–90, and Kardiner, A., and Linton R., *The Individual and His Society* (New York, Columbia University Press, 1939).

23. Faris, E., *The Nature of Human Nature* (New York, McGraw-Hill Book Co., Inc., 1937), Chap. 24.

24. Bell, Daniel, "The Theory of Mass Society," *Commentary,* 22 (July, 1956), pp. 75–76.

25. Seeman, Melvin, "On the Meaning of Alienation," *American Sociological Review,* 24 (December, 1959), pp. 783–791. See also Glazer, Nathan, "The Alienation of Modern Man," *Commentary,* 3 (April, 1947); Keniston, K., "Alienation and the Decline of Utopia," *American Scholar,* 29 (Spring, 1960); Nettler, Gwynn, "A Measure of Alienation," *American Sociological Review,* 22 (December, 1957).

26. Fromm, Erich, *The Sane Society* (New York, Rinehart and Company, 1955), p. 124.

27. Whyte, William H., Jr., *The Organization Man* (New York, Simon and Schuster, Inc., 1956), p. 14.

28. Steinbeck, John, *The Grapes of Wrath* (New York, Random House [Modern Library], 1939), p. 45.

Questions for Study and Discussion

1. Distinguish between "the individual" and "the person."
2. Show how bodily structure is important to man in the development of his personality.
3. Why are hunger and sex called urges? How does society affect the ways in which they are satisfied?

4. Define personality, socialization, maturation. Discuss their interrelations.
5. Give some illustrations of unique experiences that you feel have been important in your personality development.
6. Discuss the relationship of habits, attitudes, and wishes to each other.
7. Define self, role-taking, role-playing.
8. Why are family relations especially important in developing concepts of self?
9. Discuss the typical ways persons adjust to frustrations. How does religion help to overcome frustration? Can it cause it? Why?
10. Why may an experience be frustrating to one person but not to another?
11. Is there a kind of personality that could be called normal for American society?
12. Illustrate from your experience the various meanings of alienation indicated in the chapter.

Suggested Topics for Reports

1. Examine the questions in a standard personality test and classify them according to the degree of their reference to self or to others.
2. Make a summary study of William H. Sheldon's classification of types of body structure and types of temperament. Does his "system" pay adequate attention to sociological factors in personality?

Supplementary Reading

Cooley, Charles H., *Human Nature and the Social Order*. New York: Charles Scribner's Sons, 1902.

Coutu, Walter, *Emergent Human Nature*. New York: Alfred A. Knopf, 1949.

Davis, Allison, and Havighurst, Robert J., *Father of the Man*. Boston: Houghton Mifflin Company, 1947.

Dollard, John, *Frustration and Aggression*. New Haven, Conn.: Yale University Press, 1939.

Faris, Ellsworth, *The Nature of Human Nature*. New York: McGraw-Hill Book Co., Inc., 1937.

Faris, Robert E. L., *Social Psychology*. New York: The Ronald Press, 1952.

Gesell, Arnold, *Studies in Child Development*. New York: Harper and Brothers, 1942.

Horney, Karen, *The Neurotic Personality of Our Time*. New York: W. W. Norton and Co., Inc., 1937.

Kluckhohn, C. K., Murray, H. A., and Schneider, D. M., *Personality in Nature, Society and Culture*. New York: Alfred A. Knopf, 1954.

LaPiere, Richard, and Farnsworth, Paul R., *Social Psychology*. New York: McGraw-Hill Book Co., Inc., 1949.

Lindesmith, A. R., and Straus, A. L., *Social Psychology*. New York: Dryden Press, 1949.

Mead, George H., *Mind, Self, and Society*. Ed. by C. H. Morris. Chicago: University of Chicago Press, 1934.

Newcomb, Theodore, *Social Psychology*. New York: Dryden Press, 1950.

Overstreet, Harry A., *The Mature Mind*. New York: W. W. Norton and Co., Inc., 1949.

Scheinfeld, Amram, *The New You and Heredity*. Philadelphia: J. B. Lippincott Company, 1950.

Sherif, Muzafer, *An Outline of Social Psychology*. New York: Harper and Brothers, 1948.

Shibutani, Tamotsu, *Society and Personality*. Englewood Cliffs, N.J.: Prentice-Hall, Inc., 1961.

Stoodley, B. H., *Society and Self*. New York: The Free Press of Glencoe, 1962.

Wylie, Ruth C., *The Self-Concept: A Critical Survey of Pertinent Research Literature*. Lincoln, Neb.: University of Nebraska Press, 1961.

6

THE STRUCTURAL PATTERNS OF SOCIETIES

*A**LL SOCIETIES** have a pattern of organization that includes five classes of human relationship structures, or hurelures. These are ecological entities—the land-based units of society; human groups—the psychologically bonded units of interpersonal action; institutional agencies—the regulative mechanisms of societies; organizations—the interest-promoting agencies; and collectivities—the temporary and crisis structures. These structures, in their total organization, give a society its form. Each structure has functions which it performs for the larger system.*

Every Society Has a Pattern of Organization Composed of Human Relationship Structures

The chief principles presented in the first chapter stated that all men live with other men in societies and that these societies are entities composed of *human relationship structures*. This is to say that each society has a pattern of organization composed of the structures resulting from the associations of men with each other. This is true of our complex societies and of our simple ones also—of highly industrial and commercial England and of the direct appropriation Isneg tribe in the northern mountains of the Philippines.

Men Establish a Structural Form When They Relate Themselves to Each Other

The connections between people who relate themselves to each other create an arrangement of persons that make a unit. Some units exist for only a brief time because the bonds that unite them are broken. Some groups last only momentarily for the psychological interactions between the members dissolve. Other forms exist for years because the bonds that unite them grow stronger. Some organizations have existed for centuries because the interests they serve are continuous. Such relationship units are numerous and varied in any society. Each of us knows that he belongs to many such entities—to families, churches, clubs, organizations, audiences, crowds. Human societies are

made up of these structural forms arrranged in an interrelated way that enables the societies to operate as complex units.

Relationships Are the Key Factors in the Pattern of Societies

A *relationship* is defined here as a connection established between separate things that brings them together in a condition of association that leads to their being viewed as a unit. There are many different forms in which this joining together appears in societies as well as in the universe in general. Kinship, marriage, and organization memberships are just a few of the infinitely varied forms of relationship in societies. Some quality or aspect of two or more persons or groupings of persons links them together so that they become interlocked and operate as a system. Every society—a web of such relationships—operates through the structures created by these relationships.

Societies Are Not Only Made Up of Relationship Entities; They Function Through Them, Too

All of us use society as the vehicle for expressing our experience, the relationship entities being the mechanisms we use for this purpose. Likewise, a society uses relationship units as the mechanisms through which it functions. Institutions, organization, cities, and political parties are all tools of societies—instruments for carrying on cooperative interests. Societies could not achieve their purposes without these structural forms. Each structure has some purpose for its existence.

Structures and Functions Go Together

Structures and functions automatically go together since structures are the means through which functions are performed, and functions are always accomplished by the means of structures. The value of any structure depends upon the manner in which it accomplishes its functions. When a society's operations do not proceed properly, we usually try to modify its social structures. Applied sociology consists mainly in changing structural patterns to achieve greater social efficiency. To emphasize structure to the neglect of function or to emphasize function to the neglect of structure is to recognize only one-half the equation. Structure is useless without function, and function is only accomplished through some structure. "You talk about forms," exclaimed Goethe to a follower, "as if substance could be formless; neglect form and see how long you have any substance." We can say precisely the opposite, also. The truth is that structure and function go together.

The Nature of Functions Influences the Form of Structures and Vice Versa

There is a further important aspect of the relationship between structure and function that we only mention here. (We shall discuss it in greater detail later.) The nature of the functions to be carried out influences the form a structure will take. And the form of a structure will influence the functions that it can perform.

A little reflection will show us that a football team trying to outscore its opponent could hardly succeed through a structural form that allowed each player to follow his own initiative. Nor could a research scientist for a chemical company be creative if every step he took was prescribed by the organizational unit in which he was working. It is said that one of the reasons for Hitler's defeat was that he organized so rigidly that those who had responsibility for making decisions were not given real opportunity to use their creative capacity.

It Is Often Difficult for Us to Recognize that When Individuals Relate Themselves to Each Other, They Create Distinct Forms [1]

This observation arises from three conditions: (1) The structural forms of a society are always dynamic and must be consciously held still to see their structure. We suggest that a society is similar to a motion picture film. We can thus grasp the idea that it is a multiple of structural units, although this analogy may not hold at some points. The motion picture appears as one continuous flow of action when it is operating as we know a society always is. Stopping the moving film strip allows us to see that it is actually a series of separate "shots." After analyzing each "shot," we can describe accurately the relationship of the parts to each other. A society is a continuous flow of operating structures. Hold it still for purposes of analysis and you see parts arranged with respect to each other in wholes, and these wholes joined to each other to form the framework of the larger whole.

(2) Many of the structural units of a society are spatially widespread and therefore difficult to see as wholes. It is impossible for us to bring whole communities and regions into our vision.

(3) When we interact with each other, most of our interaction is carried on through the use of symbols that do not assume physical form. Few physical connections are established which bind the separate individuals together. If every time we interacted with each other, some physical substance like a string conducted the stimulus from person to person, these interactions would result in the establishment of a physical network that would show us the web of relationships tying us together in these entities. Since this does not occur, however, it is difficult for us to see that there is a structural unity here that we can analyze in terms of its component parts. Yet we know that these interactions are as real as those of any other structural forms. We implicitly recognize these structures —groups, organizations, and others—as the only mechanisms through which our social relationships are possible. Societies are, then, from a functional point of view, the sum total of the human relationship structures in interaction.

There Are Five Major Classes of Human Relationship Structures of Which Any Society Is Composed

Students of societies have developed different classifications of the human relationship structures. These are usually based on some general characteristic the structures possess that makes the classification useful for the purpose at hand. (We shall not review them here since such an analysis is beyond our present purposes.[2]) We present a classification of these forms of association based upon the type of bond that holds each together as a structural whole. In that the bonds that hold relationship structures together differ, this gives each form a principal characteristic. They can be *classed* together on the basis of this principal characteristic. Structures may have many common characteristics with other structures, just as vertebrates have common characteristics with nonvertebrates. A principal characteristic, namely, the bond that unifies them, makes it possible to separate them into classes, however.

We observe the following five major classes of human relationship structures in all societies when viewed in terms of the bonds that unite them:

1. *Ecological Entities:* These are aggregates of people that occupy a continuous territory integrated through common social and economic activities and are able to carry on these activities as a corporate entity.

Bonds of many varieties characterize these forms. Their distinctive characteristic is that they are always people in relationship in a definable land area—a community, a neighborhood, a region; a county, a city; a society.

2. *Human Groups:* Groups are units of two or more people meeting in the same environment, or overcoming distance by some means of communication, who are influencing each other psychologically. The distinctive bond of the group is reciprocal psychological interaction. Friends in conversation, a committee in action, and children playing together are examples.

3. *Institutional Agencies:* Institutional agencies are instruments for making institutions functional. Institutions are definitely patterned, relatively fixed, and socially sanctioned procedural norms governing relationships between the members of a society. At a given time and place, the institutional agencies seem to be the most apt way of carrying out activities that have been sanctioned and formalized within the society.

The distinctive function of institutional agencies as relationship structures is to carry the regularized procedures in society, and as such they are the means societies create to achieve their sanctioned goals. Education, religion, the family, and government are all institutions.

4. *Organizations:* These are systematically arranged units of people organized to achieve specific purposes in which units each person has a formally defined role.

The distinctive bonds making organization entities are the specific purposes to be achieved and the defined roles of the members—a choral club, a lodge; a sorority; a chamber of commerce.

5. *Collectivities:* A collectivity consists of a number of people whose behavior is specifically polarized around some temporary center of attraction that stimulates interaction and unity. Interaction and unity exist only as long as the center of attraction exists.

The bond of this class of social forms is the polarization of people around a temporary center, making it serve as the relationship mechanism for crisis or unusual, temporary, and nonrepetitive occurrences in the social organization. The collectivity serves to arrange relationships for those occasions for which society has no fixed relationship device. A crowd, a mob, and an audience are illustrations.

These five classes of the forms of association are the major mechanisms through which each society operates. Their interrelationship and interdependence bind men together into large corporate syntheses in defined geographic areas to make of our societies consistent wholes.

Specific Structures Are Not the Same in All Societies

When we say that all societies operate through the same five major classes of human relationship structures, we are not saying that the structures in a particular class are the same in all societies. They *are* the same in respect to the chief principles that unify them and in the general functions they perform. The basic patterns are generally similar, yet the specific forms for accomplishing the general functions vary widely.

Differences in institutional patterns illustrate this for us. The family is an institution of all societies. Some have families of one husband, one wife, and their children. Others have families of several wives, one husband, and their children. A primary function of the family in both cases is the same—to bear and rear children to normal manhood and womanhood. The norms of the different societies sanction different procedures for accomplishing this general purpose. The specific structural forms vary.

The Concept "Hurelures" May Be Used to Signify All the Structures of Human Association

We have referred to the structures that result from the relations between men as "the human relationship structures." At various places, we have called them "forms of association." These phrases, while they are descriptive and refer definitely to the structures that result from the interrelations among men, are cumbersome. It would be helpful if we had a word that was precise and limited to one idea only that could be used to give a single conceptual expression to these phenomena.

A thing or a class of things can be given any name, and it would suffice if the users have the same understanding of its content and if it meets the above criteria. This is true for all sciences. Concepts are sometimes expressed by words which embody the names of persons or objects. In some cases, they are words from other languages or even letters from the alphabet to which a precise meaning has been given. The concept "mores" is an illustration in sociology. Here an irregular Latin noun—*mos, meaning custom*—is generally used in sociology in the plural form—mores—to mean those uniform, sanctioned, compulsive ways of thinking and acting insisted upon by the society.[3]

By taking the first syllables of the words "human" and relationship," and the last syllable of the word "structures," the word "hurelures" (hu-rel'-ures) is formed.[4] We use it to include all the forms of human association that result from the relationships among men in societies. We will use this term in this sense in what follows.[5]

The central thesis of this book, then, is that every society is structurally composed of and functions through five major classes of human relationship forms or hurelures: *ecological entities, groups, institutional agencies, organizations,* and *collectivities.* The discussion of these structures in this order provides the substance and logical order of Part III, The Organization of Societies.

References

1. Anderson, W. A., "Rural Sociology as Science," *Rural Sociology,* 12 (December, 1947), pp. 348 ff.
2. For students who wish to study classifications, see Eubanks, E. E., *The Concepts of Sociology* (New York, D. C. Heath and Company, 1932).
3. Sumner, W. G., *Folkways* (Boston, Ginn and Company, 1906), Preface, p. 111.
4. The concept, "hurelures," was first presented in "A Note on the Phenomena of Sociology," *American Sociological Review,* 6 (December, 1941), pp. 882 ff. It has three syllables—*hu* as in human, *rel* as in relative, and *ures* as in structures. It should be pronounced hu-rel'-ures, the emphasis being on the second syllable.
5. See Robert Bierstedt's discussion of "Nominal and Real Definitions in Sociology," in Gross, Llewellyn (ed.), *Symposium on Sociological Theory* (Evanston, Ill., Row, Peterson and Co., 1959), Chap. 4, pp. 121 ff.

Questions for Study and Discussion

1. Define relationship. List and describe as many different types of relationship as you can. Are relationships in societies all of one type? Why?
2. Discuss the statement that "structures and functions go together."
3. Why is it difficult to recognize the existence of structural forms when individuals relate themselves to each other?
4. Criticize the definitions given of the five classes of human relationship structures as far as you are able to at this point.
5. Compare the definitions given in this chapter with others you look up in standard sociology texts. Discuss their similarities and differences.
6. Can you think of any other classes of human relationship structures or hurelures than the five given here?
7. Look up the difference between "nominal" and "real" definitions. (See reference 5 of this chapter.) Are the definitions of each of the five classes of human relationship structures "real" or "nominal" definitions? Is the definition of "hurelure" a "real" or "nominal" definition?

Suggested Topics for Reports

1. Devise a series of diagrams which would depict a family, a fraternity, and a university as human relationship structures.
2. Prepare a graphic and textual report showing the structural and functional changes which have occurred in your college or university during the last few years. What factors have brought these changes about?

Supplementary Reading

Cooley, Charles H., *Social Organization*. New York: Charles Scribner's Sons, 1920.

Linton, Ralph, *The Study of Man*. New York: Appleton-Century-Crofts, Inc., 1936.

Merton, Robert K., *Social Theory and Social Structure*. Glencoe, Ill.: The Free Press, 1957.

Murdock, George Peter, *Social Structure*. New York: The Macmillan Company, 1949.

Parsons, Talcott, *The Social System*. Glencoe, Ill.: The Free Press, 1951.

Von Wiese, Leopold, and Becker, Howard, *Systematic Sociology*. New York: John Wiley and Sons, Inc., 1932.

PART THREE

THE ORGANIZATION OF SOCIETIES:
The Major Human Relationship
Structures, or Hurelures

7

ECOLOGICAL ENTITIES: THE LAND-BASED UNITS OF ORGANIZATION

*P*EOPLE *associated with each other in varying degrees of organization distribute themselves in relation to the land areas in such a way as to create land-based relationships or ecological units. These follow two general patterns: natural ecological entities of unplanned types with indefinite boundaries—neighborhoods, communities, regions; and deliberately created entities with fixed boundaries for definite purposes—villages, towns, cities, townships, counties, states. The relationships within and between societies are conducted to a large extent with reference to these land-based units. Processes of concentration, deconcentration, centralization, segregation, invasion, and succession determine the distinctive ecological patterns and the changes in them.*

Man Distributes Himself in Relation to Land Areas to Form Ecological Units

The underlying proposition of this chapter is that people in societies functioning together arrange themselves in geographic space in such a way as to create a pattern of land-based units of operation. These units are the *ecological entities;* this area of analysis is called *human ecology.* It describes for us the way in which human relationships are adjusted to the physical and biological environments and how they assume their patterns of distribution in space.

Plants and Animals Create Natural Ecological Units

If we could rise to a high point above the earth and peer down upon it with a wide-angled lens, we would see plants and animals distributing themselves in segregated habitats in which particular forms dominate. These organisms have adjusted themselves to each other and to their surroundings and have established uniform belts of life. The dominant forms in these belts are those which have made the most successful adaptations to the character of their environment. Plants and animals have adjusted themselves to the soil, water, and light, and to each

other and have created natural regions where particular plants and animals predominate in the struggle for survival. The Pampas of Argentina, the Mississippi Valley of the United States, the tundra of Siberia, the forests of Africa—all are areas where plants and animals have made these adjustments.

There are smaller units within the larger areas where some variations in the physical conditions have permitted other more adaptable plants and animals to take over. Marjorie Rawlings describes such a situation in a southern United States region of scrub oak: "The scrub rolled towards its boundaries like a dark sea. It cast itself against the narrow beach of swamp and hammock that fringed the rivers. The two types of growth did not mingle, as though an ascetic race withdrew itself from a tropical one and refused to inter-breed." [1]

Sometimes a different life form will invade an area and eventually change the dominant form because it makes a better adaptation. H. G. Wells cites the invasion of gulls on a stretch of moor in southern Scotland:

When the story begins, this was covered with heather, and tenanted by typical heather-moor creatures such as the red

97

grouse. In 1892, a few pairs of black-headed gulls came to nest there. . . . The owner liked the gulls and protected them, with the result that by 1905 there was a nesting colony of over three thousand. The trampling of the birds was bad for the heather, while their constant manuring of the ground changed the character of the soil. The result was that the heather vanished altogether, its place being taken first by rushes and later by coarse docklike plants. Pools of shallow water formed here and there. With the heather, the grouse disappeared; while the pools attracted teal and other duck. In 1905, protection was withdrawn from the gulls, their nests were robbed, and they decreased rapidly until by 1917 there were only a hundred or so of them left. The heather had re-invaded most of the ground, the pools were drying up, the teal had gone, and the grouse were returning. Thus in twenty-five years the ground and all its plant and animal inhabitants had changed completely, and then changed back again.[2]

Man, Also, Creates Ecological Units

We are like other animals and plants in that we have a definite linkage with our natural environments. We might well be considered "the great invader," from the point of view of other animals, for we, too, exist by exploiting the natural environments and adapting their resources of soils, minerals, plants, and animals to our needs. We should see that we have also created areas where the plant and animal forms we can use predominate, if we observed our behavior from the heights. The rice-water buffalo areas of South China, the citrus fruit region of California, and the industrial regions of England are examples.

Here and there we should also see concentrations of houses, stores, factories, warehouses, and places where hundreds or thousands of people live and work in relatively small areas. These would constitute villages, towns, and cities, and their size and organization would depend upon the nature of the environment and the activities in which the people are engaged. Roads, railroads, and telephone and telegraph wires run between them, carrying goods and messages that unite them and the open country areas into integrated units of interdependent living. Our earliest invasions took place in those areas of the planet where food could be easily obtained. The knowledge, skills, and arts we acquired were chiefly related to the problems of maintenance as we adjusted to

these regional characteristics. Our final adaptations will probably be to the cold polar regions and the desert stretches and the physical limitations they set for us. It is this patterning of man's distribution on the land that we examine now to see further how his societies are organized and operate.

Societies Are Themselves Ecological Entities

This planet on which man lives is made up of people in social relationship with each other. It breaks down into specific societies where people in distinctly defined areas with a common culture carry on a shared life based on their interdependence. The fundamental characteristic of societies as ecological entities is the reciprocal interrelationship of the components carrying on complementary functions that make possible an operating ordered whole. Sectors of a population in given territories carry on, in relation to each other, economic, political, social, and other essential functions according to the customs, norms, and values of the larger society. The cooperative activities of people within an area create a balance between individuals and groupings that is comparable to the balance that plants and animals develop in adaptation to their environment.

Man Develops Several Ecological Forms Within Each Society

As they distribute themselves in relation to land areas, human populations develop *regions*, *communities*, and *neighborhoods* as natural units of interdependence, and legally constituted *cities*, *towns*, *counties*, and *states* as purposefully created ecological entities. We shall now consider societies in terms of these ecological components.

I. REGIONS

Societies Subdivide into Regions

Regions are the largest of the three natural ecological forms within a society. Man develops them as adaptations to the physical conditions and natural resources of a geographic area. The quality of the soil, the climate, the type of plant, and animal life; the resources in the earth, such as coal, iron, oil; and the topography of the area are the elemental factors which determine the size, shape, and type of region which can develop. Men in groups determine through experience whether or not the locations are desirable. Regions begin as economic units, organized to produce foods and fibers, to make industrial products and to carry on trade and commerce. They develop a unity centered about these production activities.

The agricultural regions of the United States illustrate this process. The whole of the United States has developed into distinct regions of agricultural production: the hay and dairy region of the northeast, the corn-hog belt of the North-central states, the cotton-tobacco region of the South and Southeast, the wheat region of the West and Northwest, the sheep and cattle

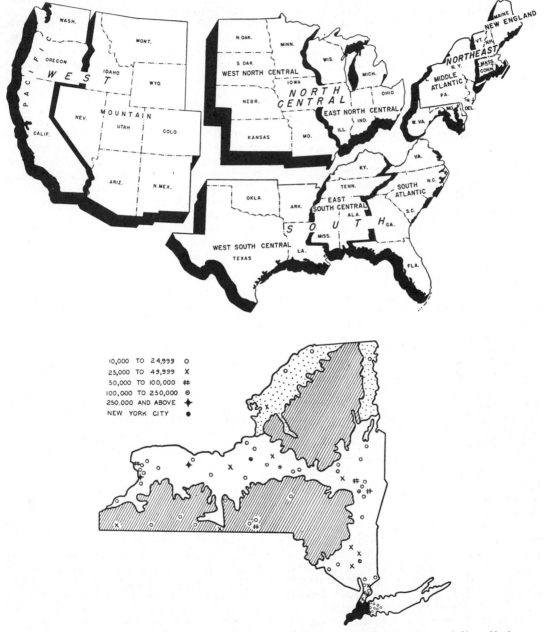

(Top) Regions and subregions in the United States. (Bottom) The cities of New York State are concentrated in its Great L Valley region.

grazing area of the West and Southwest, and the citrus and other fruit areas of the Pacific Coast.

These, of course, subdivide according to the geographic character and specialized production of a specific section. Rupert Vance describes this for the cotton belt: "Within this area differences in climate, rainfall, altitude, character of the soil, and history have given rise to subregions of cotton culture. These regions differ rather widely in the spatial distribution of what may be called human factors— black men, white men, share croppers, share tenants, small owners and planters. . . . This description of the spatial distribution of man and the artifacts of his civilization in relation to cotton lands, is, I take it, the human ecology of the cotton belt." [3]

Regions Are Constellations Composed of the Various Ecological Entities

Each region is a relatively large territorial area made up of smaller units functioning interdependently to produce the goods and services the inhabitants require. These units group together as systems like the stars of the heavens to carry on the industry, commerce, and agriculture characteristic of the region.

METROPOLITAN CENTERS   The typical pattern of modern regional organization is twofold. It includes (1) a metropolitan center around which cluster various subcenters and (2) the surrounding territory that includes the communities and neighborhoods and open country of its hinterland. The primary function of the metropolitan center is the processing, distributing, and financing of the economic activities of the region. The products of the region's industry and agriculture are assembled and distributed to the region and to other regions from the dominating metropolis through the common carriers that center there. Here, too, are located the major financing institutions—banks, insurance companies, and trust corporations, which provide the exchange needed throughout the region. The region, therefore, is the dominating metropolitan center and its supporting hinterland interacting to carry on the pursuits of human living.

SUPPORTING HINTERLAND   The supporting hinterland of the region is made up of smaller ecological forms. It usually includes, depending upon the extent of the region, other cities that integrate portions of the territory through providing such supplemental opportunities as locations for industrial plants, assembly points for raw materials, or distributing centers for finished products. Smaller cities or towns lie beyond these and serve as links in the network that ties the rural producers to urban consumers and urban producers to rural consumers. Other locality units—villages and hamlets—form the nuclei for the trading and neighboring activities of the rural population. They are the central foci of rural communities and neighborhoods. Farms and other areas, such as grazing lands, forests, and mines where the raw materials are produced, lie beyond these. In rural America, the farm will include a farmstead, where the home and other buildings of the farm family are concentrated, so that each farm family is a separate unit. This dispersed farming pattern is not the most prevalent form of farm settlement, however. Most of the farm people of the world have their homes in villages and keep their animals in their homes or in the village, while their farm and grazing lands are scattered some distance away. Thus, just as a society is a constellation of relatively large regions, so each region is a constellation of smaller ecological entities, all constituting an interrelated land-based system.

Regions Expand and Contract Due Primarily to Competition

SOME ILLUSTRATIONS   These man-made regions develop gradually from the slightest beginnings, just as do those of plants and animals. They also disappear in much the same way. Not long ago, the peach regions of Georgia and North and South Carolina did not exist. Today, they are important areas in the life of these states. In years past, the hops-producing region of the United States was in central New York. Today, there is no hops region in this section. It has moved to new areas, particularly the Pacific Northwest.

COMPETITION AS BASIC   The chief factor in this expansion is competition. Products that can do better than others in a particular territory replace those that are there. They acquire dominance in the area; the others may be completely banished. This is illustrated by changes in hops production. About 1808, a farmer in Oneida County, New York, grew some hops (he had obtained the roots from Canada) to supply a small brewery. By 1870, the diversified farming practiced in this region was gone because all the farmers were growing hops. But by 1910, this hops region had almost completely vanished. Diseases on plants, competition with a new area—the Pacific Northwest—where hops could be produced more cheaply, and competition with dairy farming, which was more stable, brought its demise. Now the area is part of the dairy region of the Great L Valley of New York.[4]

The transfer of the textile industry from New England to the South Atlantic states in the last several decades also illustrates this expansion and contraction of regions. Easier access to raw materials, an abundant labor supply, and developing power resources in the South Atlantic region were competitive factors that brought about the shift.

The Principle of Comparative Advantage Underlies Regional Developments

The Middle West is the great region of corn-hog production in the United States. The South Atlantic region is a part of the great cotton region of the southern states. But corn and hogs can be produced in the South Atlantic states; in fact, each farmer in this area usually has a patch of corn and a hog or two. More pork is consumed per person in the South Atlantic states than in any other region of the country. Most of this pork, however, comes from the Middle West.

Why does not the South Atlantic region produce the pork it needs? The answer is that corn and hogs have a comparative advantage over cotton production in the Middle West while cotton has a comparative advantage over corn and hogs in the Southeast. The farmers of the cotton region can produce relatively more cotton per acre for a larger net profit than they can corn and hogs. It therefore pays them to raise cotton and buy the pork they consume from the Middle West, while it pays the Middle-West farmers to produce corn and hogs and buy their cotton. There are alternative possibilities of production in most regions. Those present at the time are probably those that have the comparative advantages.

Regions Have Cultural as Well as Economic Uniformity

The kind of economic system that man develops in a region, whether it be farming or manufacturing, influences, to a considerable degree, his ways of living. Regions, though basically economic, are never wholly so. Their people evolve patterns of thought and action that distinguish one region from another. Attitudes toward work, people, and life in general are developed as regional traits. Regions whose soils are poor and demand constant working hardly produce the leisurely attitudes which may be found in a rich soil area, such as the tropics. What we think makes the best foods, such as rice for the Burmese, or mutton and beef for the British, are related to regional characteristics. The type of housing and of home life, schools and educational objectives, churches, and moral and religious outlooks bear the regional stamp. The supposed isolationism of the American Middle West is a regional product. Factors such as these make the region a cultural or subcultural unit.

Cultural Uniformity Evolves in a Region

The development of cultural uniformity in a region is an evolving process. The geographic environment not only has limiting influences, but also the people in the region vary considerably in social backgrounds. The geography of the region separates people at least for a period and assists in preserving differences. Time introduces new ideas and practices so that the interplay of old and new eliminates distinctive peculiarities, and the whole becomes integrated into a composite type.

The occupation of the Mississippi Valley in the United States illustrates this process. Germans, Norwegians, Swedes, Finns, English, and others brought distinct cultural backgrounds into its different sections. The interplay of these populations with each other for over a century has largely eliminated social differences between them, though some cultural islands still exist. These socially heterogeneous people have evolved a cultural similarity. It is the intermeshing of the two orders, the geographic and the social, that results in the total unified region.

Regional Organization Changes with the Changing Development of Societies

CHICAGO AND THE MIDWEST America is an excellent illustration of how the regional pattern of a society changes if the total economy of the society changes. New metropolitan centers have carved out regional provinces as this economy has changed from a predominantly agricultural to a predominantly industrial one. Chicago, for example, once held sway as the metropolis of the whole Middle West as far as the Rocky Mountains. Other cities in the area were collection centers between the open farm lands and this metropolis. The cattlemen brought their animals to Omaha or Abilene, for example, and the corn and hog buyers loaded their goods at some junction of a railway. They were destined for Chicago, where the finished products were redistributed to this region and to the East.

Ringed by satellite cities, Chicago is still the metropolitan center for the activities of a major region. Concentrated within its limits are 39 railway lines, a number of major cross-country highways, and a vast array of industrial enterprises. It has extended its bounds in every direction to include within its radius numerous cities, villages, and other civil divisions, together with the farming hinterland.

GROWTH OF METROPOLITAN CENTERS Other cities that were once subordinates of Chicago, however, are now centers for compact regions with smaller supporting hinterlands and more closely knit interdependence. Milwaukee in Wisconsin, Moline and Rock Island in Illinois, Davenport, Des Moines, and Sioux City in Iowa all illustrate this development. The hard-surfaced road, the motor truck, electric power, and new communication devices, along with intensified industry and expanded agriculture, made this possible. Where 44 metropolitan areas were counted in 1910, the United States Census counted 212 in 1960.[5]

Thus transition from old to new regional organization is inevitable wherever transportation and communication develop. Many areas of this planet are now undergoing such territorial integration because of the added possibilities of specialization in production for expanded markets.

II. COMMUNITIES

Communities Develop Within the Cities, Towns, and Open Country Areas of Regions

Societies, we see, subdivide into regions organized largely about dominant types of economic activity, but regions subdivide into smaller land-based structures. As we have noted, communities and neighborhoods are natural ones whereas cities, towns, villages, counties, and states are purposefully created ones. Our concern now is with communities.

A MAJOR FUNCTIONING UNIT The community is the local area in which most people function most completely and directly. Here is where our home is located, where our children are born, our schooling takes place, our business or work is carried on, our participation in public concerns occurs, and the primary ideals of our society are made manifest. Here it is that we obtain our greatest satisfactions from close associations with friends and neighbors. Within it our interests are harmonized with those of society as a whole. The community is the chief arena within which most of us perform, although communication and transportation have now made it possible for us to extend our association beyond its boundaries into the larger society. It is the self-sufficing area of operation for a large part of any population. Just as we belong to one family at a given time, so we belong to just one community with which we identify ourselves.

Most People in the World Live in Small Places That Are the Nuclei of Communities

Most people in the world live in relatively small places, although the trend of population movement in industrialized countries especially is toward the urban centers. This is so even for the United States, where it is often described in terms of crowded cities. Yet, in 1960, less than 30 per cent of its population lived in places of 100,000 or more inhabitants, while three of each ten live in places of less than 2500 residents and in rural areas and one in each ten more live in places of 2500 to 10,000 residents. The Census for 1960 gives 19,790 as the number of incorporated and unincorporated places in this country. Of these, 72 per cent have less than 2500 inhabitants.[6] A large proportion of the 72 per cent are the centers of functional communities.

In considering this aspect of the community, we should recognize that cities do not operate as single systems in many kinds of activity— they subdivide into functional communities. Furthermore, the rapid increase in the rural-nonfarm population in the last three decades is further evidence of the shift of residents to the less densely settled areas. This suburban trend is enhancing the development of local communities.

The Community Has Four Characteristics

DEFINITION What then is a community? A *community* is a continuous geographic area in which mutually dependent groups act together to satisfy their needs through a common set of organizations and institutions. This definition emphasizes four characteristics of this ecological form:

A Continuous Land Area (1) A community is a continuous land area, that is, it is not made up of scattered land units. This physical unity is one basis for its solidarity.

Composed of People (2) It is composed of people as are all relationship structures in society. We are dependent on each other for services because we cannot obtain our necessities or achieve our objectives by our own efforts or through the groups in which we operate alone. It takes an interrelated set of groups working together to achieve many of our goals —such as places for worship, places to buy and sell goods, and protection for life and property. Our needs and desires and the development of the machinery to satisfy them, therefore, are an additional basis for community.

Cooperate to Satisfy Needs (3) The community is the place where we cooperate to satisfy our basic needs and desires. It is true that all our needs cannot usually be taken care of within a single community. Many consumer goods are brought into the community from other communities since practically no community, except in the simplest societies, produces and manufactures all its requirements. It is necessary to satisfy some desires by going to other places. A small rural community, for example, could hardly provide classical opera for its residents.

Malinowski describes this interdependence of communities at the primitive level in the following way:

> The coastal and inland villages respectively have to rely upon each other for the supply of food. On the coast the natives never have enough vegetable food, while inland the people are always in need of fish. Moreover, custom will have it that on the coast all the big ceremonial displays and distributions of food, which form an extremely important aspect of the public life of these natives must be made with certain specially large and fine varieties of vegetable food, which grow only on the fertile plains inland. There, on the other hand, the proper substance for distribution and feast is fish. Thus to all other reasons of value of the respectively rarer food, there is added an artificially, culturally created dependence of the two districts upon one another, so that on the whole each community is very much in need of its partners. If at anytime previously they have been guilty of neglect, however, they know that they will be in one way or another severely penalized.

Each community has, therefore, a weapon for the enforcement of its rights: reciprocity.[7]

Communities may so completely provide the essential goods and services of life that we may rarely need to go outside of them—even in urban areas. It was reported a few years ago that a number of adult residents of Chicago had lived their whole lives in one of its self-sufficient communities and never visited the "Loop," the city's central area of retail business concentration.

It is not implied that all cooperation is conscious and voluntary when we say that individuals and groups act together to satisfy their needs and desires. Much of it is, but much is unconscious. We accept stores, schools, and professional and other services automatically and impersonally. A major problem in communities is to maintain a conscious awareness that the community requires us to act together to satisfy our needs.

Common Set of Organizations and Institutions (4) Because communities include a common set of organizations and institutions for satisfying needs and desires, they have a life of their own. The number of organizations and institutions in a community vary with its size and type, but most communities include the same basic ones. There are always the school, the church, and the economic agencies, such as stores, banks, and manufacturing establishments; some recreational facilities, such as movie houses and public parks; and lodges and other voluntary organizations and professional and personal service facilities. The community may be the whole society for some individuals, for here they are involved in a network of relationships that encompasses almost the whole of their lives.

Residents Develop Differing Degrees and Types of Identification with Their Community

The common life of the community is based on our common interests. We have much personal knowledge about, and are acquainted with, each other for we are residents in a relatively small area, living fairly close together where the means of communication are usually numerous. Sentiments of congeniality and solidarity are evolved, and the residents become to some degree "a body of fellows," enjoying "community of relations or feelings," as the original Latin term means. This sense grows out of the fairly long periods of residence in the community which the great proportion of people enjoy.[8]

The degree to which feelings of identification and togetherness exist differs in different communities at different times and under different cultural situations. Identification may be very strong in a small, self-contained community. This matter is important for there are many of these communities in the societies of the world today.

A MIDDLE-EAST ILLUSTRATION Afif Tannous makes the role of identification clear in his description of the Arab village community of the Middle East:

> The fellah is always conscious of the fact that he is a member of a certain community, and he knows wherever he goes people expect him to identify himself as such. A stranger is always "placed" with respect to his village, family, and church. . . . We have indicated above how the local church is identified primarily with the community rather than with the mother church. In inter-village competition or conflict loyalty to the local community asserts itself in an unmistakable manner and is expected from every individual. Practically every village has developed a sort of reputation, a general character, by which it is well known in the surrounding area.[9]

OLD ORDER AMISH IN PENNSYLVANIA Such complete identification with the entire pattern of the community is not likely in American society, except in rare instances. The Old Order Amish communities of Lancaster County, Pennsylvania, constitute such an exception. These island communities are maintained by withdrawal from contacts with the outside world and by the exercise of stern disciplinary controls within the community.

> The basic virtues in the community consist largely in maintaining the old order in social and religious life and exhibiting stability and success in a rural way of life, preferably farming. The old order in the spheres of religious and social life bespeaks adherence to the cardinal principles of the church—nonresistance, separation from the world, nonconformity to the world, avoidance of the unequal yoke, and avoidance of manifestations of pride. For the sake of maintaining uniformity and harmony in carrying these principles into effect, the church has to enforce numerous disciplines (such as proscription of the ownership of many worldly improvements and prescription of the type of clothes to be worn by each sex and all age groups) and those

who fully abide by them naturally exemplify the cherished virtues of the community.[10]

IDENTIFICATION THROUGH MUTUAL SERVICES As communities expand and direct contacts between residents decline, community identification changes from one based on primary association to one based on recognition of the interdependence of services. This situation arises as formalizing factors, such as mass media, enter and as more diversified economic pursuits take over. Personal acquaintance throughout is impossible in large communities which are made up of several neighborhoods, and where social distance and strangeness are characteristic. We recognize our relation to the community, however, in the more formally organized cooperative activities that make possible the satisfaction of our essential needs and desires within the area.

In describing the community of Irwin, Iowa —typical of the corn-livestock culture of the corn belt—Moe and Taylor say: "The community in many ways is much more a community now than it was 50 years ago. The village has become the center of the activities of the farmers, and the differences between the villagers and farm dwellers have declined. They meet together in the work and programs of the churches, the fraternal orders, and the school. The farmers' business relations in the village are on a much friendlier basis. There is general recognition that the farm and non-farm groups are dependent on each other."[11]

However, Bell, describing a southwestern Kansas county in the wheat area at about the same time, says: "Before the days of the wheat boom and rapid transportation, communities were important realities in the life of the people. The institutional activities of the people all bore relation to the community center, which in most cases was a village. . . .

"Now the conquest of space by automobiles has broken the chief bond that held the people together in communities, and this, together with economic conditions, has brought about a dispersal of the institutions. People are no longer oriented toward a specific center; the individual is now the center and looks about him in all directions."[12]

Further comments indicate that there was little identification on a community basis in this area, illustrating the extent to which readjustments to new social forces have changed community patterns in some places and are creating new foundations for community alignment.

The Community Is the Arena in Which Most Persons Acquire Their Prestige

The community plays an important role in prestige determination. Few of us are known very far beyond the community in which we live, the persons with whom we work, and our kin. Yet we wish to "count for something" with others. Our prestige must be built chiefly upon these relations. The community is the place in most societies where we can achieve it with most satisfaction.

The population is classed according to a rank system in most communities, reflecting the status structure of the society at large and revealing the local application of the various tests of social position. A study of a New York community, for example, revealed that the community used at least ten different criteria in determining the prestige of its citizens: income and level of living, occupation, nativity, political and economic beliefs, participation in organizations, family position, kinships, personal-

ity traits, clique relationships, and personal habits.[13] All communities rate persons according to traits that have become symbols for determining social position. The differential opportunities to take part in the community are, in part, a result of the prestige the community assigns to persons possessing these symbolic traits.[14] (This matter is discussed more completely in Chapter 22.)

The Typical Structure of the Community Consists of an Economic and Social Service Center, Usually a Village, and a Surrounding Farming or Residential Territory

We have pointed out that the structure of the region is composed of a dominant metropolitan center and a supporting hinterland. We may make this same characterization of communities. They have a chief focal point which is the area of concentration for residence, service, and other agencies and a supporting terri-

A pattern of rural settlement in modern America.

tory that may be the farms of the surrounding area, a residence area of families, or the residential neighborhoods into which it has subdivided.

TYPICAL FORM OF SETTLEMENT This is the typical manner of community settlement we find everywhere. Even among nomadic people, particular sites for camping, where water supply is assured and access to the natural resources of the territory is possible, are part of their organization. Fixed dwelling places became necessary as men developed settled agricultural life. Living close together for protection and cooperation make the village center inevitable. Today, the majority of the villages are fixed residence places from which agricultural lands are worked. The assembling and processing of products, at least to some degree, are also conducted in the village center. This form of settlement is generally prevalent in European, Asiatic, African, and South American societies. The farmers go out from their village residences to work their fields.

DISPERSED FARM SETTLEMENT The land is settled by scattered family holdings in some places, particularly in American society. Here the village is the service center for the surrounding territory, but it is not the residential location of farmers. Instead of providing residence for the operators of the various services, its chief function is to operate as the economic

A pattern of urban settlement in modern America.

and social integrator for its surrounding area, thus serving as the nucleus of the community.

VILLAGE SERVICES AS INTEGRATORS This integrative function of the village is illustrated by the economic and social agencies usually located there, which include retail stores; post, telephone, and telegraph offices; the railway depot; banks; professional people, such as doctors, dentists, and lawyers; schools; churches; and such organizations as lodges, granges, and other voluntary associations. The life of the community takes place in these villages, where activities are greatest, contacts most frequent, and movement much quicker than in the supporting area. Life operates almost completely within the village in those societies where it is the residential place of the population, as well as the market and social center.

The Basic Structural Pattern of Large City Communities Is Similar to That of Other Communities, but May Differ Considerably in the Type of Identification Persons Have with Them

CITIES AS CONSTELLATIONS OF COMMUNITIES Most cities began as single communities with the usual characteristics of an area of service concentration and a supporting hinterland. Their expansion, as population, economic, and social activities grew, led to their subdivision into distinct districts set apart from other areas. Today, cities are ecologically constellations of communities. The city develops areas containing specialized functions serving the whole city. An example is the area of retail concentration, in that the interdependence of these specialized areas gives the city its over-all functional unity. But sections within the larger communities operate to a considerable degree through a collection of local institutions and organizations that provide the necessary functions to permit the residents to live a large part, if not all, of their lives within them. They constitute nearly self-sufficing units.

The city community therefore is usually constituted structurally of (1) an area where retail stores and other service agencies, such as banks, are concentrated in a given place and (2) a surrounding area of residences that usually includes schools and churches. Some of the residence areas may include homogeneous population types, such as foreign-born nationalities residing in neighborhood patterns. Often natural or man-made barriers—hills, streams, and railway or streetcar tracks—separate these communities and give them definite boundaries, though usually they overlap in interstitial territories. Many city communities have had a history as independent communities before being absorbed by an expanding city. Englewood in Chicago or Boylan Heights in Raleigh, North Carolina, would be examples.

IDENTIFICATION IN URBAN COMMUNITIES A distinctive difference between large city and rural and small urban communities is shown in the identification of persons with them. Contacts are less intimate as communities enlarge, and areas take on secondary associational traits. Families live next door or in the same buildings, yet do not associate together, often not speaking to each other except, perhaps, a casual "Good morning." Many are roomers or renters with little interest in the area. Their intimate, personal relations are with those with whom they work or are otherwise associated. They are not defined by geography. The inhabitants are related to the area largely as a place to live, to work, or to obtain supplies.

Communities Change with Changing Social Conditions

Communities are not static for they change with the changing forces that play upon them. Some grow, reach a peak, then decline, while others keep on growing and may eventually become a city or a region made up of a number of communities. Once-flourishing mining areas, such as those in West Virginia, contain communities dying with the declining fortunes of the coal industry. Settlements in lumbering areas fade as the forests are cut away. On the other hand, many small communities, long stagnant, have experienced explosive growth with the coming of new industry or suburban populations. One of the most complete stories of the rise, change, and decline of a small community—Waterville, New York—is told in the references at the end of this chapter.[15] It illustrates what often happens to communities all over the world.

III. NEIGHBORHOODS

Neighborhoods Are Limited Geographic Areas in Which the Individuals and Families Are Known to Each Other and Carry on Intimate Associations Together

The third natural ecological entity is the *neighborhood*—a small area in which a limited number of individuals and families living in close proximity carry on personal and intimate association with each other. It is a geographic unit in which people know each other well by name and reputation. Common activities include visiting together, taking meals together, exchanging work, and borrowing and other forms of mutual aid. The associations are not always amicable. Spontaneous acts of kindness may give way to vitriolic quarrels, often over petty things. Neighborhood conflict is symbolized in the extreme by the notorious feud between the Hatfields and the McCoys. Paradoxically, the very intimacy of the association may increase the bitterness and duration of a quarrel.

Neighborhoods Are Sociability Entities; Communities Service Entities

The character of the neighborhood stands out clearly if we compare it with the community. Both are geographic entities. The community is usually much larger than the neighborhood, and it may be made up of several neighborhoods. The community is founded upon the social and economic requirements of its residents and the organizations and institutions to satisfy them. The neighborhood is founded upon personal acquaintance and the primary group relations that make direct social interaction its major attribute. Communities include the services necessary to make the area practically self-sufficing, whereas neighborhoods may include no social or economic services. At most, they will include only one or two, such as a church or store. Neighborhoods are units in which the residents enjoy comparatively intimate associations based on likeness in sentiments and tradition. Communities usually operate on a more impersonal, secondary basis.

The Neighborhood Is Significant Because of the Kind of Social Interaction That Exists Within It

PRIMARY GROUP ASSOCIATIONS Groups, we have pointed out, are the psychologically bonded mechanisms for functioning in a society. The neighborhood is the ecological entity where group formation takes place most frequently. The closeness of residence, the informality of contacts, the similarity of sentiments and traditions, and the usual homogeneity of occupational levels, race, and nationality facilitate the development of personal contacts on a face-to-face basis. Such primary associations influence the personalities in the neighborhood and operate as means of transmitting ideals and practices among them.

PERSONALITY FORMATION   Charles H. Cooley stressed the significance of the neighborhood in personality influence when he wrote, "The most important sphere of this intimate association and cooperation—though by no means the only ones—are the family, the play-group of children, and the neighborhood or community group of elders." [16] Many writers have reaffirmed this role of the neighborhood.

Lewis E. Lawes, the former famous warden of Sing Sing Prison, lived until he was seventeen years of age in an upstate New York neighborhood which had developed around a state reformatory. He wrote that the boys in this neighborhood grew up with the idea that the prisoners there grew were the state's criminals. The boys were not to approach too near the reformatory because something might happen. But, he continued, it was impossible to stay away from the area on Saturday afternoons when there was military drill. The martial music of the band impressed and thrilled them, and the commands of the officers and the men marching held them in rapt attention. He concluded that these experiences may have developed in him the desire to become a part of that show.[17]

Next to the family, it is in the neighborhood that children establish their intimate group relations. They absorb a large share of their ways of thinking and acting from them. From the neighborhood, most children gain the first view of their society. This, in turn, may supply the adult frame of reference for perceiving the larger social world.

ADULT INFLUENCES   Adults too are influenced by the close contacts of the neighborhood. Note that Professor Cooley emphasized "the neighborhood group of elders." Aldous Huxley described these influences by contrasting in an exaggerated way neighboring among the poor and the rich:

The rich have no neighbours in the sense that the poor have neighbors. When my mother had to go out, Mrs. Cradock from next door on the right kept an eye on us children. And my mother did the same for Mrs. Cradock when it was her turn to go out. And when somebody had broken a leg, or lost his job, people helped with money and food. . . . But you rich, you have no neighbours. You never perform a **neighbourly** ac-

tion or expect your neighbours to do you a kindness in return. It's unnecessary. You can pay people to look after you. No, you're generally not even aware of your neighbours. You live at a distance from them. Each of you is boxed up in his own secret house.[18]

Yet the rich have neighbors and are neighborly in different ways from those of the poor. Their circumstances may not require that they watch each other's children or help overcome economic setbacks. But they live by choice and associate by design with those of similar cultural backgrounds in their neighborhood. Their acquaintance with individuals and families of the same social status allows for intimate sociability in their own locality and in other neighborhoods where social status is similar. The range of their intimate associations is less restricted than that of the poor.

THREE ATTRIBUTES OF NEIGHBORHOODS   In summary, we may note three features of neighborhoods: (1) They usually have a homogeneity of social class, nationality, race, or occupational type. Their character changes or they disappear when invasion by other types occurs. (2) The forms of association within them will depend upon their cultural base. (3) Neighborhoods, like communities, may not function as a single interacting unit, though this is possible if the neighborhood is small enough. All associations of each person do not necessarily take place in neighborhoods, but there is always face-to-face, intimate, informal contact within them and more so than with individuals and families of other areas.

There Are Different Types of Neighborhoods in Rural Areas

There are, of course, neighborhoods in both rural and urban areas, and the first differentiation as to type is usually made on this basis. The neighborhood has been and still is one of the important units in rural areas. People reside in villages in most argicultural lands. Personal knowledge and intimate association are unavoidable in them. In fact, many are knit together through family ties, and others came into existence through settlement. The need to cooperate welds the people into neighborhoods. The neighborhood and the community are often the same in these situations. In their expansion, economic, social, educational, and religious services are located within the village to give it a full life. But segregation sets in and specialized areas evolve, creating several neighborhoods within the whole if the villages expand to fairly large proportions. Large rural villages with 5000 to 10,000 and more inhabitants in South China, Japan, Taiwan, the Scandinavian countries, and elsewhere have gone through this development.

FARM VILLAGE NEIGHBORHOODS IN MANY LANDS In some countries, the market town evolved as the center of exchange for rural areas. The surrounding villages are actually neighborhoods composed largely of farm families. Thus, in China, Burma and Japan, the market town is often surrounded by a number of small farm family villages that include no services except a tea house and a place of worship. Largely within its confines are the relationships of the families and individuals, which may include working together to maintain roads and bridges, to observe religious festivals, and to control fires. In historic European countries, families were largely controlled by the concerns of their village neighborhoods so that their patterns of thought and action were those of their immediate area. The novels of Reymont vividly portray this for old Russia, while a large body of literature on German and English villages does the same for these societies.

AMERICAN RURAL NEIGHBORHOODS The ecological patterns of American society are new and were not subject to strong forces of change until the Industrial Revolution. Hundreds of villages and cities in many parts of this country are not much older than the oldest residents.

The ecological patterns in American society are really still emerging. Social forces have caused constant change—especially the invention of new mechanical devices servicing an evolving machine-marketing economy.

New England Settlers in this new land brought with them the patterns of settlement to which they were accustomed in their homeland. In the New England region they settled in villages. Life had to be cooperative in order that the people might protect each other and wrest the necessities for survival from the environment. In the beginning, rules of conduct were as rigid as in the village neighborhoods of the homelands. Settlement on the frontiers became less restricted as the original obstacles were overcome and dispersion was feasible. Location in neighborhoods was a matter of choice. The problem of obtaining materials for building, exchanging surplus food and feed supplies, helping in sickness or other trials, building roads and

paths, and other common requirements created these first neighborhoods. They were village units of intimately acquainted individuals and families who shared life together almost as closely as if they were all in the same family. It was the customary unit of social control. The need to adapt in a self-sufficient organization in isolated situations led to giving and receiving services on a voluntary basis. All this mutual aid led to close integration.

The South Settlement in the South was originally in villages, also. The large land-holding class had their homes in the villages, such as Jamestown and Williamsburg, in antebellum days. The land owners commuted to their holdings. Village neighborhoods made up of cabins became the pattern of Negro settlement after slavery came. The plantation with its large dwelling house, the commissary, the school, and the cottages and cabins became a primary locality unit. Separate neighborhoods for Negroes and whites persist to the present time.

Western Areas Settlement in the Western areas was on scattered farmsteads. The necessity for protection led to building forts where the settlers retreated to in times of danger. Villages developed at crossroads and railroad points to become the service centers for these farming expanses. These villages as well as the farm lands were settled chiefly by families from European countries who made neighborhoods composed of persons of similar nationality and religion. States like Iowa, Illinois, and Minnesota were early dotted with Norwegian, Swedish, and German villages where neighboring together was the mode of life. Once established, they attracted others with similar traits. They developed their own patterns of social behavior which they were often able to maintain against outside encroachments. As late as World War I, some teaching was done in Swedish, Norwegian, or German in many of the one-room public schools that served rural neighborhoods in Iowa.

Rural Neighborhoods in American Societies Are Both Disappearing and Appearing

Neighborhoods persist in various forms in present-day rural America. It is obvious that these small units undergo changes. Shifting institutions mean the complete elimination of some, the absorption of others into enlarging communities, and the creation of new ones, especially where the geography combines with some social change to make the location of a number of families at some new point advantageous. The construction of the main automobile highways and the establishment of manufacturing enterprises in rural territory are causing changes today, just as the Erie Canal in New York created many small neighborhoods along its course when it was a chief transportation route. The subsequent building of the railroads through the Great L Valley left some of these earlier communities stranded to remain static or disappear altogether, while others grew rapidly. Many neighborhoods experiencing growth may suddenly find themselves eclipsed by others whose prospects of development seemed poorer, because the stream of life moves in another direction.

Cities Classify and Locate People in Particular Neighborhoods

The expansion of cities results almost automatically in the subdivision of territory into areas with specialized functions. Every city has its area of retail business, its chief financial section, its wholesale district, its manufacturing area, and its shipping center. Residences of a particular type also concentrate in distinct sections. In the same manner, people of particular classes, nationalities, races, occupations, or other distinctive traits locate in different neighborhoods. Some of these are neighborhoods of first settlement. Into these, immigrants from other lands almost automatically flow because they know that others like themselves are already there. The Puerto Rican area east of the Harlem district in New York City is such a neighborhood.

The rooming house area is another type of city neighborhood. Zorbaugh describes one in Chicago:

> At the back door of the Gold Coast, on Dearborn, Clark and LaSalle Streets, and on the side streets extending south to the business and industrial area, is a strange world, painfully plain by contrast, a world that lives in houses with neatly lettered cards in the window: "Furnished Rooms." In these houses, from midnight to dawn, sleep some twenty-five thousand people. But by day houses and streets are practically deserted. For early in the morning this population hurried from its houses and down its streets, boarding cars and busses, to work in the Loop. It is a childless area, an area of young men and young women, most of whom are single, though some

are married, and others are living together unmarried.[19]

We could describe other types of neighborhoods, such as those where only professional and business people reside, or neighborhoods of skilled or unskilled persons who are alike in some significant respect which causes them to select the same type of residential location.

Some large city neighborhoods have expanded and include almost all essential services so that they are no longer merely neighborhoods. The residents are able to live wholly within them, if they so desire. They thus have the characteristics of communities. Chinatown in New York City is an example. Once, a neighborhood of Chinese immigrants, it is now a large community with its own neighborhood subdivisions. But, because the residents are of one race, there prevails over the whole area the chief characteristic of the neighborhood—face-to-face, informal relationships.

IV. BOUNDARIES OF NATURAL ECOLOGICAL ENTITIES

The Boundaries of the Natural Ecological Entities Are Indefinite

THEY ARE UNPLANNED A characteristic common to all three natural ecological entities is the varying distinctness of their geographic boundaries. It is difficult at times to know where one begins and the other ends. This is to be expected since the interrelatedness in each is based on voluntary responses. These entities are unplanned. The boundaries of the region are indicated by the limits to which the dominant economic activities and mode of life have extended. Thus, the wheat region of the American Northwest can be clearly delimited to the area where wheat is almost the sole crop and where cities have developed in which activities related to its processing, distribution, and financing are focused. Likewise, activities on its periphery do not influence the operation of the region as significantly as do the activities on the periphery of the community.

The limits of the neighborhood are determined by the area of the personal associations of a cluster of families. Intimate association is more intensive within this cluster than with those outside. The limits of such association are fairly easy to define.

VARIATION OF COMMUNITY SERVICES Communities are basically economic and social service areas. These services do not have the same geographic reach. The school district may extend beyond the limits of the area from which church attendants come. Bank patrons may come to the community center from a greater distance than those who purchase hardware items. These differences in the reach that the services at the community center have—usually a village or market town in rural areas and an area of retail business concentration in the city—make the limits of the community vague. A composite line collating the areas is usually drawn to approximate the limits of the community to the area in which economic and social interrelatedness are predominant since these service areas do not coincide. Persons on the periphery of a community may relate themselves to other centers so that there is interstitial territory between communities, while those near the center of interaction will relate themselves to it almost completely. Locating the limits of communities with fairly accurate approximation has practical values since communities are often used as the geographic base for developing economic and social activities. These limits can usually be determined so that, within those approximated, a fairly unified organization of social intercourse prevails, although it is not possible to set the limits with exactness.

V. PURPOSEFULLY CREATED ECOLOGICAL ENTITIES

Men in Adaptation Create Ecological Forms Nondeliberately

Regions, communities, and neighborhoods thus come into existence naturally as operational entities where men associate with each other to satisfy needs. These entities are not planned but arise spontaneously as consequences of the relationships among people and the products of these relationships. People develop such units when they simply adjust to each other and the environments surrounding them without design. Community organization workers recognize this, as is evident in their endeavor to get residents in natural communities to be aware of these entities and to get them consciously to organize in relation to the basic problems within them.

Some Problems Require Fixed Geographic Units of Operation

But people living in association with each other face problems of relationship that can-

not wait on the slow processes of spontaneous development to create units of operation. Interrelationships need to be controlled. It is readily recognized that there must be government, which, in part, is a matter of territory. Therefore, villages, towns, cities, townships, counties, and states with fixed geographic limits are purposefully established. The limits are often arbitrarily determined, as was true of townships and counties in many midwestern states which were laid out in squares. Certain types of behavior within these areas must recognize these geographic limits. Areas need schools or fire protection or health control. School districts, fire districts, and health districts with fixed limits have to be defined. We operate in relation to these parts of our living within these bounds. We vote, for example, only at designated places in a prescribed area and vote only for officers of these areas. One of the problems in the relations of nations is the determination of the territorial boundary lines between them. Disputes as to just where they are sometimes lead to war.

Deliberately Created Ecological Entities Are Specific in Purpose

The purposeful creation of ecological units is always in relation to some definite aspect of our interrelated life. They are specific purpose areas. Counties are government units. Water districts are legally constituted units to provide adequate water supply for an area. Natural ecological entities, on the other hand, arise out of the associations that are of a more general character and involve many forms of interaction. The area of operation is determined by the practical limits to which these relationships extend. A region, for example, extends to the outside points reached by the dominant type of economic activity. The same is true for the community and neighborhood.

Boundary Inflexibility Creates Problems

The inflexibility of the boundaries of our purposefully created units, such as counties, cities, and states, leads to many problems. Our societies are dynamic and ever changing. State boundaries, for example, often hamper social controls since the coming of rapid transportation and communication. Criminal activities were relatively limited geographically when transportation was slow. Today fast-moving automobiles and airplanes as well as long-distance telephones and telegraph make criminal operations over wider areas easily possible. Our control systems are organized on a state basis. Our officers can operate only within their own specific territory. Often the apprehension of criminals is frustrated by their rapid movement across these fixed lines. The counties of which our American states are composed were defined in the days of horse-and-buggy travel. Each of these counties built courthouses and government systems to serve these smaller units. It would be possible for us to eliminate more than half of them and still have county services within easier reach of their constituencies than was true in the horse-and-buggy days. But vested interests and local ethnocentrism make consolidation difficult. Lags in the consolidation of ecological entities with fixed boundaries are thus one of today's important social problems.

VI. PROCESSES IN ECOLOGICAL ORGANIZATION

Ecological Processes Determine Ecological Patterns

The ecological organization of a society is based upon the operation of the ecological processes, which determine the spatial patterns. The processes are commonly listed as six in number: concentration, deconcentration, centralization, segregation, invasion, and succession.

CONCENTRATION Concentration is expressed in terms of density within an area at a given time. When we examine any population distribution map, we see that people concentrate at particular points like New York City, Tokyo, Shanghai, and Paris in great numbers, and at other points in lesser numbers. In such areas as farming, desert, and rugged territory we note that they are widely dispersed. The condition of the lands, the availability of transportation facilities, the natural growth and migration of people, and the type of economy all influence the extent to which populations and their utilities concentrate. New York City has one of the largest concentrations of population in the world and has actually expanded far out beyond its legal limits. It is situated, we are informed, at the most advantageous break between land and water on the North American continent. This is the front door to a large hinterland of industry and agriculture that is oriented to this point.

DECONCENTRATION Deconcentration is the tendency for people and their institutions to move away from the areas of concentration and to locate in the outskirts where more desirable space is available. The expansion of cities and towns is centrifugal. When central areas become crowded, families move outward to more open areas. Services to meet their immediate needs tend to follow, and secondary business units develop as these new areas increase in population.

One of the striking aspects of deconcentration in modern American society is the suburban movement. We have already noted that automobiles, hard-surfaced roads, and electricity have greatly accelerated the movement of people and services into suburban territory and the open country. A major measure of this trend is the very high rate of population growth outside the central cities of our many metropolitan areas.[20]

CENTRALIZATION All cities have a major area for conducting retail business. We can almost always locate the point within it where activity is greatest for usually the central banks are located there. Every small city has its crossing of "State and Tioga Streets," such as exists in Ithaca, New York. It is the intersection of two main avenues where the greatest number of persons satisfy the largest number and variety of their needs.

Frederick L. Allen described this characteristic of ecological centralization relative to finance for American society:

If there was one geographical spot in the United States that could justly be called the financial center of the country, it was the junction of Broad and Wall Streets in New York. Here, on the north side of Wall Street, stood the Sub-Treasury Building, and next to it the United States Assay Office; opposite them, on the southeast corner, an ostentatiously unostentatious three-story limestone building housed the firm of J. P. Morgan & Company, the most powerful nexus of capitalism in the world; on the southwest corner yawned the excavation where the New York Stock Exchange was presently to build its annex, and next to this, on Broad Street, rose the Corinthian pillars of the Exchange itself.[21]

SEGREGATION Segregation is the spatial separation of population and services by processes of selection relative to some chief attribute. We have just mentioned the area of retail business centralization. The typical large city may include a wholesale district, a warehouse area, a manufacturing area—to give a few illustrations of areas determined by economic attributes. The many residential districts may range from the area of elite homes to those of the poorest of our foreign-born populations ("Little Italy" or "Chinatown" are familiar names for these sections).

INVASION   The penetration into a segregated area by a different type of population or social or economic service is called invasion. This occurs continuously in societies where a residential district is penetrated by a business form, such as when automobile sales and services move into a residential district or when members of one race move into an area where another predominates. Harlem, in New York City, has passed through a whole series of invasions from different populations. Virtually every city and most rural areas have experienced some invasions.

SUCCESSION   Succession has been achieved when invasion has been completed and a new type of population or form of business has taken over a district. Such an area may take

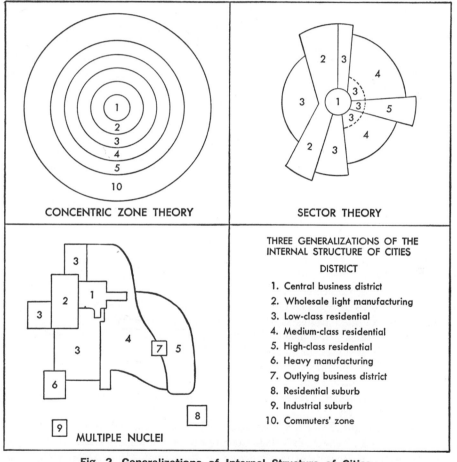

CONCENTRIC ZONE THEORY

SECTOR THEORY

MULTIPLE NUCLEI

THREE GENERALIZATIONS OF THE INTERNAL STRUCTURE OF CITIES

DISTRICT

1. Central business district
2. Wholesale light manufacturing
3. Low-class residential
4. Medium-class residential
5. High-class residential
6. Heavy manufacturing
7. Outlying business district
8. Residential suburb
9. Industrial suburb
10. Commuters' zone

Fig. 2. Generalizations of Internal Structure of Cities

"The concentric zone theory is a generalization for all cities. The arrangement of the sectors in the sector theory varies from city to city. The diagram for multiple nuclei represents one possible pattern among innumerable variations." *

* Source: Harris, C. D., and Ullman, E. L., "The Nature of Cities," Annals of the American Academy of Political and Social Science, 242 (November, 1945), p. 13.

on a new character or function. Some areas experience a series of such successions as a consequence of invasion. Louis Wirth pointed this out about the west side of Chicago where the first Jewish settlers located:

> In the course of the extension of the Jewish settlement they encountered the Irish and the Germans. As these groups moved on, the Jews followed, only to be succeeded by the Italians, the Poles and Lithuanians, the Greeks and Turks, and finally by the Negroes. Such observations as have been made in other large American cities, notably New York and Philadelphia, indicate that a similar order of succession is to be seen there. This phenomenon seems to be due, not merely to the chronological order of immigration of these various groups, but also to the relation of the standards of living of the various nationalities to one another, and to the attraction and tolerance of the successor by the predecessor.[22]

Ford, studying population succession in Chicago, indicated that the dispersion of the Negro population is unlike that for other population types because, to a certain extent, the Negro is denied the right to choose his place of abode freely.[23] Here the attraction and tolerance of the successor by the predecessor is a factor in area change.

The ecological structure of any area is, we re-emphasize, contingent upon the operation of these six processes. They bring about the patterns of distribution of people and their agencies in adaptation to geographic conditions and the cultural development that has been achieved. Three views of urban ecological structure are shown in Fig. 2 on p. 113.

Changes in Ecological Patterns Are Sociologically Important

In the chapter on social change, we will give further attention to rapid changes occurring in the ecological entities. This will stress especially urbanization, the broadening of the area of influence of cities and metropolitan regions, and the suburban movement.

References

1. Rawlings, Marjorie K., *South Moon Under* (New York, Grosset and Dunlap, 1933), p. 3.
2. Wells, H. G., Huxley, J. S., and Wells, G. P., *The Science of Life,* 2 (Garden City, N.Y., Doubleday Company, Inc., 1931), pp. 1012 and 1013. By permission of the Executors of the H. G. Wells' estate and by the authors.
3. Vance, R. B., *Human Factors in Cotton Culture* (Chapel Hill, N.C., University of North Carolina Press, 1929), p. 12.
4. Anderson, W. A., "Social Change in a Central New York Rural Community," Cornell University AES (December, 1954), Bulletin 907.
5. Thompson, Warren S., "The Growth of Metropolitan Districts in the United States: 1900–1940" (United States Government Printing Office, Washington, D.C., 1947), and United States Department of Commerce, Bureau of the Census, *Statistical Abstract of United States, 1962,* Table 10, p. 13.
6. United States Department of Commerce, Bureau of the Census, *Statistical Abstract of the United States, 1962,* Table 13, p. 21.
7. Malinowski, Bronislaw, *Crime and Custom in Savage Society* (New York, Humanities Press, 1951), p. 23.
8. Sanderson, Dwight, *The Rural Community* (Boston, Ginn and Company, 1932), p. 1.
9. Tannous, Afif I., "The Arab Village Community of the Middle East," *Annual Report of the Board of Regents of the Smithsonian Institution* (United States Government Printing Office, Washington, D.C., 1944), p. 542.
10. Kollmorgen, Walter H., "Culture of a Contemporary Rural Community: The Old Order Amish of Lancaster County, Pennsylvania," *Rural Life Studies,* 4 (September, 1942), United States Bureau of Agricultural Economics, pp. 82–84.
11. Moe, E. O., and Taylor, C. C., "Cultures of a Contemporary Rural Community:

Irwin, Iowa," *Rural Life Studies,* 5 (1942), United States Bureau of Agricultural Economics, p. 172.

12. Bell, E. H., "Culture of a Contemporary Rural Community: Sublette, Kansas," *Rural Life Studies,* 2 (1942), United States Bureau of Agricultural Economics, pp. 68–70.

13. Kaufman, Harold F., "Defining Prestige Rank in a Rural Community," *Sociometry,* 8 (February, 1945), pp. 199–207.

14. Anderson, W. A., "The Family and Individual Social Participation," *American Sociological Review,* 8 (August, 1943), p. 420.

15. Anderson, W. A., "Social Change in a Central New York Rural Community," Cornell University AES (December, 1954), Bulletin 907; Mather, William, Townsend, T. H., and Sanderson, Dwight, "A Study of Rural Community Development in Waterville, New York," Cornell University AES (1933), Bulletin 608; Williams, James M., *An American Town* (Waterville, N.Y., R. W. Williams, 1906).

16. Cooley, Charles H., *Social Organization* (New York, Charles Scribner's Sons, 1920), p. 24.

17. Lawes, Lewis E., *Twenty Thousand Years in Sing Sing* (New York, Ray Long and Richard R. Smith, Inc., 1932), pp. 12 and 13.

18. Huxley, Aldous, *Point Counter Point* (New York, Harper and Brothers, 1928), pp. 63–65.

19. Zorbaugh, Harvey W., *The Gold Coast and the Slum* (Chicago, University of Chicago Press, 1929), pp. 8 and 9. By permission of Harvey Zorbaugh.

20. For comment on the suburban movement, see pp. 727 ff.

21. Allen, F. L., *Only Yesterday* (New York, Harper and Bros., Inc., 1931), pp. 71–72.

22. Wirth, L., *The Ghetto* (Chicago, University of Chicago Press, 1928), p. 227. Copyright, 1928, by the University of Chicago.

23. Ford, F. G., "Population Succession in Chicago," *American Journal of Sociology,* 56 (September, 1950), p. 160.

Questions for Study and Discussion

1. Look up a text on plant or animal ecology and be able to indicate the areas of analysis it includes.
2. How would you describe human ecology to a person who never heard of it?
3. Distinguish between region, community, neighborhood.
4. What significance do regions have in the operation of your society? Give some concrete illustrations.
5. How does the principle of comparative advantage relate to regionalism?
6. Discuss cultural uniformity and regionalism.
7. Contrast community with neighborhood by characterizing each structurally and functionally.
8. What is meant by community identification? Is it a determinative factor in community creation?
9. Describe the social changes that have occurred in a community you know.
10. Are neighborhoods appearing or disappearing in the region where you live? Why?
11. Does the indefiniteness of the boundaries of the natural ecological entities invalidate these as human relationship structures?
12. Discuss cities, towns, counties, and states as purposefully created ecological units.
13. Differentiate between the several ecological processes.
14. Show how some of these ecological processes are operative in your home community.

Suggested Topics for Reports

1. On two outline maps of the United States, locate the standard metropolitan areas, as indicated in the United States Census for 1950 and 1960. What differences or trends are apparent? Do you find evidence of the development of *megalopolis,* the formation of belts of metropolitan areas?

2. Using the sources cited in the list of references for this chapter, prepare a summary account of the rise, change, and decline of Waterville, New York. Show how its history illustrates some of the principles discussed in the chapter.

Supplementary Reading

Clarke, George L., *Elements of Ecology.* New York: John Wiley and Sons, Inc., 1954.

Hawley, Amos H., *Human Ecology.* New York: The Ronald Press, 1950.

Kolb, John H., *Emerging Rural Communities.* Madison, Wis.: University of Wisconsin Press, 1959.

————, and Brunner, Edmund de S., *A Study of Rural Society.* 3rd ed. Boston: Houghton Mifflin Company, 1946.

Lind, Andrew W., *An Island Community.* Chicago: University of Chicago Press, 1938.

Lynd, Robert S., and Lynd, Helen M., *Middletown.* New York: Harcourt, Brace and Company, 1929.

————, *Middletown in Transition.* New York: Harcourt, Brace and Company, 1937.

Odum, Howard W., and Moore, H. E., *American Regionalism.* New York: Henry Holt and Company, Inc., 1938.

Park, Robert E., *Human Communities.* Glencoe, Ill.: The Free Press, 1952.

————, Burgess, Ernest W., McKenzie, Roderick, and Wirth, Louis, *The City.* Chicago: University of Chicago Press, 1925.

Quinn, J. A., *Human Ecology.* Englewood Cliffs, N.J.: Prentice-Hall, Inc., 1950.

Sanderson, E. Dwight, *The Rural Community.* Boston: Ginn and Company, 1932.

Taylor, C. C., *et al., Rural Life in the United States.* New York: Alfred A. Knopf, 1949.

Wells, H. G., Huxley, Julian, and Wells, G. P., *The Science of Life.* Section on Ecology. Garden City, N.Y.: Doubleday, Doran and Company, Inc., 1931.

West, James, *Plainville, U.S.A.* New York: Columbia University Press, 1945.

8

HUMAN GROUPS: THE PSYCHOLOGICALLY BONDED UNITS OF SOCIETIES

HUMAN groups are units of psychologically bonded persons through which actions in a society are ultimately carried out. The essence of this general form of relationship structure is socially defined mental interaction between two or more persons. There are many types of groups based on characteristics that differentiate them from each other, such as modes of entrance, number of persons involved, and others.

Societies develop norms or standards to govern group relationships and give them order and stability. Individuals occupying social positions that give them statuses and roles pursue their actions in terms of these norms. These norms, statuses, and roles permeate all social organization. They constitute the "social matrices" of societal structure.

I. DEFINITION AND SIGNIFICANCE

The Human Group Is the Elemental Unit for Functioning in Societies

We have surveyed the ecological structures which constitute the land-based forms of societal organization. Within these structures, many of which are broad and diffuse relationship systems, are distributed the multitude of smaller structures composed of people in more direct relationship with each other. These are the groups—the units of people whose interpersonal relations have high psychological immediacy, although the interaction will be governed by incipient, latent, or manifest social structure. These are the units through which the business of society is most concretely carried out. The management of a large enterprise may formulate its policies, procedures, and regulations, but it will be the smaller work groups which ultimately bring the finished articles through the production line. Likewise, because of the psychological proximity of the members, groups will generally have a stronger impact upon persons than will other kinds of structures.

Also, the group is the most pervasive unit in society. Life starts for each of us in a group,

the family. We all are almost constantly operating in some group or preparing to do so. Almost every experience that we have has some group connections. A most important aspect of life for both the person and the society arises when men are related to other men through direct response to mutually meaningful symbols. All through life we are entering and leaving groups, using them as they use us to carry on concerted social activities.

Groups Are Always Composed of at Least Two Persons Capable of Mental Response

DEFINITION *Groups* are units of two or more people engaging in reciprocal psychological interaction. The members may exist in the same environment or overcome distance by some means of communication.

There could be no human relationship structures (hurelures) at all if at least two persons were not in some recognizable type of relationship with each other. At least two persons are required to make psychological interaction possible.

CIRCUMSTANCES OF FORMATION Many interesting considerations arise in this connection. We pick up a book, read, and think many

117

thoughts. We are psychologically influenced by what we read and may be throughout our lives. But we are not in a group since we are not influencing the writer psychologically. The author might be a Plato or an Erasmus who passed on several centuries ago. The forming of groups with a living author is possible if the necessary circumstances are arranged.

We stop before the figure of Jefferson Davis in Statuary Hall in Washington, D.C. Here is the image of a specific man. What thoughts it can bring to us: the struggle between the American states and the ardent devotion to an area's cause. But there is no reciprocal action possible with Mr. Davis, so no group is possible. We can only wonder what his responses would be if he could now express his views.

We write a letter to a business concern, a friend, or a relative. In a few days, a letter is received in response. Or no letter may be returned. The concern or friend acts as a result of the letter. We have previously said that the letter is one of the most important communicating instruments man has devised. The act of writing anticipates a response. But is this a group situation? There is at least indirect interaction, and persons are exhibiting psychological responses. It would seem proper, therefore, to answer the question affirmatively.

It is not always possible to classify phenomena definitely at certain times. For example, it was not long ago that bacteriologists were not sure whether the tubercle germ was a plant or an animal. It possesses important characteristics of both. It is now classified as a plant since added knowledge of its characteristics became available. We need further study before we can classify definitely some situations created by the relationships of people in society. We may be sure, however, that we have a group if two or more persons are interacting directly.

Persons Do Not Have to Be in the Same Place to Form a Group

Most groups are made up of people who are in the same place, but physical proximity is not necessary to the formation of a group. Two persons talking to each other over the telephone form a group as effectively as if they were in the same room, although they may be thousands of miles apart.

The "conference call" makes it possible to connect persons by telephone throughout the country, so that they can confer with each other as if they were in the same room. Sales people make frequent use of conference calls to advise and be advised of rapid changes in business conditions. The expansion of our communication techniques is constantly increasing the possibilities of group formation.

Groups Exist Only so Long as There Is Reciprocal Psychological Interaction

When do groups cease to be groups? Groups dissolve when the mental interactions among the members come to an end. It may *seem* that a group exists after the psychological relations among the members are stopped because the *results* of the group experience do not necessarily cease when it dissolves. We may have many thoughts and perform many acts related to a group after we are separated from it. They are individual thoughts and acts, however, not interactions. There is no active relation between one mind and another. This question is further considered in the following discussion.

LATENCY NOT A GROUP CHARACTERISTIC Some careful students of social structures have contended that groups exist in active and latent form.[1] According to this distinction, groups are active when the interactions between the persons are taking place but latent when the interactions have been suspended and the individuals in the group are separated. If this point of view were correct, could we not argue that any group, once established, would continue indefinitely in a latent form? This would seem to overextend the concept of group. College classes and university seminars are used as illustrations of latent groups. It is asked if they exist as groups only when the members are in interaction in the classrooms. Our answer is "Yes." They exist as psychologically interacting units only when those who compose them are influencing each other on the mental plane. The class or seminar continues throughout the college term as a unit not because it is a functioning group but because it is a subinstitution within a larger institution. Its members come together as a class as often and as long as the prescribed institutional rules designate. It operates as a group when the teacher establishes intermindedness among the students by various techniques. This establishment of intermindedness is the real problem in classroom teaching. It must be created among the members each time the class reassembles. The ringing of the school bell, the call for attention, the assignment of tasks, and all the other methods at hand are used to make the class or seminar a single unit of interacting minds.

There is no continuous mental action going on among the members after they have separated from the class or seminar. Some members of a class or seminar might conceivably get together to work or confer, but they then form new groups. And some may never give the class or seminar a thought from one prescribed session to another. This issue might be resolved by distinguishing between active group interaction and the "residual deposits" of the experience left in the minds of the individuals.

FAMILY AS A GROUP   The family is very often referred to as a human group. A family does operate as a group with great frequency but only when its members are in psychological interaction. It is a unit of persons bound together by institutional norms and intermindedness that give it a seemingly permanent form.

A family as a single unit may often function as a single group, but it may also operate as several groups if there are more than two members in it. For example, if a family includes five persons—husband, wife, and three children—it could operate at times as a number of different groups. The father and mother may form one group, and the three children may form another at the same time. Since there are many other possible variations of these combinations, it is this circumstance that often gives a family its major problems. It is an entity of persons bound together by institutional obligations to function as a unit in many important matters. The way its members operate with respect to each other through the groups they form is, of course, at the root of family cohesion.

The trait of intermindedness makes the human group society's most general mechanism of operation. Men relate themselves to other men through communication, and the group acts whenever things need to be done. It is often the initiator of actions. The possibility of its forming and reforming facilitates the carrying out of social purposes. It is a society's instrument for completing actions.

Reciprocal Interactions in Groups May Be Those of Disagreement as Well as of Agreement

This essence of the group—reciprocal mental interaction—does not imply that interactions need to be those of agreement. There is just as much of a group when persons in the unit disagree as when they agree. In fact, the bonds may even be more emphatic because keener intermindedness is likely to be aroused in disagreement than in agreement. Disagreement can lead to constructive ends if there is frankness and honesty in our attempts to arrive at consensus.

In *All Passion Spent*, V. Sackville West described a group situation in a family where there was little agreement: "Wrangle, wrangle, she thought . . . for she had had some previous taste of family discussions; they'll wrangle for weeks over Mother like dogs quarrelling over an old, a very old bone." [2] Groups are likely to dissolve if too little agreement or consensus is maintained. But the point is that it is not the qualitative character of our interactions that determine whether or not there is a group. It is simply that there are reciprocal mental relationships of some sort among the members.

II. SOME GROUP TYPES

Human Groups Have Characteristics That Differentiate Them from Each Other

The persons composing the human group, the circumstances leading to its formation, the relations of the persons to each other within the group, and other conditions give to groups characteristics that make it possible to differentiate them from each other. Many attempts have been made to develop general classifications of groups on the basis of these characteristics. Some progress has been made. One prominent sociologist has said: "Until we take the trouble to describe different kinds of groups with the same care a biologist describes a species, genus, or family of plant or animal life, we shall fail to have any adequate understanding of the nature of the group." [3] No general classification based on detailed description has yet been produced that is in general use. Some day, when specialists in this field are more aware of its importance, a sociological Linnaeus and his coworkers will produce a classification that arranges groups with respect to each other in a systematic order. Differentiation of some groups on the basis of prominent traits emphasizing their significance and roles is made here for our purposes.

Chance Places Persons in Group Relations Constantly

SIGNIFICANCE OF CHANCE GROUPS   One of our commonest experiences is the formation of groups with one or more persons in unde-signed, unconsidered circumstances. We meet a friend or even a stranger and conversation takes place. We have no particular purpose, no pre-arranged plan. The meeting may not last more than the time it takes to exchange greetings. We are likely to conclude that groups estab-lished in this way are not significant since this is such a common experience. Most of them probably do not have important consequences, but the significance of a group does not lie necessarily in the circumstances of its creation or in the length of its existence. It lies in what takes place in the mental interchanges among its components. Groups established by mere chance may be very important from this viewpoint.

Victor Hugo's adult life, for example, was partly determined by a remark made to him by his godfather in what we could call a chance group. Hugo says: "One night—it was some great festival of the empire, and all Paris was illuminated—my mother was walking in the gar-den with three of my father's companions. . . . We saw a tall figure in the gloom of the trees. He was even then conspiring against Bonaparte in the cause of liberty, and was shortly after-wards executed. I remember his saying, 'If Rome had kept her kings, she had not been Rome'; and then, looking on me, said: 'Child, put liberty first of all.'" This sentence, accord-ing to Hugo, "outweighed my whole educa-tion." [4] This experience permeated all Hugo's writing and expressed his true sympathies for the underprivileged.

A further contemporary illustration comes from another field. Les Paul is today a renowned guitar player. One day he was fascinated by a grizzled ditch laborer playing a harmonica dur-ing his lunch break. This fourth-grade boy thought: "If I could only make music like that."

Suddenly the workman offered him the har-monica. "Go ahead, son, try it." "I can't play," Paul replied.

The old man regarded Paul for a moment. "Son, you hang onto that mouth organ, and pretty soon you'll have it licked!" Then he added nine words that were the wisest counsel Paul was ever to receive: "Don't say you can't till you prove you can't."

Les Paul tried the piano. His teacher said to his mother, "Your boy Lester will never learn music." But Les Paul was unwilling to quit. He hadn't proved to himself that he couldn't learn music. He set out to prove he could. He taught himself to play the guitar. An accident crushed his right arm. He retaught himself. Eventually, he and his partner, Mary Ford, were to develop a new musical trend with their unusual guitar and voice arrangements—all because of a chance group relation established with a wise ditch digger.[5] Such a chance group relation is a cir-cumstance where one plus one does not make two, for one idea in the mind of one person may create many ideas in the minds of others with possibly quite unexpected results.

Other Groups Form for Definite Purposes

PURPOSIVE GROUPS Some groups are formed for definite purposes and are often called inter-est or special-interest groups. It is sometimes inferred that all groups have some kind of pur-pose, that some common goal unites them. This may be true in a general sense, but there are many groups which have no definite purpose. Like spontaneous conversational gatherings, they may come together for no particular rea-son whatever. When we say that there are in-terest groups, we mean groups that come to-gether to accomplish rationally conceived goals for which they collectively wish to strive.

Societies usually include many such groups forming and reforming around every type of interest. We no doubt take part in many of them. Examples include discussion groups to consider topics of the times, such recreational groups as a foursome of bridge or of men to play a round of golf, the family meeting as a council to work out the budget for the week, several citizens meeting to advance some local community need, such as better schools, and many others representing nearly all facets of life.

The genius of democratic societies is that they allow the unhampered formation of interest groups. Initiative is stimulated, and the best thinking and acting results in the form of help-ful service when societies allow their members to promote their purposes through their own groups. One of the first things an intolerant society does is to ban the free development of autonomous groups which seek to promote some end through cooperative action.

EXPANSION OF INTEREST GROUPS The chief significance of interest groups is often in what grows out of them. Such a group may expand into an organization and even into an institu-tion if its purpose has a wider application than the interests of the group. Many of our society's permanent organizations and institutions had their origins in small interest groups. This is illustrated in the rise of a famous service organization.

Rotary International is today a world-wide civic organization with over 9500 local clubs and over 500,000 members. Its origin took place in 1905, in Chicago, when four men met at noon once each week to become acquainted, to consider how they could improve their business, and to promote community welfare. More men were brought in as interest grew. They rotated their group meetings from place to place, thus giving themselves a name—Rotary. A club was organized with officers, a constitution, a regular meeting place, and other appurtenances an organization usually acquires, as purposes become clearer and the desire to advance them grows stronger. At first, there was no thought of expanded development, but the group purposes had vitality. And today, Rotary is an international organization following the motto "Service above self."

Mode of Entrance Is Important to Many Groups

Groups may also be distinguished from each other by the way in which persons enter them. Three major ways of becoming a part of a group are voluntary joining, involuntary entrance, and selection.

VOLUNTARY GROUPS Voluntary groups are those which persons enter by choice with knowledge of what they are doing and of the objectives for which the group stands. Interest groups are usually, though not always, of this type. One joins because he has an interest in what a group promotes. That withdrawal from such groups is also on a voluntary basis is as important an aspect of group functioning as is joining. The desire to remain in a group rapidly disappears if its operation is not satisfying to the member.

INVOLUNTARY GROUPS We may possess certain characteristics, for which we are not responsible, that compel us to operate in groups based upon these characteristics. These are called involuntary groups since social conventions and traditions rather than personal choice determine our relationships. Our age and sex (girls usually do not play on boy's baseball teams) often determine participation or nonparticipation in certain groups. One's nationality or race limits group opportunities. Biological and social differences are among the strongest forces determining specific group participation. Negroes must operate in groups composed only of Negroes in certain areas of American society; the same is true of Jewish people in certain places. It is often only in ways determined by the dominant group that they are allowed to be participants in the dominant groups. Bitter personal tragedies may often result from such restrictions upon the member of a minority group.

Discrimination usually leads to the crystallization of groups that emphasize separateness. They limit themselves to their own interests. Often they function on the margin of society. The possibilities of integrating them into the total social structure are greatly reduced.

SELECTION Persons often become members of a group by being chosen; more specifically, the group decides whom it wants in its unit. Several persons, wanting to consider ways of accomplishing an objective, to work together on a common problem, or to pursue some pleasurable avocation, invite others to join them. The persons invited also make a decision as to whether they wish to be a part of this group. The criteria for the selection of members may be amiability, their ability to make a contribution, their prestige in promoting the groups interest, or other considerations. The chief matter here is the group's acceptance of the individual and the individual's acceptance of the group. Groups based on discriminate selection can develop *esprit de corps* and unity because there is community of interest and acknowledgment of common values.

Primary and Secondary Groups Are Distinguished by the Nature of the Relationships Within Them

PRIMARY GROUPS An important factor in group functioning is the nature of the relationships of the persons to each other. Groups have been designated as *primary* and *secondary* to accent this element. The originator of the concept "primary group," Professor Charles H. Cooley was particularly concerned to emphasize the group's role "in forming the social nature and ideals of the individual." He said, "By primary groups I mean those characterized by intimate face-to-face association and cooperation." Physical presence is not the point to stress since practically all groups function on a face-to-face basis. It is the intimate associations, the results of which are "a certain fusion of individualities in a common whole, so that one's very self, for many purposes at least, is the common life and purpose of that group."

"The most important spheres of this intimate association and cooperation," he claimed, "are the family, the play-group of children, and the neighborhood or community group of elders." The association in these groups "is clearly the nursery of human nature in the world about us." [6]

SECONDARY GROUPS   Other writers came to use the term "secondary groups" (Cooley never used the term) to describe those in which the contacts are more casual, segmental, and infrequent, and where the lack of intimate acquaintance leads to impersonal relations. Instances of such groups are those one might establish as a buyer with a store clerk, as student with the college registrar, or as a worker with the manager of the business. Relationships in such groups are usually formal, carried out according to accepted rules, and controlled by established norms. We have little feeling of intimacy; in fact, the circumstances are likely to cause us to have the opposite type of feeling. The way we address others in a group often illustrates this difference. We address our pastor as "Reverend" or "Father," the school teacher as "Mr.," "Miss," or "Mrs.," the physician as "Doctor." Long acquaintance and close contacts which make intimate associations natural allow us to use a person's given name without seeming improper.

An important change in modern societies is the increased dominance of these secondary groups. Primary group relationships made up much of social life when societies were agricultural, when moving about over wide areas was not so easy, and when factories and shops were smaller. Industrialization, urbanization, and wider communication have tended to establish relationships on a secondary, impersonal basis. The advantage is that we can be objective and influenced less by personal feelings in our associations. A serious disadvantage is that it can cause the loss of that vital concern for the well-being of others which prompts attitudes of service, loyalty, and the other primary ideals that are basic to a "good" society. Such institutions as the school and the church are subject to these forces. The teachers in the large central schools cannot possibly have the opportunity to build their personalities into that of their students, as could the teachers in the small schools. The minister and the director of religious education in large churches often operate on a secondary basis, carrying on their programs from afar. Even the modern social worker has difficulty maintaining close relations with his clients.

Increasing interaction through secondary relationships is a part of change in the expansion of our societies. A major task that results from this trend is promoting living in the wider world, yet retaining a concern for and interest in primary group life.

Primary Groups in Larger Organizations

The increased dominance of secondary groups tends to result in less emphasis on primary groups. We still recognize the primary group, such as the family or the play group, as the "chief basis of what is universal in human nature and human ideals." We recognize them as the supreme agents of socialization. They provide intimacy and concern and the psychological influences that we cannot do without. Durkheim and others insist that unless we have these "personal," "intrinsic" associational groups in our living, abnormal personality consequences will result. Suicide, for example, is more likely to occur among those whose primary group associations are weak than among those where they are strong.

And now we are beginning to understand that primary groups are important components in the functioning of larger organizational structures. Studies of the operation of primary groups in formal organizations, especially in the Army and in industry, have shown their significance in morale and other problems. For example, the Army studies of Samuel Stouffer and his colleagues have shown that the soldier's motivation to fight is strongly influenced by his desire and need to protect his primary group and to meet its expectations. The soldier's identification with political causes is of secondary importance.[7] The effective functioning of the Army results not simply from the controls based upon the soldier's disciplined respect for his military symbols but also from his loyalty to his immediate primary group—his "buddies." We function in our larger associational relations by responding to the prescribed requirements of these units, but we also operate significantly within them by responses to the intimate personal relations and primary group identifications that arise from the spontaneous associations created within them. These sustain us as persons through their support of our primary human qualities, such as our need for acceptance and the recognition of our own worth.

Studies of the influence of primary groups

in achieving production goals in industry, to use another example, show that where workers met in primary group situations to decide on the content of the goals and the methods to be used, sustained production goals were achieved over a long period.[8] Thus, where the spontaneous primary groups that develop within large-scale organizations are recognized, they can be used to support them. On the other hand, they can undermine an organization as well for these intimately associated groups develop understandings that operate as controls among themselves to protect each other. This may occur especially where there is concern about the requirements set by the over-head organization or management. Many other studies make us aware that primary groups are persisting entities through which our social relationships probably operate finally in virtually every social situation.

Some Groups Have Significance Because of the Number of Persons of Which They Are Composed

THE PAIR GROUP A most significant primary group type in our societies is the *pair,* or *dyad.* The pair is found in many forms, such as the married couple, friend and friend, parent and child, sweethearts, and professional or business partners. The pair differs from those two-person casual groups in which we make a brief contact, such as greeting another person in a few moments of conversation, or when we are being served briefly by some official carrying out a duty.

The pair is two persons in a repeating association involving close personal relationship. A casual two-person group may become a dyad as when a boy and girl who met only incidentally extend this meeting into repeated contacts which develop feelings and attitudes that impel continued association. Each pair relationship requires some form of contact at its origin. Whether it develops into a pair depends upon whether there are mutual interests that lead the couple to continuous primary associations.

The mutual interests that establish the pair may arise from many circumstances, but these circumstances are within the two individuals. Their relationships do not persist to satisfy conditions outside of themselves. The pair exists for itself. Edward Eggleston wrote of a dyad resulting from the biological deficiencies and efficiencies of two boys which complemented each other:

As often happens, nature had built for King Pewee a very fine body, but had forgotten to give him any mind to speak of. In any kind of chaff or banter, at any sort of talk or play where a good head was worth more than a strong arm and a broad back, King Pewee was sure to have the worst of it. A very convenient partnership had therefore grown up between him and Will Riley. Riley had muscle enough, but Nature had made him mean-spirited. He had not exactly wit—but a facility in using his tongue, which he found some difficulty in displaying, through fear of other boys' fists. By forming a friendship with Pewee Rose, the two managed to keep in fear the greater part of the school. Will's rough tongue, together with Pewee's rude fists, were enough to bully most any boy.[9]

A pair ceases to exist as a structural form if one person leaves since its reasons for being exist between the two persons only. Larger groups in continuous functioning can operate even if one or more persons drop out. If, in a pair, one person dies, the dyad is destroyed. If sweethearts or close friends disagree or move away, their relations can be severed. Married couples may separate by desertion or divorce, while any number of reasons may end a two-person partnership. A common reason for the destruction of pairs is the entrance of a third person. The presence of another person in any intimate two-person relationship is intolerable since the pair exists for itself. "Three is a crowd" in pair relations. A triangular pattern cannot usually replace it.

PERSONALITY AND PAIRS The pair can have a deep influence upon personality when the relationship between the two individuals is intimate, as in a marriage or close friendship. Of the latter, Cicero remarked: "Life would be utterly lifeless . . . without a friend on whose kindness and fidelity one might confidently repose. Can there be a more real complacency indeed, than to lay open to another the most secret thoughts of one's heart, with the same confidence and security as if they were still concealed in his own?"[10] This development of pair relationships to the point where the other person is as if he or she were ourselves gives strength and encouragement as well as dependence.

DISSOLVING DYADS The breakup of established dyads is often accompanied by strong emotional reactions. It is almost impossible to sever such a relationship on a purely intellectual basis. Jealousy and anger usually accompany the frustration of desires. Small incidents that cause jealousy or anger are sometimes magnified out of proportion to their significance and stimulate further disagreement. Control of emotions is a chief problem in preserving dyads.

Sorrow and grief also result when pairs are broken. One's personality is so completely absorbed in the other person that it often cannot survive without severe personal disturbance. This may happen when a long-lasting marriage partnership is broken by the death of one member.

PAIRS AND THE LARGER SOCIETY Pairs must relate themselves to their larger society. Some societies regulate the relationships of persons of particular ages, sexes, and other conditions, thus controlling the circumstances under which pairs may arise. Malinowski pointed out that in certain societies "every man has his permanent partner in exchange and the two have to deal with each other. They are often relatives-in-law, or else sworn friends, or partners in the important system of ceremonial exchange called Kula." [11]

Some societies allow free social intercourse and promote the possible legitimate pairs that arise. They approve marriages, business partnerships, and other dyads that advance the general welfare. Behavior patterns usually become habitual when the pair has established itself. They evolve ways of reacting so that needs are met in acceptable manners. However, some circumstance, such as a new interest or a decrease in the old, may pull the persons apart. Societies establish rules by which pairs may be dissolved to protect the society, as well as the pair, if it has critical societal importance, such as a marriage or a business partnership.

The Group of Three Persons, or the Triad, Also Has Some Characteristics That Are Significant Because of Its Number

The behavior of the group of three is radically different from that of the pair or of the larger groups. Rarely do groups of three develop the unity that is achieved in the group of two. Much of their importance stems from this fact. Simmel, the man responsible for emphasizing the significance of the *triad* and dyad, suggested that in groups of three, the third person may act as a mediator, as a holder of the balance of power, or as a divider who creates conflicts that destroy any sense of unity between any two of the persons. Since the group can exist

as a group of two if one person drops out, it is therefore less dependent upon the participation of all. This leads the three-person group to tend to separate into a coalition of two against one, as the following illustration shows. [12]

Two researchers were assigned to work together in a survey. It became necessary to speed up the gathering of data so a third person was made a part of the team. It was soon observed that only a slight increase in returns was accomplished and that there were disagreements among the three; the third person had destroyed the sense of unity. Experience often shows that the achievement of an end is better served by dyads than by triads.

The group of three is more efficient than the group of two where careful consideration of an issue is desirable. In this instance, ideas are pitted against ideas. The third person acts as a check. The usual appointment of committees of three is the common sense recognition of this principle. We should not, therefore, conclude that groups of three are always combinations of two pitted against one. Such groups develop unity by satisfying common interests that may involve differences in many cases.

Groups Made Up of Larger Numbers of Individuals Display Conditions of Creation and Control Not Found in Small Groups

The small group is founded on direct psychological interaction. If it endures, the relationships will become structured by status and role. On the other hand, the larger occasional grouping or aggregation has a transitory life which terminates when its goals have been achieved or the object of its interest no longer exists or attracts. Members of such groupings are usually focused upon some external stimulus and develop little or no definable structure. The formation and dissolution of this type of association is illustrated in Box 10.

If a large group endures over time, it usually establishes definite patterns of relationship among its components and evolves into an organization.

Groups Are Often Exclusive and Ethnocentric

A widely used and important characteristic of some groups was first emphasized by William G. Sumner when he distinguished between "we-groups" or *"in-groups"* and "others-groups," usually called *"out-groups."* "We-groups" are those to which we belong; "others-groups" are

BOX 10

Arrived at the circus grounds . . . Louie the Peeler promptly looked up Mr. Harliker and was assigned to a position near the Ferris wheel. He built a table and covered it with red cloth and on either side tacked signs saying FREE SAMPLES TO EACH PATRON TODAY. He then set up a loud-speaker and amplifier, hooked a small lapel-type microphone into the amplifier and curled the microphone around his neck. This done, he proceeded to "frame the flash." On the table he set out fancy simulated-crystal plates, bowls and pitchers, and arranged an inviting display of grapefruit, tomatoes and carrots.

As the people drifted by he displayed a magnificent unconcern in those who stopped and stared at his display. Using a pocketknife, he began to carve rosettes out of a piece of carrot. After he had made several rosettes he filled the crystal plates with water to keep them fresh. When a crowd of some twenty curious people had gathered, he suddenly looked up and said, in a confidential purring tone, "A lot of you ladies have asked me how to make these rosettes, which are a beautiful garnish for your salads when you have guests." He then proceeded slowly to sculpture a carrot, while several housewifely matrons sighed enviously.

As the crowd thickened, Louie's nervous eyes watched now one bystander, now another, but they never strayed to his nimble fingers. He started off, speaking slowly, but stepped up his tempo as he proceeded.

"Today, my friends," he said, "the firm which I have the honor and the pleasure of representing has commissioned me to distribute several samples of our line to you people here in Providence as an advertising gesture, so that you may use these handy kitchen implements and show them to your friends. After my demonstration is over, these implements will be on sale at your local department stores at the regular price from fifty cents to a dollar for each item."

He deftly slipped an intricate metal device out of a box and flashed it. Holding a potato in one hand as he talked, he explained that in Argentina the women serve an ingenious variety of stuffed potato. First they hollow out a potato in this wise—and he stabbed the potato with the garnisher, twisted it through, and then removed two interlocking spirals of potato, leaving a round tunnel right through the heart of the spud—and then they stuff it with meat, and bake. "And ladies, you don't throw away the inside of the potato.". . . Finally he came to the *pièce de résistance,* a new and improved plastic grater. He showed how harmless the plastic grater was by rubbing it against his cheek. He also stroked it with the palm of his hand. Then he peeled a potato and rapidly ran it over the squares of the grater. In a trice, the potato was grated down to a crumb and there was hardly any waste.

He now said, "I am coming to the most educational part of my little demonstration, which will appeal to every intelligent man and woman in my audience. You have probably read about the Mayo Brothers discovering carotene, the vitamin that gives you good eyesight. You have heard how the fliers in the RAF are given a glass of carrot juice to drink every day, so that they will not suffer from the night blindness. Mothers, do you realize that when you serve your family baked carrots or boiled carrots, you are losing the juice and cheating them of their necessary daily supply of carotene? With this grater you derive the full value and nourishment of the carrot."

He grated a carrot over some cheesecloth and then rolled up the cheesecloth and squeezed the grated carrot until the juice spurted into a glass. He triumphantly held the orange-colored juice aloft and said, "Mothers, give your children a glass of this to drink every morning and you can throw their eyeglasses away."

BOX 10 (*Cont.*)

He then stated, "I'm done and finished. If there are any among you intelligent enough to recognize the scientific values of what I have to offer, this grater costs one dollar, that is the regular ceiling price stamped on each and every box. . . . The price is one dollar. Who'll be the first to—ah, one there—and one here." Louie was pointing to the back of the audience. There was nobody there who had raised a hand, but this is Louie's method of turning the tip.

"One moment!" he cried. "Hold your dollar bills! Seeing that this is my first demonstration of the evening, I am going to take the liberty of giving you an extra souvenir—this marvelous little orange and lemon juicer, which.". . .

As he delineated the virtues of the juicer, Louie was throwing each of the five items into a paper bag. He whispered to me out of the side of his mouth, "I will work this tip for six sales." This seemed surprising to me, in view of the deep interest with which the tip, which now consisted of about ninety persons, had been watching the demonstration. I was sure Louie would dispose of at least twenty combinations. But when the tip had been turned and the joint had been sloughed, there were exactly seven dollar bills in Louie's fist.

"I was one off," he said. "At that, it isn't so bad. This was a cold tip; I could feel it. You get so you can feel the thought waves of the tip. I figure it is because we have them hypnotized and are in close contact with their minds. You get so you know which persons in the tip are going to buy and which are just mooches. You get so you can tell it almost to a dollar." [13]

---

those to which we do not belong. Our mere belonging, however, is not the most important thing. The way our group operates in relation to others is the really important matter. "The insiders in a we-group are in a relation of peace, order, law, government, and industry, to each other." [14] Their relations to "other" groups is one of indifference or potential and actual opposition. They are *ethnocentric*, that is, they consider their group to be superior to other groups.

Instances of in-group-out-group behavior abound in private and public life. One may see it in the relations between one family and another or between one church and another. In the newspaper one may read an advertisement like the following: "To Golfers Who Are Socially Acceptable." The advertisement described the opportunity for persons to participate in the groups of a country club with fine 18-hole golf course, tennis courts, riding stables, and restaurant. Inquiries were to be directed to an anonymous box at the newspaper. [15] An invitation to join was issued if the person making inquiry was "socially acceptable" to the in-group after it had made its investigation. If not, the inquirer was politely informed that all places were now taken and his name would be entered on a "waiting list."

ENTRANCE CRITERIA OF IN-GROUPS In-groups preserve their exclusive character by establishing, sometimes consciously, often unconsciously, definite criteria for entrance. The criteria depend upon the nature of the group. They may be wealth, family background, occupation, achievement, nationality, or a special interest. Only those who can meet the standards are admitted, and the in-group decides who meets the standards. Likewise, the in-group preserves its exclusiveness by insistence upon adherence to the standards. Persons may be dropped if they are unable to comply since the in-group forms its own rules and establishes the criteria by which they are met.

IN-GROUP DEFENSES Once established, in-groups defend themselves from attack from others-groups. They develop solidarity as a result. A group of brothers may quarrel and even fight among themselves, but when an out-group challenges them, they join as one to overcome the opposition. This is characteristic of all in-groups. It is one of the reasons in-groups are important to the accomplishment of many social ends. The "we-feeling" gives a unity that makes the force of the group effort emphatic.

IN-GROUP VALUES The in-group is often a constructive force in societies. Most of them are founded on purposes that are beneficial, though some may be based on invidious criteria and develop a snobbishness that may result in an extreme exclusiveness. The development of in-group feelings results in pride, confidence, and security. Societies ascribe status to people in terms of their in-groups and accord opportunities and roles in the society on the judgments they make of the significance of these in-groups. Persons who are recognized because of the high status of their in-groups become the leaders in community-chest drives, promotion programs of general interests, and other activities that bring them before the public. Likewise, the inclusion in an in-group of particular persons who have a high status gives the group a high status. It then achieves position in the social organization.

IN-GROUP INTERNAL RELATIONS Internal in-group relations are friendly, helpful, and loyal, often to the point of compulsion. Theodore Dreiser caught this spirit with respect to a small town social situation: "So tightly were the social lines of Lycurgus drawn, so few the truly eligibles, that it was almost necessary and compulsory upon those 'in' to make the best of such others as were 'in.' [16] In-groups are of particular significance in giving a sense of personal importance to their members. Lauren Gilfillan showed how being included in an exclusive, in-group influenced one person:

"Strike committee meetin! All men in for the strike committee meetin!"

"People were issuing from the relief kitchen, shooed from behind by an officious Stanley. Johnny got to his feet. 'What's that?' I asked him. 'Can I go to?' 'Fraid not, Laurie. Just members allowed. 'N' it takes a good long time to git elected.' " [17]

The Relationships of the Persons in Some Groups Are Systematically Arranged with Respect to Each Other; in Others, They Are Not

PATTERNED GROUPS In a sense, every group has a pattern. The relationships of person to person are systematically arranged in some; in others there is no regular order of relationship. Groups in which there is systematic arrangement of persons to each other in some form of hierarchy are *patterned* groups; those in which there is no such arrangement and in which persons function in the group on a basis of equality are *nonpatterned*. A family, a baseball team, master and servant, teacher and

Group patterns: spatial arrangement may determine the scope and form of interaction.

pupils, foreman and workers, and a military squad are some examples of patterned groups. There is a definite status the person occupies with respect to others in each of these groups so that when the unit operates as a group, the position occupied by the individual influences his functioning. Responsibility in a family, for example, is usually in the male and female head, and although ideally decisions may be a result of group consultation, parents are the final authority. Societies vary in the extent to which family heads exercise such responsibility, but in most it is theirs in one form or another.

Each player in a baseball or football team has his definite position and fixed responsibility. Each must execute his role as prescribed when the team is playing. The manager or coach in professional sports may designate plays to be executed and may even indicate what kind of ball to pitch or strike at in baseball or formation to follow in football. A soldier in a military squad may inwardly question the orders of his superior officer, but he does not disobey them.

Patterned groups are ordinarily characterized by superior-inferior rankings. The extent to which these rankings are emphasized vary with the form of the group and the society. But in all, authority moves from the top down. The group functions smoothly so long as persons in the group do not challenge these relations but retain respect for the arrangement.

A patterned type of organization is desirable where a group knows the objectives it wishes to achieve. A football team would hardly be able to cross its opponent's goal line if each player was allowed to follow his own initiative. Certainly, a squad of soldiers trying to gain a particular position in a battle would have little success if each soldier followed his own way. Most of the problems in patterned group relations are not due to the form of organization but to the way in which authority is used in them.

NONPATTERNED GROUPS Equality of position is assumed in nonpatterned groups: no one assumes authority, and relationships are informal. Persons empathize with each other in such groups. They project themselves more fully into the situations of the others and so develop an affirmative climate that is positive and constructive. Significant consequences result in such groups. The nonpatterned type of relationship is a desirable one where the group is expected to be creative and to use initiative. Creativity does not come when groups are told each step they must take. Positive results may be hoped for where members may offer suggestions and try experiments without fear of questioning. Business and research organizations recognize this. On one occasion, for example,

a young scientist was introduced into the research group of a large industrial plant. His instructions were to work *with,* not *for,* the others in the research team which was trying to solve a problem. Suggestions were freely accepted and given consideration as all thought together. The climate of this group was itself a major stimulating force to creative work. It supported the scientist's feeling about his own ability to contribute to an important problem of the group and also enhanced the solidarity of the group.

Some Groups Are Organized Horizontally; Others Vertically

HORIZONTAL GROUPS Practically all societies are stratified, some to an extremely high degree, such as the caste organization of India, and others to a slight degree as is supposed to be true of American society. The population of a society divides itself into classes as a consequence of various forces. People carry on their group relations with others influenced by this class structure and its accompanying status and role orientations. We discuss social stratification fully in a later section. We only point out now that groups often organize themselves of persons from the same levels of society, while others include persons from all levels of societies. Those consisting of persons from the same strata of society are *horizontal groups;* those from all strata are *vertical groups.*

VERTICAL GROUPS Political parties are usually composed of people from different classes. They are vertical groups. These persons work together in close relationship to promote their party's interests so that persons in them from the lowest classes may be intimately associated with individuals from the upper classes. However, these persons may have little to do with each other in other kinds of relations or groups. For example, the persons of a political group from the lower classes would hardly invite the persons in the group who were from the upper classes to dinner in their homes. They would be embarrassed to do so; in fact, such a thought usually never occurs. We form most of our groups within our own class and operate outside of our class only when some particular interest allows crossing the lines. There is an assorting process in group formation that generally puts together those of us who are similar in occupation, nationality, level of living, religious convictions, and the like.

The Growing Use of the Group as a Healing or Therapeutic Device Illustrates Its Constructive Role in Societies

Our behavior in a society is determined to a large extent by our culture. The codes of behavior or norms it adopts and the values it emphasizes become our norms and values. The sanctioned traditions and customs expressing these values and codes of behavior define the rights and wrongs for the society and for the individuals in it. We acquire these definitions from the groups that are normal to our life. Since groups are the chief links between us and our society, they are essential mechanisms for social control.

Almost every attempt to find a solution for the problem of delinquency leads to the conviction that the maintenance of the family as a cohesive group is essential to provide young people with affection, guidance, and support. This is a practical recognition that this group operates as a powerful unit to maintain the normal emotional life of its members and so to prevent conditions that lead to wrongdoing. Abandonment of a child by his family group, separation of the parents through divorce or desertion, open contentions within the home, mistreatment, and parental misbehavior will almost inevitably set the stage for abnormal behavior from youth. Fortunately, most family groups aid the development of healthy ideals, wholesome habits, and constructive behavior in their younger members.

Unfortunately, some youth live in an unstable or unhealthy family environment. Delinquency follows when they accept the values of this environment and respond unsatisfactorily to the requirements of the larger society. We must consider two elements here: the guidance of the youth and the improvement of their environment. Redirection of their group relations often serves the first need. "John Smith," fifteen years old, had a considerable variety of delinquencies. Then he started going "to a city playground," where the children knew him as a "tough guy"; however, the playground leader interested him in playing baseball and he became a member of some team. Later, he was placed in charge of groups of younger boys because his conduct since coming to the playground won him special recognition. There have been no reports of juvenile delinquency from this district during the months when the playground was open.[18]

Group methods have been applied with good results among inmates of correctional institutions. Institutional populations are broken up into small groups wherein intimate interaction can lead to common interests, the improvement of skills, and personal satisfactions. As a consequence, new goals for living help to create the satisfaction that comes from living with others without the need for harming them.

There are other conditions leading to personal demoralization which group associations often help to overcome. Persons suffering from chronic illnesses, alcoholism, heart limitations, and mental diseases often conquer their difficulty or learn to live with them through association with persons in similar conditions. Such common interest groups provide an experience that inspires members with confidence, a determination to try, and a concern for others who have similar or worse difficulties.[19]

III. NORMS, STATUSES, AND ROLES

Societies Develop Norms to Govern Group Relationships

Our fundamental proposition—that human groups are systems of psychologically related persons through which societal actions are carried out—implies interaction between the participants. Our description of various types of groups emphasizes this. The descriptions also infer that there is cooperation among the group components to attain common ends, although this does not mean that there is always agreement among the components. Families operating as groups, for example, cooperate in recurring activities to achieve common purposes in spite of disagreements.

The interactional bonds that unite persons into groups at the same time set them apart from those not in the group. Likewise, these recurring interactions on a cooperative basis give societies their order and stability, to a large extent, because people operating in groups develop standards according to which these interactions are to take place among them. These standards, in conformity to which groups and group members are to act, are their *norms*. They specify proper and improper behavior for they are the behavioral expectations of the society. We are *expected* to perform according to them whether we do so or not. In general, we are rewarded or punished as we follow or deviate from them. These sanctions may range from such rewards as a mere "Thank you" in response to a courtesy to serious punishments because we do not follow the rules about property rights or ignore other rules the society considers important.

Societies Develop Different Types of Norms

Societies develop norms about practically every aspect of our associational life. This is essential to an organized society and to group existence. Without norms, group life would be confused, disordered, and unpredictable. In fact, a normless society is hardly conceivable.

Norms, however, differ in the degree to which conformity is required. This, of course, is because deviation from them will have differing consequences. Where lack of conformity to the norm does no serious damage, feelings toward its observance may be weak. Walking on the right side of the sidewalk is a norm in American society, but people constantly disregard the practice. If it seriously hampered the movement of pedestrians, stronger feelings about it would develop and stricter conformity would be demanded. Destroying property is regarded seriously, however, in virtually all societies. The norms relating to respect for property are strong because wilful destruction would seriously damage the whole society.

Those norms characterized by low intensity of feeling and control are referred to as *folkways*. They are regarded as the proper ways and usually are the customary practices of individuals and groups in societies, although they are not compulsory. On the other hand, those norms thought essential to a society's welfare are called *mores*. They include the element of compulsion and are characterized by high intensity of feeling and control. In our discussion of government in Chapter 15, we will point out the relationship of norms to the laws which societies enact. Suffice it to say at this point that laws are norms that the society enacts and enforces as rules of the state. The norms or standards of group living permeate all the activities of societies. We will be emphasizing and illustrating them in much that follows.

Statuses and Roles Are Two Aspects of Social Positions in Group Organization

We have now stressed the fact that people operate together in groups to achieve their ends. These interactions are not only pursued according to standardized ways or norms that pattern behavior, but in terms of the positions the persons hold in their groups. Groups and other relationship structures are characterized by internal differences that constitute positions; each position represents a *status*. Thus, a family's internal organization is differentiated into positions of husband and wife, or father, mother, children. Each of these positions has, from the point of view of the society, a different status attached to it, that is, different rights and duties. "Casey" Stengel until recently served as manager of the New York Yankee baseball team. The position of manager gave him certain rights. He could remove a player, shift his position, or remove him from a game as he thought best. He could fine his players for the infraction of rules. The position also gave him duties. He had to train the players and see that they appeared at each game prepared to play. He had to represent the team in major playing decisions. These rights and duties, and many others, are a part of the position of manager of the team. As manager he occupied a status. When he was exerting his rights and carrying out his duties, he was performing his *role*. The new manager will have the same rights and duties for they are attached to the status this position has. The way he actually executes these rights and duties will be his role as the new manager of this team. So it is with all positions—those of doctors, lawyers, machinists, employers, employees, coaches, players, students, teachers, and so on.

Each position in a group's organization has both a status that is socially given and a role or pattern of behavior connected with this status that is socially expected. The execution of role expectations is role performance. Here we may point out that status and role are two sides of a single coin, namely, a social position, a complex of rights and duties, and the actual behavior expressing them.

Individuals Usually Have Many Statuses and as a Consequence Many Roles

Most people function in a number of social structures and so occupy positions that give them a number of statuses and roles. A man may be a business executive, a husband, a father, a Mason, and a golfer. He occupies a status in each one of these positions that gives him rights and obligations. As a business executive, he must care for the orderly operation of his company. This is a duty. In this, he may introduce new methods of working. This is a right. The same two elements exist in each position and influence the roles or patterns of behavior to be followed in each.

Sometimes, the rights and obligations of one position a person occupies may interfere with the rights and obligations of another. Our business executive is also a golfer. He likes the game and the companionship of the associates with whom he plays. Shall he neglect a business duty to spend the afternoon with the fellows who want him to play in a foursome? His problem is more difficult if he holds a position in government as well as in business. This competition between roles often introduces conflicts that the role occupant must resolve. He is limited to certain actions by the roles he is to perform. He must adjust alternatives to each other. This

is one of the chief behavior problems individuals have.

Individuals Do Not Necessarily Perform Their Roles in the Same Way

We re-emphasize that all social positions have a certain status with responsibilities attached to them that their occupants are expected to fulfill. They also have privileges that they are to enjoy, but the manner in which they exercise these, that is, carry out their roles, may vary with the specific persons occupying the given position. For example, one instructor may teach by the lecture method, another by discussion, and a third by some combination of these techniques. Similar variations may also be shown in the leisure-time aspects of a role. The position of President of the United States carries

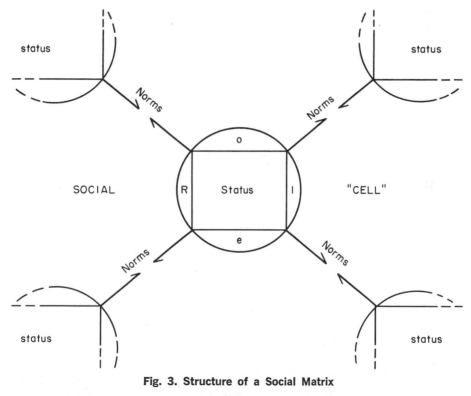

Fig. 3. Structure of a Social Matrix

Notes

(a) Social matrix = nexus of "social cells."
(b) Social cells = nexus of status, role, norms.
(c) Norms attach to status, not persons.
(d) Norms of related statuses are reciprocal obligations and rights or "expectations."
(e) Different persons may play same role in different ways.

certain vacation privileges, for instance. Former President Truman exercised these in part by taking yachting trips; President Eisenhower preferred golf; and President Kennedy enjoyed a variety of pastimes, including golfing and touch football.

Organizations and agencies may change personnel frequently because the persons occupying the official statuses perform their roles differently. Some execute them to the complete satisfaction of the members while others do not. In the one case, change may come in the form of advancement; in others, it may consist of dismissal. Efficiency in performing role requirements is a major element in group relationships.

Norms, Statuses, and Roles are the Key Structures in All Group Relations

A society, as the most comprehensive kind of relationship system, operates in an orderly fashion because group relations within it are structured by statuses, roles, and norms. In turn, these govern the actions of individual persons by specifying to them the behavior appropriate to the given statuses.

To enable the student to "see" the elemental form of social structure, we present a diagram, in Fig. 3, which shows what we may call the "social cell" within a "social matrix." [20] The explanatory notes will help clarify the concept.

References

1. Eubank, Earle E., *The Concepts of Sociology* (Boston, D. C. Heath and Company, 1932), pp. 160 ff.
2. Sackville-West, V., *All Passion Spent* (Garden City, N.Y., Doubleday, Doran and Company, Inc., 1931), p. 26.
3. Sanderson, Dwight, *Group Description* (Cornell University; reprinted from *Social Forces*, 16 [March, 1938]), p. 311.
4. Hugo, Victor, *Acts and Paroles* (*Words and Deeds*), in *Days of Childhood*, I (Paris, Michel Levy Frères, 1875–1876).
5. Paul, Les, "The Best Advice I Ever Had," adapted from the *Reader's Digest*, 70 (June, 1957), No. 422, pp. 211, 212, and 214. With permission of the *Reader's Digest*.
6. Cooley, Charles H., *Social Organization* (New York, Charles Scribner's Sons, 1920), pp. 23 and 24.
7. Stouffer, Samuel A., *et al.*, *The American Soldier: Combat and Its Aftermath*, I (Studies in Social Psychology in World War II) (Princeton, N.J., Princeton University Press, 1949), pp. 401–410.
8. Bavelas, A., referred to by K. Lewin in article titled, "Frontiers in Group Dynamics, Part I," *Human Relations* (1947), pp. 25–26.
9. Eggleston, Edward, *The Hoosier School-Boy* (New York, Charles Scribner's Sons, 1900), p. 7.
10. Cicero, Marcus T., "Essay on Friendship," *Essays on Old-Age and Friendship*, 2 (London, J. Dodsley, in Pall-Mall, 1795), pp. 35–36.
11. Malinowski, Bronislaw, *Crime and Custom in Savage Society* (New York, Harcourt, Brace and Company, 1932), Part I, Chap. 4, p. 25.
12. Spykman, Nicholas J., *The Social Theory of Georg Simmel* (Chicago, University of Chicago Press, 1925), pp. 133 ff. For recent studies of the triad, see Gamson, William A., "A Theory of Coalition Formation," *American Sociological Review*, 26 (June, 1961), pp. 373–382.
13. Zolotow, Maurice, "Pitchman," *The Saturday Evening Post*, 216 (September 23, 1943), pp. 12, 13, and 37. Reprinted by special permission of *The Saturday Evening Post;* copyright by the Curtis Publishing Company.
14. Sumner, William G., *Folkways* (Boston, Ginn and Company, 1906), p. 12.
15. *New York Herald Tribune* (March 18, 1934).
16. Dreiser, Theodore, *An American Tragedy*, 1 (Cleveland, World Publishing Company, 1947), Book 2, p. 313. Reprinted by permission.

17. Gilfillan, Lauren, *I Went to Pit College* (New York, Viking Press, 1934), p. 52.
18. Summary of "The Story of John Smith," *The Playground*, 21 (January, 1928), p. 527.
19. Kisker, G. W., "Take Your Medicine—in Classes," *Coronet*, 23 (January, 1948), pp. 165–168. See also Alcoholics Anonymous, *Alcoholics Anonymous Comes of Age: A Brief History of A.A.* (A. A. Publishing, Inc.), 1957.
20. "Relationships between persons acting in social roles constitute the matrix of social structures." Blau, Peter M., "Patterns of Choice in Interpersonal Relations," *American Sociological Review*, 27 (February, 1962), p. 41. It should be noted that there is a recent tendency to abandon the use of the term "status." See Goode, William J., "Norm Commitment and Conformity to Role-Status Obligations," *American Journal of Sociology*, 66 (November, 1960), pp. 247 ff. Diagram prepared by Frederick B. Parker.

Questions for Study and Discussion

1. Give the definition of group used in this chapter. Compare it with other definitions by sociologists. What similarities and differences do you find?
2. What is the difference between a group situation and a social situation? Is a group situation a social situation? Why?
3. Discuss the significance of physical presence in group operation.
4. Discuss groups as "active" and as "latent." Can you support the idea of "latent" groups if you follow the definition used in this chapter? Why?
5. How do agreement and disagreement influence group operation?
6. Give several dichotomous characterizations of groups and point out the significance of each.
7. Show how our society has been changing from a primary to a secondary group basis.
8. Did Louie, the pitchman, make a *group* out of a crowd?
9. Discuss the nature of the dyad; the triad.
10. Discuss the use of the group approach as a therapeutic device.
11. List the groups that you participate in in a twelve-hour day time period, indicating the type and duration of each. How many did you operate in during this period? Why did you indicate it as being of a given type? What statuses do you occupy?
12. Define norm and give some illustrations from your own behavior requirements.
13. Describe the role played by the quarterback or the goalie on one of your school teams. How does this relate him to others on the team?

Suggested Topics for Reports

1. Observe your activity during a given day and make a list of all the groups you participated in. In each instance indicate: (a) the type of group, (b) the duration of participation in each, (c) the status you occupied. Determine the amount of time you were free of any direct group participation.
2. Prepare a "social map" depicting the dyads and triads in your fraternity, sorority, dormitory, or other comparable group. Select a sample of these structures and try to determine the personal, social, and spatial bases of their formation.
3. Prepare a summary of one or more of the experimental studies in small group interaction reported in Borgatta, *et al.*, *Small Groups* or Cartwright and Zander, *Group Dynamics*.

Supplementary Reading

Bales, Robert F., *Interaction Process Analysis*. Cambridge, Mass.: Addison-Wesley Publishing Company, 1950.

Berger, Morroe, Abel, Theodore, and Page, Charles H. (eds.), *Freedom and Control in Modern Society*. Princeton, N.J.: D. Van Nostrand Company, Inc., 1954.

Brown, B. Warren, *Social Groups*. Chicago: Faithorn Publishing Company, 1926.

Cartwright, Dorwin, and Zander, Alvin F. (eds.), *Group Dynamics: Research and Theory*. Evanston, Ill.: Row, Peterson and Co., 1953.

Guetzkow, Harold (ed.), *Groups, Leadership and Men*. Pittsburgh, Pa.: Carnegie Press, 1951.

Hare, A. Paul, Borgatta, Edgar F., and Bales, Robert F. (eds.), *Small Groups*. New York: Alfred A. Knopf, 1955.

Homans, George C., *The Human Group*. New York: Harcourt, Brace and Company, 1950.

Jennings, Helen H., *Leadership and Isolation*. 2nd ed. New York: Longmans, Green & Co., 1950.

LaPiere, Richard T., *A Theory of Social Control*. New York: McGraw-Hill Book Co., Inc., 1954.

Linton, Ralph, *The Study of Man*. New York: Appleton-Century-Crofts, Inc., 1936.

Moreno, J. L., *Who Shall Survive?* Washington, D.C.: Nervous and Mental Disease Publishing Company, 1934.

Newcomb, Theodore, *Social Psychology*. New York: Dryden Press, 1950.

Olmstead, Michael, *The Small Group*. New York: Random House, 1959.

Simmel, Georg, *The Sociology of Georg Simmel*. Ed. by Kurt Wolff. Glencoe, Ill.: The Free Press, 1950.

Spykman, Nicholas J., *The Social Theory of Georg Simmel*. Chicago: University of Chicago Press, 1925.

Whyte, Wm. F. *Street Corner Society*. Chicago: University of Chicago Press, 1943.

9

INSTITUTIONS AND INSTITUTIONAL AGENCIES

*I*NSTITUTIONALIZATION *is the process of regularizing and patterning procedures in a society. As a consequence, institutions evolve as the normative complexes that relate to the major aspects of a society's activity. Societies develop many institutions and subinstitutions. All societies seem to include several basic ones: marriage, the family, education, religion, government, and economic institutions. Institutional agencies, such as schools, churches, specific families, and a host of others, are developed as instruments for the procedural functioning of these normative complexes.*

I. INSTITUTIONALIZATION

Institutional Agencies Are the Third Class of Human Relationship Structures or Hurelures of Which Societies Are Composed

We pointed out in our discussion of environmental adjustment and culture creation that societies need to have procedural ways and agencies through which their psychosocial universe can operate. We decided that the modes of thought, beliefs, customs, traditions, and other uniform ways of thinking and acting by members of a society are deemed the acceptable ways for their thinking and acting. They constitute the norms of a society and so are foundational to the society's ordered operation. They must have relationship instruments through which to express themselves. These norms are necessary to the society's ordered operation and preservation for they embody the values the people have in common. *Institutional agencies* are that class of human relationship structures that are the necessary procedural instruments. We shall describe and characterize them in this chapter as the third class of structural forms through which a society operates.

Institutionalization Is the Process of Regularizing and Patterning Sanctioned Procedures in a Society

Before we can describe institutions and institutional agencies, it is necessary for us to have an understanding of the *institutionalization* process.

Societies, we cannot repeat too often, arise out of the relationships that take place between men. In these relationships, structures are created that pattern men's ways of associating with each other. Some of these forms of association do not require definite, formal structuring for they take place between a few people for short periods of time, or under temporary conditions and on an intimate personal basis, and may not repeat themselves. Even where they repeat themselves they may not need formal structuring if only a few persons are involved and if these can operate on a person-to-person basis, make up rules for acting together as they go along, or follow the implicit conventions and standards that their society has found suitable for given occasions. For example, two motorists on a highway who approach each other act with respect to each other without establishing personal interaction

135

and association because driving on the right side of the road is conventionalized and standardized behavior in their society. They accept this patterned norm and drive accordingly.

People in societies associate together to promote or preserve common interests and values. They establish rules of conduct and develop norms for doing those things related to these interests and values that are socially binding and give their associations continuity and stability. This is what we mean by institutionalization. This process results in "a system of patterned expectations defining the proper behavior of persons playing certain roles, enforced both by the incumbents' own positive motives for conformity and by the sanctions of others." [1]

Two chief elements are involved in this process: (1) The society as a whole accepts the rules or standards and recognizes them as binding where applicable. This does not mean that each person in the society must know and accept all the norms involved in a given social system. These norms may not apply to all. Banking, which is an institutionalized aspect of the economy of most societies, is regularized through established procedures that many people, even those who use its agencies, do not know or understand. But the society, through its proper institutional agencies, knows, and its representatives seek to enforce the proper expectations. (2) The rules or standards are sanctioned so that they create a moral compulsion to act in what are considered the right ways. This again does not mean that everyone follows the sanctioned norms, but most persons accept them as the right way. They become the guide for the action of individuals in appropriate situations. Thus, most husbands and wives follow the expectation with respect to fidelity to each other.

Societies Institutionalize a Wide Variety of Social Practices

Every society institutionalizes social practices, that is, regularizes and patterns activities within it so that they become the formal and established ways of carrying on with respect to them. Gift-giving, the celebration of such events as birthdays or holidays, providing mothers' pensions, procreation, nursing the sick, and an almost endless variety of business practices have been institutionalized in societies so that the institutional patterns constitute a major part of

the social systems. Some institutionalized practices we shall point out are so important to societies that they develop definite institutional agencies through which they are made effective.

II. INSTITUTIONS

Institutions Are the Normative Complexes Relating to the Major Aspects of Our Social Activity

We have just quoted Parsons' statement that institutionalization results in "a system of patterned expectations defining the proper behavior of persons playing certain roles, enforced both by the incumbent's own positive motives for conformity and by the sanctions of others." These are the *institutions*. In whatever society we are studying, we soon discover that major essential aspects of its social structure influencing daily life constitute these complexes of institutionalized norms. Whether it be the capitalist economic system of the highly industrialized West or the direct appropriation economic system of some migrating tribe, configurations of norms are established, formalized, and regularized to bring about conformity in behavior. And so it is with all other major aspects of the social systems operative in a society.

Individuals Conform Because These Institutionalized Norms Have Been Internalized

We pointed out in the chapter on the person in society (Chapter 5) that a major consequence of the socialization of the individual is that he absorbs the norms of those influencing him so that they become internalized within him and become basic motivators in his behavior. He would not feel "right" if he did not conform to these normative institutional complexes. His own feelings or conscience would trouble him.

Individuals Also Conform Because Their Society Enforces the Institutionalized Norms

These complexes of norms are socially sanctioned. Disobedience brings disapproval from those who are most immediately involved and ready to condemn. It also comes from the whole society where its interests are involved. Therefore, societies operate in orderly fashion because of the individual's own attitudes and the pressures of the social organization about him.

The Chief Institutions of Societies Grow Out of Their Cardinal Needs and Interests

There are several classes of continuing needs and interests that develop these normative complexes or institutions in almost every society because they are cardinal needs and interests of the society.

MAINTENANCE   There is first the interest in, and the need for, maintenance. The people of every society must have food, clothing, shelter, and other necessary supplies. The society develops what Sumner calls the "maintenance mores" to regulate and expedite production, distribution, and preservation of goods and services. The economic institutions of production, distribution, contracts, property, and exchange are created and standardized around these maintenance concerns.

MARRIAGE AND THE FAMILY   The human race must regulate the sex drive and must perpetuate itself by cooperative forms of relationship between the sexes. Marriage and the family become institutionalized in each society to care for these needs. Marriage standardizes sex relations, and the family provides protection and care for the offspring and marriage partners.

RELIGION   Religious institutions provide the means whereby beliefs are expressed about the incomprehensible universe. They provide recognized forms of worship and organizational activities that give a sense of security and "oneness with the eternal verities."

GOVERNMENT   The institution of government unites the citizens of a given territory under a common network of socially sanctioned regulations that ensure conformity to its own rules. It provides the means for regulating relationships within the society and the means of protecting from aggression without. There is a host of institutions within a government that perform specific functions providing many public services related to these general functions.

EDUCATION   Each new generation must be made ready for life in its society. The young are introduced to the tools of knowledge, accumulated experience is transmitted in order to help them adapt to the organizational operation of the society, skills required for them to earn a livelihood are developed. These tasks are primarily those of the educational institutions, for which schools operate as chief agencies.

IMPERATIVE TO SOCIAL ORDER   These institutions are foundational in most societies since they are imperative to the maintenance of the social order. Societies cannot operate without each of them. They grow almost automatically out of the relationships established among men through generations of striving to meet their common needs. Groping and tentative at first, the practices become accepted procedures, evolve sanctions and compulsions, and are finally crystallized into formal relationship patterns or institutionalized complexes. They may be modified over time according to the rational procedures of the society.

SUPPORTING INSTITUTIONS   Societies develop *supporting* and secondary institutions in addition to these basic institutionalized complexes. These operate to assist the chief institutions or to channel a specific function. The institution of "engagement," for example, supports the marriage and family institutions of our societies through its prior declaration of marriage intentions. It may, in a sense, be considered a part of the marriage institutional complex.

Contracts support business institutions and other relationship situations that need formalization.

Societies institutionalize practices intentionally, at times, to make aspects of their culture more effective. Workmen's compensation, social security, and city-manager plans of government are examples of institutions purposefully developed to express specific ways for us. These are called *enacted* institutions for they are deliberately established in contrast to *crescive* institutions, like the family, which is the result of long periods of growth and unconscious formation. Actually, the enacted institutions root themselves in the folkways and mores. Their establishment represents the deliberate systematization and institutionalization of usages already in the social tradition. This tendency for societies to enact institutions as a result of study is constructive since it gives institutions greater flexibility and overcomes, to a degree, the tendency toward a rigidity that often makes the institutional instruments creatures of conservatism and vested interests.

III. INSTITUTIONAL AGENCIES

Institutional Agencies Are the Instruments for Procedural Operation in a Society

Institutions, to function effectively in a society, must develop "executive" agencies, which are the instruments for procedural operation.

Only a portion of the many relationships among members of societies are controlled and made functional by institutions. Many of our associations occur in groups and organizations that bind men together in ways that do not involve our society's institutional system. We often group or organize about concerns that are significant to ourselves only and may not involve our whole social order.

An institution comes into play primarily when its nature causes society at large to be interested. The interests of societies themselves, as well as those of the individuals who compose them, must have consideration. The patterned, normative ways of acting that express the chief interests and concerns of a society apply to all persons in the society. None of us is exempt from their dictates. All—rich and poor, aged and young, upper class and lower class—must express these interests and concerns according to the institutions our society has developed. No one of us, for example, is exempt from respecting the institutionalized rules regarding property rights or the form of the family that society sanctions. The institutions that serve economic and industrial needs, governmental requirements, and family, religious, and educational ends—to suggest again the chief ones—operate among all classes as procedural complexes of the total social order. They support the whole social system, and the members of the society are expected to support the social system through them. They are known to all of us whether or not we follow their prescribed rules and fixed forms. Some individuals may never marry, but they are aware of, and recognize, the institution of marriage and its required expectations.

Institutional agencies are, therefore, definite entities through which the institutions can be made operational in a society. They exist in concrete form as units of people related to each other to give expression to these institutionalized complexes that are to be followed. Much more than individual behavior patterns, they are products of the relationships between all people who take part in their production and operate in them to carry out these normative purposes. Education of its members is a basic interest and need in each society. It expresses itself institutionally in definite normative complexes that emphasize the need. The normative complexes are made effective through some agency, chiefly schools in most societies. Government is a generalized need in society for it is institutionalized in established, sanctioned norms to maintain order and peace. Government is an institution. A government is an institutional agency. Education as a cultural need and value is an institution, whereas schools to meet these needs and values are institutional agencies.

Institutional agencies exist independently of particular persons and properties. Persons and properties help to implement the system of relationships necessary to satisfy the functions for which our institutions are established. But societies are not dependent upon particular persons or properties for their continuity. Particular persons come and go, and apparatus changes. Universities as educational agencies change their presidents; churches get new pastors; governments have different executive, legislative, and judicial personnel. Buildings and other materials are replaced and new ones added. But the system of sanctioned relationships between *some* persons and properties survives to achieve their institutional ends. Functionaries are necessary to our institutional agencies; particular functionaries are not.

Institutions and the Institutional Agencies Serve as Social Control Mechanisms

Societies not only approve the general ends embodied in normative complexes, they also establish the methods to be used in attaining them. Institutions and institutional agencies are created as social control mechanisms. Through them, sanctioned forms of behavior are brought to bear on all persons. The rules they support for our behavior are an embodiment of what our society considers morally proper. They provide the machinery for good behavior within the society. We are judged to be good or bad citizens to the extent that we follow the society's expected norms. Social status is achieved in the community, in part, as a result of our behavior in these agencies. The accommodation of the interests of people to each other is facilitated through them.

These sanctioned practices have the force of moral judgments since they are recognized as right practices. Each generation is educated, in part, through the institutional agencies to recognize these practices as the standards of their society. Each generation usually follows them without question, automatically assuming that any different procedures are wrong. Each child in a particular society soon recognizes that the type of family in which he lives, for example, is the proper type of family and that other family forms are improper. So it is with the other aspects of living in a society. Each child has built into his personality, through functioning in its institutional agencies, the society's conception of right and wrong about the major concerns of living. Each new generation, through participation in its institutional agencies, is indoctrinated with these proper practices that have been previously sanctioned.

Many Sociologists Do Not Differentiate Between Institutions and Institutional Agencies

Following the work of Talcott Parsons, particularly, we use the concept "institution" to mean the normative patterns of established practices. Institutional agencies are the social systems through which these express themselves. A number of sociologists, recognizing the close integration of these normative complexes and the systems through which they are made effective, do not distinguish between them. Indeed, the common practice is to refer to schools, churches, libraries, and many others as the institutions of society for it is through these that the normative patterns function.

We feel, on the other hand, that the reality in social organization is more clearly discerned when it is recognized that agencies, such as schools or libraries, are relationship structures with specific functionaries and equipment that come into being to put into actual practice the basic expectations of the society so that its values may be promoted and preserved. All societies seek to preserve their cultural values and maintain their social order. Complexes of norms to express these are evolved. Agencies through which these norms can be concretely expressed become a part of the social system of the society.

Institutional Agencies Develop Some Characteristic Properties

Institutional agencies as means for implementing the institutionalized norms of a society, develop type parts which are usually characteristic of most of them.

STANDARDIZED PROCEDURES First, an institutional agency is usually a relationship structure of members of the society following standardized procedures. Institutions standardize the norms. The agencies are set up to make it possible for all in the society to act as expected with respect to them. Families as human relationship entities have a common form in a society. Each of us is expected to adopt this form

and act devotedly toward it. A government as an agency to maintain order includes rights and obligations its citizens are to operate by in standardized ways. And so also for other institutional agencies.

PHYSICAL PROPERTY Second, there are physical properties that serve as equipment. Institutional agencies require material means in their actual operation to make the usages functional. The family has its residence with household and personal utilities; government its capitol and other service buildings and properties; education its schools and books; religion its churches, ceremonials, and instructional equipment; industry its factories and shops.

FUNCTIONARIES Third, there are functionaries, persons delegated to carry out the sanctioned behavior patterns of our institutions. The principals and teachers in the schools; priests and preachers in the Church; elected and appointed officials in the government; owners and managers in industrial institutions are exemplar. They operate as the specialized personnel to promote and direct the operation of the institutional agencies according to their sanctioned ways.

ORAL OR WRITTEN SYMBOLS Fourth, there are oral or written symbolic forms that codify and preserve the expected patterns of institutional relations. Rules and laws specify the various obligations of marital partners and members of the family. The marriage license gives the sanction of the society to our marital relation. Charters, constitutions, and ordinances contain the rules of governmental units. Creeds and sacred books express the beliefs of our religious bodies. School laws and curriculums are the guideposts for education. Articles of incorporation, franchises, and contracts specify the ways economic and industrial enterprises are to operate.

SYNTHESIZING SYMBOLS Fifth, there are symbols that synthesize the relationships within our institutional agencies and express them in a representative form. The wedding ring of our married couples in the West or the way the hair is dressed by women in some oriental societies is a symbolic announcement that the persons are married; flags, national anthems, and seals are collective representations of the state; the cross and the crescent are symbols of religions; pennants, school colors, and school songs represent educational institutions; and trade-marks and advertising slogans are representatives of our economic and industrial institutions.

These five type parts, related to each other in unified wholes, give each institutional agency the necessary apparatus for operating. An institutional agency is effective to the degree that it correlates these parts so that there is good administrative organization functioning through efficient physical apparatus.

Institutional Agencies Develop Rigidity

Institutional agencies become fixed because they are mechanisms through which societies operate with respect to their institutionalized norms. They are the established instruments for the integration of the society about the societal norms. This relatively permanent form is attained because the patterned norms of the society are themselves fixed and relatively permanent. The institutional agencies are their conservers as the instruments through which these norms function. As conservers, they must develop stability or have little utility. Ends cannot be achieved through forms that are constantly changing. There is little order in a society if, for example, the pattern of government is constantly changing. Since institutions and institutional agencies are conservative and resist change, they have utility as societal instruments of control.

CHANGE COMES ONLY UNDER STRONG PRESSURE Once an institutional agency attains its form, it clings to that form tenaciously. Any modification has to be in harmony with its total structure. Thus, the monogamous family, monotheistic religion, the corporate form of business, once developed, have persisted for centuries. Sanctioned by the society at large and serving as the bulwarks of its values, they persevere in the essential forms which they attained. They change only under the severest pressures.

Specific conditions in a society tend to uphold this perseverance. Vested interests develop to retain them once they are established. Institutional functionaries, trying to keep them from changing, usually believe strongly in the institutions and their forms; they themselves may be deprived of some privileges if changes come.

The institutions are carriers of the morally right ways so they are often not challenged because we fear a sense of guilt from such action. Few persons dare to criticize the family or the Church as institutional agencies since such attacks on agencies considered sacred may offend the community and draw condemnation.

Efforts made to bring about changes cause the old to reassert itself with new vigor. The functionaries and other supporters of the old ways present strong arguments urging the retention of the older established pattern. There is strong opposition when the newer type of marital relations with its free choice of mates by the parties involved meets an older type where parents select the marriage partner of their offspring. The meeting of one form of aggressive religion with another results in renewed energy on the part of both, and especially on the part of the one extant in the area.

Then there is the general inertia and conservatism of the people influenced by an institution and its representatives. The old way is the best way to most people unless it is actually costly. Because few of us think through what is involved in following the fixed institutional forms, we do not raise questions about them. Most of us are content, through long conditioning, to accept the authoritarian implications in each of our institutions and institutional agents and view with surprise any challenge to them.

Institutions and Their Agents Do Change, However

Institutions and their instrumentalities will change even though they are relatively permanent. Stable institutions are required for they are a society's procedural norms. The agencies are devices used to meet society's universal interests and needs cooperatively. They must be stable since these interests and needs are themselves relatively permanent. Both institutions and agents will change, however, with changes in the culture of a society since they are forms within the culture. These changes, which may be of two types, are in their structural patterns and in their specific functions.

STRUCTURAL CHANGES Changes in structural patterns are illustrated by most of our institutional agencies. All have probably changed over the centuries. The monogamous family form of our present-day western societies grew in many instances out of the polygamous family systems of preceding societies. Our democratic governmental forms often had autocratic or tyrannical systems as their forebears. The factory system of manufacture carried on by our corporations is only a recent invention. Its predecessor, the guild, no longer survives.

Changes in the total structural pattern of our institutional agencies rest ultimately on changes in our institutions. Thus, over periods of time the society develops and sanctions new views about some institutionalized practices. Trustworthy knowledge and experience are perhaps the strongest forces in this regard. They are substituted for the questionable in the traditional content of the institution. Slavery, once a sanctioned institution in most societies, has disappeared almost completely. New knowledge, experience, and attitudes about people and work made this institution untenable.

Our institutional agencies change with changes in our way of living. The Industrial Revolution with its overpowering technological upheavals gave western societies new approaches to a host of interests. New conditions of work, to use one illustration, led us to new conceptions of the welfare of workers. New institutions and institutional instruments related to these responsibilities, such as the labor union, have been established.

CHANGES IN CONTENT AND FUNCTION Changes in the specific functions of our institutional agencies often take place without changing their general structure. Governments were almost wholly regulative and protective in their earliest developments. Today, they engage in many activities that we once thought were functions of other agencies. The development of economic facilities like electric power and the purchase and sale of crops were once functions of private business. At one time, we thought that governments were not supposed to be in business. Aid to needy individuals, once the function of the family and neighbors, is now engaged in on an extensive scale by governments, and we accept this. Our families once performed economic, educational, and religious functions; today, these are performed chiefly through other institutional agents. Our public schools were private institutions, and education was a commodity. Those who wished it for their children bought it in private schools. Today, our societies say general education is essential for all. Our elementary and high schools are largely publicly supported, and our children are required to attend. Our higher education in universities and colleges was once provided by churches; today, in America most of our colleges and universities are publicly supported or are operated as nonsectarian, privately endowed institutional instruments. The interaction of many forces brings about transfer of functions that goes almost unnoticed by the majority of us.

Institutional Agencies Sometimes Become Self-Perpetuating

There is always the danger that the maintenance of our institutional devices is their chief end because of the vital roles they play in the prescribed standardized procedures for operation in a society and because of their protected position. It is forgotten that the justification for their existence is that they serve as means to ends. Thus, they may tend to form the substance and engage in the exercise of unchanging self-perpetuation. This danger faces educational agencies where a fixed, rigid curriculum promoted by vested interests allows for no change. It is also true of churches where systems of symbolism have attained a protected status that makes them untouchable. These inflexible patterns resist examination and make us followers of routine rather than inquirers after truth.

Ritual and ceremonies invested with sanctity often overshadow the true institutional goals and focus attention not on what the institution can do for us but on what its agencies can do for themselves. Our agencies lag behind our changing societies. They may then yield their real functions to other agencies or to new forms of the same institutional instruments. It is essential that our institutional agencies constantly redefine their roles in relation to the trends in the society in order to adjust their operation to the course of institutional changes. Emphasis upon the institutional agencies themselves is detrimental when it hinders constructive social change and crushes individual expression and growth.

The Institutional Agencies Are Interrelated and Interdependent

When we consider specific institutional agencies, such as churches, schools, and families, we may create a sense of separateness among them. However, in societies they are bound up with each other and form a related whole that is part of the total structural system of the society. Churches, for example, are composed of families and use them to further their objectives. They solicit aid from business and schools and support the objectives of government, schools, and other institutions. The family and marriage as institutional complexes are sanctioned by Church and state, and the state regulates them through laws that define responsibilities. They are ultimately related to the economic agencies, and their forms are decidedly affected by demands of the productive system. No institutional agent operates as a distinctly separate entity in a society; their interlaced cooperation gives the society its consistency.

MERGED INSTITUTIONS This interrelationship is so intimate in some societies that the institutional forms are actually merged. In Japan, the emperor as head of the state was also the godhead. Shintoism was a religious system supporting a state and was a part of the state. Crop planting and harvesting in China were part of the religious, as well as the economic, practices; in fact, no part of living from producing to consuming was separated from the religious institutions. Institutions and their instruments are interwoven so completely with immediate objectives in primitive societies that separateness is impossible. The family is often not only a child-bearing and -rearing agency, but an economic, educational, and governmental one as well.

One institutional agency may occupy a dominant role in the functioning of a society under such conditions. The Church became a governmental and educational agency in medieval Europe by absorbing or dominating family and economic institutional functions. The doctrine of the separation of state and Church is applied in some societies to make it impossible for churches to obtain control of government and schools. The institutionalized family predominated over economic, religious, and governmental agencies to such an extent in oriental societies, particularly in China, that economic activities were family controlled, religious practices reflected family ties as in ancestor worship, and government was patterned after the family. The philosophy that made the institutionalized family dominant in China through centuries was expressed by Mencius: "The root of empire is the state, the root of the state is in the family, the root of the family is in the person of its head."

In a totalitarian society, the government controls all other institutional agencies and abolishes those it deems harmful to its purposes.

Institutional Agencies Often Perform Latent as Well as Manifest Functions

Institutions as complexes of sanctioned norms serve societies by standardizing procedures with respect to cardinal needs and interests that are their chief cultural values. The institutional agencies are the instruments through which they operate. The standardized procedures are the intended functions of institutions. Robert Merton calls these the *manifest functions* of these structures. However, he properly points out that social forms perform other functions that are not necessarily intended in their basic purposes. These are often not clear, yet they sometimes account for much of the prevailing pattern of behavior within institutional agencies. He terms these unintended and unrecognized functions as *latent functions.*[2]

Merton points out that the economic agencies produce goods for the manifest purpose of satisfying need for these goods. But people buy automobiles or choice articles of food not only to satisfy their needs but also to heighten social status.

Churches not only transmit basic moral and religious instruction—their manifest functions —but sociability, recreation, and many others often unintended and often unrecognized. Yet, these latent functions often influence the agencies and persons operating within them much more significantly than their manifest functions.

Illustrations of such latent functions could be multiplied for each of our institutional agencies and for our other structural forms as well. We must consider them because they often are as important in the operation of our societal forms and in the behavior of people associated with them as the manifest functions.

References

1. Parsons, Talcott, *Essays in Sociological Theory,* rev. ed. (Glencoe, Ill., The Free Press, 1954), p. 35.
2. Merton, R. K., *Social Theory and Social Structure* (Glencoe, Ill., The Free Press, 1957), Chap. 1, pp. 19–84.

Questions for Study and Discussion

1. Give an illustration of institutionalization connected with some agency, such as the school.
2. What is an institution? Compare the definition we are using with those in three other standard texts in this field.

3. Show how institutions are founded on continuing interests and needs in societies from your own knowledge of a specific institutional agency.
4. Distinguish between institution and institutional agency.
5. Discuss institutions as relationship structures serving a total society by contrasting them with structural forms that serve only some segment of a society.
6. Distinguish between manifest and latent institutional functions. Give illustrations of some latent functions performed by your college or university.
7. Point out the "type parts" institutional agencies usually include and show their relationship to each other.
8. Give an illustration of an institution that has changed and indicate the factors that caused the change.
9. Under what circumstances must institutional agencies redefine their roles in a society or yield their functions to other agencies?
10. Give some concrete illustrations of the interrelatedness of institutional agencies.

Supplementary Reading

Chapin, F. Stuart, *Contemporary American Institutions*. New York: Harper and Brothers, 1935.

Cooley, Charles H., *Social Organization*. New York: Charles Scribner's Sons, 1920.

Feibleman, James K., *The Institutions of Society*. London: George Allen and Unwin, Ltd., 1956.

Hertzler, Joyce O., *Social Institutions*. Lincoln, Neb.: University of Nebraska Press, 1946.

MacIver, Robert, *The Web of Government*. New York: The Macmillan Company, 1947.

Panunzio, Constantine, *Major Social Institutions*. New York: The Macmillan Company, 1939.

Parsons, Talcott, *The Social System*. Glencoe, Ill.: The Free Press, 1951.

————, *Essays in Sociological Theory*. Rev. ed. Glencoe, Ill.: The Free Press, 1954.

Rose, Arnold, *The Institutions of Advanced Societies*. Minneapolis, Minn.: University of Minnesota Press, 1958.

Sumner, William G., *Folkways*. Boston: Ginn and Company, 1906.

Whyte, William H., Jr., *The Organization Man*. New York: Simon and Schuster, Inc., 1956.

Williams, Robin M., *American Society*. Rev. ed. New York: Alfred A. Knopf, 1960.

10

THE DOMESTIC INSTITUTIONS: MARRIAGE

MARRIAGE is the institution sanctioned by societies to establish durable bonds between males and females and to permit sexual intercourse for the implied purpose of parenthood and the establishment of a family. Thus, marriage inaugurates families.

Marriage and the Family Are Primary Institutions in All Societies

We have pointed out that all societies carry out their chief functions through basic institutions that are essential to effective operation. We shall study first marriage and family institutions, which are a common system of relationship units.

The family is regarded as a primary institution in every society; indeed, it was probably the original institution of human society. All the societal forces are used for its support and protection for, through it, societies perpetuate themselves, both biologically and culturally.

For good reasons, marriage, as the relationship institution that inaugurates the family, has concerned societies at every stage of their development also. It is the institutionalized system that secures the perpetuation of the human species and the population of particular societies through sanctioning and controlling sex mating.

Marriage and the Family Are Distinct Institutions

MARRIAGE Marriage is the sanctioning by a society of a durable bond between one or more males and one or more females established to permit sexual intercourse for the implied purpose of parenthood. It is a special type of sanctioned person-to-person relationship. Established at a particular time, it may, under certain conditions, be terminated at a particular time when socially approved. However, the society's ex-

pectation and the agreement of the persons married are that the bond will continue throughout their natural lives or until some socially defined condition arises in which the expected roles cannot be performed. "Till death us do part" is implied in each marriage in our society. Monogamous marriages cease with the death of either of the married partners. The public announcement in the marriage ceremony which sanctions the bond informs the society of the proper right of the married persons to carry out their intentions. Persons so united are no longer to be sought by others for such purposes. Thus marriage sanctions the relationship of men and women as husbands and wives and notifies the rest of society of this relationship.

THE FAMILY The family is a kinship grouping formed by the bonds of marriage, blood, or adoption and composed of husbands and wives and husbands or wives, together with their biological or legally adopted children, if any. This definition includes the nuclear family of a married man and woman with their children which is the usual family form, the broken family of one parent and the children, the married couple who may not have borne or adopted children, the unmarried couple with or without children who have lived together long enough to be considered husband and wife by law, and a man with several wives or a woman with several husbands, with or without children.

Families grow out of marriage because the

normal consequence of marital relations is the birth of children. The long period of infancy and childhood requires care and training—the mother, too, has long periods of pregnancy—so the survival of mother and children rests in considerable part upon the attention they obtain. This is particularly true for the human species for children are usually born single and overlap in their development. Such a circumstance demands that there be close and helpful relationships between husbands, wives, and children for long periods of time in order to survive. Societies bind the members of the family together in strict obligations to each other, as to rights and duties enforced by custom and law, for the survival of societies depends upon the survival of offspring. Rights and duties in the family bind the parents to each other in matters beyond the marriage obligation. They bind parents to the children beyond the provision of primary needs and the children to the parents and to each other, at least for aid in case of need. Thus, the family emerges as a social institution, the behavior of its members expressing socially prescribed forms of action.

The Normal Status for the Majority of the Adults in Different Societies Is the Married One

STATISTICS OF MARRIAGE   The statistics from different countries on the proportions of the population married support the above proposition. These figures, as far as they are attainable, indicate that in European nations the proportion of the population of marriageable age that was actually married ranged from about 55 per cent for females in France to 69 per cent for males in England. It is estimated that 85 to 88 per cent of the population of England marry at some time. In the Scandinavian countries, 81 per cent of the males and 79 per cent of the females 35 to 49 years of age were married. Only 8 per cent of the males and 11 per cent of the females over 50 years of age in Italy in 1936 had never married. The oriental countries indicate similar ratios; for example, it is reported that in India only 0.1 per cent of the persons 35 to 44 years of age would not marry.[1]

The proportions of the males and females fourteen years of age and older who were married were 69 to 65 per cent, respectively, in the United States in 1961. This is nearly seven of each ten persons over fourteen years of age. Approximately 79 per cent of the males and 73 per cent of the females 20 years of age and over were married in this year.[2] Adult Americans have a favorable attitude toward marrying as is indicated by the fact that nine of each ten persons who reach marriageable age will ultimately marry.[3]

The proportion of the adult population in the United States that is married has been steadily increasing. Only 53 and 55 per cent, respectively, of the males and females fourteen years of age and over were married in 1900. These proportions were 69 and 66 per cent in 1960, and each decade had an increase for both sexes over the previous one.[4] These changes are due to the increasing tendency to marry at earlier ages and the increasing tendency to remarry when a first marriage has been dissolved.

The Extent of Remarriage Indicates a Favorable Attitude to Marriage

The extent to which remarriages occur shows that Americans look upon the married state with favor. Almost one in each five marriages that occur in the United States is a remarriage for one or both of the persons. One in each eight persons who is married has been married more than once.[5] The chances of marriage by those who have already been married and are eligible for another are greater than those for single persons. This is true for both our divorced and our widowed. These persons have a favorable attitude toward marriage which is not destroyed by the previous marriage. Three-fourths of all our ever-divorced persons remarried within five years after their divorce. One-half of the men and one-fourth of the women of all our ever-widowed persons remarried within five years.[6] Data for England and Wales indicate that about two-thirds to three-quarters of those obtaining a divorce ultimately remarry.[7] Other societies show similar experiences.

We get a strong indication of the stability of marriages in American society when we note that, in addition to remarriage, the great proportion of the American population go through life with only one married partner. Four of each five men and fully nine out of each ten women married after 21 years of age do so.

Marriages Take Two Major Forms: Monogamous and Polygamous

The form in which marriage originally appeared is not known to us. Its origins, like those of many of our other social forms, are hidden in the unfathomable past. It probably did not originate as a single form but developed in different ways in different situations. We know this to be true of marriage forms today for a number of different types are found in contemporary societies. We can subsume these under two general types: monogamous and polygamous. Monogamous marriages are unions of one man and one woman, while polygamous marriages include the union of several mates.

POLYGAMY Polygamous marriages, which we shall briefly mention, are of three general types: polyandrous, or the union of one woman with several men; polygynous, or the union of one man with several women; and group marriages, which unite several men and several women.

Polyandry Polyandrous marriages occur among some primitive people due chiefly to the scarcity of women. This scarcity, in turn, is associated with poor economic conditions and female infanticide. Polyandry exists on a small scale in Tibet, among some tribes in India (see Box 11), and in other scattered areas. It usually represents the right of younger brothers to have access to the wife of the older brother, but, in some cases, it takes a nonfraternal form.

Polygyny Polygynous marriages are much more common than the polyandrous ones. Economic conditions are important determinants here, also. Other wives may be obtained to share the labor when the household and field work of a first wife are difficult. Certain African

tribal chieftains have several wives for work purposes. Prestige results from having several wives where economic conditions are good. Thus, the rich and powerful are often polygynous. More than one wife is approved where family lineage is traced through the males, as is done in China, and sons are necessary to prevent its destruction. Wars also sometimes create a scarcity of men and influence polygynous practices.

Group Marriage Group marriage occurs in rare situations—usually between a group of brothers and a group of sisters. Some tribes in India, New Guinea, and the Hawaiian Islands sanction it, but it is not the usual marriage form even among these tribes.

MONOGAMY The monogamous union of one male and one female is the prevailing form of marriage in practically all societies because most males are not able to support more than one female and their offspring. It is the form of marriage sanctioned by law, religion, and the mores in most modern societies. Certain conditions make this form meet the needs of our present-day societies. The two sexes are about equal in number in the general population so that other forms, if generally prevalent, would upset this relationship, and fewer marriages would be possible. Relationships between the mates are more intimate where there is a single

---

BOX 11

In the high Himalayas, polyandry has the sanction of immemorial legend. According to the *Mahabharata*, the great epic poem of India, Arjuna the Bowman, third of the five sons of King Pandu, won Draupadi, daughter of the King of Panchala, by shooting five swift arrows through a ring hung in mid-air. But Arjuna's mother Kunti told him, "All things must be shared." So the five Pandu brothers all wed Draupadi and went to live in a grand palace with crystal floors. Last week in Jaunswar Bawar, a region in the northern tip of India, the legend of Arjuna the Bowman and the whole practice of polyandry were being put to test.

Like many race myths, the legend of Arjuna clothes a simple economic fact: in the upland valleys, existence depends upon a limited number of tiny terraced fields and the careful balancing of population against food reserves. Each family avoids dividing its meager tillage in ever-diminishing lots among its progeny by having the younger sons share the wife of the eldest son. Not only does this practice reduce the number of children in each generation, and keep each property permanently within the family, but it has some other curious results. Polyandry, for some reason not wholly accounted for by anthropologists, reduces the fertility of wives, and produces an abnormal ratio of male to female births. In Jaunswar Bawar, where men outnumber women four to one and more than 60,000 people practice polyandry, only one birth was reported last year.[8]

husband and wife. This intimacy probably allows the two personalities to blend in a mature affection founded upon appreciation of each other's personality, though it is sometimes not a completely sufficient foundation for lifelong marriage. Jealousy is one of the major factors that creates tensions in polygamous marriages; monogamous marriages do not eliminate this possibility, but they make it less likely. Also, property arrangements are managed more easily and its transfer probably carried out more judiciously in monogamous marriages than in other forms.

THE SANCTIONED FORM IN THE WESTERN SOCIETIES   Contemporary societies in the Western world feel so strongly that the monogamous family is the proper form of marriage that they make polygamous forms illegal. We judge a person who marries a second mate before legally severing the relationship with the first to be guilty of bigamy and subject to punishment. Warden Lawes expresses the viewpoint both of our society and of the injured parties when he tells of the prisoner in Sing Sing who had married several trusting ladies. When the wives discovered his multiple marriages, they prosecuted. Society also prosecuted. He found himself as a result within the walls of Sing Sing.[9]

Societies Set Restrictions on Marriages by Establishing Rules Governing Certain Aspects of the Relationship

Marriage is closely governed by societal controls because it is the accepted system for assuring the perpetuation of the species and the maintenance of society. Societies recognize it not only as an institution devised to suit the purposes of the marriage mates but also those of the society as well. One major concern of societies is with the kinship, racial, and religious relations of prospective mates.

EXOGAMY   *Exogamy* is the system that restricts marriages to persons outside of specific groupings. The limits may be the family, the kinship grouping, or the race.

The most universal of these exogamous rules holds that marriage mates should not be close blood relatives. Incest, as such a relationship is called, is forbidden by all societies and, with rare exceptions (see Box 12), has existed as far back as evidence can be obtained. The reason for the origin of the taboo is not known. Various theories have pointed to the adverse effects of inbreeding, the lack of sexual attraction between persons reared in intimate association, and the desire to maintain parental authority. But none of these is a wholly satisfactory explanation. How far into the kinship group the incest taboo extends varies with the society. Marriage of fathers and daughters and mothers and sons is the most widely spread prohibition; then comes marriage between brothers and sisters. In most Western societies, the taboo extends as far as first cousins, although such marriages may not be forbidden by law.

ENDOGAMY   *Endogamy* is the system which restricts marriages to persons within prescribed limits. Marriages in American society between the white and Negro races is forbidden in most states. Although our society generally seeks to prevent it, mating occurs between whites and Negroes, as is evidenced by our mulatto population. But neither white nor Negro races generally approve it. Usually, it takes place in the lower social classes and at the instigation of white males. (See Box 13.)

The rate of racial intermarriage is low even where it can take place legally. In Los Angeles County, California, where there is a large population from all races, there were only 56 interracial marriages per 10,000 marriage licenses

---

BOX 12   BROTHER-SISTER MARRIAGE IN ANCIENT EGYPT

. . . In the Pharaonic period the Egyptian kings sometimes married their sisters or half-sisters. . . . There is one fairly certain case and several possible cases of commoners who married their sisters in the Pharaonic period. In the Ptolemaic period many of the kings married their sisters or half-sisters, but there is no evidence of such marriages among the commoners. During the period of Roman rule, however, there is very strong evidence that brother-sister marriages occurred among commoners with some frequency. These consanguine marriages among the commoners were probably used as a means of maintaining the property of the family intact and preventing the splintering of the estate through the operation of the laws of inheritance.[10]

BOX 13

"Some of the leaders of one of the civic boys' club organizations met to discuss whether or not they should integrate the various branches of their club. In the office where they happened to be meeting a Negro boy was working. He was not in the discussion, no business there at all as far as these men were concerned, but he overheard all the argument. Didn't speak a word until after a while one of the white men said: 'Well, one thing we're not going to have is niggers marrying our daughters!' Then the boy said, 'Now wait a minute, mister. You mean Negroes aren't going to be marrying your wife's daughters. We've been marrying *your* daughters for a long time.' " [11]

---

issued in a period of 30 months. This is a rate of a little more than one-half of one per cent of all the marriages.[12] This does not indicate a strong tendency to intermarry racially.

Religious groupings within societies seek to prevent marriages outside of their own communion. It is almost a necessity to marry within the faith in most Catholic societies. Protestants, while not forbidding such marriages, commonly discourage them. Because the family is the keystone in the structure of Judaism, marriage is viewed as a sacrament in which the rearing of a family and promoting its moral adherence to the religious system is to serve God. Thus, to preserve itself, the Jewish faith emphasizes marriage within the communion. Marriage outside the faith in the Mohammedan Middle East is almost impossible, while in India marriage of Hindus is endogamous in the caste.

Endogamy functions to preserve the unity of the group and the distinctive quality of its life. Also, because the married pair would have a common background, their adjustments in marriage would be facilitated.

Societies Show Concern About the Age at Which Youth Marry

PERMISSIBLE MARRIAGE AGE The concern of societies is also expressed in the establishment of an age at which marriage is allowed. In most societies, the minimum permissible age is usually set at the time at which sexual maturity (puberty) is reached. Marriage is permissible at young ages in primitive societies where living is relatively simple and youth learn the ways of life early. In some societies, such as traditional India, marriages before puberty are sanctioned, but, in such cases, sexual relations are not considered proper until after puberty. The age at which a valid marriage can be contracted in European countries ranges between twelve years in Czechoslovakia and Hungary

to twenty-one years for males and eighteen years for females in Denmark and Sweden. It is eighteen years or older for males and fifteen years or older for females in most of these countries, however. The permissible age without consent of parents is twenty-one years for males in 44 of the 50 states and at least eighteen years for females in all 50 states in the United States.[13] The permissible age with the consent of the parents is two to three years lower in all the states, but in no state is it lower than fourteen years for either sex, except in Washington where it is twelve years for females.

The age at which people marry, however, is usually higher than the permissible age. For example, the median age of first marriages for brides in the United States in 1959 was 20.2 years; for grooms, 22.7 years.[14] These average ages at first marriages are about two years higher than the permissible age.

MARRIAGE AGE DECREASING However, the median age at which both males and females marry in the United States has decreased steadily from 1890 to the present time. The median age at first marriage was 26.1 years for males and 22.0 years for females in 1890. There was a decrease of about three years for males and two years for females during this period. Each of the intervening decades between 1890 and 1960 showed a decrease.

These increasingly youthful marriages are causing some serious concern because of their contribution to increases in birth rates and divorce rates. (See Box 14.)

EXPECTATION OF MARRIAGE Girls, particularly, are expected to marry by the time they reach a certain age in some societies and among certain classes in American society. They can hardly postpone marriage in many places beyond the early twenties without causing personal and family embarrassment.

Randolph reports, for example, in *The*

Ozarks that "early marriages are the rule in the hill country. Many mountain girls are wives and mothers at fifteen and sixteen. A girl of twenty is well past her first bloom, and not likely to get a desirable husband; when she reaches twenty-five she is on the cull list, and at thirty she is definitely an old maid." [16] There is still some inclination in American society to consider unmarried women in their late twenties and thirties as "queer old maids." However, our attitude is changing rapidly because the modern woman has an opportunity to make a valuable social contribution through a career other than marriage.

The age at which men marry is not a matter of serious concern in most societies since they are the dominant sex and are expected to initiate the marriage proposal. They may be considered queer, unpatriotic, or selfish if, however, they remain bachelors.

Most societies make it virtually impossible for the women to propose marriage, even though they are expected to marry. This puts girls at a disadvantage, especially where mates are freely selected. Women freed from economic dependence upon men and altered conceptions of women themselves may eventually bring change in these folkways.

WOMEN MARRY YOUNGER THAN MEN Women are generally younger than men at the time of marriage, with the age difference usually averaging from one to three years. Men prefer women younger than themselves and women prefer men who are older. As the age at marriage increases, the preference is for persons of even wider differences in age. One serious consequence of the greater age of the husband at time of marriage is that the wife may have an abnormally long period of widowhood since the mortality rate for men is higher than for women.

AGE DIFFERENCES AND MARITAL HAPPINESS It has not been factually proven, although often asserted, that wide differences in age at marriage are unfavorable to marital happiness. Some studies indicate, in fact, that these differences are not unfavorable to success in marriage.[17] Differences in experiences, the operation of fixed habits, maturity of motives, and progress in moving from physical attraction to congeniality are probably more important to success than differences in age.

Societies Are Making Some Starts in Assuring Eugenic Marriages

Societies are beginning to require evidence of freedom from health limitations, venereal diseases particularly, before issuing a license to marry. About four-fifths of the states in the United States require a blood test. At least one

---

BOX 14 TEEN MARRIAGE SEEN CAUSING PREMATURE DOMESTICATION

Anthropologist Margaret Mead warned today that the growing trend toward teen-age marriages could have serious consequences on the future of America.

Early marriage, she said in a copyrighted interview for *U.S. News & World Report,* is now more prevalent in the United States than almost any area of the world.

"Early student marriage is domesticating boys so early they don't have a chance for full intellectual development," she said. "I think it's bad for women, too."

She noted that there was a "tremendous" number of broken marriages in the early age group, but parents share a good part of the blame for the trouble, she said.

Reacting to their own uncertainties stemming from wars and depressions, she said, parents in effect tell their children: "Take some enjoyment in life while you can get it. The future is totally uncertain."

As a result of this attitude, she said, parents "are driven to conniving with the youngsters in . . . early 'going steady.' They push the boys as well as the girls into courtship as early as possible and underwrite the marriage."

"If we retire into a kind of fur-lined domesticity, in which everybody in the country is concerned only with his own little family, and his own little house," she said, ". . . it is going to curtail seriously the contribution that we can make as a nation to the development on this planet." [15]

requires a doctor's examination for venereal disease of all male applicants.

States also prohibit the marriage of insane or feeble-minded persons. However, most of the laws only provide for the annulment of such marriages if they occur. Societies still have much progress to make in providing for adequate eugenic protection.

Societies Everywhere Recognize the Importance of Marriage by the Ceremonial Rites They Establish in Connection with It

THE WEDDING Marriage is actually begun by the conduct of legal or religious ceremonies or both. The wedding is the recognition of the significance of marriage to societies and to individuals through the public ceremony usually accompanying it. Such a ceremony indicates the society's control. The pageantry impresses upon the couple the importance of the commitment they are undertaking. "In the ecstatic solemnity with which she swore her faith to him, the ordinary sensibilities of sex seemed a flippancy" is the way the religious ceremony affected Tess d'Urbervilles.[18]

The ceremony has no such quality in some instances. C. G. Norris revealed this in his novel, *Seed*. He told of the young couple who got their license from a City Hall Clerk who directed them to the chambers of the Judge across the hallway. The Judge removed his cigar, pushed himself up in his chair, read several sentences hurriedly, asked a few questions, got their signatures and attached his own, pocketed his fee, extended superficial congratulations, and bid the couple good-bye. In a brief few minutes, the couple was out in the hallway again, looking at each other in confusion in an effort to understand that they were now a married couple.[19]

THE LICENSING AND CEREMONY The formal permission to marry usually required by societies is expressed through a license issue, which then makes it mandatory for persons to meet age and health regulations. The wedding must occur before witnesses so that proper certification and registration are effected. Legally sanctioned and publicly admitted marriage is important because of property and other rights and obligations that are immediately effective when the marriage is a fact. Thus, the permanence of the obligations of the contract is established beyond question, and they cannot be freely discarded. Public sanction and public acceptance make them binding.

The wedding also indicates that two persons are fused in a new life. The exchange of gold rings, the mixing of blood, and drinking from the same vessel or eating together a common piece of food, such as mystic bread, are all symbolic of the union. The ceremony also expresses the good wishes of relatives and friends. Rice-throwing and gifts of food and other helpful items are expressions of these wishes. It often signifies, also, the joining together of two families or clans by the giving away of a daughter or son to the other.

RELIGIOUS RITE The marriage ceremony is a religious rite in many societies. Judaism and Christianity in the West developed the idea that marriage is a sacred institution. It has long been a holy sacrament with the Jews, in which each Jewish man and woman has a part in realizing the promise of Jacob that his seed should be scattered over the earth. Marriage and child-bearing are religious obligations for them.

In the early development of Christianity, sex was looked upon as an evil that needed to be controlled and purified. Marriage was a sacred bond sanctioned by God and the Church. This view has been supported more or less rigidly by Christian bodies. Some do not recognize yet the possibility of dissolving a marriage. Protestant religious bodies are fairly liberal in this respect, but all emphasize the sacred character of the relationship. These views, when accepted, serve as supporting social controls.

Mates for Marriage Are Obtained by Two General Methods: Through Arrangement or Through Freedom of Choice

The selection of mates must obviously precede marriage. Mating, of course, was carried on in the early associations of people long before ceremonial marriage appeared. Marriage developed in human societies, in part, as a means of controlling mating.

ARRANGEMENTS ARE OF MANY TYPES Arrangements for procuring mates are of many types in societies where parents or some other persons with authority control the selection. Marriages have been arranged by parents for centuries in oriental and Eastern countries, such as Japan, the Philippines, and the Middle-East societies. The couple usually acquiesces without question because all girls and boys are expected to marry in these societies. Pressures are brought to bear on them if they object. Marriages have normally been arranged by parents in European countries, too, often with the assistance of a matrimonial broker. The professional matchmaker has long been a part of the marriage system among the Jews.

Henrik Van Loon describes in his story of Rembrandt, the Dutch painter, the marriages of some sons of the family in the seventeenth century: "And when it was time for us to marry, we found ourselves supplied with wives with the choice of whom we had nothing to do, but who had been selected for us by my father, because they were good Christian women and suitable mothers for such children as it might please Almighty Heaven to bestow upon us after our lawful union.

"It happened that neither my brother nor I cared a whit for the women with whom we were thus unceremoniously thrown together. But we obeyed out of the sheer habit of obeying and we suffered the martyrdom of boredom. . . ." [20]

Two important elements are found in societies where mate selection is by arrangement. First, the social and economic position of the families to be united is an important matter. They are usually marriages of convenience, binding families together as coalitions of a common interest. Second, the desires of the children and their feelings of affection and of future happiness are almost completely ignored. However, it is the belief that love develops as part of the marriage. The fact that so many successful marriages and families are started by arrangement supports the view that previous romantic relations between the pair to be married do not necessarily have to occur to assure happy unions.

FREEDOM OF CHOICE The second method of obtaining a mate for marriage is freedom of choice. Here the selection of the mate is largely the result of personal choice based on association and the development of romantic love. Relatively free of parental or other social controls, young people must develop associations with members of the opposite sex in sufficient numbers, and of such intimacy and variety that opportunity to make a suitable choice is possible. This is not to be taken for granted. The opportunity to associate intimately with others of one's own cultural level can be decidedly limited in our increasingly secondary type of social organization where contacts may be numerous but superficial. The chances for "falling in love," therefore, may actually be few. Decisions by young people may be based on limited knowledge and perceptions of prospective mates. Possibly, hasty decisions based on physiological and emotional reactions that overwhelm sound thinking may be increased, especially where there is a strong desire for marriage accompanied by fear of losing "the desired one."

This was not so when society was predominantly rural and operated on a primary group basis. Families knew each other through close contacts under all manner of circumstances. The number of persons of the opposite sex was limited. They were of a similar social class. Their attractiveness, as expressed in physical appeal, appearance, economic and work ability, and health and vigor, was known. Their choices were thus not hard to make.

A common problem in a society that depends upon free choice and romantic love as bases of marriage is the danger that the choice will result from temporary sentimental attraction rather than from considered mature decision.

Several Factors Condition the Actual Selection of a Mate in the Freedom-of-Choice System

SEX DRIVE The selection of mates in nature is based on natural impulses. The sex drive operates as a strong force in human societies, pressing us toward sexually attractive possible mates. Marriages would hardly take place without this drive. This is nature's way of assuring the perpetuation of the species.

PROPINQUITY But the choice of the specific mate among human beings is controlled or influenced by a network of social conditions. We have already pointed out some of the restrictions that different societies set, such as selection within the race, within definite age limits, and the prohibition of incest.

A further factor influencing selection is propinquity, or the nearness, of residence. Studies show that persons marry those who are nearby in much larger proportions than mere chance could bring about. J. H. S. Bossard and M. Davie and R. J. Reeve found that in Philadelphia and New Haven over one-half the licenses to marry were issued to persons who lived within 20 blocks or less of each other.[21] A study of Columbus, Ohio, shows that six out of each ten white couples who applied for a marriage license lived within 20 blocks of each other at their first date, at their engagement, and at their application for the license.[22] It has also been found that of 2354 open-country families in New York State, 66 per cent of the husbands and wives were born in the same or a bordering county.[23] It is quite clear, therefore, that nearness to each other is a factor in determining who will marry whom. However, nearness in residence indicates other influencing conditions. People distribute themselves geographically according to nationality, race, occupation, social class, and other common characteristics. Those with similar characteristics live in similar areas, and this proximity is favorable to meeting and choosing partners of like ideals and purposes.

PURPOSEFULLY CREATED CONTACTS If young men and women live in large cities or are strangers in a community, they may need deliberately to seek out prospective partners. This often means participating in church groups, community groups, or other organizations offering possibilities of acquaintanceship. Of course, firms employing young people of both sexes provide favorable settings for making contacts. It has been asserted, too, that some young women go to college for the primary purpose of finding mates.

HOMOGAMY *Homogamy* refers to the tendency of likes to choose likes, and *heterogamy* to the tendency for opposites to choose each other. Studies of the assortive mating process, where selection is not controlled, show that "likes choose likes." Persons of similar ages, races, religious convictions, educational levels, and socioeconomic classes select each other more than they select persons with dissimilar traits. This is a further factor in marital choice.

Formal and informal groups select persons with common characteristics and purposes and bring them together. The distinctively unlike do not associate with each other intimately in primary group relations. The choices of mates for marriage come from these primary group contacts. Those of us with free choices select from those who come our way, but our social relationships send persons like us our way.

CONCEPTS OF THE IDEAL MATE One's ideas of the kind of person who would make a desirable mate also condition the specific choices he makes. Each of us is surrounded by a family and its activities. We see much of marriage as the normal condition of living among adults. We are influenced by the pressures for marriage from parents, schools, churches, literature, and social education. These forces, in addition to the pressure of our sex drives, usually result in the construction of a picture in our mind of the ideal mate. This picture is composed of one's ideas about sexual attraction, sexual ideals, physical beauty, temperament, health, desirable habits, and attitudes toward children.

The picture in our minds is built in part from experiences within our families. There is some indication that we want to marry women like our mothers and men like our fathers if our family of orientation includes a mother and father who exemplify desirable personality traits. This is the thought expressed in William Dillon's old song, rendered more or less skillfully at many a convivial gathering:

> I want a girl just like the girl
> That married dear old Dad;
> She was a pearl, and the only girl
> That Daddy ever had.

Sometimes our experiences with marital situations create a negative attitude toward marriage. The constant contact with unhappiness, poverty, or meanness lead a few of us to say, "I shall never marry anyone." But the fact that almost nine of each ten persons in the United States, for example, between the ages of 35 and 44 were married in 1961 is good evidence that such resolutions do not keep many persons from marrying. Our marriages spring from our associations. They are apt to lead us to love the person if the associations are repetitive and defects are not so serious as to destroy the attraction to a prospective mate. We usually discount defects and magnify desirable traits. We are likely to see in the associate the personality traits our ideal construct has included.

PERSONALITY NEEDS Our choices of mates for marriages are also related to our personality needs. In mate selection, we consciously and unconsciously try to find the person who seems to give us the possibility of maximum satisfaction of our needs. Psychological needs vary from person to person, of course. Basic cravings are for attention, approval, and admiration that give us a feeling of psychological security. We are likely to be drawn to another person if we find one capable of satisfying these desires. This results in a complementary comradeship and likemindedness that bridges many of the strains and frictions in our personal relations.

When young men and women are asked to express their desires they say, in effect, "We want mates we can confide in, who have respect for our ideals, who appreciate what we want to achieve and help us make important decisions, who stimulate our ambition, give us self-confidence, appreciate us just as we are, stand back of us in difficulty, admire our ability, and make us feel we count for something." [24] In other words, they want mates who know all about them yet love and admire them just the same.

The factors of nearness, the attraction of likes to likes, our constructs of the ideal mate, and our personality needs do not operate as discrete forces in our choice of a mate. Each factor is related to all the others. All the aspects of an interwoven set of personal relationships constitute a pattern of mate choice.

Intermediaries Often Influence the Selection of the Mate in the Freedom-of-Choice System

PARENTAL INFLUENCE   Parents still exert influence over mate selections in Western societies in spite of the fact that they have relinquished control over courtship and marriage and now depend chiefly upon youth to find their own marriage mates. The main reason for this is the continuing concern of parents for the welfare of their children. They want to see them make happy marriages. Marriage also establishes a bond between the husband and his wife's family of orientation, between the wife and the husband's family of orientation, and between the other relatives of these two families. The first consideration is, of course, the welfare of the couple, but these other consequences also exert influence. This is often expressed by the saying that he or she made a "good marriage," "good" referring to the hopes of parents respecting the social class, economic level, and cultural backgrounds as well as the personal qualities they desired in the mate for their son or daughter.

Parents often use their influence directly in courtship activities. They set up situations where their sons and daughters meet young people they think would make desirable mates. Sending youth to special schools, arranging memberships in clubs and organizations, and providing parties and social functions are some of the positive devices parents use to expose their children to suitable mates.

A study by Alan Bates shows that one-half of the fathers and eight of each ten mothers in a sample of 136 young married couples exerted influences on the sons in courtship proceedings. Almost seven of each ten fathers and almost 100 per cent of the mothers exerted in-

fluences on the daughters.[25] Eighty-five per cent of the parents of 195 children in 97 families in New Haven, Connecticut, said they expected their children to select mates from backgrounds like their own and sought to influence them to do so by providing a "proper" dating and courtship environment and by using persuasion, appeals to loyalty, and threats to withdraw economic support, if necessary, should they decide to marry outside their class.[26]

OTHER RELATIVES AND FRIENDS   Sometimes, brothers and sisters as well as other kin are important intermediaries in mate selection. A brother introduces a chum to his sister or vice versa; other kinsfolks, such as married cousins, arrange contacts between unmarried cousins and sisters-in-law or brothers-in-law so that courting may at least get started. Close friends also serve in a similar way. The function of the intermediary in these relations usually does not extend beyond arranging the first contacts.

MATRIMONIAL AGENCIES   Many marriageable persons have difficulty in making contacts that might lead to marriage, especially in large cities where secondary relations and anonymity prevail. Several types of matrimonial agencies offer to serve as intermediaries in such settings, some voluntary and others for a fee. Organizations often promote "introduction" or "lonely" persons clubs, "dating" service, and matrimonial bureaus for youth. At one time, a television program using a Univac sorter brought together couples who were seeking mates by matching their characteristics and desires. Commercial matrimonial bureaus exist in all large cities from which, for the payment of fees, men and women may procure the names of persons who are seeking mates through the agency. Occasionally in America, and more commonly in other societies, "matrimonials" are run in newspapers in the effort to find eligible prospective mates. (See Box 15.) The widespread use of these various agencies suggests that they perform a useful service.

Marriage Is Preceded by Courtship and Betrothal

COURTSHIP   Whether the mates are selected by arrangement or by freedom of choice, there is usually a period of time before the marriage that allows for making choices and arriving at the decision to marry. The relationship that occurs in this period is referred to as courtship, wherein those who are making the decision can test the desirability of the marriage. Courting

BOX 15

WANTED beautiful, fair, bride 18/20 B.Sc. or M.B. for Ahluwalia boy 26 (Clean shave) Engineer in British concern emolument Rs 1100/00 per month. Family from West Punjab preferred. Full details.

A beautiful tall healthy & cultured girl for a very handsome Sikh bachelor aged 34 years, drawing Rs 2,500/—p.m. from British firm. Father owns property worth lakhs with annual income of Rs. 80,000/—. Caste creed no bar. Girl only consideration. Correspond with photo.

BRIDE for young man of Indian descent living in Brazil. Highly educated and established in business shortly to be in India. Girl should have good secondary education. Graduate preferred. Must be willing to leave India, possibilities of some relatives following. No religious prejudices. Ample opportunity for cultural activities.[27]

actually involves a relationship between the relatives who make the decision rather than between the persons to be married, in those systems where freedom of choice is not permitted. Negotiations and arrangements in these situations follow prescribed practices, and they vary from society to society. A few illustrations indicate this variety.

Courting the family of the girl desired for a son involves the giving of ponies among the Arapaho Indians in southwestern United States. The father sends several ponies to the lodge of the father of the desired girl and ties them to the lodge stakes when the time has come for the marriage of a son. Betrothal and eventual marriage are indicated if the ponies are accepted.

In Mexico in the rural areas, "when the boy has found a girl he wants to marry, he tells his parents. His father and his mother and his godfather and his godmother all go together to the house of the girl to ask her consent. They are received by the girl and her parents." [28] Agreements and arrangements are then worked out by the families.

DATING IN SELECTION BY FREEDOM OF CHOICE In contemporary American society, where freedom of selection is the vogue, courtship involves the association of unmarried men and women who are attracted to each other and wish to explore the desirability of eventual marriage. It has its beginnings in the practice of dating. Here a boy and girl take part together in common activities that afford opportunity to enjoy each other's company. It is a "hunting period" with no specific obligation to the particular companion. It gives youth the chance for con-

tacts with a number of persons of the opposite sex. As a result, they can form judgments about the type of person whose company they appreciate.

GOING STEADY Dating regularly with one person becomes "going steady." Two persons focus attention on each other, after there has been a sorting out and elimination of their casual associates. They now find out more about each other's interests, temperament, ideals, and ambitions. True feelings and purposes appear as regular dating advances. Their frequent and intimate associations enhance their emotional, physical, and intellectual attachment and spur their feelings for each other.

FALLING IN LOVE Two persons eventually reach a relationship to each other that is described as "falling in love." Despite the precipitous experience suggested by the phrase, in only a minority of instances does it occur suddenly. "Falling in love" usually leads to an understanding that some day the couple intend to marry.

ROMANTIC LOVE American society stresses romantic love. Its youth absorb this view. All else often appears secondary to them. "Love conquers all," they often feel, but romantic love alone, while an essential ingredient, does not usually suffice to carry a couple through all the consequent circumstances of their married life. (See Box 16.) Trivialities become important and "from near at hand the whole affair dissolves into a thousand problems. Marriage in some sense disappears into the background; it is taken for granted, it is the basis of everything: but what about this stew-pan, for instance? The reality is the stew-pan," plus proper use of it, keeping attractive, keeping cheerful, forgetting, forgiving, and many more matters that call for acceptable adjustment.[31]

BETROTHAL   Formal engagement or betrothal follows "going steady" and "falling in love." This is a mutual agreement by a man and woman that they intend to marry. Sometimes, their decision is simply announced to their parents. Often, the consent of their parents is requested, which was the custom some decades ago. It still is followed by most couples, at least to the extent of their asking for approval of the decision. Betrothals are often announced to friends at party gatherings. Among upper class families, an announcement may appear in newspapers with descriptions of the parties involved and some indication of the marriage plans. The engagement ring indicates that a girl has been given and has accepted a proposal. Therefore,

other males "need not apply." The American folkways require that the proposal be made by the man. This is a part of the social heritage.

The length of the engagement period depends upon the specific circumstances under which the couple operates. It may prove, however, to be the most important period in the whole relationship for it presents new privileges to both parties. Plans for their living together are to be made, and understandings about their desires for children, the kind of home, property ownership, and many other things are to be reached. The period may protect against too hasty and unwise decisions about these matters. If emotion dominates this period, clear agreement on such matters may be postponed on the assumption that they can be solved after marriage or that they will eventually take care of themselves. This is obviously hazardous.

BOX 16   ROMANTIC LOVE

The function of "love" in modern society is peculiarly complex. With the partial disintegration of the rural-familistic system, the actual day-by-day involvement of personal relations—both in work and play—disappeared, and the improvisation and demonstration of a total *emotional* involvement became doubly important as an ideal. The emphasis on such emotional involvement was stepped up as codes of proper conduct with various kinds of persons became increasingly vague. When the behavior of husband and wife, for example, became more and more a matter to be settled in each marriage, rather than by reference to convention, the answer of the culture was to jazz up the tempo of romantic love.

The concept of romantic love rests on a myth. Two young persons arrive at an indeterminate age, meet, and a mysterious cosmic process informs each that this is the "one." They marry, and live happily ever after, constantly fulfilling in every act their *unique* relationship. Marriage becomes, then, not so much an institutional arrangement as a device by which each can secure his or her *individual* desire for personal happiness. Sadly enough, the very fact of basing marriage on romance operates to create a well-nigh universal frustration of the prized sentiment.[29]

Radio listeners in Russia can thrill to the sudsy sentiment of soap opera like anyone else. Last week Radio Moscow fed their dreams with a tender play about a collective farm boy and a girl tractor-driver whom fate had chanced to place on the same (moonlit) night shift.

Girl (letting her tractor stand idle for a moment): How wonderful it is to work on such a beautiful night under the full moon and do one's utmost to save petrol.

Boy (suddenly lost in her eyes): The night inspired me to overfulfill my quota by a higher and still higher percentage.

(In a matter of seconds the two are locked in each other's arms.)

Boy (huskily): I fell in love with your working achievements from the very first moment.[30]

A further important fact about engagement in American society is that it can usually be broken without reflecting adversely on the persons involved. If, however, the engagement has continued for some time, it may be difficult to dissolve without embarrassment or pain. But generally there is the implied recognition that betrothal is a period of testing suitability and so may be broken without stigma. This is not so in some societies for such an act is considered not only an injury to the man or woman but also to the family or clan. Damages may be exacted or physical punishment inflicted.

In American society, couples sometimes decide to marry and skip the courtship stage. Many marriages take place with only a short courtship period. Sometimes, the couple elopes when such a decision is made and foregoes the local marriage ceremony as well. The chief causes of elopements are parental objections to the marriage, the desire to avoid publicity, economy, or pregnancy.

Marriage Ceremonies Are Often Followed by a "Honeymoon"

The wedding ceremony, particularly in Western societies, is often immediately followed by a "honeymoon." It has become so much a part of the mating of two persons in some societies that it is often thought of as part of the rite. It is an indefinite period of time in which the newly wedded couple goes into relative seclusion at some place other than their normal residence. It usually involves a trip to a place where they are unknown. Its function is to give the couple an opportunity to adjust to each other in the intimacies of personal affection and the sex relation without embarrassment and harassment. Attitudes toward sex have been such in European and American societies as to make youth self-conscious about starting their married life when relatives and friends are about. This reticence expresses itself to some extent in most societies, especially with the females. But in some societies, "bedding" the couple is part of the ceremony, and a few even have witnesses at the first mating.

A honeymoon can have two specific functions. It gives the couple a chance to make their adjustments to each other under favorable conditions. It also gives a period of time for the emotional reactions of their families of orientation and of their friends to subside. The couple is therefore received into the normal operation of their communities upon their return without undue attention.

Marriage Imposes a Number of Obligations on the Partners

RIGHT TO SEXUAL INTERCOURSE Physical and emotional satisfaction from the sex act is certainly no guarantee of successful marriage, but it is a basic element in its achievement. This drive, both in men and women, is exceedingly dynamic. It promotes profoundly satisfying and constructive values when its exercise is combined with high personal ideals and sound social attitudes. Its healthy expression enhances the value of all areas of family experience. It is not only the most intimate act in all the associations of husband and wife but also the most spiritual for it represents the complete giving of self not only physically, but emotionally and psychologically to another. No other experience in married life, lest it be at the birth of a child, causes married partners to recognize so completely that they are truly one. It is just this profound, subtle nature of the act that also makes it so fraught with disappointment and heartbreak. Both proper attitude and physical adjustment are required if the couple is to arrive at the stage where the act is sought by both husband and wife because it represents their deepest desires. Physical adjustment is not a serious problem if the right attitudes are present in both partners.

One of these attitudes concerns sex itself. Western societies have thought of sex as unclean for so long that many persons suffer from a sense of guilt in the marriage relationship. The early Christian leaders, such as St. Paul, regarded sex as impure and evil. The teachings of the Church carried these ideas through the centuries and into all Christian countries. Today, however, both modernist Christian and secular thinking has emancipated sex from this traditional bondage. Sex is looked upon as an important value apart from its procreative function, and it is seen as a natural and enriching part of approved marital relations. Consequently, we are taking a more rational approach to the subject, even to the extent of providing sex instruction throughout the educational system.

FAITHFULNESS In some societies, sexual intercourse is permitted to married partners outside the marital bond. But where these extramarital relations are allowed they are governed by definite restrictions. For example, among the Bantus and other African tribes, men have full access to wives within the clan but not to those from other clans. Within some tribes, the exchange of wives is permitted but again according to specific rules. Also, among some tribes wives are loaned to visitors as a form of hospitality. In such cases, a refusal to accept may be taken as a serious insult. The rules of Western societies have required that sexual relations be limited to the married partner. Adultery has been an almost certain ground for divorce. It not only seriously complicates the relations between the husbands and wives but may also lead to illegitimate births. Western societies are so concerned about this danger that intimate friendships with persons of the opposite sex which existed before marriage are usually broken off after marriage. Samuel Butler expressed this view as far back as the middle of the nineteenth century: "A man's friendships are, like his will, invalidated by marriage—but they are also no less invalidated by the marriage of his friends. The rift in friendship which invariably makes its appearance on the marriage of either of the parties to it was fast widening, as it no less invariably does, into the great gulf which is fixed between the married and the unmarried." [32]

We continue our discussion of domestic institutions in the following chapter, which focuses upon the family.

References

1. Reported in *Marriage and Family Living*, 16 (November, 1954), pp. 293–404.
2. Calculated from United States Department of Commerce, Bureau of the Census, *Statistical Abstract of the United States, 1962*, Table 33, p. 37.
3. Dublin, Louis I., *The Facts of Life, from Birth to Death* (New York, The Macmillan Company, October, 1951), p. 32.
4. United States Department of Commerce, Bureau of the Census, *Statistical Abstract of the United States, 1962*, Table 32, p. 37.
5. Bernard, Jessie, *Remarriage* (New York, Dryden Press, 1956), p. 45.
6. *Ibid.*, p. 57.
7. Glick, Paul C., *American Families* (New York, John Wiley and Sons, Inc., 1957), p. 139.
8. *Time* (September 12, 1955), p. 41. Courtesy of *Time;* copyright, 1955, by Time, Inc.
9. Lawes, Lewis E., *Twenty Thousand Years in Sing Sing* (New York, Ray Long and Richard R. Smith, Inc., 1932), p. 253.
10. Middleton, Russell, "Brother-Sister and Father-Daughter Marriage in Ancient Egypt," *American Sociological Review*, 27 (October, 1962), p. 603.
11. Dykeman, Wilma, and Stokely, James, "Inquiry into the Southern Tensions," *The New York Times Magazine* (October 13, 1957), p. 20.
12. Burma, John H., "Research Note on the Measurement of Interracial Marriage," *American Journal of Sociology*, 57 (May, 1952), p. 587.
13. Golenpaul Associates, *Information Please Almanac* (New York, Simon and Schuster, Inc., 1962), p. 239.
14. United States Department of Commerce, Bureau of the Census, *Statistical Abstract of the United States, 1962*, Table 77, p. 71.
15. *Journal-Every Evening* (Wilmington, Del., May 31, 1960).
16. Randolph, Vance, *The Ozarks* (New York, Vanguard Press, 1931), p. 56.
17. See the studies of success in marriage by Terman, Lewis, *et al.*, *Psychological Factors in Marital Happiness* (New York, McGraw-Hill Book Co., Inc., 1938).
18. Hardy, Thomas, *Tess of the D'Urbervilles* (London, Macmillan and Company, 1952), p. 271.
19. Norris, C. G., *Seed* (New York, Triangle Books, 1930), p. 179.
20. Van Loon, Hendrik W., *Rembrandt (R.v.R.)* (New York, Liveright Publishing Corp., 1930), p. 164. Copyright, 1958, by Helen C. Van Loon.

21. Bossard, James H. S., "Residential Propinquity as a Factor in Marriage Selection," *American Journal of Sociology*, 38 (September, 1932), pp. 219 ff, and Davie, Maurice R., and Reeves, Ruby Jo, "Propinquity of Residence Before Marriage," *American Journal of Sociology*, 44 (January, 1939), pp. 510 ff.

22. Clarke, Alfred C., "An Examination of the Operation of Residential Propinquity as a Factor in Mate Selection," *American Sociological Review*, 17 (February, 1952), p. 17.

23. Anderson, W. A., "Mobility of Rural Families, I," Cornell University AES (June, 1934), Bulletin 607, pp. 19 and 20.

24. Young, Kimball, *Sociology* (New York, American Book Company, 1949), p. 333, and Strauss, Anselm, "A Study of Three Psychological Factors Affecting Choice of Mate" (Ph.D. thesis; Chicago, University of Chicago Library, 1945).

25. Bates, Alan, "Parental Roles in Courtship," *Social Forces*, 20 (May, 1942), pp. 483 ff.

26. Sussman, Marvin, "Parental Participation in Mate Selection," *Social Forces*, 32 (October, 1953), pp. 76 ff.

27. Various Indian newspapers.

28. Redfield, Robert, *Tepoztlan, a Mexican Village* (Chicago, University of Chicago Press, 1930), p. 140.

29. Green, Arnold W., "Why Americans Feel Insecure," *Commentary*, 6 (July, 1948), p. 23.

30. *Time* (October 27, 1952), p. 39. Courtesy *Time;* copyright *Time*, Inc., 1952.

31. Fallada, Hans, *Little Man, What Now?* (New York, Simon and Schuster, Inc., 1933), pp. 34 and 35. Copyright, 1933, 1961, by Simon and Schuster, Inc. By permission of the publishers.

32. Butler, Samuel, *The Way of All Flesh* (New York, E. P. Dutton and Co., 1925), p. 365. From Everyman's Library.

Questions for Study and Discussion

1. Why are marriage and the family considered to be universal institutions?
2. Distinguish between these two institutions.
3. Distinguish between the different forms of marriage.
4. What is the difference between exogamy and endogamy? What reasons can you give for the existence of these regulations?
5. What significance do ceremonial rites have in relation to marriage?
6. Look up materials for several societies where marriages are "arranged" and point out the different methods used.
7. What do you consider the strength of the freedom-of-choice mate selection method? Its weakness?
8. Discuss the significance of intermediaries in mate selection.
9. Contrast courtship procedures followed in two societies other than those mentioned in this book.
10. Describe present-day courtship procedures in your society and contrast them with the procedures used by your grandfathers and grandmothers. Consult them on this if they are available.
11. What limitations do you see in "romantic love" as a basis for marriage? What advantages?
12. What obligations can you think of which marriage imposes on the partners other than those indicated in this treatment?

Suggested Topics for Reports

1. Prepare a brief report indicating the ways in which exogamous and endogamous restrictions have operated in American society. How have these been changing in recent years?
2. From United States Census reports, prepare a graph showing the trends in age at first marriage in America from 1900 through 1960. What factors seem to be involved in these trends?
3. Make a summary of recent comment on teen-age marriage.
4. Prepare in tabular form a summary of the legal requirements for marriage in a regional sample of states of the United States. How may the variations be accounted for?

Supplementary Reading

Baber, Ray E., *Marriage and the Family*. New York: McGraw-Hill Book Co., Inc., 1953.

Bernard, Jessie, *Remarriage*. New York: Dryden Press, 1956.

Burgess, E. W., and Cottrell, L. S., *Predicting Success or Failure in Marriage*. Englewood Cliffs, N.J.: Prentice-Hall, Inc., 1939.

Himes, Norman E., *Your Marriage*. New York: Farrar and Rinehart, Inc., 1940.

Kirkpatrick, Clifford, *The Family as Process and Institution*. New York: The Ronald Press, 1955.

Landis, Judson, and Landis, Mary G., *Building a Successful Marriage*. Englewood Cliffs, N.J.: Prentice-Hall, Inc., 1948.

Locke, Harvey J., *Predicting Adjustment in Marriage*. New York: Henry Holt and Company, Inc., 1951.

Martinson, Floyd M., *Marriage and the American Ideal*. New York: Dodd, Mead & Co., 1960.

Terman, Lewis, *et al.*, *Psychological Factors in Marital Happiness*. New York: McGraw-Hill Book Co., Inc., 1938.

Westermarck, E., *The History of Human Marriage*. 3 vols. New York: The Macmillan Company, 1921.

Winch, Robert F., and McGinnis, Robert, *Selected Studies in Marriage and the Family*. New York: Henry Holt and Company, Inc., 1953.

11

THE DOMESTIC INSTITUTIONS:
THE FAMILY

*T*HE *family is the primary institution of societies. Its major functions include biological reproduction, economic sustenance, socialization and education, and the transmission of property and culture. Its functions and forms have changed over the years. Stability of the family is a major concern to societies.*

I. INTRODUCTION

The Family Is the Primary Institution
of Any Society

FORMATION The family is formed by the ceremonial marriage of males and females, resulting later in the birth of offspring. Producing children, of course, does not always occur, either because the married couple cannot procreate or because they deliberately avoid it. In certain circumstances, the couple may adopt the children of others. Legally adopted children are usually accorded the status of natural offspring and are given the same rights and privileges as those born from the marriage. The family, therefore, is a socially recognized unit of people related to each other by kinship, marital, and legal ties. In modern societies, it is normally composed of a married pair and their children. Every society implies its ultimate control over this unit by its institutionalization of marriage and the definition of rights and obligations that arise as a result of marriage and consequent reproduction.

A BASIC DIFFERENCE The family differs from other human relationship structures (hurelures) in that it results from the physiological union of two married persons who create the other members of the unit. We enter it only by birth or adoption, the latter involving the voluntary recognition of an accepted person as an offspring of the parents. The distinctive charac-

teristics of marriage, parental obligations, and sibling relations impel a society's interest in the family. Society is concerned about marriage because it is the socially sanctioned way to produce offspring for assuring its own survival; therefore, it regulates the marriage relationship. It is concerned about the parental relationship in terms of its permanence and its responsibility for the proper care of family members; thus, it makes rules governing these. It is concerned about the sibling relationships for it is in these that the habits and ideals of the future members of the society are formed and their roles defined. These distinctive interpersonal relationships make the family the primary institutional cell of a society.

Each Individual Usually Holds Membership
in Two Families During His Life

Most of us are participants during our lives in a family into which we are born and reared (our family of orientation) and a family in which we give birth to children (our family of procreation). One is a father, mother, sister, or brother in the family of orientation; a husband, wife, son, or daughter in the family of procreation. The family of orientation socializes the individual, provides for his economic and social needs, and gives him a place in the society. The individual has children of his own in the family of procreation and has the responsibilities of providing for them. Thus, we are usually members of two families.

This Chinese extended-family group spans four generations.

FAMILY OF ORIENTATION Membership in the *family of orientation* is generally involuntary. We cannot choose the family into which we are to be born. Our position in this group is thus assigned and usually unchangeable.

FAMILY OF PROCREATION The establishment of a *family of procreation* means that one or the other or both of the partners must leave the family of orientation. The pattern generally followed in America today—the neolocal system— means that the married couple establishes a home apart from both families of orientation. This, however, is not the most common arrangement in societies. Murdock's study of residence systems in 250 societies shows that 58 per cent follow the patrilocal system in which the wife leaves her family of orientation to live in or near the family of orientation of the husband, 15 per cent follow the matrilocal system where the husband comes to live in or near the family of the wife, 7 per cent follow the neolocal system where the couple establishes a new home separated from both parental families, and 20 per cent follow various other practices.[1]

The Place of Residence Has Considerable Influence on the Functioning of the Family of Procreation

When the family of procreation is a part of a *patrilocal* or *matrilocal* system the activities of the husband or wife may be subjected to greater parental control. The husband's work may be directed by the father, and the wife may be subject to the mother-in-law. The advantage of the system is that, in providing for all the members of the large family, it may assist the newly married couple in getting established.

AMERICAN ATTITUDE In American society, the newly married couple is expected to leave the parental abode and establish a home of its own; not to do so is sometimes considered a sign of failure. Traditionally, the pattern is the single-dwelling place occupied by the family owning it. Although many newly married couples may rent a house or apartment, until they are ready or able to build or purchase, home ownership is the hope and ambition and, to a spectacular degree, the fact for the large proportion of America's families today. The downward trend in home ownership was abruptly reversed by the "housing movement" following World War II. Between 1940 and 1960 the proportion of owner-occupied housing units increased from 44 per cent to 62 per cent.[2] It is evident that owning one's place of abode is a widespread value in American society.

INFLUENCE OF INDIVIDUAL HOME The family home, owned or rented, is an important element in family living. Since it is the child's world during his growing years, its appearance influences his outlook. A teen-age youth whose home was a shabby, unkempt place expressed his inner feelings as he sat in an ordinary but comfortable chair in a settlement house parlor: "How nice you have it here. Comfortable chairs, nice lamps, good magazines, and the place so clean. I wish we had a living room like this in my house."

Homeownership promotes family solidarity. Most homeowners do not own their properties outright except after a number of years, but, whether the property is clear of debt or is being paid for over a period of years, it nevertheless is "owned," both in the eyes of the purchasers and of others. The process of acquiring a home, with its attendant upkeep, directs a substantial amount of income toward this goal. A growing sense of security characterizes the family as the task is being accomplished. "Did I write you in my last letter," says a young lady, "that our little home will soon be our very own? We have just three more payments to make, and I just can't tell you how happy we are we took your advice and bought our home."[3] The attachment to a house that increases over the years is described by Edith Wharton for one husband who was writing at his desk in his home, when he heard a voice say, "This used to be one of the old Cesnola rooms." At once his mind reverted in memory to the important things in his life that had occurred in that room; the news from his wife that she was to have their first child; the christening of their eldest son by a venerable old friend who was Bishop of his church;

Dwellings: the sod hut of an Eskimo family, a Burmese family and home, and a typical "long house" of an extended patrilocal Congolese family.

and many other events that made the room and the house priceless to him.[4]

II. FAMILY FUNCTIONS

The Family Has Definite Functions Ascribed to It as a Social Institution

The family everywhere is controlled, sustained, and protected by the society's mores and laws. Societies use the family in whatever form it has developed to perform definite functions which each ascribes to it. Some of these functions could be performed in other ways and by agencies other than the family—some the family performs only in part—but by and large the family is the most efficient human relationship structure devised by society for accomplishing certain essential functions.

BIOLOGICAL FUNCTION The basic ascribed function, the bearing of children, has already been presented in some detail in our discussion of marriage as the institution that inaugurates the family. The importance of this function is re-emphasized by indicating that the preservation of the species is the end on which all other ends of life are dependent. The family, therefore, has assigned to it the most important function to be discharged in any society.

SOCIALIZING FUNCTION The second ascribed function is rearing children to the stage that the society considers to be normal manhood and womanhood. Here the family has the task of transforming a bit of impulsive biological flesh that can respond, learn, and grow into a socialized participating member of society. This means organizing and regulating habits and patterning actions that are acceptable to the society. This the family does by the use of parental authority and parental affection until the children accept rights, privileges, and obligations, not as demands and deprivations but as opportunities and self-imposed responsibilities.

SUSTENANCE FUNCTION The third function societies expect the family to perform is to provide sustenance for the family members. Food, clothing, shelter, and other necessities could be provided for a society's members in other ways than through the family. Societies, however, usually give this task to the family. Other institutional patterns could hardly provide the daily care and personal protection that families give by their homemaking, nor could they do it in the intimate ways that are so significant in personality-building. Family housekeeping provides necessary nutrition, a sanitary abode, a place for relaxation, and direct attention to illnesses and other personal requirements. A breadwinner—usually the husband; the bread dispensers—husbands and wives together; and a housekeeper—usually the wife, operating together in a home to provide care for dependent offspring, compose the institutional pattern most societies think best suited for these important tasks.

PROPERTY TRANSMISSION   A fourth function given to this institution is the holding and transmission of property. Families almost surely accumulate such personal property as land and other real estate, goods, money, and other forms of wealth to which they have recognized title. The use and transmission of this property is usually prescribed by rules of the society. The rules vary from society to society, but in general property is held and its use determined by the recognized head of the family, whether it be a male- or female-type of social organization. In some societies, family rights to land are limited, and the right of disposal rests in the clan or tribe. The ownership and use of land are main elements in family functioning and chief factors in maintaining its unity where the society is an agricultural one.

The industrialization of societies has lead to the creation of property forms that did not previously exist. Societies make rules about the inheritance of the family estate, whether it consists of real or personal property, for the purpose of giving protection to family members and conserving the interests of the society. While from a philosophical viewpoint, Aristotle's suggestion that the main question is not who owns property but how property is used may be sound, most families are concerned with its ownership and transmission since ownership usually determines the right to its use in most societies.[5]

CULTURAL TRANSMISSION   A fifth function societies universally expect families to help perform is to pass on the cultural heritage. They do not depend upon the family to do this alone because all the associations and associates outside of the family lend a hand in instilling the social norms in the members of the family. But the family is the first institution to get the opportunity to transmit the ideals, beliefs, and values of a society to the pliable mind of the growing child. It introduces the child to the world of meanings by which it is to order its life in the larger society. The family serves as "the natural and convenient channel of social continuity." Where it does this effectively it is the whole social world in epitome to the child.

The Family Performs Some Specific Functions for Its Individual Members

PRIMARY GROUP OPERATION   One of the significant characteristics of the family as a social institution is its functioning as a primary group, made possible because it usually includes only a few persons. The members are bound together by blood ties, usually live in the same household, eat and sleep under the same roof, and have mutual responsibilities imposed by kinship connections supported by social regulations which demand frequent, intimate contacts. Thus, we are related to each other in a family by the vital problems each of us has relative to goals, status, and values. Social distance is eliminated, and spontaneous associations predominate. It is the one institution in which we operate throughout our whole life in intimate, personal, primary group contacts based on sympathy and solicitude. The reciprocal dependence and close associations of family members have no parallel in any other human relationship structure.

PERSONALITY INFLUENCES   The family serves its individual members in distinctive ways because of these unique primary relationships. First, it develops basic personality, which emerges from the prolonged, unaffected socializing contacts that direct our undisciplined responses into a character pattern. Not only is the family the womb in which our nature as a person is created, we become a reflection of this environment. Because family members become our models, our imitation of their behavior begets like responses in us. Their self-control, habits of honesty, truthfulness, kindness, practices of orderliness, cleanliness, and aesthetic appreciation are all reflected in our character.

SOCIAL POSITION   Second, our family bequeaths a social position to each of us. The family into which we are born has already acquired a social position that is "known" in the community. This "knowledge" is a part of the heritage with which we must live.

An important factor in transmitting status to family members in Western societies is the quality of behavior families exhibit and the extent of their participation in community activities. We are fortunate if our families bequeath to us the respect of the society because of their accomplishments and behavior. When our family is already in disrepute because of unacceptable forms of behavior, we have to start out in an environment that sets handicaps for us. Even more unfortunate is the likelihood that our own personalities will be damaged by the influences of such relationships.

In the conjugal system, however, not much stress is placed on family names and tradition. In some small segments of the society, family name is considered important, as among the so-called First Families of Virginia, the aristocrats of Boston, or wealthy families who have or are striving to attain social recognition. But there is no societal pattern that makes the inheritance of family background a key to open the door of respect or opportunity to us. We may earn them, in spite of limiting conditions, in a society where each family is on its own.

PSYCHOLOGICAL NEEDS   A third specific function the family performs for the individual is the satisfaction of basic psychological needs. In general, the behavior of the individual in society is motivated by basic physiological urges, particularly hunger and sex, and by acquired desires built on inherited equipment from stimulations of the environment. As we have noted earlier, one of the most commonly used listings of these desires is that of Thomas and Znaniecki who classify them as (1) the desire for security, (2) for social recognition, (3) for new experience, and (4) for intimate response.

Each of us wants a sense of *security*. The uncertainties of life create anxieties and fears that lead us to strive for conditions that eliminate them.

Job security, for example, is certainly an important value in the lives of workers. If it is threatened in any way, anxiety and poor morale result. Economic insecurity, which has traditionally beset old age, has been reduced by our modern social security programs. The feeling that we "belong" and are accepted in our various groups satisfies this need in a somewhat different way.

We also want to be *recognized*, to count for something with other people. Many of our activities are founded on the desire for admiration. The student who works to win an athletic letter or a Phi Beta Kappa key is exhibiting the force of this desire.

We also want *new experiences*. Life has little novelty for many of us. Our job is routine, and our daily round of habitual activities gets monotonous. A function of the motion picture, the television, or the mystery story is to allow us to have new experiences vicariously. A large number of students were asked what they would

do if they were free to follow their desires and did not have to worry about cost. The answer from an overwhelming majority was, "We would travel; we would go places and see things." The billions spent annually in travel by people everywhere attests to the force of this desire and expresses a curiosity about the larger world stimulated by limited or vicarious experience.

But we want, in addition, *intimate response*. We want to count with some other persons for what we actually are. We need associates in whom we can completely confide. Curiously, it appears impossible for us to develop many friendships to the point of complete intimacy where another person can be, as Aristotle puts it, an "alter ego," or other self.

Relationships between the members of the family can develop to the point where this form of union arises through loving and being loved. Here loyalty can be complete, and even adversity can have a uniting effect. To achieve complete reliance and constancy in family life, its members remove all restraints upon sentiment; in so doing, they receive profound and lasting satisfaction. As William Wordsworth put it:

> We live by admiration, hope, and love;
> And even as these are wisely mixed
> In dignity of being we ascend.[6]

III. CHANGES IN THE FAMILY

The Family Like Other Social Forms Has Been Undergoing Changes

We pointed out in Chapter 8 that institutions change, both in structure and function. A cardinal fact in today's life is the rapidity of social change. The family, like other institutions, must make adaptations to new cultural conditions for it also operates in the larger cultural system. Much has been written about "our changing family," with some students going so far as to suggest that it might possibly be abandoned. Only a few persons take such an extreme view, but all students recognize a number of significant changes in its structure and functioning. We now consider these changes particularly from the viewpoint of Western societies. Modifications of similar types are, of course, occurring in other societies as well. For example, in Japan the large family household is disappearing with the growth of cities and industries. For centuries, the married sons lived with their parents in the large patriarchal family, but now they are establishing homes of their own. The desire to maintain the large household is still present, but cultural changes are causing these important modifications.[7] Similar changes were going on also in China before the Communists came to power.

Several Specific Factors Are Basic in Bringing About Changes in the Family

INDUSTRIALIZATION   Four specific factors associated with these changes should be presented before we discuss them. The industrialization of the economic system should be mentioned first. There are three consequences of this process that are especially significant for the family: (1) The factory system dispersed the employment of family members and thus broke up the family as a working unit. (2) The money basis of operation through which each worker received his own wages tended to support individualism. (3) The enormous increase in the number and variety of available jobs released women from their economic dependence on man.

URBANIZATION   The second force is the urbanization of societies. It is not so much that larger proportions of the population live in urban centers (63 per cent in 1960 in the United States; 15 per cent in 1850), but that urbanization makes for a degree of homogeneity in the values and experience of people. Under its influence, cultural islands tend to disappear because they have great difficulty withstanding the impact of the general social order where they do survive. The patriarchal family can hardly survive in environments where the idea of equality has spread throughout the social structure. On the other hand, the impersonality and anonymity characteristic of urban life create detachment from established standards and tend to change them. These forces change family standards, also.

DEMOCRATIC IDEALS   A third force is the growth of democratic ideals. The ideas of freedom and equality of opportunity supplanted autocratic doctrines of individual and class privilege. Equality before the law most clearly expresses the broad ideal. We have fallen short of extending democracy to all relationships, yet, as James Bryce remarks, "taken all in all, [it has] given better practical results than either the rule of a man or the rule of a class."[8]

It was almost certain therefore that these ideas would influence family organization and operation. The European patriarchal system could not continue in a frontier land like America where women and children were as important as men in maintaining the family as the basic unit of survival. Paternal authority and the submission of women and children had to give way. Its foundations were further weakened by the growing economic independence of women. (See Box 17.)

RELIGIOUS VIEWS   Changes in religious interpretations also have played a role in effecting change in the family. Christian theology had interpreted God as a father, but the picture often painted him as a demanding and punishing father. Often this view had been used to justify a control by the male family head that demeaned other family members—women especially were regarded as inferior. Newer interpretations of the character of God have changed such notions.

The religious attitude toward sex and the family has undergone change. No longer are the sex relations of husbands and wives regarded as sinful. Attitudes toward controlling family size are slowly changing, also. The Methodist Church, largest of the American Protestant denominations, voted, in its 1956 General Conference, that "planned parenthood, practiced in Christian conscience, may fulfill rather than violate the will of God." Other denominations have recently adopted the same position. Such changes in religious thinking profoundly influence family operation since it is one of the powerful social disciplines.

The Average Size of Families Has Decreased in American Society

EXTENT OF CHANGE   A first important change in the family institution relates to its size, which has been declining steadily. The average number of persons in each family in 1790, the date of the first United States Census, was 5.8 persons. In 1960, it was 3.68.[10] From 1930 to 1957, the average size of households declined from 4.11 to 3.42 while the median size dropped from 3.40 to 3.02.[11] Moreover, the changes in the proportion of families of different size emphasize this decline in average size. Over recent decades, families of moderate to small size have been supplanting large families in this society.[12]

FACTORS RESPONSIBLE   Two factors have been chiefly responsible for the long-run decline in the average size of the biological family: lower birth rates and the survival of increasing numbers of aged people. The past decline in the child-bearing function in the American popu-

BOX 17   ROLE-REVERSAL?

Today's educated young men want wives who are their equals in intellect and education. But the educated gals have a different idea. They want husbands who will dominate them. This all came out in a recent survey of college students.

So who'll have their way?

The men, naturally. When they say they want wives who are their equal they are saying they don't want the responsibility for being the big, strong, he-men who are heads of their houses.

They want wives who can make decisions, balance budgets, handle the children without bothering the papas, help the men get ahead by being social assets, and, if necessary, manage jobs with one hand and a home with the other.

Today's young men don't want to be boss because they don't want that much responsibility. Why marry clinging vines when they can marry girls who can be depended on to carry at least half of the load and maybe more?

The girls are going to be disappointed, all right, if they really think they are going to find husbands who will dominate them.

The modern woman is often accused of being too domineering for the good of the family. She is blamed for the fact that at home she rules the roost.

But the truth is that the modern woman has become head of the house because the modern American male doesn't want to be head of the house.

He has found it is much easier to turn the management of the family over to his wife than to take the responsibility himself.[9]

---

lation is vividly revealed by comparing the proportion of young children in 1800 and in 1950. In 1800, there were 1342 children under five years of age in the population per 1000 white women 20 to 44 years old. The figure had dropped to 551 a century and a half later. Moreover, between 1940 and 1960 the proportion of women of child-bearing age (15–45) in the total population declined from 24.3 per cent to 20.1 per cent, while the proportion of people 65 years of age and older increased from 6.0 per cent to 9.2 per cent.[13]

PURPOSIVE CONTROL   The most significant factor associated with this decrease has been the purposive decision by married couples to limit the size of their families. Several hundred million dollars' worth of birth-control materials are used each year to accomplish this. Birth control is now almost a part of the folkways of the society. The majority of people accept and use it, although it is opposed by some religious bodies. Behind this use is the desire for a good level of living that is more attainable if there are not too many children for whom to provide.

In earlier periods, children were an economic asset. Working on the farm or in industry from an early age, they helped their families to gain economic security. A number of factors, however, have changed this condition. School and child-labor laws raised the age at which a child may begin to work. Changes in production methods, especially mechanization, made it increasingly difficult for children to find remunerative work. The need for help from children on farms, for example, has steadily decreased. At the same time, the cost of rearing a number of children seriously affects the family budget. The expense of rearing children up to eighteen years of age in urban families ranged from $7766 for families with $2500 incomes in 1935 to $31,000 for families with annual incomes of $10,000 in 1950. Tarver estimates that the cost of rearing and educating a farm child at 1954 prices through age eighteen was more than $15,000.[14]

Recent years have seen a reversal of these fertility trends (the so-called "population explosion"), which may indicate that young couples now feel that larger families can be enjoyed without serious sacrifice in levels of living since working conditions and social security programs make the economic outlook less precarious. It may also indicate that married couples want larger families as early as circumstances permit. The assertion that married people do not want children has probably never been true for any significant proportion of the population.

FAMILY MAINTENANCE BY THE AGED The survival of increasing proportions of our aged population and their maintenance of independent homes also influence the average size of the family. In 1900, only 4.2 per cent of the population was 65 years of age or over; in 1960, the proportion had more than doubled (9.2 per cent).[15] This aging of the population has increased the proportion of two-person families.

Aged couples wish to keep their own homes. Public programs of old-age security and increasing accumulations of savings make it possible for more older people to accomplish this. The result has been to reduce the average size of the family in the society at large.

The Manner of Providing Family Sustenance Has Changed

ECONOMIC FUNCTIONING A second change is in the way the family operates to provide for itself. Not long ago our society was predominantly agricultural, our population was rural, and our families were producing units in which each member had a definite assignment in the productive enterprise. Families, even those living in villages and towns, worked together on the farm, in the store, or in the home to produce a living for the family. Earnings usually went into the family fund. Beers points out that as late as 1929 farm youth in New York received only small sums as farm wages, spending money, or allowance during a year. At least four out of each ten youth did not receive any money and nine out of each ten did not receive as much as 50 dollars in the year.[16]

Today, the members of the family work at a variety of separate occupations to earn the living for the family. Even farming has become so completely mechanized that it has ceased to be self-sufficient.

Families increasingly buy their meals in restaurants and hotels, have their clothes laundered by outside agencies, and have their houses or apartments cleaned by commercial concerns. Our society now has a machine-marketing economy in which goods are produced with machines for a market and the money proceeds used for further production and consumption needs. The family is now much like the general society. Individual family members work at separate jobs producing goods for the market, for which they are paid wages or salaries and with which they buy the necessary consumption materials for their family. The production of consumption goods like bread, butter, and clothing is turned over to specialized establishments. The family members find employment so they can furnish these necessities. The children usually contribute to the family budget by paying some sum for board and room after they begin to work. The function of providing sustenance still remains a family one, only the manner of its provision has changed markedly.

MARRIED WOMEN WORKING Wives and mothers certainly worked to help the economic status of the family in pre-industrial days. They did farm chores, made all meals, preserved food, cared for the garden, cared for all clothing, clerked in the store, ran the post office, or handled the telephone exchange. Practically all this work was done in the home or within easy reach of it and was part of a family economic enterprise.

In 1890, 14 per cent of the nearly four million women fourteen years of age and over in the labor force were married. By 1960, of the 23 million women in the labor force, 60 per cent were married.[17] This increase in the proportion of married women employed outside the home has taken place at a more rapid rate than the increases in our population.

The earnings of these married women who work are important contributions to family income and help account for the better levels of living enjoyed. In the past, most married women worked to supplement the meager incomes of their husbands. Today, larger proportions are motivated by the desire to maintain or promote a higher standard of family living.

The most serious problem connected with a working mother is providing for the care of children in her absence. Under older conditions, the working mother was usually near at hand, and her children often helped her. Now the work of the mother takes her to the factory or office and away from her home. Some other person or organization must watch over the children if they are small. Wives with preschool children, however, work outside the home in only 10 per cent of the cases. That older children are commonly left to their own devices is a factor related to youthful delinquencies.

Relationships Within the Family Have Become More Democratic

CLOSENESS OF FAMILY RELATIONS The family has always been an institution characterized by close relationships among its members. Survival in early families depended upon this cohesion. A major reason for the development of patriarchal forms—with authority vested in the oldest male—was to assure unity. Relationships were intimate, although their chief characteristic was obedience to the head as overlord.

Initiative by the members was allowed scant opportunity to develop. Such families protected themselves by presenting a solid front when their welfare was jeopardized. They also provided security since care for their members, especially the aged, was an essential family obligation. This does not mean that genuine affection and pride were lacking in these families. Many maintained these sentiments particularly where parents used their authority wisely. The Frake family as described in *State Fair* is an example. They were all proud of each other. They were not egotistical about the family, but they were especially happy to be a part of it. The wife regarded her husband and children with great admiration, and the husband always felt his wife to be young and attractive. The children rejoiced in their unusual parents.[18]

CHANGE IN THE NATURE OF THE RELATIONSHIPS Changes in the relationships among family members do not necessarily mean either greater or lesser intimacy of the interaction; rather, it is the nature of the relationships that has changed. Our families are moving from units of persons loyal to each other out of obligation to units of persons loyal to each other because of more spontaneous affection and devotion.

This change has not been easy to achieve. The deep-rooted, authoritarian ideas that the father has a heaven-given right to rule, that children are to be seen and not heard, and that the wife is to be obedient are difficult to eliminate. The conception of family relationships based upon the authority of principles is slowly replacing that based on the authority of persons. The emancipation of women and the assignment to children and young adults of a larger role in the operation of the family are big steps toward the ideal of a cooperative family life in which there is equality between husband and wife and where the personality of each member is respected. This development discards such autocratic attitudes as a father expressed in the following: "I'm goin' at four o'clock," said Ezra. "And I don't want to hear any more from any one . . . about the election. It's none of the business of the women an' boys."[19] It produces a condition in which the members are united in feeling and creates "an unconscious harmony that has nothing to do with authority."

The Formal Education Function Is Discharged by the School

AMERICAN FAMILY NEVER A FORMAL EDUCATIONAL AGENCY The family never operated in American society as a formal educational agency. In early colonial days, formal education was for the well-to-do, who paid for it themselves. Youth were sent to Europe for advanced schooling. Special higher schools to train in theology and law were set up but were attended by only a few. Most boys received their training for life by working with their fathers or some other adult to whom they were apprenticed. Girls were trained at home. The family was really the important agency of vocational preparation in the earliest days of American society. It still is an important educational agency in socializing family members, but the family has given the school the task of preparing youth for adult occupations and activities.

PUBLIC SCHOOL BEGINNINGS The institutionalization of education to include the whole youth population began in the seventeenth century. The general use of public-supported schools did not take place, however, until the nineteenth century. Today, in American society we require public school attendance of all youth from seven to about sixteen years of age, for a period of eight or nine months of each year. The child, then, is removed from the home for a considerable part of his developing life and given over to specialized training by specialized teachers with specialized equipment. It is impossible for individual families to provide all of this.

The school does not replace the home as the social and affectional center of the child's life. Rather, the school supplements the family while providing knowledge and experience which the latter cannot.

Recreational and Avocational Activities Have Changed in the Family

EARLY RECREATIONAL ACTIVITIES Our families have always taken part in recreational and advocational activities. Early American families found fun and relaxation in family calling, picnicking, church and community sociables, meals with relatives and friends, dancing, swimming, fishing, hunting, trapping, ice-skating and many other pastimes. Spatial separation, limited communications, and the seasonal demands of occupations tended to promote pleasure-seeking as a family. But when a family had arrived at a community picnic or a church supper, or had relatives or friends in for meals, they did not act together as a family. The men moved off to themselves, the women grouped together, and the young people soon separated from their parents. They broke down their activities by sex, age, and interest. Most of their recreation was, of course, homemade.

TODAY'S RECREATION Recreational and avocational programs promoted by voluntary organizations, by business and industry, and by governmental units, plus the development of commercial recreation, have been added to modern living. They supplement family life. Their growth is a result of increasing population, the ease of transportation, more available leisure time, their relatively low cost, and the development of passive and vicarious participation. Nearly 20 million "fans" attended major league baseball games in America in 1961. This is only a small part of the total commercial amusement activity in our society in a year. It indicates nothing of the vastness of the participant avocational programs of our innumerable voluntary organizations. It tells nothing of the amount of our leisure time spent watching television's 54 million sets in use at the beginning of 1960 or listening to radio's 55 million home sets in the same year.

Three conclusions that we often draw about these new developments are (1) that they are participated in by the individual family members without reference to each other, (2) that most of the activity is simply observer participation, and (3) that most of it goes on outside the home. These conclusions deserve at least brief critical examination.

Parental Participation It is easy for us to overlook the extent to which fathers play "catch" with their sons in the backyard, teach them how to "bat," kick a football, swim or fish, or the ways mothers may work with daughters in Girl Scouts or other activities. Millions of fathers and mothers work as advisers and coaches in the programs of our voluntary organizations. Almost all fathers and mothers attend the activities of their children out of pride of parenthood and a desire to encourage their offspring.

Observer Participation Upheld The assumption is also made that there is something wrong with observer participation and that true value can be realized only through active participation. Observer participation, however, may be the most beneficial kind for persons who should not try to perform because of age or other limitations. Modern homes, of course, are often not suited to many of the forms of present-day recreation, but our facilities are vastly increased in the community. The home television set has become a standard fixture, but reading to family members is not altogether a lost practice in American culture. Automobiles, while they are often used for individual purposes, frequently require family decisions about their use. Annual vacations almost always involve the whole family.

Participation as a Family Characteristic Studies of both formal and informal social participation show that they are characteristic of modern families. Where husbands participate in social and recreational activities, wives usually do; where parents participate, their children do, also. This is particularly true of self-initiated activities engaged in for pleasure. Families in all stages of the family cycle engage in a large number of informal recreational activities together, including visiting and taking meals with others, auto-riding, picnicking, and attending shows. These, combined with the new opportunities in commercial recreation, probably give our families more group recreation than ever before available.[20]

Religious Practices of Family Members Have Changed

MEMBERSHIP IN CHURCHES If statistics on church membership are indications, American families are interested in religion. The most recent report (1961) shows that about 60 per cent of the people of the United States are affiliated with the 319,000 local churches.[21] Church membership was estimated at only 10 per cent in 1790.

American churches have been expanding with our expanding society. In their early beginnings, churches held services when itinerant preachers or lay ministers were available. Sunday schools for instructing the children became part of the programs. Strong emphasis was placed upon such practices as family prayers, daily Bible reading, and grace at meals. In early American society, these developed as family religious rituals to supplement regular church worship. It was believed that regular worship should be conducted by ordained preachers who visited only infrequently.

WEEKDAY CHURCH ACTIVITIES Organizations involving weekday activities have multiplied with the expansion of our churches. Churches now have units for all age, sex, and married groupings. Practically all of these begin their activities with some worship. At the same time, the occupational diversity of our family members and the need to meet different time schedules make the maintenance of common family worship in the home more difficult than when the family worked together in the same place.

There is little evidence to support the statement that there is either an increase or decrease in religious practices by our families. It is correct to conclude that our rate of affiliation with religious institutions indicates that our participation in religious worship is extensive in America. It is probably reasonable to say that family participation in religious activities is also widespread.

Kinship Interdependence Is Still an Important Aspect of Modern Family Relations

CONJUGAL FAMILY OPERATION Our discussion of the family has considered it as a *conjugal* unit, that is, as a unit of husband, wife, and their offspring. Most Western societies are organized about this family form. Constituted of interlocking conjugal families, they are surrounded by relatives—grandparents, aunts and uncles, nieces and nephews—who are blood relatives and "in-laws" to whom they are bound by marriage. Other societies may be organized around the *consanguine family*, which includes "a nucleus of blood relatives surrounded by a fringe of spouses" called the extended family.[22]

A basic trait of the modern Western family is thus its operation as a conjugal unit that is largely separated from relatives. It stresses the unity of the spouses. Each such family normally has its own household and lives a fairly separate life that involves economic self-support, separate occupational activity, and often geographical distance. Because contacts with relatives are infrequent, the individual family must largely rely upon itself and its own initiatives. The responsibilities of the members are first and foremost to each other and only secondarily, if at all, to other kin.

RESPONSIBILITIES OF RELATIVES Kinfolk also need recognize no basic responsibilities to a particular family since they are operating their own conjugal families. However, the constant subdivision of kinship relations within our society does not mean there are no social relations between relatives. It appears from several sources that there are interrelations and much interdependence among them. The fact that these are voluntary and not obligatory, except as society itself defines limited responsibilities in cases of serious need, accounts for the prime difference between conjugal family systems and consanguine ones. Families have interlocking responsibilities in consanguine systems, while in conjugal systems relatives, even parents, are not expected to intrude.

MUTUAL AID BETWEEN RELATIVES Several studies indicate that, although each conjugal family is independent, there is still considerable mutual aid among them, especially with parents and their children. In a study of 195 parent-child relationships in 1950, 79 per cent of the parents had given some financial aid to their children in the purchase of a home, the purchase of household equipment, landscaping, or vacations. The parents expected to be included in some of the activities of their children's families in return and to receive some personal attention. The flow of financial aid was in one direction—from parents to their children. The children reciprocated by showing their appreciation.[23]

In a study of 723 Detroit, Michigan, families in 1954–1955, 69 per cent of the families had both given and received help from their relatives, 10 per cent had received help, and 14 per cent had given help. Only 7 per cent of them had neither given nor received help. Aid included baby-sitting, help during illness, financial aid, business advice, help in getting employment, help with housework, and gifts. Sixty-five per cent of the parents gave help to their children, 46 per cent of the children gave help to their parents. Fifty-four per cent of the brothers and sisters gave each other help. Only 17 per cent received help from other relatives. Parents, children, and siblings exchanged help more than distant relatives. Over-all, then, parents give help to their children more than children give help to their parents.[24]

Similar patterns of interdependence are indicated for farm families. In a study of 150 farms in Iowa, it was found that family arrangements were important for seven out of ten farmers beginning a farm operation. Over half of the farmers relied on their relatives to locate a farm to begin on. Farm operators whose parents or parents-in-law were farm owners were likely to begin operations through family arrangements and were likely to begin earlier than farm operators whose parents were not farm owners.[25]

SOCIAL RELATIONSHIPS Interrelations between kin are not limited to forms of aid. Other associations are widespread. Of 961 families in villages and rural counties of New York State, two of each three associated in informal activities with at least one family which was related to them, while one in each five associated only with families related to them. Three-fourths of the related families with whom associations were carried on involved their parents, their children, or their siblings. Kinship also holds families in association with each other over wider geographic areas than do friendships.[26] But interrelations between kin do not extend significantly beyond the circle of parents and their children's families.

IV. THE FAMILY CYCLE

Families Pass Through a Series of Characteristic Stages

CHANGE IN COMPOSITION Most analyses, including our own, treat the conjugal family as if it were a relationship form that remains constant in composition through its existence. But it is obvious that it changes continually. Each family has a definite beginning with the marriage of a couple and a definite end at the death of the last spouse. Between these two points, the family undergoes change in composition as children are born, grow up, and leave the home, and as the husband and wife themselves grow old and pass away. The life of a family is subject to biological processes that give it a fixed beginning and a fixed end. The family, to a greater degree than other institutions, is controlled by an organic cycle.

CHANGES IN OPERATION It is also inevitable that each aspect of the family's operation will be altered as it undergoes these changes in composition. Needs, wants, goals, internal family relations, and community relations cannot escape the impact of these fluctuations. The process is a continuum. But it is possible for us to divide the continuum into stages in which there are certain dominant characteristics. One of the

earliest of these sequences was devised by B. S. Rowntree. He plotted the life cycle of the poorer families in England in relation to a poverty line. His analysis shows a period of comparative prosperity after marriage until there are two or three children. Then comes a period of poverty until the first child is about fourteen years of age and begins to work. While the children earn, they contribute to a second period of prosperity. Then the family may again sink into poverty when the children marry and leave home.[27] Others have described the family cycle using other measures as a basis for their divisions. All, however, devise some system of marital, child-bearing, and child-rearing periods which are then related to social factors to show how the stages influence them.[28]

A CLASSIFICATION OF FAMILY STAGES A classification of the stages in the family life cycle developed at Cornell University recognizes six family periods based on the age of the children: [29]

1. The Pre-Child or Early Husband-Wife stages—wife is less than 45 years old.
2. The Young-Child stage—all children are less than 10 years old.
3. The Young-Older Child stage—some children are less and some older than 10 years of age.
4. The Older-Child stage—all children are 10 years of age or older.
5. The Post-Child or late Husband-Wife stage—wife is 45 years of age or more; no children at home.
6. The Widow-Widower stage—one of the mates not living and all children away from home.

Families must make adjustments to the changing ages of members, the number in the family, varying economic conditions, housing needs, and other circumstances that arise as they pass from one stage to another. For example, the social participation in formal organizations and in informal activities is significantly different from stage to stage. Relationships within the family and with other persons, organizations, and institutions reflect the influence of the stage of its development.[30]

V. THE YOUNG AND THE OLD IN THE MODERN FAMILY

The Child's Family Role Has Changed

Samuel Johnson insisted that "the rod produces an effect which terminates in itself. A child is afraid of being whipped, and gets his task, and there's an end on't; whereas, by exciting emulation and comparisons of superiority, you lay the foundation of lasting mischief." [31] Thackeray once observed: "I never saw people on better terms with each other, more frank, affectionate and cordial, than the parents and the grown-up young folks in the United States. And why? Because the children were spoiled, to be sure." [32]

These statements imply opposite views—both of which have been held in our society—of the position of the child. Our early American heritage accepted the authoritarian European position in which strict submission of children to their parents was the rule. "Spare the rod and spoil the child" and "Children are to be seen and not heard" were harsh dicta expressing the norm. This view, however, has succumbed to the modern American pattern of family democracy. The child's role in the family has therefore changed significantly—some would say drastically. Now children are considered as recognized personalities with potentialities to be tenderly developed. They are accorded the right to challenge their elders with sharp queries as to why, how, and what. Their questions, wishes, and views are felt to deserve thoughtful, if not obsequious, consideration by parents who presumably are in agreement on their purposes. Many a modern parent, feeling that the "filiocentric trend" has gone too far, can sympathize with Sam Levinson who complains, "When I was a boy, I had to do what my parents wanted me to do. *Now* I have to do what my children want me to do. When am I ever going to do what *I* want to do?"

In any event, in at least the middle-class model, children are seen as inexperienced explorers who seek to discover their own social roles under the gentle, and often confused, guidance of their most immediate and intimate associates.

The Changing Pattern of Family Functioning in Western Societies Has Created New Conditions for the Aged

POSITION OF THE AGED IN CONSANGUINE FAMILIES In the consanguine family system the problems of the aged are no more serious than those of the other members. All prosper or suffer together. Respect for the aged members is a basic characteristic of this system. "Honor thy father and thy mother" expresses the veneration of the elders in the traditional consanguine group. [33] The Chinese book of filial piety said: "It [filial piety] commences with the service of parents; it proceeds to the service of ruler; it is completed by the establishment of character." The system of ancestor worship that dominated China's social life for centuries grew from this philosophy. It gave their aged a position of respect that led them to look forward to the coming of old age when they could be cared for and honored by their sons.

POSITION IN EARLY AMERICAN FAMILIES The position of the aged in our society presented no serious problems so long as we were chiefly agricultural. As old age arrived, farms, stores, or other business activities were transferred to sons or sons-in-law. As late as 1885 to 1900, 59 per cent of the sons of farmers in New York counties followed their fathers' occupation, with a large proportion of them taking over their families' farms. [34] Parents continued to live in their farm house, in a smaller one nearby, or with some of their married children. The care of the parents, where necessary, was clearly a responsibility of their sons and daughters.

CHANGES IN RELATIONSHIPS OF AGED A number of social changes today present new problems for the aged. The separation of family of orientation and family of procreation is characteristic of our nuclear family. The strong sense of responsibility for parents that once prevailed has weakened decidedly. Our industrial system puts a premium on youth, so more and more older workers become jobless. Sudden retirement in a society where there is little preparation for it and the frequent absence of avocational interests leave many elders with little to do and little to do with. Increased mobility that scatters their sons and daughters to places of work and residence far from the family home and the engagement of their children in forms of work they do not share can create in the elders a deep sense of loneliness. (See Box 18.) Parents with a European cultural background may feel that their Americanized children reject them and their cherished values.

Social distance between generations is created when a rise in social position takes the children out of the parental social class and often leaves the parents with the feeling that they have no family at all. Financial help may be needed, but if it is proffered, perhaps reluctantly, by the children the aged parents may suffer an embarrassing sense of dependency. If simple economic need is complicated by physical

---

BOX 18   FRIENDSHIPS IN OLD AGE

The effects that widowhood or retirement have on the friendships of older people [are] found to vary with the prevalence of these changes in status within the age, sex, and class structure in which the individual is located. In those groups where widowhood and retirement are relatively rare either change in status places the individual in a deviant position among his peers, differentiates his interests and experiences from those of his associates, and thereby exerts a detrimental effect on friendships. In those structural contexts, however, where these changes in status are prevalent, it is the still married or employed individual who occupies a deviant position in relation to his peers and whose social life therefore tends to become more restricted.[35]

---

and mental illness, the suffering may become intense.[36]

SIZE OF THE AGING PROBLEM   The size of the problem of the aged in American society increases with each succeeding decade. In 1900, one in each 25 persons in the United States was 65 years of age or over. A half century later, one in each twelve was of these ages. It is estimated that the proportion will increase to about one in each ten by 1970. The population 65 years of age and over increased over fourfold in a half century, while the total population increased twofold.[37]

AGING, WORK, AND SECURITY   Accompanying this increase is a significant decrease in the proportion of the older male population that is in the labor force. Over 60 per cent of the males 65 years of age and over were in the labor force in 1900. It was only 46 per cent in 1950, and by 1970 it is expected to be about 38 per cent. This means that increasingly larger numbers and proportions of the aged males will no longer be economically productive. The development of the social security program has much significance in this regard. Since it allows persons to look forward to their older years without fear of serious want and dependency, it should be effective in removing one of the heaviest psychological burdens of the aged. It also may be a stimulant to more careful planning for the declining years.

HEALTH AND THE AGED   Health is another problem facing the older population. Medical needs and costs become larger burdens in later years. Health and medical advances have added years of life and have enabled increasing numbers of older married couples to enjoy their declining years together. The proposed program of "Medicare" would improve their circumstances still further. These advances in health

and economic support should establish a social and psychological security among the aged that offsets considerably the consequences of their alienation from the younger generation. Old age should be a pleasant experience, and aged persons, often shouldered from the scene, should have so satisfying a position that they thoroughly enjoy it.

VI. THE BREAKUP OF FAMILIES

The Breakup of Families Is as Much a Concern of Societies as Is Their Formation

The family may dissolve as a consequence of death, separation, desertion, or divorce. The ideal expectation of society is that it will endure until death breaks the relationship, and the great majority of marriages do so endure. Legal obligations, social controls, and the bonds of affection that develop between the married couple and between them and their children serve as strong cementing forces.

It is too much for us to expect, however, that all families will run their normal course. The variety of circumstances under which marriages take place, the differences in personalities, and the innumerable problems that prevent acceptable adjustments lead some families into crises that precipitate dissolution. For this reason, societies provide rules under which the marital relationship can be terminated in an acceptable way.

GRANTING DIVORCES   The granting of divorces is a society's responsibility just as is the granting of permission to marry. Societies control divorces primarily to protect marriages and families. Marriage is the only civil contract in Western societies that cannot be broken by mutual consent. Agreement by both parties to a divorce is construed as "imposing on the court," and the request for judicial action is denied. The premise upon which divorce is granted is that one of the married partners is guilty of acts upon the other that justify breaking the marriage. Divorce is denied if both parties are guilty of behavior that would justify breaking the marriage if one of the parties were guilty. Nor are divorces granted upon the confession or unconfirmed testimony of couples. Such testimony must be supported by witnesses. The society seeks thus to support its own concern for the preservation of its families. It approves divorces only to protect itself from possibly greater harm. These controls may not be complied with completely in actual practice, but they do indicate the society's basic concern about this institution.

Divorce Is Widely Recognized

Divorces are easily obtained in many primitive societies where marriage is largely a matter of custom and is not rigidly binding. This is especially true where consanguine forms predominate or where the rupture comes before the birth of children. Sometimes, a divorce is effected by a partner by the simple act of taking leave of the other.

Divorce became more difficult to obtain as Western societies advanced through historic stages in which the conjugal family system began to emerge and in which the doctrines of Christianity imposed restrictions upon the dissolution of marriage. Divorce was seen as a threat to the conjugal family because adequate support for the wife and children would be difficult to arrange. Traditional Christianity considered marriage a sacrament and not to be dissolved by any other means than death.

In the modern era, social and religious changes have brought about widespread changes in the practice of divorce and in the attitudes toward it. Some of these are indicated in the discussion which follows.

Divorces Have Increased Rapidly in American Society

DIVORCE RATES Our civilian population of 127 million persons fourteen years of age and over in the United States included, in March, 1961, 2.4 per cent divorced persons, or more than three divorced for each 100 married persons. At the beginning of the century, divorced persons constituted only 0.4 per cent of the 51 million population of persons fourteen years of age and over. So the ratio of divorced persons to those of marriageable age has increased six times in a period of 60 years. During these six decades, the total population of marriageable age increased 2.5 times, while the number of divorced persons increased 15 times.[38] American couples, particularly since World War II, resort to divorce much more frequently than in earlier periods. Although laws governing divorce have changed little, it is evident that the conditions leading to divorce, as well as the attitude toward divorce, have changed remarkably in America. Comparative data show that divorce rates in the United States are considerably higher than those in other countries.

Divorces Occur More Generally in the Earlier Years of Marriage

Slightly over six of each ten divorces in the United States in 1955 took place during the first ten years of marriage. Over four of each ten occurred during the first five years. Only one in eleven took place after 25 or more years of marriage. The second and third years show the greatest risk of divorce since about one in five occur in this two-year period. One in fourteen, however, took place before the first year of marriage was over.[39] These facts indicate that if married couples can get past the early critical years of adjustment, the chances of divorce decline rapidly.

Divorce Occurs More Frequently Among the Childless

A large proportion of the persons receiving a divorce in American society are childless. The presence of children in a family may give a married couple a strong purpose that stabilizes their relationships. Also, Burgess and Locke point out that children and their care are important factors in the reconciliation of some divorced couples.[40] It is not known, however, whether childlessness is more common among divorced persons than among married persons with the same duration of marriage and related characteristics. All that can be said is that a large proportion of divorced persons are childless.

The Control of Divorce Is a State Responsibility in the United States

GROUNDS FOR DIVORCE The grounds for granting divorces in American society are determined by each state. These vary from states that recognize no grounds or only one, such as adultery, to those that recognize many. The grounds most generally recognized are cruelty, desertion, adultery, nonsupport, a felonious crime, and incompatibility. The large majority of American divorces, about two out of each three, are granted on the grounds of cruelty and desertion. These are found in state laws more generally than other causes. However, these "causes" often bear only slight relation to the circumstances that lead to divorce. Over eight out of each ten of American divorces go uncontested, that is, the accused fails to challenge the action when it is decided that divorce is necessary. Persons who live in states with strict divorce laws often establish residence in a state which is less stringent. Nevada, with its Reno, is noted for the ease with which persons may establish residence for divorce purposes. In 1959, its divorce rate was fifteen times the rate for the country as a whole.[41] As one moves into the West and South, divorces are granted more freely than in the more conservative East. A long campaign to establish uniformity in our divorce laws has so far been unsuccessful.

Social Changes Have Led to the Increased Use of Divorce in American Society

INDUSTRIALIZATION   A number of social changes in our society have had the dual effect of weakening the stability of the family and encouraging the use of divorce as the way out of an unhappy marriage. First is the industrialization of our society. Having freed women from dependence upon men, it has given them a status more nearly equal to that of men. The new occupational world of production and service jobs has made husbands economically less necessary to women and wives less necessary to men. Neither of them must marry nor stay married to solve their economic problems. Neither must accept personal relationships in circumstances that are considered unbearable to them. Industrialization does not cause divorce, but it does weaken the conditions that often held the family together in spite of its difficulties. Rural families that operate as economic units hold together better than urban families and less frequently end in divorce. The loss of this economic bond has probably had the consequence of allowing family differences to be magnified out of proportion to their real significance.

RELIGIOUS ATTITUDES   Variations in religious attitudes also influence the extent of divorce. England, which is as industrialized as America,

has a divorce rate much lower than America. The opposition of the Church of England to divorce is a strong factor in contrast to the more liberal attitude of the Protestant churches in America. Catholic countries, also, have, in general, lower divorce rates than Protestant ones.

EQUALITY AND INDIVIDUALISM   New viewpoints dominate our social order and create conditions that stimulate divorce. The stress upon equality and individualism introduces a condition of freedom that emphasizes our right to change our choices. Henrik Ibsen made Nora, the wife, express this individualistic view when her husband, in the discussion of her determination to leave her family, said: "Before all else you are a wife and mother." Her response: "That I no longer believe. I believe that before all else I am a human being, just as much as you are—or at least that I should try to become one. I know that most people, however, agree with you, Torvald, and that they say so in books. But henceforth I can't be satisfied with what most people say and what is in books. I must think things out for myself, and try to get clear about them." [42]

Cooley summarized the force of these new viewpoints on our families as follows:

> As regards affection, present conditions should apparently be favorable to the strength of the bond. Since personal choice is so little interfered with, and the whole matter conducted with a view of congeniality, it would seem that a high degree of congeniality must, on the whole, be secured. And indeed, this is without much doubt the case: nowhere, probably, is there so large a proportion of couples living together in love and confidence as in those countries where marriage is most free.
>
> Yet it is not inconsistent to say that this aim at love increases divorce. The theory being that the contracting parties are to be made happy; then, if they are not, it seems to follow that the relation is a failure and should cease: the brighter the ideal the darker the fact by contrast.[43]

COMMUNITY RESPONSIBILITY   A consequence of our philosophy of freedom and individualism may also be the loss of our sense of community responsibility. The public says, "It is not our business. Each family is on its own." The stabilizing support of the family by the community is lost if this is coupled with high family mobility within and between communities and if the family has shallow roots in our institutions and organizations.

The Real Causes of Divorce Lie in the Functioning of the Family

HUSBAND-WIFE RELATIONSHIPS   The real causes of divorces lie in the operation of the family—in husband-wife relationships—even though social changes make divorces easier to obtain. They do not lie in dissatisfaction with the family as such if the increasing rate of family formation is indicative. In 1900, 59.9 per cent of our males and 58.7 per cent of our females fourteen years of age and over were married. In 1960, in these same categories, 70 per cent of our males and 67.8 per cent of our females were married.[44] The same situation exists with remarriages. More than six out of seven divorced persons remarried in recent decades.[45]

The grounds societies recognize as sufficient to justify dissolving a family show that the difficulties lie in the relationships within it: cruelty, desertion, and nonsupport. But why should there be such relationships between persons who have joined together to maintain a family? A basic reason is the inability of two individuals with different personalities to adjust to each other acceptably. The ability to make such interpersonal adjustment may be undermined by (1) uncontrollable interferences, such as economic difficulties or parental intrusion; (2) wide differences in education and religion; (3) serious personality defects, such as alcoholism or psychopathic tendencies; and (4) personal disappointment in the results of marriage itself.

Annulments Also Dissolve Families

An annulment is a ruling by a court that no marriage ever existed and so was void from the beginning. The grounds on which annulments are granted are force, fraud, under age, and mental incapacity. Property claims, alimony, and other rights do not exist since the marriage is ruled never to have taken place. Most American annulments, which equal about 3 per cent of our total divorces, are granted in New York State and California.

Separations May Eventuate in Dissolving the Family

A large number of families presumably existing at a given time are at least temporarily not existing as complete units because one of the spouses has left the home. "Separated" persons may be away from the family because of legal permission, usually a period before divorce is made final, because they intend to obtain a divorce, or because of estrangement resulting from marital discord. There were 862,000 married women and 1,242,000 married men separated from their spouses for one or another of these reasons in March, 1956.[46] This is 2.6 separated spouses per 100 married persons. These separated persons probably represent a large proportion of the families in which break-up will be permanent. At least, they represent families in which relationships are tenuous. Legally separated spouses are still responsible for the care of their families. Desertion may be an attempt to avoid this responsibility.

There are other families in which spouses are separated from the home for relatively long periods of time due to employment, military service, recent migration, or incarceration in institutions. Most of these families are only temporarily inconvenienced, but the condition of separation sets the stage for the introduction of circumstances that could lead to break up.

VII. FUTURE OF THE FAMILY

Two Views of the Future of the Family May Be Taken: a Pessimistic One or an Optimistic One

A pessimistic view of the future of the family institution emphasizes the exceedingly high rate of family breakdown, especially in America, our overemphasis upon the individual and his right to complete freedom, the unwillingness of parents to assume responsibilities with regard to each other and their children, the loss of many functions that helped to bind family members to each other, and the lack of any effective public concern to assist families in trouble. This reasoning suggests that our family as an institution is approaching a crisis that will lead to collapse.

An optimistic view recognizes the rapid changes that this institution has experienced during recent decades and its consequent instability and weakness. But it would argue that these are evidences of a transition stage in which the family is moving to a firmer basis that assures greater permanence and stability because of finer relationships among its members. Entrance into marriage primarily on an affectional basis, the reduction of economic pressures, and the voluntary bearing and rearing of children would appear in the long run to provide the soundest foundation for an enduring family. It would have within itself the basic resources for its own stability.

References

1. Murdock, George Peter, *Social Structure* (New York, The Macmillan Company, 1949), p. 17.
2. United States Department of Commerce, Bureau of the Census, *Statistical Abstract of the United States, 1962,* Table 1071, p. 758.
3. Drucker, Saul, and Hexter, Maurice Beck, *Children Astray* (Cambridge, Mass., Harvard University Press, 1923), p. 369.
4. Wharton, Edith, *The Age of Innocence* (New York, Grosset and Dunlap, 1920), p. 347.
5. Aristotle, "Ethics," *The Student's Oxford*, 5 (New York, Oxford University Press, 1942), Book IX, pp. 1163 ff.
6. Wordsworth, William, "The Excursion," *The Poetical Works of William Wordsworth*, 5 (London, Macmillan and Company, 1896).
7. Matsumiya, Kazuya, "Family Organization in Present-Day Japan," *American Journal of Sociology*, 53 (September, 1947), pp. 105 ff.
8. Bryce, James, *Modern Democracies*, 2 (New York, The Macmillan Company, 1921), p. 562.
9. Millet, Ruth, "Are the Men Abdicating as Heads of Their Homes?," Newspaper Enterprise Association, *Journal-Every Evening* (Wilmington, Del., August 6, 1960).
10. United States Department of Commerce, Bureau of the Census, *Historical Statistics of the United States, 1789–1945* (1949), Series B171–181, p. 29, and Bureau of the Census, Series P 20, No. 106 (January 9, 1961), p. 2.
11. United States Department of Commerce, Bureau of the Census, *Historical Statistics of the United States, Colonial Times to 1957* (1960), Series A 225–263, p. 16.
12. Glick, Paul C., *American Families* (New York, John Wiley and Sons, Inc., 1957), Table 17, p. 30.
13. United States Department of Commerce, Bureau of the Census, *Historical Statistics of the United States, Colonial Times to 1957* (1960), Series 1337–68, p. 24, and *Statistical Abstract of the United States, 1962,* Table 18, p. 26.
14. Tarver, James D., "Cost of Rearing and Educating Farm Children," *Journal of Farm Economics*, 38 (February, 1956), pp. 144 ff.
15. United States Department of Commerce, Bureau of the Census, *Statistical Abstract of the United States, 1962,* Table 3, p. 6.
16. Beers, Howard W., "The Income, Savings and Work of Boys and Girls on Farms in New York, 1930," Cornell University AES (May, 1933), Bulletin 560.
17. United States Department of Commerce, Bureau of the Census, *Historical Statistics of the United States, Colonial Times to 1957* (1960), Series D26–35, p. 72, and United States Department of Commerce, Bureau of the Census, *Statistical Abstract of the United States, 1962,* Table 294, p. 225.
18. Strong, Phil, *State Fair* (New York, The Century Co., 1932), pp. 111 and 112.
19. Quick, Herbert, *The Brown Mouse* (Indianapolis, Ind., Bobbs-Merrill Company, Inc., 1915), p. 194.
20. Anderson, W. A., "Rural Social Participation and the Family Life Cycle," Cornell University AES (January, 1953), Memoir 318.
21. United States Department of Commerce, Bureau of the Census, *Statistical Abstract of the United States, 1962,* Table 46, p. 46.

22. Linton, Ralph, *The Study of Man* (New York, D. Appleton-Century Company, 1936), p. 159.
23. Sussman, Marvin B., "The Help Pattern in the Middle Class Family," *American Sociological Review*, 18 (February, 1953), pp. 22–28.
24. Sharp, Harry, and Axelrod, Morris, "Mutual Aid Among Relatives in an Urban Population," in Freedman, Ronald, *et al.*, *Principles of Sociology* (New York, Holt and Company, Inc., 1956), pp. 433 ff.
25. Rohwer, Robert A., "Social Relations in Beginning as a Farm Operator in an Area of Prosperous Commercial Farming," *Rural Sociology*, 14 (December, 1949), pp. 325 ff.
26. Anderson, W. A., "Some Factors Associated with Family Informal Participation," Cornell University AES (March, 1953), Department of Rural Sociology Bulletin 36.
27. Rountree, B. S., *Poverty, a Study of Town Life* (New York, The Macmillan Company, 1902), pp. 160 ff.
28. Lively, C. E., "The Growth of the Farm Family," Ohio AES (1932), Bulletin 51; Loomis, C. P., "The Growth of the Farm Family in Relation to Its Activities," North Carolina AES (1932), Bulletin 298; Kirkpatrick, E. L., "The Life Cycle of the Farm Family," Wisconsin AES, Bulletin 121; Loomis, C. P., and Hamilton, C. Horace, "Family Life Cycle Analysis," *Rural Sociology*, 1 (1936), p. 180; Duncan, O. D., "Analysis of Farm Family Organization in Oklahoma," Thesis for Ph.D. degree (Louisiana State University, 1941 [unpublished]); Blackwell, G. W., "Correlates of State of Family Development Among Farm Families on Relief," *Rural Sociology*, 7 (1942), p. 161; Miner, Horace, "The French-Canadian Family Cycle," *American Sociological Review*, 3 (October, 1938), p. 700; Bigelow, Howard F., "Money and Marriage," in Hill, Reuben, and Becker, Howard, *Marriage and the Family* (Boston, D. C. Heath and Company, 1942), p. 382; Abrams, Charles, and Dean, John P., "Housing and the Family," in Anshen, Ruth N., *The Family: Its Function and Destiny* (New York, Harper and Brothers, 1949), p. 314; Glick, Paul C., *American Families* (New York, John Wiley and Sons, Inc., 1957), Chaps. 3 and 4.
29. Anderson, W. A., "Rural Social Participation and the Family Life Cycle," Cornell University AES (January, 1953), Memoir 314, pp. 7 and 8.
30. *Ibid.*, pp. 11, 13, and 15.
31. Boswell, James, *The Life of Samuel Johnson, L.L.D.* (New York, Random House [Modern Library], 1931), p. 20.
32. Quoted in Cooley, Charles H., *Social Organization* (New York, Charles Scribner's Sons, 1920), p. 361.
33. Sorokin, P. A., Zimmerman, C. C., and Galpin, C. J., *A Systematic Source Book in Rural Sociology*, II (Minneapolis, Minn., University of Minnesota Press, 1931), p. 71.
34. Anderson, W. A., "The Transmission of Farming as an Occupation," Cornell University AES (October, 1941), Bulletin 768, Table 1, p. 19.
35. Blau, Zena S., "Structural Constraints on Friendships in Old Age," *American Sociological Review*, 26 (June, 1961), p. 429.
36. On the relationship between occupational and geographical mobility and family relationships, see Litwak, Eugene, "Occupational Mobility and Extended Family Cohesion," *American Sociological Review*, 25 (February, 1960), pp. 9–21, and Litwak, Eugene, "Geographic Mobility and Extended Family Cohesion," *American Sociological Review*, 25 (June, 1960), pp. 385–394.
37. United States Department of Commerce, Bureau of the Census, "Estimates of the

Population of the United States, July 1, 1957," *Current Population Reports*, 1957, Series p-25, No. 170, p. 1.

38. Computed from the United States Department of Commerce, Bureau of the Census, *Statistical Abstract of the United States, 1962,* Table 32, p. 37.

39. Computed from Jacobson, Paul H., *American Marriage and Divorce* (New York, Rinehart and Company, 1959), Table 71, p. 145. See also Monahan, T. C., "When Married Couples Part," *American Sociological Review*, 27 (October, 1962), pp. 625–633, which shows that "the first year is the hardest."

40. Burgess, Ernest W., and Locke, Harvey J., *The Family* (New York, American Book Company, 1945), p. 639.

41. United States Department of Commerce, Bureau of the Census, *Statistical Abstract of the United States, 1962,* Table 75, p. 70.

42. Ibsen, Henrik, *A Doll's House* (London, Walter Scott Press, 1900), p. 166.

43. Cooley, Charles H., *Social Organization* (New York, Charles Scribner's Sons, 1920), pp. 365 and 366.

44. United States Commerce Department, Bureau of the Census, *Statistical Abstract of the United States, 1962,* Table 30, p. 35, and Glick, Paul C., *American Families* (New York, John Wiley and Sons, Inc., 1957), pp. 131, 104, and 109.

45. Nimkoff, M. F., "The Family in the United States," *Marriage and Family Living*, 14 (November, 1954), pp. 390 ff.

46. United States Department of Commerce, Bureau of the Census, "Marital Status and Family Status: March 1956," *Current Population Reports*, Series P-20, No. 72, Table 1, p. 9.

Questions for Study and Discussion

1. How does the family differ from all other human relationship structures in mode of entrance?

2. What is the difference between the two types of families of which most individuals become members?

3. Which is the more common type of family residence as indicated by Murdock's study? What advantages and disadvantages do you see in each type?

4. Point out the major functions the family performs for society.

5. Point out the major functions the family performs for individuals.

6. How have each of these functions been changing in societies in the last century and for what reasons?

7. What factors have been associated with the changing size of American families?

8. How do you look at the problem of married women working? Do you think it is a beneficial or detrimental situation? Why?

9. Differentiate between conjugal and consanguine family systems. Name some societies where each type is predominant. Why do you think these differences exist?

10. What stages of development do families pass through in their cycle from establishment to dissolution? What do you consider to be the major problem in each of these stages?

11. Why has the problem of the aged become so acute in Western societies?

12. Compare the extent of divorces in various countries. What reasons can you give to explain these differences?

13. What social changes have led to the increase in divorces in the United States?

14. Are you optimistic or pessimistic of the future of the family in your society? Why do you hold this opinion?

Suggested Topics for Reports
1. Examine some of the many materials on modern suburbia to determine if a distinctive type of family pattern is emerging.
2. Make an analysis of the arguments for and against a uniform divorce law for the United States.
3. Make a first-hand study of the organization and types of services performed by a family guidance clinic.

Supplementary Reading
Anshen, Ruth N. (ed.), *The Family: Its Functions and Destiny*. New York: Harper and Brothers, 1949.

Bernard, Jessie, *American Family Behavior*. New York: Harper and Brothers, 1942.

Burgess, Ernest W., and Locke, Harvey J., *The Family*. New York: American Book Company, 1945.

Cavan, Ruth Shonle, *The American Family*. New York: Thomas Y. Crowell Co., 1953.

Cummings, Elaine, and Henry, William E., *Growing Old: The Process of Disengagement*. New York: Basic Books, Inc., 1961.

Ginzberg, Eli (ed.), *Values and Ideals of American Youth*. New York: Columbia University Press, 1961.

Glick, Paul C., *American Families*. New York: John Wiley and Sons, Inc., 1957.

Goode, William J., *After Divorce*. New York: The Free Press of Glencoe, 1956.

Smith, Ernest A., *American Youth Culture*. New York: The Free Press of Glencoe, 1962.

Sussman, Marvin B., *Sourcebook in Marriage and the Family*. Boston: Houghton Mifflin, 1955.

Waller, Willard, *The Family: A Dynamic Interpretation*. Rev. by Reuben Hill. New York: Dryden Press, 1951.

Winch, Robert F., *The Modern Family*. New York: Henry Holt, 1952.

Young, Kimball, *Isn't One Wife Enough?* New York: Henry Holt and Company, Inc., 1954.

Zimmerman, Carle C., *The Family of Tomorrow: The Cultural Crisis and the Way Out*. New York: Harper and Brothers, 1949.

12

EDUCATION: SOCIETY'S FORMAL
SOCIALIZING INSTITUTION

S CHOOLS *are transmitting agencies handing on a body of accumulated knowledge thought valuable as preparation for living in society. This knowledge passes from primarily adult populations to succeeding generations on a selected basis. Societies differ in their convictions about educational needs. Some constant problems of all societies get the attention of schools.*

I. EDUCATIONAL BACKGROUNDS

Youth Everywhere Is Subjected to "Schooling"

OUR YOUTH GETS SPECIAL ATTENTION In 1961, 94 per cent of the 46 million boys and girls five through seventeen years of age in the United States were enrolled in a school.[1] Similar figures with perhaps not as high proportions are found for other societies. Every society, even where there are no formally organized "schools," gives its young people special attention. Societies take the initiative in this respect and for definite reasons. We have stressed the fact that each society gives particular attention to the family for it must perpetuate itself. Also, to transmit its social heritage, if it is to survive as a social order, each society develops an educational system to train its youth. The society's values, norms, and ways of adjusting to its technology are transmitted to them through it. The older generation passes; the newer generation is the conserver of our indispensable skills and forms. There must be conscious training of the young for their adult roles to maintain the society.

SOCIALIZATION AN ESSENTIAL Individuals themselves could not easily survive if they did not learn the ways of adapting to the environment. They must be socialized, that is, they must consciously and unconsciously adopt the ways of their societies. They must necessarily learn the ways of producing food, clothing, shelter, or avoiding danger and illness, and of adjusting to the groups about them. There are no other ways to acquire them. Youth learn the best for youth is teachable, but they might not learn well if they were left to their own limited resources. All societies assume that they will function more effectively if their members learn the materials and techniques and the ideals and values that are essential for their welfare. Therefore, they subject their youth to instruction to give them the experience and principles enabling them to adjust to various situations. Societies, therefore, create educational institutions—schools—as devices to assure the survival of their culture through their youth. What shall be taught and how it shall be taught depend upon the type of society and the stage of its own cultural development.

Primitive Societies Use Both Informal and Formal Methods in Schooling

EDUCATION DESCRIBED Education in the broad sense is the social process by which an individual learns the things necessary to fit him to the life of his society. Much of this learning comes to him from taking part in the activities of his society. Every experience is, in a sense, educative. Primitive societies depend greatly upon the almost unconscious transmission of their skills and knowledge through youth participation in daily life with adults. The individual learns and assimilates by imitation of others in a simple society.

FORMAL METHODS   In addition to informal methods, there is also formal instruction in teaching the young the skills of producing crops, caring for animals, handling tools and weapons, shooting game, making cloth, and cooking food. They do not have schools in our present-day sense. Their parents are their teachers; their classroom is wherever the task is to be performed. Indian parents teach their sons to shoot game while on the hunt; to plant their corn while in the field. Their tribal lore, religious beliefs, and sacred customs are often handed on by highly formal methods. Special houses that admit only the men are the places where, in some tribes, the growing males are taught the stories of their tribe that they must learn. Only special persons can teach them and only at designated times. The youth are formally initiated into manhood when they have learned the material and performed the required ceremonial acts. They are then full-fledged members of the adult society with its privileges and responsibilities. Some tribes have similarly institutionalized schooling to prepare the girls for their places as wives and mothers.

The educational aims in primitive societies can be accomplished early because skills and knowledge needed to fit into their culture are limited. At an early age, the young men can acquire the knowledge the older men think necessary, so formal education ceases early. The ceremonials of initiation commonly mark the end of their formal education.[2]

Ancient Civilizations and European Societies of the Early and Middle Periods Developed Formal Schooling Agencies

ANCIENT SOCIETIES   China, Egypt, Persia, Greece, and Rome had formal educational institutions that were not for the masses, but for special classes. In China, the formal system was limited to preparing scholars, who, in learning the classics and the characters for writing, were recognized as the persons suited to direct the society. Schools were set up in Egypt in connection with the courts to instruct the children of the kings and of the court personnel. Their purpose was to train youth for court service by instructing them in writing, reading, etiquette, and national history. The Greek city-states trained their young men to serve the state. The Spartan system emphasized physical development of potential warriors, but the Athenian system also emphasized training for government office. Both states trained their youth in patriotism and community welfare, underscoring especially physical perfection and individual initiative. However, the schools reached only the sons of a small group of citizens, who were companioned by an adult serving as the supervisor of their schooling. Rome had schools that trained their boys in fighting ability, the art of simple living, and services as citizens. Rome extended its schooling, however, to include commoners, who were trained particularly for trades and commerce.

MIDDLE EUROPEAN PERIOD   The middle European periods saw the formal education of youth devoted particularly to service to their Church. Monastic schools developed by the Church emphasized withdrawal from an evil world and the development of spirituality. But because many monks so trained believed in productive work, they developed agriculture and the arts and, by copying, preserved such valuable documents as the Latin classics. These activities did not touch the world at large directly, but the monastics did serve as social models for they were highly visible. For example, the Jesuits developed a highly organized system of monastery schools, centered about asceticism and obedience to their superiors. These included as many as 750 units and over 200,000 youth in

"Rhythmic teaching" in African Bwami society: by means of the dance, the initiates are instructed in the proverbs of the tribe.

Europe, as late as 1800. Reactions to the dominance and doctrines of the Church brought Luther's and Calvin's advocacy of other types of schools for youth. Both promoted universal education for children to be supported by the state. The Sturm schools grew from these ideas to stress reading the Latin classics, letter-writing, declamation and disputation, and religious training. These schools became the models for the secondary schools in Europe and the Latin-grammar schools of the early American period.

Education Became Necessary in the Western World After the Fifteenth Century as New Forces Influenced Conditions

EMPHASIS ON THE VALUE OF KNOWLEDGE The invention of printing, the increase in ocean-wide commerce, and emphasis upon the value of knowledge by thinkers like Francis Bacon and Comenius were among the developments that led to a stress on education. The guild system of production and apprentice training and the growing interest in man's own nature also acted as powerful stimuli to the creation of schools to serve the general population.

The Industrial Revolution stimulated the idea that the education of youth should have utility—that it should prepare them for living in a commercial and industrial world. Darwin, Huxley, and others pressed for schools organized to teach young people how to control the natural elements as well as human nature. It became apparent that societies could be more successfully served by a population that was literate and formally trained for its duties than by one of opposite cast. When education became recognized as a necessity, its promotion and institutionalization followed.

Schools in Early American Society Developed in Response to Rapid Change

SOCIAL CHANGE The expansion of formal education resulted from changing social needs. The growing complexity of society made its members realize that informal processes were inadequate to help youth meet the challenges of rapid changes. The need for professional, technical, and industrial training, as well as instruction in the liberal subjects, compelled the development of an extensive educational system.

EUROPEAN INFLUENCE Our early American schools took their patterns from their European counterparts. Latin-grammar schools, which em-

phasized religious instruction and the Latin classics, were promoted by the colonists and the churches at first. The motive was to train young men for college, which, in turn, was to prepare men for the ministry and law. (The girls were trained at home.) Because instruction in religion and the classics was to serve primarily the purposes of religion, our schools at the outset were supported by the Church and the families whose children received instruction.

PUBLICLY SUPPORTED SCHOOLS The tempo of industrial, commercial, and agricultural developments and the recognition of the need for an educated citizenry in a democracy brought demands for schools to educate all youth regardless of social class. The Massachusetts Bay Colony passed a law as early as 1647 to support schools by taxation. Other colonies followed this lead, but the development of our public school systems was slow. However, leaders in the new nation, like Jefferson, Paine, and Adams, advocated schooling for all youth without regard to birth or wealth, and men like Horace Mann and Henry Barnard lent their support to tax-supported universal education. In 1835, Pennsylvania established a state system of tax-supported elementary schools. State after state followed until the principle was accepted throughout the young nation.

"HIGH" SCHOOLS Higher education in America followed a similar development. Latin-grammar schools were supplanted by academies, first supported privately or by Church bodies. Their function was to extend training beyond the elementary schools for youth who could afford to pay the tuition. A number served as preparatory schools for college. The growth of the middle class increased the demand for public support of secondary schools that would provide higher training to all youth who desired it. The publicly supported "high school" was the answer. Established slowly at first, with only 100 in existence in 1860, a century later there were nearly 25,000.

COLLEGES Harvard, established in 1636 and founded primarily to train clergymen, was the first college in America. Most of the early colleges that followed were established by Church bodies and supported by tuition fees, gifts, and denominational grants. State-supported institutions of higher learning came into existence slowly. The control and support of Church-established schools eventually passed into the hands of professional and business persons who were interested in the expansion of secular and specialized professional programs to meet the needs of the expanding economy. Control and programs in American colleges and universities are now, therefore, predominantly secular, supported either by public taxes or private endowments and gifts.

II. EDUCATIONAL CONVICTIONS

Societies Develop Convictions About Education That Undergird the Development of Schools

There are folkways behind this institution that express the "convictions" of the society concerning the values of education and the way they should be implemented. These "convictions," while they allow for wide variation in types of educational agencies, programs of teaching, and specific aims, form the framework of the societal reasoning which supports and shapes the given system. America is an excellent illustration of this process. As its educational system evolved, certain convictions became paramount, and are now the criteria by which we judge the character of our schools and the use we make of schooling opportunities.

EDUCATION CAN SOLVE PROBLEMS The underlying conviction in America is that education is a "cure-all" that can solve most of the social problems of our society and lead the way to human betterment: "Educate the youth and our delinquency, crime, and other difficulties will be taken care of." "I want my children to have a better chance than I, therefore I will make what sacrifices are needed so that they can get an education." "Youth with the best education make the most money." The Kiplinger letter of December 24, 1955, for example, citing figures from the Tuition Plan, indicated that a college graduate's lifetime earnings were $268,000, a high school graduate's $165,000, and an elementary school graduate's $116,000. This would make a college education worth about $100,000 more in a lifetime than a high school education and $150,000 more than an elementary school training. The cost of a college education was put at $9,000, and the Tuition Plan president is quoted as saying: "These figures clearly indicate that a college education is the best investment parents can make for their children." An educated citizenry, by this reasoning, can assure itself of security and be the foundation of a strong democratic society. This is our American faith in education.

EDUCATION FOR ALL The second conviction is that everyone should be educated. We have no maximum standards, but we do have minimum standards in this regard. The least education that is required for anyone is the ability to read and write. The force of this conviction is indicated by the rapid decline in illiteracy in America. In 1870, one in each five persons in this society was unable to read or write in English or any other language. In 1959, this was true only of one in 45 persons fourteen years of age and over.[3]

Society assumes the right and duty to educate children. Parents may decide what schools children will attend, but they cannot decide whether or not the children will attend. Society has instituted compulsory school attendance for young people under specific ages. In American society, such rules are made by the states. How widely they have become a cultural trait in our society is shown by the fact that all states in the union have such rules, usually covering children from seven to fourteen or more years of age.

The tremendous expansion in attendance, facilities, and expenditures that are now invested in schooling in the United States is further evidence of this view. For example, 83 per cent of the youth from five to seventeen years of age attended elementary and secondary schools in 1960. They were taught by 1,387,000 teachers paid an average salary of $5,174 each. The total expenditures for teachers' salaries was over $7 billion. Our average total expenditure per pupil based on average daily attendance was $472. In 1900, only 72 per cent of those from five to seventeen years of age in the population attended similar schools. They were taught by 423,000 persons at an average salary of $325. Total expenditures for teachers' salaries were $138 million, and the average expenditure per pupil was only $20.[4] Higher education shows even more dramatic evidence of this expansion. In 1899–1900, our college enrollment was 237,-000; in 1960, 3,600,000—more than fifteen times as great. Income for higher education was $35 million in 1899–1900, but nearly $5 billion in 1958.[5] America believes in mass education. Its desire to provide it is almost a national compulsion.

EQUAL OPPORTUNITY FOR ALL A third conviction, which has become a symbol of our democratic society, is that opportunity to obtain education should be equal for all. In the early days, the aristocratic class provided schooling for their children but showed little concern for the educational opportunities of the masses. The conviction that this new society should not include a distinctively separate educated class came with the growth in size and control of the business and commercial classes. As schools were created and communities were faced with the task of supporting them, the emphasis was upon educating all children regardless of social differences. "One person is as good as another," "All men are created equal," and "The rifle and the axe made all men equally tall" were slogans that had meaning in such matters as educational opportunity. Getting an education was thought to be the way to take advantage of opportunities in this "land of opportunity."

As a consequence, our present-day schools reach all the way across the population. It is ideally classless schooling. Virtually all children in our society attend. The schools are open to all; all may attend them so long as the capacity and desire are present.

Opportunity in Higher Education Nevertheless, there is an inequality involved here. The application of the principle of equal opportunity has been more difficult in relation to higher education. Economic considerations are uppermost. In spite of state-supported institutions with small or no tuition, of scholarships and other forms of aid, costs put college education out of the reach of many youth who have superior mental ability and are desirous of having such training. Economic considerations determine for many young people the extent to which they can realize their educational goals. The society would need to develop a plan that enables those of superior capabilities to achieve their aims if this inequality is to be overcome. McCormick makes a reasonable suggestion in this regard: "No doubt the best that can be expected is that the government should try to make it possible for all young people, regardless of their family situation, to compete for public scholarships which will enable as many of the competent to attend college as the public feels it can support." [6] In spite of the inequalities, however, nearly four million persons were enrolled in our colleges and professional schools in 1961. In 1960, nearly one in each five persons from sixteen to 24 years of age was enrolled in college. [7]

State Support Varies There are other inequalities. Some spring from the way in which the institutions are controlled. There is no single pattern of control since each state develops

its own educational system. Private organizations develop schools, also, and receive approval if they meet standards set by state education departments or other supervisory bodies. Our public schools, of course, play the most important role in respect to opportunity.

Inequalities arise in the whole society from the differences in the ability and willingness of the various states to support the schools. In 1960, the average amount of current expenditures per pupil in average daily attendance in the public schools of the United States was $375. In New York State, highest in the nation, it was $562, exactly one and one-half times the average for the nation. In Mississippi, lowest in the nation, it was $206, slightly more than one-half the average for the nation. The ten states with the highest average expenditures per pupil, all in the North, Middle, and far West, spent nearly twice the amount of money per child as the ten states with the lowest average expenditures, all in the Southeast and South. [8] These differences reflect regional variations. The states of the South and Southeast have less wealth and lower incomes than other regions yet have maintained two parallel school systems, one for the whites and one for the Negroes. Furthermore, they also have a larger ratio of children to adult population than other areas and so must educate relatively more of the nation's youth than do most states. Their smaller available resources are divided over a relatively larger school population so their expenditures are much lower per pupil. The results are shorter school terms, poorer facilities, and less well-trained teachers. This failure to provide equal opportunities with other states means a failure to use the full talent potentials within all states. This is a loss to the entire society.

Racial Inequalities Other inequalities are based on race. Negroes have less opportunity for education than do whites, particularly where a dual system of schools operates. Negroes 25 years of age and over had completed nearly three years of less schooling than our white population of comparable age in 1960. The proportion of those who had had any college training was less than half that of the white population 25 years of age and over. [9] These differences in educational opportunities mean that the educational level of our whole society is lower than it might well be.

Occupational Inequalities There are also inequalities in educational opportunities for children of various occupational workers. Over one-half of the children of professional workers go to college. Only one in 20 of the children of unskilled laborers do so.[10] The average years of schooling attained by professional persons from 35 to 44 years of age as of March, 1957, was four or more years of college; of craftsmen, two years of high school; and of laborers and service workers, only an elementary schooling. Men of these ages who received money incomes under $2000 had completed only a grade school training, while those receiving $8000 or more had completed high school or more.[11] These variations are the result of both differences in financial resources and differences in the valuation of education and the motivation to achieve it.

Federal Aid   Programs of federal aid to education are designed to reduce inequalities among the states. This assistance, it is argued, is only fair since people are citizens of the nation as well as of particular states. They do not remain in the state of birth but migrate from state to state. Some states are paying for the education of youth for other states, and it is felt that federal aid could help equalize the burden. Objections to federal aid have not been overcome among those who fear federal control of our school systems. Aid is provided to the states by the federal government for many educational purposes, but no general aid has been forthcoming. It is likely to be available in the near future.

CONTROL BY THE PEOPLE   The fourth conviction, which expresses a general principle of democracy, is that education should be controlled by the people. De Tocqueville, the French philosopher, after traveling in the United States, wrote in about 1831: "The American Revolution broke out, and the doctrine of the sovereignty of the people, which had been nurtured in townships took possession of the state: every class was enlisted in its cause; battles were fought and victories obtained for it, until it became the law of laws." [12] The sovereignty of the people has been a supreme law in American society from its beginning.

Control of education by the people became a basic conviction because of the belief that schools were the cradles in which democracy was to be nurtured. In pioneer days, people themselves took the initiative in establishing schools in response to their own sense of need. Recognizing that youth must have the tools of knowledge—reading, writing, arithmetic—the people organized school districts on their own and built one-room, one-teacher schools that children in their neighborhoods attended. The "school district" became the ecological unit of organization and operation. The "one-room, one-teacher school" is today still the local school unit in many neighborhoods. It existed generally until the 1920's, when the automobile and improved roads made consolidation possible. Furthermore, the people created "the school board," or "the school trustees"—a small number of local citizens elected from among themselves into whose hands they placed the control of the school as their representatives. The board of trustees was responsible for the school property, hiring the teacher, making the school budget, and presenting these to the people for approval. School boards are the controlling bodies in our public school systems to this day. The people also decided upon the way education should be supported. These historical developments firmly established a major characteristic of today's American public school system—ultimate control by the people.

Changes in Administrative Patterns   Changing social circumstances have, of course, made changes in this elemental pattern necessary. Increased population density and changes in the ideas about the amount and type of schooling needed to prepare young people for life meant enlarged schools with richer curricula. Our city schools and rural school districts have grown to large size and require more administrative oversight. Superintendents of school district systems, principals of schools, teachers of special subjects, and special schools have all come into existence. School boards cannot oversee property, instruction, and budgets directly, so authority must be delegated to others especially qualified. Elected school boards are still the final authority, but they must necessarily operate at considerable distance and depend upon their employed personnel for guidance.

Rural schools have not grown as far away from the people as have our city schools. But even here, controls must be left to professionals because of the complexities of consolidation, the problems of supervision, the adequate preparation of teachers, the broader programs of instruction, and the more extensive property holding.

Public Participation   There are ways in which the people can directly influence school operation in addition to electing school board members, even though expansion in size and program has made our school operations a specialized business. The voluntary organization of parent-teacher associations to consider school problems is one such way. The creation of citizen's organizations to promote school interests or taxpayer's associations to consider school costs can act as citizen groups to influence the decisions of school boards.

State Departments of Education A further development related to the control of schools resulted from the creation of state departments of education as states began to offer financial aid to school districts on the condition that they conform to standardized state requirements. At first, the duties of such departments were chiefly advisory and clerical, but as they proceeded to establish teacher certification, organize suggested curricula, give approval to school buildings plans, and support each measure with state aid programs, their influence became strong. In large measure, this has been beneficial for it has raised standards in all areas of school operation. At the same time, final authority in decision-making still rests with the people at the local level through their representatives.

EDUCATION SHOULD BE SECULAR A fifth conviction is that public education should be secular. This conviction rests upon two other principles that undergird American society: the separation of Church and state and religious freedom. No view has been more strongly defended in American society than that citizens be free to follow the religion of their choice. The principle of the separation of the state and its agencies from all religious activities has been strongly entrenched in our culture to avoid any possibility that the government and its agencies might be used to promote particular religious systems. Public schools, therefore, are expected to be neutral in religious matters and to avoid religious instruction lest doctrinal teachings enter.

Private Schools This principle, of course, does not prevent the establishment of privately supported denominational schools having the right to teach religion. In October, 1957, 13 per cent of all enrolled students up to 34 years of age were in private denominational schools. Most of these are parochial schools of the Catholic faith.[13] The youth of America are overwhelmingly in public schools (84 per cent), but private institutions do include a considerable proportion (16 per cent).

Our private elementary and secondary schools are supervised by state departments of educa-tion in the same manner as the public schools. Families who prefer to send their children to a denominational school must, nevertheless, pay taxes in support of public schools since these schools are available to all citizens.

Private denominational schools are most active in the elementary and college fields. Almost 15 per cent of all elementary school students are in denominational schools. Only about 9 per cent of the high school students are in denominational schools, however. Our private colleges and professional schools have just over one in each three persons enrolled. Our denominational colleges, representing both Catholics and Protestants, have 14 per cent, while private colleges have 21 per cent.[14] Religious bodies developed higher institutions early in the history of our society to provide leadership for their Church enterprises. They continue this practice today.

Religious Instruction In recent years, an interesting development has taken place in some states with reference to religious instruction. It has been deemed proper to allow children in our public schools to go to their respective denominational churches or some designated place not a school during specified school hours for religious instruction. It is not possible to predict how far this practice will develop. At the present time, about one-fourth of our public schools have provisions for such religious instruction.[15] In 1962, the Supreme Court's decision that the recitation of prayers in public schools was unconstitutional has also raised some far-reaching questions.

III. EDUCATIONAL OBJECTIVES

Schools Perform Two Basic Functions for Society's Youth

Schooling serves a society by assisting in socializing children so that they will absorb the social values, beliefs, and norms of the society in order to operate effectively with others in the society. This is a vital function of school. There are two important functions that our schools perform in accomplishing this generalized end.

TOOLS OF KNOWLEDGE One is to provide children with the tools of knowledge. A child must have tools if he is to learn, which makes it emphatic that he know how to read, write, spell, and master arithmetic. A common criticism of modern schools is that they do not teach young people to use these tools effectively. This reaction reveals some measure of prejudice and lack of adequate investigation because examination shows that modern youth have considerable competence in these areas.

Mastering these basic tools demands considerable repetition and practice until their use is automatic. Since such repetition and practice can be uninteresting, a major problem in instruction methods is devising ways for children to acquire these tools with economy of time and effort, yet without loss of interest. Many adults conclude that today's instruction is faulty because older methods depended so much more upon straight memory exercise than do present ones.

As education proceeds, it involves the acquisition of suitable additional tools. Each body of subject matter develops its symbol system through which analyses are made. Facts are presented and relationships expressed by these symbols. For example, mathematics is a primary system no physicist or chemist can be without. As any science evolves, quantification of its material is more and more essential. Vocabularies describing clearly the phenomena with which each field of study is concerned are also tools for description and analysis. Their adequate acquisition makes knowledge more easily acquired and used.

TRANSMITTING ACCUMULATED KNOWLEDGE
The second basic function of our schools is transmitting to the oncoming generation a body of accumulated knowledge which the older generation thinks will be valuable. What shall be taught for the most effective intellectual and social development of the young is often a difficult question. Tradition, fashion, and vested interests influence the content of curricula and often make adaptations to new conditions difficult. Rapid social change often makes much learning unusable and creates the need for new knowledge and approaches.

There are at least three fundamental matters that must concern educators: (1) the nature of facts and their relationships, (2) principles, and (3) objectives. The basis of sound learning is the possession of a body of demonstrable facts. Proper thinking can hardly be pursued without a foundation of fact. It is often suggested that teaching consists too much in giving facts and demanding their retention. Factual material is, however, essential. But facts are soon forgotten unless they are used in relation to other facts. Indeed, their major use is to establish relationships, and, when this is done, the principles by which phenomena operate can be demonstrated. One major end of knowledge is to understand the principles by which phenomena of the universe operate. This is the scientific approach, which gives meaning to the life-processes. Herbert Spencer emphasized correctly that those who have never attempted to study scientific works know little of the rhythmic beauty that is in them. He points out that it is exceedingly sad to see how many men are not interested in these marvelous phenomena, but engage only with trivial matters and care not to understand the way the universe operates.[16] A chief purpose of instruction is to instill in the learner a love for the scientific spirit as he deals with any relevant subject matter.

Educational theorists who deal with objectives are confronted with several interlocking issues of great sociological importance. These issues are contained in three questions which have spurred much discussion but no final answers: (1) Should the schools stress vocational preparation or "liberal" education? (2) Should education emphasize intellectual development or the personality and social adjustment of the student? (3) Should educational agencies reflect and preserve the social *status quo* or actively influence the direction of social change? Our educational efforts are likely to remain confused until we find some satisfactory answers to these questions.

The School Also Functions as a Social Selector

All our children do not complete school, and some even fail to finish elementary grades al-

An "open air" primary school in a jungle area of eastern India.

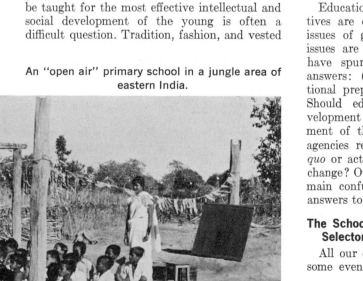

though the law requires attendance to a certain age. Children, of course, have different mental capacities. Except in extreme cases, however, all of them enter school. But the essential condition that will allow them to remain is the ability to cope with the training the school program presents. Children are graded on the quality of their work. They are "passed" from grade to grade or held back according to their ability to meet standards. Because the work is also graded to fit what is considered to be the ability of the average student, it is too easy for students of superior intelligence. They may waste time, get bored, and rebel if greater challenge is not provided. On the other hand, those with low intelligence and motivation may show the same reactions. In fact, they are more likely to do so than are the brighter students.

EXTENT OF SELECTION   Selection, while not a manifest function of our schools, is clearly an unintended or latent function. It advances or drops children from the system in terms of their ability to pass its requirements. Of each 1000 children who were in the fifth grade in American schools in 1934–1935, fewer than one-half graduated from high school in 1942, only one in each eight entered college, and only one in each 20 graduated in 1946. Thus, nineteen of each 20 children in the fifth grade in 1934–1935 dropped out of school before completing a college education. Nine years later (1943–1944), slightly over one-half of each 1000 fifth-grade youth graduated from high school, and

one in each five entered college. Three years later (1946–1947), just over one-half of each 1000 fifth-graders later graduated from high school in 1954, and just over one in each four entered college. The latest data, covering the period of 1951–1959, show that 58.2 per cent, or 582 of each 1000 fifth-graders, graduated from high school and that 308, a little less than one in each three, entered college.[17] The selective process is relatively rapid as children progress from grade schools through high schools and colleges. We may note, however, a general improvement over the decades.

REASONS FOR DROP-OUTS   Why our young people drop out of high school is suggested in the reports of 231 high school principals in Massachusetts. Of nearly 6000 students, 41 per cent left because they preferred to work; 21 per cent because they lacked interest; 10 per cent because of economic needs; 6 per cent each because of parental suggestion, a transfer to other schools, or entrance into military service; and the other 10 per cent because of school failure.[18] Nearly half (47 per cent) of those who dropped out during the 1952–1957 period had IQ's below 89.[19]

The two chief reasons given for six out of ten of these drop-outs (preference for work and lack of interest) suggest a fundamental principle in our education, namely, that the chief point of contact in holding our students must be his own interests. (See Box 19.)

BOX 19

A ten year old boy, who presented his parents with a dreary report card, did not feel a bit chastened or inferior. Instead, he said, "I'd like to give the teacher an exam. I'll bet you I could ask her lots of things I'll bet she doesn't know." Whereupon he listed the questions he would ask his teacher. The long list included:

How can you tell a GMC or a Mack truck from a Ford truck from the rear?
What food can you put at a bird-feeding station that even grosbeaks like?
What is the horsepower of a Caterpillar bulldozer, Model D-8?
What do they use an 0-4-0 locomotive for?
What is a Phelps screwdriver?
What do you feed a pet garter snake?
What is the best way to start a car when the starter's stuck?
How do you tell grouse from pheasant tracks in the snow?
What's the difference between a Christie and a jump turn on skis?
Why do some trucks have dual rear wheels?

"There," said the young man, "is an exam I could pass easy." [20]

CONSEQUENCES OF SELECTION A major consequence of the sifting function in our schools is that it distributes youth within our larger society, placing those with the greater abilities and training in higher positions and those with the lesser abilities and training in lower ones. There are, of course, exceptions as other conditions, such as wealth, social class, and family position, counteract the selective effect of the schools. But amount of schooling serves as an important determiner of who shall have the opportunity to fill the higher positions. A person with only elementary schooling will have little chance to work as an engineer, for example. Amount of schooling thus facilitates movement up the social scale and gives the person a social status which improves his competitive chances to use his abilities.

Educational achievement also influences personality. It has some effect in inducing young people to strive for the higher, rather than the easier, goal. Few college graduates could accept with satisfaction the work of an unskilled or semiskilled laborer. But individuals who are selected out in the early years of schooling are too often content to accept limited opportunities. The main challenge of this selective process is to see that it operates so that those who do have superior abilities are not discarded because of conditions over which they have little control.

There Are Certain Constant Problems in Life Which Education Can Help Each Youth to Meet

PHYSICAL WELL-BEING The maintenance of physical well-being is essential to satisfactory living for each individual. The laws of health and the habits of wholesome living can be taught. To recognize that to conserve our bodies is a vital duty and that upon it depends much of the pleasure and productivity of a person is one of the vital lessons schools can help youth learn.

VOCATIONAL TRAINING A second constant problem is that of providing the means for living. Each person needs an occupation from which he can earn enough to support adequately himself and those dependent upon him and in which he makes a contribution to social well-being. Our elementary and secondary schools can help youth discover that honorable work gives both a living and a life. They can assist them in deciding on suitable vocational goals and steer them to subject matter that gives them foundations for their proper start, although they can hardly train, except in special schools, for specific vocations.

Where vocational education is the center of a secondary school program, tools, machines, and other equipment are provided to train youth to fill useful occupations in their communities. Subject matter is adapted to their vocational ends, while, at the same time, instruction is given in subjects that will prepare them for a useful life in society.

ADJUSTMENT TO PEOPLE A third constant problem of youth is adjustment to people as they operate in the structural units of their society—the home, the school, the community: a social-civic aim. One of the most important lessons for youth is how to get along with others. This is more complicated in our mobile, secondary society of today than in the relatively static, primary society of yesteryear. Developing ethical standards and maintaining right social relations can be taught in school. What is more important, they can be actually demonstrated in the many group and organizational relationships in which the child is involved in the school. Our schools are miniature societies demanding the same basic adjustments as the world at large demands; the task is chiefly one of teaching and demonstrating proper social controls. The child is a member of society, so he is taught that his actions are subject to the same disciplines that maintain order, and that his freedom must not impinge upon the rights of others. The aim is the development of the self-controlled person.

PREPARATION FOR FAMILY LIFE A fourth constant problem is the preparation of young people for family life. Marriage and family living are the normal conditions for practically all individuals. Yet, one of the serious omissions in our secondary schooling is preparation for parenthood and family management. Someone has suggested that if a person in a future century examined the curriculum of our schools he might well say: "This must have been their program for training their celibates." For a long time our attitudes toward sex hindered any objective consideration of family life problems in the schools. It was thought that no preparation was needed in these matters, although they involve the most important relationships between married couples and are essential to the care of children. Now it is being recognized that these relationships are subject to direction and that there are physical and intellectual principles related to them that our schools can transmit with highly profitable effects upon youth.

LEISURE TIME Our fifth constant problem has to do with leisure time. The industrialization that has created our mechanically operated societies has also increased the leisure time available to virtually all people. Not long ago, little consideration was given to our avocational pursuits when it was thought that play was morally wrong and that earning a living should consume our time. Today, avocations must be a part of normal living. Wholesome avocations release us from the strains of an intense work world. But they do more than this for us. They give us a feeling of exhilaration and spontaneity for in them the person is acting just for the sheer fun of it.

Only the beginnings of avocational programs have been made in many school programs. Much of the recreation in the schools has consisted of sports and team games. Though exceedingly beneficial, many times they limit the number of students who may participate. Likewise, avocations have too often been considered only in terms of play. Any constructive activity that gives us pleasure and release is a proper avocation. Our schools must develop concrete programs for the guidance of avocational pursuits lest the new abundance of leisure time be spent fruitlessly or in activities that are socially detrimental.

IV. SCHOOL AND COMMUNITY

The School Has an Opportunity to Serve Communities in Many Ways

SECONDARY ASSOCIATION IN THE SCHOOL Our schools are institutional agencies of the neighborhood or community. But they often stand aloof from the rest of the community life because of the rapid change from a primary to a secondary group basis of social life. When neighborhoods and communities were small and when the one-room or small elementary schools predominated, the school was the community center. Local citizens known to all were the trustees. Teachers knew the parents and, in fact, often lived in their homes. They took part in local community activities, and their pupils often grew up under their sole instruction. Today, elementary and high schools of our cities and the consolidated schools of our rural areas have developed large student bodies, multiple instruction and extracurricular programs, and specialized subject-matter teachers. They have themselves become institutional agencies operating primarily on a secondary basis. The expansion of all areas of school program has resulted in increased emphasis upon school operation and lessened attention to neighborhood or community relationships.

TEACHER-PUPIL RELATIONSHIPS This shift in our schools from a primary to secondary basis of association and the almost complete concentration on internal operation have many consequences. Teacher-pupil relationships can hardly have much intimacy when the teacher instructs large, constantly changing classes, unless pupils take the initiative or the teacher develops a particular interest in some of them. The burden of the teacher's own routine work often precludes close associations. Yet, the teacher seeks to transmit ideals and motives vital to youthful development. Too often this influence is exerted "at a distance." Important values may not be imparted because of the weakened personal impact of the teacher upon the pupil.

PARENT-TEACHER RELATIONSHIPS Parent-teacher relationships may also be impaired by these circumstances. Not only is the teacher busy; parents are also, and they often leave school problems to school people. While parents and the community at large may show little concern for the teachers personally and hardly make them a part of their life, they often expect standards of behavior from them that they do not require of other persons and which they themselves do not follow. Even today, teachers may be criticized if they smoke, attend local dances or clubs, or fail to take part in local church activities. Often these restrictions lead to parent-teacher friction because modern teachers want to live normal lives in the community. They do not feel that they must be different from others.

COMMUNITY RELATIONS AND THE SCHOOL Schools bear the marks of the neighborhood or community in which they operate and transfer these marks to youth. In many communities, ideals are high, and a major task of our schools is to help maintain them. In some, the school may rise above the community and exert its influence to better it. The pupil-to-pupil relationships in school associations reinforce the ideals absorbed in the community and bring them into the classrooms. The school seeks to reinforce behavior which supports high standards and to redirect behavior which deviates from acceptable social norms. Society has always expected the school to perform the latent function of promoting high ethical standards.

The school may relate itself closely to the community in two other ways: (1) by using the resources of the community in its programs, or (2), by providing resources to the community that the community does not now enjoy. There are important aids for pupil instruction in practically every locality. Business men, factory managers, members of the professions, skilled mechanics, and others often help bring subject matter alive with presentations, demonstrations, and field trips. They can thus develop closer ties with the schools. On the other hand, the school can provide the community with sports,

drama, music, and library facilities. It can serve as a center for public meetings and promote within the school numerous community activities, such as beautification programs, chest campaigns, Red Cross activities and other concerns of the community as a whole.

ADULT EDUCATION PROGRAMS   A final way in which the school extends itself into the community is through its adult education activities, which are usually called "extension" or "continuation" education programs. This type of service has expanded with the growing need of modern adults for further knowledge and training which, in turn, reflects the demands and challenges of a dynamic and expanding social order.

References

1. Computed from the United States Department of Commerce, Bureau of the Census, *Statistical Abstract of the United States, 1962*, Table 143, p. 114.
2. For fuller discussion, see Mead, Margaret, "Education, Primitive," *Encyclopedia of the Social Sciences*, 5 (New York, The Macmillan Company, 1937), pp. 399–403.
3. United States Department of Commerce, Bureau of the Census, *Statistical Abstract of the United States, 1962*, Table 153, p. 120.
4. *Ibid.*, Table 154, p. 121.
5. *Ibid.*, Tables 170 and 171, p. 132.
6. McCormick, Thomas C., *Sociology* (New York, The Ronald Press Company, 1950), p. 439.
7. United States Department of Commerce, Bureau of the Census, *Statistical Abstract of the United States, 1962*, Table 171, p. 132.
8. *Ibid.*, Table 141, p. 113; Table 175, p. 136.
9. *Ibid.*, Table 148, p. 117.
10. United States Department of Commerce, Bureau of the Census, Chap. B, "Education," *Census of Population, 1950* (Special Report P.E. 5B) (1953), Table 11.
11. United States Department of Commerce, Bureau of the Census, "Educational Attainment: March, 1957," *Current Population Reports* (December 27, 1957), Series P-20, No. 77, pp. 4 and 5.
12. De Tocqueville, Alexis, *Democracy in America*, 1 (New York, Henry G. Langley, 1845), p. 58.
13. United States Department of Commerce, Bureau of the Census, "School Enrollment: October, 1957," *Current Population Reports* (February 13, 1958), Series P-20, No. 80, p. 2.
14. *Ibid.*
15. "Ten Criticisms of Public Education," *Research Bulletin 35* (National Education Association of the United States, December, 1957), No. 4, p. 171.
16. Spencer, Herbert, *Education* (New York, D. Appleton and Company, 1929), pp. 72 and 73.
17. United States Department of Health, Education, and Welfare, Office of Education, "Statistical Summary of Education, 1953–1954," *Biennial Survey of Education in the United States, 1952–1954* (1957), Chap. 1, p. 10. United States Department of Com-

merce, Bureau of the Census, *Statistical Abstract of the United States, 1962,* Table 146, p. 116.

18. Mack, A. Russell, "A Study of Drop-Outs," *The Bulletin of the National Association of Secondary School Principals,* 38 (February, 1954), No. 200, pp. 49–51.

19. United States Department of Commerce, Bureau of the Census, *Statistical Abstract of the United States, 1962,* Table 151, p. 119.

20. "Cross-Examination," *Reader's Digest,* 58 (May, 1951), No. 349, p. 118. (From "Topics of the Times" in *The New York Times,* February 12, 1951.) By permission of *The New York Times* and *Reader's Digest.*

Questions for Study and Discussion

1. What, briefly stated, are some chief reasons for subjecting youth to "schooling"?
2. Discuss the significance of formal and informal methods of education among primitives. Within modern societies.
3. What types of formal education existed among ancient societies and among European societies in the Middle Ages? What were their purposes?
4. How did social changes influence attitudes toward education in Europe and in America after the fifteenth century and after the Industrial Revolution?
5. Explain the convictions that prevail in American society relative to educational opportunity, educational control, educational administration, and educational support.
6. What indications are there of educational inequalities in American society? How do you think these can be overcome?
7. How important do you consider the latent functions schools perform when you compare them with their manifest functions?
8. What are some implications of the statement that "the school is an institution of the neighborhood or community" for school administration? For the neighborhood or community?
9. What problems of the schools do you consider to be most important in the Western societies of today?

Suggested Topics for Reports

1. From census data, prepare a graph showing enrollment trends for elementary, secondary, and college levels from 1900 through 1960. What interpretation can you make of the trends?
2. Make a study of one of the school integration crises which have occurred since the 1954 Supreme Court decision that racial segregation in public education violated the Constitution.
3. Make a critical examination of the arguments for and against federal aid to education.
4. Consult the catalogues of your college issued over the past fifteen years and trace the growth of new courses and curricula in the college program. Which have been dropped? Indicate how these curricular changes reflect changes in American society.
5. If they are available to you, study the records of the recent "drop-outs" in a local school system. What can you infer from the data concerning intelligence, motivation, family background, and social class level?

Supplementary Reading

Brookover, Wilbur A., *A Sociology of Education.* New York: American Book Company, 1955.

Cook, Lloyd A., *Community Backgrounds of Education.* New York: McGraw-Hill Book Co., Inc., 1938.

Counts, George S., *The American Road to Culture: A Social Interpretation of Education in the United States*. New York: The John Day Company, 1930.

Hollingshead, August B., *Elmtown's Youth*. New York: John Wiley and Sons, Inc., 1949.

Lieberman, Myron, *Education as a Profession*. Englewood Cliffs, N.J.: Prentice-Hall, Inc., 1956.

Report of the President's Commission on Higher Education, *Higher Education for American Democracy*. 6 vols. Washington, D.C.: United States Government Printing Office, 1947.

Thayer, V. T., *The Role of the School in American Society*. New York: Dodd, Mead & Co., 1960.

Waller, Willard, *The Sociology of Teaching*. New York: John Wiley and Sons, Inc., 1932.

Wilson, Logan, *The Academic Man*. New York: Oxford University Press, 1942.

Znaniecki, Florian, *The Social Role of the Man of Knowledge*. New York: Columbia University Press, 1940.

13

RELIGION: THE MORAL
AND SPIRITUAL INSTITUTION

THE Church is the institutional agency which transmits the moral and religious principles related to ultimate societal and individual values. It is the agency of the institution of religion. Religion, a universal institution, is a complex of ideas, emotions and procedures expressing beliefs in supernatural powers.

Religion Is a Universal Experience with Man

On a mission to their city, St. Paul said to the Athenians that he perceived that in everything they were very religious. We, too, can perceive that people everywhere give explicit or implicit evidence of religious interests. Whether it be in a rural village of Japan, a jungle area in northwest India, the crowded streets of Cairo, or along Fifth Avenue in New York City, the outward evidences of this interest meet us in the form of a little shrine before which a peasant woman is devoutly kneeling, a group of men carefully placing offerings before animal images on a dirt altar, the constant passing in and out of a great mosque by a line of men, or the tolling of bells from the spire of a magnificent cathedral.

The testimony is that religion is universal. Every society known to man possesses religious practices and institutions. In every tribe and nation man worships and prays. The earliest periods of man's existence also yield evidences that he worshipped.

"As far back as the Mousterian period, thirty thousand years ago, certain practices were being observed by the Neanderthal race of western Europe which modern savages observe in obedience to the dictates of their religion. When these people of the Mousterian laid away their dead, they put some of their belongings with them. When existing nations do this, it is invariably in connection with a belief in the continued existence of the soul after death. We may reasonably conclude therefore that even

in this long-distant period human beings had arrived at a crude recognition of the difference between flesh and spirit; in short, religion had come into being." [1]

Religion Arose as One of Man's Solutions to His Problem of Survival

The origins of religion are hidden in the dimness of the past. Its universality, however, warrants the suggestion that it grows out of man's responses to his experiences. Life is struggle. It was struggle for early man in a world he little understood. Food was scarce; animals were dangerous; pain was common; age, sickness, and weakness came; death, the inability to respond in any form to comrades, was mysterious. When he slept he was often in a world of bliss or pain with all the good things and good people or bad things and bad people he experienced in his waking hours. Where had he been; what other world was that, which had not yet been called the "dreamworld"? Life was an incomprehensible thing to him. Great storms and beautiful calms, long periods for things to grow and long periods for things to die, periods of abundance and periods of scarcity filled him with wonder and confusion.

How could he resolve all this wonderment and give it meaning? He would have had no need to resolve these enigmas if there had been no strange occurrences, no serious dangers. He required some interpretation of what occurred to him in order to have hope and confidence in the face of his own insufficiency and awe at the happenings in the world about him. How was he to explain the events that seemed to be meaningful actions of "something" that caused them? They must be the works of powers outside of himself to which he must adjust. Surely, he must be right when others had similar experiences and came to similar conclusions. There must be powers that plan these actions to which he must adjust. In his attempt to do this, he came to believe in gods or God—supreme forces with infinite powers. He joined with others who believed likewise because they had had similar experiences. Together they worshiped, they prayed, they made sacrifices. In other words, just to believe was not enough; something had to be done about it. So religion became a set of beliefs about God or gods, man's relations to them, his efforts to adjust to them, and his expectations of help from them.

Religion Expresses Itself in a Diversity of Forms.

Man pays homage to the universal controlling forces in an untold number of ways. He does it in terms of his own ability to conceive of them. In his efforts to grasp more concretely his own notions of these forces, he creates symbolic representations of them, even though he may believe that they are formless or shapeless like the great God Mahadeo of India. He may make tablets which represent the spirits of his ancestors or take forms from nature like trees, cows, the sun, the moon. On the other hand, he may give them no specific form. But he may state his beliefs in his creeds and exemplify them in his liturgies as fitting conceptions of his ideas and as proper forms of their expression. It may be true that some believe the physical representations their hands have made possess powers in themselves. The more likely notion, however, is that they stand as symbols of these powers, or that they are not the powers but that the powers reside in them in some manner.

Two conditions stand behind this diversity in man's religious expression: the variable experiences of men and the variable conditions of the environments. The two go together for men always have their experiences in an environment and are particularly dependent upon their social environment. Since both factors vary from place to place, man's beliefs and practices vary likewise. For example, the religious forms of the Maria Ghonds in the forests of West India are widely different from those of our Midwest agriculturalist of the American corn belt be-

cause their environments and particularly their cultural backgrounds are widely different. Yet both have a common religious problem—how man is to adjust to the spiritual forces he assumes to be influencing his life.

Religions Consist of Four Primary Components

BELIEF IN SUPERNATURAL FORCES Each religion, regardless of its form, contains four basic elements. First is the belief that supernatural forces—powers outside of man and his observable world—exist and influence human conditions and events. Some call these forces God; others call them gods; yet, others leave them nameless, simply recognizing them as forces in their universe requiring adaptations. Whatever they are called, their basic characteristics in belief is that they are controlling forces so far as man and his destiny are concerned.

MAN'S ADJUSTMENT TO SUPERNATURAL FORCES Second is a set of beliefs as to how man may adjust to these forces. Man is dependent upon them. His proper relationship to them involves his acknowledgment of his dependence on forces and obedience to what he thinks the forces require of him. As a consequence, religions include outward acts, prayers, hymns, creedal recitations, and other forms of reverence, usually performed with other people and in public. Worship, many people say, is the true essence of religion. Among primitive folk, failure to perform these acts is considered offensive to the gods or God. It is thought that such failure, because it is deemed a sin, may bring disaster to a person and his society. Therefore, individuals feel guilt, and society inflicts punishments. In modern society, too, the failure of people to acknowledge God is generally considered sinful.

ACTS DEFINED AS SINFUL In human development, relationships between people were defined as right and wrong and were given not only moral but also religious meaning. This leads to the third primary component of religions, namely, the definition of certain acts as profane and sinful. Such acts destroy man's harmonious relationships with God or the gods and also create his sense of guilt. Man brings upon himself the disfavor of the controlling forces, both by failing to acknowledge them properly and by committing certain acts unacceptable to them. "And what doth the Lord require of thee, but to do justly and to love mercy, and to walk humbly with thy God?" [2] This quotation from the ancient Hebrew Scriptures sums up both the reverent and the moral aspects of religion as they usually appear in religious systems.

SOME METHOD OF SALVATION Man needs some method by which he can regain harmony with the gods through removal of guilt, since he does not always keep the commandments or "do justly." A fourth primary component of religions appears: redemption or a method of salvation. The forms this component takes also vary widely. The Buddhist hopes to attain salvation by being absorbed in the godhead and entering Nirvana. This absorption in the godhead and the extinction of the conscious individual give a state of eternal felicity. The Christian has a redeemer in Christ, the Son of God, who gave His life for man's sins. The Hindu seeks release from the bondage of Karma, which is the joy or suffering he undergoes as a result of his actions in this life. This he may accomplish by recognizing the inadequacy of the senses, by his striving for the higher goal, and by the practice of inner spiritual contemplation.

These components take many other forms, but the examples indicate how several major religions make provision for the attainment of spiritual goals.

The Church Is the Institutionalized Expression of Religion

DEFINITION OF THE CHURCH Institutional agencies, we previously learned, are formalized mechanisms which regulate the activities of the members of a society with respect to their cultural values. Religion is the institutionalized set of beliefs we hold about supernatural forces. Our effort to adjust to them formalizes and regularizes itself in the Church. The *Church*, then, consists of a number of people holding the same religious beliefs who are united for their observance, together with the accessories thought necessary for this purpose.

ACCESSORIES Numerous accessories develop to perform selected functions in Church operation. Some of the more important ones need consideration. Beliefs are usually formulated into *creeds*, which are brief codified statements of the essential ideas of the faith. They serve to reiterate the accepted ideas of the Church so that the followers will develop strong loyalty to them and so conform to them in practice. In some churches, recitation of the creed is part of each worship service. Since it contains inviolable ideas, the creed in time becomes a fixed

expression that can be changed only with great difficulty.

Ritual also is a characteristic of religious expression of churches. It functions in part to impress the worshipper with the sanctity of the situation. By influencing him emotionally, it puts him in a receptive condition for the intended instruction. The body of rites and the ceremonials attached to them focus attention on the act of worship and help to make the worshipper a willing respondent. They also serve to enhance the unity among the believers since they are congregational acts. All are one in the performance of the ceremony. The observance of the Lord's Supper, for example, achieves an individual dedication to the practice of Christian principles, but it also emphasizes that this is done with fellow-believers who are making a like dedication.

Churches also house *sacred objects*. Writings that contain the religious works of a people are sacred. The Koran of the Mohammedans, the Veddas of Hinduism, and the Bible of the Christians are all sacred objects to be treated with reverence. The cross, the crescent, the altar, the images of saintly persons, and the saffron robe of the monk are a few of the things that serve as collective representations of religion. What gives these objects their sacred character is what they stand for. They symbolize the essence of the spiritual, call forth attitudes of reverence and loyalty, and unite those with similar views.

Some religious bodies minimize creeds, rituals, and sacred objects and emphasize a rational approach to the spiritual. Even among these, some formal organization is necessary to give their conceptions vehicles for conveyance.

Ritualism May Be Dysfunctional Some critics argue that there are dangers in the development of too great emphasis on these ritualistic elements. One alleged danger is that they may be considered to have efficacy in themselves, whereas they are only external symbols of the really efficacious. Ritual and ceremony, it is averred, can destroy what is really vital when they become dominant ends in themselves.

A second presumed danger is that the overt routines of the churches may become the chief preoccupation. The mechanical execution of standardized practices may claim the chief attention of the personnel. Real objectives may thus be hidden in the perfunctory performance of ritual, which could result in an artificiality that may mean destruction or division. Morris

People may worship in a village church or in a great cathedral like Notre Dame in Paris.

Hindus points to this element in the Orthodox Church in Russia. He says: "I once attended a lecture in Moscow by Archbishop Vvedensky, perhaps the most eloquent clergyman in Russia and one of the most scholarly. . . . Among other things he said: 'The extraordinary Byzantine glitter of our Orthodox services has been our greatest curse. Our church has striven after external gorgeousness at the expense of inner virtue, after showy splendour at the cost of spiritual perfection. It acquired pomp, power, riches, but lost its soul. Only now are we beginning to realize what a feeble spiritual infant our Orthodoxy has been. That is why it is disintegrating.' History corroborates the learned clergyman's diagnosis." [3]

FUNCTIONARIES Religious institutions also have *functionaries*. Churches, like other agencies, must operate through persons. Among simple people, where religion is a family or clan matter, the spiritual forces are communicated through the clan or family head. He prescribes the ceremonies and leads them. The priesthood probably arose as a separate class, in tribal societies, from the delegation of religious duties by the tribal heads to particular persons. Priests became persons set apart because they dealt with sacred matters of vital consequence for the whole society. They became leaders in the community through serving as prophets, guardians of the holy places and objects, and conductors of the tribal rituals. Special training for the functions and special modes of living, such as residing apart from the rest of the community, gave added prestige to their office. Priests were probably the first class of professionals developed by societies.

Organized churches today have trained functionaries of various grades depending upon the extent to which their system has grown. Preachers, priests, or pastors are the functionaries who conduct services, visit parishioners, perform various rites, and, in general, supervise the work of specific churches. There are also over-all supervisors, such as superintendents and bishops, who represent the general body of believers in administration and promotion. Other functionaries are used as more services are developed. Missionaries, for example, are trained personnel whose primary business is to carry the beliefs of their religion to nonbelievers at home or abroad.

A major problem with religious functionaries is the maintenance of contacts with the laity. Priests, preachers, or ministers, as agents of the supernatural, tend to be set apart. Some religions effect this separation deliberately, although others insist that religious leaders are no different from any other persons, that they are simply professional persons following the vocation of the religious teacher. But the religious leader often takes on these characteristics as formalism grows. As a consequence, the social distance between leader and follower may widen to the point that a superstitious attitude develops toward the leader and his office. The somber dark clothing with clerical vests and turned collars make these functionaries marked persons in the daily relationships of society, and priestly robes clearly separate their wearers from the masses. Aside from the military, religious functionaries, with some exceptions, are the only occupational class who wear the garments of their office while they are "off duty." This magnifies the separation between religious leaders and the laity and creates a distinction that may discourage easy informal association.

The Church as the Institutional Agency of Religion Performs Several Distinctive Functions for Societies

FOCUS ON ULTIMATE VALUES The distinctive function of the churches is to focus on ultimate values and to make them guiding forces in our affairs. The Church's stress upon the holy in the universe, and its constant call for man to seek it, set aspirations for the whole society. Ultimate values subordinate and energize our other values and bring them into accord with a higher idealism. An ultimate value stands as a constant demand to respect the spiritual and to acknowledge it in our attitudes and actions.

Loyalty to moral and spiritual values is a force that unifies and solidifies a society. It binds men together in allegiance to them and leads them to acknowledge each other as "brothers." By providing for society a cohesive element that can pervade the whole, it thus contributes to the unity of society and strengthens its other institutions and organizations. In no basic institution is the religious element completely absent.

MAINTENANCE OF SOCIAL STANDARDS A second function stems from the preceding one, namely, support for the moral standards of the society. Religions generally include definitions of socially acceptable behavior. Thus, they define the good. They also set ideals for behavior, such as those expressed in conceptions of the

People may worship before a simple shrine in a forested area, or before a statue in Japan, or in a Buddhist temple, such as the Shew Dagon in Burma.

golden rule, the brotherhood of man, and the infinite worth of the individual.

AGENCY OF SOCIAL CONTROL   A third function of the Church is its service to social control. Religions emphasize, in one form or another, the consequences resulting from behavior. Rewards or punishments follow approved or disapproved actions, constraining the believer to follow the moral codes. Religion and the Church support the folkways and mores of societies by placing the powerful sanctions of the supernatural behind them. They make certain forms of behavior not only offenses against society but against God as well. "Thou shalt not steal" is not only a social regulation but a religious command. Disobedience brings condemnation from the spiritual forces and from society.

An even more important aspect of the social control function of the Church is the positive one. Since the Church presents an ordered framework for wholesome living, those who relate themselves to it absorb this framework. It provides a model for living and so influences the quality of life by holding up ideals and by helping to inculcate them as habit patterns. This is an especially important contribution to the development of youth.

PROMOTION OF WELFARE FUNCTIONS   A fourth function of the Church is the promotion of welfare, philanthropic, and other civic services. The extent to which this is done varies widely among churches for it is commonly a secondary or latent function. It may extend from aiding indigents with temporary relief to maintaining agencies for orphans, hospitals for the ill, and homes for the aged. Often, church facilities include social and recreational centers that serve their congregation and their neighborhood. The promotion of public lectures, community entertainments, plays, and other forms of social activity are also contributions which churches make to constructive associations. The Church has, therefore, stimulated societies to develop social work programs in many areas. Hospitals are an excellent example because it was the Church which first entered this field as a religious service.

FRIENDSHIP FUNCTION   Churches, as congregations of believers, are ideally organizations of friends. This friendship function is a vital service to adults but an even more vital one for youth. No other institution offers any better opportunity for youth to associate with other youth who are motivated by high purposes. It often functions as a place for them to find their mates and as the only place for friendly association available to newcomers to the community.

LITERATURE, ART, AND MUSIC   The Church also functions constructively in relation to literature, art, and music. The desire to laud and please the gods has led people to extol them in song, sculpture, painting, and architecture. Some of the world's most beautiful monuments are buildings erected to the glory of the gods. Vast cathedrals, beautiful altars, shining pagodas, and artistic images express man's desire to portray his conceptions of the supernatural in aesthetic and inspiring ways. The sacred writings stimulate an appreciation of beautiful prose and poetry. Religious themes are the inspiration for some of man's finest paintings, and the desire to sing praises has led to the creation of some of the world's greatest music.

The Church Also Performs Three Distinctive Functions for Individuals

MENTAL AND EMOTIONAL CONTRIBUTIONS   Religions perform services for individuals in the mental and emotional realm. The most important of these is certainly their concept of man himself. Developed faiths can give men a sense of their own worth: "The soul of the believer is worth more than all the earthly kingdoms." If we believe that God himself makes sacrifices to serve us and that every man has worth in the eyes of the Divine, we are exalted as the noblest thing in creation. Because no other part of a social order idealizes man in this way, the emotional drive to try to make it a reality is very strong. Religion helps many believers to answer baffling questions concerning the meaning of their existence. It provides links with the eternal and offers a completeness to life beyond the finiteness of present existence.

EMPHASIS ON MORAL VALUES AS PERSONAL GOALS   The second function is to induce individuals to translate the highest moral values into personal goals. Thus, it provides persons with the moral initiative that they must have. No other institution stands so consistently before us, challenging us to achieve in ourselves these moral and spiritual values which we recognize as the firmest foundation of social order.

LIFE'S DISAPPOINTMENTS MADE BEARABLE   The third personal function is to make disappointments and sorrows in this life bearable. No one goes through life without suffering and without knowing uncertainties. Some of our hopes are unattainable, our ambitions are blasted, and even our own behavior is often frustrating. Sometimes disaster befalls. It is religion and the Church that point to more durable objectives in these circumstances. Such doctrines as immortality and the forgiveness of sins serve the individual by helping him to achieve psychological adjustments and peace of mind. Worship with others who share a common faith gives assurance, courage, and self-confidence. In other words, the maintenance or re-establishment of mental composure is an important therapeutic service the Church may perform.

The Great Religions Include the Populations of the World

The population of the world was estimated to be about 2,800,000,000 in 1960. Although statistics on religious affiliation are of questionable validity, the estimated distribution of this population by religious faith may be indicated.[4] The followers of Christianity are the most numerous (31 per cent). The Moslems are the second largest group (15 per cent). Hindus and Confucianists are about equal in numbers (11.6 per cent and 10.5 per cent, respectively). Buddhism and primitive religions follow with about 4 to 5 per cent each. Shintoism and Taoism have between one and 2 per cent each. The Jewish faith is followed by less than one per cent of the world's population. About one in each five persons follows some religious faith other than these or none at all.

AREAS OF CONCENTRATION Christianity is the faith of the people of the West, its area of concentration being in Europe and North and South America. Hinduism, Confucianism, and Buddhism are faiths of Asian people, while Mohammedans and the followers of primitive religions concentrate in Asia and Africa. None of the great religions except Christianity has as yet made strong inroads into Europe or the Americas. On the other hand, Christianity has made only small inroads in Asia and Africa.

Christianity Is the Dominant Religion of American Society

SOCIETIES USUALLY HAVE A DOMINANT FAITH Some societies adopt their religious system officially. Some Middle-East societies, for example, declare themselves Moslem, while some European societies have officially adopted Christianity. Others emphasize religious freedom but, because their culture is integrated with a dominant religious system, they are considered followers of that particular faith. American society serves as an example of a civilization that has a definite Christian orientation.

AMERICAN SOCIETY IS OVERWHELMINGLY CHRISTIAN That American society is oriented toward Christianity is shown by the fact that of 96 per cent of the population fourteen years of age and over who reported a religion in March, 1957 (latest year for which data are available), 92 per cent declared themselves to be Christian, 3 per cent Jewish, and one per cent followers of some other faith. Only 3 per cent reported no religion, and one per cent gave no report. This does not mean that 96 per cent of the population are members of and attend a Christian church. However, many associate themselves with a church and use its name, thus indicating that they consider themselves followers.[5]

MEMBERSHIP IN RELIGIOUS BODIES In 1960, the total membership in American religious bodies constituted 64 per cent of the population. Of all these, 56 per cent belong to Protestant churches, 37 per cent to Roman Catholic, and 5 per cent to Jewish congregations. The remaining proportion (3 per cent) are Eastern Orthodox or Old Catholic and Polish Catholic. Four bodies—Baptists, Methodists, Lutherans, and Presbyterians—include over four out of each ten members of our Protestant bodies, with Baptists and Methodists far outnumbering the other denominations.[6]

CHANGE IN CHURCH MEMBERSHIP In the United States, membership in churches has been increasing rapidly in the last century. Only 16 per cent of the population were church members in 1890; in 1960, 64 per cent. This increase, while it is almost startling, does not necessarily indicate increased active participation in church programs. The fact that many more people belong to churches indicates affiliation, but that there is a comparable increase in participation does not follow.

The Church in American Society Has Divided into Many Sects and Denominations

OVER 250 RELIGIOUS BODIES The diverse interpretations that we have made of Christian beliefs has led to the development of many divisions within this faith. The 1962 *Yearbook of the American Churches* lists 259 religious bodies. These include many subdivisions based on nationality or language differences or some distinctive cult notions and have small numbers of followers. There are, for example, such groupings as "The Social Brethren," with 1500 members, and "The Triumph the Church and the

Kingdom of God in Christ," with 67,000 members. The large denominations also include many subdivisions. The largest Protestant denomination, the Baptist, has no fewer than 26 subdivisions, including such tiny units as the "Christian Unity Baptist Association" and the "General Six Principle Baptists."

THE SECT A sect is a group of people committed to socioreligious conceptions that vary from those generally held in the society. Under the sanction of divine authority, it adheres zealously to these principles. The sect is exclusive, often withdrawing from the larger community so that it may practice its different ways without hindrance. It cannot be tolerant of views other than its own, either among its adherents, over whom it exercises strict control, or among those outside its fold. It jealously guards its identity.

The Amish as a Sect The Amish, a Christian sect totaling about 35,000 adherents located chiefly in Pennsylvania, Ohio, and Indiana communities, illustrate these characteristics of the sect. Their chief doctrine is that persons become Christian by an inner regeneration of soul proved by outward behavior. They are obligated to adhere to prescribed practices that will make them God-fearing and obedient Christians and first-rate farmers. They commonly worship in their homes rather than in churches, publish no literature, and do not try to extend their teachings. They dress plainly, travel by horse and buggy, and avoid other forms of worldly display. The strictly orthodox do not use automobiles, tractors, electricity, or telephones. Their way of life requires that they live apart from secular society. Everything they do is inseparable from their religion because they do not differentiate between the sacred and the secular. These practices give them a deep sense of rightness with God and the universe. They have survived for several centuries, transmitting their strict teachings from generation to generation and creating a strong social solidarity.[7]

THE DENOMINATION A *denomination* is a collection of churches operating under the same system and following in general the same viewpoints. It has accommodated itself to society. Denominations usually have their beginnings as sects. The Methodist denomination, for example, originated as a group of dissenters within the Church of England. They withdrew to practice their distinctive ideas of conversion, salvation, and holiness. Over a period of time, they became accommodated to society. The sharpness

of their distinctive doctrines diminished, the original issues disappeared, the strong emotional attachment weakened, and clear-cut meanings lost their force. Today, as the second largest Protestant denomination in the United States, membership requires only that one avow a belief in Jesus Christ as the Son of God and as one's personal Savior. There is a wide range of interpretation within the denomination, confusing its members as to what its distinctive doctrines are.

THE AMERICAN SETTING ENCOURAGES DIVISION The American setting is ideal for the multiplication of sects and denominations. The cultural heterogeneity of the population, the complete freedom of religious expression, emphasis on individualism and independence, and the absence of authoritarian leadership in religious matters are all circumstances that contribute to this disparateness. Beyond these, our doctrine of the separation of state and Church makes it impossible for civil authorities to enter into church relationships or to check their multiplication.

There Are Some Evidences of Broad Religious Unity in American Society

HAS ONLY ONE MAJOR RELIGION Major differences are not as numerous and wide as they appear in American society, notwithstanding this proliferation of denominations and sects. We have noted that Christianity is the only major religion in the society. Only one per cent of the people report association in any of the other major religions of the world. Those who do are immigrants who have brought their religion with them. There is more diversity of major religions in a society like India where Hinduism, Mohammedanism, Buddhism, Christianity, Sikhism, and Jainism are significantly represented.

THREE OF EACH FOUR MEMBERS ARE IN FIVE DENOMINATIONS Seventy-seven per cent of all church members in America belong to only five different religious bodies: Catholic, Baptist, Methodist, Lutheran, and Presbyterian. The rest are scattered among the other 250 bodies. Eighty-eight per cent of all Protestants belong to only eight different denominations; 12 per cent are scattered among all the others.

DENOMINATIONALISM LOSING ITS MEANING Denominationalism today hardly has the same meaning that it had three-quarters of a century ago. Broadened conceptions of the essentials in religion eliminated many of the bases for division. Most American Christians have ceased to lay emphasis upon the form and now consider chiefly meaning and reason. The ministers of our churches tend to de-emphasize divisive doctrinal matters. Christians may change membership from one denomination to another without noticing many doctrinal differences. Loyalty to a given denomination is probably more the result of habit and tradition than anything else. Changing from one regular Christian church to another seems not to mean any vital change in religious outlook.

COOPERATION BETWEEN CHURCHES   Unity and cooperation are also exhibited by the churches in local communities. Promotion of united programs in religious training, recreational activities, and other public services are common. The community church, the federated church, or the larger parish illustrate the union of several different denominational churches into one unit. This development is likely to occur where existing churches are weak or where the convictions of the members of the various churches lead them to promote union.

CHURCH MERGERS   What is happening to individual churches is also happening among church bodies and, to a degree, because of it. A number of mergers within and between denominations have taken place since the early part of the century. Lutheran bodies have effected several mergers. The Christian and Congregational churches are united. The Methodist Episcopal, Methodist Episcopal South, and the Methodist Protestant churches merged into the Methodist Church. In recent years, there have been significant attempts to bring about mergers of several of the major denominations themselves.

COUNCILS OF CHURCHES   Other evidences of growing unity exist in the development of national, state, county, and city councils of churches. Widespread in our land, these interdenominational units promote common activities through many departments and committees, such as those for religious education and weekday religious training, and social action programs, such as migrant labor betterment. An over-all organization, the National Council of Churches of Christ in America, is the representative of cooperating Protestantism in the society as a whole.

INTERFAITH COOPERATION   There are also many illustrations of cooperation between Christianity and Judaism. The National Conference of Christians and Jews promotes social and economic reforms for the whole society. In local areas, too, these groups often work together to advance social changes.

CONDITIONS PROMOTING UNITY   Two general conditions have brought about the movement toward unity. Cultural differences are disappearing. Religion reflects these changes, and since it cannot be isolated from other aspects of the interrelated whole, it too experiences the disappearance of uniqueness.

New attitudes toward differences in religious beliefs have also appeared. The growth of tolerance has led to a greater willingness to take account of the purposes of others, to respect the views of others, and to recognize that righteous character is not the exclusive virtue of any particular creed.

There Are Some Differences, However, Between the Major Religious Expressions and Within the Protestant Denominations

DIFFERENCES IN AUTHORITY   Although there are evidences of unity and cooperation among our churches, there are still some significant differences between them. Catholic and Protestant churches, for example, differ on the matter of authority. Catholicism, with a system of rigid ecclesiastical organization, makes the Church an absolute authority by Divine institution and establishes the Pope as God's representative on earth. Man approaches God and achieves spiritual aid, therefore, through the medium of the Church and its functionaries. Protestantism, on the other hand, emphasizes direct relationships between man and God. It views the Church as a humanly created institutional agency to minister to the spiritual life of individuals. Catholicism depends upon an authoritarian position in its relations to its constituency, while Protestantism depends upon the voluntary association of its constituents. This difference accounts, to a considerable extent, for the unity of the Roman Catholic Church as exhibited in its parish system, and the diversity of character and control among Protestant denominations and sects.

MODERNISM VERSUS FUNDAMENTALISM   Perhaps the most important difference within present-day Protestantism is found between fundamentalism and modernism. These are contrasting interpretations cutting across the Protestant viewpoint. They are found in all denominations. Fundamentalism bases its doctrinal position on a literal interpretation of an inerrant, infallible Bible. It holds that what is written in the Bible is literally true and comes as a statement from God himself. Modernism, on the other hand, approaches this problem from an historical point of view. It views the Bible as a body of religious writing that came out of the daily life of many people in their efforts to solve their spiritual problems. Modernism rejects, therefore, prescribed authority. It finds the truth by historical methods that depend upon freedom of intellect. It reconciles its beliefs with the findings of history and natural science. It accepts the Bible as the guide for our religious life but, at the same time, it is not bound by literalistic interpretations. It recognizes many of the Biblical accounts to be in conflict with the findings of science and to represent, from the historical point of view, only the earnest attempts of earlier peoples to describe the majesty of God as they saw it.

The major emphasis in fundamentalist churches is upon repentance for sin and conduct of a righteous life so that one may be saved in the life hereafter. Modernists stress the righteous life no less but stress it as a social value serving to help us in the building of a finer social order and better personalities.

Where these cleavages will eventually lead remains for the future to decide. Some persons consider the fundamentalist approach a failing cause. There are, however, persons who are receptive to a positive, authoritarian view because it offers a certainty and finality of belief that its adherents seem to need. Modernism, which does not have this characteristic of finality in its teaching, tends to subordinate supernaturalism and does not emphasize everlasting happiness as a reward. Some question whether this more sophisticated approach has the appeal of older ideas and whether a church that deals primarily with personality and social problems can motivate strong personal loyalty and participation.

Social Changes Have Required Readjustments in Our Churches

CHANGES TAKE PLACE The history of the Church is the history of an institutional agency that, like all other agencies, is relatively rigid and inflexible. Yet it has been compelled to change or lose its vitality. Questioning of religion is often discouraged or condemned because it deals with ultimates, which are based on faith and not subject to testing, and because it is presented as revealed and sanctioned by supernatural forces. But changes in social situations impinge upon viewpoints and compel reconsideration and readjustment. Religion is, like all other institutions, a conserving agency. It cannot constantly alter its ideas of the controlling forces, the nature and purposes of man, and the spiritual norms it establishes, lest it destroy completely its own stability. Yet religion, in order to survive, is compelled to modify its beliefs and practices if it is to meet the needs of the times.

SCIENCE AND THE SCIENTIFIC METHOD Several major developments have compelled changes in religion and the Church. Probably the most momentous one has been the development of the scientific method. The long, bitter conflict between science and religion has been alleviated by the recognition that they are two approaches having different but not necessarily incompatible objectives. Religion deals with our relations to the omnipotent forces that we believe are supreme in the universe and which give meaning and purpose to our lives. Science deals with the relationships that exist in the natural world, which includes man. It seeks to understand nature and life as fully as possible by discovering their characteristics and the principles by which they operate. There is no incompatibility between being a man of religion and also a man of science if these objectives are recognized. Early religious writers gave colorful and imaginative descriptions and explanations of the origins of the universe and its operations in extolling the character and purposes of God in His universe. Some were plainly symbolic; others were in terms of the knowledge and the beliefs of the times. They were limited, partial, and untrue in terms of our later knowledge. But early interpreters of these writings considered them correct descriptions of the origin of the natural world. The earth was considered the center of the universe, with the heavens revolving about the planet; in the depth of our earth was hell. Human history was confined to 6000 years. Man's salvation depended not only on righteous behavior but also upon his acceptance of these ideas.

Scientists came forward to show clearly that the earth is not the center of the universe, that the universe extends in space beyond imagination, and that it has existed for eons of time. They traced man's evolution as a natural creature and showed the universe to be a vastly greater and more marvelous thing than the small contracted system earlier interpreters envisioned. Instead of regarding man as a sinful creature, fallen from purity, science sees him as a striving being, exerting his energies to reach ever greater heights of physical, mental, and moral perfection.

The Church, however, held on to a static theology. It violently attacked those who questioned in any way these early formulations, refused to admit that these descriptions were based on the limited knowledge of the times, and insisted that the earth was made primarily to extol the majesty of God. They resisted vehemently all efforts at reformulation or reconciliation.

The modernist decries the refusal of the fundamentalist to see that science gives us new and expanding knowledge of the world in which we live by producing new truths about the uniformities and laws of nature. Science makes a great contribution to religion through its spirit, which is essentially a continuous search for truth. It believes that if one knows the truth, no matter where it leads, it will truly set one free. But even more than these, its ever enlarging conceptions of the world, man's place in it, and its laws of growth give us a new sense of the spiritual forces that operate in it.

SCHOLARS WITHIN THE CHURCH Scholars within the Church are themselves bringing forth materials that make religious beliefs more reasonable. Many approach the study of the Bible from the historical point of view, by describing the times and circumstances under which the books were written, together with handling problems of authorship, purposes, and message. Setting conceptions in their historical context makes possible a view of the expansion and change of ideas about the nature of God and the meaning of the religious messages. Religious writers are showing how these ideas enlarged from the limited notions of tribal peoples to the profound conceptions of Jesus and His followers. These presentations make untenable the older, literal interpretation of religious documents and have led to the discovery of meanings and values that were not apparent in the old tradition.

COMPETING SOCIAL ATTRACTIONS Churches have also been forced to adapt to increased competition from new social attractions. Not many decades ago, churches had almost a complete monopoly on the social life of their communities. This was generally true when society was largely agricultural, when communities were small, and associations were primary and face-to-face.

Under these circumstances, churches were centers of sociability as well as of religious instruction and worship. The forms of sociability were carefully determined, the activities on Sunday having been especially controlled. In the early days, attendance at church services was obligatory, and most types of recreation were forbidden. Many communities had church-sponsored laws forbidding the playing of such games as baseball or the reading on Sunday of such secular materials as newspapers. Commercial forms of recreation were practically nonexistent.

Today, the churches are confronted with an impressive array of competing facilities and activities. Movies, television, the motor car, commercialized sports, and the golf course take many people away from Sunday services. The modern church no longer holds the central position in community life that it formerly enjoyed.

Population growth, industrialization, and different attitudes toward the use of Sunday and toward recreation have changed the position of the churches in these matters. The churches, while often speaking out against competing activities, exercise little influence over them. The exception is found in the few states which still have so-called "Blue Laws," but vigorous campaigns are now being carried on to have these repealed.

The churches have responded to this challenge in two opposite ways. Some insist that the churches should not attempt to "meet the competition" and argue that it is not the business of these institutions to serve as centers for sociability and recreation. To do so would lower their standards to worldly or secular levels.

Other churches, in effect, attempt to cope with the competition by absorbing it ("if you can't lick 'em, join 'em"). Some of these have developed social and recreational services which overshadow the traditional religious emphasis, which is generally the inclination in modern "suburbia." [8]

The Nature of the Church Gives It Some Problems Other Institutional Agencies Do Not Have

A VOLUNTARY ORGANIZATION There is an important difference between the Church and other institutional agencies that affects its operation. Participation in its programs is voluntary, and in most societies people are not required to belong, to attend, or to support this agency unless they so desire.

In some societies, the use of the services of the temples or the priests is like the use of other commodities. If one wishes to use them, he purchases them for a price. There are few congregations of worshippers with responsibility for support of these agencies. The temples or monasteries are operated by professional religionists whose support comes from voluntary contributions and income from services, endowments, and real property. In some cases, they rely on appropriations of government. In some European societies where there is a state Church, citizens pay taxes for its support, but this does not involve compulsory attendance or membership. "Free" churches often organize in these societies on the basis of voluntary support of their adherents.

There are no compulsions for the support of religious agencies in American society, unless we consider the expectations of the community or the Church itself or the influence of family and social heritage as compulsions. Even these cannot insist that support be given. This voluntary support is not characteristic of other basic institutions like the family, education, and government.

Churches must therefore build up their own sources of financial support. As a consequence, they must devote a good deal of time to recruiting members and raising money. Depending upon contributions may sometimes affect the positions that churches take on critical issues of social or economic justice. The fear of alienating contributors can induce ministers and other officials to take "safe" positions on important questions.

Understandably, also, churches have competed with each other for members and funds. The movement toward mergers and interchurch cooperation will reduce this problem.

LAY LEADERSHIP Another consequence of the voluntary character of the Church is the importance of lay leadership. A major character-istic of Protestant Christian churches is their organization as congregations of believers having varying degrees of responsibility for the local church. The scope of responsibility ranges from the complete control exercised by autonomous local congregations who hire their own professional personnel and operate their own program to the more authoritarian units in which high officials appoint ministers and otherwise control the local church activities.

Effective lay leadership and active lay participation can produce a deep loyalty and enthusiasm which will support a strong local enterprise. The genius of many churches lies in the active acceptance of responsibility by the local laity.

Would One Religious Creed for One World Be Possible?

Someone has said that "above all religions is religion." The history of religion indicates that it diversifies into hundreds of different forms because of varying cultural conditions and the human responses to them. Religion is one of man's deepest experiences and one of society's chief control mechanisms. It is often asked whether there are general beliefs that would make possible the development of a creed for one world, so that men of all kinds could unite to use the power of religion for the common good of all.

Religions have evolved over the centuries from primitive animisms to noble monotheisms. Their growth has varied and their adjustments have been slow and difficult. But is it not conceivable that eventually common principles could be synthesized into universal conceptions that express the basic beliefs held by all men in such a way that they can unite to achieve their common ends? Such an objective would undoubtedly be considered Utopian by most persons. The idealist, at least, could aspire to develop a unified religion which might undergird a unified world.

References

1. Kroeber, A. L., *Anthropology* (New York, Harcourt, Brace and Company, 1923), p. 171.
2. Micah 6:8.
3. Hindus, Maurice, *Humanity Uprooted* (New York, Jonathan Cape and Harrison Smith, 1930), p. 23. By permission of Jonathan Cape Ltd., London.
4. *The World Almanac and Book of Facts, 1962* (New York, New York World-Telegram

Corp., 1962), p. 719. (Data from the *1961 Book of the Year* of the Encyclopaedia Britannica.)

5. United States Department of Commerce, Bureau of the Census, *Statistical Abstract of the United States, 1962*, Table 45, p. 46.
6. *The World Almanac and Book of Facts, 1962* (New York, New York World-Telegram Corp., 1962), pp. 705–706. (These and the following data are from *Yearbook for American Churches, 1962*, National Council of Churches of Christ.)
7. Hostetler, John A., *Amish Life* (Scottsdale, Pa., Herald Press, 1952).
8. See, for example, Winter, G., *The Suburban Captivity of the Churches* (New York, The Macmillan Company, 1962).

Questions for Study and Discussion

1. Does the fact that religion seems to be a universal experience of men today and seems to have been from earliest times indicate that it is instinctive?
2. How would you explain this fact of universality?
3. What factors do you consider most significant in explaining the great variations in religious expressions?
4. Can you add any other components that seem to be basic to religions in addition to the four stressed in this chapter?
5. Give a definition of a church and contrast it with a sect. How do sects arise? Did Christians once constitute a sect?
6. Discuss the role of functionaries in the operation of churches.
7. Discuss the role of the Church in societies in terms of their manifest and latent functions.
8. Do you regard as sound the arguments presented in this chapter that indicate a broad religious unity in the American society?
9. What do you understand to be the important differences between modernism and fundamentalism? Can such differences be resolved?
10. Do you think science and religion are incompatible? Discuss pro and con.
11. Point out some changing conditions in societies that have made changes in the churches necessary.
12. Is religion just a significant type of social control or does it have other values?
13. Discuss differences between the Church and other institutions that result in important problems for the Church that other institutions do not have.
14. Defend or oppose the thesis that communism is a religion.

Suggested Topics for Reports

1. Consult the books by Vernon and Wach listed in the supplementary readings for this chapter and prepare a statement indicating the distinguishing features of the sociological approach to religion.
2. Prepare a study of an Amish, Mennonite, or Doukhobor community with a focus on the problems in its relations with the secular culture of the larger society.
3. Make a comparative study of an old church in a central city and a new church in a modern suburban community.

Supplementary Reading

Durkheim, Emile, *The Elementary Forms of the Religious Life*. London: George Allen and Unwin, Ltd., 1915.

Hoult, Thomas F., *The Sociology of Religion*. New York: Dryden Press, 1958.

Lenski, Gerhard, *The Religious Factor: A Sociological Study of Religion's Impact on Politics, Economics and Family*. Garden City, N.Y.: Doubleday and Company, Inc., 1961.

Lynd, Robert S., and Lynd, Helen H., *Middletown*. New York: Harcourt, Brace and Company, 1929.

Neibuhr, Reinhold, *Christianity and Power Politics*. New York: Charles Scribner's Sons, 1940.

Sperry, Willard L., *Religion in America*. New York: The Macmillan Company, 1946.

Vernon, Glenn M., *Sociology of Religion*. New York: McGraw-Hill Book Co., Inc., 1962.

Wach, Joachim, *The Sociology of Religion*. Chicago: University of Chicago Press, 1943.

Weber, Max, *The Protestant Ethic and the Spirit of Capitalism*. Tran. by Talcott Parson. New York: Charles Scribner's Sons, 1930.

Yinger, J. Milton, *Religion in the Struggle for Power*. Durham, N.C.: Duke University Press, 1946.

———, *Religion, Society, and the Individual*. New York: The Macmillan Company, 1957.

14

ECONOMIC INSTITUTIONS:
THE SELF-MAINTENANCE AGENCIES

*I*NDUSTRY *and economic institutions provide the maintenance materials for a society through the production and distribution of needed and desired goods, by the combined use of capital, labor, land, raw materials, and managerial ability.*

The Economic Institutions Are Pivotal in Societies

The first order of business in any society is its self-maintenance. There must be food, clothing, and shelter so mere survival makes work imperative. We must obtain these necessities even if it means no more than picking them from the ground or a bush. Usually, it requires much more than the mere taking to satisfy our elemental needs since we are in competition with other animals and because our environment is so niggardly. A vast part of the population of the world is bound by the chains of economic necessity. Many have little opportunity to live for much else than to satisfy their elemental necessities.

The human animal strives to attain a level above the mere satisfaction of his elemental needs. His development leads to the growth of a cultural environment from which he acquires new needs beyond mere subsistence. As human beings, then, we come to live on the plane of choices—of selecting deliberately among our expanding possibilities. But a good number of our possibilities are narrowly restricted. Since most of the goods and services we want are scarce in varying degrees, we must make choices between scarce items in terms of the value we place on some as compared with others we desire. Economic institutions arise out of the determinations we make with respect to the goods we need and want in terms of the alternative possibilities. Our available choices are based on the complex of techniques, ideas, norms, and values that develop from our adaptations to our environment.

Economic Institutions Perform Several Essential Functions

INSTITUTIONAL INTERRELATIONSHIPS The functions which economic institutions perform are interwoven with the functions of all other societal institutions and agencies, for they arise to satisfy societal wants and needs. Societies are systems operating as integrated units. How property is produced and used is related to government, the family, religion, and almost all other parts of our system. For example, we cannot use an automobile in any manner we wish. We are limited by the rules of the road, the desires of our family, and the ethical and moral principles of our community.

Production Production by various economic agencies of the goods needed and wanted requires organization of the productive resources. Decisions must be formed as to what the productive organization shall "make," whether it is to be food products and in what quantity and quality, or television sets and in what quantity and quality. Here the problem of alternatives arises in relationship to the type of society. In a free enterprise society, supply and demand are supposed to be the regulating forces. The form which produced goods take and how much is produced are determined by what the market will take. Those directing the economy in a totalitarian government may decide that some goods are more necessary than

209

Subsistence technology in a primitive society: Banyanga women pounding cassava, a diet staple; Mongo hunter and equipment; Eskimo whale-hunting party.

others—heavy industrial equipment for further production, for example, rather than consumption items for the people. There are many degrees of economic control in societies that range from the free market system to complete societal control. The extent of the control varies in a given society from time to time, depending on the circumstances and the values that appear more important at the time.

Distribution Food must be distributed after we produce it. One aspect of this function is called marketing, which is the process of getting goods to the user. Some call this the creation of place-and-time utility. As specialization and division of labor increase, the mechanisms for distribution are increasingly necessary and intricate. The problem of distribution in a simple society is also simple because the society is usually self-sufficing. The number of links in its marketing chain are few. The family in the simple society satisfies its needs almost directly. Goods pass through many hands in a complex society until they reach the persons who buy them with their medium of exchange—money which they have earned from their particular roles in the economic system.

Adjusting Production to Consumption The third function is the adjustment of production to consumption. The market can consume certain quantities of goods within a given period. Values decline and waste ensues if we produce more than we can use. A method for bringing the two into a reasonable equilibrium is essential. Our demands in relation to our supplies are supposed to take care of the adjustment in a free economic system. The society may develop programs to control the process if production and consumption are seriously out of adjustment and there are large surpluses. This situation, which arises chiefly when there is overproduction, can be illustrated by the United States' post-World War II support programs developed to compensate for surplus agricultural production. The production machinery is stimulated to meet consumption requirements if there is not enough production to satisfy them.

Production Is the Basis of Economic Activity

We must produce most of the goods and services required to satisfy our needs and wants. The skill and techniques we possess, then, must be applied to the resources of nature in order to appropriate them for use. Our success in doing this demands that we cooperate and accommodate to the social life about us.

Nature, though the source for satisfying our needs, is often a reluctant giver and a formidable destroyer. These circumstances are major forces in the creation and maintenance of our social order and the adjustment we make to it.

Different Systems of Economy Are Followed by Societies

A CLASSIFICATION Societies follow different types of economic systems, ranging from direct and simple procedures to indirect and complex ones, in the variable forms of their cultural development. Although they have been described in various ways, one classification commonly used includes the following types: (1) direct appropriation, (2) pastoral, (3) agricultural, (4) handicraft, and (5) industrial. In traditional analysis, these were regarded as evolutionary stages.

Direct Appropriation Economy In a direct appropriation economy, man uses what nature provides in its original form—berries, nuts, fruits, grains, animals, fish, and other natural products. Because he has to wander from place to place to assure himself of adequate supplies, he does little processing and storing. He hunts and fishes with various equipment, which could start him on the road to tool-making. Bows, arrows, and slings are probably the first forms of private property.

Pastoral Economy Man makes use of animals for multiplying his food, clothing, shelter, and draft needs when he discovers that some of the animals he formerly killed can be tamed. Now he begins to transform natural products. The domestication of animals gives him a more certain supply of food. Still a nomad, he must move about to provide food for his herd and flocks. He continues to eat the edible fruits, grains, and berries supplied by nature, but his concept of private property now encompasses group ownership by families and clans. There may be individual ownership, but communal ownership is the predominant property pattern.

Agricultural Economy Man is induced to settle down when he finds that he can cultivate some of the foods he had formerly consumed in their wild state. Also, his flocks may in some ways limit his movement. Now domesticating plants as well as animals, definite plots of ground are designated as growing and living areas, and permanent dwellings appear. Property in animals, land, tools, and houses becomes more clearly private.

Handicraft Economy The care of land and animals, the construction of dwellings and barns, and the growing requirements in clothing, furnishings, and tools are more than one man and his family can effectively handle. Others have more aptitude than he in making shoes, repairing equipment, and building structures. Specialization and division of labor come into existence. Economy begins to operate by his assigning work to others and his paying for it in goods or in direct money payment. Natural products are the raw materials for the making of goods. Their processing by craftsmen becomes general. The handicraft stage makes private property predominant. Men produce goods which they directly own, or they give services for wages with which they buy goods to become their own.

Industrial Economy Man's power sources in these previous economic systems are largely his own strength. He makes some use of animals to transport grain or pull loads, but this is limited. In an industrial economy, he applies power sources other than human or animal, such as running water, steam, gasoline, and electricity. He creates a machine system that produces goods for a market which are purchased by people with money earned in wages or salary. This system is the present-day machine-marketing economy.

CHANGE IN ECONOMIC STAGES There are still some societies in each of these stages of economic production. Erroneously, some older scholars assumed that every society must pass through each of them. Societies skip some of these stages, primarily because their environment does not lend itself to them or because borrowing from other cultures makes it possible to pass over a stage. Each economy develops out of antecedent cultural conditions. For example, the development of the industrial economy had taproots in the handicraft production system that preceded it. The goods of the handicraft era were made in the homes of the master workmen, but the merchants who sold them began to supply raw materials and tools to further production. They hired workers who became their employees, wrested the control of making and selling goods from the craftsmen, and laid the groundwork for the factory system. Pure forms of these production systems are exceptions; each has features of the preceding forms. This continuity is characteristic of

Subsistence technology in a peasant society: grinding grain and spinning thread.

cultural transmission. Production in each form of economy involves, however, the same factors of operation, some division of labor, and some control of property. Economic institutions evolve about them.

A Constant Set of Factors Enters the Production Process of a Society, No Matter What Economic Stage It Is In

RAW MATERIAL Each of the economic systems, no matter how simple or complex, uses five factors of production: raw materials, labor, land, capital, and managerial ability. We list raw materials first. It is not necessarily inferred that we create new materials when we say that we "make" something. We may simply change the form of materials possessing certain properties that nature provides. The materials in their original state are *raw* materials, and man works these to make his goods. For example, he cuts trees, makes lumber from them, and uses the wood to shape useful goods ranging from toothpicks to beautiful paneling for many-roomed buildings. He is simply changing the form of a raw material.

LABOR We are exerting labor when we use our energy to make these objects. No production occurs without the use of some human labor—even modern automation does not eliminate it completely. It is a factor of production whether it is exerted directly on the object or indirectly to create the means for production. A fair proportion of the value of any commodity represents labor's contribution. Just what this proportion is has been an issue in many labor disputes in the past.

LAND Land always enters the productive process as a factor, either as a raw material in production, as a source of raw materials, or as a place where productive activities are carried on. The farmer uses land chiefly as a raw material, combining its chemical properties with those of seed, fertilizer, and labor to produce the food supplies of a society. His farm, too, is a place where his productive activities are carried on. Also, land is a source of raw materials. The miner, the fisherman, and the forester use it as a source for extracting materials to be processed into consumable goods. Productive activities must be carried on at some place. Factories, warehouses, and all other equipment that enters production must rest on land.

CAPITAL Capital is that which we have saved from our enterprise to make possible further production. We require greater quantities of saved resources to support production as a society expands and becomes more complex, and as the process spreads over longer periods. Tools, machinery, and factory buildings must be provided and then replaced when worn out. Even the primitive man's oxen will eventually die and his hoe break or wear out. He must save in order to have capital for replacements. Capital requirements are a major factor in present-day production processes where machinery, factories, stocks of materials, and workmen's wages or salaries must be supplied.

MANAGERIAL ABILITY Raw materials, labor, land, and capital must be combined in proper proportions to give the best net return. This is perhaps the most important task in the production process. Managerial ability is the factor that provides this combination. In simple economies, the operator may provide several of these elements so that he is laborer, capitalist, and manager operating his own enterprise—changing the form of some raw material at his own place into his consumable goods. The farmer today is still laborer, capitalist, and manager (the two latter functions are becoming more significant as farming becomes more mechanized). Today's complex production system divides these functions so that it contains laborers, managers, and capitalists as separate categories. Many of today's economic problems come from this division of labor and function. Out of it, however, have grown many of society's institutions.

The Economic Institutions of Western Societies Have Been Produced by the Machine-Marketing Economy

We discovered in Chapter 2 that the Industrial Revolution created a new pattern of conducting economic activities in Western societies. The institutionalized norms of previous economies led to the crystallization of most of our present economic institutions. The machine-marketing economy gives dominant roles to some of them in the present economic life. These are the concern of our following discussion.

Property Is a Pre-Eminent Institution in the Economy of Societies

The first of these institutions is property. We create property, things that satisfy needs and wants, by the use of the factors of production. Property consists of goods and services that a society gives an individual or group of individuals the exclusive right to possess, use, and dispose of. They are "one's own" as the Latin *proprietas* implies. Property may be tangible or intangible. Tangible items constitute most of our property, but society often gives an individual or group of individuals the exclusive right to intangibles that have value. For instance, someone invents a new material, and a society grants a patent, the exclusive right to use this material for certain periods of time. The owners can demand payment for its use from others during such a period. Copyrights, good will, and secret processes are intangible properties.

DIFFERENCES IN OWNERSHIP This right to possess property differs in various societies; in some, it may rest in the whole society. The animals that are killed in the hunt belong to the whole tribe in some direct appropriation societies. In these, everything the tribe or any member of it has is common property, except wives and the weapons of the males. In some societies, ownership of some property may be public, and other property may be private. Some of the land used for grazing belonged to the whole community in our early New England colonies—"the commons," it was called. But most of the land was private, possessed by particular individuals who were permitted to use it as they chose and dispose of it as they wished.

Private Property An outstanding characteristic of economic life in the democratic societies of today is the prominent role of the institution of private property. In the democratic system, the society itself does not try to be a property owner except of the land, buildings, and equipment it uses for its governmental operations, together with the atmosphere, waters, land, and other natural resources that it protects for free use. It encourages individuals and groups of individuals to use the factors of production to produce property for their exclusive use and to dispose of it as they desire. The prize offered is the possibility of accumulating wealth, that is, goods that have utility and command value, especially exchange or money value.

Societies in Which Private Ownership Prevails Support the System with Other Institutional Patterns

FREE ENTERPRISE, EXCHANGE, AND CONTRACT A society based on a private property system supports it with the institutions of free enterprise, free exchange, and free contracts. The society relies upon these institutions, normative complexes related to competition and agreement, to make sure that wealth is not accumulated without competition. They allow us to seek it in any *legitimate* way we choose—freedom of enterprise—and to dispose of it wherever and however we can—freedom of exchange. The freedom of enterprise and of exchange involves freedom of contract—our right as individuals or groups to agree to act with respect to each other relative to a specified matter in a definite way, which indicates what rights and obligations we have in respect to each other. These agreements make relationships impersonal and

objective. Practically all economic relationships are based on such oral or written contracts. Society supports their validity when they are made in due form.

This completely free and open struggle to obtain by competition possessions of wealth is the heart of the free enterprise system. Competition between legitimate enterprises is depended upon to regulate the whole economy. Society tries to protect us against such activities as fraud and theft, which are excluded from the rivalry. Prices for shoes or grain, for example, rise and bring increased production to meet demands if there is a shortage. Wages rise and more workmen are attracted if a particular form of labor is scarce. Thus, market prices are the controlling factor, determining by their fluctuations how much of particular goods and services should be produced.

OPEN MARKET The operation of these institutions assumes that competition is completely free and "our market" open to all. It assumes that there are no efforts to restrict the supplies of goods and services or to control them in a given direction. Thus, consumers, by buying for their needs in a rational way, and producers, by creating according to these needs, set up a demand-and-supply situation in which an equilibrium price determines what is produced. Such conditions never completely prevail in modern societies. Consumers do not always act rationally. They buy, in part, according to desire rather than to actual need. They are influenced by fads, fashions, and high-pressure salesmanship. Also, producers cooperate to control production and prices out of self-interest. There are commercial and trade associations, farmer's cooperatives, professional associations, labor unions, and many others—all of which limit competition to promote their own economic well-being.

The logic of the free enterprise, competitive system, wherein what is produced for use is determined by supply and demand, has had strong appeal. But modern societies have reached the stage where perfectly competitive economies do not exist and where the public interest requires protection. This is accomplished in two general ways: (1) by government regulations that prevent combinations presumed to be opposed to competition and (2) by regulation of combinations that are injurious to the interest of the public. These matters lead us to a consideration of the characteristics of the modern capitalistic economy.

There Are Several Major Characteristics of the Modern Private Property Economy

The modern machine-marketing economy has a number of major characteristics: (1) Machines are concentrated primarily in factories to produce goods in quantity. We have "mass production." (2) The system breaks the productive activities into small parts, thus creating a high degree of division of labor. (3) The subdivision of activities leads to the creation of specialized occupations and the de-personalization of the workers. (4) Workers are organized into labor unions to protect their interests. (5) Corporations are the major organizations for production, with their ownership and management separated. (6) Large-scale, mass production requires financing for its operational purposes, thus creating extensive financial organizations to supply money and credit needs. (7) Small businesses represented by individual proprietorships and partnerships are numerous, particularly in agriculture and merchandising. (8) The whole system is closely interdependent so that any major change in one part immediately influences the operation of the whole. (9) Governments intervene to protect the public interest, prevent undesirable combinations and regulate desirable ones, and control the relations among the parts.

The Corporation Is the Pivotal Institution of This Economy

CONTROL OF BUSINESS We shall use the American economy as our illustration of modern economic systems. We may characterize it as operating through many small businesses and a relatively small number of large corporations. The total number of businesses in this society in 1959 was over eleven million. Eighty-two per cent of these were sole proprietorships, and 9 per cent more were partnerships. Although corporations—about one million in number—constituted only 9 per cent of all our businesses, they are the chief form of business operation when we measure them in terms of business transacted. Of all the receipts of these businesses in 1959, the corporations received 75 per cent; individual proprietorships, 17 per cent; and partnerships, 8 per cent.[1] The corporations employ the majority of gainful workers and produce virtually all (estimated at over 90 per cent) the manufactured goods of the society. They control most of the financial resources of the country. Smaller businesses compete for a diminished part of the total market as "big business" becomes dominant in production, distribution, communication, and finance. Corporations are at the center of today's economy, and smaller enterprises gravitate about them.

CORPORATION DEFINED A corporation is a voluntary organization of persons operating under the laws of a state and through a charter granted by a state for the purpose of handling property or other interests for the benefit of those who compose it. It is a legal entity with the right to own and dispose of its property, make contracts, and conduct business or other interests in its own name. Perhaps the most famous description of this relationship entity is that made early in our national history by Chief Justice Marshall of the Supreme Court of the United States:

> A corporation is an artificial being, invisible, intangible, and existing only in contemplation of law. Being a mere creature of law, it possesses only those properties which the charter of its creation confers upon it. . . . Among the most important are immortality, and, if the expression may be allowed, individuality; properties by which a perpetual succession of many persons are considered as the same, and may act as a single individual. They enable a corporation to manage its own affairs, and to hold property without the perplexing intricacies, the hazardous and endless necessity of perpetual conveyance, for the purpose of transmitting it from hand to hand.[2]

OWNERSHIP IN CORPORATIONS Corporations are not new forms of doing business. They arose in relation to public enterprises that required considerable capital. Their method of acquiring capital began to be used by other production enterprises, and the modern corporation grew from this. Capital to supply corporation needs is derived chiefly from the sale of stocks. Those who own shares in the business of a corporation are its owners. Their ultimate responsibility for the operation of their business is discharged by electing a board of directors which is charged with company management and the formulation of the policies to be followed. In 1962, there were seventeen million shareowners in the corporations of the United States. Some corporations, such as American Telephone and Telegraph Company, have hundreds of thousands of shareholders, although the great majority of them own only a small number of shares.

Ownership, then, is divided into many small units and is of a highly impersonal character, which is a great change from the individual type of ownership that marked the societies of past centuries. It introduces a new system of property rights into society. No stockholder can claim any particular part of the property or holdings of a corporation as his own, even though he is part owner. It is an entity to be subdivided only by the proper legal decision of all its owners and by duly authorized legal procedures.

CORPORATION CHARACTERISTICS There are three chief features of corporations. The first is that the owners of a corporation have only limited financial liability for it. This is set by law at the value of the stock they own. They lose no more than they have invested if their corporation should go bankrupt, and they are not liable for the debts of the corporation itself. Stock shares can be transferred from person to person, giving the corporation a continuity regardless of the particular persons who own it. The second feature is the wide dispersal of ownership. Dispersion is inevitable when companies sell millions of shares of stock to a great number of people. The result is that only a few of the stockholders know much about their business. The stockholders' main concern is to obtain returns from their investments. The role of the owners of corporations, therefore, is quite different from that of the single owner of a business. The single owner must not only be concerned about the profits on his investment but also about every other aspect of his operation, if he is to have any assurance of profits at all.

The third feature of corporations is the concentration of management in an hierarchical pattern. While stockholders are responsible for the operation of their corporation, they perform this function indirectly, by delegating management to a board of directors. The board usually employs salaried managers who have specialized training and skill. These, in turn, direct their subordinates who, in turn, pass their orders and suggestions "down the line" until the operations are accomplished. Policies are handed down by the group at the top. Thus is formed what we describe as a bureaucracy.

SOCIAL SIGNIFICANCE The social significance of the corporation parallels its economic influence. It is an ingenious device to coordinate under unified management the resources and energies of people in order to make possible large-scale, economic activities requiring much capital and labor. The gigantic enterprises of our time bring huge numbers of workers into single organizations and reorder their relationships. They are responsible for technical advances and research findings that are almost impossible for small enterprises. They are a major factor in the creation of our unparalleled standard of living since they have reduced the prices of goods through low production costs, large output, and volume sales. And they have an immense impact upon the local community, the region, and the nation.

Small Business Has a Significant Role in This Economy

Of major concern to the nation is that small business in the American economy is being crowded out in an unequal struggle. Over nine of each ten business enterprises are of this type, if we assume that sole proprietorships and partnerships are, in the main, small business. Small businesses furnish a livelihood for a significant proportion of persons in the labor force. They are found in all types of endeavor but are concentrated chiefly in the distribution field and in services. They represent a large part of the economy's total activity, a significant part of our business investments, and a large number of people who are risking their resources to make a living and concurrently to serve society. One student concluded that while "small business cannot have its stability insured, the complexity of our economy makes new demands for regulation in the common interest so that small business can have a rightful place in the competitive market." [3]

The Character of the Competition Has Changed

CAPITAL REQUIREMENTS LIMIT COMPETITION A foundation principle in the free enterprise system is that wealth should not be accumulated without free competition. But the problem of maintaining a free competitive system became increasingly difficult in the American economy as it developed from a predominantly agricultural to an industrial system and as corporations grew in size and scope. Completely free competition, if it ever existed, has now disappeared. It is virtually impossible for those who might desire to enter certain types of production to do so just for the simple reason that capital requirements are out of reach. Even in farming, capital requirements for machinery and land are an important factor for those individuals desiring to enter it. If we consider automobile manufacture as an example, we find it took from $250 to $500 million to build a single automobile factory, even in 1951.[4] This is a far cry from the early days of Henry Ford and his first cars.

Differences in resources for developing new technical inventions that reduce costs of production and give lower price advantages also make competition unequal. Moreover, small businesses can hardly compete with the great corporations in marketing activities. They must confine themselves largely to economic fields where they do not compete directly, as in distribution and services. The activities of many small business units consist in distributing the products of the great corporations.

INTERCORPORATION COMPETITION What of competition between the great corporations themselves? To many, they seem to operate as monopolies. This appears to be correct where the corporation controls a major share of the market for a particular good. For some time now, three great automobile corporations—General Motors, Ford, and Chrysler—have had from 80 to 90 per cent of the production in this field. The "independents"—three to seven of them—have had what was left. These big corporations do not try to compete directly with each other by cutting prices (they advertise their prices, "the lowest prices of the low priced three," or use other slogans to emphasize the fairness of their prices). But they try to get the market by outadvertising, outstyling, or outdoing each other in the quality and services offered. They compete with each other, not by price-cutting, but by bidding against each other for the buying market.

COUNTERVAILING POWER What keeps the few great corporations from agreeing on prices and pushing them up to make even greater profits? Here Galbraith's principle of "countervailing power" operates. He illustrated this by pointing out that "Sears, Roebuck & Company was able, by exploiting its role as a large and indispensable customer, to procure tires from Goodyear Tire and Rubber Company at a price from twenty-nine to forty per cent lower than the going market."[5] Thus Goodyear's power was decidedly weakened, not by another rubber company, but by its customer. Chain stores have also been able to compel food manufacturers to lower their prices by using their buying power as pressure.

Kaplan summarized these operations by saying: "In our economy big business undertakes the major role of coordinating individual efforts and resources into collective achievement. This is a function that must be undertaken under modern technology, whether by private enterprise or by the state. In the United States it has been possible so to mix dispersion with centralization that the major job can be left to private competition under government regulation. Big business has not merely been kept effectively subject to a competitive system; on the whole it has also made an essential contribution to its scope, vitality, and effectiveness."[6]

The Cooperative Method of Doing Business Endeavors to Introduce a New Concept of Profit Distribution

PATRONAGE DIVIDENDS The only significant new form of conducting business to be introduced into the private enterprise system of industrial societies is the cooperative. The cooperative does not do away with the private enterprise system but seeks to change it in relation to the distribution of profits. The cooperatives are like corporations in that they organize the factors of production so as to obtain the greatest net profit. Corporations pay for the use of capital with dividends on the stock owned by the various holders after all other costs are cared for. The profits are divided among their shareholders at a return per share. Cooperatives, on the other hand, pay for their use of capital at a predetermined fixed rate just as they pay for the use of the other factors of production. Their profits are distributed to the users of the enterprise as a patronage dividend in proportion to the amount of business each patron has contributed to it. Profits are determined only after all costs, including those for the use of capital, are paid.

True cooperatives have other principles—such as one vote for each member—but the primary difference between them and the corporations is in their method of distributing profits.

SPREAD OF COOPERATIVES In 1844, this form of business operation started with a retail store in Rochdale, England. It expanded to include wholesale buying, manufacturing, transportation, and housing. It has spread in several European countries, such as the Scandinavian group, until now significant proportions of most types of business are cooperatives. It has had its greatest growth in the production, marketing, and consumption of agricultural products.

The Individual Worker Achieves a New Social Position in Our Industrial Economy

What of the workers in our economic system? We emphasized in our discussion of societies and their cultural antecedents (Chapter 2) that the Industrial Revolution ushered in a new social class structure in Western societies and changed social relationships in the economic world. Industrialization contributed to the ultimate disappearance of the manorial form of organization. The tenant serfs who had been bound by custom and tradition to their manorial lords became free and independent workers. Other occupational activities had also been fixed by custom and tradition so that the son of a mason, carpenter, or other freeman or freeholder almost automatically followed in the footsteps of his father. Industrialization, however, made workers free to sell their skills wherever they could to best advantage. Moving about from one job opportunity to another became characteristic. New types of work and skills appeared, and ascribed position gave way to achieved position.

But the free position of the worker was not altogether to his advantage. The employer also was free. In the feudal system, the lord saw to it that his people were given protection and provided with the necessities of life. The entrance of free enterprise allowed him to employ whom he would for as long or short a time as he desired without further obligation. Therefore work, wages, and working conditions could become uncertain matters. In the early periods of industrialism, they certainly were. Thus, while the new economic order made the achievement of new status and power possible to the masses of workers, it gave them problems relating to their well-being that have been critical in Western societies ever since.

The New Freedom of Workers and Employers in Industrial Societies Required the Development of New Social Relationships

CHANGING ECONOMIC OPERATIONS The application of machinery to the processing of goods and the development of an industrial society dependent upon a world-wide market thus changed the older occupations and created many new ways of making a living. It concentrated workers in factories and cities under the supervision of employers who organized work into minute subdivisions and specializations and workers into single-operation performers. The industrial worker no longer makes anything completely—he only contributes a step or so to its making. The assembly-line technique has been refined to the point where workers integrate hundreds of repeated machine operations that combine dozens of parts and processes to produce a single product. Under automation, that is, the control of manufacturing machines by automatic devices, the worker only feeds instructions to machines which relay them to manufacturing units. The major task of workers in this system is thus reduced to the maintenance of the machines.

IMPERSONALITY OF THE WORKER The most striking consequence of these industrial developments is the increasing replaceability and impersonality of the worker in machine production. He can be replaced at any time and almost by anyone because he does a single task that can be learned in a short time. The significance of his task, though important to the product, is lost in the total process. Any personal skill, cleverness, or exceptional craftsmanship he may possess is submerged in the impersonal operation of his machines. Many decry this "subservience" of the person to the machine which, they feel, produces human automatons with low aspiration and poor morale.

UNCERTAINTY OF EMPLOYMENT A further consequence of this development is the relative helplessness of the individual in contracting for his services. The free-enterprise economy demands freedom of contract. The worker is free to let his services to whom he will. On the other hand, the employer is free to hire whom he will. Labor is one of the factors of production for the employer to be used in such quantity and of such quality as to give, in combination with the other factors of production, the greatest net profit. No other obligations are imposed except to pay wages for the hours of work given. No concern for regularity of employment or other conditions that face the worker are to be imposed upon the employer any more than the employee is to be concerned whether the enterprise makes a profit. Uncertainties concerning job opportunities and adequate income create deep fears that have continuously plagued the worker. Wages, regular employment, hours in the working day, and conditions of work have been the traditional problems of the workingman.

A few decades ago, a young boy worked in a factory where powder kegs, lard cans, and other buckets were manufactured from sheet iron

and tin. The enterprise employed several dozen men working at machines, most of them married and with families. Each noon these men assembled on the shipping dock to eat their lunch. This boy still vividly remembers that the conversation always came around to the questions of how long the job would last, who would be laid off first, what were the possibilities of a wage increase, whether or not the plant would shut down after a particular job was completed. What still is particularly remembered after many years is the fear that always haunted these workers. Fathers were afraid they might not be able to earn what their families needed; single men, that they could not pay their board and room or get married. There was no assurance of a job or of wage increases, to say nothing of better work conditions, unemployment care, or health protection. A man who hurt himself was sent to a doctor, but if he was away from his work too long, he lost his job. There was no agreement about anything except that the worker was to work so many hours each day at so much per hour if his work was satisfactory, and that he would be paid weekly. There was no organization of the workers, so each man was dealt with separately. The insecurity that characterized the employees of that can company was typical of worker insecurity prevalent throughout industry. No one was to blame—this was a free enterprise system. But the most serious defect in the whole operation became more and more apparent as the system developed, namely, the unequal bargaining position of the workers in relation to that of the companies.

Collective Bargaining Is Now a Basic Institutionalized Principle

Workmen attempted to meet these problems by organizing. Their employers had the advantage in that a single or, at most, a few persons were involved in making their decisions. The employers were also organized into national associations. Many trade associations had come into existence, and chambers of commerce promoted the interests of the industrial enterprises. The attempts of the workers to organize were opposed by various means, to the point

Technology in the American machine-marketing economy: wheat harvested by diesel-driven combines; manufacture of business machines; a factory complex.

that some of their organizations were declared illegal. But the right of workingmen to organize was eventually recognized as this social movement in America persisted and gained the support of the national government in the New Deal era. Collective bargaining, in which one or more individuals represent the larger group of workers in negotiations with their employers to discuss hours of work, working conditions, wages, and other interests, is an established sanctioned principle in society. Although labor groups participate in political activity, the main energies of the American labor movement have been used chiefly to organize the workers to increase their bargaining power. In contrast, their European counterparts use political organization to promote their purposes. Although never realizing its full potential, the American labor union movement has enjoyed substantial success despite persistent and sometimes spectacular difficulties.

The Labor Union Is the Formal Organization Responsible for Promoting Collective Bargaining

The strength of the labor unions, however, does not lie solely in the number of workers organized. Their greatest power lies in the critical character of the economic activities they have been able to unionize almost completely. These now include all forms of transportation, steel manufacturing, building trades, mining of coal and metal mining, automobile and aircraft industries, newspaper printing plants, publishing companies, and communications industries. A nationwide strike, the ultimate collective behavior weapon of unions, in any one of these fields could cripple our total economy. The public, through its government agency—the National Labor Relations Board—uses its powers to maintain acceptable industrial management-labor union relations.

BENEFITS OF UNIONISM The development of the labor union has given the workingman a bargaining representative that places him on a fair footing with those who employ him. It has also given him an organization wherein it is possible for him to identify with others like himself. Here he may work with others to solve common problems. This situation has not been long enough in American society to create a real labor class with an awareness of its own possible strength. Craft unionism, as promoted by the American Federation of Labor, unified workers within a given craft but often the unions fought each other. (For example, carpenter's unions often fought plumber's unions over the right to perform tasks in construction jobs.) Consequently, craft unions were not always united to achieve common goals. The industrial union, represented by the Committee for Industrial Organization—(CIO)—brings together in one union all the different workers in an industry. This kind of mass union, which can disrupt an entire industry, makes possible a maximum exertion of worker strength.

Labor has thus developed in the union an organization that makes it more capable of meeting the concentrated power of the corporations. Over the years, unions have increased their power through membership loyalty and the wealth acquired from membership dues, welfare, and pension funds. They have increased in membership and gained benefits for the workers, such as effective grievance procedures, seniority regulations, nondiscriminatory employment policies, closed shops, sick leaves and vacation pay, to say nothing about better wages and work conditions.

PROBLEMS OF THE UNIONS Responsibility in the labor unions, as in all large-scale organizations, must be delegated. The individual member cannot exercise it directly, so he depends upon the integrity of the leaders he selects. The rapid expansion of unions created an opportunity for unscrupulous men to take advantage of their leadership positions and to eliminate any effective opposition to their control. The democratic processes upon which the unions were founded were not adequately protected.[7] Instances of leadership corruption are well authenticated, and effective opposition within many labor unions is wholly absent. Government regulation may need to be extended because the autocratic domination and vicious dishonesty that may creep into unions injures not only the unions but the society as well. Society found it necessary to regulate corporations and business enterprises in the public interest. Unions, now so crucial to the operation of our total economy, seem to need regulation in the public interest also.

Some students see a bleak future for organized labor. Without question, a major threat is automation. This amazing technological development is making the need for large masses of unskilled workers a thing of the past. A well-known labor analyst states that ". . . automation is drying up the fields of historic union strength. . . . It eliminates large numbers of

blue-collar jobs in manufacturing and transportation, thus chipping away the bedrock of union enrollment."[8] At the present time, organized labor is finding it very difficult to hold its former share of the work force. This decline in strength could be offset by a more successful effort to organize the expanding ranks of white-collar workers.

The Occupational Structure of Society Changes with Changes in Industrial Organization

INCREASE IN GAINFUL EMPLOYMENT The machine-marketing economy has resulted in marked changes in the occupational structure of our society. The proportion of persons fourteen years of age and over in the civilian labor force who were employed stood at 94 per cent in 1962. Over the decades, there has been a steady growth in the proportion of persons gainfully employed in spite of the fact that military service, continued education, and employment regulations cut down the number of youth available to the labor force, while our industrial system and social security programs encourage persons over 65 years of age to retire from their work.

CHANGE IN PROPORTION OF WORKERS The most striking change since the beginning of the century is in the proportion of our employed workers engaged in agriculture—a decline from 32 per cent of all workers in 1910 to only 7 per cent of the employed civilian labor force in 1962. The application of power machinery to farming has made it possible for a very small part of the working population to produce all the food and fiber the total American population requires and still have a tremendous surplus. At the same time, the proportion of unskilled workers has declined markedly—our machines now dig the ditches and do other drudgery jobs that require little skill. Semiskilled workers have remained fairly constant while clerical and sales workers have almost doubled in the 40 years. Our proprietors, managers, and officials, along with professional persons, have also doubled. The number of women fourteen years of age and older in the employed civilian labor force doubled between 1940 and 1960 [9] because of the expansion of machine, clerical, sales, and other forms of work that women can do as effectively as men. These occupational changes show that there has been a continued development toward a technical economy, using highly trained workers with superior mechanical equipment and creating a society in which want for basic necessities would appear to be unnecessary.

Occupations Make It Possible for the Individual to Obtain Essential Subsistence and Also to Make a Contribution to Social Well-Being

SOCIAL CONTRIBUTION OF WORK Those employed in any occupation must be able to earn from it at least enough to take care of themselves and those dependent upon them. This necessity was one of the major motives prompting labor union development; for some, it is the only motive. Yet, work has significance beyond its subsistence function. It is the basic channel through which most adults gain their social identity, participate in society, and make their contribution to its well-being. As we note later, it is also a key factor in the person's social status in the society. Unfortunately, these functions of work are too often not realized. Many jobs are so specialized and mechanically routinized that the workers find little interest in them and fail to see their contribution to the larger society. Moreover, pressures within the work group or exerted by the union may frustrate the individual who wishes to maintain a high standard of quantity and quality in his work. Indeed, where men are organized they are often not permitted to work up to their full capacity. The bricklayer may, for example, be allowed to lay only so many bricks per hour or the painter to cover only so many square feet of surface per day. Further, many persons are enticed by the promise of easy gain into such pursuits as gambling and drug peddling which have only injurious effects upon society.

SOCIAL SERVICE MOTIVE There are, on the other hand, occupations which stress the social service motive and seek to subordinate the emphasis on economic gain. The doctor, clergyman, nurse, social worker, teacher, and artist, to name some, recognize that their work must of necessity supply a livelihood but that it must be motivated by a spirit of service. This spirit is difficult to create among workers who must struggle to obtain a fair return for their work. It is almost impossible for this spirit to prevail throughout the work world because the economy makes gain the uppermost value. Those in the professions have an advantage in this respect since they are usually not employed by organizations whose purpose is to make money from their services, but by persons whose aim is to obtain a service from them. How to develop the attitude that work may promote the good life because it performs services for others and so makes it possible for each worker to have pride and satisfaction in his occupation is one of the problems of the social system.

Occupational Placement Occurs in Several Ways

CHANCE OR ACCIDENT American workers are distributed through more than 15,000 major forms of work. The question is, how do they find their way into them? Obviously, there are several channels and influences. One of these is chance or accident, as is illustrated by the experience of a great painter.

Marie McCall describes how a trivial incident started Jean Millet on his life work. She says Millet was returning from Mass with his father one Sunday, when he saw an old man on the roadside. He quickly drew a charcoal picture of the man on a wall. Millet's father immediately recognized the old man, for the likeness was a striking one. He then and there decided that Jean must study painting. So the father and son visited a leading artist in Cherbourg to ask his advice. At first, the artist, a Monsieur Mouchel, would not believe that the drawings the father presented had been done by this farm lad. When, however, he was convinced that they had been, he scolded the father severely because he had kept the boy at farm work so long.[10]

Chance is a common factor in occupational selection as well as in specific job placement. Indeed, its frequency would indicate the lack of adequate vocational counselling. Chance alone, of course, would rarely be the basic factor. Rather, it would most often serve to crystallize or precipitate a pre-existing latent disposition. In a sense, as someone has said, "Chance favors the prepared individual."

CONSCIOUS PLANNING The selection of an occupation at the higher skilled and professional levels involves more conscious deliberate choice and preparation. Here there is a definite and deeper commitment to a specific career instead of a general disposition (or necessity) to enter any kind of "job" that promises a living wage. In making a choice, the person may be influenced by parents or other relatives, friends, teachers, past work experiences, or vocational counselors. The last may provide the soundest basis of choice because these professionals are able to reveal to the individual his relevant interests and capacities and to direct him into the most promising occupational areas.

In most cases, occupational selection follows a series of vague or definite decisions made over a period of years. The future significance of many of these "choices" may not be apparent at the time they are made, as, for example, a general preference for mental rather than physical activity. Occupational choice, then, is a process of growth, play of circumstance, opportunity, and increasing particularity of decision. Some students regard it as a largely irreversible process in which compromise is an essential aspect of each decision.[11]

Occupational Selection Also Takes Place as a Result of the Operation of Societal Forces

PHYSICAL QUALITIES We not only choose our occupations; in a sense, society selects us for occupations. The environment offers job opportunities, but it also sets job limitations. The selective processes in societies are usually three, based chiefly on individual qualifications for the acceptable performance of given kinds of work.[12] Occupational selection may be influenced by the physical qualities of the individual. Slight persons of limited strength can hardly engage in work requiring the handling of heavy objects like chests and boxes of freighted materials. Persons who are physically unattractive can hardly hope to be successful as actors unless the unattractive quality is exploited. Clerical jobs do not require physical strength but call for finger-and-hand dexterity. Physical factors probably enter in some degree into every occupational selection.

MENTAL TRAITS Selection of workers is also based on mental qualifications. Persons with a low mentality can hardly succeed as engineers or top business managers. On the other hand, many routine jobs require little mental ability. Indeed, too much mental ability could sometimes be a handicap to performance and job satisfaction. Over the broad range of occupations there is probably not a close correlation between mental ability and successful work performance. Indeed, William James, the psychologist, often insisted that most people use only a small proportion of the mental capacity they possess. Given the average requisite intelligence, occupational achievement is more largely a result of such factors as determination, reliability, and ability to adjust to others. Recent studies have shown that job failures of college-trained people are more often due to defective social adjustment on the job than to lack of competence.

OCCUPATIONAL PRESTIGE Society's evaluation of occupations can also influence the person's occupational choice. This is not surprising since occupation represents the "key" status to most adults. It is a basic factor in the social standing or prestige that people may enjoy. Numerous researches have revealed the differential prestige that society accords to various occupations: [13] the rankings are remarkably consistent over the years.[14]

These reports generally show that professional workers and high government officials are given the highest ratings; business men, manufacturers, merchants, and farm owner-operators are in the next highest grouping; skilled trades, such as machinists and carpenters come next; clerical positions, such as bookkeepers and secretaries next; while unskilled workers are universally ranked lowest. "There is a relatively invariable hierarchy of prestige associated with the industrial system, even when it is placed in the context of larger social systems which are otherwise differentiated in important respects," conclude Inkeles and Rossi, after comparing occupational prestige in six different countries: United States, Great Britain, New Zealand, Japan, Germany, and the Union of Soviet Socialist Republics.[15]

The prestige of an occupation derives from the attitude that members of the society have toward it. In no precise sense, this evaluation is based upon some judgment of the contribution the occupation makes to the society, the influence or power of the persons who are in it, the skill and training it requires, and the financial remuneration it offers. The prestige dimension of the occupational system will influence, at least in a general way, the person's choice of a career.

Occupational Activities Have Significant Influences upon Those Who Engage in Them

PHYSICAL EFFECTS How does prolonged employment in a given occupation affect the worker? First of all, it may affect him physically. The bookkeeper develops humped shoulders, the soldier or sailor a definite posture, the musician soft hands and muscles, while the plumber develops hard muscles and calloused hands. It is often possible for a perceptive person to guess correctly a stranger's employment from his physical characteristics.

Many kinds of work carry serious physical hazards in the form of disease, poisons, or possibilities of accidental injury and death. The high incidence of hazards in modern industry has led to two major developments: vigorous safety programs within American industry and the workmen's compensation program controlled by the government.

MENTAL OUTLOOK   Prolonged experience in an occupation influences one's mental outlook. Workers become identified with their occupation. Each occupation tends to develop an ideology and a distinctive form of discourse or argot that the member absorbs. The worker relates himself to his occupational peer group and work clique through acquiring a status and a title within them. His work gives him a definite role in the total operation.[16] He interprets his relations to the larger society in terms of these occupational activities and sees his world through the eyes of his occupational experiences. The military man is likely to interpret experiences from the point of view of command and obedience, the farmer from the position of the essential producer, or the attorney from the position of the sacredness of the law. Long association with one occupation often limits a person's outlook or frame of reference for perceiving the rest of society. One of the major sources of difficulty in human communication today is this diversity of occupational orientations with their unique and often esoteric "languages."

SOCIAL RELATIONSHIPS   A third type of occupational influence is related to the worker's social relationships. The financial remuneration from employment is a major determinant of the level of living workers may maintain. This in turn bears upon the locality in which they will live and so relates to ecological patterning.

The unskilled workman can hardly afford to live in the same neighborhood where professional people reside, and the professional people do not usually live among unskilled workers. Workers at the same occupational levels usually reside in similar neighborhoods and associate with each other. Their friendships are among those in similar occupational categories. Recent research shows that such residential proximity of people on similar occupational levels is not determined directly by sheer economic competition. Rather, it seems to be a function of differences in "style of life" which, of course, is correlated with level of education and income.[17] In any event, similarity of occupational levels is supported by similarity of residential levels. Some degree of social solidarity is thus created within the various occupational strata. This becomes a basic factor in social class behavior as is shown in studies of social stratification. (Box 20 indicates another social aspect of occupation.)

Other Economic Ideologies Challenge the Private Enterprise System

CONFLICT AND STRUGGLE MOTIFS   In its time, the private enterprise system has been challenged by ideologies of the Left and Right—of radicalism and reaction. The former include syndicalism, socialism, and communism. Each of these sees the members of the worker class pitted against the capitalist controllers of the economy. The workers can achieve security and the just rewards of their labor only by offsetting or destroying the power of the dominating, exploiting capitalist class. Struggle and conflict are the constant themes of their ideology. On the other hand, the rightist systems are illustrated by fascism in Italy, Naziism in Germany and Falangism in Spain. Fascist systems are in part reactions against the labor movement in its various forms.

BOX 20   CAREERS AND SOCIAL PARTICIPATION

Data suggest that chaotic experience in the economic order fosters a retreat from both work and the larger communal life. Even a taste of an orderly career enhances the vitality of participation: compared with men who have chaotic work histories, those who spend at least a fifth of their worklives in functionally-related, hierarchically-ordered jobs have stronger attachments to formal associations and the community. Their contacts with kin, friend, and neighbor are at once more integrated, wide-ranging, and stable. Their "occupational community" is stronger.[18]

SYNDICALISM   "Syndicalism," the French term for trade unionism, holds that in the struggle with the owner class, trade unions have a special role to play in the establishment of a collective society. The trade unions are to crystallize the class consciousness of the workers, fire their determination to control, and portray their role in the revolution which will establish the collective ownership of all property. The conventional governments are to be abolished, and in their stead the society is to be organized about autonomous production and distribution associations. The state is to consist of these syndicates or organizations of workers through which each individual can express himself economically, politically, and spiritually.[19] Syndicalism had considerable vogue in France, especially in the 1920's and 1930's. It waned as Marxian socialism and communism grew in strength.

SOCIALISM   Socialism too is rooted in the idea of class struggle. Marx and his coworker Engels held that in the free enterprise system all of the methods used to increase production are at the expense of the laborers who are being exploited. The lot of workers is one of increasing misery as capital accumulates and its domination of labor increases. The increase of wealth at one end means the increase of misery at the other until those exploited can stand the condition no longer, rise up, destroy the capitalist order, and establish the socialist system of a classless society. The new society is inevitably to be born out of revolution in which an equitable distribution of income and power can be assured.

Fabian socialism, as developed in England, did not accept the idea that the socialist society would come only by revolution. It sought the classless society and the equitable distribution of income through education and gradual legislative reform. Other Continental groups also supported the development of socialism through social reforms, predicting that these reforms, "creeping socialism," would come gradually so that it would be difficult to say when the industrial society passed from capitalism to socialism.

IS SOCIALISM INEVITABLE?   The basic question about the inevitable establishment of socialism hinges on the accuracy of the prediction that the working class will become more impoverished, that the middle class will disappear, and that wealth will be ever more concentrated in the hands of the few. Economists point out that the real income of workers, as measured by

purchasing power, has steadily increased for over a century and a half. It more than doubled during the last century. It is today higher than ever before, so that the theory of the increasing misery of the workers does not hold.[20] The workers' level of living has vastly improved over earlier periods, especially when one adds to increased real income all the other social benefits societies now provide, such as fire and police protection, education, sanitary environments, roads, and many others.

There are those who point out that, although workers are actually much better off than under previous conditions, obvious differences still exist between them and the more privileged. This condition is sometimes called "relative deprivation." These differences, it is believed, create a psychological dissatisfaction and a drive for more advantage. A worker illustrated this attitude when he said, as a company boss rode by in a big shiny car, "That's what makes me mad. We do all the work. He only rides around and bosses. He lives in a swell house. They pay us well and we have cars, but we earn it. Yet we can't have anywhere near what he and his family has." This psychological factor may be more important in determining changes in the economic system than actual differences in incomes.

It does not appear that the middle class is disappearing. It would seem, rather, to be expanding as the modern economy adds to it technicians, scientists, managers, new professional groups, and many others whose level of life and opportunity has improved. We could surmise that socialism would have difficulty in displacing the present system so long as these circumstances prevail. (For an ironic view of our economy of abundance, see Box 21.)

COMMUNISM   The underlying belief of communism is that society should ultimately become classless after a period of preparation under "the dictatorship of the proletariat," or propertyless people. There must be no private property in such a state. All property must be state owned since it belongs to all the people. Production and distribution are the functions of the state operating through councils or "soviets" of workingmen in urban areas and of peasants in the rural districts. The local soviets are to be represented in provincial and regional soviets and these in an all-state soviet. Such a society demands complete planning, not only with respect to economic matters, but to every

BOX 21   THE AFFLUENT SOCIETY: A SURFEIT OF HONEY?

[Only] the most dyed-in-the-wool Pollyannas, the most direct descendants of Dr. Pangloss, could look about them and say that this is, after all, the best of all possible worlds. Superficially (I hope it is only superficially) the Baron's castle is something of a shambles. The sad and undeniable truth is that prosperity has made monkeys of far too many of us. . . .

What happens? People get to thinking that they had better pluck the fruit while there is still time, and having plucked it, they happily squirt its juice into other people's eyes. They worry about getting more money until they get it, or more goods until they can find a way to put off the day when they will have to pay for them, and then look around and find that their friends have everything they have. Everybody's name becomes Jones. But most of all, plucking the fruit gives them a convenient and well-sloganed reason for not thinking. Their pattern of behavior is known as "supporting the national economy." They can be satisfied that their role as consumers is essential to the national well-being. No one ever did his social duty with so little apparent strain or inconvenience.

No one, on the other hand, ever got so worried about "the meaning of life." Ask the clergy. Ask the psychiatrists. Ask *King Henry the Fourth, Part One:* "They surfeited with honey and began to loathe the taste of sweetness, whereof a little more than a little is by much too much." Ask your best friend. Ask Bridey Murphy.

Put in its rudest terms, prosperity produces not only plenty but curiously empty values and a national uneasiness. It produces strange kinds of personal economic competition in which symbols like the automobile and the freezer represent a burning desire for status. Cars get gaudier; hi-fi sets get hi-er, beer can openers become mink-bearing, open fields are swallowed up to make future slums, slums are torn down to make parking lots; pastures become drive-in movies; drive-in movie operators provide heaters so that one does not have to desert his status symbol even in winter. Artists and architects, writers and musicians worry about hits and their spoonfuls of gravy rather than about their art. Everybody, or nearly everybody, gets tense about the unknown—about flying saucers and foreign relations, about tomorrow, especially about tomorrow.[21]

---

other concern of life as well. It is the ultimate function of the soviets to do this planning.

The leaders in the Union of Soviet Socialist Republics (U.S.S.R., or Russia) place their planning program under the Council of the People's Commissars. The Council is served by a State Planning Commission and other boards or commissions that control defense, banking, man power, education, standards of production, co-operatives, and other major areas of the society's operation. This system is in accord with Lenin's position that the transition from a capitalist to a communist society requires a "political transitional period" in which these agencies represent the dictatorship of the proletariat.

Russia has actually been operating in this political transitional period since 1917. The first aim was to industrialize the society and collectivize the farms. Property was expropriated by the state without compensation on the ground that it rightly belongs to the people. The Communist party has been able to keep control of the total society by repressing or eliminating opponents of its program, and by controlling the press, the educational system, the military, and the apparatus for election to office. A small dictatorial minority, therefore, has become the ruling class, which uses its power to force acceptance of the Communist system.

FASCISM   Fascism is a politicoeconomic system. The central concept is the supremacy of a national state embodied in its elite and represented by a single person. The power of the state is transcending and unchallengeable, and the life of the society is totally dominated. The economic organization of the society, therefore, is subordinated to the maintenance of state power.

The system approves the basic institutions of capitalism, including private production and property, to the extent that they serve the interests of the state. To implement their control of economic activity, the fascist states established corporations in heavy industry, manufactures, and marketing. These corporations decide the goals of production which are coordinated through a Council of Corporations under the Ministry of Corporations. Unquestioned obedience to the decisions of those in authority is exacted, for they represent the elite of the state and are regarded as the only persons qualified to determine the good of the state. Thus, the economic system is a hierarchy of authority flowing from the top down. Private property, free exchange, and union organization are permitted only so long as they can be fitted into the production and employment programs for creating national self-sufficiency.

Otherwise, the corporations assume control. The Italian Labor charter of 1927 states: The corporate state considers that private enterprise in the sphere of production is the most effective and useful instrument in the interest of the state. . . . State intervention in economic production arises only when private initiative is lacking or insufficient, or when the political interests of the state are involved. This intervention may take the form of control, assistance or direct management."

The challenge of these economic ideologies, especially communism, inevitably compels us to consider the problems of changing social systems (see Chapter 23). Economic systems do not remain static. The remarkable modifications of the original form of capitalism demonstrate its adaptation to new conditions. What further changes in this and other systems will occur can only be determined by an uncertain future.

References

1. Computed from the Department of Commerce, Bureau of the Census, *Statistical Abstract of the United States, 1962*, Table 646, p. 488.
2. *Dartmouth College* v. *Woodward*, 17 U.S. (4 Wheat.) 518, 636 (1819).
3. Kaplan, A. D. H., *Small Business: Its Place and Problems* (New York, McGraw-Hill Book Co., Inc., 1948), p. 248. This is a study made for the Committee on Economic Development.
4. Bain, Joe S., "Economics of Scale, Concentration, and the Condition of Entry in Twenty Manufacturing Industries," *American Economic Review*, 44 (March, 1954), Table 7, p. 36.
5. Galbraith, John K., *American Capitalism* (Boston, Houghton Mifflin Company, 1952), p. 125.
6. Kaplan, A. D. H., *Big Business in a Competitive System* (Washington, D.C., The Brookings Institution, 1954), p. 248.
7. See, for example, Faunce, William A., "Size of Local and Union Democracy," *American Journal of Sociology*, 68 (November, 1962), pp. 291–298.
8. Raskin, A. H., "The Squeeze on the Unions," *Atlantic Monthly*, 207 (April, 1961), p. 56.
9. Data in this section are from United States Department of Commerce, Bureau of the Census, *Statistical Abstract of the United States, 1962*, Table 280, p. 215.
10. McCall, Marie, "Education Through Paintings," *Popular Educator*, XI (1940), No. 7, p. 5564.
11. Ginzberg, Eli, and associates, *Occupational Choice* (New York, Columbia University Press, 1951), p. 185.
12. Pitirim Sorokin develops this in detail in his *Social Mobility* (New York, Harper and Brothers, 1927), pp. 202 ff; Counts, G. S., "The Social Status of Occupations," *School Review*, 33 (1925), pp. 16–27; Davis, J., "Testing the Social Attitudes of Children in the Government Schools in Russia," *American Journal of Sociology*, 32 (1927), pp.

32–47; Anderson, W. A., "Occupational Attitudes and Choices of a Group of College Men, I and II," *Social Forces*, 6 (1927–1928), pp. 278–283, 467–473; Anderson, W. A., "The Occupational Attitudes of College Men," *Journal of Social Psychology*, 5 (1934), pp. 435–465; Kriesberg, Louis, "The Bases of Occupational Prestige: The Case of Dentists," *American Sociological Review*, 27 (April, 1962), pp. 238–244.

13. *Opinion News*, IX (1947).

14. Deeg, M. E., and Patterson, D. G., "Changes in Social Status of Occupations," *Occupations*, 25 (1947), No. 4.

15. Inkeles, Alex, and Rossi, Peter H., "National Comparisons of Occupational Prestige," *American Journal of Sociology*, 61 (January, 1956), pp. 329–339.

16. Becker, Howard, and Carper, James W., "The Development of Identification with an Occupation," and "Elements of Identification with an Occupation," *American Journal of Sociology*, 61 (January, 1956), pp. 289–298, and *American Sociological Review*, 21 (June, 1956), pp. 341–348, respectively. See also Hollingshead, A. B., "Behavior Systems as a Field for Research," *American Sociological Review*, 4 (December, 1939), pp. 816–823; Inkeles, Alex, "Industrial Man: The Relation of Status to Experience, Perception, and Value," *American Journal of Sociology*, 66 (July, 1960), pp. 1–31; Dibble, Vernon K., "Occupations and Ideologies," *American Journal of Sociology*, 68 (September, 1962), pp. 229–241.

17. Feldman, A. S., and Tilly, C., "Social and Physical Space," *American Sociological Review*, 25 (December, 1960), pp. 877–884.

18. Wilensky, Harold L., "Orderly Careers and Social Participation: The Impact of Work History on Social Integration in the Middle Class," *American Sociological Review*, 26 (August, 1961), p. 521.

19. *Encyclopedia of the Social Sciences*, 13–41 (New York, The Macmillan Company, 1955), pp. 496 ff.

20. The classic study of changes in the real wages of workers in the United States is that of Douglas, Paul H., *Real Wages in the United States* (Boston, Houghton Mifflin Company, 1930); Garver, F., and Hansen, A. H., *Principles of Economics* (Minneapolis, Minn., Perine Book Co., 1947), also discusses socialism and worker situations in Chap. 23, pp. 567 ff.

21. Lynes, Russell, *A Surfeit of Honey* (New York, Harper and Brothers, 1957), pp. 123–124; 131–132.

Questions for Study and Discussion

1. Why have economic institutions developed without planning and guidance so generally when they are so pivotal in societies?

2. Discuss the production and distribution of economic goods as sociological problems.

3. Compare the advantages and disadvantages of the direct appropriation form of economy followed by some primitive societies with those of our modern industrial economy.

4. What are the roles of the five factors of production in a society's economic system?

5. Discuss the institutions supporting the individualistic property systems of some society.

6. What is the essential difference between the corporation and the cooperative as forms for doing business?

7. Competition is often said to be "the life of trade." How do present-day conditions influence its operation?

8. What are the major constructive activities of labor unions? What have become chief problems in them?

9. Report on the changes in the occupational structure of American society in the last half century.
10. How do most persons get into their jobs? Discuss the factors influencing this.
11. How may occupations influence workers physically, mentally, socially?
12. How extensive is the workmen's compensation program in your state or country?
13. Distinguish between syndicalism, socialism, communism, and fascism.

Suggested Topics for Reports

1. Analyze the occupation of doctor, lawyer, minister, or other professional within the framework provided by A. B. Hollingshead in his article, "Behavior Systems as a Field for Research." (See reference 16.)
2. Interview several industrialists and labor union leaders concerning automation and compare their reactions. Is any basis of accommodation discernible?
3. Examine a number of issues of the employee-relations magazine of a large company and identify what seem to be the elements of its socioeconomic ideology.
4. Study the public relations department of a large firm and report on its organization, purposes, and activities.
5. Trace the growth of "fringe benefits" in an industry. Is there any basis for the assertion that through them modern industry is promoting the pattern of the welfare state?

Supplementary Reading

Bendix, Reinhard, *Work and Authority in Industry*. New York: John Wiley and Sons, Inc., 1956.

Berle, A. A., and Means, G. C., *The Modern Corporation and Private Property*. New York: The Macmillan Company, 1934.

Douglas, Paul H., *Real Wages in the United States*. New York: Houghton Mifflin Company, 1930.

Dubin, Robert, *The World of Work*. Englewood Cliffs, N.J.: Prentice-Hall, Inc., 1958.

Galbraith, John K., *American Capitalism*. Boston: Houghton Mifflin Company, 1952.

———, *The Affluent Society*. Boston: Houghton Mifflin Company, 1958.

Gardner, B. B., and Moore, D. G., *Human Relations in Industry*. 2nd ed. Chicago: Irwin Press, 1950.

Ginzberg, Eli, and associates, *Occupational Choice*. New York: Columbia University Press, 1951.

Gouldner, Alvin W., *Patterns of Industrial Bureaucracy*. Glencoe, Ill.: The Free Press, 1954.

Hickman, C. Addison, and Kuhn, Manford H., *Individuals, Groups and Economic Behavior*. New York: Dryden Press, 1956.

Johnson, E. A. J., *Some Origins of the Modern Economic World*. New York: The Macmillan Company, 1936.

Kaplan, A. D. H., *Big Business in a Competitive System*. Washington, D.C.: The Brookings Institution, 1954.

———, *Small Business: Its Place and Problems*. New York: McGraw-Hill Book Co., Inc., 1948.

Likert, Rensis, *New Patterns of Management*. New York: McGraw-Hill Book Co., Inc., 1961.

Moore, Wilbert E., *Industrial Relations and the Social Order*. 2nd ed. New York: The Macmillan Company, 1951.

Nosow, Sigmund, and Form, William H. (eds.), *Man, Work, and Society: A Reader in the Sociology of Occupations*. New York: Basic Books, Inc., 1962.

Tawney, Robert H., *Religion and the Rise of Capitalism.* New York: Harcourt, Brace and Company, 1926.

Veblen, Thorstein, *The Theory of Business Enterprise.* New York: B. W. Heubach, Inc., 1923.

Weber, Max, *The Theory of Social and Economic Organization.* Tran. by A. M. Henderson and Talcott Parsons. New York: Oxford University Press, 1947.

Whyte, William F. (ed.), *Industry and Society.* New York: McGraw-Hill Book Co., Inc., 1946.

15

GOVERNMENT: THE OVER-ALL CONTROL INSTITUTION OF SOCIETIES

G OVERNMENT *is a society's over-all control institution providing regulatory direction within the society and protection against aggression from without. The state is its major agency. Governments vary with different cultural settings.*

Government Is a Normal Consequence of Relationships Among Men

Government, a complex of procedural norms for societal control, is another of the basic social institutions present in all societies. The circumstances out of which it arises are the need for over-all control of the individuals, groups, organizations, and institutions of which societies are composed; the need for over-all representation between the components of one society and those of another, and the need for representation between societies themselves, is a further *raison d'être*.

It is possible to handle most relationships informally when societies are small and simple. Even in complex societies, informal controls operate so that our attitudes, customs, and community opinions direct our behavior toward conformity. However, as societies increase in size, both in area and population, their growing complexity and the necessity of their adaptations to other societies require more formal methods of handling relationships. Government is the institution of a society for handling these over-all relationships.

There Are Several Theories About the Origins of Government

DIVINE RIGHT   The origins of government as an over-all control are hidden in the darkness of the past. There are several theories that center about its objectives which throw light on their origins. One of the earliest, now almost completely abandoned, is that of divine origin. This theory invested priests, chieftains, and kings with sacred powers, particularly because it was thought that societies resulted from supernatural design. The Hebrews, for example, emphasized the rule of God over their society. Laws and commands were made in the name of Jehovah. The Christian heritage also led rulers in European nations to claim their positions by divine right. As late as this present century, the Emperor Wilhelm maintained that he was ruler of Germany by divine right. In the Orient, the Japanese emperor was one of many rulers who was thought to be a divine person, deriving his authority therefrom. This theory has been discarded, however, in practically all societies, just as it was discarded in Japan after World War II.

CREATION OF NATURAL INSTINCTS   "Man is by nature a political animal" and "It is evident that the state is a creation of nature" were the statements of Aristotle in which he summarized the idea that man's innate traits led him to establish government.[1] The fact of our association together certainly had bearing on the development of this institution, although it cannot be held that instincts led us to associate.

CREATION BY CONTRACT   Three European philosophers of the seventeenth and eighteenth centuries supported a social contract theory of the origin of government. Each held a different conception of the nature of man. Hobbes thought that man was brutish and full of fear lest others excel him, so the state of nature was always "a war of all against all." Locke thought men were persons of reason and that the state of nature was one of mutual aid. Rousseau held that everything was good as it came from the hands of the Creator but degenerated under man. From these different viewpoints each suggested the necessity for government. Hobbes held that men so endangered each other in the state of nature that they banded together for self-preservation under an absolute ruler. Rousseau argued that government originated by contract in which men turned themselves over to the sovereignty of the general will. Locke said we contracted with each other to form a commonwealth in which the "collective body created by social pact" is designed to protect our equality and rights and to improve upon the benign state of nature.[2]

We must not, of course, infer from the symbolic phrase "social contract" that men living together in a state of nature, no matter what it was like, suddenly and rationally agreed to set up a government. It is more reasonable to see this institution as the result of gradual social growth rather than a relatively sudden creation.

In any event, the social contract theorists influenced European societies for two centuries. Locke's theory, especially, through its stress on equality and the rights of men, had much influence upon Thomas Jefferson and the writing of the American Declaration of Independence.

MIGHT AND FORCE   Might has also been advanced as the creator of government. The theory holds that men who were stronger and more clever imposed their will on the weak and more stupid and subjected them to their rule. This presupposes that those imposing their wills were already organized into some kind of unity where power and authority to control were allocated to some persons. Men certainly have governed by might, but to do so they had to be previously organized in some way.

The counterpart of this theory is that people established government to control persons who sought prestige and power. No doubt one of the factors leading to cooperation between men was that of self- and community protection.

GEOGRAPHY   Geography has also been advanced as the basic factor leading to governments. People living together develop a sense of unity in solving their common problems within a territory. For example, nomadic people who travel within a given area and need to obtain their living from its resources unite in systematic ways to meet these needs. Certainly, territory is a conditioning factor in the creation of government. Once defined, it is a major element in the operation of government. Protection from outside aggression is a major function of present-day governments.

KINSHIP   MacIver finds the origin of government in the family and kinship. They are the earliest patterned groupings of people with authority already established in the family head. It is necessary, however, to expand this order on a wider scale to involve the larger community as population increases and economic and other problems arise, so that standards and control may prevail throughout.

DIVISION OF LABOR AND SPECIALIZATION   The advantages of division of labor led men to get together in social groupings, according to an economic view. As a consequence, they established controlled relationships in which all were the greater benefactors. Government thus became an institution to achieve these advantages. A different economic view is that government was established by those who had acquired control of wealth to make sure they could retain it. Both of these viewpoints are limited. Primitive man hardly had the foresight to recognize the advantages of specialization with so little experience in group associations. The second explanation is a gross oversimplification.

Government Institutions Are the Result of Cultural Development

Each of these theories of the origin of government has limitations. Most of them are justifications of forms of government actually in operation. The proponents reasoned back from current conditions to find origins and inferred certain characteristics in man and societies for which there is little evidence. Furthermore, each is a monistic theory placing the causal condition for this social institution in a single force. Social forms are never the consequence of a single causal condition but are results of the interrelationships among a number of conditions. Governmental institutions are no exception.

CULTURAL DEVELOPMENT   Today, students of societies hold that government is the result of cultural developments in which specific functions related to over-all social control in a society have been assigned to a specific social structure. Governments are institutions growing out of social relationships in which all of the forces mentioned in traditional theories play a part. MacIver sums up this view in the following way: "Government is a phenomenon that emerges within the social life, inherent in the nature of social order. Man's social nature is a complex system of responses and of needs. In the relation of man to man everywhere there is the seed of government. It takes different institutional shapes according to the interplay of these relations." [3]

The State Is the Major Governmental Agency

STATE DEFINED The over-all control system of a society is spoken of as the government of a given state. (We speak of the government of the German state, for example.) A state is that agency in a society that is authorized to exercise coercive control within a given territory. It is not necessarily coterminous with the society, though it may be. An expanded definition of the state holds that it is a politically organized body of people occupying a definite territory and living under a government entirely or almost entirely free from external control and competent to secure habitual obedience from all persons within it—in other words, possessing both external and internal sovereignty. [4]

POLITICAL ORGANIZATION "People politically organized" is the first component of the state and infers that a related body of people believe that certain aspects of their relationships to each other should come under the control of all. It is recognized that personal drives need restraint lest conflicts result and that relationships with other groupings require representation. So two universal purposes, regulating relationships within the society to assure obedience to cultural norms and providing defense against external dangers, lead to organization in order to handle relationships more effectively. People give up some of their independence for the added security that joint action provides. Plato considered that the ideal number of people to be organized in this all-embracing way was 5040. Today millions of people are organized in single states, which makes the internal problems of states more complex and the external problems more pressing. Small states are often dominated by the larger, while the larger states often intensify their activities to protect their sovereignty from external threats. People born in a state ideally accept citizenship with its obligations of allegiance and privileges of protection as a matter of course. The state assumes that all persons born within it are members. The citizens may

hardly notice the manifold ways in which the state influences their behavior. However, they can go on day by day only because of its manifold activities.

TERRITORIAL LIMITS Modern states occupy a "definite territory." Contained within geographically limited and legally defined areas, they are ecological entities. Some of the chief ways in which the land areas of states have been acquired is by settlement, by conquest and annexation, and by purchase or exchange with some other states. States, therefore, are limited areas fashioned out of land bodies. They are created units rather than units defined by social interaction and cultural patterns delineating natural regions. Usually, the territory of a state is continuous, but there are some states that have widely separated territories. Pakistan is an example of a recently created state where the land area is divided into two parts separated by about 1500 miles. The United States, including distant Alaska and Hawaii, is another example.

Territory is one of the powerful elements in governmental life. Many wars have resulted from disputes over territorial possessions and conflicting territorial claims. States are highly sensitive to any intrusions upon their territories by either hostile or friendly aliens. Furthermore, there are few places on this planet where territorial movement is completely free. Permanent or temporary movement from one state to another involves complicated procedures regulated by strict rules.

SOVEREIGNTY AND POWER The state possesses "both external and internal sovereignty." The core of state organization is the right to use force in the protection of a society's interests. The state has supreme control in a given area; no other power is above it. This principle is expressed in John Jay's statement: "Nothing is more certain than the indispensable necessity of Government, and it is equally undeniable, that whenever and however it is instituted, the people must cede to it some of their natural rights in order to vest it with requisite power." [5] It may punish the citizen who commits offenses by depriving him of things that he values, even his right to live. Theodore Dreiser described a mother before a prison where her son was soon to be executed: "She paused for a moment a little later in a small parking place beyond the prison to stare at the tall, gray walls, the watch towers with armed guards in uniform, the barred windows and doors. A penitentiary. And her son was now within—worse yet, in that confined and narrow death house. And doomed to die in an electric chair." [6] So may the state exact the ultimate penalty.

This over-all entity would be ineffective if such power were not available. It is not the actual use of force that serves as the important deterrent. It is rather that it can be used when necessity demands. Most of us are not affected directly by this right since we are law-abiding. We are affected indirectly since it is our guarantee of protection.

A Government Is an Institutional Agency for Carrying Out the Activities of Over-All Control

A GOVERNMENT AS MEANS   A state, as a politically organized and geographically limited body of people that possesses the right to use power to preserve its values, must have instruments through which to operate. Governments are these instruments. They consist of the persons and agencies designated to carry out the state's purposes. All the citizens of a state are not part of a government, but they usually have some choice in deciding who and how the state shall be "run." A government includes only those officials and departments who are elected, appointed, or employed to determine, interpret, and carry out the regulations of the state or its subdivisions.

Fundamental to this governing process is the regularization of the power these authorized individuals and groupings can legitimately use over members of their society as they exercise their functions. A government as the means for carrying out the purposes of the state justifies its authority by showing that it is properly founded on the cultural values of the society. Only in this way can it achieve and maintain the stability that is essential to its monopolistic use of coercion in the territory of its jurisdiction. A government must show in some way that this authority comes from the people or their operations would not be accepted, except by the use of physical forces. Reports indicate that the use of force is necessary in mainland China because its government tries to establish a new social system that has no real roots in the culture of the people.

A government's sole purpose is to act as the instrumentality through which the state serves its citizens. One of the problems of government is the tendency of its divisions (departments and bureaus) to become ends in themselves, dedicated to their own self-preservation even after the services they once performed are no longer required. William Penn stressed this tendency early in our American history: "It is too common an Error, to invert the Order of Things; by making an End of what which is a Means, and a Means of that which is an End. Religion and Government escape not this Mischief: The first is too often made a Means instead of an End; the other an End instead of a Means." [7]

CHANGING GOVERNMENTS   Governments change because governments are means. Most states have provisions for change either at certain times or under certain conditions. Some change frequently. The government of France is an illustration of a great state where the government has changed repeatedly since World War II. Such a situation introduces instability in the society since governments determine policies. Policies can hardly be consistent when they change frequently. States, on the other hand, do not expect to change. They imply perpetuity. No state ever provides for its own termination since every state expects to be perpetuated.

The Directives for Governments in Operating the State Are Embodied in Laws

LAWS AS RULES FOR OPERATING   Laws are rules of the state that specify its regulation of individual and community activities. Such legislation usually includes the penalties for its violation. These laws are the directives that a state adopts to guide those who are responsible for operating the government and for controlling the behavior of its citizens. They have general application, being relevant to all persons alike in order to promote orderly and just operation.

Laws are usually enacted by legislative bodies and are expressed in written statutes. There are some common laws, however, whose origin lies in custom rather than in statute, but most common laws eventually are defined in written statutes.

Laws as Crystallized Customs and Traditions Some laws come into existence as the crystallization of customs and traditions that are regarded as binding. Such laws are basic because they are the consequences of behavior found valuable in the past. Because we feel that they are proper, we give them added strength by deliberately providing for their enforcement through the agencies of the state. Thus, laws grow out of the folkways and mores, the sanctioned ways of acting that a society has already been following. They prescribe how the governing persons may use their legitimate authority and exercise their power to make effective these impersonal rules of the society.

Other laws are enactments of legislative bodies which apply to changing conditions and the new needs of a society. They are the rules which are enacted as a society grows in size and complexity.

LAW-MAKING AN EXPANDED ACTIVITY Rapid social change creates many new situations to which customary ways are hardly applicable. Auto and air traffic and the complex operations of large corporations are cases in point. The tempo of change provides little time for new "ways" to be developed and crystallized into laws. Dynamic societies must thus depend heavily upon formally designed regulations of new relationships. The resulting proliferation of law may give the impression that we have become addicted to controlling all behavior by legislative means. It is reported that America now has more than two million laws on its statute books!

CONSTITUTIONS Most states have written constitutions recognized as the supreme law of the land. These are specific documents that outline the rights of a government and of the people so that certain guarantees are assured to both. They usually cannot be overruled by any law-making body, but they can be interpreted by courts, however. The provisions of the laws have not always carried the same meaning, and different interpretations are possible, depending upon the viewpoint the interpreters hold. Constitutions do change slowly because their provisions are broad and allow reinterpretation to meet changed conditions. They consist not solely of their original articles but also amendments, judicial interpretations, modifying statutes, and practices that have been added through time. The American Constitution is the ultimate basis for judging the legality of any law a legislative body enacts. The Supreme Court of the United States has the final power to determine whether laws are made in pursuance of the provisions of the Constitution.

Certain Personal Rights Have Been Made Inviolate in the American Constitution

CIVIL LIBERTIES The founders of the American state were so concerned lest laws be made that interfered with personal life that they wrote into the Constitution restrictions upon the reach of government into the realm of civil liberties. There was precedent for this in the English Magna Charta obtained in 1215 from King John and in the English Bill of Rights of 1689. The First Amendment to our Constitution says: "Congress shall make no law respecting an establishment of religion, or prohibiting the free exercise thereof; or abridging the freedom of speech or of the press; or the right of the people peaceably to assemble, and to petition the Government for a redress of grievances." The Fourteenth Amendment as interpreted by the Supreme Court puts similar restrictions on the states of the Union. It says no state shall "deprive any person of life, liberty, or property, without due process of law." [8] These provisions guarantee our rights of freedom of religion, of speech, of the press, and of assemblage.

PROCEDURAL GUARANTEES Definite "procedural" guarantees were also incorporated in this basic document to make sure that our citizens were given the protection of law. They include, among others, our right to know why we are under detention and to be given, when accused, equal protection with all others through "due process of law."

Governments Perform Many Functions

Governments perform many functions in serving a society's needs for regulation and protection. These functions evolve around laws since states operate primarily through laws and are "governments of laws rather than men." The functions of governments as institutional agencies are described as *legislative,* or the making of laws; *executive,* or putting the laws into effect; and *judicial,* or interpreting and supporting the enforcement of the law.

LEGISLATIVE FUNCTION No present state is small enough to allow the direct participation of the citizens in the making of the rules which govern them. Nor are the problems that arise simple enough for the citizens to have information that will provide them with intelligent opinions about them all. States are usually complex units with many interrelated problems. Law-making, therefore, is commonly delegated to elected bodies that serve specifically for this purpose. The members of such groups are presumed to have more or less expert knowledge.

National Legislative Bodies Most states have a national legislative body, such as a Parliament or a Congress, to make rules that apply to the state as a whole. The importance attached to this agency in a society like ours is indicated by the fact that the first article in the Constitution says that "All legislative powers herein granted shall be vested in a Congress of the United States, which shall consist of a Senate and House of Representatives." [9] This two-bodied unit enacts the legislation for the nation subject to approval by the President. This later proviso makes the President of the country also a party to legislative enactment.

Other Legislative Bodies There are subunits in our several states, such as counties and cities, having powers that are exclusively theirs. They also have legislative bodies that make laws covering the special problems that are not provided for in the laws of the larger units. There are over 100,000 government subunits in American society which have the right to make some regulations. We thus are subject to the particular laws that each of these units can properly make.

Legislation and Geographic Location The American institution of government is based upon geographic location. Our elected personnel represent the people of a given area. Our Congressmen are peculiarly sensitive, for example, to what their people "back home" think of the measures they support. This often makes it difficult for the legislator to serve the larger social interests in the face of the specific expectations of their constituency. Our citizens vote only within their defined districts.

This basing of governmental organization on geographical units has many other important sociological influences on political functioning. Perhaps the most significant is that it can determine who will have the political advantages in societies where representation is based on political party elections. If those in political control can set the boundaries to voting districts so as to assure the distribution of voters favorable to themselves, they can control legislative bodies and government operations for long periods of time. This practice, engaged in American national, state, and local politics continuously, is called gerrymandering after Elbridge Gerry, governor of Massachusetts in 1812, who reorganized the voting districts of his state so that the Republican party was assured of political control.

Reapportionment takes place in American society each ten years following the taking of the federal Census to determine the number of seats in the House of Representatives each state is to be allowed. This gives the party in power the opportunity to organize electoral districts in such a way as to favor the election of representatives and other officials that are of their party. Thus, government control and power are often determined by political objectives.

There also may be changes in legislative, and so in government, operations resulting from significant shifts in type of population from one area to another. Louis Harris points out in his study of the Republican party that the shift of white-collar workers to suburban areas may decidedly influence the results of elections.[10] In like vein, the shift of population from rural to urban areas has brought about a need for reapportionment of legislative representatives from these areas.

Pressure Groups and Lobbies Representation by locality also results in activities by groups having interests not defined by geography. Interests not limited to given areas come into existence as our societies expand. These groups must create organizations to promote their interests since there are no ways for them to obtain direct representation in legislative bodies. Farmer's organizations, labor unions, chambers of commerce, veterans' organizations, religious bodies, racial and nationality organizations, to indicate a few, organize to achieve desirable legislation by seeking to influence area representatives. Lobbying, as this activity is called, is now recognized as a legitimate procedure regulated by national and state governments in a society. In the American society, lobbying is a big business.

These "pressure groups," as they are called, play a distinctive role by pressing for the interests they represent. They are a form of representative government based on problems and issues rather than geography. They try to create favorable public opinion and to influence the electorate to bring pressure on their representatives. They prepare bills and furnish materials to support them when they are introduced to a legislative body. They get outstanding persons to appear before hearings and interview persons who can influence the legislators. These pressure groups are so powerful, especially where they cooperate together for a common interest, that some analysts say that our American government is government by pressure groups. If the projects they press for are in the public interests, such groups can be strong forces in promoting action because they represent a more functional approach to our legislative needs than does the one based on territory. Some say, however, that they represent every interest but the public interest.

JUDICIAL FUNCTION The second function of government, that of interpreting and enforcing the law, is the role of the judicial system. People and groups break laws by committing crimes. They have disagreements about contracts. They have differences over the meaning of laws and questions as to whether or not a law is proper. These and many other issues require decisions. The business of the courts is to enforce the criminal laws and to make decisions in civil cases. Criminal and civil cases are the two general forms in which legal problems arise.

Federal Courts Our federal courts, including a Supreme Court and "such inferior courts as the Congress may from time to time ordain and establish," have jurisdiction in crimes or civil disputes involving interstate relationships.

State and Minor Division Courts The different states, counties, and cities have courts also to enforce the laws within their jurisdictions. A chief principle in the judicial system is that an individual accused of a crime has the right to be judged by his fellows of equal position. The judge presides over and conducts the case in such situations but a jury, commonly of twelve citizens, decides the guilt or innocence of the person on trial.

Courts as Law Makers One significant manner in which the American judicial system differs from others, such as that of Great Britain, is that the courts can declare acts of Congress, state legislatures, local governments, and executives constitutional or unconstitutional. Our Supreme Court declared the National Industrial Recovery Act of 1933 unconstitutional. It has

Decisions by the United States Supreme Court have had a profound effect upon American life.

taken the same action on laws supporting racial segregation. The only thing Congress can do in such a situation is to revise the law to meet the objections since the Supreme Court is the final arbiter. Because the courts declare laws unconstitutional, they enter the field of lawmaking to that degree.

Due Process of Law The citizens in any state must depend upon their judicial system to protect their rights under the law. Societies provide for such protection by limiting the states from depriving persons of certain rights without "due process of law." This usually involves the right of an accused to a defense against charges, to a fair trial including relevant witnesses who can be cross-examined, and to an appeal if the decision is unsatisfactory.

EXECUTIVE FUNCTION The third function of governments is to administer or put into operation the laws of the state. In simple societies, the making and administration of laws may all be effected by a chief or council of persons who designate citizens to perform certain duties. This is impractical in complex societies. Proper administration requires specialized officers and agencies which become more numerous as states become more specialized.

Chief Administrative Officer The chief administrative officer is usually the head of the state. In some instances, heads of state are largely symbolic. The actual administrative head may be a prime minister or other official. A cabinet of officers, each heading an administrative department, is usually developed to advise on policy. They also serve under the chief executive as responsible administrative officers because government operations are so numerous and involved. The President's Cabinet in the United States includes ten persons, each heading an executive department. There are also special branches for specific tasks.

BUREAUCRACY Government agencies grow rapidly as their tasks increase. They also become self-perpetuating units that develop into separate institutional agencies. This growth is known to us as bureaucracy. Its characteristics have been outlined by Max Weber:

> Each official has his own bailiwick—a sphere within which his conduct is limited by rules or laws.
> Each person is assigned official duties, certain fixed jobs.
> Authority to issue orders is lodged in specific offices and officials operating under specific rules.

Each office is supervised "from above" by a higher authority.

Levels of authority are arranged in pyramid-fashion.

Management depends on written records for its authority; the individual is custodian of, not a substitute for, the written records.

Office management is highly specialized and trained.

Official duties have first call on the official's working time.

Conduct of the office is regulated by general rules. These rules are:

—Stable; they do not normally change overnight or over a period of time.

—All embracing; they try to anticipate every type of situation that may arise.

—Learnable; they can be readily understood and mastered through study by officials.[11]

This description stresses division of labor, hierarchical control, fixed patterns of communication, and dependence on fixed rules and records as characteristic of bureaucracies. The major purpose of this patterning is to secure efficiency in the execution of work. The worker is depersonalized in carrying on his work by being subject to service systems under which most jobs are classified. It would be impossible to handle such numbers of people and such large amounts of business on a person-to-person basis. Fixed rules and regulations that must be their guideposts are "red tape" to the average citizens who are accustomed to direct dealing. They are annoying when their rigidity tends to delay action which is felt could be executed immediately.

Formal organizations in which positions and actions are controlled in detail result whenever activities are large scale. Bureaucracy is characteristic of large corporations, manufacturing enterprises, church bodies, and nationwide labor organizations, as well as of government. The major problem in such circumstances is to devise means whereby they do not become self-perpetuating ends, persons do not become mere automatons and service to the public remains their chief goal.

The top administrators in bureaucratic organizations must use their initiative, but often they must make concessions to the demands of the powerful to control their departments. They must perform acceptably for their chief executive, remain in the good graces of their legislative bodies, and still please their public. They may thus become primarily concerned with strengthening their own position rather than with serving the public.

POLICY DETERMINATION In executing the policies laid down by Congress or other major legislative bodies, administrative agencies may actually influence the determination of policy. They do so by requesting desirable legislation. The increase of controls over different aspects of our social life by governments is largely the consequences of demands from the public for more services. These demands are reflected in the legislation which government divisions press on Congress. This constant pressure for increasing assistance results in more government.

GOVERNMENT IN BUSINESS AND SOCIAL SERVICES As a result, governments become operators of such business enterprises as electrification projects, do research on many products and problems, operate testing laboratories and statistical bureaus, maintain museums and art galleries, and provide health and hospital services. There is practically no major area of our societal operations today in which the government is not active in some form, if not directly, then indirectly, through regulation. It has absorbed functions from other institutions which can no longer perform their tasks. Old-age assistance, for example, can hardly be provided on a local or family basis as the number of older people grows speedily. In all of this, the chief consideration must be the interest of the public and the well-being of individual citizens.

Governments Are Supported Primarily by Taxation

Governments must be supported if they are to perform their functions for their citizens. Taxation or the levying of compulsory charges against persons and property is the major means which governments must employ. Tribute exacted from conquered people once formed an important part of government support. In modern times, it has not been a major source of support, although theoretically the victors in internation struggles can claim indemnities from their defeated opponents. An ostensible irony following World War II has been the award of financial aid by the victors to the vanquished.

Generalized taxes on citizens and their property are the foundation of government maintenance today, and they cannot be avoided. The failure to pay the sums assessed is often punishable by confiscation of property and by imprisonment. Sometimes, imprisonment for tax

THE FEDERAL ADMINISTRATIVE ORGANIZATION

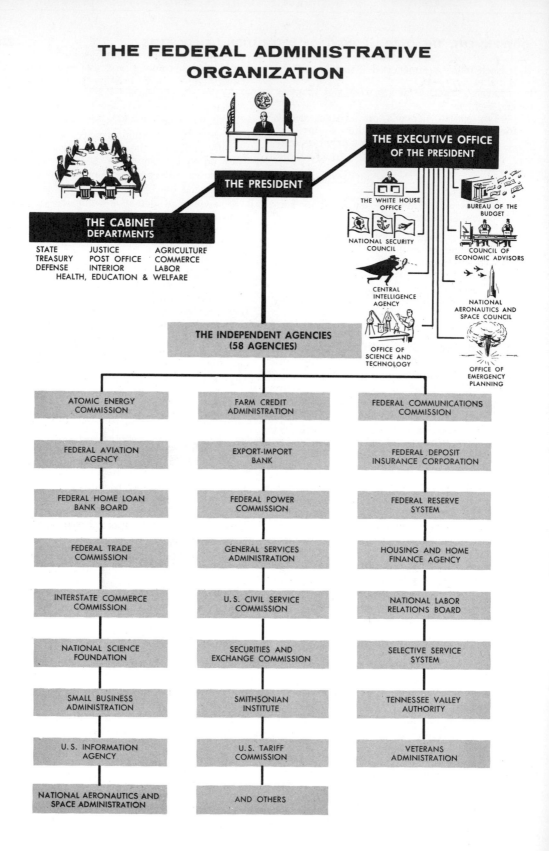

THE PRESIDENT

THE CABINET
DEPARTMENTS

STATE   JUSTICE   AGRICULTURE
TREASURY   POST OFFICE   COMMERCE
DEFENSE   INTERIOR   LABOR
HEALTH, EDUCATION & WELFARE

THE EXECUTIVE OFFICE
OF THE PRESIDENT

THE WHITE HOUSE
OFFICE

BUREAU OF THE
BUDGET

NATIONAL SECURITY
COUNCIL

COUNCIL OF
ECONOMIC ADVISORS

CENTRAL
INTELLIGENCE
AGENCY

NATIONAL
AERONAUTICS AND
SPACE COUNCIL

OFFICE OF
SCIENCE AND
TECHNOLOGY

OFFICE OF
EMERGENCY
PLANNING

THE INDEPENDENT AGENCIES
(58 AGENCIES)

ATOMIC ENERGY COMMISSION	FARM CREDIT ADMINISTRATION	FEDERAL COMMUNICATIONS COMMISSION
FEDERAL AVIATION AGENCY	EXPORT-IMPORT BANK	FEDERAL DEPOSIT INSURANCE CORPORATION
FEDERAL HOME LOAN BANK BOARD	FEDERAL POWER COMMISSION	FEDERAL RESERVE SYSTEM
FEDERAL TRADE COMMISSION	GENERAL SERVICES ADMINISTRATION	HOUSING AND HOME FINANCE AGENCY
INTERSTATE COMMERCE COMMISSION	U.S. CIVIL SERVICE COMMISSION	NATIONAL LABOR RELATIONS BOARD
NATIONAL SCIENCE FOUNDATION	SECURITIES AND EXCHANGE COMMISSION	SELECTIVE SERVICE SYSTEM
SMALL BUSINESS ADMINISTRATION	SMITHSONIAN INSTITUTE	TENNESSEE VALLEY AUTHORITY
U.S. INFORMATION AGENCY	U.S. TARIFF COMMISSION	VETERANS ADMINISTRATION
NATIONAL AERONAUTICS AND SPACE ADMINISTRATION	AND OTHERS	

evasion is used to punish criminals when other methods fail. This was the case with Al Capone, the famous gangster leader. Our government prosecuted him for income tax evasion rather than for his other crimes.

FORMS OF TAXATION Taxes take many forms. Taxes on the incomes of individuals, levied on a sliding scale based on the principle of ability to pay, provide over one-half of the federal government tax income in American society. Taxes on the income and profits of corporations provide 30 per cent. Excise taxes—a percentage added to the price of products being sold—add 13 per cent, while all other taxes, such as those on inheritance, provide 3 per cent.[12] Income from the earnings of individuals and corporations, therefore, is our basic source of revenue for maintaining our federal government. In some societies, this graduated tax is used to modify inequality in incomes.

American states also collect taxes for their support. Fifteen per cent of their tax collection in 1953 came from intergovernmental revenue; 14 per cent from general sales, use, or gross receipts; 12 per cent from service charges; 11 per cent from gasoline taxes; 10 per cent from individual and corporate taxes; and 6 and 5 per cent, respectively, from insurance trust revenue and motor vehicle and operator's licenses. The other one-fourth came from a variety of other taxes. Our states use more forms of taxation to obtain their revenues than does our federal government.

Governments Take Several Forms

Societies may develop as many forms of ruling organization as their varied cultural backgrounds and their immediate circumstances may require. The elements in governing may be combined in numerous patterns. Therefore, governments appear in many forms based on some primary element which characterizes them.

CLASSIFICATION OF GOVERNMENTAL FORMS One of the most important of these variations is in the way the governing power is distributed. Aristotle (384–322 B.C.), from his study of 158 states, classified normal governments as monarchies, or rule by one person; aristocracies, or rule by a few; and democracies, or rule by the many. If these normal forms are perverted,

Top levels of bureaucracy in the Federal administrative organization.

monarchies become tyrannies, aristocracies become oligarchies, and democracies resort to mob rule. Aristotle was critical of democracy, but he felt that the potential capacity of the citizens for sound collective judgment could assure the success of this form.

MacIver modernized Aristotle's classification. He considered all government forms either as oligarchies, with rule by the few, or as democracies with final authority resting in the many. The reasoning with respect to oligarchy is that there can be no government by one person since he must be supported by others.[13] Gaetano Mosca in *The Ruling Class* carries this view further by saying that all governments are oligarchies since they are dominated by an elite to whom the majority defer and who rule because they control the means through which governments operate.[14]

Lincoln Steffens supported this view of Mosca in the following characterization of European and American governments:

The skeletons of all the governments of Europe that I saw into were as like one another and as like the skeleton of American government as the bony structures of human beings are alike—and as unlike as the apparent constitutional framework. . . . There were Kings in England and Italy, an emperor in Germany, presidents in France and the United States, but there were premiers, too, and parliaments and bosses. In England and Italy they were notoriously figureheads, hats or crowns upon the heads of premiers, who in their turn were the agents of the temporarily adjusted economic interests which composed the throne and literally dominated the government just as in the United States a boss like Mark Hanna directed, when he would, his president—just as political bosses controlled governors, mayors, legislators in the interest of most active businesses, which the boss represents.[15]

TWO DOMINANT FORMS OF GOVERNMENT CLAIM ATTENTION TODAY Today, our major attention is drawn to two dominant forms: totalitarianism, in which the control is in the hands of one or a few persons and society's policies and programs are dictated; and democracy, in which political power is widely diffused among the governed by the process of representation. These forms are in a struggle to capture the loyalty of nations. Citizens in many states are in a quandary as to which form they should adopt. A distinguished leader in an Asian country has said,

"We do not know whether finally to adopt the slow, educative method of your democracies or the speedy, autocratic system of the communists. We do know this, the communists are working diligently among our masses with glowing promises that they make exceedingly enticing." [16]

Democracy Is Government by the People

FOUNDATION PRINCIPLES Democracy rests upon the proposition that sovereignty, or the ultimate power in a state, resides in the citizens. Man, it is asserted, is born free and equal and the inheritor of certain inalienable rights of which he must not be deprived. One of these is the right to determine how he is to be governed. It is axiomatic in democratic governments that all citizens have equal political privileges which only they can exercise and which they cannot transfer to any other person. Likewise, it is foundational that rule of the majority shall prevail, this majority to be expressed by the direct voting of citizens or expressed for them through their chosen representatives. A third principle is that the citizens have means for inducing the government to meet their needs. At the least, citizens can vote unwilling and inefficient officials out of office. Government is the servant of the people.

Democracy assumes that its citizens have opinions about public affairs or will get them through study and that they will exercise their privileges for the public good. People are not compelled in this respect but act voluntarily. Democracy also assumes that problems can be solved by the use of intelligence and that the combined judgment of the electorate will in the long run be sound when it is informed. The citizen depends upon his representatives to indicate what is desirable, but he makes the decision about its acceptability.

Basic Social Values This governmental form is based upon two social values of democratic culture. These are equality and liberty—freedom to act as we wish so long as we do not inflict injury upon others. These values were part of the early American tradition and have persisted among us ever since. The Puritan fathers stressed the equality of all believers—"Ye are all one in Christ"—and a doctrine of Christian liberty founded upon the inward conviction of the believer. They held that truth could be arrived at by free discussion.

New England local communities were democratically organized. Persons were equal and free to express their convictions in their own meetings where majority decisions prevailed. The pioneer conditions under which the early colonists lived reinforced the necessity of cooperating together as equals. Equality of opportunity, if not equality of position, and the opportunity to achieve position became cardinal principles with them in this society. Democracy was thus established as these principles of equality and liberty were incorporated as ideal habits of thought and action within the developing system.

DEFECTS IN DEMOCRACY Democratic governments are often criticized for certain defects. The first of these is that the citizens do not fully exercise their rights nor accept their obligations. Democracy, it is asserted, presupposes an intelligent citizenry that recognizes its duties, is intelligently aware of issues, and acts with respect to them in the public interest.

Voting Voting is a paramount right and obligation in a democracy. Through it, we choose the officials who are to represent us in determining policies and programs. It is a main opportunity for the citizens to influence their government. The obligation to vote, however, is not fully discharged in most elections. The percentage of eligible American voters who fulfilled the obligation in Presidential elections over the last three decades ranged from 51.5 per cent in 1948 to 63.8 per cent in 1960.[17] These elections usually bring out the heaviest vote, but other interim and local elections bring out smaller numbers of voters. Such evidence indicates a significant amount of political indifference among us.

George Bernard Shaw, while admitting that democracy has "much less humbug about it than many older institutions," criticizes its dependence upon voting in the strongest terms: ". . . Our solution of the political problem is Votes for Everybody and Every Authority Elected by Vote, an expedient originally devised to prevent rulers from tyrannizing by the very effectual method of preventing them from doing anything, and thus leaving everything to irresponsible private enterprise." [18]

Our voting practices are also criticized from the qualitative viewpoint. Emphasis, it is said, is upon the number of votes without regard to the persons who do the voting. Primary elections, where candidates are named, are participated in chiefly by persons in political party organization. Most of our voting, it is asserted, is by political party, little by issues. The voters often do not give equal attention to the proposals of the different parties so that they can make few comparisons and arrive at carefully considered judgments about issues. Election campaigns consist in a large measure of praising one's own side and condemning the other. Studies show that voting by political party is consistently followed by seven to eight out of ten voters, regardless of the circumstances or candidates. These conditions, coupled with apathy on the part of so many voters, mean that the whole process of democratic government is jeopardized. Few would deny that criticism is justified. Strong public interest and public opinion are important factors in making democracy work.

Leadership A further criticism of democracy is leveled at leadership. In a small state like Athens, or in a small New England town, each citizen could express himself directly about governmental problems as they arose. This is not possible in large societies and communities having complex relations and problems. In these, citizens must necessarily express their wishes through representative units that often seem far away and out of touch with local situations. In other words, government by the people is government for people through representatives. Two crucial problems arise here. One concerns the quality of leadership and the other the possibility of removing leaders who are not truly representative or qualified.

The criticism of democracy on this score is that, by and large, only the less capable persons are interested in government careers, and they are easily dominated by special interests or by what they think the masses want. Good government can be achieved only by able leaders who are neither class conscious nor interest-controlled, but who follow convictions honestly arrived at after careful thought and thorough study. Democracy must produce leaders who not only follow but who can create opinions. No society rises higher than the level of its leadership. Political leaders in democracy must be of the people but also of a level of competence higher than the average and unafraid to give direction to their thinking.

Bryce's Conclusions on Democratic Government

A succinct summary of the workings of democratic governments is given by James Bryce in his exhaustive study of modern democracies:

I. It has maintained public order while securing the liberty of the individual citizen.

II. It has given a civil administration as efficient as other forms of government have provided.

III. Its legislation has been more generally directed to the welfare of the poorer classes than has been that of other governments.

IV. It has not been inconstant or ungrateful.

V. It has not weakened patriotism or courage.

VI. It has been often wasteful and usually extravagant.

VII. It has not produced general contentment in each nation.

VIII. It has done little to improve international relations and ensure peace, has not diminished class selfishness (witness Australia and New Zealand), has not fostered a cosmopolitan humanitarianism nor mitigated the dislike of men of a different colour.

IX. It has not extinguished corruption and the malign influences wealth can exert upon government.

X. It has not removed the fear of revolution.

XI. It has not enlisted in the service of the State a sufficient number of the most honest and capable citizens.

XII. Nevertheless it has, taken all in all, given better practical results than either the Rule of One Man or the Rule of a Class, for it has at least extinguished many of the evils by which they were defaced.[19]

Bryce frankly stated further that democratic government cannot be assumed to be the final form of government. He also added: "No government demands so much from the citizen as Democracy, and none gives so much back. . . . The statesmen and philosophers of antiquity did not dream of a government in which all men of every grade should bear a part: democracy was for them a superstructure erected upon a substructure of slavery. Modern reformers, bolder and more sanguine, called the multitude to power with the hope and in the faith that the gift of freedom and responsibility would kindle the spirit self-government requires." [20]

Totalitarian Governments Concentrate Power in One or a Few Persons

The concentration of power in one or a few persons in totalitarian states is not dependent upon the consent of the governed but upon the capacity of a few persons to achieve control by various means. The operation of the state is dictated by the small group at the pinnacle of power, and regulations are handed down through officials. Usually, questioning of the ideas and practices of the rulers is not tolerated. Freedom of expression by the individual or the press is denied. Autocratic systems cannot allow questioning and survive; they must be omnipotent. Failure to obey is met by strong discipline, not only to punish offenders but to serve as warnings to others. In totalitarianism, obedience is the supreme law to be enforced by the use of police powers.

Totalitarian systems seem to appear most commonly in societies already conditioned to autocratic rule. The cultural backgrounds of Germany, Italy, and Russia, each of which has experienced totalitarianism, are examples. None of these had had experience with either democratic values or democratic government.

Totalitarianism has a rigidly patterned social organization. This pattern allows no place for unrestricted or uncontrolled associations. In fact, it eliminates all those which it fears may undermine loyalty to its system. It subjects all social groupings to the designs of the state. Such organizations as are allowed are those which the government establishes and controls to support the opinions and practices of the system.

Totalitarianism in Russia Claims to Be Democratic Because Its System Desires to Lift All People to One Level

OBJECTIVE OF RUSSIAN TOTALITARIANISM Totalitarianism in Russia today is of particular interest to us because this system exists, it is asserted, to establish true democracy. This is implied, in part, in the official name of the state, the Union of Soviet Socialist Republics. The union of republics suggests that each republic of which the state is composed has authority to operate as a free unit. Soviet means "council," which is the unit of governmental organization. Village and city "councils" are the primary units of local government, and their members are elected by all the citizens. The Communist party members function in the soviets, which are found in each republic. The members are appointed by the supreme Soviet of the Union Republic, which also appoints members of the Presidium, the executive committee of the supreme Soviet. Other authorities, such as the courts and the commissars, are also appointed by the supreme Soviet. The controlling personnel, therefore, is appointed by a relatively small

body, the composition of which the Communist party leaders determine.

There is a hierarchy of control in each member republic and in the Union of Republics dominated by the Supreme Council. The decisions of the Supreme Council, which are executed by the commissars, are the supreme law. All citizens and officials are pledged by their constitution to obey them. The Communist party, the only political party allowed, is tied to the administrative divisions and dominates them by use of its police organization.

The system cannot be changed by the people since only one ticket of political candidates is ever allowed. They are nominated from above by the Communist party. This is justified on the ground that these candidates are pledged to work for the interest of the people. This, it is asserted, is the most democratic basis on which governments can be founded. If other parties were allowed, it would mean a return to competition that might usher in a struggle against socialism. It is said the people renounced this competition when they legitimately established the Communist state. The use of force to compel acceptance of programs is then justified by arguing that the present period is a necessary first stage to remove those who will not conform. True democracy will thus be achieved after the state has educated the populace to the values in the system, when all indications of exploitive capitalist ideology have been destroyed, and when no social classes remain. Even the state will "wither away," according to Communist doctrine, since the people are accustomed to following the elementary rules of social life that will eliminate all exploitation. There will therefore be no need of a state or a government.

Political Parties Are the Link Between Government and Citizens

ROLES OF POLITICAL PARTIES Political parties have evolved as organizations, as the means whereby candidates are nominated and elected. They play an especially important role in societies which permit the citizens to decide who will be nominated and elected to office. Societies usually do not stipulate the methods of selecting and electing candidates. For example, in the new American state, no provision was made for the choice of candidates for government offices beyond the positions of President and Senators. As a consequence, political organizations —"parties"—consisting of persons holding certain views and promoting certain interests came into existence. They function as devices to advance political ideas and aims, to develop "platforms," to select candidates, and to carry on campaigns promoting their programs and candidates for office. The ultimate aim of a political party is to win and keep control of the government. This is implicit in our references to an English government as "Conservative" or "Labour," or to an American administration as "Republican" or "Democratic."

POLITICAL PARTIES ARE QUASI-OFFICIAL ORGANIZATIONS　Political parties are not official organizations that states have created. They may be regarded as quasi-official in the sense that states sanction, regulate, and permit them to offer candidates for public office if these candidates meet the prescribed qualifications. Their membership as organizations includes cross-sections of the population holding common beliefs about issues. The Conservative and Labor parties in Great Britain contain larger proportions of one economic class than of others. In the United States, the Republican party seems to include more conservative and business people, while the Democratic party includes more liberal and working-class people. But each of these parties includes members who have the characteristics imputed to those of the opposite party. This is particularly true where circumstances have led sections of the country to support one political party predominantly—such as the "solid Democratic South" or the Republican Midwest. Here tradition is a strong factor in determining the party affiliation of the people.

TWO-PARTY SYSTEMS　The number of political parties in a society varies from one to many. England and the United States are illustrations of societies where the two-party system prevails. The advantage of the system is its capacity to present more clearly cut issues and fewer candidates instead of a multiplicity of positions on issues and a wide array of candidates. The losing party will always have some of its representatives in the legislative branch to serve as a "loyal opposition," which can force the majority party to consider its position and to make concessions to it. Under these conditions, political power is never completely in the hands of one of the parties.

Attempts to organize third parties in these countries have not met with much success. Such attempts have usually led to the absorption of the third party by one of the larger ones, which takes over its program. The third-party effort may perform a valuable service through inducing the major parties to modify their programs and positions. This points up another characteristic of the two-party system. Parties are not so rigidly committed that they cannot change their principles and strategies in adaptation to new problems and circumstances. This gives the political system flexibility.

Party Loyalty　Party loyalty in the two-party system is obtained in several ways. The organization itself is built in a hierarchal manner that begins with local precinct and ward units in cities and extends to county units, then to state committees and state conventions, and finally to a national committee and national conventions. Persons and groups providing financial support have considerable influence since political campaigns are costly. Persons who have committed themselves to the party organization cannot easily shift from one party to another. The voter may shift his vote, depending upon his desire to support given candidates or issues, but usually personal ties and traditional associations hold most people to party lines. Persons soon lose any status they may have enjoyed within either party if they shift back and forth from one to the other.

The strongest force keeping party members in line are the favors which winning candidates can dispense, the most important being jobs. Elected officials appoint, or have considerable influence in the selection of, public officials ranging all the way from the members of a president's cabinet to postmasters in small villages. Civil service systems, of course, place many jobs under permanent appointments presumably beyond the reach of party politics. Yet, many positions are still appointive, especially those in local and state systems. These are dispensed as rewards for political services. There are other favors too, such as appointments to party committees or to represent a unit of government on some board or commission. These are often not permanent jobs and carry little compensation, but they are honors that bring the party worker to the attention of the public. Loyalty on a local basis is built by party workers who give aid to persons in need or see to it that social services are made available to them.

Keeping Party Loyalty　Elected officials always work to retain the loyalty of their followers. They use part of their time in visits with those who elected them. Their variable reception at home is illustrated in David Grayson's report about a Congressman who was busy strengthening his position in his district. The Congressman had spoken at meetings of his followers in his community. The Republican paper described the results by referring to the Congressman as "The Honourable Arthur Caldwell." It stated that he was given a most enthusiastic hearing by a large and sympathetic audience. The Democratic paper, on the other hand, referred to him as Arty Caldwell, the Republican boss who was mending his political fences. It stated that he spellbound a handful of henchmen rather than a large and sympathetic audience.[21] The successful politician will always keep in touch with his supporters at home and perform services for them in the state or national capitol.

MULTIPARTY SYSTEMS   France is an illustration of a state that has operated with a multiparty system. She had six main parties in 1955. The chief argument for this system is that in any given time there are many issues and that each issue has many sides (issues are highly important factors in government). Because it was felt that all these issues and views should be openly espoused the great variety of parties developed. But where many different shades of opinion are represented by distinct political parties, it is necessary for them to work out coalitions among their elected legislators and executive officials in order to carry on government at all. Much "behind the scenes" maneuvering is involved since compromise is difficult to effect in the open. Such governments tend to change rapidly for a consistent policy is difficult to maintain. The voters are bewildered by the number of viewpoints presented and the multiplicity of candidates and parties they must assess. The overwhelming victory of the de Gaulle party in the 1962 French elections seems to have shattered the multiparty system in that country. Whether this remarkable development will lead to one-party government remains to be seen.

ONE-PARTY SYSTEM   Russia is a society with a one-party political system—the Communist party. Germany and Italy were one-party states under Naziism and fascism, but these two governments have disappeared. The arguments supporting the one-party system is that only one party can truly represent the interests of the people, therefore only one party should be allowed. This gives the party leaders a monopoly on all political activity and creates a governing elite impossible to remove peaceably. The limitation in this system is the rigid insistence that the given method of governing the society is to the best interest of the people and is therefore inviolate. The people have no peaceful opportunity to change it or its leaders, a philosophy that is directly contrary to the conviction that political power resides ultimately in the people. The value to the dictators of having one party is that it gives a semblance of popular approval of their policies and programs. The dictators can at times create favorable public support by education and propaganda, especially if promises are fulfilled and some benefits to the populace are forthcoming. As Machiavelli put it, the best protection the dictator can have is not being hated by his subjects. He said, "If they hate you, no fortress can save you, for when once the people take up arms, foreigners are never wanting to assist them."[22]

The Politician Plays an Important Role in Our Party System

ATTITUDE TOWARD POLITICIAN   The political party, as the link between the people and their government, created the occupation of politician. He devotes his energy to advancing his party's interests and to advancing himself by helping it gain and hold power. This occupation frequently suffers from an unsavory reputation because of the unscrupulous activities in which politicians have sometimes engaged. The party machine, the inner circle that obtains control of a political party in a city or state, has often been guilty of unethical practices. As a consequence, the occupation often attracts only those who are unscrupulous or those having little knowledge or preparation for governmental careers. One of the serious limitations of democratic government is that so much of it is in the hands of poorly qualified persons with no training in the science of government.

LAWYERS AS POLITICIANS   The legal profession has traditionally been closely associated with government. Lawyers serve in significant numbers in the legislative and other branches of government. This can be a very fruitful relationship since professional training and experience in the law is clearly a desirable asset to a servant of government. The valuable contributions of lawyers in government service are abundant. Lawyers, however, are also human, and they too may exploit their positions to pervert the processes of government to personal and group advantage.

H. G. Wells was acidulous in describing the

role of the lawyer as a professional politician in England:

> Law is the basis of civilization, but the lawyer is the law's consequence, and, with us at least, the legal profession is the political profession. It delights in false issues and merely technical politics. Steadily with the ascendancy of the House of Commons the barristers have ousted other types of men from political power. The decline of the House of Lords has been the last triumph of the House of Lawyers, and we are governed now to a large extent not so much by the people for the people as by the barristers for the barristers. They set the tone of political life. And since they are the most specialized, the most specifically trained of all the professions, since their training is absolutely antagonistic to the creative impulses of the constructive artist and the controlled experiments of the scientific men, since the business is with evidence and advantages and the skillful use of evidence and advantages, and not with understanding, they are the least statesmanlike of all educated men, and they give our public life a tone as hopelessly discordant with our very great and urgent social needs as one could well imagine.[23]

This statement, exaggerated though it is, emphasizes again the necessity of keeping political activity on a high ethical plane so as to attract the best qualified people to government service. This is important in any society, but especially so in a democracy.

An International Political Organization Is Essential to Mankind's Future Well-Being

ONE WORLD It is not just a rhetorical statement to say that societies operate today in one world. There is hardly one modern society whose activities in commerce, trade, and other cultural relationships remain within its own confines. Science, medicine, religion, and other human values are international for they do not know of state borders. Markets are now world markets, created by a flow of goods between all nations. Economically self-sufficient nations no longer exist.

Included among many other illustrations of the interwoven character of modern societies would be the international postal system, international system of weights and measures, international narcotics agreements, international telegraph and communication union, international aviation organization, and code of international laws. There are dozens of international societies dealing with the common interests of humanity. Each of these accents the advantages of cooperation among all societies.

Internationalism in the political area has, however, not kept pace with the growth of internationalism in other areas. Nations that are confronted with serious problems involving interstate relations too often use war as the final recourse for settlement. The policy of strong nations is to develop such fighting strength that they will not be challenged. Each era of peace, therefore, has been a period of armament races, as they are called, between these strong nations. Organizing the nations in a balance of power so that no one nation or group of nations has the strength to conquer one or all of them is usually part of the preparation. They are efforts to achieve equal or superior military strength. Nothing underscores more forcibly our need for a broader international political orientation and organization than does the threat of war.

INTERNATIONAL FAILURES OF THE PAST Despite such historic efforts as the League of Nations and the United Nations, we have so far been unable to evolve any really adequate machinery for analyzing international disputes and for suggesting and enforcing peaceful compromises for their solution. Such disputes are usually deemed to be only the concerns of the countries involved, though in many cases they soon involve other nations. War is the accepted method of arriving at final solutions when other methods fail. It is assumed that wars are inevitable because nations will not compromise. Many have rationalized them in terms of man's fundamental make-up. He is said to possess fighting instincts that cause him to war. Now we recognize no such inherited drives, and we know that wars come from limitations in our social systems. Warrior classes have been characteristic of nations, fighting prowess has been glorified, and military castes have often controlled the political operation of societies because war has been deemed necessary. It was the military class in both Germany and Japan that led these nations into the struggles of World Wars I and II.

WAR AS A PROCESS Nations proceed to prepare their people for war if a problem arises that seems insoluble by other methods. They lay the issues before their people so that it appears as if the enemy is completely in error, is unreasonable and uncompromising, and is violently hostile. Mobilization is begun, economic forces consolidated, and a mood created that leaves fighting as the only solution believed to be honorable.

The state takes over completely when war comes. All activities are geared to conquering the enemy. Restrictions are placed upon citizens in all the areas deemed essential to this end, including food, materials important to fighting, and the movement of persons. People must participate in the war effort as those in complete command determine.

When wars end, as they must, if one side is completely defeated, peace terms may be exacting. In recent times, because nations are so completely interwoven with each other and so much of the total economy of the world is dependent upon the economy of all, compromises are devised in the attempt to recreate peacetime conditions as quickly as possible. However, as happened at the end of World War II, some states may completely disappear or be brought within the orbit of a conquering state and the pattern of their government completely changed. For instance, democratic Czechoslovakia is now a Soviet Communist satellite.

Right to Declare War More and more we question the right of nations in the family of nations to declare war to solve problems. War often creates more problems than it solves. It seems wholly incompatible with any reasonable system of morals and religion.

STATE SOVEREIGNTY The major factor in this dilemma of nations not yet attaining a fully international outlook is the principle of state sovereignty. States are the largest units in which political control operates, and the people recognize no higher authority than the state. Loyalty to the state is a supreme societal value. Nationalism, the body of ethnocentric beliefs and convictions about our own state, has been a major characteristic of modern times. It received strong impetus after World War I with the enunciation of the principle that nationalities who speak a common language and share common historic traditions have a right to organize their own states. Many new states came into existence as a consequence, making nationalism a world-wide principle. Millions of people who are subject folk as a result of the colonial imperialism of the nineteenth century now demand their right to independent national existence. This principle stands as a roadblock to the development of the larger principle of an effective international control system. No nation-state, once having developed its own

political unity, gives up what seems to be its independence by submitting to decisions made by other states. This symbol of complete freedom was so strong that when the United States had to make a decision about joining the League of Nations, it rejected membership even though its own President had been its primary designer and exponent. National sovereignty remains as a major obstacle to the success of the United Nations.

There can be little doubt that the people of the world want peace. Even a state like Russia, the leaders of which openly insist that their form of government and pattern of living must eventually dominate the societies of our world, hopes to accomplish this by peaceful means. The development of international laws, covering even the conduct of war, emphasizes our desire for peace. Efforts by voluntary associations to organize international units to promote peace as well as the activity of militant pacifists exhibit this strong desire. But the cultural differences between nations, the problems arising from the differential possession of resources, and the great differences in living standards between them serve as barriers. Fears and anxieties created by racial, religious, and national attitudes and the ambitions of particular states and their leaders to gain positions of power impede the development of genuine confidence among states. In fact, these forces lead many Americans and others to believe that real security lies more surely in strong military preparations and in alliances with other nations than in over-all international associations.

It thus seems evident that an effective association of nations with power to enforce peaceful relations between nations can be built only over a long period of time. Perhaps we are making some progress toward this goal. World War I proved conclusively that the balance-of-power principle was not effective enough to prevent war. The League of Nations was a serious attempt to create a political structure that could preserve the values of individual states and cope with aggressive imperialism. But lack of support by member states and the isolationist attitude of the United States brought about its collapse.

World War II stressed again our need for an effective international political body. The United Nations was the result. It has a fundamental weakness as a control device in that its recommendations are not binding on a member nation and are ignored when they are contrary to what members consider their national interests. Nor is there any genuine police force at its disposal to enforce its decisions. It does not even have the cooperative financial support of its members. These weaknesses can hardly be overcome without some reorganization to reduce the veto power and other limitations to the authority of the United Nations. Many still insist that, if the United Nations is given strong support by its member nations, it can develop good will and a sense of world community that will lead to an effective institution serving the purposes of international control. The steps taken, even with their weaknesses, direct us toward a goal mankind must eventually reach if it is to survive.

References

1. *The Politics of Aristotle* (Oxford, England, The Clarendon Press, 1885), p. 4.
2. Locke, John, "An Essay Concerning the True Original, Extent, and End of Civil Government," *The English Philosophers from Bacon to Mill*, ed. by E. A. Burtt (New York, Random House [Modern Library], 1939), pp. 437 ff.
3. MacIver, Robert M., *The Web of Government* (New York, The Macmillan Company, 1947), pp. 20 and 21.
4. *New Dictionary of American Politics*, ed. by Smith, E. C., and Zurcher, A. J. (New York, Barnes and Noble, 1949), p. 356.
5. Jay, John, *The Federalist, No. II*, in *Harvard Classics*, 43 (New York, P. F. Collier and Son, 1910), p. 203.
6. Dreiser, Theodore, *An American Tragedy*, 1 (Cleveland, World Publishing Company, 1946), Book 2, p. 357. Reprinted by permission.
7. Penn, William, "Some Fruits of Solitude," in *Harvard Classics*, 1 (New York, P. F. Collier and Son, 1909), p. 348.
8. *Constitution of the United States*, First and Fourteenth amendments.
9. *Constitution of the United States*, Article 1, Section 1.
10. Harris, Louis, *Is There a Republican Majority?* (New York, Harper and Brothers, 1954).
11. Summarized in Weinberg, O., and Shabat, M., *Society and Man* (Englewood Cliffs, N.J., Prentice-Hall, Inc., 1956), p. 611; and from Weber, Max, *The Theory of Social and Economic Organization* trans. by A. M. Henderson and Talcott Parsons (New York, Oxford Press, 1947), Section III, pp. 324 ff.
12. *Facts and Figures on Government Finance, 1954–1955* (New York, The Tax Foundation, 1954), p. 125.
13. MacIver, Robert M., *The Web of Government* (New York, The Macmillan Company, 1947), pp. 20 and 21.
14. Mosca, Gaetano, *The Ruling Class* (New York, McGraw-Hill Book Co., Inc., 1939), p. 50.
15. Steffens, Lincoln, *Autobiography* (New York, Harcourt, Brace and Company, 1931), p. 705.
16. From a confidential conversation with the senior author.
17. United States Department of Commerce, Bureau of the Census, *Statistical Abstract of the United States, 1962*, Table 497, p. 373.
18. Shaw, George B., *The Apple Cart* (New York, Brentano's, 1931), p. XII. Permission granted by the Public Trustee of G. B. Shaw Estate and the Society of Authors, London.
19. Bryce, James, *Modern Democracies*, 2 (New York, The Macmillan Company, 1921), p. 562.
20. *Ibid.*, pp. 608 and 609.

21. Grayson, David, *Adventures in Friendship* (New York, Grosset and Dunlap, 1915), pp. 207 and 212 ff.

22. Machiavelli, Niccolo, *The Prince,* in *Harvard Classics,* 36 (New York, P. F. Collier and Son), p. 71.

23. Wells, H. G., *An Englishman Looks at the World* (Stuttgart, Germany, Bernhard Tauchnitz, 1914), pp. 54 and 55.

Questions for Study and Discussion

1. What theory of the origin of government seems to be the most valid to you?
2. What is the difference between the state and the government?
3. What is the relationship of law to government and the state?
4. Discuss the three traditional functions of governments. Point out changes which have occurred in these in American society.
5. What do you understand by bureaucracy in government? What positive and negative roles do you see it performing in government?
6. How do separation of powers and checks and balances relate to the concentration of powers?
7. Discuss the merits of different governmental forms.
8. Consider the functions of political parties in government and discuss the merits of the various party systems.
9. What are your attitudes toward politicians? Why?
10. What are the possibilities for an international government as you see them?
11. What are the chief obstacles to its establishment?
12. How do you think the rapid development of man's relations to outer space will affect international relations?

Suggested Topics for Reports

1. Select one of the new African nations and examine the cultural and social problems bearing upon its efforts to become a modern state.
2. Make a study of the way in which population changes in your state have affected the apportionment of representatives in the state legislature.
3. Prepare an outline statement drawing parallels between the problem of unifying states within a nation and the problem of unifying nations within an international governmental organization.

Supplementary Reading

Anderson, William, *American Government.* New York: Henry Holt and Company, Inc., 1942.

Berelson, B., Lazarsfeld, and McPhee, W., *Voting: A Study of Opinion Formation in a Presidential Campaign.* Chicago: University of Chicago Press, 1954.

Blau, Peter, *Bureaucracy in Modern Society.* New York: Random House, 1956.

———, and Scott, W. R., *Formal Organizations.* San Francisco: Chandler Publishing Company, 1962.

Bryce, James, *Modern Democracies.* 2 vols. New York: The Macmillan Company, 1921.

De Tocqueville, Alexis, *Democracy in America.* 2 vols. New York: Vintage Books, 1954.

Heberle, Rudolph, *Social Movements: An Introduction to Political Sociology.* New York: Appleton-Century-Crofts, Inc., 1951.

Key, V. O., Jr., *Polities, Parties, and Pressure Groups.* New York: The Crowell-Collier Publishing Co., 1952.

Leighton, Alexander, *The Governing of Men*. Princeton, N.J.: Princeton University Press, 1945.

MacIver, Robert M., *The Web of Government*. New York: The Macmillan Company, 1947.

Michels, Robert, *Political Parties*. Glencoe, Ill.: The Free Press, 1949.

Millikan, Max F., and Blackmer, Donald, L. M., *The Emerging Nations: Their Growth and United States Policy*. Boston: Little, Brown and Company, 1961.

Mills, C. W., *The Power Elite*. New York: Oxford University Press, 1956.

Mosca, Gaetano, *The Ruling Class*. New York: McGraw-Hill Book Co., Inc., 1939.

Presthus, Robert, *The Organizational Society*. New York: Alfred A. Knopf, 1962.

Riesman, David, Glazer, Nathan, and Denny, Ruel, *The Lonely Crowd*. New Haven, Conn.: Yale University Press, 1950.

Thompson, Victor A., *Modern Organization*. New York: Alfred A. Knopf, 1961.

Ulmer, S. S. (ed.), *Introductory Readings in Political Behavior*. Chicago: Rand McNally Company, 1961.

Verba, Sidney, *Small Groups and Political Behavior*. Princeton, N.J.: Princeton University Press, 1961.

16

ORGANIZATIONS: THE INTEREST-PROMOTING STRUCTURES

O*RGANIZATIONS are that class of human relationship structures wherein people purposefully associate in systematically arranged units to promote and achieve some common purposes or interests that are not specifically expressed in the institutions. Each member has a formal status and role in his organization.*

Organizations Are the Fourth Class of Human Relationship Structures or Hurelures of Which Societies Are Composed

We have discussed in the last seven chapters, the structural mechanisms—institutions—by which societies regularize the behavior of the people through normative complexes that relate to the forms of behavior thought essential to a society's preservation. We have, however, many interests that are not specifically expressed through institutions. Institutions are the sanctioned procedures through which a society's fundamental values are realized, but there are innumerable specific values which supplement or implement the general ones of the society. These bring people into reciprocal relations with each other, creating important structural forms that constitute parts of the total social system. These forms are organizations.

A DEFINITION *Organizations* are associations of individuals through which certain value-oriented interests are satisfied. They are systematically arranged units of people in which each person has a formal status and role.

Organizations Have Several Essential Characteristics

The human relationships structures of a society, like all other phenomena, form distinct classes only when they possess some essential properties that differentiate them from all other relationship forms. Organizations as a class possess several distinctive properties that mark them off from the other relationship forms.

CLEARLY DEFINED LIMITS A first distinguishing characteristic is that organizations have clearly defined limits prescribed by the interests to be satisfied. Organizations always limit themselves to the pursuit of some definite goals. The purpose uniting people in organizations is the achievement of these defined goals. In highly developed societies, organizations arise to promote interests in almost all areas of life. People quickly find that it is easier to achieve their goals through deliberate cooperation than without it. We cannot, in fact, achieve most of our goals without cooperation. Organizations, then, are devices for combining the efforts of a number of individuals to achieve more effectively their common goals.

The limiting quality of organizations is the specificity of their interests. Organizations do not come into existence to do just anything; they always have some definite ends. Organizations usually dissolve if their goals are achieved and the reasons for their continuance no longer exist. The organizations that were created by women to achieve universal suffrage in American society dissolved after their right to vote was made part of the Constitution. Organizations may, however, find new goals to justify their continuance after they have achieved the particular purposes for which they were originated. For example, a labor union, having attained its end of higher wages and better working conditions, may shift its attention to educational, welfare and, political goals.

Organizations May Develop an Institutional Character Organizations may become institutionalized and supported as part of the socially sanctioned institutional system of the whole society if their objectives prove to be values for the larger society. Early American agriculture saw the development of a number of organizations for promoting scientific experimentation and practices, such as the Agricultural Society of South Carolina and the New York Society for the Promotion of Agriculture, Arts, and Manufactures. These organizations carried on technical experiments, and their work dealt with values that were important to the whole society. They led to the development of the United States Agricultural Society in 1852, out of which came the United States Department of Agriculture established in 1862 as part of the government's institutional system.

Purposes Are Set Forth in Constitutions Organizations are developed to serve every major interest of a modern society: economic, religious, educational, scientific, recreational, philanthropic, professional, literary, artistic, political, and others. But in each instance, whatever the general area of their operation, they are concerned with some definite purpose or purposes related to it. These purposes are customarily set forth in the constitution and bylaws or the charter of the organization in a formal, definitive, and consistent manner.

PURPOSEFUL DEVELOPMENT A second characteristic of organizations is their purposeful development. Human groups often form casually, sometimes without an avowed purpose, from the interrelations of two or more persons. They exist only so long as the persons are actually interacting with each other. Organizations, however, always arise out of purposeful concerns. They are creatures of design having specific value-orientations. Groups may become organizations; crowd activity may in time lead to the creation of organizations—whatever their origins, organizations grow from specific purposes. Individuals with a common interest, no matter how they come together, may decide to join together to promote their interest. They agree to form a unit for achieving an end.

Coercion Is Used in Some Societies In some societies, organizations are set up and individuals compelled to join them. Young people, for example, were pressed to join youth corps in

Germany under the Nazis. Governments in autocratic societies often decide what organizations they think will further their interests, abolish those they do not favor, and create new ones and promote membership in them. But again, organizations are created as social forms for specific purposes, whether membership is forced or voluntary.

FORMAL STATUS AND ROLE

Individuals Are Members of Organizations A third characteristic of organizations is that each person in them has a formal status and role. The term "members" *must* be used to designate the persons who belong to an organization, although it is often used in a common sense way to designate persons who are parts of human relationship structures other than organizations. In becoming members, persons accept definite privileges, powers, and obligations related to the activities of their organization. The act of joining is usually accompanied by some kind of ceremony designed to impress upon the initiate the distinctiveness and meaning of the new status he is assuming. Likewise, membership distinguishes recognized participants from nonparticipants by some degree of social distance. The member of a fraternal organization, for example, enters a status which sets him apart from others. As a member of the order, he may exercise specific rights and responsibilities and participate in its ritualistic and other activities from which nonmembers are completely or largely excluded.

Members Are Representatives The member of an organization is a representative of his organization. He must represent it as prescribed by the code of behavior for the membership. Each organization has standards of member conduct, written or implied, reflecting the character and purpose of the organization. The Boy Scout, the Odd Fellow, the gun club member, and the trade union member, for example, all follow prescribed norms of conduct that are distinctive to the organization and supported by its system of control and discipline. This conformity to distinctive norms and values will tend to generate an identifying ethos in each organization.

SELF-CONTAINED ADMINISTRATION Each organization also has its own self-contained administrative structure. Persons united to achieve definite objectives must have a pattern for coordinating their activities. Each member is not allowed to go off in his own direction. Therefore, a new organization must first establish an administrative system with definitions and positions for control to guide it toward the values determined upon. This gives a framework within which its activities are conducted and assures the continuity of the organization regardless of the persons who are members of it.

CONSTITUTIONS AND BYLAWS Practically all organizations describe their purposes, conditions for membership, and their administrative structure in written instruments commonly called constitutions and bylaws. These state how its functionaries are to be chosen, how replaced, and what responsibilities they have. Methods of membership admission, exclusion, replacement, and identification are specified so that those who are "of the organization" are recognizable to each other. An organization is commonly recognized as an entity by the public, as well as by its membership, through a name which is commonly stated in the opening sentence of its constitution and through such symbols as badges, buttons, headgear, uniforms, and the properties it acquires. All of these unify an organization so that it functions as a distinctive unit.

LOCAL AND OVER-ALL ORGANIZATIONS

Relationship Between Them Many organizations are units of larger organizations. For example, a local community or county health organization may be a unit in a state- or nationwide health organization. The local unit has its own self-contained structure so that it can operate, however, without such a relationship. A local tuberculosis, cancer, or mental health organization usually is related to a larger association, but nothing need prevent it from operating as an independent organization. Since organizations with similar purposes find advantages in cooperating, they often set up over-all organizations to obtain these benefits.

Mutual Obligations One of the problems that arises between over-all organizations and their local units concerns their mutual obligations. Usually, a charter or contract between a local organization and the over-all organization describes the obligations of each. Local organizations sometimes find their obligations to the over-all organization unacceptable and withdraw, while over-all organizations sometimes drop local units if they do not fulfill their contract agreements. National college fraternities have dropped local chapters because they admitted persons to their membership who were unacceptable to the national body. Some local civic clubs have withdrawn from their parent

organization because of policies and practices that they did not deem proper. The local organization might need to change its name or some of its activities, but it could continue to operate for it possesses its own self-contained administrative structure.

CONTROLS IN ORGANIZATIONS

Defining Authority The development of lines of authority and control within an organization is associated with this self-contained administrative structure. The right to make judgments, to take action, and to have these accepted is recognized. The constitution or charter is the control instrument communicating such authority. It establishes at least a minimum set of functionaries whose powers are described. Most organizations have a chief officer, president, or chairman; an assistant chief officer or vice-president to "take the chair" if the chief officer is not available; other assistant officers as the objectives require; a secretary to keep records; and a treasurer to receive and dispense income. Other officers may be designated, depending upon the particular organization. Thus, authority is located and ranked according to the organization rules.

VARIATION IN AUTHORITY

In Decision-Making The granting of authority to direct its members, to perform acts in its name, and to represent it with nonmembers varies with the organization. In some, such as social and recreational organizations, a functionary must receive instructions from the members before carrying out acts that obligate them. He is an executive only. Total membership is the decision-maker. On the other hand, an individual, once given a prescribed status, may make final decisions in some organizations. The ranking officer, such as the master of a Masonic Lodge, is given complete authority to make decisions for the organization. In the one case, judgments are made by the members; functionaries simply carry them out as instructed. In the other case, judgments for the organization are made by the functionaries. (See Box 22.)

Committees Organizations often use selected groups of members, called committees, to represent them in special activities. Because some organizations have permanent concerns with respect to their major interests, they appoint or select several of their members to operate continuously relative to these. Such committees are called "standing committees." When matters not previously planned for arise, and for which

---

BOX 22   AUTHORITY AND VOLUNTARY ASSOCIATION

The ideology of voluntary social groups in America tends to be anti-authoritarian. The constituency of these groups is distrustful of centralization and further rationalization of their organizations. However, to achieve the imperative goals of these voluntary associations bureaucracy is necessary, social tension increases, and the problems of authority and power become increasingly acute.[1]

---

no administrative provision has been made, a committee of members may be appointed or selected to represent the organization—either to act for it or recommend action to it. Many organizations set up "executive committees," usually consisting of their officers and several persons from their membership at large, so that they may operate between the times of their set meetings. They are given authority to represent the organization in these periods and to take such action as appears justified within the limitations prescribed.

Leadership Is an Important Factor in the Life of an Organization

Partly because of their largely voluntaristic character, organizations are dependent upon effective leadership to a greater extent than are some other types of hurelures. Their fluctuations in vitality over a period of time are closely correlated with the variations in the quality of leadership. Successful leadership is generally characterized by the ability to make the organization's goals seem significant, to initiate or energize the actions of others, and to inspire confidence and enthusiasm in the members. If leaders fail to facilitate goal achievement in these ways, the organization will almost certainly become moribund or collapse.

BASIC FUNCTIONS OF LEADERSHIP

Direction   If we reduce the functions of leadership to the basic essentials, these would be direction and the maintenance of morale. The effective leader devotes himself to the direction and supervision of the activity of others, rather than to try to perform it all himself. This requires that he delegate work to others who have competence in given areas, instead of assuming full responsibility for detailed execution. This principle will not only lead to greater efficiency in the organization but also will enhance the sense of participation in the members.

Morale   The leader must be able to direct the structure so as to focus upon the desired ends. This is especially crucial when the organiza-

tion's goals are only vaguely understood and the motivations of the membership are complex and varied.[2] Beyond giving the members a clear, strong sense of common purpose, the leader must employ such measures as are required to give them a feeling of personal worth and fulfillment, to maintain a spirit of unity, and to sustain enthusiasm. These are all elements of group morale, the maintenance of which is a vital function of leadership.

CHARACTERISTICS OF LEADERS   Listings of leadership traits abound in traditional studies which usually assumed that such characteristics combine to form a model detached from social contexts. These abstracted listings are of doubtful value. We have come to realize that the leader is always, in significant measure, a function of the situation in which he operates. This implies that a person who is a successful leader in one situation might not be in another. To a degree, we may say that the situation creates the leader. One student has suggested three related qualities of leadership that would be generally transferrable from one situation to another. The leader, says Von Tungelin, is (1) interested in the people; is (2) interesting to the people; and is (3) interested with the people in the solution of their problems.[3] A leader who has these qualities is likely to be effective in any organization.

Organizations May Be Classified from Several Viewpoints

PRESCRIBED VERSUS VOLUNTARY ORGANIZATIONS   In totalitarian societies, as we have noted, organizations are almost wholly government sponsored or sanctioned. They are usually established and directed by government officials, and membership in them is often compulsory. Others, except those operating "underground," are tolerated only if the government believes they will advance its purposes. Under these circumstances, organizations will rarely arise as spontaneous expressions of the interests of people themselves.

Organizations arise out of whatever interests the people may have in societies where freedom of thought and action is permitted and valued. In such societies, organizations express an amazing variety of interests. They range from those to preserve the memory of a deceased person or a past event to those to prevent some possible future activity from taking place. The purpose of each may be classified according to each major interest that motivates people. Such categories as religious, educational, economic, and occupational are only a light sampling.

MOTIVES IN JOINING ORGANIZATIONS

Personal Satisfaction There are two elemental motives which lead people to join organizations. One reason is to provide personal satisfaction. We join such organizations as card clubs, dancing societies, and recreational associations for the personal pleasure we derive from such activities. A Pennsylvania study points out that the greatest benefit people reported receiving from their organization memberships was the friends they made. The pleasure from social contacts served as the justifying value.[4]

Service Motive The other motive we have is to help in social services. We join labor organizations, improvement leagues, hospital aid societies, and hundreds of others because we are interested in what these organizations try to accomplish in society. Often, our membership in an organization will serve both these purposes so that our motivations cannot be sharply separated. Many, for example, belong to civic clubs, such as Rotary or Kiwanis, or a fraternal organization, such as the Shrine, because they provide pleasurable contacts, friends, and fun, and also carry on constructive social service programs.

Mixed with these manifest motives is the desire, often thinly disguised, to climb the social ladder by joining the "right" organization. The "status seeker" has become an arch symbol of our time, and, incidentally, easily lends himself to satire: Nunnaly Johnson, the movie producer, reports that his original level of association in rural Georgia was so low that he considered the people who lived along Tobacco Road to be the country club set! Some would call this "inverted snobbery."

ORGANIZATIONAL OPERATION Another approach to the typing of organizations is suggested by the degree of secrecy with which they operate. From this viewpoint, we can identify open organizations, secret organizations, and organizations with secrets.

Open Organizations A golf club, a business association, an improvement league, while limiting participation to their members, usually carry on all activities in the open. In fact, they desire to have the public know about them so that new members may be attracted and the public be made aware of their services.

Secret Organizations At the other extreme, there are wholly secret organizations. Here the purposes are known only to the members, their activities are kept secret, and in some instances, their members are not known to each other except by secret signs. A main factor in the maintenance of such organizations is the existence of key leaders whose power and authority take on mysterious qualities because of the autocratic pronouncements they issue and the fact that their own identity is hidden.

Organizations with Secrets Such completely secret organizations are not widely prevalent in Western societies. There are, however, many "organizations with secrets" (many lodges are of this nature). Most of them make no secret of their purposes or their membership because they make the public aware of what they stand for in their journals, in public meetings, and by other methods. A Masonic lodge, for example, gives aid to many indigent people, helps maintain hospitals for children and homes for the aged, and promotes any service within its capabilities that will help its fellow citizens. The members are readily recognized from the symbols they wear. Their headquarters are often used for public functions. The same is true of virtually all other fraternal bodies—but they do have secrets. Most of these are associated with their ceremonials that emphasize the moral, ethical, or religious principles the organization promotes. They are especially important in introducing the novice to the personal and social purposes of the organization and guiding him symbolically "toward the light," as well as reminding the members of their obligations. The ceremonial oath is used to ensure the preservation of their secrets.

ADMISSION TYPES A third classification of organizations may be made on the basis of the openness of membership. Organizations may be described from this viewpoint as inclusive, restricted, and exclusive.

Inclusive Inclusive organizations are those that admit to membership anyone who expresses an interest in the organization's purposes and who meets other requirements. A citizen's association for good schools, a neighborhood improvement society, or a community recreational association are illustrations of such organizations.

Restricted Restricted organizations are those that admit only persons who conform to predetermined qualifications that characterize both the applicants and the organization. A carpenter's union admits only qualified carpenters, a merchant's association only merchants, and a medical association only doctors.

Exclusive Exclusive organizations limit admission through selection by the current members of the organization. Some social clubs, fraternities, civic clubs, and honorary societies come under this category. Choice of their members depends altogether on selection by the organization, though certain qualifications in the candidates are essential to consideration.

These characterizations of organization types are not always mutually exclusive. A given organization may be both an organization with secrets and exclusive, as is true of most fraternal organizations. The characterizations do, however, indicate major differences between them.

Organizations Are Numerous and Large Proportions of the Population Belong to Them in American Society

A GREAT PROLIFERATION It is not known how many organizations there are at a given time in a society, such as the American. There have been some estimates based on surveys, but they are only estimates, however, since most of the studies use different definitions of organizations or set limitations on size or other conditions that may exclude many of them. There is little doubt that they are numerous, though. As far back as the 1830's, de Tocqueville, the French philosopher, commented: "Americans of all ages, all conditions, and all dispositions constantly form associations. They have not only commercial and manufacturing companies in which all take part, but associations of a thousand other kinds—religious, moral, serious, futile, extensive, or restricted, enormous or diminutive. The Americans make associations to give entertainments, to found establishments for education, to build inns, to construct churches, to diffuse books, to send missionaries to the antipodes; and in this manner they found hospitals, prisons, and schools. If it be proposed to advance some truth, or to foster some feeling by the encouragement of a great example, they

form a society." [5] James Bryce pointed out that "associations are created, extended, and worked in the United States more quickly and effectively than in any other country." [6] This is part of the genius of the society, for it is through their organizations that the people not only provide many of their satisfactions and handle many of their local problems but also provide much of the stimulus for solving state and national problems. As de Toqueville puts it: "In democratic countries, the science of association is the mother of science; the progress of all the rest depends upon the progress it has made." [7]

LARGE NUMBER OF ORGANIZATIONS TODAY Much evidence shows that the number of organizations in American society is very large. One study lists 5000 *national* organizations in American society in the early 1950's, and the author did not consider the list complete. [8] A study of Minneapolis and St. Paul found 3000 different organizations in those cities. More than 500 organizations were found in Litchfield County, Connecticut; 428 in Goodhue County in Minnesota; 815 in Fairfield County, Ohio, including churches and church-affiliated organizations. [9] Other county studies give similar results. There are 3068 counties in the United States. There would be well over 500,000 organizations of all types in American society if we suggest a conservative figure of 200 as the average number of organizations in each county. It is fair to say that there is a great abundance of organizations throughout the society, even if this estimate of the number is dubious. It is a rare place where a citizen cannot find an organization to meet his needs. It is still true that he may, as de Tocqueville pointed out, organize one if he cannot find it: "Americans are the most peculiar people in the world. In a local community a citizen may conceive of some need which is not being met. He goes across the street and discusses it with his neighbor. A committee begins to function on behalf of his need and you won't believe this but it's true: all of this is done without reference to any bureaucrat, by the private citizens on their own initiative."

A PATTERN FROM EARLY DAYS Organizations have always been used in American society to influence the course of our social development. As tools of democracy expressing the views of both majorities and minorities, they were as important—if not more so—in the days when the society was predominantly agricultural as they are now, when it is predominantly industrial. From precolonial to present times, the farmers and small town residents united in local, sectional, and national organizations to handle their problems, thus bequeathing to us a pattern of citizen initiative that has always served as the stimulus for the development of such organizations in urban centers.[10]

MEMBERSHIPS IN PROPORTION TO TOTAL POPULATION   What is probably the proportion of the population that belongs to organizations? The Detroit profile study shows that in 1951, 63 per cent of the population belonged to at least one organization other than the church.[11] In Lansing, Michigan, 85 per cent of a sample studied belonged to one or more organizations, while in the North Lansing fringe, 69 per cent belonged to one or more organizations.[12] In four neighborhoods in San Francisco, 75 per cent of the men belonged to at least one organization.[13] Of over 2000 persons in a Pennsylvania community, only 2 per cent had no formal participation, that is, did not belong to or did not operate in any organization.[14]

In a New York county, only 3 per cent of the farm owners and 18 per cent of the tenants did not belong to at least one organization, while in two other counties 55 per cent and 69 per cent of all the family members belonged to at least one organization. Only 14 per cent and 6 per cent, respectively, had no family member in any organization.[15] Most studies show that two or more of every three persons belong to one or more organizations other than those connected with our churches. We must conclude that a significant additional number of persons carry out their organizational activities in churches and in churches alone when we remember that membership in churches is one of the most extensive forms of voluntary association in the society and that the churches include organizations for most age and sex groupings. The proportion of individuals who belong to organizations is at least three out of every four persons over twelve years of age and probably more, if the church organizations are included.

Organizations Play Four Significant Roles in Democratic Societies

CHARACTERISTICS OF OTHER DEMOCRATIC SOCIETIES   Our illustrations of the creation and activity of organizations are from American society because information about them is most available here. Other democratic societies also have many organizations with similar characteristics. In any society where they exist, organizations play significant roles and make positive contributions to the society and to the individuals within it.

Promotion   One function of organizations is promotion. Basically, all organizations are promotional in the sense that they are purposefully created to forward some end. Many are specifically promotional in that they are created to quicken a definite phase of the social organization.

In the semiarid sections of Arizona, the possibilities of an agriculture producing a variety of crops on a year-round basis depended wholly upon their water supply. Nowhere was the individual so limited and organization so necessary to provide a measured flow of water. Because no government control existed, mutual organizations were established to create irrigation districts to obtain it. The families of an area promoted their development together and made possible a successful agriculture. They also stimulated government concern in the problem and achieved government supervision of irrigation districts to make possible an even more efficient operation for them.[16] Private organizations often serve a society by stimulating general interest in problems, as well as solving their own particular problems. They can experiment with various approaches to test the effectiveness of given methods and so provide stimulus, standards, and models to more official agencies which are not free to assume risks nor free of the reviews public agencies must undergo.

This function of promotion is especially important in societies where new political, social, and economic problems are of pressing character. Organizations that are not dominated by a specific political, social, or economic viewpoint but represent the general social welfare are of great value. The Grange in the United States, for example, accomplished many important things in American society between 1870 and 1880, when there was rapid western expansion. These included such matters as the regulation of railroads, the establishment of a United States Department of Agriculture, and local community cooperation.[17] Organizations that promote specific viewpoints or programs also contribute by bringing these before the public for its consideration. Thus, they are vehicles for directing and achieving change.

Opportunity to Participate A second function of organizations is to provide opportunity for all segments of the population to participate in the society's operation. Democracies require the participation of individuals in organizations to achieve their goals. Cliques or government agencies may quickly assume the ascendancy in areas where the citizens do not accept this responsibility. Organizations can operate more satisfactorily in many areas since cliques or government agencies may have vested interests, while organizations can be interested in the social whole.

Organizations are exceedingly important in making local minority opinions and programs vocal. In most communities, as studies of community power structure show, the control of activities and policies often resides in dominant interest groups that have little incentive to change the existing patterns of organization and control.[18] Organizations of minority groupings, such as taxpayer's associations, traffic associations, beautification societies, and others can make suggestions and exert pressures that often effect desirable changes in static situations.

Personal Benefits to Participators Organizations contribute values directly to those who take part in them. They operate by rules, usually by majority rule. They make a contribution by developing individual readiness to abide by authoritative decision whether they are made by an individual or group of individuals with authority. Respect and consideration for the positions of others, tolerance of different views honestly promoted, willingness to enter into open discussion governed by rules without prejudice, and objective consideration of suggestions are some of the socializing lessons that come from working in organizations. There is no better socializing experience in which to absorb the qualities needed to engage in deliberative considerations than in the sessions of a fraternal society, a civic club, a farmer's association, or similar organizations.

Organizations lead to familiarity with the workings of the society because they usually deal with societal matters. The millions of men and women who hold labor union cards, and through their organizations hope to improve their work and other conditions, are necessarily conscious of the larger social whole, since these organizations make their adaptations to it. Men and women who are active in political party organizations must learn the workings of the larger social system if they hope to be successful. Students who take part in the organizations of their college cannot avoid acquaintance, in some measure, with the social processes that make adjustments possible among the members within the limits of their organizations. Organizations serve indirectly as social control mechanisms by helping their members to learn the techniques of social adjustment.

Regulative Function We have seen that a basic purpose of institutions is the regularization of behavior. As a fourth function, organizations strive to regularize activities. The behavior of members within and without their organizations is governed by rules. Members of lodges, for instance, must conform to their ritual requirements during meetings and live up to their norms in outside associations. All organizations, even a simple recreational association, have prescribed rules by which they regularize membership behavior according to their norms.

Periods of Unrest and Crisis Promote the Creation of Organizations

PROMOTED BY DISSATISFACTIONS Although organizations come into existence at any time a group of people have an interest to promote, they tend to multiply when there is unrest or discontent. If a condition thwarts or perplexes them, they are likely to form an association to deal with it. (See Box 23.) Often, too, new organizations appear as reactions against existing ones. Neighbors who are left out of social activities form a club of their own. College students who do not "make" a fraternity develop their independent society, or a nationality grouping creates its nationality organization. The National Association for the Advancement of White People arose as a counter to the National Association for the Advancement of Colored People. The organizations thus created may not deal directly with the real causes of unrest but simply be an outlet for the feelings that have been curbed. Such organizations are likely to be short-lived and disintegrate quickly, unless they develop purposes that have enduring value.

MULTIPLIED BY CRISES Periods of crisis also see the multiplication of organizations. Depressions lead us to create more business associations, chambers of commerce, community councils and other forms for working together. Wars necessitate the development of close integration of activities. Organizations quickly spring into existence in democratic societies to perform the

BOX 23

Negroes are more likely to be affiliated with formal voluntary associations than whites, especially at the lower-class level. Negroes who are affiliated with voluntary associations are much like whites who are affiliated. . . . Negroes are active in association because they are not allowed to be active in much of the other organized life of American society. The organizations of Negroes follow a pattern that is a generation behind the general American pattern. The greater affiliation of Negroes may be related to the looser ties that characterize the extended family structure of the Negro, especially the lower-class Negro. Finally, the voluntary association may function in much the same way as the Negro church to provide the Negro not only with an opportunity for self expression and status recognition, but also with an avenue to compete for prestige, to hold office, to exercise power and control, and to win applause and acclaim.[19]

public tasks that are essential to the war effort. Knitting and bandage units, first aid classes, civil defense units, and Red Cross societies are activated. The established organizations often find it necessary to adapt their program to crisis requirements. Lodges may serve as units of some war organization, such as the Red Cross, and the recreational organizations may become civil defense associations. If the crisis passes, many of these special organizations disappear, and those that adapted their programs return to their former activities.

THEIR COORDINATION A major problem in periods of crisis is the coordination of rapidly forming organizations. Over-all councils often come into existence to serve as coordinating agencies. They may be constituted of representatives of the individual organizations and serve to direct the activities so that competition and conflict are avoided. Such councils often hold over after a crisis to continue their coordinating function. Indeed, even in peacetime, community councils need eventually to be established for the coordination of the many special interest groups.

There Appears to Be a Maximum Number of Organizations Most Individuals Take Part In

THREE ORGANIZATIONS PER PERSON It has been found that 87 per cent of the farmers in four New York counties belonged to three or fewer organizations in the first of the Cornell studies of organization membership. Other Cornell studies have shown that 70 per cent or more of the people in the rural areas belong to no more than three organizations. Other rural and urban studies confirm this ratio.[20] We may tentatively generalize that three is the maxi-

mum number of organizations in which most people take part. The extent of their interests, the time available, and the costs probably all enter this determination. But most people who belong to organizations are not members of as many as three. About one-half belong to no more than one organization; three-fourths to no more than two. The suggestion that most people belong to too many organizations does not appear to be true.

MEMBERSHIP IN ONE ORGANIZATION A STIMULUS TO MEMBERSHIP IN OTHERS Individuals who are active in some organization have taken their first step toward activity in others. The evidence for this observation is found in studies of the membership of almost 3000 New York farmers and in studies of Farm Bureau and 4-H Club memberships. The proportion of the members who belong to a given organization who are also members of other specific organizations is always higher, by 10 to 20 per cent, than the proportions of people who belong to the specific organizations but who are not members of the given organization. For example, 66 per cent of the farmers who belong to the Farm Bureau also belong to a church, 53 per cent belong to a Grange, 30 per cent belong to a lodge. Of the farmers who do not belong to the Farm Bureau, only 47 per cent belong to a church, 26 per cent to a Grange, and 13 per cent to a lodge. The same is true for the membership in each specific organization. Members of the Farm Bureau belong to an average of four organizations, nonmembers to only slightly more than one organization. Women of the Home Bureau also average a total of four memberships, while nonmembers of the Home Bureau belong to only one organization.[21]

Other Participation in Organizations, in Addition to Belonging, Is Essential to Developing Them into Cohesive Entities

FUSION OF MEMBERS THE GOAL Other aspects of participation, in addition to belonging, are important to organizations. One must be a member to play a role at all. But taking part in the activities of organizations, such as attending their meetings, helping with programs, serving on their committees, and participating as officers, are also essential to their success. The objective of any organization is to fuse its members into the organization, that is, to get them to identify so completely with its programs that they are agents of their organization for the realization of its objectives. The objective of individuals in an organization is to make it an agency for the realization of their purposes.[22] These objectives focus our view upon the central problem of any organization, namely, the creation of a cohesive entity. The extent to which we follow up "belonging" with "taking part in" is an indication of this process. How much we attend, hold office, or serve our organizations on committees and in other ways indicates the degree to which fusion has taken place. There are numerous studies of local people that give data on each of these matters.[23] Organizations meet varying numbers of times per week, month, or year, depending on their type, while their office, committee, and other responsibilities are limited in number. As a consequence, there is an inevitable selective process which brings those who are most thoroughly identified with an organization to the forefront since they show the greatest degree of conformity to their organization's norms. They are the fully participating members. Their morale is high since they are involved in the significant activities of their organization. Most organization members are only partial participators.[24] The more an organization satisfies personal needs and desires by its programs, the more its members will integrate into it. If a member's own participation is not vital to him, he will take little part and soon drop out.

Participation in Organizations by Individuals in American Society Is, to a Considerable Degree, a Function of the Extent to Which Their Families Participate

PARTICIPATION A FAMILY TRAIT When husbands belong to organizations, wives usually do also, and where husbands and wives belong, children usually will. Belonging and taking part in organizations is chiefly a family trait. This does not mean that all the members of the family are included in the same organization or organizations. It means that the family is a unit in which the participation behavior of the whole family has a positive or negative influence upon the participation of each individual in the family. We give one statistical finding to substantiate this. Chapin participation scores for the individual members in 1176 families were correlated with the average participation scores of the rest of their family members to see what relationship the participation scores of the individual family member had with those of the rest of the family as a unit. We see that the relationship of individual participation to family participation is a high one from the fact that the coefficients of correlation range from $+0.68$ for the scores of the daughters and the rest of the family members to $+0.74$ between the wives and the rest of the family members. Likewise, the relationship between the scores of the individual family members is consistently high, ranging from $+0.55$ to $+0.76$.[25]

SPECIAL INTERESTS TOO OFTEN THE EMPHASIS Many organizations give little thought to the significance of primary group influence on participation. Organizations are accustomed to working in terms of their special interests and usually approach persons in terms of these special interests. But individuals who have special interests often do not express them when there is little stimulation from their family to encourage their participation.

One illustration emphasizes this. Missionaries seeking to make converts often approach their prospects on an individual basis and experience little success. Their effort to pull individuals away from their socializing environment is an almost fruitless one. This principle is constantly violated in promotion work in rural areas, also. Rural workers try to get boys into the Scouts or the 4-H Club and give little thought to their family or peer groups. It is almost impossible to keep people in programs for long without the support of their primary socializing agencies.

The Wife or Mother Is the Family Member Who Supports Organization Participation Most

WIVES AS THE BEST PROMOTERS The suggestion that participation in organizations is largely the result of family participation practices leads to the question, "Do some family members exhibit this trait to a greater degree than others?" The studies at Cornell show that the wife and mother is the most active organization promoter in families, that daughters are next, sons next, and husbands and fathers last. This statistical conclusion that the wives and mothers show most interest in organizations and take most responsibility for promoting them with their other family members is in accord with practical experience.[26] If it is desired to obtain greater participation by a family, the initial approach can probably best be made through them.

There Are Other Correlates with Participation in Organizations

GREATER MALE MEMBERSHIP Studies of factors and characteristics of participation show somewhat varying results. There are, nevertheless, several characteristics of participation that appear to be general for American society. Practically all studies report that more men than women belong to organizations. This is not because there are more organizations for the men than women, but that the women's organizations are usually small. The women, however, are more active than the men in their organization.

SOCIOECONOMIC STATUS Participation is directly related to socioeconomic status. People who have the highest incomes, have the most education, are home owners, and are of the business, proprietor, and professional classes participate in organizations more extensively than do persons in other classes. (For example, see Box 24.) This is true of both urban and rural residents. This greater participation reflects the participators' social status and the community's acceptance of it. The lack of participation by the lower-class members is a reflection of their acceptance of an inferior social status. A community bestows participation positions upon upper-class persons and withholds them from the others. The community status gained or inherited from personal, economic, and social success often makes it unnecessary for persons in the upper class to put forth efforts to gain organization membership or positions of leadership in them. These are often thrust upon them.[28]

FAMILIES IN CHILD-REARING STAGE Participation is higher for the families with children than for those without children. It is often said that caring for the children or earning the family living takes so much of their attention that parents do not have the time or energy left for organizations. Actually, parents increase their participation as one way of encouraging their children. Children also introduce their parents to organizational activities.[29]

MIDDLE AGE AS "BEST" PERIOD Organizational participation is highest between the ages of 30 and 55 years. Thereafter, it declines for both males and females.[30] By the middle years, people have become socially established and are striving for expression in their larger relationships. They have achieved experience and a community status and are undoubtedly stimulated to activity by their school-age children. The later years are those of declining energy for most people, and their accomplishments, if any, have been completed by this time.

Organizations Follow a Growth Pattern

The development of organizations follows a growth pattern of rather definite stages.[31] The length of these is, of course, related to the type of organization and the influence of societal conditions upon them. But the stages seem to be relatively clear-cut, most organizations experiencing each of them in turn.

PERIOD OF CULTIVATION Every organization must have people who are interested in its purposes. These people are not difficult to discover. Several individuals express their interest in

---

BOX 24 SOCIAL CLASS AND PARTICIPATION IN ASSOCIATIONS

Women on upper-class hospital boards in Chicago belong to more, more prestigeful, and more metropolitan associations than do women on middle-class boards. They join their boards earlier, enjoy greater gratification, are more active, and are more committed to the board. The board role is linked to family and class responsibilities for the upper-class women, whereas it is subordinate and supplementary to the domestic role for the middle-class woman.[27]

some social condition and spontaneously form the nucleus of an organization. However, some purposes require promotion to convince people of the value of an idea. Thus, there follows a period of interest cultivation, which varies with the type of organization proposed, the obligations required, and the acuteness of the problem. Lively interest may arise speedily if there is a new condition or an old dissatisfaction that creates a cause to be promoted. It may be only a matter of finding persons who see the possibilities and will accept leadership, if the action involves introducing locally a unit of an established organization that already has defined and developed programs.

Importance of Promoters The promoters are important in this stage. Most local social, recreational, and avocational organizations are started by people in the community who have an interest and have the confidence of the residents so that the latter will want to associate with them. Or they may be persons from the outside, either amateurs or professionals, who come in for the express purpose of promotion. Civic organizations are established in this way. An individual member or a group of members of an organization, such as the Lion's Club, may approach qualified men in a community, tell them about the organization, get them to survey the community, suggest possible members, and suggest a meeting of prospects for informal consideration. The objective is to get the prospects to want the organization.

Professional Promoters Professional promoters, such as union organizers, must find in their prospective members compelling conditions that make it possible for them to change individual views into collective action. Union promoters, while they follow no set rules, look for circumstances that enable them to emphasize those aspects of unionism that are attractive. The union is an abstraction to most workers who have little experience with it. Success in organizing them will depend to a considerable degree, therefore, on the personality of the organizer.[32] This is also true of most promotional efforts by professionals. Although the tactics are important, the promoter must sell himself to sell his organization.

Creating Enthusiasm During the period of cultivation, activities are informal, the participation spontaneous, and the roles are not defined. A committee may be established to recruit persons as a nucleus to consider forming an organization and try to arouse the interest of others. If enthusiasm runs high, many of them may be emotionally moved to request the creation of an organization.

PERIOD OF FORMATION Organizations do not achieve their purposes through sentiment, nor can they operate informally. They must build a structure through which they can achieve their goals. At a first meeting they may name a temporary chairman. Then a committee on constitution and by-laws is set up after discussion of the purposes and the form of the organization has taken place. The constitution and by-laws, when adopted, state the purposes in definite form. Membership qualifications, dues, officers, committees, elections, number of meetings, and changes in the constitution are provided for. The organization now has its form. It is ready to go about its tasks.

Guidance in Formation Guidance is an important factor in the period of formation. The promoters and individuals who have had some experience may provide it if it is a local organization. If it is an organization that is part of a national association, professional promoters may provide the guidance. Most national organizations have suggested constitutions that can be followed. Some organizations, such as lodges, are granted charters that prescribe the form of organization to be followed.

PERIOD OF NORMAL FUNCTIONING

Program-Planning An organization does not usually remain on an intense level of enthusiasm. Its work has to be done under conditions of normal functioning. Emotions soon subside, and interest may require continuous feeding. Officers must be aggressive and plan effectively so that the programs and activities do not become dull or trivial. They must involve the membership in vital ways. Members usually tire of the same pattern of operation, particularly if they have no part in it. This is true even of the organizations with prescribed rituals that are often beautiful in symbolism. The large proportion of the members of organizations are onlookers who will soon drop even this passive role if there is little to maintain their interest. One way to hold their enthusiasm is promoting other benefits that are not directly related to the specific purposes of the organization, such as social activities and entertainment for the members, their wives, and children. This encourages family support of the organization and also gives the members additional reason for remaining loyal. The responsibility for this effort falls on the inner group of officers or leaders.

Control of Cleavages Cleavages in the organization may arise from conflicting conceptions of the organization's goals, from the management of the organization, or from failure to press rapidly enough toward achieving the purposes. It may be felt that the leadership is lacking in ability, or that certain members have secret ambitions which they are seeking to realize. Such tensions are overcome, to some extent, by fixed rules that define positions and procedures carefully.

Interorganization Competition Competition and conflict with other organizations require attention, also, for organizations are units of the society. The judgments of others have considerable bearing, particularly when people have multiple memberships. Conflicts may arise within individuals because of the conflicts in the goals of the different organizations to which they belong.

Overcoming Ossification A further problem of organizations is to keep them from becoming ossified. In the early stages of their normal operations, changes in membership, program, and procedures are not too difficult to obtain. The relationships have not become highly formal, and the roles have not become rigidly standardized. But as time goes on structure tends to become fixed. The basis for decision-making rests on what has been done in the past, causing members to become less and less involved. Finally, they cease to attend. New members accept the operations as they find them or become inactive after a short period. The organization loses its adaptability. The situation may become chronic, especially if the inner core of members have leadership positions that give them vested interests. Organizations that started as young people's associations, for example, continue to operate, but the members may be those persons who joined at the beginning and have actually become old people. The organization still follows its original pattern, forcing the young people to develop a new organization.

The prevention of ossification may be aided by provisions that limit the tenure of officeholders. Provisions for periodic study of the purposes and operation are helpful. Few organizations, once established, ever seriously try to discover those purposes that are really significant in the light of the new conditions at the time. Activity too often is aimed simply at preserving the organization.

PERIOD OF DECLINE AND PASSING

Objectives Accomplished Some organizations disappear because they have accomplished their objectives. The National Foundation for Infantile Paralysis has been a successful national organization in providing aid for those afflicted with poliomyelitis. The discovery of the Salk vaccine, which provides protection against the disease, virtually eliminated the necessity for this organization. It must find some other purpose or pass out of existence after completing a few years of most important service. Many organizations do survive because they find new goals for old ones.[33]

Transfer of Functions Some organizations pass because their functions are taken over by other organizations or institutional agencies. This is particularly true in periods of rapid social change when new organizations are created to deal with new conditions. For example, new organizations in education are increasing because of rapid population increases and the competition with Russia in the field of science. Citizens set up new organizations in addition to the already existent ones, such as the Parent-Teachers Associations, to consider the school curriculums, other programs, and to suggest changes. These may become permanent, although they may soon die if the schools meet the problems or if the Parent-Teachers organizations absorb them.

During the depression years of the 1930's, a movement proposing to provide pensions for all elderly persons gained widespread popularity, especially among the aged. "Townsend clubs" were organized across the land to influence state and national legislative bodies to provide such pensions. Membership in the thousands of units reached 2¼ million in 1936. Twenty-five years later these organizations had all but vanished. Membership totaled only 56,000, a drop of 97.5 per cent after 25 years. The units that continue are aged people's sociability organizations.[34] The problem of the security of the aged was taken over by state and national governments. The Federal Social Security program now meets these needs, causing the Townsend organizations to disappear because they are deprived of the value-oriented purpose that sustained them.

Loss of Importance As conditions change, organizations also become inactive and die because they have lost their importance to their members. Attention is focused on other activities. The new Farm Bureau organization is more inviting than the old farmer's club, while the neighborhood improvement association in the city has more challenge than a woman's book club. Organizations cease to operate, in the main, when they are deprived of their original purposes and cannot devise adequate substitutes, and when they provide inadequate satisfactions to their members so that they do not command loyalty.

Organizations Get Their Support from Various Sources

DUES AND FEES Organizations must find means of support since they are groupings of people joined together voluntarily to satisfy some common purposes. The most universal method used is to require payment of dues and fees. Virtually all organizations require their members to pay annual dues, an amount of money from each member which is calculated to meet their budget requirements. Many organizations also require a fee upon entrance, which is calculated to cover the costs associated with making the person a member. The costs could pertain to such items as certificates of membership, national organization fees if it is an affiliated organization, and membership buttons or other symbolic materials that are presented to new members. Some organizations, such as social clubs and fraternities, that wish to maintain their exclusiveness set an abnormally high entrance fee and high dues to serve as barriers to membership. The nonpayment of dues over a period of time is almost universally accepted as grounds for dropping a person from an organization.

EVENTS AND SPECIAL ACTIVITIES Events and special activities are promoted by some organizations that need more money than comes in from their normal channels. Dinners, barbecues, baked goods sales, rummage sales, card parties, dances, concerts, sponsored events (like professional football and baseball games), and the sale of materials from which a commission is gained serve this purpose. The patrons receive some benefit from such activities that is considered to be worth the price they paid.

SOLICITED CONTRIBUTIONS Many organizations have programs that income from these sources cannot support. They may have no large operating membership or may conduct programs that require all the attention of their workers. The Boy and Girl Scout organizations, voluntary health associations, senior citizen's organizations, and welfare organizations that provide some community service are illustrations. These depend upon solicited contributions from citizens in the communities who are willing to support such causes.

ENDOWMENTS AND BEQUESTS Endowments also are a source of support for organizations. Such funds are usually provided by persons of wealth who take a special interest in an organization.

Bequests also provide funds. One of the problems with bequests is that they sometimes include conditions that hamper the operation of an organization. Careful consideration is properly given to all gifts that are made with conditions attached, to make sure that they do not impose limitations on the free functioning of the organization in relation to its goals.

Organizations Are Significant as Intersociety as Well as Intrasociety Structures

Our analysis of organizations as the fourth class of human relationship structures has been limited so far to those in given societies. In the modern world, however, many organizations are becoming international in scope and are establishing intersociety relationships. People with common interests that extend beyond national boundaries join together to promote their common interests for the welfare of all mankind.

MANY INTERNATIONAL ORGANIZATIONS There are more than 1000 such international organizations in existence today. They deal with almost every kind of interests from religion to recreation, cancer to labor problems, child welfare to international peace. Their importance is so great that the United Nations has directed its Economic and Social Council to make consultative arrangements with many of them to get expert information from those that have special competence.

The twelve major areas in which such organizations exist include business and finance, communication and travel, labor, agriculture, arts and sciences, press, education, religion, social welfare, sports, peace, and international law.

A FEW EXAMPLES Some examples of these international organizations are the International Chamber of Commerce, International Federation of Trade Unions, International Confederation of Students, World Council of Churches, Associated Country Women of the World, Institute of International Law, Pan European Union, and Rotary International.

The functions these organizations perform include meeting some specific international need, molding public opinion on international problems, and developing national understanding on fundamental issues.

Their great value, of course, lies in their promotion of common interests of all mankind that contribute to better intersociety relationships.[35]

Organizations Operate as Major Elements in the Control System of Societies Through the Influences They Exert

We have made inferences in the preceding pages concerning ways in which organizations operate as controls in the society and on the citizenry. There is no possible way of measuring their total effect. The fact that they constitute a major class of a society's human relationship forms and appear in relation to all aspects of social life is an indication of their major influence.

SOME ILLUSTRATIONS Perhaps the best way to indicate these influences is to illustrate the accomplishments of a few organizations in society in general, and of local communities in particular, and their effect upon individuals. Any organizations that have had continuing programs can be used, and we can multiply examples from our own experience. Health organizations are a good starting point if we select at random and for no other purpose than that of illustration.

Health Not long ago tuberculosis was one of the most common killers in American society. Its control has been almost completely accomplished in this society, although it still is a serious menace since infection is easy. The local tuberculosis associations, the state associations, and the national association must be credited with much of this achievement. The returns from Christmas Seals, which have supported these organizations, made possible the educational activities, research programs, and hospital support that have been primarily responsible for this conquest. This same story is now being told for cancer, cerebral palsy, polio, and mental diseases.

Agriculture In the field of agriculture, the Patrons of Husbandry, or the Grange, as it is commonly called, has already been referred to as being responsible for major accomplishments. For over three-quarters of a century, this organization with its local, county, state, and national units has emphasized a family approach in the rural areas that has added much to the economic, recreational, educational, and legislative level of living in the rural areas and, by indirection, to the society as a whole.

Politics Political parties are organizations that aim to educate the public on the political issues and present candidates for the political offices. American political life is actually the story of the operating political organizations, working in communities, states, and nation where Democrats, Republicans, socialists, free-silverites, prohibitionists, and others have banded together to get control of the government through their organizational activity to make their viewpoints the way of life in the society. Formal organization was the only possible way for them to exert this influence.

Labor Labor unions with their millions of members have become, over the years, such powerful organizations that they can exert great influence on the course of the economy. Their activities in behalf of the workers have been so effective that today millions enjoy work conditions and incomes that were undreamed of a half century ago.

The League of Women Voters, the Parent-Teachers Associations, the Women's Christian Temperance Society, Alcoholics Anonymous, fraternal bodies, the Federal Council of Churches, the innumerable business organizations, and hundreds of others have all, in their fields, promoted interests that have had wide influence throughout the whole society. A major attribute of democratic societies is their use of organizations to foster their social interests.

References

1. Harrison, Paul M., "Weber's Categories of Authority and Voluntary Associations," *American Sociological Review*, 25 (April, 1960), p. 232.
2. Sussman, M. B., "The Calorie Collectors," Mimeograph paper from Western Reserve University; modified version of paper presented April, 1955, at Midwest Sociological Society at Des Moines, Iowa.
3. From personal notes.
4. Brown, Emory J., "Who Take Part in Rural Organizations?" Pennsylvania State College Agr. Exp. Sta. (June, 1953), Progress Report 103.

5. De Tocqueville, Alexis, *Democracy in America,* 2 (New York, J. Langley and Henry G. Langley, 1843), p. 114.

6. Bryce, James, *The American Commonwealth,* 2 (New York, The Macmillan Company, 1910), pp. 281–282.

7. De Tocqueville, Alexis, *Democracy in America,* 2 (New York, J. Langley and Henry G. Langley, 1843), p. 118.

8. Fox, Sherwood D., "Voluntary Associations and Social Structure," Unpublished Doctoral Thesis, Harvard University (December, 1952).

9. Riecken, H. V., Jr., and Whetten, N. L., "Rural Social Organization in Litchfield County, Connecticut," Storrs Agr. Exp. Sta. (May, 1948), Bulletin 261, p. 59; Alexander, Frank, and Nelson, Lowry, "Rural Social Organization in Goodhue County," Minnesota Agr. Exp. Sta. (February, 1949), Bulletin 401; Lively, C. E., Smith, R. C., and Fry, Martha, "Some Aspects of Rural Social Organization in Fairfield County, Ohio," Ohio Dept. of Rural Ec. (July, 1936), Mimeo. Bulletin 91, p. 10.

10. Taylor, C. C., *The Farmer's Movement, 1620–1920* (New York, American Book Company, 1953).

11. "Detroit Area Study," *A Social Profile of Detroit* (Ann Arbor, Mich., University of Michigan Press, 1952), pp. 13 ff.

12. Beagle, J. A., and Schroeder, W., "Social Organization in the North Lansing Fringe," Michigan State Univ. Agr. Exp. Sta. (Sept., 1955), Tech. Bulletin 251, p. 26.

13. Bell, W., and Force, M. T., "Urban Neighborhood Types and Participation in Formal Associations," *American Sociological Review,* 21 (Feb., 1956), p. 33.

14. Buck, R. C., and Ploch, L. A., "Factors Related to Changes in Social Participation in a Pennsylvania Rural Community," Pennsylvania State University Agr. Exp. Sta. (August, 1954), Bulletin 582, p. 14.

15. Anderson, W. A., "Rural Social Participation and the Family Life Cycle—Part I, Formal Participation," Cornell Univ. Agr. Exp. Sta. (January, 1953), Memoir 314, p. 31, and Anderson, W. A., and Plambeck, Hans, "The Social Participation of Farm Families," Cornell University Agr. Exp. Sta. (March, 1943), Rural Soc. Mimeo. Bulletin 8, pp. 7 and 23.

16. Tetreau, E. D., "Social Organization in Arizona's Irrigated Areas," *Rural Sociology,* 5 (June, 1940), pp. 196–198.

17. Anderson, W. A., "The Granger Movement in the Middle West," *Iowa Journal of History and Politics,* 22 (January, 1924), pp. 3–51.

18. Hunter, F., *Community Power Structure* (Chapel Hill, N.C., University of North Carolina Press, 1953).

19. Babchuk, Nicholas, and Thompson, R. V., "The Voluntary Associations of Negroes," *American Sociological Review,* 27 (October, 1962), p. 647.

20. Axelrod, M., "Urban Structure and Social Participation," *American Sociological Review,* 21 (February, 1956), p. 15, and Bell, W., and Force, M. T., "Urban Neighborhood Types and Participation in Formal Organizations," *American Sociological Review,* 21 (February, 1956), p. 28. There are also many others.

21. Anderson, W. A., "The Membership of Farmers in New York Organizations," Cornell University Agr. Exp. Sta. (April, 1938), Bulletin 695, p. 22. See also "Farm Women in the Home Bureau," "Farmers in the Farm Bureau," and "Farm Youth in the 4-H Club," Cornell University Agr. Exp. Sta., Dept. Rural Sociology, Mimeo. Bulletins 3, 4, 13, and 14.

22. Argyris, Chris, "The Fusion of an Individual with the Organization," *American Sociological Review,* 19 (June, 1954), p. 267.

23. For references to studies of participation of urban population, see Wright, C. R., and Hyman, H. H., "Voluntary Association Memberships of American Adults," *American Sociological Review*, 23 (June, 1958), pp. 284 ff, and Rose, Arnold, *Sociology* (New York, Alfred A. Knopf, 1956), Chap. 10, p. 303. For extensive bibliography on studies of participation of rural population, see Anderson, W. A., "Bibliography of Researches in Rural Sociology," Cornell University Agr. Exp. Sta. (August, 1957), Rural Soc. Publ. 52, pp. 109–115.

24. Anderson, W. A., "Types of Participating Families," *Rural Sociology*, 11 (December, 1946), pp. 355 ff.

25. Anderson, W. A., "The Family and Individual Social Participation," *American Sociological Review*, 8 (August, 1943), p. 421.

26. Anderson, W. A., "Family-Member Roles in Social Participation," *American Sociological Review*, 8 (December, 1943), p. 719.

27. Moore, Joan N., "Patterns of Women's Participation in Voluntary Associations," *American Journal of Sociology*, 66 (May, 1961), p. 592. By permission of the University of Chicago Press; copyright, 1961, by the University of Chicago.

28. Anderson, W. A., "Family Social Participation and Social Status Self-Ratings," *American Sociological Review*, 11 (June, 1946), pp. 253–258.

29. Anderson, W. A., "Rural Social Participation and the Family Life Cycle—Part I, Formal Participation," Cornell University Agr. Exp. Sta. (January, 1953), Memoir 314, p. 40, and Wright, C. R., and Hyman, H. H., "Voluntary Association Memberships," *American Sociological Review*, 23 (June, 1958), p. 292.

30. Mayo, S. C., "Social Participation Among the Older Population in Rural Areas of Wake County, North Carolina," *Social Forces*, 30 (October, 1951), pp. 53–59.

31. Kolb, J. H., and Wileden, A. F., "Special Interest Groups in Rural Society," Wisconsin Agr. Exp. Sta. (December, 1957), Bulletin 84, pp. 74–79.

32. Karsh, B., Seidman, J., and Lilienthal, D. M., "The Union Organizer and His Tactics: A Case Study," *American Journal of Sociology*, 59 (September, 1953), pp. 113–122.

33. Sills, D. L., *The Volunteers* (Glencoe, Ill., The Free Press, 1958).

34. Messinger, S. L., "Organization Transformation: A Case Study of a Declining Social Movement," *American Sociological Review*, 20 (February, 1955), pp. 3–10.

35. The materials for these paragraphs are taken from White, L. C., *International Non-Governmental Organizations* (New Brunswick, N.J., Rutgers University Press, 1951).

Questions for Study and Discussion

1. Distinguish between an organization and an institution.
2. All human relationship structures have organization. Does this make them organizations?
3. Describe an organization to which you belong in terms of the essential characteristics that distinguish an organization from other hurelures.
4. Discuss the characteristics of, and the roles of, leadership in organizations.
5. What open, secret, or organizations with secrets do you know about? Describe one of each type as far as you properly can.
6. Make a list of the organizations you know exist in your home community or neighborhood. Classify them by type.
7. What roles do the organizations you belong to play in your activities? In those of your community?
8. Discuss the conditions under which organizations are likely to arise.

9. Discuss the problems of participation that characterize an organization to which you belong.
10. Describe the growth pattern of an organization you can get information about.
11. Discuss the problem of organizational support.
12. Describe an international organization you have investigated.
13. Discuss organizations and social controls.

Suggested Topics for Reports

1. Study a local organization (or a local unit of a national organization) to determine the latent functions it is performing.
2. Study a student organization that is coming into existence on your campus and one that is declining or passing out of existence. In both instances, show the processes which are operating.
3. If there is a Council of Social Agencies or some comparable organization in your community, make a study of its structure and mode of coordinating the activities of its member organizations.
4. Examine the "write-ups" of a sample of persons in *Who's Who in America* and make a classification of the national, regional, state, and local organizations of which they are members. Do you find any evidence of social class gradations among them?

Supplementary Reading

Angell, Robert C., *The Integration of American Society*. New York: McGraw-Hill Book Co., Inc., 1941.

Berger, M., Abel, T., Page, C. H., *Freedom and Control in Modern Society*. Princeton, N.J.: D. Van Nostrand Co., Inc., 1954.

De Tocqueville, Alexis, *Democracy in America*. 2 vols. New York: Henry G. Langley, 1843.

Dubin, Robert (ed.), *Human Relations in Administration*. Englewood Cliffs, N.J.: Prentice-Hall, Inc., 1951.

Ferguson, Charles W., *Fifty Million Brothers*. New York: Farrar and Rinehart Co., 1937.

Hausknecht, Murray, *The Joiners: A Sociological Description of Voluntary Association Membership in the United States*. Totowa, N.J.: Bedminster Press, 1962.

Hunter, F., *Community Power Structure*. Chapel Hill, N.C.: University of North Carolina Press, 1953.

Lipset, S. M., Trow, M., and Coleman, J. S., *Union Democracy*. Glencoe, Ill.: The Free Press, 1956.

Sills, D. L., *The Volunteers*. Glencoe, Ill.: The Free Press, 1958.

Tannenbaum, Robert, Weschler, I. R., and Massarik, F., *Leadership and Organization*. New York: McGraw-Hill Book Co., Inc., 1961.

White, L. C., *International Non-Governmental Organizations*. New Brunswick, N.J.: Rutgers University Press, 1951.

17

COLLECTIVITIES: SOCIETY'S TEMPORARY AND CRISIS STRUCTURES

COLLECTIVITIES, *such as crowds and audiences, are those aggregations of people who are polarized around some temporary center of attraction that gives them unity. This unity exists only so long as the center of attraction exists. They arise out of disturbances to the routine of living, through efforts to introduce variation in routine living, or from the absence or deterioration of social controls.*

I. CHARACTERISTICS OF COLLECTIVE BEHAVIOR

Collective Behavior Varies from the Uniform and Customary Patterns of Behavior in Societies

We have seen that society, as a self-maintaining system, depends mainly upon four classes of structural forms, or hurelures: groups, ecological entities, institutional agencies, and organizations. These forms regularize action in societies according to the established norms, statuses, and sanctioned roles that are commonly known. Societal operation is orderly, for the most part, because the behavior of the people follows the expectations in the norms and conventions that these structural forms sustain.

There are some kinds of social behavior, however, that are not so completely regularized. People act in crowds, mobs, audiences, and in other areas in a manner which is usually outside of the established rules, is often short-lived, and is only weakly structured. They have few rules of operation but develop them as the occasion requires. This behavior, which sociologists have termed as "collective behavior," and the structural entities through which it expresses itself, as "collectivities," often violates or exceeds our sanctioned behavior. These terms are somewhat misleading since all human relationships represent aspects of collective (that is, social) behavior. They are established in our

usage, however, and are employed in this limited sense. *Collectivities* are, then, the fifth class of hurelures, or human relationships structures, of which a society is composed. We now consider them.

Collectivities Have Several Major Characteristics

DEFINITION We may define a *collectivity* as a number of persons whose behavior is specifically polarized around a temporary center of attraction that leads to interaction and a unity which exists only as long as the center of attraction exists.[1]

POLARIZATION This definition indicates several characteristics of this class of hurelures. The distinctive feature which differentiates it from other human relationship forms is the *polarization* process. Some event or circumstance operates as an attracting agent, a polestar, toward which individuals are drawn and with respect to which each is interacting. Someone's automobile crashes against a tree, or a fire breaks out in a building. A crowd assembles within moments, merely to observe or perhaps to help. Some conditions in the society are felt to be wrong or injurious. People join together to change them, and a social movement, such as prohibition, for example, is born. A concert group comes to town. The public is advised and an audience is assembled. These events or circumstances which generate polarization usually represent deviations from, or additions to, the regular operation of the society. Automobiles are not supposed to crash, employers are not expected to take advantage of workers, and concerts are not part of the daily routine of our lives. Each is an occasion for collective action. Each provides a specific center of attraction and a point of sharp focus. We must understand this integrating process which fuses separate units into a whole.

RANDOM HUMAN COMPONENTS Collectivities consist of people in interaction just as do all other human relationship structures. But who are the people composing a collectivity and how do they become parts of it? The definition simply says "a number of people." The human components of collectivities are random. They are individuals who happen to be attracted by the center of polarization, the polestar. They are not selected or elected, nor do they often premediate participation. Anonymity is a chief characteristic of these persons. This condition may persist in a collectivity until it finds direction and develops into an organization. The persons in a crowd watching a Fourth of July celebration are largely anonymous. The persons in a mob remain anonymous and often only a few—those who take over leadership roles—may become known. It is important to note that anonymity will often encourage irresponsible action by the members of a collectivity.

NO PREVIOUS STRUCTURE A third characteristic is the common absence of a previously existing structure. Collectivities are largely unanticipated because the polarizing stimuli are not developed in a systematic way in advance, though conditions may exist that eventually lead to structuring. In most instances, the polarizing factor just happens, and the aggregation of people about it occurs as a product of the moment.

This is clearly seen, for example, in a crowd that assembles about a fire. It may not be so clear in an audience that is watching a professional baseball game. Here, because some established business organizations, which "own" the teams, plan to attract their audiences, they set polarizing conditions. But what specific audiences this produces depends upon the operations of the polarizing factors in relation to the conditions under which they operate. A specific audience may be small as measured in numbers if the teams are playing poor ball, if the weather is murky and threatening, or if economic conditions are bad. The previous audiences do not determine the succeeding audiences; each is polarized by the way in which the factors influence those who are potential participants at the moment. This is uncontrolled and unpredictable except within broad limits.

TEMPORARY AND SHORT-LIVED Collectivities are usually short-lived because the polarizing factors are usually temporary. Crowds and audiences break up as soon as the incident that brought them into existence is over. When the fist fight is through, the assembled crowd dissolves. A social movement has no need for further existence when its promoters have gained their end and their objective is incorporated into the normal structure of society. When the question is no longer pertinent, publics that debated it cease to argue. Most collectivities are random and fleeting although some, such as social movements, must operate over long periods of time to effect, if ever, the changes they work for.

STANDARDS OF BEHAVIOR Each type of collectivity determines its own standards of behavior. Most of the norms emerge in the operations of the entity. There are some practices that are common in the operation of the same type of collectivity, but these are not necessarily the formal norms. The crowd usually stands in the seventh inning of a baseball game, but it is not necessary to do this. Baseball or football players are cheered at any time during a game, but a tennis player is cheered only after he makes a point. How the collectivity will act emerges largely from the circumstances under which it operates. Norms are of their own making and may contradict the accepted norms of a society.

NONREPETITIVE COMPONENTS A sixth characteristic is that collectivities rarely reappear with exactly the same components after they dissolve. Their composition is nonrepetitive.

Crowds, audiences, or a mob may be brought together by the same *type* of polarizing factor, but those who compose them are not necessarily or usually the same persons. The polarizing factor itself usually has different characteristics, even if it is of a similar type. Each fire that attracts a crowd is unique as to extent, place, and time. Each concert that assembles an audience, even if by the same person or persons, has its distinctive traits as to program and other conditions. Each cause that sparks a movement is distinctive, so that in each instance the collectivity is itself unique. The same people repeatedly operate in organizations or institutional agencies in relation to established goals, but this is not true of collectivities. Each polarizing force attracts its own specific constituents. Baseball or football teams have their regular "fans," but each time the teams bring together an observing audience, the persons that compose it are different persons, except for the regulars who constitute a continuing core. This is one reason why, for example, college students organize cheering sections where all the students sit together. The heterogeneous composition of each football crowd requires these devices to speed up the development of interactional unity.

POSSIBILITY OF PERMANENT STRUCTURES Collectivities serve primarily to arrange relationships in situations for which society has no ready relationship structure. But the people who compose them may develop groups or organizations to promote certain ends if the polarizing factors include permanent values to the society. Until recently, for example, fires in the rural areas were fought by quasi-crowds organized into bucket brigades. Organizations to control fires in these environments have evolved speedily from this relatively unorganized collective action to patterned fire-fighting companies. Publics consider the merits of public registration for voting, their opinion is crystallized, and the registration is adopted or rejected as suitable to the situation. Organizations develop to promote or oppose it, as a consequence of this collective action.

Collectivities Are Produced by Distinctive Social Conditions

EFFECT OF DISTURBANCES IN ROUTINE LIVING A first social condition out of which collectivities are created are disturbances in the routines of normal living. Some of these disturbances create immediate responses. Because they differ in intensity and extent, they result in individual and collective responses of different intensity. A casual crowd may assemble about a street performer, such as a man with his monkey and grind organ. Only momentary attention is given to this. The loosely organized crowd dissolves rapidly, and the man and his monkey move on.

An unexpected disaster—the tornado of May twenty-fifth, 1955—leveled Udall, Kansas, and left the survivors temporarily stunned and panic stricken. As they recovered from shock, organization rapidly emerged. Every available resource was brought to bear to give the injured immediate aid. But in this initial stage, people rushed about in all directions until reorganization by authoritative controls was effected. Later, the process of rebuilding a destroyed community led to the creation of an almost completely new one.

DELIBERATELY PLANNED VARIATION Some variations are deliberately planned to introduce change in the routine of living or to prevent undesirable collective action. Communities organize home-coming celebrations, local and county fairs, athletic contests, and other collective activities that cut through the cake of custom. These create crowd and audience situations that serve to release people from the monotony of their daily tasks and satisfy more fully their basic desires. These are important functions of collective recreation and the collective enjoyment of such entertaining presentations as plays or sports events. A dull social environment can lead to widespread boredom, unrest, and possibly more dangerous consequences.

ABSENCE OR COLLAPSE OF SOCIAL CONTROLS Most collectivities, however, result from the absence or collapse of social controls. The lack of established controls in pioneer communities, for example, usually encourages various forms of collective behavior on both sides of law and order. In the American "Wild West," individual criminals and outlaw gangs sprang up to exploit the weakly structured society (as modern television daily reminds us). The community, however, countered with the posse, a band of armed people immediately organized to protect the community. That it did not always mete out true justice is shown in *The Oxbow Incident*. In any event, these were almost automatic reactions in the uncontrolled social situations. The collectivities which were created often functioned as the only effective control mechanisms. Not every Dodge City had a Marshall Dillon.

A collectivity may even serve as a deliberative unit if the social organization does not provide control devices to handle unexpected occurrences. One of the writers witnessed an accident, in a narrow street in a Chinese rural village, in which a cart knocked over a fruit stand, spilling and severely damaging the fruit. A crowd quickly encircled the scene. The owner and the cart driver scolded back and forth. Members of the crowd started asking questions and making comments. They soon "took charge," determined responsibility, assessed the loss, and imposed the penalty. Consensus was arrived at, the injured and the injuring party agreed to the suggested solution, and the cart driver paid (after claiming some of the damaged fruit), and went on his way. The crowd disbanded immediately. If a similar incident occurred in American society, the police would have taken control, and the crowd would simply have been a curious collection of onlookers. But even in America, if no police appear, members of a throng will sometimes react like the Chinese crowd.

Collective behavior, usually of a destructive sort, results if the formal social controls collapse. And this may happen even in a small sedate community. For days, during the fall of 1962, the quiet college town of Oxford, Mississippi, was the scene of some of the most vicious and destructive mob action ever seen in an American community. (See Box 25.) The tragic violence, which shocked national and international sensibilities, arose from the bitter resistance of students and other Mississippians to the admission of a Negro to the state university. Local and state officials were unable or unwilling to cope with the breakdown of law and order. The intervention of federal officers and troops was required to resolve the issue and to re-establish the semblance of social control. No doubt, the moral and sociological residue of the action will endure for years to come.

Another example, of historical interest, comes from a proud city in the North. The Boston police strike, which removed effective controls from this city in 1919, let loose gang rioting, crowd looting, collective destruction of property, and attacks on persons. While here and there, an individual dared to loot alone, practically all this activity was carried out by crowds, much of it surreptitiously. This did not abate until Governor Calvin Coolidge ordered

---

BOX 25   JAMES MEREDITH AT "OLE MISS"

"I was sure that if I were killed, somebody else would take my place someday." These were the thoughts of James Meredith as he stood at the very center of a historic national crisis with the world watching.

From eight o'clock Sunday, September 30, 1962, until nine o'clock the following morning, a second American Civil War was fought on the campus of the University of Mississippi and in the nearby small town of Oxford, Mississippi. Although the final outcome was never in doubt, there were moments when even the President of the United States, listening to reports of the battle over an open telephone line into a university building, wondered whether the forces he had committed would be overwhelmed. In the end, 500 United States marshals and 60 Mississippi National Guardsmen, along with bayonet-wielding U.S. military police, beat off a mob of 2,500 Mississippians, and several critical issues were settled on the spot. It was determined that the state of Mississippi could not successfully defy the Federal Government. It was also determined that 29-year-old Negro James Howard Meredith would attend the University of Mississippi.

Students began kicking and rocking a car occupied by television cameraman Gordon Yoder and his blond wife, who happened to be from Jackson, Mississippi. "Nigger-lovin' Yankee bitch," the boys screamed. One Ole Miss coed giggled nervously and asked her date, "Lord, Joe, what are they gonna do to that woman?" "Kill her, I guess," the boy said. "She's a nigger lover, isn't she?" Finally three state troopers hurried Mrs. Yoder away.

How could a civilized country have allowed this situation to develop? Who was to blame? More important, what effect had this had on the people of Mississippi, and on the rest of the troubled South?[2]

in the state militia and formal social controls were re-established.

Collective uprisings, such as revolts and revolution, may result if a social system and its controls are unjust or brutal. In disturbed conditions, people live under continuous uncertainty as to what the future portends. Beneath the overt manifestations, there is usually a stage when attitudes toward the control system become crystallized into deep-seated dissatisfaction and general unrest. Respect for law and faith in the old order dissolve. At this juncture, the prevailing mood of the mass may crystallize into a spirit of revolution which promises a new social order.

Social Unrest Is the Sociopsychological Condition in Which Most Collectivities Are Developed

RESTLESSNESS AND EMOTIONAL CONTAGION Our discussion so far has indicated that collectivities are created chiefly when the normal operation of the society is disrupted and urgent needs are not being satisfied. The consequence is the creation of social unrest which, when developed to high intensity, expresses itself in collective actions. At the initial stage, when movements are without focus, individuals feel uneasy and restless. *Social unrest*—aimless, uncertain movement seeking some form of release ("milling in the herd")—develops as individual restlessness is transmitted back and forth within the group or society.

DESPERATION OUT OF DISSATISFACTION People cannot be restless for long without developing discontent from their inability to remove their frustrations. It is an easy step from discontent to desperation. We have the urge to act in a state of anxiety and fear. "Why don't we do something?" is the inevitable question. Action often comes rapidly for emotionally aroused people because they are driven to attack or eliminate the source of their frustration.

Michael Gold describes the development of a tenement rent strike against a rapacious landlord in New York City. His tenants had developed a high state of restlessness. When someone suggested a rent strike, the other tenants agreed enthusiastically. They gossiped about it with each other, indicating how they would swear at the landlord and how they would refuse to pay the rent they thought exorbitant. These interactions created feelings of animated tension during the days before the landlord called for the rent.[3]

Here were the conditions to which social unrest leads. A possible solution, a rent strike, was suggested. There was constant chattering about it until each sympathetic person was quick to respond to the suggestions of the others, intensifying their state of rapport. Constant communication about their rent situation, the polarizing factor, achieved collective excitement. The feeling was contagious. It united the whole tenement into a single collectivity bent on a common achievement. This same emotional contagion characterizes stampedes, riots, mobs, and other collectivities. The social psychologist analyzes the process in terms of "circular response."

II. FORMS OF COLLECTIVE BEHAVIOR

Crowds Are Common Structural Forms for the Expression of Collective Behavior

CROWDS DEFINED Crowds, audiences, publics, and social movements are the chief structural forms in which collective behavior finds expression. All are types of collective behavior involving a number of people whose common behavior is polarized around a center of stimulus. Each type varies from the other, however, in ways that will be apparent in our discussion.

The *crowd* is the most common form of collectivity. It is that form of collectivity in which a number of people are brought together in a particular place by their concerted attention to a common stimulus to which all react in a manner which creates an affinity among them.

A Number of People with Focused Attention We should first note that a crowd usually consists of a relatively large number of people. There are situations in which a few people meet each other, act together, and depart, such as happens during the meetings of friends or acquaintances. We have already described these as temporary groups in that they are face-to-face entities bound together for a short time by psychological interaction. Crowds, however, usually involve relatively large collections of persons.

But the mere presence of a large number of people in a particular place does not make a "true" crowd. People on a bus, in a public park, at a fair, where each person has his attention focused on his own activity and is going his own way, constitute not "true" crowds but aggregations. They are mere collections of people with no kind of union among them except physical presence. But let an accident occur, say someone swimming in the park lake calls for help, and at once the individuals focus, there is interstimulation, and a crowd is created that is much more than a number of people gathered at the same place.

Physical Presence A second characteristic is already apparent: the persons composing a crowd are physically present. Dispersed individuals are brought together in a particular place. The moment disperson takes place the crowd ceases to exist.

"Occasion" Entities Crowds are "occasion" entities. A number of people gather together because they are all attending to a common stimulus. There is no previous plan for assembling that arises from the crowd members themselves. In a strict sense, this feature would hold even if the crowd emerged from an audience.

Heterogeneous and Anonymous Since a crowd may include persons of all occupations, ages, sexes, and races, it tends to be heterogeneous and anonymous in character. No one can tell beforehand who will make up the crowd. The members may represent any social class and have widely varying social values. One may observe these conditions when several thousand people are assembled to watch a Fourth of July celebration with its band music, group marching, and fireworks. The "occasion" brings them together. A community representative has organized the celebration. People of every social class come, representing rich and poor, ignorant and learned, old and young. All are equals in the crowd, sitting where they would and doing pretty much what they wish. Some smoke, others eat popcorn or peanuts, and most simply sit and watch. Within twenty minutes after the occasion is concluded, the area is completely empty. We may presume that there was little personal acquaintanceship among those present.

Affinity Between the Persons—A crowd is characterized by "an affinity" of the heterogeneous persons composing it for the duration of its existence. This creation of fellow feeling results from the sharing of a common experience and the implications it has for each member. The cries of a person in distress while swimming introduces excitement in each person in the crowd. This is spread to the others by rapid talking, crying, and other forms of communication that may reach to our unconscious feelings of danger, fear, and unhappiness. Repressed feelings are released if swimmers make a rescue.

All cheer as a collective unit. Their feelings are of the same kind now expressing a sense of cohesiveness. A sort of social contagion resulting from these stimuli has been created by the release of individual restraints. It manifests itself in common feeling tones and actions that pervade the crowd and engulf the individual.

Division Possible Not all crowds are unified in the sense that the people in them view the polarizing situation in the same way. Divided into two or more partisan segments, such crowds are sometimes called factional.[4] The whole crowd is a unit in its polarization about a football game, for example, but it is usually factional. One faction favors one team, and the other faction supports the other. It operates as a single crowd, however, since the actions of one part influence the actions of the other. When the game is on, the moods of each faction vacillate with its progress, giving it a common pattern of action.

Crowds, then, are collectivities composed of a number of physically contiguous persons focusing attention on a common polarizing center, stimulating each other, and creating an affinity that expresses itself in dominant feeling tones and moods.

Four Types of Crowds May Be Identified

Crowds may be typed in terms of the objective of the crowd, the focus of crowd action, and how the crowd arose. We shall describe four general types—casual, action, expressive, and conventionalized crowds—and characterize each from several points of view.[5]

CASUAL CROWDS Among the most common are *casual crowds* since there are so many incidents in daily life that can create them. A curious performance on a street corner, smoke from a residence, an altercation between two neighbors, a street accident, and many other incidents serve as their polarizing forces. The panel members on a television show asked the chief lifeguard at Coney Island whether a person would be arrested if he disrobed on the beach. The answer was "Yes." The next question was, "On what charge?" The answer, "Inciting a crowd to collect." Such crowds last only a short time and have little organization. The movement to and from them is rapid, and interstimulation is weak.

ACTION CROWDS The *action crowd* is one whose attention is focused on some external objective that it deals with collectively. The motive is to relieve strong emotional tensions by some form of overt action. The persons in the action have a common purpose. Numbers add strength and support to this purpose while achieving the purpose itself requires the support of the crowd. Numbers give the individuals a feeling of power, but, at the same time, their sense of personal responsibility is lost.[6] Such a crowd is highly suggestible. By acting in response to aroused feelings rather than to logical reasoning, it gives free play to emotions that are normally held in control. Slogans, harangues, and shouting are important as stimulants to action because there is little critical consideration of issues. The action itself is virtually predetermined by the nature of the

inciting circumstances that created the sense of injury, oppression, or fear which must be relieved.

The lynching mob described in Box 26 reveals the virulence of these processes, as it centers on a person who had committed a revolting crime. People were excited by it. They talked about it to each other, describing as best they could what had happened. As they talked, they added embellishments which brought excitement to a high pitch. Some made threats which were taken up by others. The rapid interactions and the reciprocal physical and mental stimulation generated a readiness for action. The crowd decided to do something

---

BOX 26

Suddenly I became conscious of that sense of alarm which is always aroused by the sound of hurrying footsteps on the silence of the night. I stopped work and looked at my watch. It was after eleven. I listened, straining every nerve to hear above the tumult of my quickening pulse. I caught the murmur of voices, then the gallop of a horse, then of another and another. . . . We saw men moving in one direction, and from the mutterings we vaguely caught the rumour that some terrible crime had been committed. . . .

I went out and, following the drift, reached the railroad station. There was gathered there a crowd of men, all white, and others were steadily arriving, seemingly from all the surrounding country. How did the news spread so quickly? I watched these men moving under the yellow glare of the kerosene lamps about the station, stern, comparatively silent, all of them armed, some of them in boots and spurs; fierce, determined men. . . . The impression made upon me was that everything was being done in quite an orderly manner. In spite of so many leaving, the crowd around the station continued to grow; at sunrise there were a great many women and children. . . .

Before noon they brought him in. Two horsemen rode abreast; between them, half dragged, the poor wretch made his way through the dust. His hands were tied behind him, and ropes around his body were fastened to the saddle horns of his double guard. The men who at midnight had been stern and silent were now emitting that terror-instilling sound known as the "rebel yell." A space was quickly cleared in the crowd, and a rope placed around his neck, when from somewhere came the suggestion, "Burn him!" It ran like an electric current. Have you ever witnessed the transformation of human beings into savage beasts? Nothing can be more terrible. A railroad tie was sunk into the ground, the rope was removed, and a chain brought and securely coiled around the victim and the stake. There he stood, a man only in form and stature, every sign of degeneracy stamped upon his countenance. His eyes were dull and vacant, indicating not a single ray of thought. Evidently the realization of his fearful fate had robbed him of whatever reasoning he had ever possessed. He was too stunned and stupefied even to tremble. Fuel was brought from everywhere, oil, the torch; the flames crouched for an instant as though to gather strength, then leaped up as high as their victim's head. . . . Some of the crowd yelled and cheered, others seemed appalled at what they had done, and there were those who turned away sickened at the sight. I was fixed to the spot where I stood, powerless to take my eyes from what I did not want to see.[7]

about it. Action upon some common object was demanded.

As the crowd moved toward its object, self-appointed, accepted leaders—usually the most vociferous persons—gave instructions as to how they were to proceed since their action had no rules. These leaders served to increase the emotionality of the mob by crystalling hate, fear, and moral indignation. They may have even suggested that the actions they had called for were actually too good for the offender. Everyone was swept along by the contagion in the situation, even those who were present only out of curiosity. They found it almost impossible to withdraw, even though they inwardly disapproved.

The specific act of lynching was accompanied by cheers and yells. Others turned away in fear. People had virtually lost their individuality and were hidden in the mob. No one of them, except the most hardened, would have undertaken the act if he had to do it on his own.

The act over, the mob rapidly disintegrated, each person going where he could be alone or with only a few confidants. All keep silent about their act. The action of the mob was the achievement of a collectivity that felt it had righted a wrong. Individuals justified their participation on the ground that they were handing out deserved punishment because the law moves too slowly and others need to be warned in an emphatic way.

A run on a bank is an illustration of an action crowd in which the motive is clearly to serve individual purposes. In such a crowd there is no leadership. Each person is on his own and after his own. There is little thought of other persons. Preserving his own possessions is the polarizing factor in this type of action crowd. Someone starts a rumor—rumors often create crowds—after seeing a crowd near the bank. No one tries to find out why the crowd was there. Once the rumor spreads that a run has started, all possibility of changing the focus of attention of the crowd is gone. The bank officials who try to give assurance that their bank is solvent might be lying. Some are afraid to take a chance; therefore nobody does. The attitude of each heightens the attitude of the others. Here the crowd dissolves only when all of those in it, who fear the worst, have been satisfied.

In another kind of action crowd the people are concerned chiefly with their own safety. But, here too, the action of each individual intensifies the action and reaction of others.

Panics, such as sometimes occur in theater or hotel fires, are tragic examples of the disaster and death that may befall people who are gripped by terror. In such cases, action leading to the rapid dissolution of the crowd consists in irrational flight to escape impending disaster. One of the most remarkable instances of mass panic in American history was precipitated by a radio program reporting a fictional invasion of the earth by men from Mars. In crises of this nature, the threat of disaster so excites each person that rational consideration of possible alternatives is destroyed and ordered control is impossible.

EXPRESSIVE CROWDS   John Galsworthy, in the *Forsyte Saga,* gave a splendid example of an *expressive crowd.* This was a crowd which was not directed toward some external object but toward the release of tensions that had accumulated from the situation in the society or from personal experiences. Mafeking, a town of 6000 persons in South Africa, was besieged during the Boer War for 215 days. British troops held out until reinforcements relieved it. The receipt of this news in London set the stage for this expressive crowd action:

> He [Soames] wandered thus one May night into Regent Street and the most amazing crowd he had ever seen: a shrieking, whistling, dancing, jostling, grotesque, and formidably jovial crowd, with false noses and mouthorgans, penny whistles and long feathers, every appanage of idiocy, as it seemed to him. Mafeking! Of course, it had been relieved! Good! But was that an excuse? Who were those people, what were they, where had they come from into the West End? . . . The whole thing was unspeakable! These people had no restraint, they seemed to think him funny; such swarms of them, rude, coarse, laughing—and what laughter! Nothing sacred to them! He shouldn't be surprised if they began to break windows. . . . They were hysterical—it wasn't English! And all about the relief of a little town as big as Watford, six thousand miles away. Restraint, reserve! Those qualities to him more dear almost than life, those indispensible attributes of property and culture, where were they? It wasn't English! No, it wasn't English! [8]

This type of crowd has as its objective the relief of the participants' own pent-up tensions by unconventional expressions of their joy. Their laughter, their dancing, and their teasing of onlookers are a collective projection of their own joy in various ways and on objects associated with it. The more they shout, dance, and tease, the more intense their reactions become, for each act serves as a stimulant for further reactions. Their restraints are gone, and expressions of their feelings are ends in themselves. They become collective as the people dance and sing.

Other circumstances may create expressive crowds, especially where relief has come after relatively long periods of worry and fear. The expression of collective ecstasy in rhythmic dancing and singing are symbolic of the common unity that exists in these crowds. Religious revivals, where people attend meetings night after night, give opportunity for unconventional expressions that relieve tensions in these ways. In the revivals that were led by John Wesley during early colonial days, these external expressions of internal feelings often were so strong that the preacher had to caution restraints. But their own presentations dramatized the personal problems of their followers and created the emotional conditions that burst forth in expressive reactions.

CONVENTIONALIZED CROWDS　The fourth type of crowd is that which operates according to the conventions of the society and is called a *conventionalized crowd*. The polarization of the activities of large numbers of people around a common objective creates human relationship structures of great force. "It would be amazing if such a potent force," to quote Kingsley Davis, "were not socially utilized in some way." [9] It is utilized in the crowds that a society deliberately organizes.

There are often conditions in societies that organized crowd behavior helps to correct. The Fourth of July in the United States was traditionally celebrated by the uncontrolled shooting of fireworks from early morning till late at night. Injuries and deaths often occurred. In time, community after community outlawed the indiscriminate sale of these dangerous fireworks and substituted forms of crowd action, deliberately organized, such as parades with marching bands, floats, military units, and supervised fireworks displays. These served the function of joyful expression through the removal of personal inhibitions, yet under controlled conditions that minimized the dangers.

Neighborhoods which have been plagued with irresponsible gang pranks have handled some of their problems through the organization and direction of youth activities in which crowd occasions, such as dances, can permit the same emotional release that pranks formerly provided. Such planned crowd activities often prevent undesirable gang situations from arising. Community baseball leagues, such as the Kiwanis and Little League programs, are outlets for youth as well as adult crowd expressions. They may also serve to inculcate the norms and values of the society and to prevent the possibility of many antisocial activities. The mid-week and Saturday night band concerts in local parks in old-time rural communities were crowd occasions that created ordered sociability and yet allowed the release of pent-up feelings.

Audiences Are Probably the Most Common and Important of the Conventionalized Crowds

AUDIENCES DEFINED　We define *audiences* as collectivities of individuals meeting at a particular time and place and polarized, in their collective reactions, to a common object or event. Audiences include, not only collectivities of listeners, but also groups of spectators of all kinds. The term does not, however, apply to such scattered collections of people as those who are listening to a radio program, watching a television show, or reading the same evening newspaper. These are particular types of publics. Audiences include groups assembled at theaters, concerts, public lectures, formally organized sports events, radio and television studio performances, and congregational church services, to give some varied examples.

Certain Classifications of Audiences Give Insight into Their Characteristics

Typing audiences as (a) active or (b) passive emphasizes that audiences are usually people who are quiet listeners or observers of some polarizing performance. They behave according to rules that control their reactions. They are active only at certain times and then in specific manners. Clapping or other forms of approval are given by audiences at definite times—for instance, only at the conclusion of a number during a piano recital. At times approval or disapproval is shown spontaneously. A speaker may even seek approval from his audience for positions he is advancing, but in general, prescribed conduct patterns are followed in each type of audience. If they are violated, they at least cause embarrassment. If violated too completely, they cause the breakup of the audience. The conventionalized crowd then becomes a mob.

Madison Bently classifies audiences on the basis of the degree of integration within them as (a) heterogeneous, or gathered for occasional discourse or event; (b) homogeneous, or gathered for a common purpose, need, or request; and (c) primed, or gathered because previous association, common interests, sentiments, and needs have existed and are implied.[10]

Kimball Young classifies audiences as (a) information-seeking, as in the public lecture or classroom; (b) recreation-seeking, as in attendance at a play or concert; and (c) conversional, where people come to be converted or have their beliefs strengthened. His classification stresses the motivations that bring people into audiences.[11]

Polarization Is the Central Process in Audience Operation

The chief characteristic of any audience is the common expectation of the members with respect to the event which brings the audience into being. Therefore, people assemble at the appointed time and place. Polarization of the audience is the central process in its functioning. This has two aspects: (a) the creation of an all-to-one relationship between the auditors or spectators and the focus of their attention— the lecturer, musicians, or entertainers; and (b) the breaking down of any conditions within the assembled audience that interfere with the all-to-one relationship, such as reading of newspapers or visiting with friends before the event begins.

GAINING ATTENTION   The first step in achieving this all-to-one relationship is to gain the attention of those who compose the audience. The individuals in the audience are to be primarily passive recipients of what is to follow in a one-way communication process. Communication among the members themselves is eliminated. The center of their polarization is the area of stimulation; the observing individuals constitute the area of response. Physical patterning is important to this end. Audiences are usually fitted into a predetermined physical setting. The size and shape of the assembly place, the arrangement of the seats and lighting, and the central performance area set limits to this patterning. Assembly places for audiences are usually designed to facilitate the all-to-one relationship desired. The audience forms a pattern within these limits, further accentuating

Polarization in three types of audience: a conference audience; a student audience watching College Bowl Quiz; a college football audience.

the polarization. The 50-yard line is the preferred place at a football game, the back of the auditorium at an indoor band concert, front seats at a lecture program.

Attention is gained by an activity that indicates that attention is called for—the lowering of lights, the raising of curtains, the blaring of trumpets, or the rising of the chairman.

CREATING INTEREST Attention having been gained, interest must be built up. This will depend upon the nature of the performance. Speakers often create interest by presenting ideas in introductory remarks that their audience likes to hear. Skilled performers employ various techniques for extending initial attention to continued interest.

MAINTAINING THE ALL-TO-ONE RELATIONSHIP Attention must thus be followed by strengthen-

ing the all-to-one relationship. An audience must be able to hear and see what is going on. A pleasing voice, commanding appearance, and attractive scenery are important factors. The performance itself, to be effective, should have clarity, dramatic qualities, change of pace, and other such attributes. Emotional stimulation usually induces polarization more effectively than the purely intellectual. The nature of the particular audience determines the steps to be taken to achieve its polarization. Getting the attention of the heterogeneous crowd demands much preparation, whereas the primed type may only need to be called to order.

The tactics of audience control are often well demonstrated in political conventions and political rallies. (See Box 27.) Totalitarian states show great skill in this endeavor. And, in Amer-

---

BOX 27

[In his youth, the senior author attended a political rally in Chicago to hear Theodore Roosevelt speak for the presidential candidacy of Charles Evans Hughes. He reports:]

The building which held fifteen thousand persons was crowded when we arrived. The building was oval shaped so that the audience completely encircled a raised stage which stood at one end so that each person could see and hear. Red, white, and blue bunting decorated all parts of the building and the stage was decorated with flowers and American flags. We found good seats in the top balcony behind the stage. Two bands, one at each side of the platform, were playing the popular music of the day. Persons were conversing in small casual groups throughout the hall.

At the appointed time, the bands struck up the *Star Spangled Banner*. This was the first step in polarizing this large crowd into a single all-to-one audience. It served to break up the small conversation groups and eliminate passing to and fro. The crowd stood. All hats were removed.

As soon as the playing of the national anthem was over and before the crowd could again break up into small groups or individuals could be otherwise distracted, the Mayor of Chicago, William H. Thompson, began to speak. He praised the United States for its wonders and the Republican party for its role in helping to achieve this nation's greatness. The audience liked to hear this. They gave him attention and became interested for practically all of them were Republicans. After Mr. Thompson eulogized the Republican party, he began to discuss the accomplishments of Theodore Roosevelt, the evening's speaker. He referred to Mr. Roosevelt as a man of vigor and determination who used these traits when necessary. He then referred to Mr. Roosevelt as "the man with the big stick" to dramatize these characteristics. Then he stooped down behind the podium, picked up a cotton-stuffed shillalah, and waved it vigorously before the audience which, by this time, was cheering loudly. At this signal Mr. Roosevelt, surrounded by escorts, came from a side entrance into full view of the people, marched across the floor and up the stairs where he took his place beside Mr. Thompson who was still waving the shillalah. The whole audience was now wildly cheering its acclaim. This was the next step in welding this crowd into a single audience clearly polarized about this center of activity.

BOX 27 (Cont.)

Mr. Thompson gave the shillalah to Mr. Roosevelt who began to wave it as the cheering started to subside. This increased the applause and focused greater attention on Mr. Roosevelt. The cheering subsided after some minutes. Mr. Roosevelt then put the shillalah on the podium in full view of the audience and, before their attention could be shifted to other things, he began to speak. The crowd had now been unified into a single entity polarized around one point. It reacted at various times in the course of Mr. Roosevelt's speech with approval by hand clapping and shouting.

During the course of his speech, Theodore Roosevelt told what he would do in the case of Mexico if he were President of the United States. The Mexican government had threatened to confiscate the oil holdings of American companies in Mexico. Someone in the audience yelled out, "What would you do with Germany?" The Germans had just sunk the Lusitania. A number of Americans had perished and much American property had been lost. Mr. Roosevelt was at first taken aback by this question, shouted so loudly that all in the hall could hear it. But he stopped speaking and replied: "If you will let me finish what I want to say about Mexico, I'll tell you what I would do with Germany!" He then finished his comments on Mexico, put his notes on the desk before him, straightened back his shoulders, and said: "Now I'll tell you what I would do with Germany. If I were President of the United States and Germany touched any American property, I would immediately seize every German vessel in an American harbor, I would put a gun on the front end of each one, and send a note to the Germans telling them that the next time they touched any Americans or American property, every boat was going to the bottom of the sea."

Pandemonium broke out. Hats were thrown in the air. Flags waved. People shouted. This crowd was acting under the mental and emotional impact as a single unit. Its cohesiveness was developed to its highest pitch. If Mr. Roosevelt had suggested any physical action, this audience would have reacted as one person. Even hecklers became part of his approving audience. Shortly after this demonstration, Mr. Roosevelt concluded by reiterating with force his main theme . . . that the election of Charles Evans Hughes would assure this country of his kind of forceful government. With this the audience arose, gave a prolonged ovation, and then rapidly dissolved. This purposely created human relationship structure had performed its objectives for an expectant audience.

---

ica, manipulation has become such a fine art that audiences in television studios can be induced to laugh and applaud on cue.

III. MASS BEHAVIOR COLLECTIVITIES

Societies Have Developed Mass Behavior Characteristics

The industrialization of economic processes, the growth of cities, the more intense competition between nations, and the development of techniques of communication have made modern societies more and more subject to expressions of collective behavior. An important characteristic of today's social life is the behavior of men in the mass.

This condition shapes a major policy in authoritarian societies where newspapers, radios, motion pictures, magazines, and television are all devoted to the continuous promotion of their viewpoints on a mass basis. In such societies, persuasion is made more effective by restricting population movement and controlling collective gatherings. In a totalitarian society, such as Communist China, people must have special permits to travel beyond their own districts. This isolation makes mass communication more effective since it exposes many individuals to the same persuasions at the same time and makes it difficult to counteract them.

The masses are bombarded by these devices in democratic societies, also. The heterogeneous character of the social organization exposes dispersed individuals from all walks of life to the play of these one-way forces. As a result, those who may be interested are often puzzled. They respond without being able to orient their actions to those of others because of their isolation and anonymity. They make selections on the basis of their own needs. Today's advertising, for example, appeals to separated individuals or their immediate families and aims at their particular needs.

DEFINITION OF MASS   A *mass* is a number of individuals who are responding *as individuals* to the same stimulus in a similar way.[12] It is more than a mere collection of persons since it has a common focus of attention and similar responses. It is not a collectivity, however, since the persons are not in true interaction. A mass is composed of anonymous individuals who have no common customs or traditions by which their individual reactions to the stimuli are governed. They act as the result of mass persuasions and their own suggestibility. Mass behavior expresses itself in free societies in booms (see Box 28), rushes, crazes, fads, and fashions. Chain letters, the hula hoop, hot-rod racing, the twist craze, and frisbee disk-throwing are all examples of this "hysteria" behavior. (See Box 29 for a recent collegiate manifestation.)

Mass Communication Makes Publics Possible

Not only do societies have expressions of mass behavior in such forms as booms, fads, fashions, and crazes, they also create publics where there is freedom of expression and of beliefs.

A *public* is that form of collectivity which includes a number of dispersed and nonorganized individuals who are faced with an issue about which there may be differences of opinion. There may often be a desire to achieve collective judgment by the discussion of alternatives.

Publics are exceedingly significant in democratic societies because of their function. They arise by spontaneous reaction to debatable issues. They are the arenas for considering public problems. Issues are discussed, with individuals not only expressing their own but also endeavoring to influence the opinions of others. The right to criticize opinions and to endeavor to change them is recognized as legitimate. This is one of its important differences from crowds. Behavior in the crowd is pointed in one direction. Since there is usually no discussion, it expresses emotional impulses and not reflective deliberation. Behavior in publics is also pointed in one direction, but it strives to achieve a common direction by moving towards a collective decision through discussion in which issues are considered, opinions compete, and views are modified. The decisions of publics are rarely unanimous, but because democratic societies depend upon public expression and majority opinion, publics are important in creating sound opinions and bringing forth facts relevant to the issues. Rumor, unfounded suggestions, and

---

BOX 28   FLORIDA LAND BOOM

[The scene is Miami, Florida, in the year 1925.] There was nothing languorous about the atmosphere of tropical Miami during that memorable summer and autumn of 1925. The whole city had become one frenzied real-estate exchange. There was said to be 2,000 real-estate offices and 25,000 agents marketing house-lots or acreages. The shirt-sleeved crowds hurrying to and fro under the widely advertised Florida sun talked of binders and options and water-frontages and hundred-thousand dollar profits; the city fathers had been forced to pass an ordinance forbidding the sale of property in the street, or even the showing of a map, to prevent inordinate traffic congestion. The warm air vibrated with the clatter of riveters, for the steel skeletons of skyscrapers were rising to give Miami a skyline appropriate to its metropolitan destiny. Motorbusses roared down Flagler Street carrying "prospects" on free trips to watch dredges and steam shovels converting the outlying mangrove swamps and sandbars of the Bay of Biscayne into gorgeous Venetian cities for the American homemakers and pleasure-seekers of the future. The Dixie Highway was clogged with automobiles. . . . People were sleeping wherever they could lay their heads, in station waiting rooms or in automobiles.[13]

BOX 29   PIANO LESSON

Jimmy Durante would be the first to admit that he would never qualify as a deep student of scientific theory. But last week, one of the Old Schnozz's nightclub specialities—piano wrecking—was becoming the newest college campus craze, and all in the name of science.

Unlike Durante, who tears pianos apart with his bare hands, collegiate wreckers use axes, sledge hammers, iron wedges, crowbars and brooms. Working against the clock, the students must batter a piano into pieces small enough to be passed through a hole in a board 20 cm. (7.87 in.) in diameter. The sport got its start at Britain's Derby College of Technology, where the best time was 14 min. 3 sec. Then, at Caltech, members of the Reduction Study Group claimed the piano-demolition championship by crippling a keyboard in 10 min. 44.4 seconds. But records are made to be broken. Last week students at Detroit's Wayne State University reduced an old fraternity piano into kindling in 4 min. 51 sec.

Unlike cramming bodies into telephone booths or rotating in Laundromat dryers, piano reduction is supposed to be scientific team tomfoolery with a high purpose. Explained Caltech Piano Reducer Robert W. Diller, head of the team: "Piano reduction has psychological implications which are pretty dear to us. It's a satire on the obsolescence of today's society. We're sending out a brochure to see if we can get competition started all over the world. We'll start with the Paris Conservatoire and the Juilliard School of Music." [14]

---

emotions may be the dominating forces controlling the action in other forms of collective behavior. Publics must have a solid factual and deliberative character. Their behavior is more rational than other forms of collective behavior. Publics, Gabriel Tarde said, are the products of the printing press which makes the range of opinions extend far beyond the local community to include the whole world.[15] Today, mass communication devices extend their scope with miraculous speed to every remote spot so that ideas almost instantaneously reach everywhere.

Publics Have Five Developmental Phases

Foote and Hart indicate that each public has five developmental phases: [16] (1) The first is the *problem* phase. Here people recognize an issue and indicate concern about it. (2) The second is the *proposal* phase. Here some action seems necessary, and proposals are considered pro and con. This is the preliminary discussion phase in which experiences are shared and compromises worked out. (3) In the third or *policy* phase, there is consideration of plans of action and commitments relative to them. (4) In the fourth or *program* phase, decisions are put into action. This phase changes a public into an organization with specific memberships and definite roles assigned to accomplish the objectives. Discussion has ceased, at least temporarily. The public is now promoting a position. Other agencies also may accept the position and promote it. The public as a discussion collectivity then ceases to exist. It now may be called a pressure group. (5) If the objectives are not accomplished, an *appraisal* phase may follow. Consideration of further actions calls the public into existence again.

ADHERENTS AS PROPAGANDISTS   Issues that have not been resolved and have continuing interest result in continuing publics which new adherents may join and from which old ones may drop. The adherents of a public are an amorphous body of people. They do not interact with each other directly nor do they meet together. Therefore, a public represents a changing constituency, depending on the interest. Each member approaches the issue in terms of his desires, knowledge, and sometimes prejudice. Prejudice may be so strong in some persons that they do not reason or recognize facts. They are propagandists. One of the problems of the public is to avoid becoming a pressure group before the issues have been fully considered.

Publics Create Public Opinions

DEFINITION OF PUBLIC OPINION The objective of a public is to arrive at a prevailing collective opinion concerning an issue. When such a composite point of view is reached as the result of discussion, it may be called a public opinion. Someone has said: "Nothing is stronger than public opinion. Given the facts, nothing is wiser." Davis has pointed out that a public opinion held by thousands or millions may ruin or enrich an industry, start a war, produce a revolution, or overthrow a government.[17]

THE IMPORTANCE OF FACTS We must not conclude that the discussion creating public opinion is always deliberate and reasoned. Sometimes rumors, falsehoods, lack of information, and mere hearsay constitute the material on which the discussion is founded. Correct opinions cannot, therefore, always be assured. Faulty opinions may be changed by more adequate factual materials, as well as by actual change in the situation as the public perceives it. For publics and public opinions to do their most constructive work, therefore, facts should be accessible for they are the elements from which sound opinions are formed.

Several Means of Communication Are Mediums in Forming Public Opinion

Publics obtain the materials for the formation of their opinions from many sources. Whatever bears on the issue may contribute, whether it be valid data, falsehoods, gossip, rumor, or primary group influences. (See Box 30.) The major sources are the mass systems of communication: newspapers, magazines, radio, television, and movies.

NEWSPAPERS Despite competition from other media, the printing press is still probably the most effective force influencing publics and creating public opinions. Newspapers, especially the daily ones, provide the publics with the general and special information that enters into opinion-making. World events, local events, business conditions, sports activities, and social affairs all have their informational columns in the newspapers. Pages of advertising advise the buying public of what may be purchased. Each of these channels helps us to crystallize our views on the issues at hand through giving factual data and reporting the varied interpretations and views. Editorials enter directly into the process of opinion formation by stating definite positions on issues and giving evidence to support them. However, they usually present a biased view which supports only their own position. Chain journalism, whereby a single corporation with centralized control publishes several newspapers in different cities, has meant the passing of much personal journalism. Some deplore this because they feel it produces "soulless" newspapers under the domination of corporations, while others view it simply as the passing of self-appointed leadership. It is a matter of judgment whether the newspaper is still the promotional prophetic agency Carlyle described it to be: "There is no church sayest thou? The voice of Prophecy has gone dumb? This is even

---

BOX 30 PUBLIC OPINION AND THE PRIMARY GROUP

Interaction in primary groups performs an essential function in the formation of public opinion. Research on small groups shows their significance for the generation and maintenance of opinions. Panel studies of elections show the importance of personal influence in opinion change. Opinion leadership in the community can be distinguished from opinion initiation in primary relations. In a public, as distinct from a mass, there is a disjunction between personal interests and group expectations. Types of adaptation to these two determinants of public opinion are pro, con, ambivalent, undecided, and uninformed. The typical history of a public passes through stages characterized by mass behavior, public controversy between organized factions, and institutionalized decision-making. In each stage primary groups perform generative and relay functions within larger structures. The consequence of continued interaction is sharpening, crystallizing, and polarizing of opinions. Persons who are ambivalent, undecided, and uninformed change in the direction of conformance to primary group expectations. Interests are redefined to accord with expectations.[18]

---

what I dispute: but in any case, hast thou not still Preaching enough? A Preaching Friar settles himself in every village; and builds a pulpit, which he calls a Newspaper. Therefrom he preaches what most momentous doctrine is in him, for men's salvation; and dost not thou listen, and believe?" [19] While the newspaper may not function as powerfully today, it is no doubt still a major creator of public opinions.

MAGAZINES   Magazines, especially weekly news magazines, may be classed with newspapers as instruments in the formation of public opinion. This is especially true of those which select articles from the wide range of magazines and journals and digest their most pertinent ideas and facts. While the process of selecting and briefing introduces bias, the fact of selection by famous periodicals adds prestige to the articles and enhances their influence in opinion creation.

RADIO   Radio perhaps became the second most important instrument in forming public opinion during the several decades of its existence. It is now almost universally present in the homes of the Western world and in community centers in practically all other parts of the world. Its advantage is the immediacy with which messages may be broadcast. No significant happening occurs which is not broadcast within minutes. Inability to read is no barrier since the human voice carries the messages. Its reach extends to all persons within the sound of the broadcaster's voice.

The radio serves as a chief source of news and other information for many people who do not subscribe to newspapers or magazines. It also provides entertainment, most of which emphasizes the basic norms, such as honesty, fair play, and justice. The fact that it penetrates all social, economic, and other barriers with the same message means that it is a powerful agent for developing opinions about public problems. This activity is all the more significant when these are presented by a person who has gained the respect of the public so that the speaker's own voice becomes the medium of the message.

TELEVISION   Television, in adding sight as well as sound to mass communication techniques, is placed in a powerful position to influence public opinions. We not only hear but see the sources of news and views. Growth in the use of television in American society is indicated by the increased number of homes with sets. In New Brunswick, New Jersey, a city of 40,000 inhabitants 30 miles southwest of New York City, fewer than two families out of each 100 had television sets in 1948. In 1954, 76 families of each 100 owned sets.[20] Eighty-eight per cent of all households in the United States had a television set in May, 1960.

Few studies of the effect of television on public opinion have as yet been made. We can expect that investigations under way will reveal in full measure the potent influence of this instrument on opinion formation.[21]

MOTION PICTURES   Movies as a communication device influence publics by portraying aspects of the social world in which the audience lives, thus crystallizing pictures in their minds of what this world is or ought to be. The pictures, like radio and television, tend to confirm the sanctioned norms because they are kept within the limits of our sanctioned activity. Their influence on public opinion is usually an indirect one. Motion pictures, however, can paint images in the minds of their viewers that are distorted or wholly erroneous, especially when they are shown to audiences having little knowledge of the culture of the society portrayed. Thus Middle-East and oriental people tend to build up a picture of an American society filled with gangsters, Indians, cowboys, cocktail parties, and "hot-rodding" youth who have few, if any, serious ambitions.

The capacity of the commercial motion picture directly to influence public opinion on serious problems appears to be quite limited. This is not surprising since the movie is viewed primarily as a source of entertainment. One study of the attempt of a commercial movie to influence public opinion on infantile paralysis found that the film appealed only to a limited public, which considered it propaganda.[22] (The study summarized in Box 31 shows somewhat different results.)

Propaganda Attempts to Control Publics and Public Opinion

DEFINITION   *Propaganda* is the deliberate use of communication to induce people to favor one predetermined line of thought or action over another.

Publics arise around unresolved issues which in turn generate varied opinions. Since opinions represent attitudes rather than empirical evidence, they are subject to manipulation by the techniques of the propagandists. These agents strive to persuade people to accept one side of an issue and to reject others.

BOX 31

Experimental subjects who saw the motion picture "Gentleman's Agreement" were more likely to show reductions in the expression of anti-Semitic sentiments than control subjects who did not see the film. Moreover, there was a reduced but still considerable carry-over effect with regard to anti-Negro prejudice. Those who correctly perceived the theme and who reacted favorably to the film were more likely to show a reduction in anti-Semitism than those who did not. These factors, in turn, were inversely related to anti-Semitism. Initial anti-Semitism was directly related to absolute reductions in AS scores but was inversely related to proportionate reductions relative to the maximum reduction possible for each individual.[23]

Propaganda is not necessarily antisocial or immoral. Sometimes, valuable social ends, such as national loyalty in wartime, fluoridation of drinking water, and fair economic practices are attained by attitude persuasion.

Propagandists Must Deal with Three Divisions of the Population

Efforts to induce publics to accept a given end, thus eliminating reflection and bringing about action, must recognize that divisions of the population may have different attitudes toward these ends. First are those who are *favorable* to a position—the task here is to reinforce the views of these persons. Then there are those who are *disinterested*—the problem here is to create attitudes that overcome the lack of concern. The third subdivision includes those who are opposed or *unfavorable* to the position.

ATTRACTING THE DISINTERESTED Individuals in the first and third groupings above have already reacted either positively or negatively to the objective. The interest of those in the second group needs to be aroused. The advertiser knows that his first job is to gain attention. The main technique for accomplishing this is to associate his objective with a personal concern. People attend to things that have to do with their welfare. Attention may be captured by views which are presented in a sincere manner which generates personal involvement.

The success of Soviet propaganda in the colonial world is, in a sense, based on this approach. The Russians challenge these people, not to become Communists, but to oppose the imperialists who are oppressing them and to oppose those foreign powers who are frustrating their national aspirations. At the same time, they elaborate the image of the Soviet Republics as lands of free people who have been liberated from their imperialist oppressors.[24]

THE UNFAVORABLE The unfavorable group resists or has rejected the objective. Resistance is an attempt to neutralize the appeal of the suggested objective. Rejection is the dismissal of the proposal completely. Overcoming resistance and rejection is probably better accomplished by meeting the arguments against the proposal rather than by presenting only those arguments that support it.[25]

THE FAVORABLE The favorable grouping consists of those who help to develop the arguments which support the issue. Their positive action probably provides the best reinforcement of their own position.

Propaganda Employs a Variety of Techniques

A CLASSIFICATION Propagandists use an extensive repertoire of techniques to influence behavior. Davis points out that "they all involve either the control of fact or the control of interpretation."[26] Others appeal chiefly to the feelings through the manipulation symbols. Lee has classified these techniques in the following way:

A. Basic procedures
  1. Selecting the issue
  2. Case-making or card-stacking
  3. Simplification
B. Use of omnibus words (basic propaganda shorthand)
  4. Name-calling
  5. Glittering generality
C. Techniques of identification
  6. Transfer
  7. Testimonial
  8. Plain folks
  9. Band wagon

D. Strategic techniques
    10. Hot potato
    11. Stalling [27]

Explanation of These Techniques The propagandist first selects and states the issue on which he stands, orders his facts or falsehoods to support this issue, and reduces them to simple forms often expressed as slogans. This is his basic procedure.

Name-calling and *glittering generalities* short-circuit rational discussion by arousing biased and oversimplified responses. Opposing ideas, individuals, or institutions are given evil labels, whereas supporting ones are treated as virtuous.

Transference is the association of an issue with some universally respected symbol, such as God or the flag. *Testimony* exploits the statements of honored persons in support of issues in a manner that lends prestige to the propagandist's point of view. The *plain folks* technique seeks support for a program by implying its close connection with the ordinary people. The *band wagon* device implies that everybody is supporting it.

The technique of the *hot potato* involves the use of some incident that is interpreted to the disadvantage of the opposition, while *stalling* is a play for time which causes the opposition to lose enthusiasm and support.

The Propaganda Programs of the Nazis and of Russia Illustrate the Use of These Techniques

Both the Nazis and the Russians stated their basic themes in the simplest terms. Hitler and Goebbels held that the intellectual capacity of the masses was so restricted that propaganda must be uncomplicated and focused on few opponents. The objective was to unite the masses in hatred of "democrats," "plutocrats," "bolshevists," and "Jews" who were keeping the racially pure, industrious Germans from attaining their rightful place in the sun. In Russia, the masses are taught to think and accept a Marxian economic view of life. Brief, dogmatic, simple, and constantly repeated assertions of historical materialism, class war, and proletarian leadership form the crux of their powerful propaganda. Bourgeois idealism, romanticism, and morality are presented as outdated modes of thought. Marx is the savior of the people, Lenin his chosen emissary—examples of transferring.

Nothing is asserted more often than that all actions are for the sake of the people. This identifies all programs with and for the people. Name-calling and glittering generalities and slogans, expressed in cryptic fashion, reiterate the positions. "Common good before personal advancement" ("Gemeinnutz vor Eigennutz") was the theme of Herr Hitler's propaganda while "destroy the power of the Jews" ("Juda verrecks") translated their racial attitudes into a simple formula. "Capitalists" and "imperialist aggressors" are terms used to characterize democratic powers, while the U.S.S.R. is designated as "the peaceful, powerful friend of the people." The completely monopolized systems of communication concentrate on their propaganda lines in these many ways, dinning their messages into the people by mass media, face-to-face meetings, public assemblies, and posters.

Propaganda Is a Tool Used in Most Areas of Social Life Today

Politics, business, religion, and other major aspects of social life use propaganda to promote their interests. To protect themselves from error, the public must develop the ability to recognize what is based on truth and what is based on falsehood. Fortunately, there is some safety in competing propaganda. The dangers of misleading the uninformed public are lessened when opposing propagandists present conflicting views. Such incongruities will induce critical questioning and closer study of the issues.

IV. SOCIAL MOVEMENTS

Social Movements Are Distinctive Forms of Collective Behavior

In a strict sense, social movements are to be distinguished from so-called mass movements exemplified by booms, manias, collective hysteria, and other forms of spontaneous emotional behavior which may surge through a society. Although the social movement may be accompanied by expressive behavior, its development is marked by defined goals and the progressive growth of structure which leads to stable forms and the patterning of collective emotion.

DEFINITION AND CLASSIFICATION We may define a *social movement* as a form of dynamic pluralistic behavior which progressively develops structure through time and aims at partial or complete modification of the social order. It is directed *against* something, which is the condition the movement seeks to correct, and also directed *toward* something, which is the goal the movement strives to realize.[28]

Social movements have been classified in various ways by students of collective behavior. These represent the varying purposes and perspectives of the writers. We suggest a working classification based upon three criteria which are not mutually exclusive:

1. *Relation to the primary values and norms.* If a movement strives for changes which are in accord with the mores, that is, if it accepts the basic values of the society and tries only to eliminate behavior which is inconsistent with them, we may call it a *reformative* social movement. The campaign for woman suffrage is an example. If, on the other hand, the movement challenges the primary values and seeks to replace them by a new set, the social movement is *revolutionary*. The Communist movement illustrates this mode.

2. *Scope.* If the social movement is engulfing in scope, that is, aims at changing the entire society in accord with the basic tenets of the "new order," it is called *totalitarian*. Fascism and communism are illustrations. When it aims at changing only a part of the society, it is a *segmental* social movement. The temperance or prohibition movement is an illustration.

3. *Method.* Although it is impractical to make arbitrary distinctions between types of social movements upon the basis of the methods employed, there are some conspicuous differences in strategy associated with the two types. The reformative-segmental movement is likely to rely on the more rational procedures of public discussion, propaganda, education, and legislation. The revolutionary-totalitarian form depends upon the more dramatic, emotional, extra-legal devices. The former might be said to use *persuasion*, the latter *conversion*. Changes advocated by the first type tend to be effected by peaceful, gradual, democratic means, whereas the methods of the second are spectacular, violent, or coercive and authoritarian.

COMPONENTS AND STAGES   We have said that a social movement develops over time. If it matures as a full-fledged movement, it will reveal certain characteristic components and generally recognizable stages. These components and stages may be briefly identified in outline form:

1. *Social unrest*—social maladjustment, discontent, anxiety, frustration, and possibly random behavior and emotional contagion. This condition will usually be created by social change which disrupts traditional structures and routines.

2. *Emergence of leadership*—often a multiplicity of leaders, one of whom usually becomes ascendant.

3. *Definition of issues and problems*—clarification (and often oversimplification) of the problem and the issues, done by the leader for the followers.

4. *Formation and propagation of the ideology*—dissemination of a more or less systematized body of tenets, beliefs, goals, and ideas which provides the intellectual structure or rationale of the movement.

5. *Program, organization, and strategies*—formation of policies, creation of local and national organizations, and development and use of propaganda, pressure, and other techniques of persuasion or coercion.

6. *"Capture of power"*—gaining control of the government or effecting basic legislative changes.

7. *Institutionalization*—establishment of or integration of the news patterns within the basic structure of the society.

Neither components nor stages should be taken as separable, distinct elements of a social movement. The components are interrelated, and the stages overlap in varying degrees. The outline, however, may provide the student with a working framework for analyzing one or more of the many social movements which have developed in modern times.[29]

References

1. Anderson, W. A., "Rural Sociology as Science," *Rural Sociology*, 12 (December, 1947), p. 352.

2. Massie, Robert, "What Next in Mississippi?" *Saturday Evening Post*, 235 (November 10, 1962), pp. 16 and 18. Reprinted by special permission of the *Saturday Evening Post;* copyright 1962, The Curtis Publishing Company.

3. Gold, Michael, *Jews Without Money* (New York, Liveright Publishing Corp., 1930), pp. 249–250.

4. Turner, Ralph, and Killian, Lewis, *Collective Behavior* (Englewood Cliffs, N.J., Prentice-Hall, Inc., 1957), p. 85.
5. Blumer, Herbert, "Collective Behavior," in Lee, A. M. (ed.), *New Outline of the Principles of Sociology* (New York, Barnes and Noble, 1951), Part 4, p. 178.
6. LeBon, Gustave, *The Crowd* (London, T. Usher Unwin, 1896), pp. 25–38.
7. Johnson, James W., *The Autobiography of an Ex-Coloured Man* (New York, Alfred A. Knopf, 1951), pp. 184–188.
8. Galsworthy, John, *The Forsyte Saga* (New York, Charles Scribner's Sons, 1927), pp. 672–673. This illustration suggests the role of cultural differences in collective behavior.
9. Davis, Kingsley, *Human Society* (New York, The Macmillan Company, 1949), p. 351.
10. Bentley, J. M., "A Preface to Social Psychology," *Psychological Monographs,* 21 (1923), No. 4.
11. Young, K., *Social Psychology* (New York, Appleton-Century-Crofts, Inc., 1946), p. 400.
12. Turner, Ralph, and Killian, Lewis, *Collective Behavior* (Englewood Cliffs, N.J., Prentice-Hall, Inc., 1957), p. 167.
13. Allen, Frederick L., *Only Yesterday* (New York, Harper and Brothers, 1931), pp. 270–271.
14. *Time* (March 1, 1963), pp. 64–65. Courtesy of *Time;* copyright, 1963, by Time, Inc.
15. Park, R. E., and Burgess, E. W., *Introduction to the Science of Sociology* (Chicago, University of Chicago Press, 1921), p. 868.
16. Foote, N. H., and Hart, C. W., "Public Opinion and Collective Behavior," *Group Relations at the Crossroads* by Sherif, M., and Wilson, M. O. (eds.) (New York, Harper and Brothers, 1953).
17. Davis, Kingsley, *Human Society* (New York, The Macmillan Company, 1949), p. 357.
18. Baur, E. Jackson, "Public Opinion and the Primary Group," *American Sociological Review,* 25 (April, 1960), p. 208.
19. Carlyle, Thomas, *Sartor Resartus* (New York, E. P. Dutton and Co., 1929), pp. 189-190. From Everyman's Library.
20. "When Television Comes to Town," National Project in Agricultural Communications, East Lansing, Mich., Michigan State University (July, 1955), No. 2.
21. See, for example, Lang, K., and Lang, G. E., "The Unique Perspective of Television and Its Effect; A Pilot Study," *American Sociological Review,* 18 (February, 1953), pp. 3–12. The evidence indicates that the exposure which Kennedy received in the Kennedy-Nixon television debates influenced public opinion to his great advantage.
22. Hulett, J. E., Jr., "Estimating the Net Effect of a Commercial Motion Picture Upon the Trend of Local Public Opinion," *American Sociological Review,* 14 (April, 1949), pp. 263–275.
23. Middleton, Russell, "Ethnic Prejudice and Susceptibility to Persuasion," *American Sociological Review,* 25 (October, 1960), p. 679.
24. Katona, P., "Soviet Propaganda to the Colonial World," *Yearbook of World Affairs,* 9 (1955), pp. 149–173.
25. Lumsdain, A. A., and Janis, I. L., "Resistance to Counterpropaganda Produced by One-Sided and Two-Sided 'Propaganda' Presentations," *Public Opinion Quarterly,* 17 (1953), pp. 311–318.
26. Davis, Kingsley, *Human Society* (New York, The Macmillan Company, 1949), p. 160.
27. Lee, Alfred M., "The Analysis of Propaganda: A Clinical Summary," *American Jour-*

nal of Sociology, 51 (September, 1945), p. 133. By permission of the University of Chicago Press; copyright, 1945, by the University of Chicago.

28. Abel, Theodore, "The Pattern of a Successful Political Movement," *American Sociological Review,* 2 (June, 1937), p. 348, and Abel, Theodore, *Why Hitler Came to Power* (Englewood Cliffs, N.J., Prentice-Hall, Inc., 1938), pp. 120 ff.

29. For some cases, see Abel, Theodore, *Why Hitler Came to Power* (Englewood Cliffs, N.J., Prentice-Hall, Inc., 1938); Cantril, Hadley, *Psychology of Social Movements* (New York, John Wiley and Sons, Inc., 1941); and Heberle, Rudolph, *Social Movements* (New York, Appleton-Century-Crofts, Inc., 1951).

Questions for Study and Discussion

1. Illustrate the major characteristics of a collectivity.
2. Describe the conditions under which a crowd that you have observed came into existence.
3. Characterize crowds and give concrete illustrations of several types.
4. Diagram the physical pattern of a large audience of which you have recently been a member.
5. Define a "mass" and give some examples of mass behavior.
6. Compare a mass with a public.
7. Discuss the roles of newspapers, magazines, radio, television, and other mass communication media in creating public opinion.
8. Discuss the characteristics and uses of propaganda in modern societies.
9. Why do there seem to be fewer social movements in America today than there were a generation ago?

Suggested Topics for Reports

1. Report on the formation and behavior of a crowd which you have observed or participated in. Deal with the underlying and precipitating factors which brought it into existence, the process of emotional contagion, and other elements of collective behavior discussed in the text.
2. Diagram the physical pattern of a large audience of which you have recently been a member and describe the techniques employed to achieve polarization.
3. Describe one or more of the college fads (or crazes) which have received national notice in the last twenty years (for example, students swallowing gold fish, crowding into telephone booths, conducting "panty raids," or demolishing old pianos). How would you explain the appearance of such phenomena in the college community?

Supplementary Reading

Gittler, Joseph B. (ed.), *Review of Sociology.* Section on Collective Behavior by Herbert Blumer. New York: John Wiley and Sons, Inc., 1957.

Heberle, Rudolph, *Social Movements.* New York: Appleton-Century-Crofts, Inc., 1951.

Hoffer, Eric, *The True Believer.* New York: Mentor Books, The New American Library of World Literature, Inc., 1951.

Katz, Daniel (ed.), *Public Opinion and Propaganda—a Book of Readings.* New York: Dryden Press, 1954.

Lang, Kurt, and Lang, Gladys E., *Collective Dynamics.* New York: Thomas Y. Crowell Co., 1961.

La Piere, Richard T., *Collective Behavior.* New York: McGraw-Hill Book Co., Inc., 1938.

LeBon, Gustave, *The Crowd.* London: T. Usher Unwin, 1896.

Lee, A. M. (ed.), *New Outline of the Principles of Sociology*. Section on Collective Behavior by Herbert Blumer. New York: Barnes and Noble, 1951.

Lippman, Walter, *Public Opinion*. New York: Harcourt, Brace and Company, 1922.

Merton, Robert K., Fiske, Marjorie, and Curtis, Alberta, *Mass Persuasion: The Social Psychology of a War Bond Drive*. New York: Harper and Brothers, 1946.

Park, Robert E., and Burgess, Ernest W., *Introduction to the Science of Sociology*. Chicago: University of Chicago Press, 1921.

Sherif, Muzafer, *An Outline of Social Psychology*. New York: Harper and Brothers, 1948.

Taylor, Carl C., *The Farmer's Movement, 1620–1920*. New York: American Book Company, 1953.

Turner, Ralph, and Killian, Lewis, *Collective Behavior*. Englewood Cliffs, N.J.: Prentice-Hall, Inc., 1957.

Whyte, William H., Jr., *Is Anybody Listening?* New York: Simon and Schuster, Inc., 1952.

Von Weise, Leopold, and Becker, Howard, *Systematic Sociology*. New York: John Wiley and Sons, Inc., 1932.

18

INTERRELATIONSHIPS AND INTEGRATION:
THE MUTUAL ADJUSTMENT OF STRUCTURES

T*HE five classes of relationship structures present in a society are so interrelated and interdependent upon each other that the society operates as an ordered system supporting a set of common values. The commonly accepted values of a society serve as the chief forces in societal integration.*

A Society's Structural Forms Are Interrelated

In Chapter 6, we stated that societal forms are "arranged in an interrelated and interdependent way with respect to each other so that societies operate as wholes." Any particular society is a constellation of structural units—groups, organizations, institutional agencies, collectivities, ecological entities—so interrelated that it operates as an interconnected system supporting a set of common values. So far, the treatment of each of the major structural components of societies has emphasized its particular characteristics and functions, although the view of societies as integrated systems based on common values has been stressed repeatedly.

One may have the impression that a society is merely as mass of separate individuals, or just heterogeneous aggregations of people, existing autonomously, rather than a constellation of persons bound together and dependent upon each other in systems of interrelationships that combine to constitute a total functional structure. In this chapter, we show how the "parts" of societal systems are interrelated so that they constitute a continuing entity wherein dissimilar forms, and the individuals who compose them, operate in response to common expectations, norms, and goals that are the essence of the social heritage.

The Characteristics of "Systems"

We may think of a system as a combination of a number of separate parts united by a form of interdependence into a functional whole. The heating system in a home or a modern apartment house consists of a central heat producing unit—the furnace—which is itself a combination of many parts—boiler sections, grates, thermostats, and others. Then there are lead-off and return pipes to carry hot water or steam from the furnace and back to it; radiators to absorb and disperse the heat carried to them into the rooms; valves to regulate the flow of heat from the radiators; and thermostats to start and to shut off the system. These parts constitute a system when they are combined in an appropriate manner so that each can carry out its function in the integrated whole.

Systems, whether they relate to a material or nonmaterial aspect of living, have functions that are the purposes for their existence. Heating systems obviously are to provide warmth. Societal systems are to achieve ends the society considers valuable. Each part of a system also has functions in this whole. These functions of a part of the system are its roles, that which is expected of the part in the whole.

Functioning in social systems, both of the whole and of the parts, expands into other significant relationship elements that we will treat when we consider social action and social change.

Societies Are Integrated in Different Ways

TIGHTLY WOVEN SYSTEMS The government in totalitarian societies controls social life so completely that each structural form and those who compose it are completely coordinated with the aims these societies support. Thus, the schools, churches, economic agencies, organizations, and all manifestations of collective behavior are subsumed under the policies and controls of this governing institution. It regulates or manages them. It abolishes or forbids their operation where control is not feasible. This system of state and government dominance, which represents one extreme in the unification and integration of societies, may be characterized as a "closely woven" type of integration, to employ Embree's term.[1]

An Illustration   Communist societies illustrate such tightly integrated systems. There is only one political party, and it controls all other organizations, imposing its regulations on all, including families. It controls all communication channels, thus directing each sanctioned agency's activities through its official hierarchy that heads up in the leaders and the inner circle. The system arranges all elements of the society in a stringently controlled pattern. No challenge to its power or the system of values that defines its aims is tolerated. It achieves its integration by constant threat or the use of force.

LOOSELY STRUCTURED SYSTEMS   On the other hand, some societies are "loosely woven." Two oriental societies that are so structured are Thailand and Ceylon. The societal norms are expressed in these by a wide range of alternative channels of conformity. Social behavior that does not conform to them is condoned, since the offenses against the society are ill-defined and the enforcement of legal and moral precepts are laxly carried out. The values of social organization that give them permanence and solidarity are undeveloped, giving their group life an informal character with ill-defined relationships in which social roles are subordinated to individual roles.[2] This loose structure does not imply that the society is poorly integrated. "On the contrary, the loose integration is a functional one, allowing not only variation in individual behavior, but also in national behavior. . . . A loosely integrated structure such as the Thai may adjust to external cultural influences with less drastic overall changes than a more rigid structure such as the Japanese or Vietnamese."[3] Allan Holmberg also describes "loose structuring" in the society of the Siriono of Eastern Bolivia, while B. J. James does it for the Chippewa Indians.[4]

The Type of Integration Influences Functioning

It is not implied here that societies can be placed on a continuum of integration ranging from "closely woven" to "loosely woven." This may eventually be possible. We give the illustrations to show that there are different types of integration of the structural systems of societies and that these influence their operation significantly.

This relationship has significant theoretical value as well as a practical importance for analyzing societal structure and functioning. Social change in societies with different types of integration presents different kinds of problems. A society where loose application of standards is tolerated will absorb change in a manner that differs from one requiring close adherence to norms. The possibilities of directing organizations, institutions, groups, and individuals vary widely in relation to the type and degree of social integration. Different attitudes toward the structural forms of societies will lead to differences in the procedures for introducing changes and in the mechanisms for their acceptance. Tennant, a student of cultural change, wrote of the Sinhalese: "They are by no means the plastic substance which such a description would suggest—capable of being molded into any form, or retaining permanently any casual impression —but rather a yielding fluid which adapts its shape to that of the vessel into which it may happen to be poured, without any change in its quality or any modification in its character."[5] The characteristics of the social organization of this society, as an example, had to be discovered before it could be understood, to say nothing of bringing about changes in it. This is true for each society. A knowledge of its structural pattern and the character of its integration is basic to understanding it. This is the foundation for intelligent social control.

Commonly Accepted Values Are the Chief Integrating Forces in Societies

Societies depend mainly upon the development of loyalty to a common set of values that serve as the chief integrating forces in a society. Such values evolve over long periods of time as core elements of the culture. They are transmitted from generation to generation as the core elements upon which the whole culture and its parts are to act. We evolve structures, particularly institutions and institutional agencies, as instruments for their implementation. These structures form webs of relationship units that preserve and promote these values. There are always some persons and groups in most societies who do not accept or follow these values and their norms nor operate through their approved structures. They are the anti-social people and cause, in part, the social problems of societies.

When basic changes occur in a society, as when a new technology is introduced into the economy, the basic values and norms that are prescribed may become inadequate or the structures serving them—schools, churches, and governments—may no longer function effectively. Then new social forms are created, or old ones are readjusted, to develop and express a new consensus around the altered basic values. The process serves to maintain or re-establish the integration.

Integration Is Based on the Functions Performed by the Human Relationship Structures

Our study of each of the five classes of human relationship structures (hurelures) pointed out the functions each performs in promoting the accepted values of a society. This, in turn, results in a common awareness of sharing that promotes the unity of the whole society. Every society is characterized by a division of labor in the upholding of its values. The different human relationship structures are the mediums of operation for this division of labor. They interact to support the normative order by carrying out functions acceptable to the society and suited to its pattern of organization.

This can be illustrated by recalling the major values that undergird the American society, as described in Chapter 2 on the cultural heritage of a society. Here it was shown that the supreme value of the individual, the possibility of a social order of fair play and justice, and freedom in religion, political, and economic life were underlying values that determined the quality of this society. The basic human relationship structures evolved to support these values. Democratic government, publicly supported schools available to all, religious freedom as an inviolable trait of the social order that allows religious institutions of every variety, and property institutions and the agencies for their protection and development all operate as struc-

tures for their support. They are causally related to each other and develop mutual consistency with each other.

Each of the structural forms supplements the others in its promotion of these values. The schools stress participation in, and loyalty to, the government. Government authorizes the schools and makes regulations about their programs, support, and attendance. Industry aids the schools by grants and other forms of support. Religious institutions are encouraged in the schools and protected by the government. And government regulates such industries as public utilities and banks in the interest of public welfare. Voluntary organizations arise in relation to nearly all these values in the support of the essential purposes of the society. These structural forms are not independent units; rather, they are interdependent, and they interact upon each other to achieve the shared values of the social system.

Integration Is Illustrated in the Changing of the Functions of the Structural Forms

COMPLEMENTARY FORMS Structural forms come into existence to perform functions in relation to social values. Churches as institutional agencies, for example, operate to promote character-building by developing a sense of relationship with the Divine. Thus, purpose is not lost, even though churches take on other functions, such as providing opportunities for recreation and sociability or aiding those who are distressed by emotional or economic problems. Other institutions and organizations of the society have the function of character-building, also. The work of schools, Boy and Girl Scouts, and many other organizations supplement, and are often correlated with, the work of churches in this respect. The churches organize and support Scout units, while Scouting promotes the church activities among its youth. Thus there is supplementation of effort in attaining common goals.

LOSS OF FUNCTIONS In some instances, relationship structures lose some of their functions to other structures almost completely For some time, the Church in American society provided almost completely the elementary and higher education available in the society. Academies and colleges were almost all Church agencies in colonial days. Today, the public elementary school, the public high school, and the publicly supported and privately endowed colleges and universities have taken over this function. Of course, the shifting of this function has been gradual because churches still support some educational institutions, but this function is now primarily assumed by the public schools.

The family is another example. It once provided its members with protection, economic opportunity, education, recreation, and old-age care, as well as offering a home and personal affection. Protection is now largely a responsibility of communities and states, through police, courts, and other officials. The family is no longer a production unit. Youth find their work in service and productive agencies outside of the family. There is still some occupational transmission from fathers to sons, but it is slight. Education is now a task of the schools. Recreation is provided by such clubs and organizations for youth as the baseball and football leagues, Camp Fire Girls, and others. Moving pictures and many commercial activities take the adults outside of their homes for much of their leisure activity. The care of the aged is increasingly a matter of public responsibility as programs of social security expand.

The family still remains the agency for providing sanctioned sex relations, care of offspring, and guidance in personality development. It now only supplements other agencies for many of the functions for which it previously had primary responsibility, causing it to be increasingly dependent upon other structures to provide for certain essential services. These interrelationships often lead to closer association among these agencies.

ADDITION OF FUNCTIONS Some of the agencies of a society lose functions. Others add them. The loss of economic functions by the family in Western societies has meant their addition as functions of industry. Production of goods, financing of business operations, and marketing of products are all functions the economic system has taken over from the family. Few families, even among farmers, market their products to consumers in a direct way. They usually take only the first step in the marketing chain by bringing their raw materials to a wholesale center from which it moves through the further steps of processing, distributing, storing, and retailing. All of this involves many new related agencies and subagencies tied together in a system of intermeshed units dependent on each other for different specializations.

Changes in the Functions of Structures Indicate That Integration Is in Part the Consequence of Differentiation and Specialization

The complementing of functions and their shifts from one social structure to another stresses the principle that integration results from diversity and specialization. Interdependence increases as societies become more and more complex and activities more differentiated. Integration is necessary where the elements are linkages in the social system. As the economic system expanded and acquired new functions which other institutions or organizations gave over, government became related as the regulative link representing the public interest. Government exercises controls relative to prices, work conditions, hours of labor, and other aspects of the economic order that the family once controlled. It now meshes with the economic order at hundreds of points. Thus institutions, organizations, and other structural forms become intertwined as they operate together to serve the purposes of society and to develop orderly and integrated societal unity.

Social Structures May Not Change Although Their Functions Do

REASONS FOR PERSISTENCE The organizational patterns of structures often persist, once their forms have crystallized, though their functions change. This is true for several reasons, even if some of the functions they performed have been lost. Each structure usually performs some distinctive function or functions other structures cannot perform, or perform as well. The family has lost many of its functions to other agencies, but none has been able to take over its biological or psychological functions because they cannot perform them as well. Some of the functions structures perform may become even more significant as changes take place. The function of providing intimate association by the family for its members, for example, takes on greater significance, and this structure becomes more important because societies have moved increasingly to a secondary type of organization. Moreover, structures can often take on additional functions without the necessity of changing their patterns. They do not need to change, although they can and do if the additional purposes require it.

PERSISTENCE PROMOTES REGULARITY AND ORDER
This persistence of structural forms is important to the interrelationships and integration of societies. Orderly and continuous operation would be difficult if these forms were constantly changing. The structural forms themselves may require little attention because there is this persistence. Attention can be devoted to the activities to be performed by the structures.

Persistence of Structures Leads to Conservatism and Stagnation

Although structures of a social system make it possible for it to operate in an orderly way, they may also become so rigid that they will not adapt to change. Because the established structures have proven their utility, individuals and groups not only generate strong feelings of attachment but also develop vested interests in them. They often block change.

CHINESE SOCIETY AS AN EXAMPLE The structural pattern of Chinese society persisted for twenty centuries without significant change. It was organized around the institution of the civil service examination, which constituted the gateway to political position, social prestige, and economic success. It preserved the conservative aspects of Confucianism and the dominant position of the literati. The institution was relatively democratic in that it made the examinations open to nearly all. Since it absolutely prohibited any changes in the system, it preserved the unity of Chinese social organization so thoroughly that cultural inertia and stagnation marked the society for centuries.[6]

This persistent adherence to structural patterns that are presented as sacred and maintained by those with vested interests is a major factor in the stagnation of many societies. Any society faces the problem of maintaining the resiliency of its ideas and forms, lest its social structures become so rigid that they can be altered only by violent means.

Mutual Adjustment Within Human Relationship Structures

Our discussion of the integration of structural forms has dealt broadly with the relationship of structures to each other. When we narrow our focus we see also that groups, organizations, and other structures have internal bonds that integrate and unify the component parts of each into a coordinated pattern.

CONCERT BAND AS AN ILLUSTRATION If we select any specific structure, we should be able to see that it is bonded by various functions that make it a unified entity. We select a concert band as an illustration. The objective of this organization is to produce harmonious concert music through a variety of instruments. Each part has its own function to perform in the production of the finished product. A number of individuals playing a variety of instruments make a successful band only when each independent performer coordinates his playing with that of the others, so that each player supplements or complements the others. If each structure is to persist in a society, it must possess such functional interrelations which hold the parts together in a pattern of mutual adjustment.

THE HINDU JAJMANI SYSTEM The Hindu caste system is the chief integrating structure of the society of India. Each individual in the Hindu system has a fixed social and economic position established by his birth in a particular caste. An interesting aspect of this total system is the manner in which hereditary occupations are integrated with each other in a system of mutual interrelationships that orders the economic life of the society. The Jajmani system requires that each caste within a village give certain economic services to the families of the other castes: a carpenter repairs buildings, a barber cuts the hair, and so on. But the workers "do not necessarily perform these services for everyone. Each man works for a particular family or group of families with which he has socially hereditary ties. His father worked for these same families before him and his son will continue to work for them, the occupation or service being determined by his caste. The family or family-head served by an individual is known as his *jajman,* while the man who performs service is known as the *jajman's kamin* or *kam karne-wala* (literally, worker)."[7]

This system operates without much exchange of money; grain and other supplies are the chief payments for services. It provides hereditary jobs for the village castes and a stable labor supply for the region covered. The advantage of such a system is the security it provides the castes, which in turn, results in peace and contentment.[8] Every caste, from the Brahman to the Chamar, is somehow integrated into the social and ceremonial round of the community and is given some opportunity to feel indispensable and proud.[9] Lewis and Barnow came to a different assessment of this system, pointing out that it leads to the exploitation of the workers by their jajman.[10] Our interest in the matter is that it is an excellent example of the way one aspect of a total social system is effectively integrated.

References

1. Embree, J. F., "Thailand—A Loosely Structured Social System," *American Anthropologist,* 52 (April–June, 1950), p. 182.
2. *Ibid.,* pp. 181–193, and Ryan, B. F., and Straus, M. A., "The Integration of Sinhalese Society," *Research Studies of the State College of Washington,* 52 (December, 1954), pp. 179–227.
3. Embree, J. F., "Thailand—A Loosely Structured Social System," *American Anthropologist,* 52 (April–June, 1950), p. 191.
4. Holmberg, A. R., "Nomads of the Long Bow—The Siriono of Eastern Bolivia," *Institute of Social Anthropology, Smithsonian Institution* (Washington, D.C., 1950), Publication 10, and James, B. F., "Some Critical Observations Concerning Analyses of Chippewa 'Atomism' and Chippewa Personality," *American Anthropologist,* 56 (1954), pp. 283 ff.
5. Quoted in Ryan, B. F., and Straus, M. A., "The Integration of Sinhalese Society," *Research Studies of the State College of Washington,* 22 (December, 1954), pp. 221 and 222.
6. Cressey, Paul F., "The Influence of the Literary Examination System on the Development of Chinese Civilization," *American Journal of Sociology,* 35 (September, 1929), pp. 250–262.
7. Lewis, Oscar, and Barnouw, Victor, "Caste and the Jajmani System in a Northern Indian Village," *Science,* 83 (August, 1956), pp. 66 ff. Reprinted by permission of *Science.*
8. Wiser, W. H., *The Hindu Jajmani System* (Lucknow, India, Lucknow Publishing House, 1936), p. 187.
9. Opler, M., and Singh, R. D., "The Division of Labor in an Indian Village," *A Reader in General Anthropology,* Coon, C. S. (ed.) (New York, Holt and Company, Inc., 1948), p. 496.
10. Lewis, Oscar, and Barnouw, Victor, "Caste and the Jajmani System in a Northern Indian Village," *Science,* 83 (August, 1956), p. 77. Reprinted by permission of *Science.*

Questions for Study and Discussion

1. What are the main objectives in societal integration?
2. Describe a "tightly woven" societal system other than that of Russia.
3. Discuss the relationship of structure to function in social systems.
4. How do the changing functions of the structural forms of a society relate to its integration?
5. Why may a human relationship structure persist even though it loses many of its functions?
6. Illustrate the transfer of social functions and show how they influence societal integration.
7. Discuss the relationship of conservatism to societal integration.
8. Describe the existence of integration in an organization or institution in which you operate.

Suggested Topics for Reports

1. Select any one of the basic social institutions (family, education, economic organization, government, religion) and in outline or chart form show the major functional interrelations between it and each of the other four institutions.
2. Select any two of the five basic social institutions and show how their functional interrelations have changed in recent times.

Supplementary Reading

Angell, Robert C., *The Integration of American Society*. New York: McGraw-Hill Book Co., Inc., 1941.

Linton, Ralph, *The Study of Man*. New York: Appleton-Century-Crofts, Inc., 1936.

Merton, Robert K., *Social Theory and Social Structure*. Glencoe, Ill.: The Free Press, 1949.

Ogburn, William F., and Nimkoff, Meyer F., *Sociology*. Boston: Houghton Mifflin Company, 1958.

Panunzio, Constantine, *Major Social Institutions*. New York: The Macmillan Company, 1939.

Parsons, Talcott, *The Structure of Social Action*. New York: McGraw-Hill Book Co., Inc., 1957.

Riesman, David, *The Lonely Crowd*. New Haven, Conn.: Yale University Press, 1950.

Sorokin, Pitirim, *Society, Culture, and Personality*. New York: Harper and Brothers, 1947.

Williams, Robin M., *American Society*. Rev. ed. New York: Alfred A. Knopf, Inc., 1960.

PART FOUR

THE OPERATION OF SOCIETIES:
Social Action and Interaction,
Social Differentiation, Social Stratification,
Social Change, and Social Control

19

SOCIAL ACTION: THE OPERATIONAL PROCESS

SOCIETIES *are always in action, never static. All the structures of a society have social purposes—values they serve to satisfy. The action forms in any society are those of "inter" actions. Interactions are of three types: cooperation, competition, and conflict. Interactions lead to accommodations through compromise, conversion, tolerance, arbitration, truce, or subordination. They lead to assimilation through fusion of interests and values.*

I. THE CHARACTERISTICS OF SOCIAL ACTION

Meaningfully Oriented Human Actions Are the Elements in the Operation of a Society

The previous chapters have dealt with the *structures* of societies. The understanding of society, however, requires that we see more than the static pictures of its structural forms. We must also view society in terms of the behavioral processes associated with the forms. Therefore, we now turn to *social action*. The distinction between social structure and social action is analogous to the difference between a still shot in a movie (showing structure) and the flow of the running film (showing action). Figuratively, we have been looking mainly at "still shots" of society by examining structures and their relations and organization.

A society as an integrated unit acts through its parts. Human actions, when meaningfully oriented to those of others through the use of a common set of symbols, are *social* actions. They constitute the elements in the operational process of a society. The simplest of the social actions is the reciprocal influence of two individuals in contact. At the other end of the continuum are the reciprocal actions that occur within and between complex human relationship structures, such as in industry and government. Explanation of these actions within and between structures is essential to the understanding of a society.

A UNIVERSITY AS AN ILLUSTRATION The meaningful actions among the differentiated parts of human relationship structures make them dynamic wholes in which the action of each part is oriented to, and coordinated with, that of the others. We use a university as an illustration.

Universities have functionaries, such as deans, teachers, clerks, and janitors; equipment, such as classrooms, laboratories, books, eating places; organizations, such as fraternities and special interest clubs; and regulatory elements, such as rules, grades, degrees. What binds all of these into an entity with a common core of functions and a "boundary" that leads us to think of it as a university? It is that these persons and relationship forms act in coordinated programs according to the norms designed to achieve the purposes for which this structure and its parts were created. In these actions, each person, group, organization, or other relationship unit has its status and role. These define their privileges and their responsibilities to the ends or values to be achieved. Students confer with registration officers who help them work out programs of study; professors meet classes, give instruction, and guide study; coaches drill teams that play games which are attended by university people and other persons. In many other ways, a multitude of interlocking activities carried out according to rules and regulations—often published in handbooks—constitute the university in action. Notice that all the verbs in the sentences above denote action: "confer with";

301

"work out programs"; "meet classes"; "give instruction"; "drill teams"; "play games"; "attended"; "carried out." Notice also that they imply communication that results in interactions among people in definite situations.

The Basic Actions in a Society Are Those of "Inter" Action

Actions that have significance to the functioning of a society are those that take place between people and among various groupings of people. These "inter" actions constitute the basic relationships through which a society operates. There is no society nor are there any societal structures except when there are "inter" actions—activities *between* persons to form groups and *between* groups when formed. Therefore, we cannot state too strongly that interaction is the foundational process in any society and that the types of interactions that take place influence the character of the society. They provide the possibilities for orderly and constructive association or for disorderly and destructive consequences. The types of interactions that take place within families, schools, the community, or the whole society have profound consequences on their operation, for it is through these interactions that the direction of human behavior is determined. It is clear that the types of interactions within a society vary in form and in their consequences. They interpenetrate in complex and numberless ways. Some are consciously directed toward specific goals, while others may have no predetermined objectives.

Human "Inter" Actions Are Based Chiefly on Societal Norms That Express the Stable Patterns of Societies

Human relationships are always directed outwardly from the person. We are constantly dealing with other people by responding to them as they respond to us. These interactions exist not only in the awareness of individuals but also, in most instances, are expressed in the sanctioned patterns characteristic of the social structure of the society. This has been shown in our study of the structural components of societies. These express the social norms or standards. The individual functioning in and through them reacts according to these norms. Interaction with friends, enemies, partners, parents, team associates, husbands, or wives— and an infinite number of others—almost automatically causes us to recognize different rela-

tionships. Because this is true, we bring forth expected patterned responses according to the relatively stable forms of interaction that have been established in the culture of our society. It is with these reciprocal, patterned, stabilized forms of interaction that we are chiefly concerned. It is through these that societies operate.

II. THE FORMS OF SOCIAL ACTION

Interaction Takes Three Major Forms

As a result of their contacts, individuals and groups ranging from simple two-person units to complex institutional agencies may interact in three major ways: they may cooperate, they may compete, or they may engage in conflict. We shall first discuss each of these forms of interaction as if each took place in an independent way, realizing, of course, that in most social situations it does not do so.

A. COOPERATION

Cooperation Permeates All Areas of Social Life

Cooperation is the form of social action in which two or more individuals or groups work together jointly to achieve common goals. It is the type of activity upon which societies depend to maintain their stability. It is the form of interaction which makes unified social achievement possible because, in contrast to competition and conflict, it is the form of social action in which all participants benefit by attaining their goals. It recognizes that "in union there is strength." Cooley goes so far as to say that the central fact of history is the gradual enlargement of social consciousness and rational cooperation.[1]

Cooperation permeates all aspects of a social organization from the maintenance of personal friendships to the successful operation of international programs. It appears wherever social and personal ends may be advanced. Boys cooperate in games, men in business, workers in production, public officials in community controls, and so on, in an endless variety of beneficial activities that make possible an integrated social life. This striving together to achieve desired values is ever present so that, unless we consciously look about to observe it, it proceeds unnoticed. But when we stop to look, we see that the existence of roads, health and sanitation systems, postal systems, religious activities, and every other aspect of social organization is founded on mutually helpful relations among people. It occurs spontaneously in relation to most of the wants of life; it is promoted consciously where forces tend to frustrate it.

Cooperation Is Brought About by Several Circumstances

INDIVIDUAL GAIN Working together to achieve common values results first, perhaps, from the desire for individual benefits. The impossibility of solving many of our personal problems alone causes us to work with others. Our own security depends upon cooperating with others.

ALTRUISTIC MOTIVES Striving together also results from the desire to give aid. We join together voluntarily to put out a fire, to rescue persons in danger, or to take part in pleasurable associations. Many of society's organizations are founded on principles of mutual aid that promote the sharing of experience as a part of daily life. We develop a spirit of altruism that leads us to cooperate to benefit our fellows as well as ourselves.

COMMON PURPOSES Cooperation also reveals itself in the devotion to common purposes. A group of people, believing that a community needs a new library, join together to achieve it. Another segment, believing strongly that atomic bomb testing should be stopped, work together to create a public opinion that will demand its elimination.

SITUATIONAL NECESSITY Cooperation also results from necessity. It would be impossible to operate a modern factory, a large department store, a county government, or an educational system if the divisions and branches in each did not work together in interlocking units to achieve their objectives, and if individuals in the systems were not able to carry out their responsibilities. The complexity of many enterprises with their division of functions makes cooperation indispensable. Theodore Dreiser illustrated this need in a factory line operation when he pointed to the problem of the new machine operator in a production line: "The pieces of leather came from the girl at the machine to her right, and were passed on to the girl at her left. Carrie saw at once that an average speed was necessary or the work would pile up on her and all those below would be delayed." [2]

ACHIEVE LARGER GOALS Cooperation is often required for the achievement of larger values.

Sumner has called this "antagonistic cooperation":

> It consists in the combination of two persons or groups to satisfy a great common interest while minor antagonisms of interest which exist between them are suppressed. The plants and animals of the desert are rivals for what water there is, but they combine as if with an intelligent purpose to attain to a maximum of life under the conditions. . . . Madame Pommerol says of the inhabitants of Sahara that the people of the towns and the nomads are enemies by caste and race, but allies in interest. The nomads need refuge and shelter. The townspeople need messengers and transportation. Hence ties of contact, quarrels, fights, raids, vengeances, and reconciliations for the sake of common enterprises of plunder.

Antagonistic cooperation is the most productive form of combination in high civilization. It is a high action of the reason to overlook lesser antagonisms in order to work together for great interests. [3]

Cooperation Is Goal-Oriented and Conscious

Individuals and groups always work together in cooperative action to achieve some material or nonmaterial value. It is the joint performance of a task that leads to a desired end, whether the joint performance is supported voluntarily or by compulsion.

Goal orientation implies that we are actuated to operate together through a common interest in the result to be achieved. It may be working at the same task, such as solving a mathematics or chemistry problem. Or it may be doing one part in a series of operations, each of which is necessary to achieving a goal (for example, each member of a baseball team playing his position in order to have a game). Much cooperation depends upon our working together doing different coordinated tasks, that is, the labor is divided up so that each has his share. Thus, cooperation is generally on the conscious level. Those who pay taxes to support municipal services like fire protection, for example, are aware that they are cooperating with others in a desirable common goal, whether they wish to do so or not.

MAINTAINING COOPERATIVE CONSCIOUSNESS The sense of cooperative striving may be dimmed as societies grow and communities take over more activities that are performed more efficiently by specialized personnel and departments. Also, as cooperation is expressed by in-direct support, as in the payment of taxes, di-rect responsibility is eliminated. Keeping the citizenry aware of the cooperative nature of a societal enterprise is a problem as societies de-velop more and more of a secondary character.

This is also true of business cooperatives. Many cooperatives are now so large that the di-rect involvement of the members is difficult to achieve, except in the use of economic services. Their interest in emphasizing the cooperative features dies out. The problem is one of devis-ing methods of bringing the membership into more meaningful contact with the operating mechanisms, so that their own roles are recog-nized as significant. Continued awareness of social roles is essential to positive cooperation.

B. COMPETITION

Competition Also Is Universal and Continuous

DEFINITION *Competition* is that form of so-cial action in which we strive against each other for the possession or use of some limited mate-rial or nonmaterial good.

EXPLANATION Competition is no less uni-versal than cooperation, mainly because most of the desirable material and nonmaterial goods exist in limited quantity. It is just this limited existence of things in relation to the numbers striving for them that makes competition gen-eral and serves as a basis of selection. For ex-ample, the number of workers in American so-ciety who are looking for jobs at any one time now number from three to four million per-sons. This is normal unemployment. Available workers outnumber available jobs, therefore competition for work exists continually. Even air and water, usually considered to be free, now enter the competitive field. Those who operate industries, manage airlines, irrigate fields, and increase commerce compete fiercely for these two elements. Cities and states now regulate their use so that, in the competitive struggle, equitable distribution can result.

Such striving, which is an effort to outdo others who are seeking the same goals, ranges all the way from getting bread to making reli-gious converts. Upon it may rest security, sta-tus, and power. We engage in it when we think we can achieve more by struggling for some-thing than by pooling our efforts and dividing the product.

The Dominant Patterns of the Society Influence the Extent to Which Competition Is Allowed

Societies vary in the extent and manner in which competition is allowed to operate. In open-class societies, where status is commonly *achieved,* competition is given a vital role. Here prestige is accorded to persons who compete successfully. People who climb to the top in their occupations, or who gain wealth, receive considerable recognition in American society where status achievement is a major value. Our society steadfastly believes that this is possible for any person who has the capacity and will exert himself.

In those societies where status is *ascribed,* competition is allowed only between persons and groups in the same class or caste. Even within a caste there are often restrictions on competition for work, as is true in the patron system. In some societies, competition is not a significant process, especially where there is general availability of the basic necessities of life and the social organization does not depend upon personal initiative or the exercise of power over others.[4]

Competition is not open to all alike, even in societies where competition receives major em-phasis. Negroes may not compete with whites in many areas of the United States for occupa-tions, political positions, or places of residence. There may be a technical right, but practical opportunity is made impossible by customs and traditions. A society may also control compe-tition in certain areas, especially the economic, to protect what it considers vital services. Sub-sidies to airlines, tariffs for economic protec-tion, civil service regulations in government jobs, and minimum wage laws are a few ex-amples.

Competition Results from Several Motives

REASONS FOR We compete with each other for the same basic reasons that we cooperate with each other: both are actions to attain given goals. The goals in competition are gen-eralized as striving against others (1) for ma-terial objects and (2) for nonmaterial prestige. Material objects are usually scarce and com-peted for because the environment is limited or because the society has given them status value, which makes them symbols of achievement. Money, wives, animals, beads, and shells are major goals of competition in various societies.

Nonmaterial goods that have prestige value, and thus give status and power, are scarce, too, because the society makes them so. Their successful attainment carries with them recognition of superiority. Champion, captain, president, or a Phi Beta Kappa membership imparts a high prestige position in our groups and communities. The same is true of competition between groups and organizations, since recognition, status, and power are equally motivating forces among them.

VALUES OF COMPETITION Societies encourage competition to promote effort and efficiency. People seem to work hardest when they are individually rewarded for producing better quality or larger quantities than their fellows. Competition increases the level of achievement by raising the level of aspiration.[5] It makes success more desirable and failure more odious.

HARMFUL POSSIBILITIES On the other hand, competition between unequals can be harmful because it creates discouragement. Societies try to equalize competitive conditions to control the striving for goals. Miriam Van Waters believes this is true in the American school situation: "It is increasingly being recognized that competition is a poor instrument in the school room. Pressure of competition has caused untold, unproductive suffering among children, and has contrib￵￳ed to delinquency. Such suffering is unproductive because it harms the loser, and cannot make him any brighter, it injures the winner because it makes him conceited. The modern progressive school sets the child a task which uses all his ability, the exercise of which is its own reward." [6]

Competition may also be harmful if goals are trivial. Many would not agree with the following analysis by Ludwig Lewisohn, but it is a view we should consider:

> In one respect only did I fail to achieve a complete conformity. It was in a matter of games. . . . Football and baseball and basketball were all competitive—aimlessly competitive. And this struck me then, as it strikes me now, as incomprehensible and odious. As an experienced college professor I later confirmed the deliberate judgment of my boyhood: competitive, inter-school or collegiate athletics weaken the mind by assigning purely fictitious values to trivialities; they rob the best of our youths of the joy and health of the body by setting upon that joy and health something akin to a horse-jockey's outlook and a gambler's corruption.[7]

Competition is harmful also where it is allowed to destroy the energy and capacity of those competing. Here is an illustration from industry: "The peculiar bitterness of all this was that Jurgis saw so plainly the meaning of it. In the beginning he had been fresh and strong, and he had gotten a job the first day; but now he was secondhand, a damaged article so to speak, and they did not want him. They had got the best out of him—they had worn him out, with their speeding up and their carelessness, and now they had thrown him away." [8]

Competition may also lead to false promotion:

> If these were the principal causes of Coolidge prosperity, the salesman and the advertising man were at least its agents and evangels. Business had learned as never before the immense importance of it to the ultimate consumer. Unless he could be persuaded to buy and buy lavishly, the whole stream of six-cylinder cars, super-heterodynes, cigarettes, rouge compacts, and electric iceboxes would be dammed at its outlet. . . . The advertiser must plan elaborate national campaigns, consult with psychologists, and employ all the eloquence of poets to cajole, exhort, or intimidate the consumer into buying—to "break down consumer resistance." . . . The salesman must have the ardor of a zealot, must force his way into people's houses by hook or by crook, must let nothing stand between him and the consummation of his sale.[9]

Excesses in advertising have forced society to introduce controls so that unfair, fraudulent, and dishonest practices are not perpetrated on the public.

Competition Is Goal-Oriented and May Be Conscious or Unconscious

CONSCIOUS COMPETITION That competition is just as goal-oriented as cooperation is obvious from the action that expresses it. Our striving against others is for some objective. The grocery storekeepers located in the neighborhood know there is a total amount of trade available there. Each proprietor strives to get as much of it as he can, fully aware that the other grocers are doing the same thing. His focus is therefore upon the goal: to get as much of this trade as possible. His focus is not upon the other grocers with whom he is competing; rather, he tries to gain the trade by superior quality, better prices, or some other advantage.

Doctors, jewelers, bankers are usually on friendly terms with others in their work, but they put forth their best efforts to get the trade or business for themselves.

Achieving goals in some situations may mean eliminating others completely. There is only one winner in a tennis championship. Only one suitor finally gets the girl. But even here the focus is on the goal. This competition, where there is a keen personal sense of striving, is designated as *rivalry*. Competition that is so personalized that we develop a strong eagerness for it acts as an incentive to increase effort. Such rivalry is often an avenue to conflict.

UNCONSCIOUS COMPETITION Much competition occurs when those competing have little knowledge of who or where their competitors are—or even if there are any. This is not a consequence of the nature of competition but largely the result of limited communication. Farmers in the eastern belt of the cotton South were not aware that new competing areas of production were being opened in western Texas, where lower costs of production were possible. But they soon became conscious of them as the prices of cotton dropped because of the large increases in production. One of the practical aspects of acting in a competitive situation is awareness of the nature and extent of the competition. Business concerns soon face difficulties unless they keep aware of the development of new competing enterprises, new products, alternative materials, and competing advertising. The makers of woolen goods, for example, are conscious of their competition with such new materials as synthetic fibers. They try to meet it by presenting the merits of their woolen goods.

Societies Restrict the Operation of Competition

Hardly any type of competition is allowed to operate in an unrestricted manner. We often say that all is fair in love and war, yet all is not fair in most competitive situations—not even in love and war. Restrictions are imposed by rules of custom and tradition, or norms are consciously made by societies to control cheating, fraud, and force. This is the only way in which societies can act to control competing interests. Societies pass restrictions to prevent monopolies. Antitrust laws aim to prevent companies from controlling so much of the business that others cannot compete at all.

In virtually all other situations, competition is controlled at least in part. All sports have their rules. The professional's baseball bat has definite limits as to materials and length, while in basketball certain actions between players are "fouls." The rules determine fair play, and competition proceeds according to them.

There Are Many Efforts to Avoid Competition

Competition does not always operate, even when it is supposed to proceed under the "rules of the game." In many situations, there are attempts to avoid competition in order to protect gains. Business concerns operating in the same field agree to charge the same prices for similar goods, pay the same wages for similar work, or not to operate in the same geographic areas.

Workmen also seek to avoid competition. To protect gains, they make rules restricting the number of apprentices who may enter a field of work in a given time or the amount of work a person can turn out in a day.

In some situations, competition does not get a chance to operate completely because trade associations, knowing the public's consuming capacity, try to prevent too much production so that prices can be maintained. Association rules that bar advertising for clients also tend to limit competition in some professions.

C. CONFLICT

Conflict Is Social Action to Achieve Goals by Conquest

Conflict, the third form of social action, is interaction in which individuals and groups endeavor to achieve their goals by eliminating other contenders. It is also goal-oriented. But unlike cooperation and competition, it seeks to capture its goals by making ineffective the others who also seek them. It is a form of struggle like competition, but in conflict the struggle is directly between individuals and groups. If the opposition is made powerless, the goal is automatically won. Conflicts between individuals and groups range from fights between two persons with fists or weapons to wars involving millions of people and unlimited quantities of armaments. The use or threat to use such materials for destruction is aimed at eliminating or neutralizing the opposition in order to take the goal. Each party to a conflict tries to avoid being neutralized. Conquest may be achieved without the use of violence in some cases. The threat of violence may be sufficient to neutralize the opposition where the odds are greatly in favor of one of the opponents.

Conflict Is Conscious and Personal

The interaction in conflict is conscious since contenders try to achieve goals by conquest. Whether it be a fight between boys or a war between nations, each is clearly aware of the adversary. The struggle is, or tends to be, personal since each is trying to overcome and to avoid being overcome. Feelings are involved also, for such activity generates anger and fear since it is an attempt to hurt or frustrate. Hostility prevails between the foes. When the conflict is between numbers of people who are fighting for their community, clan, or their nation, the interaction may be extreme and pitiless, as many wars have illustrated. The individual enemy personifies the whole opposition. There can be no mercy for him since his opposition is threatening to destroy the whole system with which we identify and which gives us our position and security. Whether the conflict is directly personal or vicarious, it is the form of social interaction in which feelings play a major role. The goals for which conflict began may be forgotten as the conflict proceeds, our feelings intensify, and the effort to destroy increases.

Conflict Is Not Necessarily Overt Violence Between Persons

Conquest is attempted in many ways other than by the use of force. A physical and psychological sabotage of programs, the so-called war of nerves, the use of deceit on the ground that the goal justifies the means, secret agents who undermine morale—all are forms of strategy that today's conflicts involve.

Conflicts Are the Result of the Clash of Opposing Interests That Are Socially Created

CONFLICT NOT INHERENT It used to be assumed that we sought to achieve goals by conquest because men inherited a fighting instinct. No such inherent tendency is now recognized by students of man. This easy explanation may therefore be summarily dismissed.

DIFFERENCES IN INTERESTS Individuals and groups operate in relation to their interests. They live in societies where these do not remain fixed. The aspirations of men and societies often change as conditions change. The desire to retain a situation or to change it sets up circum-stances that create opposing interests that incite conflict. Cattlemen and farmers in the American West often fought over the attempt to fence the land. Here a changing social situation caused the paths of incompatible interests to cross. Collisions resulted. The movement of populations in response to increasing need for productive lands has often made people clash in trying to preserve their different interests. The residents oppose the "invaders," so conflict ensues until defeat, victory, or an accommodation between them is achieved.

VALUE OF GOALS The seriousness, or extent, of conflicts will depend chiefly upon the value the contending parties place upon their goal. Some conflicts have lasted many years because of the importance placed on the goal or because the struggle has inflicted damage or injured feelings that cannot be overlooked or assuaged. Feuds are of this nature. Direct damage and injured feelings that must be avenged cause these conflicts to endure. The feud between the house of Capulet and the house of Montague, made famous in *Romeo and Juliet,* had lasted from ancient times and was settled finally only by the death of the two lovers. Hatred had been engendered, and the grudge endured. It is this emotional character that often makes conflicts last far beyond the time when the original battle was joined. The individuals involved are representatives of their group and are committed to fight. The conflict is a group conflict, not a personal one, which demands that the fight continue. Being of an intermittent nature, it breaks out anew when some incident acts as a trigger. Most conflicts continue in this fashion unless one of the opponents is completely eliminated or a satisfactory settlement is achieved. Secondary factors may perpetuate the conflict, although the attainment of some goal has been the original motive.

Conflict Tends to Increase the Solidarity Within the Contending Parties

MORALE It is almost axiomatic that societies or groups within them must develop strong cohesion when they seek to gain goals by conquest. The fact that their opponents are intent upon conquest from which they would suffer loss means that, from a personal and societal point of view, solidarity is essential. Creating a strong morale that consolidates the forces for the struggle is therefore a major aspect of conflict pattern-building. It is relatively easy to create such morale because the struggle involves a contest with the outcome usually in doubt. Uncertainty, fear, and anger heighten feeling and purpose. Contentions within the groups are subordinated to the cooperation necessary for realizing the groups' objective of overpowering the opposition.

Morale Created by Trickery Sometimes, to unify a society, conflicts will be created with outsiders who are made to appear as enemies. A significant illustration of this is the Franco-German war of 1870–1871. Bismarck, the Chancellor of Germany, was bent on consolidating the German states. After making sure his armies were ready for war, he gave a dispatch, which he had received from King William of Prussia, to the German press in such a form that it appeared to the people of the German states that their king had been insulted by the French ambassador. He then re-edited the dispatch and sent it to the French press in a form to make it appear that the French ambassador had been insulted by the German emperor. The report had the effect in France, to use Bismarck's own words, "of a red rag upon the Gallic bull." France, in immediately declaring war, was depicted as the aggressor. The German states responded with complete cooperation, and France was quickly overcome. But more important to Bismarck was the immediate union of the German states and the quick proclamation of the German Empire. Bismarck's stratagem had worked.

Societies Seek to Prevent Internal Conflicts

Conflict can be dysfunctional in a society since it seeks its goals by conquest. Societies depend in general upon cooperation and controlled competition to give them ordered accomplishment. Conflict offers one way of maintaining order when adequate means of adjusting contending interests are absent. The threat of conflict was often the only means of protecting interests in early pioneering days.

LAW AS REGULATOR Societies, however, try to prevent damaging conflicts by developing social codes that anticipate their occurrence. Law and its associated agencies are a society's chief means of preventing the general use of conflict to solve problems. Regulatory rules are set up in areas where conflict is likely to arise and serve to prevent conflict by defining and enforcing the expectations of the society in the given situations. Laws defining property and personal rights state what the society requires.

As a result, many possible conflicts never arise.

WAR AS INTERGROUP CONFLICT War, the most violent form of intergroup conflict, is probably as old as human society. It is such an immense subject for sociological discussion that no brief statement is adequate. We will only note the five main types of armed conflict found in historical and prehistorical societies: the ritualistic or ceremonial wars of certain primitive societies,[10] religious wars, wars of conquest, civil wars between divisions of a state, and international wars common to recent times.

Modern warfare is the ultimate form of human conflict. It has become supernational in scope and completely lethal in consequence. That mankind must organize effectively to control it or face extinction is the paramount platitude of human history.

III. DIAGRAMMATIC COMPARISON OF THE FORMS OF ACTION

There Are Three Common Components in Each Form of Social Action

Social actions, whether they are cooperative, competitive, or conflictive, have three common components: values toward which actions are oriented, human relationship structures oriented to each other in some degree for the achievement of these values, and an actional pattern orienting the human relationship structures to the values and to each other.

The important difference in each action form is the way the action pattern is oriented to the attainment of the values and to the human relationship structures designed to achieve the goals. The human relationship structures in cooperative action, whether they be groups, organizations, institutional agencies, or others, are positively oriented to each other so that they act together through common means to attain the desired goals or values. They work together with positive interaction focusing upon goal attainment (Fig. 4A).

Each human relationship structure in competition focuses positively upon achieving its values or goals. Relationships between the structures are indirect and negative. In this form of action, while each competitor may be aware of others also seeking the goal, direct interaction between them may be entirely absent (Fig. 4B).

Interrelationships in conflict involve direct and negative interaction between each contend-

A. Cooperation

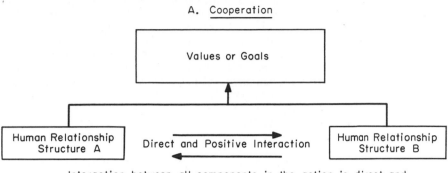

Interaction between all components in the action is direct and positive.

B. Competition

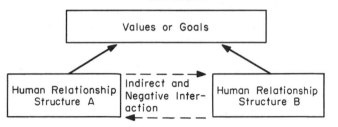

Interaction between human relationship structures is indirect and negative; action toward goals is positive.

C. Conflict

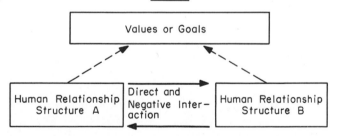

Interaction between the human relationship structures is direct and negative. Toward the goals it is reduced, since eliminating the opposing human relationship structure assures the goals.

Broken lines indicate goals temporarily secondary.

Fig. 4. Forms of Interaction

ing human relationship structure. The focus on goal attainment is secondary since it will be achieved automatically if the opposition is eliminated (Fig. 4C).

Thus, the means employed by human relationship structures to achieve their desired values or goals differ in each form of social action. It is the means employed to achieve values that makes them different types of action.

IV. INTERRELATIONS BETWEEN THESE FORMS

The Forms of Social Action Are Usually Interrelated

Our treatment of the three forms of social action up to this point might leave the impression that each operates without any relationship to the other. Actually, in most situations they are closely intertwined and related to each other in many ways. For example, two competing football teams cooperate to set up and play the game for their pleasure and that of an audience. Within each team, there is cooperation between players in the execution of the plays. There is competition between players for a place on the team. Conflict may occur between the players when tempers flare in the intense competition of the game. This simple situation is characteristic of practically all social interaction for few social situations occur in "the pure" form of cooperation, competition, or conflict alone. Competing business enterprises cooperate to expand the total business in their area. Competing organizations group together to advance a cause. Conflicts almost always involve cooperation. War is not simply the action of some individuals to destroy other individuals; it entails the cooperative action of individuals and groups, many of whom are competing with each other in the process, to carry on the conflict. Intergroup competitions or conflicts always involve intragroup cooperation.

DOMINANCE OF AN ACTION FORM A social situation may be dominated more by competition than by cooperation, or by conflict than by competition. As we have noted, however, most social situations involve more than one of these action forms. In a United Fund drive, competition may predominate among teams organized to see which can raise the largest amount of money in a cooperative effort to support social agencies. In one sense, competition is dominant; in another—the joint effort to raise funds—cooperation is dominant.

One Form of Social Action May Grow into Another

Competitive interactions may easily pass over into conflict when persons or groups struggle to appropriate an undue share of a value or goal. Here the objectives may be forgotten, and direct action on the competitor is taken to eliminate him. Competition between laboring groups for jobs has often led to conflict, where one is willing to accept conditions the others reject and compromise is not acceptable.

Competition may become cooperation where competitors discover that pooling their resources and services could result in a greater total return than each can obtain separately. Many business consolidations result from such a discovery.

It is often difficult to distinguish between social actions in a society, especially between competition and conflict, when rivalries are intense. Many times, this is true of labor-management relationships. Collective bargaining, which is a competitive device used by labor for bettering its work conditions, may involve the use of the strike as one of its potent weapons. Thus, it often cannot be distinguished from conflict. The strike, a form of action to force management's acquiescence, often degenerates into acts of violence when its objective is not achieved.

One Form of Action Is No More Fundamental to Societal Functioning than Another

Each society makes use of all three forms of social action. It may emphasize that one form is more desirable than another. It may exert controls to limit the free operation of competition and conflict. Yet, all these are used in the operation of a society and in relations between societies. Social philosophers have sometimes argued that one or the other form is the most fundamental. It has often been stressed that in Western societies competition and conflict are the basic forms of social action. The Darwinian theory of struggle for survival in the world of nature, and the *laissez-faire* doctrine in economics that argues that free competition provides the best productivity, are ideas that dominated the nineteenth century. They became the major viewpoints in interpreting societal actions.

Reactions to this view insist that mutual aid is as significant to the survival of all forms of life, and especially human life, as is competition or conflict. Now it is generally recognized that, depending upon the situation, all three forms operate in varying balance.

V. ACCOMMODATION: THE ADJUSTMENT OF SOCIAL ACTIONS

Social Interactions Require Adjustment

Accommodation is the achievement of adjustment between people that permits harmonious acting together in social situations. It is the termination of competing or conflicting relations between individuals, groups, and other human relationship structures. It establishes a state of agreement so that people may work together, even though certain differences may separate them.

Accommodation is viewed by some sociologists as a process. Here we view it as the result of social action or the operational processes. As groups and individuals interact with each other by cooperating, by competing, or being in conflict, they may arrive at adjustments so that further interaction is in concord. This adjustment is an end product, a result where further action together can proceed in an orderly manner. Thus, while it properly may be conceived of as a process, it can also be viewed as a result that makes further positive social action possible.

The prevailing condition in modern societies is one of accommodation. Individuals and groups adjust to each other and to the requirements of their society so effectively that they can continue to operate in relation to each other without serious rivalries. Samuel Butler said: "All our lives long, every day and every hour, we are engaged in the process of accommodating our changed and unchanged selves to changed and unchanged surroundings; living, in fact, is nothing else than this process of accommodation; when we fail in it a little we are stupid, when we fail flagrantly we are mad; when we suspend it temporarily we sleep, when we give up the attempt altogether, we die." [11]

Accommodation Is Achieved in a Number of Ways

COMPROMISE   There is a number of readily recognized relationship forms that are used by societies to achieve adjustment and to make effective working together possible. Compromise is one of the most useful. In a *compromise*, each contending party agrees to make concessions that allow them to reach agreement. This mutual conceding until all parties are satisfied or reconciled is a common procedure in contentious situations. The exchange of goods practically always involves compromise. Persons buy and sell to each other when they agree on a price. An interesting example of this is the "bargaining" between buyers and sellers in some oriental countries where one-price systems do not exist. Compromises in labor-management disputes prevent the more serious struggles of strikes and lockouts.

The foundations for destructive actions are laid when contending parties are unwilling to make concessions. This is one of the serious difficulties when different ideologies or philosophies of life are in conflict. Some are founded on principles that cannot allow compromise, lest they be completely destroyed. This is the danger in all dogmas and a reason why resulting struggles about them are so severe. The proponents believe they must either conquer or die.

CONVERSION   Accommodation is also achieved by *conversion*. Here one of the interacting parties accepts the views or actions of the others as its own. This is the form of accommodation usually related to religious beliefs. Indeed, religious groups often deliberately propagate their beliefs so that others will see them as the only true beliefs and become followers. Maurice Hindus describes this form of accommodation as it took place with a Russian Orthodox believer. (See Box 32.)

The permanence of such accommodation

BOX 32

He had been Orthodox, and, like all the Orthodox, he had since the Revolution been weakening in his faith. Once at a fair two men got drunk and started fighting, and one cracked an empty bottle over the other's head, knocking him unconscious, so that the police came and took him away to the hospital. A crowd gathered and the people began talking about the fight, an elderly woman arguing that if these men had had God in their hearts they would never have fought, for they would not have touched liquor. . . . She explained that she was a Baptist and talked about her faith. . . . Orthodox people just did things without knowing why they did them; but Baptists were different. They reasoned about everything. Well, this woman set him off thinking with the result that, some time later, he himself became a convert to the Baptist faith, and now he knew that real religion meant cleanliness, kindness to all living things, simple worship anywhere, in a house, in the open field, or even in a barn, industry, humility, abstaining from resistance and violence, no wars, no bloodshed, and the brotherhood of all people and all classes the world over. That was real religion.[12]

often depends upon the convert's opportunity to associate with those who hold the new beliefs he has accepted. A problem of converts in the mission fields is one of holding to their new views in the midst of their native community life. The building of converted religious groups in differing cultural settings has often required separating them from their native culture and surrounding them with a social milieu organized about their new beliefs.

TOLERANCE *Tolerance* may effect accommodation where compromise and conversion do not. In this circumstance, the contending parties decide to bear with each other, but the basic issue is not eliminated. Each party holds to its position and agrees "to live and let live." Less-

ing, the German author, in his drama, *Nathan the Wise*, makes a strong plea for accommodation through tolerance as the result of a bitter theological conflict in which he had engaged. He calls for tolerance in such controversies since noble character belongs to no particular creed, but to all creeds, as set forth in the parable of the wonderful ring. (See Box 33.)

ARBITRATION The adjustment of social interactions is sometimes accomplished by *arbitration*. Here the contending parties submit their problem to third parties who act as supposedly neutral mediators. They judge their problem on the merits of the case, bringing the contending parties to a point where they deliberate over differences with some objectivity. One of the

---

BOX 33

[Saladin, the Sultan and Mohammedan, addressing Nathan, the wise Jew, says:]

"Since so great your wisdom,
"I pray you tell me what belief, what law
"Has most commended itself to you."

[Nathan then tells him the story of the ancient man who owned a priceless ring with secret power of giving favor to the one who wore it. He gave it to his best loved son enjoining him to pass it on to his best loved son. But the son had three sons, all of whom he loved equally. To solve the dilemma of which son to give the ring, he has two additional identical rings made.]

And e'en the father cannot tell his own.
Relieved and joyful, summons he his sons,
Each by himself; to each one by himself
He gives his blessing, and his ring—and dies. . . .
The father was scarcely dead, when each brings forth his ring,
And claims the headship. Questioning ensues,
Strife, and appeal to law; but all in vain.
The genuine ring was not to be distinguished;—
As undistinguishable as with us
The true religion.

[The judge reveals what happened and enjoins tolerance upon each of the three sons.]

"Go, therefore," said the judge, "unless my counsel
"You'd have in place of sentence. It were this:
"Accept the case exactly as it stands,
"Had each his ring directly from his father,
"Let each believe his own is genuine. . . .
   "Let each one
"To his unbought, impartial love aspire;—
"Let gentleness, a hearty love of peace,
"Beneficence, and perfect trust in God,
"Come to its help." [13]

roles an international organization, such as the United Nations, performs is that of mediation. It often prevents serious consequences by getting contending nations to arbitrate before conflict takes place.

TRUCE In some conflict and competitive situations, suspension of relations is agreed upon for a period of time. A truce is usually made to allow time for the consideration of proposals for settling issues. It does not indicate that the issues are settled; it only allows a period of time to probe the possibilities of settlement. Such a period is known in warfare as an armistice. Both sides agree to cease their fighting to discuss terms of peace. It therefore is only a temporary accommodation for paving the way to a permanent one.

SUBORDINATION Accommodation also serves to structure the relationship of victor to vanquished as the outcome of conflict. An unequal status between contending groups usually means submission to a subordinate position for the conquered party.

One of the keenest forms of struggle among societies today arises from the striving of colonial peoples to extricate themselves from their subordinate position in a political empire. England, France, and the Netherlands have attempted to work out relationships with their colonies so that the latter will remain in their commonwealths. The colonies usually demand complete independence. In some instances, accommodations are worked out which keep the colonial unit within the empire on a basis of equality and independence. In others, the break is complete, and the formerly subjugated areas become full-fledged independent powers.

Accommodation by subordination is effective under two conditions. One occurs when the dominant party is so strong that the subordinate party is forced to accept. This is seldom a final or satisfactory accommodation for the stronger party must be constantly ready to use force should rebellion occur. If the condition persists long enough and the status gives substitute satisfactions, the drives to regain a former position may lose their force.

Subordination is also successful where these relationships are a part of the sanctioned social heritage of a society. In military relationships, the recognition of subordination, which extends from the highest ranking officers down to the private soldier, is part of the sanctioned pattern through which this system operates. There is constant striving in military organization to change one's rank so as to obtain the benefits of the higher positions.

Rigid subordination systems, which stratify whole populations and assign individuals to a particular social position from which they cannot escape, have developed in some societies. The most extreme example is the Hindu caste system. Here individuals not only learn to know their place, their place is a predetermined one that has been fixed by the society. It is governed by rigid conventions that make movement from one level to another almost impossible. Even in democratic societies, relatively rigid subordination systems may exist. The relations between the commoners and the aristocrats in English society, between white landowners and "the poor whites" in some American states, and between our white and Negro citizens are illustrations.

A major concern of the dominant parties in a subordination system is to induce those in the subordinate status to accept such a position without resentment so that the favored groups may enjoy the fruits of their superior position without jeopardy. Often this means depriving the subordinates of opportunities that might bring them to question the relationship. Educational opportunity, for example, is often withheld from subordinates, a practice rationalized on the grounds that the subordinates are biologically inferior and that endeavors to educate them would be futile. And when a system of subordination is strongly supported by the belief that it is ordained by Divine will, it becomes almost impossible to change.

Accommodation Is a Requisite Condition for Integrated Social Action

Effective accommodation allows parties to act together without discord so that they can move toward the achievement of their goals with a minimum of interference from each other.

When the interacting units in a social order reach accommodation through compromise, toleration, arbitration, and subordination, they can become related to each other in harmonious ways. This is the goal toward which interrelationships strive, although an harmonious state is probably never completely achieved at any time within a society or between societies. But it is the condition that must generally exist to allow social structures to operate. The question as to whether the accommodations are the ultimately desirable ones is to be decided on ethical grounds. It often happens that the accommodations achieved are considered unfair or that they have been nullified by changes in the conditions under which they were established. Because this leads to further contentions, most accommodations are probably never final. Societal relationships are ever changing, requiring new accommodations continuously.

VI. ASSIMILATION: THE FUSING PROCESS

Assimilation Implies the Complete Merging of Divergent Cultural Groupings Within a Society

Successful accommodation sets the stage for an additional consequence of human interactions, namely *assimilation*. This implies the complete merging and fusion of two or more bodies into a single common body, a process analogous to digestion, in which we say that food is "assimilated." Walter de la Mare stated it succinctly in a four-line ditty:

> It's a very odd thing
> As odd as can be
> That whatever Miss T eats
> Turns into Miss T.

Assimilation in social relationships means that the cultural differences between divergent groupings of people disappear. Thus, they come to feel, think, and act similarly as they absorb new common traditions, attitudes, and loyalties and consequently take on a new cultural identity. We see the process operating among ethnic groups which enter a society with their own society's culture. The processes that lead to accommodation develop favorable attitudes toward the host group. The results are an acceptance of the common goals, common attitudes, and common loyalties that make the culture of the host society their own.

Complete Assimilation Is Difficult to Achieve

The complete union of divergent cultural groups does not take place until such distinguishing characteristics as race and nationality are eliminated. Divergent groups can accommodate to each other so that they function in the main through the common cultural life. But the elimination of social distance takes place exceedingly slowly because an entering group may wish to remain separate or a receiving group may not wish to share its common traditions and attitudes. For example, the Jewish people in most societies are able to carry on their distinct way of life, which does not promote their assimilation. Many of those who are assimilated do not favor the idea of a separate Jewish culture within the larger culture. But there are those, however, who maintain accommodative relations to the non-Jewish society without becoming assimilated within it.

Accommodation without assimilation is also possible under other circumstances. Coughlin has given us the example of the Chinese in Bangkok, Thailand. These immigrants have established themselves in a privileged economic and social situation, by assuming the role of commercial go-betweens who funnel imported consumption goods to the people through their wholesale and retail outlets. The local populations exhibit little aptitude for these commercial activities. The Chinese are able to avoid assimilation because of their favorable economic position, their own desire to retain their values, and their nonacceptance by their host society.[14]

Many Nationalities Are Assimilated into Other Cultures, However

A striking example of the process is the way in which the many nationalities have been assimilated into American society. This has occurred within a relatively short time because of two circumstances. One is the extent to which amalgamation between these nationalities has taken place. The other has been the existence of free public education throughout this land.

AMALGAMATION   The biological process of mixing different peoples, usually ethnic and national groupings, by intermating is referred to as *amalgamation*. In American society, the kindred stocks that settled this land intermarried with great abandon, thus crossing their varying biological characteristics. Carl Carmer's description of this for one community could be repeated scores and scores of times in reference to other nationalities: "Frenchmen and Germans and Indians and Americans, all the people who remained on the site of the colony, gradually merged into the people who now live in the typical little Southern town. Aside from the Gallic names of a few families there is nothing about the inhabitants to recall the character of their ancestors."[15] At the same time, these migrants entered the various occupations developed in the land, eagerly sought education, discarded their Old World traits, and took on American ways—all in order to become incorporated into the new social system. This amalgamation, which had the support of the society's mores and which thoroughly mixed the various nationality stocks, served to speed up assimilation, especially of the second and subsequent generations until, in many areas, all traces of the older cultures have disappeared.

PUBLIC EDUCATION Public schools have played a powerful role in this assimilative process. The children of immigrants always want to become Americanized. This desire has often been difficult to fulfill because of the unwillingness of many Americans to accept them and to share their way of life on a basis of equality. Also, the process has often been impeded by the parents who wished their offspring to follow the ways of the Old World. But, from the beginning, public schools threw all classes together, stressed equality of opportunity, and operated on a primary, face-to-face basis. This hastened assimilation and helped to mold the oncoming generation into the common life of the new country.

This has not been a forced process. The culture was absorbed quietly by those exposed, both consciously and unconsciously, and appropriated as the heritage of all. Assimilation takes time because it involves the slow process of replacing once vital values by other values that must become just as vital.

Cultural history abounds in illustrations of migrating populations which have been assimilated by other societies. The early Jewish immigrants into China are an interesting example. They amalgamated with the Chinese population and became Chinese in features, language, dress, and customs. Their Chinese roots now run back so far that little that is Jewish mark them. They are completely absorbed by this culture. The story is told of the American Jew who was travelling in China. On one occasion, he attended the services of a synagogue in the city he happened to be visiting. As he departed, the Chinese rabbi asked him: "You Jewee?" The visitor replied "Yes." At that, the rabbi exclaimed, "That's funny, you no lookee Jewee!"

Assimilation Has Two-Way Consequences

The common opinion is that when migrating people move into a society and are assimilated they take on the culture of the new situation and give up their own. This is only part of the interplay. Those who move into the society also contribute, as well as receive, cultural materials. The movement of Middle-East Mohammedans into the Far East led them to accept much of the culture of the areas they invaded. On the other hand, they have spread their religion into these areas until many regions have given up their native religious systems for the new one. Many people now follow the religion of the invaders, just as invading Greek culture came to dominate the eastern Mediterranean area about the time of Christ. Greek philosophy was so potent that it influenced profoundly the point of view of early Christianity and became a blending of the two. The outcome of assimilation may actually be a fusion of two or more cultures into a new one that has a distinctiveness of its own.

We have indicated that crossbreeding and public education are important factors in promoting the assimilation of different cultural groups within a society. Wherever toleration makes opportunities available for economic, educational, and social advance, conditions are good for the rapid assimilation of newcomers. This acceptance makes possible intimate contact with the receiving culture. It also overcomes forced social isolation and eliminates the superior attitudes of contempt for the newcomers which, in turn, could create social barriers that make accommodation difficult.

References

1. Cooley, C. H., *Social Organization* (New York, Charles Scribner's Sons, 1920), p. 113.
2. Dreiser, Theodore, *Sister Carrie* (Cleveland, World Publishing Company, 1954), p. 40. Reprinted by permission.
3. Sumner, W. G., *Folkways* (Boston, Ginn and Company, 1906), p. 18.
4. Mead, Margaret, *Cooperation and Competition Among Primitive Peoples* (New York, McGraw-Hill Book Co., Inc., 1937).
5. May, M. A., and Doob, L. U., *Competition and Cooperation* (New York, Social Science Research Council, 1937), Bulletin 25, pp. 88 ff.
6. VanWaters, Miriam, *Youth in Conflict* (New York, Republic Publishing Company, 1925), p. 104.
7. Lewisohn, Ludwig, *Upstream* (New York, Boni and Liveright, 1922), pp. 74–75.

8. Sinclair, Upton, *The Jungle* (New York, Viking Press, 1950), p. 124.

9. Allen, F. L., *Only Yesterday* (New York, Harper and Brothers, 1931), pp. 168 and 169.

10. See, for example, Matthiessen, Peter, "The Death of Weake," *Harper's Magazine*, 253 (October, 1962), No. 1349, pp. 53–60.

11. Butler, Samuel, *The Way of All Flesh* (New York, E. P. Dutton and Co., 1961), p. 343. From Everyman's Library.

12. Hindus, Maurice, *Red Bread* (New York, Jonathan Cape & Harrison Smith, 1931), pp. 162–163.

13. Lessing, G. E., *Nathan the Wise* (New York, Holt and Company, Inc., 1888), pp. 110–118.

14. Coughlin, P. J., "The Chinese in Bangkok: A Commercial-Oriented Minority," *American Sociological Review*, 20 (June, 1955), pp. 311–316.

15. Carmer, Carl, *Stars Fell on Alabama* (New York, Farrar and Rinehart, 1934), pp. 110–111.

Questions for Study and Discussion

1. Define social action and describe a structural form in terms of its social actions.

2. What is meant by saying that "the basic actions in a society are those of 'inter' action"?

3. Define cooperation, conflict, competition. Give a specific illustration of each from a situation of which you were a part.

4. Discuss the positive and negative consequences of war as a form of social conflict.

5. Give some concrete illustrations where conflict, competition, and cooperation are all involved in an interactional situation.

6. Give some concrete illustrations where one form of social action grew into another.

7. Discuss several chief methods by which accommodations are accomplished.

8. Illustrate the failure of accommodations and the renewal of conflict and competition.

9. Give an illustration of the assimilation of some European nationality grouping that you have had contact with or have read about.

10. Contrast the assimilation of the Negro into American society with that of the American Indian. Are they being assimilated or just accommodated? What is the difference in these concepts?

11. There are many organizations like the Sons of Italy in American society. Do you think such organizations help or hinder assimilation?

Suggested Topics for Reports

1. Analyze an instance of competition in a manner that illustrates the appropriate part of Figure 4. Do the same for conflict and cooperation.

2. Survey the relations between your college or university with others to determine the various ways in which they compete, conflict, and cooperate with each other.

3. Examine the organization and operation of the United Nations from the point of view of its accommodative and cooperative functions.

4. Make a comparative study of the assimilation of a northern European and a southern European nationality group in American society. What factors have made for differences in their experience?

5. Make a report on one of the following organizations: National Conference of Christians and Jews, National Association for the Advancement of Colored People, the Anti-Defamation League.

Supplementary Reading

Cooley, Charles H., *Social Process*. New York: Charles Scribner's Sons, 1918.

Eubank, Earl E., *The Concepts of Sociology*. Boston: D. C. Heath and Company, 1931.

Heron, Alexander, *Why Men Work*. Stanford, Calif.: Stanford University Press, 1948.

Keller, Albert G., *Societal Evolution*. New York: The Macmillan Company, 1915.

Kropotkin, Peter, *Mutual Aid*. New York: Alfred A. Knopf, 1909.

Lewin, Kurt, *Resolving Social Conflicts*. New York: Harper and Brothers, 1948.

May, Mark A., and Doob, Leonard U., *Competition and Cooperation*. New York: Social Science Research Council, 1937.

Mead, Margaret (ed.), *Cooperation and Competition Among Primitive People*. New York: Social Science Research Council, 1937.

Nelson, Lowry, *Rural Cuba*. Minneapolis, Minn.: University of Minnesota, 1951.

Park, Robert E., and Burgess, Ernest W., *Introduction to the Science of Sociology*. Chicago: University of Chicago Press, 1921.

Ross, Ellsworth A., *Principles of Sociology*. New York: The Century Company, 1930.

Schermerhorn, Richard A., *These Our People: Minorities in American Culture*. Boston: D. C. Heath and Company, 1949.

Znaniecki, Florian, *Social Actions*. New York: Rinehart and Company, 1936.

20

SOCIAL ACTION AND BIOLOGICAL DIFFERENCES

D*IFFERENCES between people made socially significant by a society must be accommodated to make social interaction functionally effective. Socially significant differences arise out of two types of variation among men: biological and cultural. The chief biological variations are age, sex, individual differences, and race.*

I. BACKGROUNDS

Socially Significant Differences Must Be Accommodated to Make Interaction Functionally Effective

Our previous chapter on social action stressed the idea that the fundamental form of social action is "inter" action. It expresses itself in cooperation, competition, and conflict. Integrated social action can take place when, by compromise, conversion, arbitration, toleration, or subordination, individuals, groups, organizations, and other structural units accommodate themselves to each other.

Our next two chapters will show how differences among the individuals who compose the various structural forms in societies are given social significance. These socially significant differences are conditioning factors in actions that take place in a society. There must be, therefore, accommodation on the basis of these social differences in order that these dissimilar parts of a society may function together effectively.

Socially Significant Differences Arise Because of Two Types of Differences in People: Biological and Cultural

Differences within the population which give rise to socially significant differences are related to inherited biological traits and to socially acquired characteristics. Differences in age, sex, mental capacity, and race are the chief bio-

logical determinants of social differences. Differences in occupation, education, wealth, cultural traits, such as language, religion, and nationality, and other socially produced characteristics form the other basis for differentiations. A process of sorting and selection goes on that places individuals and groups in their different social positions when societies have given such differences social importance. These carry with them defined statuses and roles and create distinctive functions that are applicable to them. Groups within each society, therefore, are differentiated from each other because of the roles they perform in relation to their own aims and to those of their society. They become integrated with each other because the statuses, roles, and functions assigned are correlated with the purposes of the society.

Societies Determine What Differences Have Social Significance

It is important that we understand that these original differences are not significant until the society makes them so. There are no biological characteristics or social traits that possess a predetermined social meaning; rather, a given society will determine what particular qualities it will recognize. This imputation of meaning varies from society to society and within the same society from time to time. Possession of wealth is given a strong differentiating power in some societies, but in others it is of little significance. In some societies, birth order is an important basis for differentiation, as in China and Japan where the oldest male is given certain specific responsibilities and privileges. In the United States, it is of little significance in these respects. The differences that exist between societies are, therefore, in part, the results of the differentiating factors stressed within each. The factors which are stressed arise out of the interrelationships of cooperation, competition, and conflict. The end result is the distribution of functions and ranks or roles and statuses that make it possible for a society to operate as a unified whole. Our recognition of those differences that have social meaning, therefore, is important to our understanding of the way societies are organized and operate.

Societies Are Increasingly Differentiated as Their Cultures Expand

In primitive societies, relationships are predominantly primary, face-to-face, and intimate. The chief unifying force is kinship. Members of these groups share common rights and obligations on an undifferentiated basis. The geographical areas are usually small, and economic sustenance is obtained by common action so that constant contacts enforce the solidarity of the society. The bases for differentiation increase as societies develop new commercial and industrial methods. As specialization and the division of labor grow, as new occupations develop and occupational organizations come into existence, as communication broadens and contacts extend, and as secondary associations become more dominant, the differentiating circumstances increase.

This increasing expansion of cultures leads to the formation of new groupings and becomes the foundation for a widening process of differentiation. Societies develop so many diverse tasks as they change that they must have systems of assigning positions to them to prevent disorder, to take advantage of the division of labor, and to direct the social organization so that it operates as a unit. New differentiations, as they occur, must also be embodied in the structure of the society so that they function according to the societal norms. The differentiated parts of a society become distinguishable from each other because they perform different functions and are ascribed ranks and roles in relation to the society's other parts. This process of developing socially significant differentiations is a universal one, though its forms vary from society to society. The student may discover some of the implications of this process if he will compare the positions of old-time country doctors and modern space engineers.

Different Social Statuses and Roles Result from Socially Significant Differences

The chief consequence of the establishment of socially significant differences in any society is the assignment within it of different statuses and roles to the persons or groupings of persons possessing them. We have already pointed out that a status is a position assigned by a society to the person on the basis of a socially significant difference. The persons or groupings occupying the differentiated positions have the status. The reader will recall that each status carries with it obligations and rights, duties and privileges. Since in the social system, the duties and obligations that statuses possess are carried out by roles that people play, these roles are interwoven with statuses. They are the active expressions of statuses.

Statuses Can Be Acquired in Some Societies; This Is a Strong Motivator

Statuses are part of a fixed system of social heritage in some societies because those people are established in a specific position, usually from birth. The social order usually makes it impossible or difficult for them to change their position.

The channels for movement up or down the status ladder are open in other societies on the principle of equal rights and opportunities for all. The individual may use his ability to achieve the status to which he aspires. Thus, competition is introduced between aspiring persons and becomes a major factor in obtaining efficiency. Aspiring individuals perform the roles of their present statuses as satisfactorily as their ability allows so as to deserve promotion, while those already occupying desired positions use their abilities in such a way as to retain or improve their high positions. Competition is not between the statuses, but between individuals aspiring to obtain them. Pitching on a college baseball team does not compete with playing first base. Each position has a definite status and role on the team, but individuals may compete to become the pitcher, rather than the first baseman, because they may think this position carries greater prestige with it. The governorship of a state does not compete with the Presidency of the United States. However, one may aspire to a governorship to help prove his fitness for the higher status.

II. BIOLOGICAL FACTORS IN DIFFERENTIATION

A. AGE

Age-Grading Establishes Our Relationship to Society

Differences in age, sex, mental capacity, and race are biological characteristics that are given social significance by different societies. They carry with them different statuses and roles. Age differences are among the generally recognized biological differences on which statuses and roles are assigned. The classification of individuals by age is usually not made by specific years but by periods of years.

Age by years among primitive tribes is often not known. Puberty or the physiological transition from childhood to manhood and womenhood commonly forms their chief line of demarcation. Later, tribal rituals and ceremonies advance individuals to adulthood with its statuses and roles. The specific number of age classes may vary with tribes. Each age class has its distinctive rights and duties. Age-grading in primitive societies is significant in that it establishes the individual's relationship to his whole society. It thus determines his participation in a specific part of the culture by conferring on him the statuses and roles that are assigned to this age division.[1]

Age differences also determine many of our relationships to the larger system in modern societies. Attainment of a specific age is necessary to enjoy the privileges of attending school, voting, marrying, holding certain public positions, and many legal rights and responsibilities.

Age periods are clearly differentiated. Those commonly distinguished are childhood, adolescence, adulthood, and old age. Statuses and roles for these periods are definite, although the lines of demarcation between the periods are variable, particularly as they apply to specific individuals.

CHILDHOOD This period usually extends from birth to twelve or fourteen years af age, the time when the physiological capacity to reproduce appears. It is often subdivided into infancy and late childhood, with infancy extending to six or seven years of age. It is a period of complete dependence, during which responsibility for maintenance rests wholly with others, especially other family members. The infant performs an unassigned latent role, namely, that of solidifying the family by motivating its purposes and giving it happiness, thus making it a more efficient institution of the social order. The infant has little other status in the society except as a future responsible citizen.

Late childhood is still one of dependency but with rights uniquely its own. Aside from attending school and beginning the process of conditioning to responsibility, childhood is primarily playtime. Treatment of the sexes is much alike in early childhood, although the process of directing each sex toward its appropriate role is stressed. Conformity to adult patterns is initiated but not enforced. However, questioning and expression of opinions are prerogatives of the child around which the activities of the family often center. "There seem to be broad tendencies toward permissive discipline in certain respects and toward an idealization of childhood," as Williams[2] put it for American society.

The American child has not always enjoyed this favored position. Our Puritan forefathers brought with them the relatively severe authoritarianism of their European partriarchal systems. They looked at children as sinful creatures in need of strict discipline. They were to be formed into proper adults as quickly as possible. Play was sinful; work was good.

Attitudes have changed through time, however. Children are now not only the concern of the family but of the society. There is little question about the primacy the child enjoys today. Ideally, he is given a status enabling him to develop his personality through playing roles in which initiative and spontaneity are stressed.

ADOLESCENCE Adolescence is a transitional period between the childhood and adult statuses. It generally begins with puberty, which is marked by rapid body growth and the appearance of secondary sexual characteristics, and culminates in physical and social maturity. It commonly extends from about twelve or fourteen years of age to 21 or 22 years of age. An adolescent can begin to assume all the roles of manhood and womanhood in this period. He is able not only to express his sex capacities, but also to perform adult work and carry adult responsibilities. In past generations, the assumption of adult activities began at an earlier age than today. An historical example illustrates the older pattern. George Washington took over the management of his family estate at fifteen years of age. He checked all accounts, sold slaves, and directed the affairs of this enterprise. At seventeen, he was considered fit for public office and was made assistant public surveyor of Fairfax County, Virginia. By nineteen, he was involved in many other adult responsibilities. This was not uncommon for youth in Western societies several generations ago. The passage-of-puberty rites in primitive societies is also accepted as the attainment of social maturity with the statuses and roles that accompany it.

The major task of the adolescent in achieving these statuses and roles is the development of social maturity. Learning to work with others in larger social situations and acquiring the knowledge essential to a constructive career are involved. Developing skills essential to a chosen occupation, evolving acceptable attitudes toward the opposite sex, developing a self-confidence that will make him properly independent of the close parental supervision of his childhood, and absorbing ethical ideals that will support his completed socialization are also necessary.

The adolescent faces two major problems in achieving this development: his own inexperience and sense of insecurity and his achievement of a smooth emancipation from parental control. Youth do not face these problems in societies where the process is planned and definite *rites de passage* govern the transition. In such simpler societies, youth make the change as a normal part of their adjustment. In American society, no directed program for making this transition exists, and expectations are vague. The societal expectations involve going to school, getting a job, finding a mate, and establishing a family. Only going to school is clearly defined; the others are indefinite. Consequently, the adolescent's understanding as to how to prepare for his roles is not clear. He must often do the best he can without clear direction from parents, teachers, or friends. He is, as a result, often confused, emotionally upset, and fails to grow in responsibility. Having a good time, especially in association with the opposite sex to which his orientation is expected, may become his primary goal if this occurs.

This adaptation is even more difficult when the family is not able to give him assistance. The American small family system is built on the expectation that the adolescent will get a

job after he is schooled, will get married, and will leave the parental home. Parents are usually anxious to give their children aid in making this transition, although sometimes they are overanxious to do so. At the same time, they may well be out of touch with many aspects of modern adolescent behavior. In such instances, youth often question parental suggestions or not even seek them. Youth may even reject parental suggestions altogether, when parental values are different from those of the larger society. This occurs especially with immigrant families. A youth may thus be faced with a serious parental conflict just when he needs parental guidance most.

ADULTHOOD Adulthood, reached when a society confers full social responsibility upon us, is the period of life for which childhood and adolescence are the preparation. It is usually attained around the age of 21 years in Western societies. In America an interesting problem arises from the fact that society claims that, although political majority is not reached until 21 years of age, one is mature enough to bear arms at eighteen. Youth argue that if eighteen years is mature enough to bear arms, then this should also indicate sufficient maturity to assume all other adult roles.

A review of their activities and responsibilities makes obvious the central role of adults in a society. As parents, they create and support the family institution through which new members of society are produced and socialized. They supply the greater proportion of productive workers and professionals in the society. They direct and maintain the major social activities, agencies, and programs without which society could not endure.

Because adulthood is accompanied by greater control and power, it carries the most prestige of any age group. The power structure in societies rests predominantly upon adults.

THE AGED The determination of who are the aged is more difficult than determining who are the young and who are the adults. In categorizing this stage, societies differ according to their character and the social situations to which their members must make adjustments. Changes in physical characteristics in later years—gray hair, slower walking gait, loss of physical strength, and stooped shoulders—all indicate the aging that reflects itself in physical behavior. It may be inferred that old age has set in when these changes are accompanied by loss of mental vigor, when ambitions are focused on retaining the *status quo,* and when conservatism directs thinking. But we vary greatly in these respects. Some persons of 65 years of age have more physical stamina and mental alertness than others who are much younger. There is no definite time that societies recognize as marking the dividing line between adults and the aged. We fix arbitrary ages for many purposes, an example being retirement from occupations. But these vary for the same occupations within the same society and between societies as well.

The major element in determining who are the aged lies chiefly in the character of the society. The status which the elders have depends to a considerable degree on this factor. In pre-Communist China, for example, the aged were highly respected under their family and ancestor worship system. A father was commonly considered old at 50 years of age. Retirement at this age was definitely planned if there were sons to care for him and the mother. In primitive societies, functions are often divided according to age. The younger are the hunters and warriors, and the older make up the governing council for it is believed that age gives wisdom and knowledge of the ways of the tribe. Gerontocracies, or governments by the elders, are not uncommon among the primitives. The alderman-mayor system of government, while no longer emphasizing old age as a qualification for office, may have originated in this manner. Alderman is the German word for "older man." Also, mayor means major or "older man."

The aged are at a disadvantage in maintaining the pace in Western societies, where industrialization and individualism dominate the economic system and speed and rapid change intensify all aspects of the social organization. They are retired from their jobs almost abruptly with little provision for maintaining any satisfying contact with them. This often carries with it the invidious judgment—or so the retired persons believe—about their fitness for further work. Since their society thus judges them to be old, they often conclude that they are truly old and are ready to be placed on the shelf.[3] There is also the loss of position in the community. The young business and professional men take over the positions of leadership in community affairs which the older ones once held. Close ties with the members of their family, too, are severed. The conjugal family system results in small independent units of husbands, wives, and children, with little place for the aged parents in them. Although the aged parents no doubt prefer to live independently, this loss of intimate associations with responsibility is a heavy blow and adds to the sense of uselessness. Their plight is truly difficult, if not desperate, if they also are dependent upon others for economic support.

Societies are now recognizing their responsibility to the aged under these changed circumstances. Federal, state, and local governments are cooperating in programs for them in both economic and health areas. Activities that provide social and psychological relationships are developing in organizations for the aged. These provide hobby, recreational programs, and job opportunities for them that fit their capabilities through part-time and casual work programs. The situation presents a great cultural lag for this problem has come upon societies with suddenness and is increasing with great rapidity. At the beginning of this century, only one in 25 persons was 65 years or older in the United States. In 1960, one in each eleven was in this age group. The expectation of life at birth in 1900 was only 47 years; today, it is 70 years. Our society has yet to devise educational and avocational programs that effectively prepare people for retirement by helping them develop the intellectual and spiritual resources to meet this inevitable period of their lives.

B. SEX

Sex Differences Are Stressed Early in Life

The biological division of the human species into two sexes, male and female, has no doubt always determined differences in their social relationships. The fact that the roles of each of the sexes in biological reproduction are so significantly different means that societies almost certainly would have created different statuses and roles for each of them. The inescapable determination by nature that the female shall conceive, give birth, and provide the nourishment for human offspring as her primary biological role, and that the male shall have only a secondary part in this process, sets the stage for differentiating the social world into two divisions where the statuses and roles of each are associated with these functions.

These differences are so vital in societies that they begin to express themselves in the earliest years. Though infants are not greatly differentiated for the first one or two years of their lives, the first question about a child upon birth has to do with its sex. All the prejudices about the roles of each sex begin unconsciously to operate as soon as this is known. Conscious effort to make a male into a man and a female into a woman starts as soon as talking and walking begin. Different forms of dress, toys, and activities about the home tend to stress the roles each is to play. In some societies, where the masculine role is especially valued, the clothing of young males is constructed so that their sex organs are visible as an announcement that a child is a son. Sex differences are stressed especially in relation to preparation for adult roles when adolescence is reached. Basic schooling is somewhat the same, but it usually is directed toward feminine roles for the girls, especially homemaking, and toward male occupational activities for the boys. The schooling of adolescents and older youth is often conducted in separate institutions, thus emphasizing the differences in their roles.

The Attitudes Toward and the Handling of the Sexes Differ in Almost All Societies

Sex differences express themselves in adulthood mainly in attitudes, in economic responsibilities, in public activities, and in moral standards. These patterns are determined culturally, but it is this inherited sex difference that underlies these determinations.

In virtually all societies, males have been the controlling sex. This is not because men are biologically more durable than women—the evidence indicates that the opposite is true. Men generally have greater muscular strength than women, although they do not live as long as women and are more susceptible to disease and illness. Nor are males more intelligent than women. Evidence does not show that the two sexes differ widely in mental capacity. Gross inherited biological characteristics do not account for the commonly observed differences.

The role of the female in the reproductive and rearing process is the major factor in the development of attitudes toward women. Females are hampered in their activities by their childbearing and child-rearing responsibilities, particularly during the process of childbearing, which is long and cumbersome. The female's need for protection and support during her vulnerable years leaves her largely dependent upon the male. Many different views of the statuses and roles to be given women have grown out of this circumstance in primitive and

Sexual division of labor in a simple African society: pottery-making is woman's work; making a fish trap is the man's job, but only a woman can use it.

modern societies. Most of these have resulted in woman's subordination.

Women have little status in many primitive groups. Some societies even deny them any role other than that of a tool to be used by men. In others, they have been regarded as incomplete or defective creatures—for example, the early Christian Church held them responsible for original sin. These attitudes have changed slowly, however. Woman has not been held in low regard in all societies. She has often been held in high esteem as the mother, especially of sons, and the director of household organization. But she has attained equal rights with men in only a few societies, even today.

The Traditional Role of the Male Has Been That of Breadwinner and Protector; of the Female, Homemaker and Housekeeper

"The woman's place is in the home." This oft-repeated statement expresses the traditional attitude toward the role of females. In most societies, the woman is expected to marry. The society thinks something is wrong if she fails to marry, have children, and care for a home. Her family and relatives may press her to acquire a mate. Her marriage is arbitrarily arranged in some societies which believe it to be the only proper condition for a female. The inference is that the rest of the occupational world belongs to the males. This attitude has existed generally in our tradition until the modern expansion of machine production. The Industrial Revolution created an occupational world in which women can find employment and thus achieve economic emancipation. Much of the division of labor based on sex has dis-

appeared. Females now enter all kinds of occupational activities in increasing numbers, although inequalities based on sex still persist. The whole range of occupations is usually not fully open to women. Most of them are employed in clerical, sales, secretarial, nursing, school-teaching, and certain factory positions. Their proportions are small, however, in such areas as the professions, administration, business, and engineering. (See Box 34.)

Commonly, women are paid lower wages than men for the same type of work. Several rationalizations support this practice: Women do not have the economic responsibilities men have. They should not be given the same pay, lest it invite too serious competition with men. Males are more efficient than women, so they deserve more pay. Women without families to support can live on less than men. Finally, it costs more to operate enterprises employing women, so costs of production are higher. These arguments are largely spurious justifications rather than factually supported truths. They persist, perhaps, because they help to maintain male dominance.

One of the problems of the female in industrial societies is that she must often prepare

---

BOX 34

In 1642 the master and fellows of Christ's Church, Oxford, decreed that the serving maids at the college should be of *"horrible visu,"* and ever since there has been a curious prejudice against women at the male residential colleges, especially against women teachers. (David Riesman, the Harvard sociologist, has attributed such refusal to learn from women to a "male vanity culture" based on "fear of homosexuality.") This irrational hostility was brought home in traumatic fashion last year to Dr. Jessie Bernard, Visiting Professor of Sociology, who had been chosen to "break the sex barrier" (her own title): the first woman to bear that title at Princeton, an institution so implacably anti-feminist that it is the only university in the world (except Catholic University in Washington, D.C.) which refuses to admit women to its graduate school. She met a stern, relentless resistance from a substantial proportion of her sophomores, who adopted some sort of philosophy of *"elles ne passeront pas."* Mrs. Bernard is a distinguished scholar, and in the typical objective posture of the social scientist turned this experience into teaching material, delivering this lecture which analyzed the anti-petticoat fever of the class as a sociological phenomenon. Back at Penn State and unscarred from her memorable encounter with the Tiger, she philosophically observes that she intends to send her son here and admires Princeton tremendously—but it's no place for a lady (to teach).

It seems to us that this lecture is, to use a barbarous sociological word, "insightful"—it tells us things about ourselves that we didn't realize before, and in its detached, no-nonsense manner, illustrates the academic mind at work, abstracting meaning from everyday experience.—*Ed.*[4]

for two careers, one from which she can earn a living if she does not marry, the other for a life as wife and prospective mother. A further issue arises from the woman's hope or effort to combine marriage and a career. Much has been written about this question. A currently popular view holds that the earlier termination of the childbearing period today permits a woman to enter or re-enter a career when she is still relatively young.

Women Are Usually Limited in the Public Activities in Which They Take Part

Public activities are largely in the hands of men, in part because they are constantly in contact with the outside world through their occupations, while women are usually more closely associated with their homes. A few women have gained political positions in Western societies, but the men control overwhelmingly—there were fewer than 20 women in the Eighty-seventh Congress of the United States, a body that included over 500 members. Several women entered the House of Lords in England for the first time in 1958. Women can take no part in public affairs in some societies, such as those of the Middle East. In American society, the Nineteenth Amendment of the Constitution gave women full rights to vote. They do not, however, take part in political life to the extent that was expected. This suggests that, even in those societies where women have equal rights in many legal respects, they are not yet integrated into public activities as equals of the men.

Sex Differences Express Themselves in the Moral Standards Governing the Behavior of the Sexes

Moral precepts are the standards of good or bad behavior which society imposes upon individuals and groups. The application of these precepts to males and females differs sharply. Actual experience in most societies has resulted in one set of standards for men and another for women—the so-called double standard. The common demand that women observe the norms of chastity and fidelity probably arose out of the proprietary attitudes men traditionally held toward women. Galsworthy let Soames Forsythe express this view toward his wife:

Gratitude was not a virtue among Forsythes who, competitive, and full of common-sense, had no occasion for it; and Soames only ex-

perienced a sense of exasperation amounting to pain, that he did not own her as it was his right to own her, that he could not, as by stretching out his hand to that rose, pluck her and sniff the very secrets of her heart.

Out of his other property, out of all the things he had collected, his silver, his pictures, his houses, his investments, he got a secret and intimate feeling; out of her he got none.[5]

As the modern Western woman gains greater equality with men in all areas of life, including the sexual, it appears that the double standard is passing. We are not prepared to say what the new standard will be.

C. INDIVIDUAL DIFFERENCES

Variations in Mental Traits Influence Social Differences

Variations in the mentality, temperament, and other traits grounded in the biology of individuals also influence the placement of persons in various social statuses. The low-grade moron obviously has little chance of becoming a teacher. The phlegmatic young man could hardly win a place on his football team, even though he had the size and strength. Such variations in abilities clearly help to determine the positions individuals will hold in a society, although they do not usually function as precisely as sex and age differences.

Intelligence Is of Primary Importance

Intelligence is of primary importance in determining the statuses and roles of individuals in societies. Intelligence consists of those inborn mental potentials that are elicited through the cultural tools and influences of society. The amount of intelligence that we possess is inferred from the extent to which we can use, in meaningful ways, the cultural tools of our society. Thus, intelligence is the extent of our ability to learn from our own experience and from others. Through this capacity we become able to reason, to solve problems, to adapt to situations, and to select stimuli for response.

Francis Galton was among the first to emphasize the importance of inherent intellectual differences in determining the status and roles of individuals. He said: "It is in the most unqualified manner that I object to pretensions of natural equality. The experiences of the nursery, the school, the University, and of professional careers, are a chain of proofs to the contrary. I acknowledge freely the great power of education and social influences in developing the active powers of the mind just as I acknowledge the effect of use in developing the muscles of a blacksmith's arm and no further." [6]

Quetelet, the Belgian statistician, made it clear that the measures of the physical traits of a homogeneous grouping of people distribute themselves about an average in a more or less bell-shaped curve. He held that mental traits are distributed in the same way. Francis Galton accepted this principle and stated it thus: "All variable human characteristics are distributed according to a normal curve of frequency distribution. Characteristics of individuals are distributed along this curve according to their frequency of occurrence, equally above and below the median with respect to distance along the base line." [7]

Binet, followed by Terman and others, devised tests to measure intelligence. They developed the Intelligence Quotient (IQ), chiefly to distinguish normal from subnormal children. The IQ, which provides the chief objective data available on general intelligence, is actually a measure of the combined influence of heredity and environment. The importance of providing the environmental conditions that make possible the full development of potential cannot be overstressed. Inherent ability will not emerge automatically; it is rarely, if ever, fully developed in any normal person.

The Extremes in Intelligence Illustrate How Differences Influence Functioning in Societies

The significance of differences in intelligence can be illustrated by the extremes in mental capacity and the relation of intelligence to occupations and to leadership in society.

THE MENTALLY LIMITED   The intelligence of the true feeble-minded cannot be greatly increased. A society may need to segregate those who get into trouble or who cannot care for themselves because of their limitations. Sterilization is often suggested to prevent the reproduction of these types. Genuinely feeble-minded couples do not usually produce normal offspring, but they do multiply at high rates, causing their offspring to be cared for at considerable cost. The evidence shows that feeble-minded persons with a mental age of eight to twelve years may be trained to be self-supporting. They can also be trained to establish the attitudes and habits that enable them to manage their own affairs with ordinary success.

THE MENTALLY SUPERIOR   Inherent qualities of the germ plasm are also responsible in part for the attainment of success in the performance of social roles. Eminence is related to inherited biological traits. The studies of Francis Galton, Havelock Ellis, Frederick Woods, the Stanford Studies of Genius, and of others support this observation. This does not pit hereditary traits against environmental influences, but it does mean that, to have high success in adapting to the demands of society, there must be inherent potential qualities in the germ cells. The statement of MacIver is appropriate here: "Heredity—the germ cells—contains all the potentialities of life, but all of the actualities are evoked within and under the conditions of environment." [8] We repeat that combined influences of heredity and environment produce the person. Nature-nurture are joint operators —together they produce the efficient or inefficient.

There Is a Positive Relationship Between Intelligence and Occupational Level

Some occupations require more intelligence than others. In the long run, persons of superior intelligence will enter those occupations which require the most intelligence, while persons of inferior intelligence will be drawn into those that require the least. This proposition would hold, even when other factors may also affect occupational choices. It would be especially true in societies where occupational roles are achieved and opportunities are not restricted to certain persons or classes.

Many studies using different tests have investigated the soundness of this proposition. One study of occupational selection and intelligence in rural areas of Missouri used the Ohio State University Intelligence Test with high school students and their fathers and mothers. The authors reported their conclusions as follows:

[We find] rather consistently that the professions other than teaching and the student category rank first, second and third in all classifications where they appear. These occupations tend to attract a disproportionate number of persons of high intelligence and consistently to show the highest average scores. Next follows clerical work, which selects high score women relatively more than high score men. Sons and daughters of clerical workers both ranked third although high score wives did not seek out clerical husbands.

Male subjects who entered military service, as well as women who married service men, ranked somewhat above the average for the sample as a whole, with a rank of four in both series. Persons who entered business and sales, as well as the sons and daughters of fathers in these occupations and the women who married men at this occupational level, ranked consistently close to the average of the groups as a whole. Perhaps this is partly due to the considerable diversity of this category, which includes proprietors and managers of substantial business affairs, small entrepreneurs, and sales people at all levels.

Consistently ranking at the bottom of the scale in each of the five series were manual workers, both skilled and unskilled, personal service workers, and farmers. Between these classes differences in test performance were insignificant.

Taking all three groups together, there seems to be a distinct tendency for the brighter boys and girls in rural areas and in small towns in Missouri, to find their occupational levels in the higher prestige occupations, especially the professional groups, while those who perform more poorly on tests are more likely to become manual workers and farmers with somewhat lower rankings on the prestige scale.[9]

It is clear from this and other studies that there is a positive correlation between measured intelligence and occupation followed.

Intelligence and Leadership Are Also Related

Intelligence is related to leadership in societies, if intelligence is defined as the intellectual quality of individuals resulting from the impact of environment on inborn capacity. Those with higher intelligence coupled with energy, motivation, and tact have a better chance to direct and stimulate the activities of others—which is what leadership is—than do those of lower intelligence. Leadership is the product of a number of interacting factors, including the particular situations. We cannot safely talk about leadership traits in general. Persons of intelligence exhibit those characteristics, which, in given circumstances, create a following—groups of disciples—without which there is no leadership. Intelligence is the factor that helps the leader to employ physical qualities, sociability, temperament, and other traits in such a way that others accept him as their guide. Butler indicated an aspect of this capacity when he said of one of his characters: "Perhaps his main strength lay in the fact that though his

capacity was a little above the average, it was not too much so. It is on this rock that so many clever people split. The successful man will see just so much more than his neighbours as they will be able to see too when it is shown them, but not enough to puzzle them."[10]

D. RACE

The Development of the Social Significance of Race Differences Is Recent

"The noblest, the most highly gifted in intellect and personal beauty, the most active in the cause of civilization, is the Arian race."[11] This statement, made over a century ago by Arthur De Gobineau in his *Inequalities of the Races*, epitomizes the character of the racist viewpoint. This view holds that the struggle between races and the achievements of the fittest of them is the basis of human progress. The first volume of this four-volume work was translated from French into English in 1856 by H. Hotz, an American slaveowner who dedicated it to American statesmen. It is probably the most influential work ever published in support of the superiority of the white race. It has been the foundation on which other racial exponents have elaborated. It gave support to Negro slavery in America and later influenced the passage of American immigration legislation discriminating in favor of peoples from northwestern Europe. It provided justification for Hitler's ideas on German supremacy. One author went so far as to say that De Gobineau must be considered one of the greatest of God-inspired heroes, saviors, and liberators sent by Him across the ages.

This belief that race determines the psychological and cultural traits of a people is a modern one. It received its pseudoscientific impetus from these nineteenth-century works. It had, however, found some root earlier in European minds when colonial expansion brought Europeans in contact with people of other races. Race was not a basis for social discrimination among Greeks and Romans and the peoples who conquered each other in the Mediterranean Sea area. Each of these populations considered themselves to be a chosen people—just as the Chinese considered themselves to be a chosen people and the Temple of Heaven in Peking the center of the earth. But their differences were not founded on color of skin or hair or shape of head but upon differences in modes of life. Other people who became Greeks or Romans in behavior and took on Hellenic and Roman character did not suffer social exclusion on account of their race or color.

It is difficult to determine when differences of skin color, hair color, shape, and other physical traits began to influence man's social relations. The Christian world held that man as a special creation of God was a single species. Non-Europeans began to be considered an inferior subspecies of man as Europeans, through commerce and trade, came in greater contact with others, and as slavery became a common practice. Montesquieu made the European slave master of his time say: "These creatures are all over black, and with such a flat nose that they can scarcely be pitied. It is hardly to be believed that God, who is a wise Being, should place a soul, especially a good soul, in such a black ugly body." . . .[12] Echoes of this sentiment still resound in the twentieth-century world.

Linneaus, the Swedish botanist, and Blumenbach, called the father of anthropology, classified mankind into various races in the last part of the eighteenth century. The development of racially conscious nations was rapidly accentuated when De Gobineau and his followers presented their ideas in the middle of the nineteenth century and gave them the appearance of scientifically supported analyses.

Race Is a Biological Concept

RACE DEFINED   *Race* as a scientific concept "applies solely to the biological grouping of human types."[13] It refers to groupings of people "which share in common a certain set of innate physical characters and a geographical origin within a certain area."[14]

THEORIES OF ORIGIN   The view commonly held by most physical anthropologists is that mankind is a single biological species that has differentiated into several subspecies. The division of the single species into subspecies resulted from mutations, natural selection, adaptations, migrations, and isolation over long periods of time that allowed distinctive traits to become predominant. This is the single-origin theory of races. It holds that man originated from a common ancestral type that appeared somewhere between the eastern end of the Mediterranean Sea and India, or perhaps even in Africa. He subsequently moved about, underwent mutations, and gradually developed varied physical characteristics by processes of selec-

tion, adaptation, and inbreeding. Mankind has the same general characteristics in spite of these differences. The fact that normal offspring are produced by interracial matings would demonstrate the common physical character of all men.

Some anthropologists hold that man appeared in several different areas. He presumably multiplied his distinctive traits in these areas as a result of natural selection and adaptation over long periods of time. This is the multiple-origin theory.

It is impossible to be certain about the origin of human races since it is hidden so far back in prehistoric times and because the evidence is so fragmentary. It is clear, however, that there are great divisions of mankind living predominantly in common geographic areas and characterized by hereditary physical traits that serve as the basis of classification into races and subracial categories.

Classification of the Races Has Followed a Number of Patterns

Linneaus designated four subspecies of men:

Europeans, light, lively and ruled by rites,
Asiaticus, stern, haughty, ruled by opinion,
Afer [African], cunning, slow, ruled by
    caprice,
Americanis [American Indian], tenacious,
    content, ruled by custom.

These divisions do not constitute a valid classification since people with these traits can be found anywhere.

Blumenbach (1775) named five races based on skin color: Causasian, or white; Mongolian, or yellow; Ethiopian, or black; American, or red; and Malayan, or brown. Classification by skin color has been the most popular method. Many anthropologists have added other traits, such as shape of the head or cephalic index; hair form, such as straight, wooly, or curly; gene frequencies; and blood groups. But skin color stands out as the most obvious difference on which to base a classification. The red and brown races are now included in the yellow race, so that the three principal races recognized today are the Caucasoids, or white race; the Mongoloid, or yellow race; and the Negroid, or black race. Box 35 gives the principal physical characteristics of these three races. Figure 5 gives a traditional classification with the principal subdivisions.[16]

BOX 35 PHYSICAL CHARACTERISTICS OF THE THREE MAIN RACES OF MANKIND [15]

Trait	Caucasoid	Mongoloid	Negroid
Skin colour	Pale reddish white to olive brown; some dark brown.	Pale yellow to yellow-brown; some reddish brown.	Brown to brown-black; some yellow-brown.
Stature	Medium to tall.	Medium tall to medium short.	Tall to very short.
Head form	Long to broad and short: medium high to very high.	Predominantly broad; height, medium.	Predominantly long; height, low to medium.
Face	Narrow to medium broad; no projecting jaw.	Medium broad to very broad; cheekbones, high and flat.	Medium broad to narrow; frequent projecting jaws.
Hair	Head hair: colour, light blond to dark brown; texture, fine to medium; form, straight to wavy. Body hair: moderate to profuse.	Head hair: colour, brown to brown-black; texture, coarse; form, straight. Body hair: sparse.	Head hair: colour, brown-black; texture, coarse; form, light curl to woolly or frizzly. Body hair: slight.
Eye	Colour: light blue to dark brown; occasional side eye-fold.	Colour: brown to dark brown; fold of flesh in inner corner very common.	Colour: brown to brown-black; vertical eye-fold common.
Nose	Bridge usually high; form, narrow to medium broad.	Bridge usually low to medium; form, medium broad.	Bridge usually low; form, medium broad to very broad.
Body build	Slim to broad; slender to rugged.	Tends to be broad; occasional slimness.	Tends to be broad and muscular, but occasional slimness.

Race Is a Powerful Societal Fact When Endowed with Social Meaning

The importance of these race differences in our understanding of societies lies in the fact that they condition our associational patterns. They are one of the strongest forces influencing the relationships of people within and between societies because the differences have

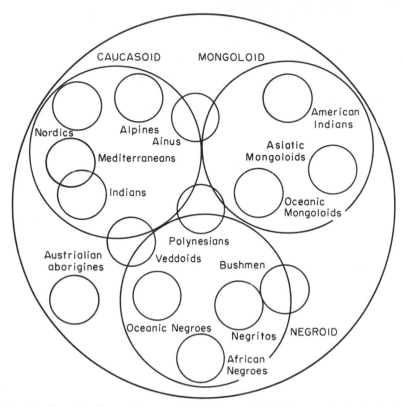

Fig. 5. Classification of Races. (According to A. L. Kroeber.) (Traditional)

been given connotations of superiority-inferiority that often make it difficult for them to live together amicably. There is little possibility that men can act together anywhere in full harmony when a superior-inferior relationship exists. These hereditary differences serve as a basis of prejudice which is passed from generation to generation with amazing persistence. The essential conditions for conflict are at hand where prejudices lead to discrimination and segregation.

The Statuses and Roles Which Individuals and Groups Can Enjoy Are Profoundly Affected by Attitudes Toward Race Differences

The statuses based on race are ascribed by the dominant elements of the society in which physical differences are given social meaning. In this respect, race is similar to other biological differences, such as age, sex, and inherited capacities. But there is an important difference between the statuses ascribed to races and

those based upon other biological differences. Race differences are considered neither by the victims of prejudice nor by informed people to be significant differences. Color of skin, color of eyes and hair, shape of head, blood types, and other bodily variations, they insist, do not result in different capacities that influence functioning. There is little or no evidence, they maintain, that there are important differences in the mentality of the races that affect their behavior. They hold that prejudiced attitudes are the result of factually unfounded beliefs which serve to support a sense of superiority in the dominant group. What are we to say of these views?

Bodily Traits Are Not Determinants of Achievement

COLOR OF SKIN   The history of man shows that people of each skin color have achieved high levels of culture. Dark-skinned people built the civilizations of Persia, Syria, and Egypt. The civilization of the Chinese—Mongolian people—was built long before European whites had emerged from the tribal state. Negroes in Africa invented and used iron tools and evolved great political kingdoms, such as ancient Ghana in West Africa. Indians in Central and South America built the Aztec, Inca, and Mayan cultures long before the Spanish invaded their areas.

Skin color is the result of the presence in the body of two chemicals, carotene and melanin. Carotene gives a yellow tinge, melanin a brown. Together, with the pinkish tinge from the blood vessels, these give different color shades to the skin. All people have in their bodies some of these chemicals, which are carried in the genes. When genetic changes or mutations produced dark-skinned or light-skinned people, natural selection favored those best adapted to various environments. They multiplied and occupied their respective geographic regions.[17] Quite possibly, color differentiation was affected by *social* selection, a process in which a cultural preference favors those with a given skin color. In any event, different skin colors are found among the most advanced and the most primitive peoples. They do not in any direct way influence their achievements.

HEAD FORM   Head form is sometimes considered important as an indicator of differences between subraces. Head form is described by the cephalic index, or the ratio of the width to the length of the head. Racial groups are classified as long-headed, or doliocephalic, where the ratio is below 75; where it is 75 to 80, as medium-headed, or mesocephalic; and where it is above 80, as round-headed, or brachycephalic. Within the white race, Nordics are mostly long-headed, middle Europeans or Alpines are round-headed, and Mediterraneans are medium-headed. Long-headed Nordics were believed to possess superior mental capacity and a nature that was creative, energetic, and independent. The round-headed people were supposed to be of average intelligence and energy, but lacking in leadership. But the important point is that these long-headed shapes are not peculiar to the Nordics. They are found in the other white populations and in those of all colored people. There has been a wide variation in achievement among them all.

The size of the brain also has been cited as indicative of achievement possibilities. But this trait varies widely with body size and build within each race. Brains of all sizes are found in all races. Some of the world's most brilliant

people have had small brains. One of the world's largest brains belonged to a London idiot.

BLOOD TYPES   A common belief about race is that if the blood of the races is mixed, people take on the physical and mental characteristics of those from whom they received it. Such ideas as "blood is what counts" influence the attitudes of many people. This is a holdover from the time it was thought that hereditary traits were transmitted through the blood. Now it is known that hereditary traits are transmitted through the genes, and genes of different blood types are present in all the races.

There are four blood types—O, A, B, and AB. Blood type O can be successfully mixed with A, B, and AB, but the other three cannot be generally mixed, except in certain combinations, without clotting or clumping that may cause difficulty or death. These four blood types are found in people throughout the world regardless of their color, nationality, or race. No race, therefore, has a distinctive blood type.

Many other physical characteristics have been studied in an effort to ascertain their relationship to the achievements of races. None seems to result in any consistent correlation. To use them as indicators of race capacities or behavior can hardly be justified.

Are Some Races Superior to Others in Intelligence?

It has been assumed in some quarters that races differ in inherent mental capacity. Is it not possible that the races differ in their mental capacities, just as they differ in their physical characteristics? Two questions need answering: (1) What has been found relative to racial mentality? (2) To what extent is intelligence influenced by environment and opportunity? (See Box 36.)

When mental tests are given to large populations, differences in the scores spread over a wide range, with most of them falling around a central position or average. These tests show that wide differences in the intellectual capacity of individuals exist in any general population. Are these differences correlated with racial factors? A major difficulty encountered in such comparisons is the practical impossibility of controlling the conditions that influence intelligence. The tests measure not only innate capacity but what happens to it after individuals are born. Intelligence tests given all white and Negro soldiers in the American Expeditionary Forces in World War I showed white soldiers

BOX 36

People may be equal without being alike. . . . Equality is a precept, similarity or dissimilarity is a precept. Strictly speaking, science does not tell us whether people should or should not be equal, but it does show what consequences result from equality or inequality of opportunity. . . . The decisive point is, however, that nobody can discover the cultural capacities of human individuals, populations, or races until they have been given something like an equality of opportunity to demonstrate these capacities.[18]

[While Oxford, Mississippi, was still reverberating from the crisis precipitated by James Meredith's effort to enroll in the state University, two other American Negroes of lowly origin were making their way to Oxford University, England. The *Time* magazine reports:]

This year not one but two of 32 U.S. Rhodesmen are Negroes. Culled from 544 formidable candidates nominated by colleges across the country, they had to meet Cecil Rhodes's requirement that each of his scholars be "the best man for the world's fight." Few young men have already fought so well:

John E. Wideman, 21, the son of a Pittsburgh waiter, is a senior majoring in English literature at the University of Pennsylvania. Wideman won the campus creative-writing prize, last month got his Phi Beta Kappa key, this year captained Penn's undefeated basketball team. Last week, hours after hurdling the Rhodes selection committee, Captain Wideman led Penn to victory over Vanderbilt, topped his team's scoring with 18 points. His Oxford agenda: language and literature in order to teach college English.

Joseph Stanley Sanders, 20, born in a south Los Angeles slum, is the son of a city garbage-truck driver. Stan's big brother Ed chose one way up—boxing—and died after being knocked out in his ninth profight. Stan's way led to top marks at mostly Negro David Starr Jordan High School, thence to a full athletic scholarship at Whittier College, where his size (6 ft. 4 in., 204 lb.) and blinding speed (9.8 sec. for the 100-yd. dash) made him an All-America end in small-college football. He also kept A-minus grades in his political science major, was student-body president. Turning down pro football offers, Stan will pursue Oxford's famed "PPE" (philosophy, politics, economics), aims to become a lawyer. He is Whittier's first Rhodes scholar.[19]

---

to score higher than Negroes. But Northern soldiers, including both white and black, scored higher than Southern soldiers, both white and black. And Northern Negro soldiers scored higher than Southern white soldiers.[20] Other studies have shown that Northern Negro children in New York City, having the same schooling as the white children, test much higher than Negro children in the segregated Southern schools.[21] Franz Boas, the anthropologist, having reviewed these and similar findings, concluded that it is not possible to prove that these differences are due to innate mental traits. He then said, "I believe the present state of our knowledge justifies us in saying that, while individuals differ, biological differences between races are small. There is no reason to believe

that one race is by nature so much more intelligent, endowed with great will power, or emotionally more stable than another, that the difference would materially influence its culture."[22]

This issue remains unsettled. Scientific or pseudoscientific efforts to substantiate the claim that the races differ in inherent abilities continue to appear in print.[23] We would insist, however, that even scientific proof of the existence of such differences would provide no justification for discriminatory practices in a democracy.

The Races Cannot Be Considered Pure Types

CONTINUAL INTERMIXTURE None of the competent students of race considers the three major races or subspecies of mankind to be pure types. From earliest times, men moved about, intermarried, begot children, and produced hybrids because there were few prejudices to limit their intermixture. The fact that couples from any race could produce offspring is evidence that we are a single species. Mixtures are fertile and result in fertile hybrids. Crossings take place rapidly when the contacts between migrating populations are not antagonistic. The offspring show few physical differences from the parent stocks, when the mixing is between nearly related racial types.

Mixing Stimulated by Migration Man's history may be described by his movement about this planet and by his intermixture with populations already established in habitable areas. Waves of people came into Europe from the east and southeast after the Christian era started and moved across the continent, mixed with the native peoples, settled down, and became the basis for the modern population stocks of Europe. The inhabitants in the Mediterranean Sea area moved across the eastern end of this sea into North Africa to trade, to war, and to mix with the people of these regions. Mongolian people from Asia moved into Africa. Arabs moved across North Africa and mixed with the Negro populations. Later, these mixed people moved into Spain and became part of this population. Mongolians from Asia swarmed across Europe again and again. White populations that came to America intermixed with Indians of both northern and southern continents, and Negroes have mixed with both Indians and whites. These mixtures continue today throughout most of the world.

WHITES MOST MIXED The white population is probably the most mixed of all. The Mediterranean Sea area, Europe, and the Atlantic Ocean were for centuries the pathways for the movement of innumerable populations which amalgamated into hybrid stocks. Neighboring peoples mixed constantly to form new populations like the Alsatians of Alsace-Lorraine. Americans are a polyglot people for they are a mixture of all the racial groupings that formed the chief populations of Europe as well as of America itself. These continual intermixtures indicate that the idea of pure races is a fiction. The purest races are to be found in isolated places like aboriginal Australia, where peoples have inbred for long periods of time. Mixed populations can consolidate their physical characteristics into uniform types in isolated situa-

tions. There is little possibility of developing a pure racial type, however, where the populations are constantly moving.

NO PROOF OF INJURIOUS RESULTS FROM MIXING What is the effect of such race crossing? If we limit ourselves to its biological consequences, it can be said that there is no proof that race-crossing has injurious physical and mental results. Some students of race say that it has beneficial effects in that it makes possible the combination of a greater variety of inherited traits that improve the physical and mental qualities of the offspring.

In concluding this discussion of the physical aspects of race, we should note that the most modern physical anthropologists are seriously questioning the validity of traditional racial concepts, measures, and classifications. It is even suggested that the term "race" be abandoned altogether.[24] We can expect that this change will not only alter the biological approach to human types but will also modify our thinking about the social implications of race.

Race Differences Are Strong Barriers to Cooperative Social Action

Despite the absence of proof that biological differences between races determine variations in intellectual and social behavior, they do serve as a basis of prejudice and discrimination which lead to segregation and conflict. Cooley remarked on this tendency: "Two races of different temperament and capacity, distinct to the eye and living side by side in the same community, tend strongly to become castes, no matter how equal the social system may otherwise be. The difference, as being hereditary, answers in its nature to the idea of caste, and the external sign serves to make it conscious and definite."[25]

Attitudes of Superiority Are the Chief Factors in Maintaining These Barriers

Although facts may deny it, there nevertheless is the *belief* held by the dominant races that they *are* superior, that other races *are* inferior, and that the privileged status the former enjoy is justified because of their superiority. The dominated races may *believe* just as strongly that they are the physical and mental equals of other races, if given the opportunity; that the attitudes of the controlling races are rationalizations; and that they have a just right to equal status in the social order. Prejudiced attitudes are almost impossible to counteract or eliminate because they have crystallized over long periods of time as parts of the cultural heritage and are thus inculcated in individuals through socialization. They become stereotypes or fixed pictures in our minds which may be applied indiscriminately to all members of another race.

We recall vividly how such prejudice became part of the mental life of two white girls whose parents were Northerners. They lived in a Southern white community adjacent to a segregated Negro neighborhood for a time. Small Negro children played across the road not far distant. Every now and then these four- and five-year-old white girls would be found playing freely with the Negro children. They knew nothing of race differences or prejudice until they began to attend an all-white school. Soon they were making disparaging comments about Negro children because they were now taking on the attitudes of their schoolmates. Playing with the Negro children ceased, and only contacts with Negro servants remained. These were relationships of dominance. Through association with Southern white companions, these children became as strongly stereotyped in their relations with Negroes as any child born and reared in the South. Interestingly enough, in spite of intellectualizing the situation, these stereotypes still express themselves in the attitudes of these young ladies.

So long as a dominated race accepts the conclusion that they are inferior and with it the pattern of relationships that follows, no problem arises. But all the elements of race conflict are present when the dominated race begins to feel that, because its position is the consequence of unwarranted prejudice, it is being unfairly discriminated against. Walter White, a former executive secretary of the National Association for the Advancement of Colored People, said in a public address some years ago: "The Negroes in the United States must keep a chip on their shoulders if their conditions are to receive attention from the American public." He was asserting that unless Negroes themselves are aggressive, no one would endeavor to better their situation. "Sit-in" strikes and "Freedom-Rider" activities are examples of this aggressiveness.

Prejudice Leads to Discrimination; Discrimination to Justification

PREJUDICE A biased attitude toward persons or situations taken before complete or accurate evidence is available or considered is called a prejudice. It thus constitutes a prejudgment that may, of course, be favorable or unfavorable. It often becomes fixed and rigid and remains as a disposition even after its falsity is proved. This is one of the difficult problems in race relations for, even though scientific evidence is presented, the prejudiced attitude inhibits its acceptance. Such evidence is simply ignored or distorted—and apparently occurs even among people at higher levels of education. Dr. Donald Young tested about 450 university students some years ago to see how much a semester's course in American race relations resulted in changed prejudices. Questionnaires were completed by the students at the first and last sessions of the course. His conclusion was that a term of teaching did little to alter race prejudices which had been formed through long periods of time.[26] Some one has said that prejudices are like nails: the harder you hit them, the deeper you drive them.

DISCRIMINATION Prejudice expressed in action is *discrimination*. Discrimination deprives its victims of rights or privileges that are generally enjoyed by others in society. This may occur on a racial basis in any area of society: education, employment, housing, political activity, recreation, or personal services. Often, the purpose of discrimination is to make serious competition from the subordinate group impossible, causing discrimination to be related to race differences in an indirect way. Race may be used as a justification for unfair action when threatened competition arises. Negroes may not be given employment, for example, because they do not qualify educationally. Their lack of education is used as an explanation, when actually the reason is race prejudice. The expression of race prejudice is indirect and camouflaged in such a case. To complete a vicious circle, the low level of education and employment may be used as evidence of the Negro's inherent inferiority.

JUSTIFICATION Those who discriminate hardly ever admit it. We do not consider *our* actions discriminatory. To justify them, we have "satisfactory" explanations, which usually take one or more of four forms: (1) Those discriminated against deserve this treatment because they are inferior and incapable. (2) Such action is taken for self-protection since equal status would make the inferiors arrogant and overbearing, and they would destroy the values of the society. (3) The controls we use are actually beneficial to the "inferiors" who are ignorant, lack ambition, and must have guidance. (4) Discriminatory controls are perfectly natural, anyway, for it is inevitable that there should be superiors and inferiors. (See Box 37.)

Minority Reactions to Discrimination Are Varied

PSYCHOLOGICAL DISORGANIZATION AND OPPRESSION REACTIONS   What reaction would a white man have if he came to a town in a Southern state where only Negroes lived and was confronted with a neatly painted sign that said: "White man, don't let the sun go down on you in this town"? Negroes in America have seen such signs in some white towns.[28] What reaction would the white man have if colonies of Chinese built a section in a Western city, such as Denver or London, and then posted signs in its parks that said: "No dogs—No white people"? The converse of this once occurred in Shanghai, China, where white men did put up signs in the parks that said "No Chinese—No dogs." [29]

At the very least, such discriminatory actions as these cause bewilderment and resentment. They often arouse more serious psychological reactions. Victims of prejudice and oppression may lose self-respect and suffer inner conflict and personal demoralization as a consequence. Racial minorities, subjected to severe and continuous frustration, tend to develop persistent and exaggerated emotional states called oppression psychoses. These mental states, characterized by anger, suspicion, and insecurity, may unify even factional segments of minorities into cohesive groups hostile to their oppressors. Frustration and fear are likely to provoke aggressive actions and these, in turn, invite counterattack by the oppressing forces. Thus, the mental and emotional states of two races may be so inflamed that conflict may erupt almost spontaneously.

ACTIVITY THROUGH ORGANIZATIONS   Having little faith that the spontaneous good will and the avowed democratic philosophy of the dominant group will improve their lot, oppressed minorities, in time, organize for education and action to eliminate prejudice and discrimination against them. Over the years, in America, numerous associations, commissions, and committees have formed to promote programs of education, publicity, economic pressure, and legal action to induce the dominant group to grant greater equality of rights and opportunities. A primary function of the National Association for the Advancement of Colored People is to publicize cases of discriminatory treatment and press for their correction. Through agitation and court action it has succeeded in eliminating many injustices in the American Negro's position.

Other organizations, such as the National Urban League, the National Negro Congress, the Congress on Racial Equality (CORE), and Negro newspapers and journals not only protest but also develop educational programs among both the Negro and white communities. There is also cooperation with other organizations, such as the National Interracial Conference, Commission on Interracial Cooperation, and the National YMCA and YWCA. These activities spread ideas that emphasize working together for better understanding and for cooperative programs that will eliminate hostility.

These organizations tend to be of two general types—the one aggressive and demanding, the other cautious and educational. They represent divisions of opinion within the racial minority as to which is the best organizational approach.

DIRECT AGGRESSION   Years of accumulating tension between the Negro and white popula-

---

BOX 37

[Ironically, those who hold to categorical evaluation and separation of races sometimes cite as support Kipling's line: "East is East and West is West and never the twain shall meet." Actually, the poem urges the judgment and acceptance of men on the basis of individual merit:]

Oh, East is East, and West is West, and never the twain shall meet,
Till Earth and Sky stand presently at God's great Judgment Seat;
But there is neither East nor West, Border, nor Breed, nor Birth,
When two strong men stand face to face, though they come from the ends of the earth! [27]

---

tions of Chicago exploded in one of the most violent race conflicts in American history. (See Box 38.) It was difficult for these races to live side by side, constantly encroaching on each other's privileges, without periodic conflicts. There had been gang fights over many points of contention, which intensified mutual resentment as competition and misunderstandings grew in many political and economic areas. A point had been reached where a minor incident precipitated a large-scale violent conflict.

Minority peoples who are already suffering from feelings of enforced inferiority and unfair oppression can hardly remain placid while further acts of injury are inflicted. In many racial situations, the dominated group feels that it has no other recourse in meeting discrimination than by direct aggressive action. The cards are usually stacked against the minority. The cause of the controlling party is considered just and that of the minority in error. The minority is often deprived of any legal rights to challenge the position of the dominant group. Compromise seems impossible and the blind fury of physical attack the only alternative.

Such, for example, seems to be the case in South Africa, where about 3 million white people dominate 11 to 12 million native colored people and a quarter of a million Indians. Here the nonwhites are completely barred from many public places and from entire sections of some cities. Nearly half of the natives live in areas set aside for them under the practice of apar-

theid (segregation). Violent anger and action are the predictable results.

Aggression does not always mean physical conflict. Negroes have used their vote where possible to elect persons, white or colored, who promise to get them fair treatment. In some cities and states in the United States, they have staunchly supported and brought about the election of municipal and state officers, thus showing their political effectiveness. The boycott has also proved to be a potent weapon in many race conflicts, as its use in some American states and in India has shown.

SUBMISSION The opposite reaction to aggression is submission. Often a significant element in a racial minority will simply accept their condition and remain apathetic. This may be due to several circumstances. Some reason that they can do little about their conditions and that trying would only make their burdens heavier. Others reason that their submission will bring them favors, especially economic ones. Still others have made accommodations which are satisfactory to them, and they do not wish to disturb them. For a significant proportion, especially where contacts with the majority are few, submission is hardly submission. It is simply conforming to the order of things that always existed. This is the way it always has been, and they give thought to no other. Some rest on their conviction that somehow a better day is coming and that it is best for them just to wait and hope.

BOX 38

One sultry afternoon in the summer of 1919 a seventeen-year-old colored boy was swimming in Lake Michigan by a Chicago bathing beach. Part of the shore had been set aside by mutual understanding for the use of the whites, another part for the Negroes. The boy took hold of a railroad tie floating in the water and drifted across the invisible line. Stones were thrown at him; a white boy started to swim toward him. The colored boy let go of the railroad tie, swam a few strokes, and sank. He was drowned. Whether he had been hit by any of the stones was uncertain but the Negroes on the shore accused the whites of stoning him to death and a fight began. This small incident struck the match that set off a bonfire of race hatred. The Negro population of Chicago had doubled in a decade, the blacks had crowded into white neighborhoods, and nerves were raw. The disorder spread to other parts of the city—and the final result was that for nearly a week Chicago was virtually in a state of civil war. There were mobbings of Negroes, beatings, stabbings, gang raids through the Negro district, shootings by Negroes in defense, and wanton destruction of houses and property. When order was finally restored it was found that fifteen whites and twenty-three Negroes had been killed, five hundred and thirty-seven people had been injured, and a thousand had been left homeless and destitute.[30]

Submission is the despair of those within a racial minority who want to alter the situation. No change is forthcoming in intergroup relationships unless the dominated press for it. The apathy of subjugated people is often difficult to overcome.

PROVING ONE'S WORTH Nothing is more important to individuals than their respect for themselves. This is also true of racial groups. Reactions are strong when discriminatory relationships hurt racial pride. "We'll show them, then recognition cannot be denied," is the motive. This was the emphasis of Booker T. Washington. He constantly argued that Negroes should make themselves successful in their occupations and prove themselves competent in their academic and professional pursuits. Then, recognition and status would follow, and discrimination in relation to opportunities would cease. This attitude is still evident in some Negro school and college programs today.

One explanation of the success of Negroes in athletics is this desire to prove their worth. They can compete on equal terms with others in these activities, and the desire to prove their worth stimulates them to the extra effort that often brings great success. Althea Gibson, the Negro tennis champion, perhaps without recognizing the implication, said that the reason for her success was that she always wanted to be somebody.[31] Other examples can be found in all modern fields of sport.

ESCAPING FROM THE PROBLEMS Many members of minority races have thought that the solution of their problems lay in some form of escape. Marcus Garvey won a following some time ago by proposing that the Negroes in America return to Africa. It was argued that the United States was not the Negro's nation. Neither politics, religion, nor education could solve their problems in America because they could not achieve proper recognition either by force or pleading. A return to Africa, the native home of the Negro, was the only way left to them. In Africa, the American Negro could teach the native Africans their ways of civilization and, there, build states of their own.

This type of argument has recurred from time to time. However, segregation in different states or separate colonies is an impractical solution. Minorities do not really wish to be separated nor does the majority wish to have them separated except in certain kinds of relationships. Separation tends to occur between groups and within them as they adapt to each other on the basis of economic, religious, social, and racial distinctions. Racial groups oppose segregation that is imposed in a compulsory manner through laws, intimidation, or violence. These methods infer inferiority. Segregation takes place as a natural consequence of interrelationships, even where regulations have not compelled it. Efforts to escape separation occur when it is felt that there is no other way to avoid intolerable discrimination.

The rapid migration of Negroes from rural states of the South to the large cities of the North in the United States is, in part, an attempt to escape from a difficult situation. Occupational opportunities for semiskilled and unskilled labor in the North have made this possible. But escaping can solve these problems only temporarily because they tend to be recreated in the new situation in a very short time. Race problems, long relatively absent in Northern cities, have become acute as a consequence of this migration.

BIOLOGICAL ABSORPTION There are those who contend that the only ultimate way to solve the racial minority problem is through biological amalgamation. Even where races are culturally assimilated, they argue, the prejudice against color makes impossible equal acceptance in their intimate social relations. Therefore, the only way out is the elimination of the racial factor by biological fusion. The opposition to racial mixture in some societies is so strong that advocacy of such a program as a practical solution is almost unthinkable. Such prejudice does not prevent acceptable intermarriages in some societies; in others, it is strongly resisted.

Passing Racial absorption is facilitated in some measure by the phenomenon of "passing." Hybrid individuals who have the physical traits of the dominant race to such a degree that they are hardly distinguishable from them may either be taken for, or purposefully pose as, members of the dominant group. How extensive this practice is in a society like America is unknown. The estimates vary widely. There is usually no disposition on the part of the "passer" to become permanently identified with the dominant race. It is used only in occasional situations where their privileges are restricted.[32]

Hybrids Have the Distinctive Problem of Adjusting to Two Social Situations

Race mixture takes place in every society where two or more races live in the same area.

Practically all students of race relations emphasize this tendency. Wirth and Goldhamer have said, "It is doubtful whether two races ever lived within the confines of a single society without the process of race mixture setting in." [33] Mixing is usually not ignored by most societies, though it causes no problem in some. Crossing with American Indians results in little, if any, loss of status in American society, but crossing with Negroes is strongly opposed throughout. This opposition is shown by the fact that 29 states have laws forbidding interracial marriages. In many states, a person is classed as a Negro and must function with Negroes if it can be shown that he is any degree a mixed type. Hybrids, therefore, must react to the pressure of two social systems, often not knowing where or how to make the most acceptable adjustments.

Robert Park first used the expression "marginal man" to denote the hybrid individual. He described him as "one whom fate has condemned to live in two, not merely different, but antagonistic cultures." And both of these cultures may be antagonistic to him. A dominant white culture, where there is strong race prejudice, rejects him and compels him to find a place, if possible, in the dominated race. This is the most frustrating experience he has for it deprives him of the privileges of the controlling elements of his society. The dominated group may reject him also if it has strong antipathy to mixing. As a consequence, hybrids are an intermediate grouping with no established place in their society. They are the victims of an almost outcaste position for which they are not responsible. This has been the state of the Anglo-Indians since the British left India after World War II.

There Are Differences Between and Within Societies in the Treatment of Races

Differences in race make little difference in social relationships in some societies. They do not stand in the way of economic, political, or social advancement. This is true in several of the South American (Brazil, Argentina, and Uruguay are examples) and Asiatic countries. "What is important in these countries is a man's social and economic attainments. An educated, well-to-do, and cultivated person is highly regarded whatever his color." [34]

Race attitudes and treatment vary widely within societies. Westie's study of Negro-white status differentials and social distance in a Midwest American city shows that social distance between these races is "least where both Negro and white have high socio-economic status. Social distance is greatest where both Negro and white have low socio-economic status." [35] However, there are areas where prejudice is so strong that few associations are possible on any other basis than that of superiority-inferiority.

The concept of "social distance" is used to express in measurable terms the extent of personal and social association that results from race and other forms of social consciousness. This term is used to apply to those forms of social consciousness discussed in later sections of this book.

References

1. Linton, Ralph, "A Neglected Aspect of Social Organization," *American Journal of Sociology,* 45 (May, 1940), pp. 870–872.
2. Williams, R. M., Jr., *American Society* (New York, Alfred A. Knopf, 1956), p. 63.
3. Blau, Z. S., "Changes in Status and Age Identification," *American Sociological Review,* 21 (April, 1956), pp. 198–203.
4. Davies, John D. (ed.), "Breaking the Sex Barrier," *Princeton Alumni Weekly,* 61 (September 23, 1960), p. 3.
5. Galsworthy, John, *The Forsyte Saga* (New York, Charles Scribner's Sons, 1927), p. 59.
6. Galton, Francis, *Hereditary Genius* (London, Macmillan and Company, 1892), p. 12.
7. *Ibid.,* pp. XI and 23.
8. MacIver, R. M., *Society: Its Structure and Changes* (New York, Ray Long and R. R. Smith, Inc., 1931), p. 328.
9. Pihlblad, C. T., and Gregory, C. L., "Occupational Selection and Intelligence in Rural Communities and Small Towns in Missouri," *American Sociological Review,* 21 (February, 1956), p. 70.

10. Butler, Samuel, *The Way of All Flesh* (New York, E. P. Dutton and Co., 1916), pp. 20 and 21. From Everyman's Library.
11. Hotz, H., *The Moral and Intellectual Diversity of Races*, tran. from the French of Count A. de Gobineau's *The Inequalities of Human Races*, I (Philadelphia, J. B. Lippincott Company, 1856), p. 457.
12. Montesquieu, B., *The Spirit of Laws* (Cincinnati, Robert Clark and Co., 1886), Book XV, Chap. V, p. 275.
13. Boas, Franz, "Race," *Encyclopedia of the Social Sciences*, 13 (New York, The Macmillan Company, 1934), p. 25.
14. Department of Mass Communication, UNESCO, *What Is Race?* (Paris, Imprimerie George Lang, 1952), p. 36.
15. *Ibid.*, p. 45. Table is slightly altered from original one in Krogman, W. M., "The Concept of Race," in Linton, R. (ed.), *The Science of Man in the World Crisis* (New York, Columbia University Press, 1945), p. 50.
16. *Ibid.*, p. 42.
17. Benedict, Ruth, and Weltfish, Gene, *The Races of Mankind* (New York, Public Affairs Committee, Inc., 1943), p. 10.
18. Dobzhansky, Theodosius, *Mankind Evolving* (New Haven, Conn., Yale University Press, 1962), pp. 285–286.
19. *Time*, 80 (December 28, 1962), p. 39. Courtesy of *Time;* copyright, 1962, by Time, Inc.
20. Benedict, Ruth, and Weltfish, Gene, *The Races of Mankind* (New York, Public Affairs Committee, Inc., 1943), p. 18.
21. Klineberg, Otto, *Characteristics of the American Negro* (New York, Harper and Brothers, 1944), pp. 183–189.
22. Boas, Franz, *Race, Language, and Culture* (New York, The Macmillan Company, 1940), pp. 13 and 14.
23. See, for example, Putnam, Carleton, *Race and Reason; A Yankee View* (Washington, D.C., Public Affairs Press, 1961).
24. See Montagu, Ashley, "The Concept of Race," *American Anthropologist*, 64 (October, 1962), Part I, pp. 919–928.
25. Cooley, C. H., *Social Organization* (New York, Charles Scribner's Sons, 1920), p. 218.
26. Young, D., "Some Effects of a Course in American Race Problems on the Race Prejudices of 450 Undergraduates in the University of Pennsylvania," *Journal of Social Psychology*, 22 (October–December, 1927), pp. 235–242. It is quite clear that such studies as this one do not give true measures of the potential effect of courses on race relations on prejudice. In probably every instance, these courses are "elective," and so those students who lack strong prejudice are selected. Therefore, only small degrees of change would appear. For more recent evidence on the effect of education, see Stember, Charles H., *Education and Attitude Change. The Effect of Schooling on Prejudice Against Minority Groups* (New York, Institute of Human Relations, 1961).
27. From "The Ballad of East and West," *Rudyard Kipling's Verse* (New York, Doubleday, Page and Company, 1922), p. 268. Reprinted by permission of Doubleday and Company, Inc.
28. Carmer, Carl, *Stars Fell on Alabama* (New York, Farrar and Rinehart, 1934), p. 59.
29. Buck, Pearl, *My Several Worlds* (New York, The John Day Company, 1954), p. 64.
30. Allen, F. L., *Only Yesterday* (New York, Harper and Brothers, 1931), pp. 63 and 64. Also, see Grimshaw, Allen D., "Urban Racial Violence in the United States: Changing

Ecological Considerations," *American Journal of Sociology,* 66 (September, 1960), pp. 109–119.

31. Gibson, A., *I Always Wanted to Be Somebody* (New York, Harper and Brothers, 1958).
32. Burma, J. H., "The Measurement of Negro Passing," *American Journal of Sociology,* 52 (July, 1946), pp. 18 ff. See also, Drake, St. Clair, and Cayton, Horace R., *Black Metropolis* (New York, Harcourt, Brace and Company, 1945), pp. 159–173.
33. Wirth, L., and Goldhamer, H., "The Hybrid and the Problem of Miscegenation," in Klineberg, O. (ed.), *Characteristics of the American Negro* (New York, Harper and Brothers, 1944), p. 263.
34. Leyburn, J. C., *World Minority Problems,* Public Affairs Pamphlet No. 1932 (1947), p. 24.
35. Westie, F. R., "Negro-White Status Differentials and Social Distance," *American Sociological Review,* 17 (October, 1952), pp. 550–558.

Questions for Study and Discussion

1. Discuss the statement that "societies determine what differences have social significance."
2. What changes have been occurring in the status of the child, the adolescent, and the elder in our society?
3. What social functions are served by age-grading in a society?
4. Discuss the so-called "double standard" and give illustrations of why it is changing in modern society.
5. Does living in modern society require more individual intelligence than was needed in the past?
6. Define "race" and evaluate the theories of race origins.
7. What bodily traits are most important in endowing race with social meaning? Discuss their importance in influencing achievement.
8. Can races not be considered pure types today?
9. What is the relationship of belief to race relations? How does prejudice lead from discrimination to justification?
10. What common stereotypes do you find exhibited by your associates?
11. It has been said that "when the ledgers of a people show red, the outlook for minorities is black." Explain.
12. Has the position of the hybrid or marginal man become easier in modern society?

Suggested Topics for Reports

1. In the past, adolescence usually began with the onset of puberty. Make a study of the evidences indicating that behavior traditionally attached to the adolescent stage is today being displayed by preteen-age youngsters.
2. Make a study of the ways in which traditional sex differences in occupations, dress, speech, and other behavior are changing. What are the causes and implications?
3. Prepare a report showing the similarities in the movements for equal rights for women and equal rights for Negroes.

Supplementary Reading

Benedict, Ruth, and Weltfish, Gene, *The Races of Mankind.* New York: Public Affairs Committee, 1943.

Berry, Brewton, *Race Relations.* Boston: Houghton Mifflin Company, 1951.

Boas, Franz, *Race, Language and Culture.* New York: The Macmillan Company, 1940.

de Beauvoir, Simone, *The Second Sex*. New York: Alfred A. Knopf, 1953.

de Gobineau, Arthur, *Inequalities of the Races*. 4 vols. First volume translated into English by H. Hotz. Philadelphia: J. B. Lippincott Company, 1856.

Handlin, Oscar, *The Newcomers: Negroes and Peurto Ricans in a Changing Metropolis*. Garden City, N.Y.: Doubleday and Company, Inc., 1962.

Klineberg, Otto, *Characteristics of the American Negro*. New York: Harper and Brothers, 1944.

Komarovsky, Mirra, *Women in the Modern World*. Boston: Little, Brown and Company, 1953.

Lundberg, Ferdinand, and Farnham, Marynia, *Modern Woman: The Lost Sex*. New York: Harper and Brothers, 1947.

Mead, Margaret, *Male and Female*. New York: William Morrow and Company, 1949.

Miller, Herbert A., *Races, Nations, and Classes*. Philadelphia: J. B. Lippincott Company, 1924.

Myrdal, Gunnar, *An American Dilemma*. New York: Harper and Brothers, 1944.

Simpson, George E., and Yinger, J. Milton, *Racial and Cultural Minorities*. New York: Harper and Brothers, 1953.

Stember, Charles H., *Education and Attitude Change: The Effect of Schooling on Prejudice Against Minority Groups*. New York: Institute of Human Relations Press, 1961.

21

SOCIAL ACTION AND CULTURAL DIFFERENCES

CULTURAL *differences which influence social actions are nationality, wealth, education, occupations, and rural-urban location. As with biological differences, the consequence of attaching social significance to cultural differences is in the assignment of varying statuses and roles to individuals and groups in the society.*

Cultural Differences Have Significant Influence upon Social Action

In the preceding chapter, we sought to show how social meanings attached to biological differences in age, sex, intelligence, and race affect the social behavior of people. We now examine the ways in which social relationships are influenced by differences in such cultural factors as nationality, wealth, education, occupation, and urban or rural residence.

One function of these cultural differences is to serve as bases for differential statuses. In this respect, the following discussion provides an introduction to Chapter 22 on social stratification, the process by which people in the relevant statuses are categorized in social hierarchies or classes.

A. NATIONALITY

Nationality Differences Lead to Socially Significant Differences in Relationships

A *nationality* is an aggregation of people usually living in a common territory and bound together by common cultural traits: language, religion, traditions, and customs. Out of these come similar institutional patterns and a strong "we" feeling produced by a common way of life. The Ukrainians in Russia, the Welsh in England, the Hakkas in China, and the Flemish in Belgium are a few examples of people bound together by nationality. Common traditions and customs lead each to a consciousness of kind and a conformity to similar folkways and sanctioned norms that represent a way of

living handed down from generation to generation.

A nationality becomes a *nation* when it has achieved self-government and established its own political institutions, usually in a continuous territory. There are few nations, however, which do not include more than one nationality. A problem of the nation containing several nationalities is the adjustment of these to the common way of life.

A Universal Characteristic of Nationalities Is an Ethnocentric Attitude Toward Their Own Cultural Patterns

We pointed out that races generally think of themselves as superior; the nationalities within the nations and races also show the same self-regard. This loyalty to one's own nationality is known as *ethnocentrism*. People are ethnocentric about almost every aspect of their national life. We think the best "place" is the place where we live; the best "food" is the food we eat; the right way to think or act is the way we think and act. The ways of others are inferior. Often the smallest nationality will show the most intense ethnocentrism. Louis Adamic, describing his experience with Montenegrin peasants upon a return visit to his native land, said: "No citizen of the United States, even if he lives in the best imaginable circumstance, loved his rich and powerful country more than the average Montenegrin loves his poor, tiny, rocky Montenegro. Foreigners, with their different sets of values (if any), find it hard to understand this patriotism and incline to consider the Black Mountaineer more or less a fool and a semi-wild man." [1]

We are not to be blamed because we are ethnocentric. These ways of thinking and acting are usually the only ways we know—for us, they are the normal ways. Therefore to hold to them with pride and to oppose those who would ridicule them is a normal reaction. Unfortunately, acting on these convictions may impede the development of harmonious intergroup or international relations.

A Nationality Strives to Preserve Its Way of Life

A nationality, like a nation, strives to preserve its cultural heritage. In an alien setting, it seeks to keep alive its language, its institutions, and other elements of its traditional mode of life. This effort, however, leads to separatism and in-group loyalty. This, in turn, often creates problems in its relationship to the host or native society.

Alien nationalities tend to segregate in common residential areas in order to maintain better their way of life. Intrusions from the outside can be more easily guarded against. In this manner, "Little Italies," "Little Polands," "Little Germanies," and other enclaves have appeared like a mosaic throughout America. "If you're looking for Norwegians, you have found the right place, all right. We sift the people as they pass through here—keep our own, and let the others go." So wrote Rolvaag of the Norwegian settlers in the American Midwest. [2]

The voluntary segregation of a nationality serves as a way of maintaining pride, self-respect, and protection against prejudices. It permits the preservation of the nationality system through social and recreational clubs, mutual aid societies, native language newspapers, and other means. A nationality that is large enough to have its own social world within the larger society can effectively impede its assimilation into the larger social system.

However, the segregation of nationalities, and of races, tends to accentuate differences between them and the society in which they are residing. Consequently, intergroup conflict may be bitter and prolonged.

Patterns of Behavior Toward Nationalities

Inevitably, a native population will have certain reactions to a nationality seeking to establish itself in a society. Contacts between the two are at first indirect since neither knows the other and knows little about the other's ways. The newcomer attaches himself to others of his nationality who have already become established, or he remains aloof. Much of what the native knows about a nationality is gained through gossip. Curiosity marks attempts to know the newcomer, but ignorance of his language and customs prevents intimate associations leading to understanding and mutual helpfulness. The native develops "pictures in his mind" that may reflect not the character of the newcomer but only his own prejudice.

The immigrant is welcomed by those who can use him to their advantage. This soon creates a difficulty, however, since it means conflict with natives who fear competition for their jobs, wage-cutting, and a lowered level of living. The entrance of immigrants who may become competitors for jobs has been a basis for restrictive immigration legislation in the United States, particularly as a limit on those whose social backgrounds are most unlike those of Americans.

Conflicts develop easily when the dominant group disparages the new nationality, exploits it, and discriminates against its members. The immigrant, especially his children, soon learns to fight back. This is one of the factors in the development of the gang fights among youth in the cities containing nationality areas. Michael Gold described the situation for New York's East Side of his youth. He reported that each street was occupied by a different nationality, and that the appearance of a strange boy on it was the signal for an attack. Beatings were administered without mercy—sticks, rocks, and fists were used relentlessly. He himself suffered three holes in his head and many black eyes from such street wars. [3] In recent years, New York's Harlem has become the scene of almost daily battles involving Puerto Rican youth. These conflicts are even more vicious than those of Gold's day.

Accommodations Are Essential to Both National and Native Groups

Natives and nationalities must, in the interest of common participation in social life, work out acceptable adjustments to each other. These accommodations are not difficult to establish when discrimination is weak and opportunities for common contacts are available. Despite the persistence of ethnocentric attitudes, mutual tolerance can permit the development of fruitful working relationships between the two groups.

Stable accommodations will require reducing the major sources of conflict. If members of a nationality insist on using only their own language, communication difficulties will impede interaction and mutual understanding. Unusual religious beliefs may so antagonize the native population as to inhibit the development of cooperative relations. On the other hand, the native society may generate resentment by refusing to honor the economic and legal rights of the minority groups. Acceptable accommodations of divergent interests may not be effected until after several generations have passed. One writer has observed, perhaps with some exaggeration, that "it takes three generations of a family to own a piece of land and four generations to erase their more obvious old world characteristics." [4]

Nationalities Become Assimilated in Various Degrees

The ultimate outcome of the experience of nationality groups is usually their assimilation into the native culture. Some European nations have sought to discourage or forbid the perpetuation of alien cultural practices within their borders. The experience of Alsace-Lorraine is a case in point. On the other hand, others like Switzerland and Belgium have persisted for centuries as multinationality countries. America, although providing various programs to facilitate the adjustment and absorption of newcomers, has followed a generally *laissez-faire* policy based on the "melting-pot" theory of voluntary assimilation. A Polish national once remarked: "In Germany, we were forced to become Germans, so we remained Poles. In America, you let us remain Poles, so we became Americans."

GRADUAL CHANGE Dropping nationality characteristics and picking up new ones are usually gradual processes, although accommodations are often made with considerable speed. Since accommodation produces changes in external relations, it can usually be effected with relatively little difficulty. Assimilation, however, which involves changes in values, sentiments, and loyalties, reaches deeper levels of experience. Alteration of these internalized attitudes is a slow, gradual process, and one that can be impeded by marked language differences and strong reciprocal prejudices. Marshall, studying the interactions between the Norwegian, Polish, and Welsh nationalities and native culture in Wisconsin, found that while the original value systems of these nationalities have been greatly modified, there still persisted among them all— after 40 to 90 years—several of their major Old World traits and countless minor ones. His conclusion was that, after this period of time, "we have instead of an amalgam from the melting pot, a mosaic of cultures." America still holds many pockets of unassimilated nationalities who have remained isolated in large cities and in some rural areas.

FACTORS IN ASSIMILATION We have noted in an earlier discussion, in Chapter 19, that public school education and intermarriage among members of the second and third generations are among the major factors in assimilation. (The latter may be seen as both cause and effect of cultural absorption.) We may briefly recall their role in the process.

The public schools present the ideals and norms of the dominant culture. Immigrant children are exposed to these norms and ideals through formal instruction and through their daily association with their schoolmates or peer groups. Beyond absorbing American ways themselves, they serve as a contact between their parents and the new culture. The relationship often brings conflict between parents and the young. The children often know little or nothing about their parents' culture and quickly lose any feeling for it if they do. Usually, the children insist on being part of the New World culture. In the process, they may have to overcome both parental resistance and rejection by native youth who suffer the prejudices of their parents. These combined forces can make accommodation difficult and assimilation doubly so.

Perhaps the final step in the destruction of the dominance of the old culture comes when children of immigrant families marry across nationality lines. Nationality, other than that of the dominant culture, has little significance in the selection of mates by children of the second and third generations.

Nationalism Is the Ethnocentric Attitude of Citizens Toward Their Nation

When a nationality has achieved self-government within its own territory, it becomes a nation. (Several nationalities may so combine.) No social phenomenon has developed more rapidly and tended more to separate societies from each other in modern times than has the development of the national consciousness of so many people. There are strong national feelings in Europe and America: "There will always be an England," "America First," and "Germany Over All" express the sometimes chauvinistic sentiment. People throughout the world in Asia, Africa, South America, and the Islands of the Seas are vigorously exerting their rights to freedom as nations. The European war settlement of 1919, which established the principle of national self-determination, implied that the reconstruction of societies should be on this foundation. This is the driving ambition of almost every people who have a common historical tradition and similar culture patterns which give them a common mode of life. It is the flaming aspiration of those peoples who have lately been under the domination of others.

Strengthening of National Bonds Is a Major Activity of Each Nation

LOYALTY IS NATURAL FOR THE NATIVES The basic problem of unifying any nation is to make its citizens cognizant of their common identity and their vital interest in strong social cohesion. Unity is not difficult to achieve when the nation has a homogeneity built on common language, common religion, and common racial and cultural backgrounds. The habits built from youth in the knowledge and use of its folkways and norms, and the pride that is engendered by its accomplishments, assure loyalty to it above all others. Citizens will evince loyalties in varying degrees to their churches, communities, and voluntary associations within and without their society, but loyalty to their nation usually supersedes all. This is the consequence of firmly established attitudes which result from continued identification with all that their nation has stood for.

The calm reaction of the old Japanese grandmother to the disillusionment of her granddaughter illustrates the ready loyalty typical of those who have been born and bred in their nation's unique distinctiveness:

"Honourable Grandmother," she said, pointing to a coloured map of the world, "I am much much troubled. I have just learned that our beloved land is only a few tiny islands in the great world."

The grandmother adjusted her big horn spectacles and for a few minutes carefully studied the map. Then with slow dignity she closed her book.

"It is quite natural, little Etsu-bo, for them

to make Japan look small in this map," she said. "It was made by the people of the black ships. Japan is made large in the Japanese maps of the world." [5]

HETEROGENEOUS NATIONS MUST CREATE COHESION The problem of loyalty is significantly different when a nation is composed of heterogeneous elements from many racial and cultural backgrounds who are already possessed of strong feelings toward their own heritage. It is an herculean task to create social cohesion from these varied elements—each with its divergent ideals, hopes, and fears—and yet allow the degree of self-realization congruent with the needs of the nation as a whole.

Communication Basic No doubt, the first necessity for establishing such unity is adequate means of communication. Usually, this means a common language. Some nations are so insistent upon the basic necessity of a national language that they would compel its use by all as a condition for enjoying many of the benefits of the society. There can be no denying that the existence of a single language makes the transmission of history, laws, and usages an easier task. However, there are ample illustrations of nations strong in spirit in which several languages or dialects have prevailed for long periods of time—Switzerland, England, and Sweden, to mention a few. Many different foreign languages have been spoken in the United States. Both World Wars I and II proved that the vast majority of those who spoke a foreign language were truly loyal to their adopted country. The foreign language newspapers have been a most valuable medium of presenting American ideals. In this country, English prevails as the national language, but forcing its use upon all would contradict the ideals of the society. There is little resistance to the acceptance of a national language which is a pervasive part of daily life and which is basic to educational and other institutions of the society. Moreover, the very toleration of foreign languages may further induce their users to adopt the national language.

Knowledge of Traditions The other necessity for such a unity is the development of respect for national traditions and culture. This cannot be accomplished by demeaning the traditions and culture of others. Nothing sets persons so rigidly against the adoption of new practices or views as any action that causes them to lose their own dignity. The process of substituting one national culture for another is promoted when those involved know that they have as good a chance of self-realization in relation to their ability as have any others. Nothing gains the devotion of a people so speedily as the discovery that the traditions of the host nation insist on individual liberty and social equality.

Formal Instruction Formal instruction in a nation's ideals is usually part of its educational program, where it is absorbed by the child in the schoolroom. This learning must be supplemented, of course, by daily activities that demonstrate in practice the ideals that are taught.

Other Techniques Have Been Used to Develop Nationalism

"SCAPEGOATING" "Scapegoating" is a practice some nations have used to develop national loyalty. Usually, some group is selected as the chief cause of a nation's difficulties. This "villain" must be controlled or eliminated. The Jews have been used many times in history for this role. Hitler's Germany made the Jews responsible for the misfortunes of that nation. Anti-Jewish propaganda was the recurrent practice of other European societies. Nor has the practice of "scapegoating" been unknown in the United States. Allen described its operation in the 1920's:

> Henry Ford discovered the menace of the "International Jew" and his *Dearborn Independent* accused the unhappy race of plotting the subjugation of the whole world and (for good measure) of being the source of almost every American affliction, including high rents, the shortage of farm labor, jazz, gambling, drunkenness, loose morals, and even short skirts. The Ford attack, absurd as it was, was merely an exaggerated manifestation of a widespread anti-Semitism. Prejudice became as pervasive as the air. Landlords grew less disposed to rent to Jewish tenants, and schools to admit Jewish boys and girls; there was a public scandal at Annapolis over the hazing of a Jewish boy; Harvard College seriously debated limiting the number of Jewish students; and all over the country Jews felt that a barrier had fallen between them and the Gentiles.[6]

SUPPRESSION Another method of trying to foster national loyalty is to suppress those who outspokenly challenge the nation's ideals and way of life. Socialists and Communists have been the subject of constant attacks. All forms of radicalism that seem to espouse causes contradictory to the general national views are fought in the name of the national welfare. Purging traitors within the nation is a common method used to reinforce loyalty.

Other methods seek to develop national cohesion by the use of fear. These usually defeat their own purposes, since the loyalty they develop is easily destroyed because it rests on a negative basis.

B. WEALTH

Wealth Is an Important Differentiating Factor

It was Goethe in his *Faust* who had the beautiful Margaret say, after she adorns herself with the jewelry Mephistopheles has left in the casket:

> Were but the ear-rings mine, alone:
> One has at once another air.
> What helps one's beauty, youthful blood?
> One may possess them, well and good;
> But none the more do others care.
> They praise us half in pity, sure:
> To gold still tends,
> On gold depends
> All, All! Alas, we poor! [7]

A SYMBOL OF ACHIEVEMENT The significance of wealth as a differentiating factor among people rests chiefly on two characteristics: (1) what it represents in personal achievement and (2) what it makes possible for its owners to do. We have commonly regarded the acquisition or possession of wealth as a sign of superior ability. As a consequence, positions of prominence and of power tend to go to the rich, provided their wealth has been gained according to the accepted rules of the society. Very often even the inheritor of wealth is presumed to be a person of competence, although he had nothing to do with its creation.

The businessman acquires a special status in the machine-marketing economy where production of goods and profits is a primary goal. The ability to organize and operate a successful business—meaning, making it pay in dollars—is commonly taken as a mark of competence and the resulting social position as a symbol of achievement.

WEALTH CAN GIVE THE GOODS OF LIFE The use of wealth is also an important criterion of social differentiation. There is little question of a good standard of living if wealth is available.

Beyond this, it is the possession of things to which the society has attached status values that makes the difference. Wealth makes possible costly sports, vacations, luxurious homes and automobiles, exclusive entertainment, and servants to maintain homes and gardens. (Veblen, an astute student of the "leisure class," called all this "conspicuous consumption.") All of these are inaccessible to the large majority of the people in a society. The ability to use our time as we wish and to avoid the necessity of work are important status-giving and differentiating factors. People strive for wealth because with it they can do almost anything they wish and when they want to. Thus, Ben Johnson was led to offer some questionable advice:

> Get money; still get money, boy,
> No matter by what means.[8]

C. EDUCATION

Educational Differences Have Resulted in Social Differences in All Societies

EDUCATION HAS DIFFERENTIATED PEOPLE THROUGHOUT HISTORY Differences in education have acted throughout history as socially differentiating factors. The most extreme example of this is probably to be found in old China. Although the examination system by which the scholars and leaders of that society were picked was democratic in that it was open to nearly all, the cost of preparation limited it to those who could afford it. The possession of wealth was a differentiator here. Once social position was gained by this method, however, it was retained.

From Grecian times to the present day, the educated class has been restricted to a few who were trained for special tasks which set them apart from the unlearned masses. When they first came into existence, elementary schools taught only the simplest of beginning subjects. Entrance to higher schools had to be prepared for by special tutoring or obtained in expensive private schools. Higher education was a product to be bought but, once purchased, it brought social benefits to the few who could afford it.

AMERICAN OBJECTIVES The objective in the American society has been to provide education on an equal basis to all. Schools, colleges, and universities include in their student bodies representatives from all social classes. In general,

the educational system tends to prepare youth to work in the occupational and social class to which their parents belong. Some exceptionally able children of the lower classes get an opportunity to move up the educational ladder, but usually the system tends to select and drop students from the lower classes in the early stages of the educational program. The usual explanation for this is inferior intelligence, which is, however, only a partial explanation. Other factors, including differences in social background and opportunity, must be taken into account.

Education Is a Steppingstone to Social Benefits

Robin Williams points out that, in American society, education has become the escalator to the better-paid and prestige-carrying occupations. This is true of other societies as well.[9] It is a major reason why fathers and mothers want their sons and daughters to go to college. A majority of parents, as reported in a *Fortune* magazine survey, wanted their children to be trained for some particular occupation or profession in order to have greater earning power. Among families at the lower levels, emphasis is placed on education as the means to achieve a higher social status. The higher status families take their higher level of education for granted, as a means of maintaining their family social position.[10]

Differentials in education operate in the industrial world. Management employs college-trained men for supervisory positions rather than promoting men from the worker ranks. Men from the ranks, lacking education, often do not have a capacity for handling other men and for relating themselves effectively to the higher levels of management. This gives the educated man a decided competitive advantage in the occupational world and makes it possible for him to rise relatively faster. Men from the ranks are blocked.[11]

Educational differentials are also a factor in blocking the advance of races and nationalities. Such obstacles are greatest among the Negroes, who have been most severely restricted by prejudice and discrimination. The lower incomes of both races and nationalities are also effective impediments, since most persons in these categories cannot afford college training for their children.

These Differentials Often Create Incompatibilities Between the Educated and Uneducated

Conflict between the learned and unlearned often exists. The untrained feel envy and jealousy and often want to reduce the educated to their level. They are often encouraged in this regard by others who wish to silence the educated for usually nefarious reasons. Politicians, teachers of a narrow religion, demagogues who wish to create social discontent, and quacks who oppose scientific applications, may all strive to hinder the work of the scholar. These conflicts rapidly disappear as the educational level of the society advances and the role of scientific principles in the practical affairs of life is generally understood. Farmers scoffed at the white-collared scientist not long ago. Today, they recognize him as an important colleague. They have learned, as others have, that nothing is so practical as a scientific principle or an established truth.

Uneducated people usually cannot understand why persons who pursue learning are often willing to forego many things to strive for the values that inhere in intellectual pursuits, to become scholars, or to search for scientific truth. Indeed, people who presumably have been educated sometimes display a similar attitude.

D. OCCUPATIONS

Occupations Have Always Been Differentiating Factors

Occupations have always served as a basis of social differentiation, social status, and social identity. Even at the primitive level, some division of labor is discernible. With the historical development of societies, the various traditional crafts emerged—often associated with kinship groupings. Indeed, many surnames persisting today derive from the relationship between family and occupation. (See Box 39.)

With the decline of familism and other bases of social standing in modern times, occupation gains greater significance than ever as the person's key status. Today, in inquiring about a stranger or new acquaintance, our question, "*Who* is he?" really means, "What does he *do* —what is his job or line of work?" Interestingly enough as more men engage in highly specialized and unfamiliar tasks, they tend to become identified on the basis of company affiliation— as a "Du Pont man" or a "GE man." This, in turn, seems to lead to differential evaluation of the employee in the community.

PRESTIGE RATINGS As we have noted at greater length in a previous discussion (Chapter 14 on economic institutions), occupations are accorded differing amounts of prestige depending upon various social criteria. Occupa-

---

BOX 39   WHAT'S IN A NAME?

Abbott	Fisher	Rector
Baker	Forester	Seaman
Barber	Glover	Shepherd
Bishop	Hooper	Singer
Bookbinder	Jester	Skinner
Brewer	Merchant	Smith
Butcher	Miller	Steward
Butler	Millman	Tanner
Carpenter	Miner	Taylor
Carter	Moneymaker	Wainwright
Chamberlain	Painter	Weaver
Cook	Pastor	Woodward
Cooper	Piper	Workman
Draper	Porter	Yeoman
Dyer	Priest	
Farmer	Sawyer	

---

tional prestige is reflected in the status of the family and its individual members. Thus, the wife of a banker or lawyer is given a prestige position commensurate with the position of these occupations in the society. The role of this factor in determining social class position is indicated in the following chapter.

Although within a given society, prestige ratings of occupations seem to be remarkably consistent, there is conspicuous variation between societies. For example, the artist, musician, and intellectual have been given high prestige in other societies whereas, until recently, they have not enjoyed comparable status in America.

Generally, throughout societies, a major criterion of evaluation is the relative amount of physical or mental labor required in the occupation. Manual labor usually has a demeaning cast and hence low prestige ratings. Although their contributions are indispensable, the "hewers of wood and drawers of water" have rarely, if ever, enjoyed high esteem. Conversely, as the mental component of work increases, its prestige rating rises. Professional people, such as doctors, lawyers, ministers, professors, and business executives, rate high on all empirical scales of measurement.

Societies Reward Workers in Terms of Occupational Prestige

Societies compensate workers in different occupations on the basis of the social prestige rating and the social contribution they believe the occupation makes. Professional and managerial workers usually command the highest salaries while unskilled workers, such as common laborers, receive the lowest wages. This differential does not always hold, however. Ministers of religion and college professors are not usually compensated commensurately with other professions, although they are thought to make important contributions to their societies and are commonly given much prestige because of the nature of their work. Even the President of the United States, who occupies the highest prestige office in the land, does not receive as much compensation as do many business executives. The prestige derived from such positions seems to be considered part of the compensation and is sometimes called "psychic income." (In the special sense that "psychic" means "outside the realm of the known," it is an apt adjective!)

On the other hand, occupations that return large incomes may not carry any social prestige because we consider them antisocial. Gambling and dope-selling are not only rated low but are vigorously combatted as socially harmful.

Occupations Differentiate Ways of Living

As we have previously seen, societies dominated by the machine-marketing types of economy develop an ever-increasing number of occupations. Division of labor and specialization have reached such an extent that now nearly all occupations are specializations. This subdivision has meant increased interdependence and cooperation so that workers are closely unified in their work relations in a given occupational area, such as the complex production of automobiles. Such unification creates ways of living that are characteristic of various occupational areas. A specialization that is of a highly individualistic sort, as it is with physicians, develops common interests among the professions' workers that knit them into a certain pattern of living.

It is often said that farming is more than a way to make a living—it is a way of life. This may be said in truth of virtually all occupations that men engage in for any significant period. The occupation is a way of living, in part, because it controls the mental outlook of the workers. Each person comes to think and act in terms of his work. His interests center about it, and his values are determined by it. Indeed, his whole life is largely structured by it. (See Chapter 14.)

A consequence of this specialization is the narrowing of social outlook. We tend to see life in only one of its aspects and do not see it whole. The worker in a special field may therefore miss much that surrounds him and become limited in thought and action. It is not difficult for a scholar, for example, to lose touch with all but his own small intellectual vineyard.

The corrective for such occupational overspecialization is the development of a wider educational outlook through the creation of avocational interests that will supply it. A serious defect of the modern-day occupational world is its failure to provide constructive programs for aiding workers in avocational activities or for indicating areas where avocational values may be found.

E. RURAL-URBAN

Differences in Rural and Urban Populations Are Relative

In one guise or another through history, the "country bumpkin" and the "city slicker" have symbolized one of the oldest forms of social differentiation—and antipathy—in human society. "Rube" and "dude" have stood for styles of life almost as disparate as those of two different cultures. In this perspective, urban and rural sociologists have traditionally distinguished between country and city people on the basis of personality and social characteristics each is presumed to possess.[12]

Actually, in America at least, city and country today represent not dichotomies but poles on an urban-rural continuum. Within this broad frame of reference, we see that the specific social differences in such attributes as heterogeneity-homogeneity, social mobility, and formal and informal control would fall along a series of gradients or scales drawn from megalopolis to the open country. (See Box 40.)

To be sure, we might be justified in drawing sharp social differences between urban and rural modes if we were viewing an earlier period, say before World War I, when an almost wholly different state of the arts existed. However, the changes brought by industrialism, including those in farming, have remarkably altered older patterns and created a social milieu in which differentiation between rural and urban can be made only in the most general terms. What once were relatively clear-cut variations are merging—already have merged in many places—into integrated forms of living that do not manifest attributes that are distinctly urban or rural in character. Indeed, the social differences *within* city and country are surely as great as those *between* them.

Of course, there are some respects in which life in the country and in the large urban agglomerations does differ. But, essentially, these differences result from adaptations to forces that belong neither exclusively to the city nor to the rural area but accompany the decisive changes that have taken place in the whole culture. We shall now consider some of these differences that influence social actions.

BOX 40   RURAL-URBAN CONTINUUM

| | | | | | Metropolitan | |
| Farmstead | Hamlet | Village | Town | City | Area | Megalopolis |

→ Increasing size, density, and complexity of social structure →

Some Presumed Differences

1. Urban dwellers have more interpersonal contacts than rural dwellers.
2. Urbanites tend to interact in terms of specific social roles, whereas rural dwellers are more likely to interact as whole personalities.
3. Primary contacts are more common among rural than among city people.
4. Interaction among urban dwellers is characterized by greater anonymity.
5. Interaction among urbanites tends to be utilitarian or instrumental—use each other as means to ends.
6. Contacts among urbanites are spatially more diffuse.
7. Urban dwellers tend to be more tolerant of social differences, and more relativistic in judgments, than are rural people.[13]

The use of the terms "rural" and "urban" in current publications reveals a gross lack of agreement concerning their referents. This is interpreted as resulting from the failure to distinguish the influences upon men's actions of density and size of population, on the one hand, from the influences of culture, on the other. Although these two categories of influences cannot be severed in actuality, they must be distinguished if the nature of communities is to be perceived clearly.[14]

The Occupations of City and Country Are Characterized Both by Similarity and Diversity

OCCUPATION AND SPACE The activity that has been basic to rural-urban differences is occupation. Rural people are primarily engaged in producing food and fiber from the soil or in using products of the soil. Agriculture requires space since plants and animals can only be produced where soil areas are relatively extensive and open to nature, no matter how intensive the agriculture. On the other hand, occupations of urban residents, especially the processing and distributing of goods and services, are better pursued in relatively concentrated areas. Farms cover much territory, whereas factories, stores, and office buildings cover relatively little. Residence, too, is differentiated in that farmers live on scattered farmsteads or in concentrated but dispersed villages with their work readily accessible. Urban residents live in concentrated residential districts that also permit relatively ready access to their jobs. The suburbanite is, of course, an exception.

DIFFERENCES IN JOBS The work of farmers is somewhat similar since they produce food and fiber materials from the soil. They plow, plant, cultivate, harvest, feed, and market. City residents process and distribute many varieties of goods and provide many varieties of services that attend these activities. Therefore, their work is varied, diversified, and specialized.

But there is oversimplification here. It is difficult to see the diversification in the occupation of the farmer and the specialization of different farmers because they are physically dispersed. On the other hand, urban residents deal with a variety of goods and services in their manufacture and distribution. It is easy, though, to overlook the sameness that exists in these urban occupations. It makes little difference what is being made—machine operatives do virtually the same types of work in all factories. It makes little difference what is being sold—clerks in stores do much the same things. It makes little difference whether we are delivering groceries, coal, or flowers—we are doing much the same thing in each case. We may say here that the urban worker, whether he be bookkeeper or lawyer, is doing much the same thing within his occupation as all other persons in theirs. The city has a concentration of many different occupations requiring similar activities, however, whereas there is a dispersal in the rural area of similar activities relative to one chief occupation—farming.

Specialization Is a Characteristic of Industrial-Marketing Societies and Affects Rural and Urban Alike

It is often suggested that specialization is primarily a characteristic of the cities. The implication is that the major occupation of farming does not specialize. It is true that Washington, D.C., is primarily a government city and that its workers are chiefly government clerks of higher or lower grades; that Detroit is an automobile manufacturing center; that Hollywood is the motion picture capital of the world; that Mecca and Jerusalem are religious centers; and that Hong Kong is a commercial exchange market. But none of these shows any greater specialization than the corn-hog belt of the American Midwest, the bulb-producing areas of the Dutch low-country farm sections, or the sheep- and wool-producing areas of Australia.

Specialization is a characteristic of today's industrial and marketing civilization. It characterizes all activities, urban and rural. Specialization is necessarily spread over wide areas in agriculture and, equally necessarily, is concentrated in small areas in manufacturing, distribution, and financing. Consequently, rural areas are thinly, and urban areas densely, populated. There is, however, a far closer interdependence between the financial operators in Des Moines and the corn-hog producers of central Iowa than between the corn-hog producers of central Iowa and the citrus growers of California. The financial operators in Des Moines are, in fact, part of the corn-hog specialization, while the citrus growers have little or nothing in common with it.

The Demands of Forms of Work Differ for Rural and Urban Residents

Bierstedt has said:

> The countryside presents a sameness to those who dwell on the land. The city alters its attractions with every passing block. . . . The countryman's corner of earth imposes upon him a more homogeneous round of activity than his cousin in the city pursues. He responds more directly to hours of daylight and the hours of night, follows in greater harmony the progression of the seasons. . . . The countryman pursues his span of life in intimate relationships with the physical forces that make the day and the year, the weather,

and the wind. . . . The city man, on the contrary, performs his tasks in independence of the wind's vicissitudes and the season's change.[15]

Cannot these statements be directly reversed? The countryside alters its attractions—fields and forests, cattle and poultry; there is a change with every passing day. The city presents a sameness—asphalt streets, regular rows of immovable buildings; the same newspaper-reading travel companions; the same pattern of machines, desks, or counters—day and month, year in and year out. The countryman's corner of earth imposes upon him a heterogeneous round of activity—tilling a field, planning a farm layout, feeding animals, balancing books, repairing machines, painting buildings, marketing hogs. His cousin in the city pursues day after day and month after month the same tasks, repeated with a monotony that makes it imperative for his employers to shift him from job to job or to develop avocational after-hour activities that give him some relief from monotony. The city man responds more directly to the hours of the daylight and the hours of the night—he must catch the seven o'clock bus or he will be docked for not punching the company clock by eight. Nor can he stop until the whistle blows at twelve. This whistle makes him resume at one o'clock to continue till it blows again at five. He follows this pattern spring, winter, summer, and fall, hardly knowing that spring turns into summer and summer into fall. His country cousin gets up at five or six in the morning, but he doesn't have to report to his field at an exact moment and he may take—and usually does—the time he needs to enjoy his home-cooked breakfast. He may take the day off, especially when the crops are in, to go to town, and no one is going to tell him he cannot. His time is largely his own when winter rolls around, even to a winter vacation in a sunny climate if he has a hired man to take care of his stock.

The city contains an almost endless number of jobs. But the city man, like the farmer, usually earns his living from only one area of work. Once he has been in that work for a time, it is difficult for him to shift to another. Though the city man is not faced with capricious fates governing wind and storm, his job is usually so interwoven with other jobs that when there is a breakdown—a strike or a depression—he is in a precarious situation. And it is the city worker for whom unemployment insurance is provided.

Social Relationships Are Probably More Primary for Rural Than for Urban Residents

There are few data to prove that social relationships contain more intimate primary group contacts for the rural resident than for the urban dweller, though this is commonly asserted. The urban dweller probably has more secondary associations than the rural dweller. The simple fact of population concentration and movement in the city would account for the latter circumstance.

Yet, the implication must not be given that urban relationships are all of the secondary sort. Every city is composed of neighborhoods where many people live on intimate terms. True, they do not associate on a primary group basis with everybody in their neighborhood. Neither is this true of rural residents, although the fact that rural residents usually know their neighbors is taken to mean that they are intimate with them. Cities contain a large number of voluntary associations, clubs, lodges, and church organizations in which the city dweller finds his primary group associates. They can be as intimate and as numerous as those of the rural people. Interest groupings of every sort abound in the city. Associations are face-to-face and highly personal in these, also.

Changes Are Rapidly Reducing the Differences Between Rural and Urban People

COMMUNICATION AND TRAVEL DEVELOP SIMILARITY Not much more than a quarter of a century ago, the major emphasis in discussions of rural life was on isolation, the movement of farm people to the cities, and the characteristic physical appearance and psychological outlook of farm residents. They emphasized the independence of the farm folk and their close contacts with, and dependence on, the natural elements. The fiction of a rural mind that was narrow and limited was created out of these studies. There never really was any truth in this view, and it certainly is not true today. It is admitted that the experiences of rural and urban people were quite different in those earlier days, and that the things they worked with resulted in different attitudes. But the rural person who wears over-alls and who gawks at tall buildings in the city is no more provincial than the city resident who rarely ventures beyond the few blocks which define his day-to-day environs. The farmer who is superstitious about the right time for planting corn is no more common than the city speculator who consults a fortune-teller or astrologer before selling his AT and T stock. And the rustic who is suspicious has a city cousin who keeps one eye cocked on the butcher's thumb as he weighs out the filet mignon or hamburg.

Today, common elements in the economy (from standard products to business practices), widespread rural-urban travel, and the mass media of communication are causing even greater similarities in the thinking, dress, and modes of life of the city and country dwellers. Not everyone would be entirely happy with the change.

OCCUPATIONAL DIVERSITY Rural areas are being increasingly characterized by the same occupational diversity found in the city. There has long been a common impression that the rural areas are occupied predominantly by farmers and that all farmers fall into one occupational grouping. This view is a holdover from the past, when rural areas actually were predominantly farming areas and a large proportion of the farmers carried on the same activities. However, today the great proportion of residents in rural areas of the United States work at some occupation other than farming. Farming itself is more and more specialized as well as mechanized so that often within the same community, and certainly between communities, the interests of farmers are dissimilar. In fact, they are often competitive.

The proportions of nonfarmers to farmers in rural areas will continue to rise and occupational diversity will grow at an accelerating rate, as the movement of nonfarming people into rural areas continues and the number of farms and farmers themselves decreases due to increased mechanization. This will result, as it already has in many places, in situations where a chief task in the rural community will be the integration of residents with different interests around common community goals.

POPULATION CHANGE Rural areas are also being characterized by increased population diversity. The migration of people to the suburbs and open country is giving rural areas a more diversified population. This movement has been accompanied by the spread of urban culture. Rural areas now have practically everything the cities have and some things the cities cannot have—open space, fields, and forests. Rural areas in the United States already have electricity, automobiles, paved or improved roads, telephones, radios, and television. In addition, there are ample dwelling units with modern facilities, such as refrigerators, running water, indoor bathrooms, business delivery services, and virtually every other thing to assure a comfortable home and community life. It is not meant that *every* area or *every* family in the rural sections of the United States has these things, but rural families already have them in as large proportions as do families in the cities.

Some years ago, Dean Liberty Hyde Bailey of Cornell said, "I doubt the philosophy that would improve the open country by moving the attractions of the city into it." We do not know if Dr. Bailey ever changed his mind about this. But whether he did or not, the attractions of the city have moved into the country until today rural areas possess virtually everything our cities have. They have ready access to the city and retain their own unique values. The revolutionary changes in transportation, communication, and mechanization, with their influences on the homes and other institutional agencies in rural areas, have already created what appears to be the most attractive dwelling environment to many people.

Although cities continue to have a functional dominance in the organization patterns of societies, differences between rural and urban areas increasingly disappear everywhere. This dispersing trend will no doubt continue, spreading the population over the total area, particularly for residence purposes. Services will go with them so that what has been distinctly rural and urban can conceivably become, neither rural nor urban, but "rurban." (See Boxes 41 and 42 for some implications of suburbanism.)

BOX 41 THE "BETTER ELEMENT" MOVES OUT OF THE CITY

Data from . . . national samples indicate that the suburban belts around standard metropolitan area central cities between 1950 and 1956 became areas of increased concentration of families (1) with higher incomes, (2) whose heads had skilled or semi-

BOX 41 (*Cont.*)

skilled occupations, (3) who were engaged in raising children, and (4) who were living in more expensive housing. During this period, the areas beyond the suburban belts had greater increase in families whose heads had business or professional occupations and in moderate cash housing than did the central cities. . . . [The] increased suburban concentration of skilled and semi-skilled family heads points up a growth in suburban occupational heterogeneity as more prosperous families continue to overflow rigid central city boundaries.[16]

"Classville, U.S.A."

"Economically segregated communities are springing up," Mr. Lazarus said, noting that the suburbs were being built by middle class families who have left the cities to the rich and the poor.

The heart of the problem, he said, is that the children of these single-economic-class "ghettos" are not being properly exposed to life, and cannot be expected to "walk straight out of a social incubator and cope with a world of national and international conflict."[17]

BOX 42   Perspectives on Suburbia

The wreath that rings every U.S. metropolis is a green garland of place names and people collectively called Suburbia. It weaves through the hills beyond the cities, marches across flatlands that once were farms and pastures, dips into gullies and woodlands, straddles the rocky hillocks and surrounds the lonesome crossroads. Oftener than not it has a lilting polyphony that sings of trees (Streamwood, Elmwood, Lakewood, Kirkwood), the rolling country (Cedar Hill, Cockrell Hill, Forest Hills), or the primeval timberlands (Forest Grove, Park Forest, Oak Park, Deer Park). But it has its roots in such venerable names as Salem, Greenwich, Chester, Berkeley, Evanston, Sewickley and Rye.

In those towns and hills and groves last week the splendor of a new summer seemed, as always, to give a new lilt to life. The hills and fields triumphed with fresh green grass. In the old towns, the giant oaks and elms threw rich new shade across the white colonial mansions and the square, peaked-roofed clapboard houses. In fresh-minted subdivisions, sycamore striplings strained at their stakes to promise token cover for the bare houses of glass, steel, stone and shingle that have sprouted (19 million since 1940) as from a bottomless nest of Chinese boxes. School buses headed toward the season's last mile; power mowers and outboard motors pulsed the season's first promise. Fragrance of honeysuckle and roses overlay the smell of charcoal and seared beef. The thud of baseball against mitt, the abrasive grind of roller skate against concrete, the jarring harmony of the Good Humor bell tolled the day: the clink of ice, the distant laugh, the surge of hi-fi through the open window came with the night.

For better or for worse, Suburbia in the 1960s is the U.S.'s grass-roots. In Suburbia live one-third of the nation, roughly 60 million people who represent every patch of democracy's hand-stitched quilt, every economic layer, every laboring and professional pursuit in the country. Suburbia is the nation's broadening young middle class, staking out its claim across the landscape, prospecting on a trial-and-error basis for the good way of life for itself and for the children that it produces with such rapidity. It is, as Social Scientist Max Lerner (*America as a Civilization*) has put it, "the focus of most of the forces that are remaking American life today."[18]

BOX 42 (*Cont.*)

In suburbia we have communities without a history—without tradition. The pioneers or early settlers were staking out their homesteads at about the same time that the newcomers from Keokuk and Kankekee were loading their furniture in Allied Moving Vans. There can be in these settlements only the most diffuse connections with our cultural heritage—a heritage which is often mediated to us most concretely by local heroes and local landmarks of the past. In none of these communities did Lincoln speak or Washington sleep. No Sherman has marched through them. There will be no Williamsburg restorations in suburbia. There will be no "Our Town"—and probably not even a Thornton Wilder. Pride of place and sense of history seem to dissolve in the limited dreams of the Great Society.[19]

References

1. Adamic, Louis, *The Native's Return* (New York, Harper and Brothers, 1934), p. 131.
2. Rolvaag, O. E., *Giants in the Earth* (New York, Harper and Brothers, 1929), p. 316.
3. Gold, Michael, *Jews Without Money* (New York, Liveright Publishing Corp., 1930), pp. 42–43.
4. Marshall, D. G., "Nationality and the Emerging Culture," *Rural Sociology*, 13 (March, 1948), pp. 40–47.
5. Sugimoto, Etsu I., *A Daughter of the Samurai* (Garden City, N.Y., Doubleday, Doran and Company, Inc., 1935), p. 312.
6. Allen, F. L., *Only Yesterday* (New York, Harper and Brothers, 1931), p. 64.
7. Goethe, J. W., *Faust* (New York, Random House), p. 104.
8. Jonson, Ben, "Every Man in His Humor," Act II, Scene 5, in *Yale Studies in English* (New Haven, Conn., Yale University Press, 1921), p. 97.
9. Williams, R. M., *American Society* (New York, Alfred A. Knopf, 1960), p. 281.
10. Brookover, W. B., "Education in American Culture," in Schuler, E. A., *et al.*, *Outside Readings in Sociology* (New York, Thomas Y. Crowell Co., 1952), pp. 543–547.
11. Warner, W. L., Meaker, M., and Eells, K., *Social Class in America* (Chicago, Science Research Associates, Inc., 1949), p. 29.
12. See, for example, Nelson, Lowry, *Rural Sociology* (New York, American Book Company, 1948), p. 24, and Sorokin, P., and Zimmerman, C. C., *Principles of Rural-Urban Sociology* (New York, Holt and Company, Inc., 1929), p. 56.
13. Adapted from Hatt, Paul K., and Reiss, Albert J., Jr. (eds.), *Cities and Society: Revised Reader in Urban Sociology* (Glencoe, Ill.: The Free Press, 1957), p. 631.
14. Dewey, Richard, "The Rural-Urban Continuum: Real but Relatively Unimportant," *American Journal of Sociology*, 66 (July, 1960), p. 60. University of Chicago Press; copyright, 1960, by the University of Chicago.
15. Bierstedt, Robert, *The Social Order* (New York, McGraw-Hill Book Co., Inc., 1957), pp. 381–382.
16. Lazerwitz, Bernard, "Metropolitan Community Residential Belts, 1950 and 1956," *American Sociological Review*, 25 (April, 1960), p. 245. See also Whitney, Vincent H., "Changes in Rural-Nonform Population, 1930–1950," *American Sociological Review*, 25 (June, 1960), pp. 363–368.
17. *The New York Times* (October 17, 1962). See also Lieberson, Stanley, "Suburbs and Ethnic Residential Patterns," *American Journal of Sociology*, 67 (May, 1962), pp. 673–681.

18. "Suburbia, U.S.A.," *Time* (June 20, 1960), p. 14. Courtesy of *Time;* copyright 1960, by Time, Inc.
19. From a lecture by Frederick B. Parker.

Questions for Study and Discussion

1. What forms of minority reactions to discrimination seem to offer the most constructive ways of overcoming it?
2. In what ways is ethnocentrism a constructive force? A destructive force?
3. How many frustration encourage "scapegoating"?
4. What are the relations between patriotism, nationalism, and ethnocentrism?
5. What differences would you find between the aliens who have come to America since World War II and those who came before World War I?
6. What evidence of the decline of rural-urban differences can you note in your area?
7. What roles do differences in education play in the functioning of the community where you live?
8. What social values do you see in a college education?
9. How important are differences in wealth in the social life of your community? How do they express themselves?
10. Illustrate the prestige differences in occupations as they express themselves in your community.
11. What changes in social patterns seem to be produced by modern suburban living?

Suggested Topics for Reports

1. From US Census data, determine the rates of naturalization for major nationality groups in America. How would you account for the differences?
2. Devise a list of 25 common occupations and ask a sample of your student colleagues to rate them from one through 25 according to prestige. Calculate the average "prestige value" of each occupation and attempt to account for the differential ratings.
3. Select a city with which you are familiar, locate the new shopping centers that have appeared on its periphery, and survey the older central business district to determine the number and kinds of stores which have gone to the suburbs or gone out of business.

Supplementary Reading

Barron, Milton L. (ed.), *American Minorities.* New York: Alfred A. Knopf, 1957.

Duncan, Otis D., and Reiss, Albert J., Jr., *Social Characteristics of Urban and Rural Communities, 1950.* New York: John Wiley and Sons, Inc., 1956.

Gallaher, Art, *Plainville Fifteen Years Later.* New York: Columbia University Press, 1961.

Ginzberg, Eli, *et al., Occupational Choice: An Approach to a General Cultural Theory.* New York: Columbia University Press, 1951.

Hatt, Paul K., and Reiss, Albert J., Jr. (eds.), *Cities and Society: Revised Reader in Urban Sociology.* Glencoe, Ill.: The Free Press, 1957.

Kramer, Judith R., and Levantman, Seymour, *Children of the Gilded Ghetto: Conflict Resolutions of Three Generations of American Jews.* New Haven, Conn.: Yale University Press, 1961.

Lynd, R. S., and Lynd, H. M., *Middletown in Transition.* New York: Harcourt, Brace and Company, 1937.

Parsons, Talcott, *Essays in Sociological Theory, Pure and Applied.* Glencoe, Ill.: The Free Press, 1949.

Reiss, Albert J., *et al.*, *Occupations and Social Status.* New York: The Free Press of Glencoe, 1962.

Sorokin, Pitirim, Zimmerman, Carl C., and Galpin, Charles J., *Systematic Source Book in Rural Sociology*, 3 vols. Minneapolis, Minn.: The University of Minnesota Press, 1930.

West, James, *Plainville, U.S.A.* New York: Columbia University Press, 1945.

White, Leslie A., *The Science of Culture.* New York: Farrar, Straus and Cudahy, 1949.

Williams, Robin M., Jr., *American Society.* Rev. ed. New York: Alfred A. Knopf, 1960.

———, *The Reduction of Intergroup Tensions.* New York: Social Science Research Council, 1947.

22

SOCIAL STRATIFICATION: CLASS AND CASTE

S OCIALLY significant differences in societies lead to the stratification of populations and systems of hierarchical relationships. This process expresses itself in the formation of social classes. These develop different degrees of rigidity, ranging from open forms where movement up and down the social scale is relatively free to closed forms or castes where social position is fixed for life by social heritage. Class consciousness must exist to a relatively high degree to lead to class conflicts.

I. STRATIFICATION

Societies Stratify on the Basis of Socially Significant Differences

Virtually all societies develop systems of hierarchical relationships or *social stratification*. If no stratification existed in a society, it would necessarily have a small homogeneous population. Its occupations would be of such a nature that no significant division of labor existed, competition and conflict would be absent, and social control would rest in the whole population. It is difficult to conceive of societies meeting these conditions except under unusual or very primitive circumstances. A society can hardly exist for long without division of its social functions. Gradation of function is indicated by the power and control the husbands and fathers have over their wives and children even in the simplest societies. These gradations multiply as societies develop complexity.

The basic origin of stratification lies in the universal tendency to evaluate socially significant differences arising from biological and cultural variations among people. These socially significant variations lead to differential positions carrying different prestige and esteem values. Since some of these differences are fixed in the positions of the society, respect, esteem, prestige, and power are associated with them. Participation in a society is influenced by them because of the social inequalities they create.

A SIMPLE ILLUSTRATION A visitor was watching an outdoor basketball game in a certain community when his attention was attracted to a group of five teen-age girls who were conversing near the sidelines. He noticed particularly a sixth girl who was circling the group, laughing loudly at the comments of the other girls and trying in various ways, such as smiling and nodding approval, to become a part of the group. Her behavior was so noticeable that the visitor asked his host if there was something wrong with the girl. "Oh, no," the answer came, "she is just one of those tenant girls who lives down the road." The five others were daughters of landowners. There was no place in their group for a tenant's daughter, though she was of the same age and obviously craved acceptance. The stratification barriers based on landownership kept her out. (For a more complex satirical illustration, see Box 43.)

The formalization of these differential relationship systems places people and groups in different ranks of social superiors and social inferiors, in which the reciprocal relationships imply obligations and rights. These hierarchical ranks give societies their "successive layer" character that subdivide societies into levels of function and power.

Stratification Can Be Studied as a Structural Concept

We place our consideration of social stratification in this division of the book dealing with social action or functioning (it could just as well have been considered in the part dealing with social structure). The consequence of the layer-

---

BOX 43   SIGNS OF STATUS IN WASHINGTON

By now you likely have read, or at least read about, a book called "The Status Seekers." It is all about people who aren't content with the status quo.

The book tells us how to recognize status seekers by their status symbols. It is a best-seller just about everywhere, except in Washington.

I suspect it lost sales status here because it made people self-conscious. Few places are more status-minded, or have more status symbols, than the U.S. capital.

I have done some research on federal status seeking which I offer, in the interests of science, as a footnote to the book.

For laboratory purposes, let us divide the seekers into four classes—civil servants, bureaucrats, very important persons (VIP) and eggheads. Then let us examine their status symbols in the following fields:

Transportation to work: Civil servant—rides bus. Bureaucrat—has permit to park own car in government lot. VIP—has government limousine and chauffeur. Egghead—walks.

Office space: Civil servant—has small desk in large outer office. Bureaucrat—has large desk in small inner office. VIP—has large desk in larger inner office. Egghead—has briefcase.

Lunch: Civil servant—eats in government cafeteria. Bureaucrat—has two-hour, two-martini lunch in downtown restaurant. VIP—has two-hour, two-martini lunch in private dining room. Egghead—brings own lunch in briefcase.

Cocktail hour: Civil servant—has two beers at home. Bureaucrat—attends big cocktail party given by lobbyist. VIP—attends small cocktail party given by lobbyist. Egghead—has two glasses of wine at home.

Dinner: Civil servant—eats at home. Bureaucrat—has two-hour, two-martini dinner in downtown restaurant. VIP—attends two-hour, two-martini dinner party given by lobbyist. Egghead—cooks own dinner.

Parades: Civil servant—watches from sidewalk. Bureaucrat—watches from office window. VIP—rides in procession. Egghead—ignores whole thing.

Receptions: Civil servant—not invited. Bureaucrat—invited. VIP—stands in receiving. Egghead—invited but doesn't attend.

Travel: Civil servant—commercial airline, makes own reservation. Bureaucrat—commercial airline, secretary makes reservation. VIP—government plane. Egghead—rides bus.

Press relations: Civil servant—writes letters to editors. Bureaucrat—leaks news to reporters. VIP—holds press conference. Egghead—buys newspaper.

Congressional hearings: Civil servant—carries bureaucrat's briefcase. Bureaucrat—testifies before subcommittee. VIP—testifies before full committee. Egghead—tells VIP what to say.[1]

---

ing process in a society is the creation of structural forms—social classes. While class is an ambiguous term used in many ways, it implies strata of social positions with differences in prestige in a society.

In some societies, classes are not clearly structured and tend to be, if present, only the grouping of persons with incipient structural character. In others, they are rigidly patterned and institutionalized as in a caste system. Class implies movement up and down a social scale, as well as sanctioned normative complexes attached to social positions that have become fixed. Therefore, caste organization is an institutionalized structural system. A particular caste is an institutional agency that makes this fixed relationship system functional in a society. Because stratification implies movement up and down the social scale and is a matter of evaluation based on many possible characteristics, we discuss it in this section, recognizing that it can be approached from the structural viewpoint and, in that case, is most properly approached as an institution.

Social Stratification Performs Several Functions in Societies

The stratification or layering of societal structure into graded divisions of prestige and power performs several services in a society. An excellent presentation of these is made by Kingsley Davis and Wilbert Moore; they are restated by Davis in his *Human Society*.[2] We summarize the analysis and add one or two other functions of a general character.

(1) Stratification in societies is functionally necessary to the placement and motivation of individuals to effect the performance of their necessary social duties. (2) Since the duties associated with various positions in societies are not all equally agreeable to individuals and equally important to societies, and because some require more training or talent than others, societies must inevitably have some rewards or inducements and some ways of distributing these rewards differentially according to the different positions. The distribution of these rewards gives rise to social stratification. (3) The rewards—usually economic, prestige, and leisure—are built into the social positions so that, being unequal, they result in inequality of the positions. This is what stratification is: the organization of societies into hierarchies of status levels based upon the inequality of social positions.

This organization of societies into hierarchies of status levels serves to obtain the performance of functions needed to operate a society properly. There must be authority in government, to use the Davis-Moore illustration. Governmental officials command and citizens must comply because societies have granted this authority and fixed the responsibility. Some occupations are rewarded with high income because they are essential to a society's operation, while others are given smaller rewards because they are judged to be less important or because almost anyone can perform them. Stratification sets apart the various positions of a society in a hierarchy of status levels that regulates the relationships between the people within a society all the way through the social order. Practices appropriate to each level maintain the proper accommodations within each level and between the different levels.

Israel's Collective Settlements Illustrate the Almost Certain Establishment of Societal Stratification

An interesting illustration of the almost inevitable development of social stratification in human societies is given by the collective settlements in the new state of Israel.[3] Some 200 agricultural collectives operate on a completely communal basis where all property belongs to the commune. Members who leave have no claim to any of it. There is no exchange or labor market in a commune. Members are assigned to their work by an elected work committee, and all administrative officers and branch managers are elected for one or two years. The principles of turnover and rotation operate. The member's position in the administrative setup is not related to material returns for the basic norm is "from everyone according to ability—to everyone according to need." All commodities are distributed centrally and in kind. Meals are eaten in a communal dining hall. Children are brought up from birth in communal children's homes. Political institutions are equalitarian, each decision being made by majority vote, one vote per member. There is no economic differentiation between members.

Yet distinct social strata have emerged in this equalitarian setup. Members have developed stereotyped attitudes recognizing high and low statuses where none are supposed to exist. The stratification has arisen because managerial and other leadership positions are of vital importance to the operation of the communes. Scarcity has put a premium on capable members with leadership ability. Functional necessity keeps these valuable persons in their leadership positions. Prestige has become associated with them. Those having these positions are given high social status, which bring them recognition and emotional benefits the other members do not get, although they do not carry added economic rewards. This leads to struggles between the managerial and leadership stratum and the rank-and-file members. The leadership stratum tries to satisfy the lower stratum through "ideological education" that will result in their emotional satisfaction. But the struggle between these levels goes on.

Several Different General Conditions Have Created Social Stratification

This development of accommodations within societies on a basis of higher and lower status results from many circumstances. Stratification arises generally from (1) biological differences and from (2) cultural differences, as we have previously noted. A race, a subdivision within a race, or a sex has gained dominance over another by some means where biological differences have been given differential social evaluation. Some distinctive, culturally created condition has resulted in the granting of statuses and roles to one segment of a population in preference to others on the basis of value judgments that express the worth of the differences. These social differences result in stratification. Biological and social circumstances supplement each other in creating stratification in most situations.

CONQUEST Conquest has been one of the traditional circumstances resulting in stratification. History is replete with instances wherein war and capture have reduced people to an inferior status in a social order. Conquerors always try to benefit from their triumphs, which often means they gain new material possessions and an added labor supply. Conquered peoples are given the menial work associated with inferiority and the social positions commensurate with it. They are not allowed to have places that might lead to power nor are they given training that would free them from ignorance. The Japanese, in their control of the island of Formosa from 1895 to 1946, allowed only a few Formosans to hold positions in their government of the island higher than that of a second-rate clerk. Nor would they allow the youth to get college training except in the field of medicine. Enforced exclusion is commonly used to support stratification.

The conquered may even become chattel to be exploited in whatever manner is profitable when conquest subjects people to the lowest status level. Slavery, as this form of human relationship is designated, usually robs the subjected of the last vestiges of property and personal dignity. It has been outlawed in most civilized societies.

RACE AND CULTURAL DIFFERENCES Racial differences accompanied by cultural dissimilarity have led to stratification. The settlement of white people in areas where colored races live has seen the introduction of new stratification when the whites became dominant. South America, dominated by the Spanish; Africa by the English and French; Asia and the Islands of the Pacific by English, Dutch, and Portuguese —all have seen new lines of social demarcation established on a racial basis. India, the most

rigidly stratified of all societies, is supposed to have been subjected to a series of racial and cultural invasions that overwhelmed the native people and eventually led to the firm establishment of the caste system. The system was a consequence of the social differences imposed by the conquerors on the native peoples in lower stages of cultural development. Race is a chief factor in the American stratification system. Difference in color is always one of the most likely conditions to result in social hierarchy. Observable physical differences within a population favor stratification. Combinations of racial and cultural differences make it possible for a racial grouping to keep its superior position by holding to a distinct body of traditions that do not allow social intercourse except under circumstances that recognize the superior-inferior relationships. This occurs, for example, when the subordinate group performs menial services for the superordinate group. Contacts are then carefully limited so as to support the stratification system.

DIVISION OF LABOR Division of labor also leads to social stratification. Function and power must inevitably result in stratification, since virtually all societies are complex enough to have developed division of the essential tasks into specializations. This applies to all major areas of a society's organization so that different ranks in economic, political, educational and other aspects of a society's system develop as some of the activities associated with each are judged to be more important than others. Those operating in a given area are ranked according to the functions and powers their positions hold. Rights and privileges accompany the duties the positions impose.

SCARCITY Stratification, both economic and otherwise, as Spengler points out, is founded upon scarcity.[4] Short supply or scarcity is created whenever society differentiates positions in terms of functions and powers and assigns rights and privileges to them. This makes some positions more desirable than others for society grades them by their rewards. There are only a few corporation presidencies, church bishoprics, or government executive offices available. The standards or norms of the society prescribe greater rewards to corporation presidents than to factory operatives, to bishops than to pastors, and to government executives than to government clerks. The titles themselves indicate differentiation in the statuses and, in addition to other remunerations, are prestige rewards.

Stratification evolves from the allocation of these scarce privileges and powers.

II. CLASS

Social Stratification Expresses Itself in the Formation of Social Classes

CLASS AS A POPULATION SEGMENT A class as a population segment is defined in terms of some predominant characteristic, such as occupation, wealth, or education, to which other characteristics adjust. This kind of stratum tends to evolve its own sentiments and forms of behavior over periods of time so that individuals expressing similar sentiments and acting in similar ways are recognized as persons of the same class. *Class,* as distinct from stratum, always includes some objective feature or combination of features, such as occupation, wealth, race, or education, and some subjective features, such as similar attitudes and values that create a consciousness of kind, a mutual social recognition, and similar forms of action that are expected.

We receive our class position with its statuses and roles from our families as these positions are transferred from generation to generation as part of the social heritage. Class position may or may not be changed, depending upon the rigidity of the class system. Competition may allow the able and determined individuals to move up in the class hierarchy in societies where class organization is open, as in democratic societies, while those who lack ability or industry may lose their positions.

CLASSES RANGE FROM OPEN TO CLOSED FORMS The nature of the particular society causes the form which classes may take to vary widely. In some, class position is determined by ability to meet requirements through skill, intelligence, and motivation. In others, it is determined by a social inheritance that permanently fixes the position from which a person can only rarely escape during his life.

An open class system exists when stratification is based on competition and ability, thus making it possible for persons of varying capabilities to move up and down the social scale. A closed or caste system exists where there is little or no possibility of changing from the positions the society has determined for people. Caste is from the Latin, *castus,* meaning pure or unmixed. It indicates that all persons in a stratum are of one unmixed social heritage. Classes exhibit varying degrees of rigidity based on the number and type of limits imposed by different societies. The patterns range from the ideally open class system where functions and privileges are distributed on the basis of comparative efficiency to the tightly closed or caste system where they are based on inheritance. Neither of these systems exists in pure form.

The open class system and the closed or caste class system thus represent extremes in types. It is often suggested that the different class systems of societies would probably form a continuum based on the extent to which people acquire their class position as a result of their ability, or to which they have their positions assigned through hereditary devices. This is a reasonable possibility, although no such continuum has actually been constructed as yet.

Some Class Systems Are Presented as Illustrations

LATIN AMERICA A few class systems are chosen from those described by sociologists and anthropologists to illustrate the variety of systems in societies. Only the barest outlines are possible here.

Beals [5] outlines the character of the class divisions for Brazil, Peru, Guatemala, and Mexico. He indicates that most countries in Latin America are best described by a gross three-class system, each class containing a series of stratified groupings. (Two of his outlines are included in Box 44.) Some details are elimi-

---

BOX 44

BRAZIL *

Rural   *Urban*

Uppermost elite defines self racially
        Landholders, industrialists, bankers, high government officials, heads of church, army, many professional men, declining number of intellectuals

---

BOX 44 (*Cont.*)

Rural	*Urban*
Managerial	Managerial
Middle bureaucracy	Middle bureaucracy
Professionals, lower church and army offi- cials, teachers, small landholders, store- keepers	Storekeepers
	Some professionals and intellectuals
	Teachers
	Some service personnel and technicians
	White-collar workers

(Increasing breaching of barriers)

Negro, mulatto, and mestizo—few barriers to marriage.

Small traders	Petty civil servants
Independent small farmers	Small shopkeepers
Farm laborers	Artisans
	Working-class groups

Large groups of extremely impoverished in both rural and urban settings

MEXICO *

Rural	*Urban*
Hereditary aristocracy vanishing	High government officials
Few large landowners	Industrialists and businessmen
City businessmen and political leaders domi- nate	Some professionals and intellectuals of wealth and/or family
	Heads of church and army top managerial personnel

Storekeepers, bureaucracy, technicians, and managers, teachers, lower church and army officials	Technicians, middle bureaucracy, some pro- fessionals, and intellectuals
Small landholders	Small businessmen and industrialists
	Lower church and army officials
	White-collared workers and teachers
	Some skilled workers

Indian-plural cultures:	*Indo-mestizo:*	*Mestizo:*	*Mestizo:*
Small farmers	Culture similar to In-	Small farmers	Small shopkeepers
Subsistence farmers	dian but Europe-	Petty officials	Petty civil servants
Handicraft workers	oriented, mobility	Shopkeepers	Working-class groups
Rural laborers	easier		regularly employed
Own internal prestige system			Domestics
Horizontal and vertical mobility possible but not frequent			Impoverished Proletariat irregularly employed
			Indian in city or factory by defi- nition becomes mestizo

* Note: Continuous horizontal lines mean effective barriers to vertical movement;
broken lines mean considerable ease of mobility.

nated, but enough remains to make each outline clear.

A background of Spanish and Portuguese feudal institutions, landholding systems of peon-patron relationships, an already stratified native population, native Indian populations and/or rapidly developed mixed or Mestizo populations, the development of industrialization and urbanism, and significant rural-urban differences—all entered into the creation of these Latin-American classes.

NEAR-EAST MOHAMMEDAN SOCIETIES The stratification systems of the Near-Eastern Asian societies are based upon differentiation of religious beliefs. The Mohammedans constitute true believers in Mohammedan societies; followers of other religions are disbelievers. They are tolerated if they are "peoples of the Book," that is, of the Bible. The disbelievers are usually forced into small subsocieties within the larger society. Thus, these societies include a main, religiously directed organization with small subunits operating within them by sufferance.[6]

Social class differences in homogeneous Mohammedan rural villages can be illustrated by the pattern prevailing in Lebanon. The major factor in class differentiation within the dominant rural society is occupation. This does not apply to urban situations. The following abbreviated fivefold classification gives a fairly accurate picture of their divisions:

1. The elite: Combines part-time farmers who own much land that they rent out, professionals, administrators, retired village elders.
2. Moderate sized land operators: Operates 25 dunums (a dunum is approximately one quarter acre) of land or more. "Farmer" is the accurate and acceptable term.
3. Non-agricultural laborers: Combines those without skills such as road workers, domestics, peddlers, and those with skills such as millers, small shop keepers, blacksmiths. The category includes all those in marginal economic activities other than farming.
4. Small land operators: The more successful fellahin—combines small land operators, 11–25 dunums, and skilled agricultural laborers such as tractor drivers.
5. The ordinary fellahin: The largest membership classification. The ordinary fellahin are distinguished from their brothers in categories 1, 2, and 4 by the degree of their land and monetary poverty and their lack of skill.[7]

PREREVOLUTIONARY RUSSIA Prerevolutionary Russia was an "estate society" in which the clergy, nobility, merchants, burghers, and peasants were separated into social strata that depended on birth, and was controlled by law. There was some possibility of movement from one estate to another for a commoner could be admitted into the nobility. These estates were, however, divided into five social classes that formed the society:

1. The upper class—
   Centered about the imperial court—included higher bureaucracy, high military men, high clergy, and wealthy landed nobility.
   Birth and education were requisites.
2. The upper middle class—
   Middle grades of bureaucracy, military and professional men, clergy, business men, and owners of small estates.
3. The lower middle class—
   Urban-artisans, shopkeepers, rural clergy, lowest rank of bureaucracy, and semi-intellectuals.
4. The peasants—
   Three levels of farm peasants: those who could hire help, those who did own work, those who had also to hire out—included 80 per cent of the population.
5. The proletariat—
   Predominantly urban industrial workers—about 7 per cent of the population.

POSTREVOLUTIONARY RUSSIA ON EVE OF WORLD WAR II The class structure of Russia changed several times between 1917 and the outbreak of World War II. By the outbreak of this war, the society was divided into the following classes:

1. The ruling elite plus a few fellow-travelers —chiefly the Communist party machine with total political power, highest social prestige, and the highest incomes.
2. The nonparty Bolsheviks—
   Comparable to middle-class of industrial societies.
   Industrialists, professional men, and administrative officials.
3. The "toilers"—
   Workers, employees, peasants, and artisans.
4. The paupers—
   The disenfranchised—ascribed no social function and are impoverished.[8]

Many Different Conditions in Societies Influence the Class Structures Developed

PHILOSOPHY OF THE SOCIETY The illustrations we have given of the class structure of a few societies indicate their variety. They also imply that different conditions in the societies are related to their development. The general philosophy of the society is important to any class system. A society in which equalitarian ideas predominate evolves a class system in which people move from one class to another through their ability and initiative. These class divisions are supported by the belief that they stimulate endeavor. Therefore, they result in greater contributions to social welfare since people are more productive in a competitive situation. On the other hand, a society which subordinates individuals, families, and other groups completely to the interests of the society probably develops an hereditary class system. This is justified by such arguments as the existence of inherent biological differences between people, religious determination which defines the positions in terms of the will of God, or other forces that inevitably create differences about which it is supposed man can do little.

CULTURAL ANTECEDENTS Each society has a cultural background out of which its class structure evolves. Haiti, for example, has a cultural background of French mulatto dominance that contributes directly to the way its present two-class system evolved. It is almost certain that specific class structures will vary because their cultural antecedents vary from society to society. Some classes may have things in common with classes in other societies, but each society's unique cultural situations make it almost imperative to consider this background to understand its development. Prior class structures leave their imprint upon the development of new systems.

POPULATION HOMOGENEITY AND HETEROGENEITY The homogeneity or heterogeneity of a society's population is also a factor influencing the class structure evolved. The class structures of South American societies reflect the heterogeneity of populations, including Europeans, Negroes, Indians, and Mestizos. Although there are rough similarities between some classes, each society shows unique class differences based on its own specific population composition. Both nationality and racial heterogeneity have been deterrents to the development of clear-cut homogeneous classes in the United States. In many European societies whose populations are homogeneous, class levels extend throughout the society. These are based primarily on occupation and the possession of property.

PREDOMINANT ECONOMIC SYSTEM The economic system of a society also influences the form its class system will take. Landownership is the important factor determining class structure in societies that are predominantly agricultural. Land control has stratified the society for centuries in Lebanon, Syria, and Egypt. Landownership was the key to all prestige and power positions in Syria before 1950. The peasants, as well as their villages, were virtually the property of the landowners. Rome and Greece in ancient days had classes of patricians, plebeians, and slaves, while the Middle Ages had feudal lords, vassals, and serfs, all primarily based on land control.

The role of economic systems in class determination is the basis of the societal analysis made by Karl Marx and Friedrich Engels. They said, following the principle of economic determinism, "the history of all hitherto existing society is the history of class struggles." "Our epoch, the epoch of the bourgeoisie, possesses, however, this distinctive feature: It has simplified class antagonisms. Society as a whole is more and more splitting up into two great hostile camps, into two great classes directly facing each other —bourgeoisie and proletariat." [9]

Max Weber, the German sociologist, also conceived of class as the product of economic factors. He asserted that "property and lack of property are the basic categories of all class situations. The factor that creates class is unambiguously economic interest, and indeed, only those interests involved in the existence of the market." [10] This approach to class differentiation in industrial societies differs from that of Marx in that Weber emphasizes class as the result of economic distribution rather than of economic production. He types classes as (1) a property class—"primarily determined by property holdings," (2) an acquisitions class—primarily determined by its "opportunity for the exploitation of services on the market," and (3) the social class—"examples of social classes are: the working class as a whole, the lower middle class, the intelligentsia . . . and the classes occupying a privileged position through property and education." [11]

OCCUPATIONS Occupation is an aspect of economic systems which often influences social class structures. Rogoff compared social class determinants in the United States and France. Her major conclusion was that "of all the criteria mentioned in determining class position, occupational position is the most consistently named among the various strata" in both societies.[12] Talcott Parsons also confirmed this for the

United States by saying that "the main criteria of class status are to be found in the occupational achievements of men." [13] Richard Centers, after studying the conceptions of occupation and belief as criteria of the several social
classes in America, concluded that "despite some
differences, both in-group and out-group perceive each class—upper, middle, working, and
lower—as embracing more or less distinct sets
of occupational categories." [14]

INTERRELATIONSHIP OF DETERMINANTS We
have mentioned five factors that are strong
determinative forces in class creation. There are
others, depending upon the particular society
and the attitudes toward those characteristics
to which it attaches social significance. Classes
evolve, however, from the interrelationship of
several of these determinants. They are rarely
the product of a single factor. Cultural background, social philosophy, and economic system
interact in concrete situations to determine the
specific class formation that emerges. Some
forces are more influential than others in a
given society. However, each plays its role.

Class Structure in American Society Is of the Open Variety

In America, the factors involved in class formation have all tended to create an open class
organization. Chief among these is the democratic ideology of the society. Equality of opportunity has always been the ideal. Giving
every mother's son the chance to be President
has been one of its chief values. Although every
mother's son cannot possibly be President, the
opportunity is there, and the goal is potentially
attainable to those who have ability and high
aspiration.

The governmental organization that made social equality "self-evident" was born in an atmosphere that stressed the freedom of the individual in all the major concerns of life. The
waves of people who migrated from the working and small proprietory classes of Europe to
this new society did so to get away from hereditary class systems. The conditions of this new
region demanded initiative and ability if the
economy was to be built. It could hardly tolerate emphasis upon class distinctions that were
divisive. The opening of the frontiers to agricultural cultivation and the development of industry, commerce, and trade invited all who would
make the effort and take the risks. Every man
had the right. Wealth and honor were the rewards of those who rose to the top.

All of this led H. G. Wells to say of the
American class system:

In America, except in the regions where the
Negro abounds, there is no lower stratum.
There is no "soil people" to this community
at all; your bottom-most man is a mobile
freeman who can read, and who has ideas
above digging and pigs and poultry-keeping,
except incidentally for his own ends. No one
owns to subordination. As a consequence, any
position which involves the acknowledgement
of an innate inferiority is difficult to fill; there
is, from the European point of view, an
extraordinary dearth of servants, and this
endures in spite of a great peasant immigration. The servile tradition will not root here
now; it dies forthwith. An enormous importa-
tion of European serfs and peasants goes on,
but as they touch this soil their backs begin
to stiffen with a new assertion.

And at the other end of the scale, also, one
misses an element. There is no territorial aristocracy, no aristocracy at all, no throne, no
legitimate and acknowledged representative
of that upper social structure of leisure, power
and State responsibility which in the old
European theory of society was supposed to
give significance to the whole. [15]

If H. G. Wells were writing of America today, he would still emphasize the open nature
of this class system, although his statement
would probably be more moderate.

Today's American Class System Is Described in a Number of Different Ways

DIFFICULTIES IN DESCRIPTION Sociologists have
been trying for years to describe the American
class system. The problem is a difficult one for
two reasons: (1) Members of classes, unlike
members of associations or institutions, do not
develop formal organization but operate through
the established structures of the society according to their style of living. A church or a school
may be a predominantly class agency because
persons from a given class constitute its clientele. This implies that class membership may
have to be inferred indirectly. (2) Differentiations in open class societies change rapidly, and
definitions of class criteria vary from one community to another and one region to another.
It is difficult as a consequence to specify criteria of class differentiation that apply throughout the society. Most descriptions of the class
structure describe classes for a particular area.
We cite some of these to see what common criteria they reveal that might, in turn, give clues

to a common pattern of classes in the society as a whole.

TWO-CLASS DESCRIPTIONS

A Middle-sized City The most widely quoted study describing a middle-sized city in American society in terms of a two-class system is that of the Lynds in their books on Middletown, the Indiana city of Muncie. This city was studied by them in 1925 and again in 1935. Robert Lynd wrote:

> While an effort will be made to make clear at certain points variant behavior within these two groups, it is after all this division into working class and business class that constitutes the outstanding cleavage in Middletown. The mere fact of being born upon one or the other side of the watershed roughly formed by these two groups is the most significant single cultural factor tending to influence what one does all day long throughout one's life; whom one marries; when one gets up in the morning; whether one belongs to the Holy Roller or Presbyterian church; or drives a Ford or a Buick; whether or not one's daughter makes the desirable high school Violet Club; or one's wife meets with the Sew We Do Club or with the Art Students' League; whether one belongs to the Odd Fellows or to the Masonic Shrine; whether one sits about evenings with one's necktie off; and so on indefinitely throughout the daily comings and goings of a Middletown man, woman, or child.[16]

The Lynds' division of this population into working and business classes put 29 of each 100 persons in the business-professional class and 71 of each 100 in the working class. The major factor determining to which of these two classes a person belongs is his occupation, according to the Lynds. They say it is "the watershed down which the rest of one's life tends to flow in Middletown." [17]

A Village James West, in his study of a village he called Plainville, found that, although the people insisted stoutly that there were no classes in the village and that everyone was an equal, there was a distinct two-class system that could be portrayed in the form of a diamond shape and in which the two classes subdivided into smaller gradations within each. The upper class was composed of the honest, hard-working people. They prided themselves on these characteristics. They were thought to include about one-half of the population of 275 persons, most of whom lived on the prairie and were called prairie folk. There was a small upper level or would-be upper level in this class. The lower class was composed of the good lower-class people who worked hard, were honest, and had good morals like the upper-class people. But they lived back in the hills, did not use the best farm methods, were not well-to-do, and were not from the better families. There was also a small lower element whose way of living was not highly respected and an additional small element who "lived like animals." In addition to economic well-being, morals and manners were important criteria determining class position in this community.[18]

THREE-CLASS DESCRIPTIONS

Occupational Classes Advancing the thesis that societies stratify themselves by occupation and economic power, Cooley, Angell, and Carr said that, in the United States, classes may be divided into agricultural and nonagricultural, and that these may be subdivided into three classes each. They included in the agricultural classes (1) farm owners, (2) farm tenants, and (3) farm laborers.[19] They subdivided the nonagricultural class into (1) professional men, (2) business class members, and (3) workers.

The business class, they held, dominates American society through its economic and political power, its control over the press, its influence over the professional class, and the social prestige it possesses.

Income, Occupation, and Way of Living Merrill and Eldredge also followed what is often referred to as the traditional three-class system of American society: an upper or elite class, a middle class, and a working class.[20] They pointed out that this pattern is becoming increasingly stratified as the agencies of social mobility crystallize.

The upper class has a quasi-monopoly on economic power since it owns or controls most of the wealth of the society, especially the large corporations which dominate the business and industrial life of the nation. This class sets itself off from others by employing elements of "conspicuous consumption" the other classes cannot afford, such as yachts and breeding horses.

The middle class comprises the backbone of the business and professional groupings. They operate most of the business of the society and keep the books. Their chief motivation is to get ahead economically and socially; in fact, many are as well off as those of the upper class. But money and occupation do not completely describe these class differences. Family backgrounds and the way of living enter into the picture as well.

The working class, sometimes called the lower class or proletariat, includes factory, farm, and service workers, skilled and unskilled artisans, and those who work chiefly at manual jobs. The wearing of white as contrasted with blue collars is a symbolic differentiation between middle and working classes. But the upgrading of the incomes in the jobs the working classes hold has almost eliminated this difference. The middle class holds to personal initiative as the major factor in success, whereas the working class, accepting the necessity of following their jobs, depend on collective action to achieve better conditions. A bottom layer of the working class is a poverty grouping that lacks education and the motivation to rise. No one acknowledges to belonging here. Thus, in this analysis, we see that occupation, income, and the way of living that can accompany them are major criteria which can be used in determining the class structure.

FOUR-CLASS DESCRIPTIONS

Awareness of Class from Identification Richard Centers uses a subjective approach, that is, the person's awareness of his position in the class structure, to arrive at a four-category classification of classes as upper, middle, working, and lower. Awareness of class is thought by him to come from the individual's feelings of identification with others who have similar goals and similar economic and social backgrounds. Individuals responded to a question about which of these four classes they belonged to. Forty-three per cent indicated that they belonged to the middle class, 51 per cent to the working, 3 per cent to the upper class, and one per cent to the lower class. Two per cent did not respond.[21]

Neal Gross tested Centers' four-class system derived from the use of his closed-form question. He asked a sample of 935 persons to indicate what classes there were in Minneapolis, Minnesota. Then he asked to which of these classes they belonged. A second question was: "Some authorities claim that there are four social classes, middle class, lower class, working class, and upper class. To which of these social classes would you say you belonged?" A third question then was: "Some people say there are three social classes in Minneapolis. They call them lower, middle, and upper social classes. Which would you put yourself in?"

Gross found that the use of different ques-

tion forms about class position gives different results. The three-class question led three-fourths of the people to say they were middle class. The four-class question put the greatest proportion in the working class. The open-ended question gave a wide scattering of responses. His conclusion was that the results of research are often influenced by the methods used by the researcher, and that open-ended questions may be more appropriate in dealing with the study of class identification than such closed-form questions as those used by Centers.[22]

FIVE- AND SIX-CLASS DESCRIPTIONS Hollingshead used a five-class system in a study of youth in a county seat town he called Elmtown. It was based on the index of *evaluated participation* which the committee on Human Development, under the direction of W. Lloyd Warner, had developed. It included (1) the upper class, (2) the upper-middle class, (3) the lower-middle class, (4) the upper-lower class, and (5) the lower-lower class.

The upper class included those who combined their accumulated wealth and family lineage so as to perpetuate their position from generation to generation. Half of the upper-middle class achieved their positions, while the others inherited theirs from pioneer stock. They were the hyperactive families who attain prestige through community leadership and business success. The lower-middle class were small businessmen, farmers, independent professionals, and wage and salary workers living in the better residential districts. They were strongly conscious of their class position and resentful of the two classes above them. The upper-lower class were aware of their inferior position and resentful of attitudes toward them. They were the honest poor people who paid their debts, worked regularly, and behaved properly. They were employed on farms, in the mills, and in the shops as daily wage earners. The lower-lower class were the "scum" of the city who had little respect for law and order.[23]

These five-class divisions are based on status, standards of family lineage, wealth, occupation, community reputation, and mode of living. They involve a considerable awareness of social distance between classes. Movement between these classes is therefore difficult.

The Yankee city study by Warner of an old industrial-commercial city of Massachusetts used the same prestige-status standards that were employed in Hollingshead's Elmtown study. It described five social classes similar to those in Elmtown except that it subdivided the upper class into an upper-upper and lower-upper grouping to give a six-category classification.[24] (See Box 45.) The basis of this division in the upper class was lineage. The lower-upper class wielded more power and had more wealth, but it did not have the prestige of family history. These upper-upper families held to a status position that was based on their past heritage and scrupulously avoided recognizing the lower-upper class.

AN ELEVEN-CLASS DESCRIPTION   A final description of American class systems is that of Harold Kaufman. He used the consensus of fourteen raters selected to represent the major social groupings in a central New York community.[25] Combining their judgments in a prestige rating based on the reputation of these families on several characteristics, he concluded that he "was able without difficulty to place the community population in eleven classes," ranging from 2 per cent of the population with a one prestige rating to eight-tenths of one per cent of the population with a class rating of 6. The middle segments with ratings of 3, 3.5, and 4 included 65.9 per cent of the population.

No Over-All Class Pattern Is Discerned for American Society

The illustrations we have given—to which many others could be added—indicate clearly that there is no consensus as to the number of classes in American society. No class pattern applies throughout. The class organization varies from one region to another and even between sections within regions. There are several reasons for the absence of a distinct class pattern: the society itself is young, the population is heterogeneous and mobile, and different areas of the society are in different stages of economic and social development. Class distinctions are

---

BOX 45.   ONE METHOD OF DETERMINING SOCIAL CLASS

Warner's system is based on four major factors (symbolized by drawings below) of social prestige: (1) the house a person lives in, (2) the neighborhood in which he lives, (3) the type of job he holds, and (4) the sources of his income. Warner rates each factor mathematically. The lower the total score the higher the subject's social class. A total score of 12 to 15 puts a person in the upper-upper class; 16 to 22 means lower-upper; 23 to 37 equals upper-middle; 38 to 51 equals lower-middle; 52 to 66 equals upper-lower; 67 to 84 equals lower-lower.

3 *Type of house* is given a mathematical rating by Warner. It depends upon the size and condition of the house and the extent of landscaping around it. For example, a trailer ranks low and an elegantly kept old house often ranks over a spanking new one.

2 *Dwelling area* or neighborhood is also rated. A person with an extensive, well-kept house in a rundown area would be averaged down in his social status because of his neighborhood.

4 *Occupation* is rated according to the prestige generally accorded different jobs by people whom Warner has interviewed. Professional men like doctors and lawyers rate high; farm owners have higher status than tenant farmers; skilled workers rate over unskilled workers, insurance salesmen over auto salesmen.

3 *Source of income*, and not the amount of it, affects social standing. Inherited wealth ranks highest, with earned wealth next. Then comes profits, salary, wages, and relief in that order. A grocer getting $3,000 in profit from his own business ranks higher socially than a store manager who receives a $5,000 salary.

TOTAL 12 *Total score* helps determine person's social position. Low score indicated high status. Sample here is upper-upper class.

generally considered invidious by the population; ideals emphasize equality and minimize class differences; the criteria of social differentiation are not fixed; and there are rapid changes in the structure of the society accompanied by rapid vertical mobility. All these factors prevent the crystallization of sharply defined classes that fit the whole society. This does not deny that, in specific communities and even within regions in the society, there are sharp class distinctions that are real. The few illustrations that we have given indicate that there are. Occupation, wealth, family lineage, and style of living are the important factors in the creation of class differences where they exist. But since we apply them differently in various places, they do not constitute criteria of a common class pattern for the whole society.

III. CASTE

Caste Is the Extreme Form of Closed Class Systems

Caste is that extreme form of social class organization in which the position of individuals in the status hierarchy is determined by descent and birth. This position cannot be changed except under unusual circumstances. Therefore, it is a form of permanent positioning of people as superiors and inferiors which is based on the principle of inheritance and not upon the actions of the persons or the judgments of the society. Statuses and roles are transferred by social heritage through family lineage. Because they are accepted by each stratum as the ordained order, the society operates through a rigidly stratified system. Thus, caste is class institutionalized and carries the sanctioned norms of a society with respect to the class positioning of the people.

India Has Been the Classic Example of a Caste Society

India has operated as a closed class society for many centuries, a system which is supposed to have emerged from Brahma, the creator. Today, there are many castes and subcastes in this society that are grounded on four basic ones. The Brahmins, or priests, are the highest in the hierarchy—they came from the mouth of Brahma. The Ksatriyas, or warriors, are second—they came from the arms of the creator.

The Vaisyas, or tradesmen, are third—they originated from Brahma's thighs. The Sudras, or laborers, are the fourth caste—they came from the feet of Brahma. In addition, there are the untouchables, who are too unclean to have come from Brahma and too lowly to be included in the caste system. The untouchables scavenge and do the menial work, are excluded from the villages, and, in extreme cases, must not even allow their shadow to be thrown in the pathway of a caste person. This has probably been the most complete system of socially inherited inequality of social relationships that any society has known.

The Castes of India Have Institutional Characteristics

The categoric limitation on movement from one caste to another in the Indian system is accompanied by associated characteristics. Marriages are endogamous. There is strong opposition to marriage across caste lines. Castes follow definite occupations so that the members of each caste are united by the kind of work they do. Levels of living in the caste are largely determined by the occupational opportunities each caste possesses. The status of each caste is carefully protected, not only by caste law but by the conventions that are understood within the communities. These are openly enforced by the community. The taboos, the customs, and the institutionalized norms control the forms of contact between the castes. The all-pervading concept of ritual pollution applied to food, drink, intermarriage, and social contacts is the force that effectively operates to keep the castes separated. Each caste has a customary name that helps to set it apart.

These rules make deference between castes more easily practiced because the lower castes pay deference to the upper castes, while the upper castes must accept this deference but not return it. It is one of the religious requirements to look down upon the lower castes. Dealings between one person and another, therefore, are not based on character but upon the status of the caste to which they belong. Each caste develops its own subculture since the behavior of the individual is governed by the requirements of his caste. The doctrine says that it is better for a person to follow the dharma (religious obligation) of his own caste, no matter how low, than the dharma of another caste, no matter how illustrious.

There Are Cultural Factors Now Undermining This Indian System

Having been founded on the doctrine of re-incarnation, the Indian caste system is an integral part of Hindu religious institutions. It is a social system that is sharply defined and generally accepted by its constituents because it is religiously sanctioned as the ordained order, and the laws governing its organization and operation are clearly specified in the holy books. Such a system could probably not have dominated this society for so many centuries if the religious system had not made it sacred and inviolable.

There are cultural factors in this society that are now undermining the system. Perhaps the most important are the rapid social changes that are leading to India's industrialization and urbanization. The caste system is operative in the factories. Caste people know whom to work with and whom not to work with; what to eat and what not to eat; whom to eat with and whom not to eat with; what materials to handle and what materials not to handle. But the rapid expansion of factories and the requirements for close association between the workers are modifying many of the caste practices so that new accommodations are necessary. Movement from the villages to the cities and vice versa results in the transfer of ideas and new forms of behavior back and forth. Travel on common carriers that makes separation of people by caste difficult helps to modify the system. Communication is expanding rapidly, and isolation is diminishing. Radios and other communication devices are now in the villages. Patterns of life in other parts of the world are now known to the people. The state of enlightenment is increasing. Democratic ideas that have come into the country as an accompaniment of the new national freedom compel questions about the propriety of such rigid class separations. Christianity with its emphasis upon the worth of each soul in the sight of God has tended to raise questions about the kind of attitudes toward individuals that the caste system promotes. Perhaps no stronger challenge to the caste system has come from any source than that presented by Mahatma Gandhi and his emphasis upon the brotherhood of man and his strong opposition to discrimination against any caste, including the untouchables. These factors combined with the new spirit of nationalism

in India have introduced many challenges to the old order.

But a social system that has existed for several thousand years, while it can change with rapidity and can suffer sudden collapse, is supported by tremendous inertia, many vested interests, and a hardened cake of custom and institutional supports. It is to be expected that change, in spite of legislation and other influences, will come slowly to this stratification system.

Caste Organization Has Characterized Other Societies

Other societies, too, have been organized on a caste basis though none seems to have approached India in the completeness of its institutionalization. Greece, especially Sparta, with its stratification into the closed classes of citizens, helots, and slaves, and Rome with its patricians, plebeians, and slaves certainly approached caste societies. Medieval Europe, where the nobility, yeomen, burghers, and serfs were all hereditary and endogamous classes, certainly had castelike societal structures. Japan, too, had a caste organization in which the nobility was the top hereditary class. The military class was followed by the commoner class, which divided into three subcastes of husbandmen, artisans, and traders. Finally, there was the *eta*, or defiled folk, and the *hinim*, or outcasts.

Caste Characteristics Based on Color Exist in American Society

The traditional position of the Negroes in American society has shown some of the characteristics of a caste system.[26] These have been associated with their geographical concentration in the rural South and segregation in Northern cities, their original status as slaves, and the general opposition to their amalgamation and assimilation within the larger population. Some of these characteristics may be examined to test the extent to which familiar restrictions suggest a caste system.

AVOIDANCE PATTERN The fact of birth segregates Negroes from white society. This is a first characteristic of caste. Many of the privileges of the white population are available to them, but these vary from area to area. Negroes cannot participate freely in the total pattern of social activities. With growing exceptions, they encounter avoidance restrictions which prevent full association with the whites.

A correlate of avoidance is endogamy, another caste feature. Marriages across race lines are not generally allowed. One of the strongest antipathies in American society is directed toward marriages between Negroes and whites. Other ethnic groups have amalgamated and assimilated in the society. This is not true of Negroes. Gunnar Myrdal, in his study of the American color-caste pattern, concluded that the white man's refusal to consider any amalgamation—felt and expressed in the entire society—can be described as the common denominator in this problem. The fear of crossbreeding and intermarriage, he contended, is so great that rigid segregation is demanded to avoid inference of social equality.[27]

EXPRESSIONS OF INEQUALITY Expressions of inequality that support segregation are of many sorts. A major form consists of limited occupational opportunities. Certain forms of work are open only to whites, while Negroes are restricted to others in a manner similar to the pattern in India. Jobs available to Negroes are almost invariably the unskilled, menial, or more poorly paid ones. Negroes on farms are usually croppers or field hands employed by white owners. The relationship is one of white superiority and Negro inferiority if the work demands direct contacts. Negroes rarely serve as bosses of white workers. Individual qualities, such as training and skill, are irrelevant; the Negro is unequal, no matter what his personal traits or capabilities.

Separate institutional agencies and organizations are also expressions of inequality. Schools have been separate for whites and Negroes, especially below the Mason and Dixon line. Desegregation is only slowly coming to pass under local and national pressures.

Churches have been generally separate throughout the society. Theatres have had their "nigger heavens," and many hotels and restaurants still bar Negroes. The attitude toward separate use of public facilities is indicated in the following comment: "He went in the white people's toilet, Uncle. I ought to jail him, but I'll let him off this time. It's his first offense, I reckon. Better let it be the last."[28] Voluntary organizations, such as lodges, fraternities, and recreational associations, have operated largely on a color basis.

Personal relations also emphasize this inequality. Southern whites customarily address Negroes as Jim, Nancy, Johnson, or Smith rather than Mister, Mrs. or Miss. No white man ever tips his hat to a Negro woman. These practices imply that Negroes are not on the same social level with white people and that in daily relationships this difference is to be shown. Personal expressions of intimacy, such as visiting in homes, eating meals together, and attending social functions together, are all rigidly tabooed.

DENIAL OF RIGHTS Inequality is nowhere more flagrantly perpetrated than in the denial of the Negroes' rights as natural born citizens. Negroes have been denied the right to vote through pretext and the imposition of standards that few can meet. Most notorious of these barriers have been the poll tax and unfair literacy tests.

ENFORCEMENT OF INEQUALITY The forms of inequality between whites and Negroes are enforced, as in India, by members of the local communities, the police, and the courts. Enforcement measures include physical punishment of Negroes and ostracism of whites who violate the taboos, terrorism, lynching, and almost certain death penalties for Negroes who commit capital crimes against whites. Mass terrorism and violence may include cross burnings, gang abductions and torture, bombings, and race riots. These tactics, used in both the North and the South, serve to enforce racial separation and white dominance through a strategy of fear.

Do These Characteristics Create a Caste System in American Society?

THE POSITIVE VIEW Some argue that these relationships between Negroes and whites, especially in the South, integrate into one caste system "all aspects of white-Negro behavior: social, sexual, economic, political, education, religious, legal, associational, and recreational" and that this system "is a rigid stratification, maintained by physical, social, psychological punishments and rewards." It is even suggested that "this social caste system is more rigid than that described in the classic literature on Hindu castes."[29]

THE NEGATIVE VIEW Others say that "while there is more than a little justification" for considering our Negroes a caste in American society, "the resemblance between traditional India and modern America is, however, more superficial than otherwise." The argument is that "a true caste system is consistently supported by a total religious-social context" and that while "the Negro's inferior place in modern America is part of the mores, it is contrary to the dominant political ideology and religious precepts." Negroes, it is stated, do not accept an inferior racial status and in those areas where the forms of approach, avoidance, and deference have remained the least changed, changes are nevertheless occurring from migration, industrialization, better education, enlightenment, greater economic opportunities, and the exceedingly rapid rise of this people. This clearly indicates that America does not possess a caste system. The dynamics of the American scene escape the confines of such a rigid concept.[30] Certainly the slow but steady gains which Negroes have achieved in every sphere of life mean that the rigid separation that gives the impression of caste is disappearing.

IV. VERTICAL SOCIAL MOBILITY

Societies Differ in the Extent to Which It Is Possible to Shift from One Class Level to Another

IN CLOSED CLASS SOCIETIES Societies differ from each other to the extent in which individuals can move from one class or status level to another. Some societies are marked by practically no class shifting at all. This is true of caste societies. In fact, the purpose of caste is to prevent movement from level to level, particularly upward movement. Persons in a caste society may lose their position by breaking the rules of their caste. They would then have no relationships with any caste persons except those who have also been ostracized.

IN OPEN CLASS SOCIETIES Other societies are marked by open class patterns. Movement up or down the status ladder is virtually unrestricted. Movement up or down in such societies is based on criteria of achievement, in contrast to the permanent fixing of position by heredity. Societies that have open class systems differ in the degree and rate at which movement up or down is possible, depending upon the criteria that are effective in the society at a particular time. This movement of people upward or downward in the class system is called *vertical mobility*.

Several Factors Condition Vertical Mobility in Open Class Societies

CHANGING OR STATIC SOCIAL CONDITIONS The class structure of a society may itself change in response to altered conditions of a time. New classes may appear as old ones disappear.

Class differences were sharp in the early American colonies, for example, because they represented the European background. However, this pattern soon changed since the conquest of frontiers, the development of industry, and the development of agriculture all depended upon ingenuity, hard work, and ambition. Ability and achievement, rather than any inherited class background, were the measure of a man. If he possessed those attributes, he could climb to any height. Peasants from the lowliest European backgrounds moved to the top of the social ladder in this new society because they exhibited these valued traits. Anyone showing them, like a Michael Pupin or an Edward Bok and thousands of others in lesser degree, had a chance to move up.

The rise or fall of class structures occurs also where societies are disturbed by such external conditions as war or political, social, or economic revolution. Revolution reorganized the class structure of French society, while the Industrial Revolution reorganized completely the class structure of each of the societies it affected. There has been general upward mobility in the population in America where the technological advances have liberated increasing numbers of workers from manual labor and multiplied the opportunities in skilled, clerical, and business occupations.

On the other hand, static social conditions result in fixed class position and little vertical mobility. Where the society is at a standstill and new industries or occupations are not developed, opportunities to move up are limited to places vacated either by retirements, deaths, or resignations. Barriers are erected to restrict movement into the professions and occupations. Classes crystallize and are institutionalized if conditions remain static for long periods. Old positions are then sharply differentiated and are transmitted from generation to generation so that sons follow fathers and fathers their fathers. An hereditary class system becomes the pattern.

POPULATION MOVEMENTS Vertical mobility is stimulated when people migrate. It occurs in areas migrants have left, for this departure creates some scarcity of people to fill desirable positions that are available. On the other hand, since immigrants in a society tend to occupy positions in the lower levels, an upward thrust is given to those who were previously in the lower positions. This is illustrated by the upward **social** movement of successive ethnic groups in a city like Chicago or New York. Each succeeding wave tended to push the preceding one up the social scale. These movements of new population segments into societies are also a factor in keeping class organization flexible.

DIFFERENCES IN FERTILITY RATES   Families in the upper social classes generally have fewer children than those in the lower social classes. The Population Reference Bureau report on the reproduction rates of 1921 graduates from 50 American colleges showed that men graduates who had married had only 1.97 children per family and that women graduates who had married had only 1.70 children per marriage in their completed families.[31] Our own study of the graduates from Cornell University of the years 1919, 1920, and 1921 showed that of those who had married, the men had only 1.85 children and the women only 1.79 children per completed family.[32] Since it required 2.2 children per couple just to reproduce themselves, it was obvious that these college graduates were not reproducing themselves. Their families are representative of the upper classes. The upper classes create what Professor Pitirim Sorokin terms "a social vacuum" within the society when they do not reproduce themselves. People from the lower strata have an opportunity to move up to their positions and advance in the social scale.

Too high reproduction rates in lower-class families, on the other hand, hamper the chances of specific family members in rising in the social scale. Westoff, emphasizing this point, quoted Arsene Dumont, who saw this relationship in the 1890's. In his theory of social capillarity, Dumont claimed that "just as a column of liquid has to be thin to rise under the force of capillarity, so a family must be small in order to rise in the social scale."[33]

The Channels of Vertical Mobility Differ for Different Societies

CLOSED SOCIETIES—HEREDITY, LOYALTY   The methods by which persons ascend in the social scale vary according to the nature of the society. Closed societies depend, as has been stressed, upon hereditary qualifications. Mobility here may be possible for those who show qualities which are valued by those in power. Thus, as in England, loyal support of and participation in the programs of the ruling elite provide opportunities for moving up the ladder.

OPEN SOCIETIES—OPPORTUNITY   Ability, education, occupation, wealth, associations, luck, and personal drive are factors conditioning an individual's movement up the social ladder in open class societies. Most open class societies stress both the possibility and the desirability of achieving success. These are major values in the social organization and serve as selective forces to put people in positions for which they are thought to be fitted. Open class societies emphasize opportunity to ascend, and, at the same time, they seek to make such opportunity available to all. However, opportunities are usually not open to all. Some persons are born in lowly situations where the education necessary to climbing is not easily provided. Others cannot make contacts that are helpful. Some never develop the personal drive that is necessary to bring out their abilities or to exploit their opportunities. (See Box 46.)

MAJOR ELEVATORS   Societies stress the importance of some factors more than others in moving up the social scale. In American society, the major "elevators" to social ascent are *higher education* and the *acquisition of wealth*. The rapid development of technology, finance, and commerce resulted in a demand for technically and professionally educated personnel. Only 1.8 per cent of the persons enrolled in the schools in the United States in 1910 were enrolled in schools of higher learning, that is, beyond high school. In 1960, the proportion was 8 per cent, more than four times that of 1910.[35] This shows a realization that moving up in the occupational and social world requires advanced training. A great ambition of parents in this society is to provide a college education for their children. They often make heavy sacrifices to do so.

W. Lloyd Warner and his colleagues published a study showing that a considerable part of the American population cannot get this higher training because of economic limitations. Ninety-three per cent of a group of upper-class students, with IQ's of 110 or higher, graduated from high school. Of these, 57 per cent attended college. Of those from the lower classes, 72 per cent graduated from high school and only 13 per cent went to college.[36] Financial inability to pay for higher education is an important factor here. Other studies indicate the same selectivity.

A person can move up the social ladder in American society if he gains wealth. Money provides not only the means to maintain the level of living upper-class membership involves,

BOX 46   THE VALUE-SYSTEMS OF DIFFERENT CLASSES

The existence of stratification in American society is well known. The corollary fact—that individuals from lower strata are not likely to climb far up the economic ladder—is also known. However, what requires additional analysis are the factors that account for this lack of mobility. Many of these factors of an objective nature have been studied. Opportunity in the society is differential; higher education or specialized training, which might provide access to a high position, must be bought with money —the very commodity which the lower classes lack. Such objective factors help maintain the existing structure. But there are other factors of a more subtle psychological nature which have not been illuminated and which may also work to perpetuate the existing order. It is our assumption that an intervening variable mediating the relationship between low position and lack of upward mobility is a system of beliefs and values within the lower classes which in turn reduces the very voluntary actions which would ameliorate their low position. . . . To put it simply, the lower class individual doesn't want as much success, knows he couldn't get it even if he wanted to, and doesn't want what might help him get success.[34]

it also makes it possible for its possessor to do the things for which the upper classes give position. Those from the lower classes who acquire wealth often buy the requisites to upper-class position, which is similar to what was done in earlier times when the "new rich" bought titles. Those who wish to move upward imitate the symbols of the upper class in such things as type of residence, place of residence, dress, church affiliations, and manners and emulate the consumption standards of the classes above them. The imitation of consumption standards is a common mode of trying to make the climb upward.

V. CLASS CONSCIOUSNESS AND CLASS CONFLICT

Class Consciousness Is the Degree of Awareness Persons in a Class Have of Their Common Status

AWARENESS OF STATUS   "It is always a mistake to presume on a professional connection. We shouldn't like it if the grocer asked me to stand godfather to his son. The old English view is that a man's class is his own and that he should be proud of it."[37]

This quotation from an English novel implies that in that society there is a definite awareness of the existence of a social class system, of each person's membership in it, and of the behavior that is appropriate to each level. Not only is the awareness related to one's own place and

behavior but also to that of other persons in the class system. This is what is meant by class consciousness.

SOCIAL DISTANCE   According to some students, it is consciousness of class that really constitutes class as a social entity. Robert MacIver, for example, referred to class sentiment as "the inner aspect of class" and said that it "does indeed unite those who feel distinct from other classes, but it unites them primarily because they feel distinct."[38] A consciousness of differences that creates social distance between people is the essential feature of class. Social distance is the degree of separation between individuals and groups in different social classes that results from their perception of the status and behavioral differences among them. It does not imply that persons in one class do not like persons in other classes, but, instead, that the recognition of differences in social position prevents certain relationships. A master and a slave, a king and a beggar may be fond of each other, but their different stations make acceptable only certain types of relationships.[39]

To What Extent Does This Consciousness of Class Exist in Societies?

IN CLOSED CLASS SOCIETIES   The answer to the above question depends largely upon the nature of the society. This consciousness is exceedingly strong in a society with a closed class, or caste, system. In the Indian caste system, everyone knows his place and that of every other person in the community. Each person identifies closely with those of his own caste and feels completely separated from those of other castes. This strong sense of cleavage between these classes creates a strong feeling of solidarity within them. The fixing of social position by accepted exterior conditions and not by one's efforts leads to ready identification with those who are in the same position. Each class has its own system of thought and its common culture. It explains its position in the hierarchy as justified by the order of things.

In closed class systems, class consciousness may be intensified when change in the social order threatens those in superior positions. Resistance to change may become openly active. In India, for example, where change is challenging the old order, some groups have renewed their efforts to retain the caste system.[40]

IN OPEN CLASS SOCIETIES The extent to which class consciousness exists in open class societies depends upon the extent to which the social structure is open. Societies differ markedly in this respect as our illustrations of class structure have shown. Consciousness of class, if present at all, is weak in societies whose class structure is wide open, and where movement up and down the social ladder is relatively easy. It is difficult to create a feeling of sharp class difference in a society, such as the American, where individuals have moved rapidly from one level to another and where persons may have vital interests with all areas of the society. Workers may hold stock in great corporations. They have easy access to the cultural opportunities of the privileged. They are free to participate in the voluntary associations of communities. People who have these opportunities can hardly have sharp feelings of separation. Just as there are no clear-cut class patterns in this society, there is no clear-cut class consciousness within it.

Class consciousness, where it does exist in America, is largely confined to specific communities and areas and not common to the society in general. This variability reflects the character of American class structure itself, which is in contrast to the pattern of older European societies. Because in the Old World family heritage is a class determinant to a degree not common in America, the result is less mobility and greater class consciousness. Moreover, a traditional society, such as Germany, for example, built up an aristocratic officialdom of a thoroughly class character. It consisted of an almost

hereditary nobility composed of estate-owners (junkers, or German nobles), military men, and public officials. This older class organization gave the society a rank-order character systematically expressed in the pattern of commanding from above and obedience from below. Even after these upper classes were eliminated, the middle-class leaders who took over continued to employ the upper-class symbols. Those persons in the lower levels also continued to respond to the symbols since they had long been conditioned to them. One reason for the difficulty in establishing democracy in this society has been the inability of the people to understand that initiative is expected of all and not just of the privileged upper class. Most European societies which have a heritage of officialdom have shown relatively clear-cut class organization with strong class consciousness. The sharpness of class differences has, however, been reduced by the impact of modern industrialism.

A High Degree of Class Feeling Is Required to Generate Class Conflict

Unlike institutions or associations, classes do not develop a formal organization through which they express themselves in a unified way. Class controls are made effective by informal techniques applied by individuals and groups which insist upon the observance of the roles assigned to class members. If they are to act as units, those who compose the classes must be welded together when it is necessary to meet any challenges to interests held vital to the class as a whole. Conflict on a class basis is therefore not a common phenomenon.

In open class societies where vertical mobility is high in fact and in expectation, it is difficult to generate dissatisfaction or hostility on an interclass basis. If individuals move up (or down) the social scale in large numbers, they are not likely to identify closely with a horizontal grouping, such as class. It is doubly hard to create a class consciousness that results in conflict when the traditional privileges of the upper classes tend to filter down to the lower classes and the differences in "the ways of life" are reduced by the possession of, or the possibility of gaining, those privileges. If, for example, opportunities for education, wealth-gaining, and institutional participation are widely available throughout the society, class conflict is improbable. Moreover, if there is widespread informality and democracy in interpersonal relations among people from various social levels, interclass hostility will be slow to develop. It is, of course, difficult to determine just how much vertical mobility and diffusion of privilege are required to forestall the development of class feeling.

In closed class, or caste, societies conflict may erupt when those long held in subordinate positions rise to challenge the very foundations of the system. The French Revolution and the Gandhi-led revolt in India are spectacular examples. Such upheavals may be abetted and even instigated by sympathetic members of the upper classes. They profoundly challenge the old order and all the historical, ideological, and religious sanctions which support it. The elite groups who stand to lose their status and power may react so vigorously that a violent explosion is inevitable.

Class Conflict Can Be Generated by Associating the Loss of Vital Interests with Class Organizations

Whether the society has an open or closed class organization, conflict between classes can only be generated by linking the loss of vital privileges, or the possibility of ever achieving them, to class conditions. This is what Karl Marx wanted, and what the Communists have sought to do. In their ideology, history is to be interpreted in terms of class struggle. This position was set forth vehemently in the *Communist Manifesto:*

> The Communists fight for the attainment of immediate aims, for the enforcement of the momentary interests of the working class; but in the movement of the present, they also represent and take care of the future of the movement. . . .
> But they [the Communists] never cease, for a single instant, to instill into the working class the clearest possible recognition of the hostile antagonism between bourgeoisie and proletariat, in order that the German workers may straightway use, as so many weapons against the bourgeoisie, the social and political conditions that the bourgeoisie must necessarily introduce along with its supremacy, and in order that, after the fall of the reactionary classes in Germany, the fight against the bourgeoisie itself may immediately begin. . . .
> In short, the Communists everywhere support every revolutionary movement against the existing social and political order of things.
> In all these movements they bring to the

front, as the leading question in each case, the property question, no matter what its degree of development at the time. . . .
> The Communists disdain to conceal their views and aims. They openly declare that their ends can be attained only by the forcible overthrow of all existing social conditions. Let the ruling classes tremble at a Communist revolution. The proletarians have nothing to lose but their chains. They have a world to win.
> Workingmen of all countries, unite! [41]

Class and Caste Can Be Dysfunctional in Societies

Class and caste can be dysfunctional in societies, even though they do not result in overt conflict. Class systems of whatever degree of rigidity are systems that distribute privileges and power unequally among people. Equality of opportunity to achieve these is a cultural ideal in some societies, but even here class differentiations often make its attainment impossible.[42]

USE OF HUMAN RESOURCES The most serious consequence of class differentiation is that it makes difficult the fullest use of human resources. "The discovery, recruitment, and training of functionally important talent" is extensively hampered when access to the opportunities for developing capacities is limited by class restrictions. The loss to societies of undiscovered talent or its inefficient use is incalculable. In addition, strong class crystallization may even destroy talent completely. The competition for position often leads to difficulty within classes. Capable persons have been eliminated when they have stood in the way of the grasp for power. Purges within the upper classes, as in some revolutions, have ruthlessly destroyed talent. There is no way of calculating what societies lose through undiscovered, undeveloped, unused, or destroyed talent resulting from caste or class differences and conflict. Our imagination assures us that they are tremendous.

POWER CONCENTRATION Class and caste organizations concentrate power in the controlling classes. Decision-making is their function, and their decisions usually are made to uphold the order that supports them in their controlling positions. Since they identify their own values as the valid ones for the whole society, social change is difficult to achieve. The landowning class in some societies, through holding political control, has made it impossible to initiate reforms which would improve the lot of the peas-

BOX 47 Social Class in Political Dimension
(To Be Read Aloud by a Democrat to a Republican or
by a Republican to a Democrat)

Although to the casual glance Republicans and Democrats may appear to be almost indistinguishable, here are some hints which should result in positive identification:

Democrats seldom make good polo players. They would rather listen to Béla Bartók.

The people you see coming out of white wooden churches are Republicans.

Republicans are likely to have fewer but larger debts that cause them no concern.

Democrats owe a lot of small bills. They don't worry either.

Democrats give their worn-out clothes to those less fortunate. Republicans wear theirs.

Republicans post all the signs saying NO TRESPASSING and THESE DEER ARE PRIVATE PROPERTY and so on. Democrats bring picnic baskets and start their bonfires with the signs.

Republicans employ exterminators. Democrats step on the bugs.

Republicans have governesses for their children. Democrats have grandmothers.

Democrats name their children after currently popular sports figures, politicians and entertainers. Republican children are named after their parents or grandparents, according to where the most money is.

Republicans tend to keep their shades drawn, although there is seldom any reason why they should. Democrats ought to, but don't.

Republicans study the financial pages of the newspaper. Democrats put them in the bottom of the bird cage.

Republicans raise dahlias, Dalmatians and eyebrows. Democrats raise Airedales, kids and taxes.

Democrats eat the fish they catch. Republicans hang them on the wall.

Democrats watch TV crime and Western shows that make them clench their fists and become red in the face. Republicans get the same effect from the presidential press conferences.

Christmas cards that Democrats send are filled with reindeer and chimneys and long messages. Republicans select cards containing a spray of holly, or a single candle.

Republicans have guest rooms. Democrats have spare rooms filled with old baby furniture.

Republican boys date Democratic girls. They plan to marry Republican girls, but they feel they're entitled to a little fun first.

Democrats make up plans and then do something else. Republicans follow the plans their grandfathers made.

Democrats suffer from chapped hands and headaches. Republicans have tennis elbow and gout.

Republicans sleep in twin beds—some even in separate rooms. That is why there are more Democrats.[43]

---

ant masses. The peasants are held in a position of complete and almost hopeless dependence upon the controlling class. Counterparts of this inequitable distribution of power may be found among industrial societies. Revolution has often been the only method of destroying such imbalances because ruling classes usually do not willingly surrender privileges and power, especially in rigidly stratified societies.

CULTURAL COMPARTMENTALIZATION   When classes are sharply defined each one tends to develop a subculture of its own. A society may thus become subdivided into cultural segments having different norms. Kinsey's studies, for example, have presented evidence of social class differences in the norms of sex behavior. Extensive variations may weaken consensus and so impede societal integration. Intercommunication between social levels may be difficult. Loyalties may be divided as each class sets its own interests above the interests of the whole. Motivations to participate in the concerns of the larger society are likely to be subordinated to those associated with class interests.

PERSONALITY INFLUENCES   Class and caste may be inimical to normal personality development. Self-perception reflects the person's own image of his social status. One may wonder what the untouchable, the fellahin, the poor white, or the Negro cropper thinks of himself. Possibly, these persons give little thought to their lowly positions but accept them as a part of the natural order. One could believe that the realization that they have no significant place or prestige in the society paralyzes the urge to achievement and so smothers any aspiration for a better lot. Apathy may reach a level where survival is the only urge.

On the other hand, we may find that some who are born to the upper classes may acquire self-estimates, values, and expectations that are not justified by individual and social worth. In either of these extremes, society may again pay the costs of an incongruence between individual ability and social status.

Are Class Trends Increasing or Decreasing in the Societies of Today?

EMPIRICAL DATA ARE LACKING   Those who have studied this problem, particularly as it refers to American society, show divided opinion. Their judgments are based chiefly on opinion, since studies are so few, and based on such scattered and small communities that they do not provide adequate data to support definite conclusions about trends for whole societies.

MORE RIGID STRATIFICATION IN AMERICA? Those who suggest that class lines in America are becoming more rigid say that the conditions that fostered open class conditions and vertical mobility have disappeared. The geographic frontiers are gone, immigration has been limited, and more capital is now required to establish a business.[44] The compartmentalization of social life is more rigid, the occupational structure is tightening, and associated institutional agencies

are supporting it. The excess of upward over downward mobility has diminished and is likely to be further reduced. Class consciousness will increase as aspirations are frustrated. The urbanization of the society and the decrease in the number of farms, accompanied by an increase in commercialization of agriculture, have shifted many people from an open class system, with its opportunity to climb from farm worker to farm owner, to more definitely fixed class positions in urbanized environments. Educational preparation is of utmost importance since opportunity to move up will be largely within established enterprises. The question here is whether the educational system will itself be open enough, especially in terms of economic costs, so that those who are capable can acquire the training they need to operate in an increasingly competitive situation.

LESS RIGID STRATIFICATION IN AMERICA? Those who stress that American class differences are less rigid than formerly point out that the power elite has been splintered because they have experienced loss of monopolistic controls through expanding labor and governmental power. Possessions and occupational achievements are increasing among workers; their higher standards of living and the increased professionalization of their jobs attest to this. Such personal attributes as dress and speech associated with class tend to disappear so that it is difficult to identify people with class with any real exactness. Class is this much less well-defined today than previously.[45]

CHANGES IN OTHER SOCIETIES   We can do no more than make a general comment about trends in class stratification in other societies. There is so much upheaval in societies today resulting from two World Wars, economic depressions, the clamor of groupings for political independence, and the reorganization of their systems that many are in a state of instability and their class organizations in a state of flux. In some, processes are operating to establish a rigid class organization as in the Communist lands, while in others people are pressing for democratic organization with class emphasis at a minimum.

References

1. West, Dick, *Journal-Every Evening* (Wilmington, Del., January 13, 1961).
2. Davis, Kingsley, and Moore, W. E., "Some Principles of Stratification," *American Sociological Review*, 10 (April, 1945), pp. 242–247, and Davis, Kingsley, *Human Society* (New York, The Macmillan Company, 1949), pp. 366–377.

3. Rosenfeld, Eva, "Social Stratification in a 'Classless' Society," *American Sociological Review,* 16 (December, 1951), pp. 766–774. See also Aurbach, H. A., "Social Stratification in the Collective Agricultural Settlements in Israel," *Rural Sociology,* 18 (March, 1953), pp. 25–34.

4. Spengler, J. J., "Changes in Income Distribution and Social Stratification: A Note," *American Journal of Sociology,* 59 (November, 1953), p. 258.

5. Beals, R. L., "Social Stratification in Latin America," *American Journal of Sociology,* 58 (January, 1953), pp. 326–339. By permission of University of Chicago Press; copyright, 1953, by the University of Chicago.

6. Cahnman, W. J., "Religion and Nationality," *American Journal of Sociology,* 49 (May, 1944), pp. 524–529.

7. Armstrong, Lincoln, and Hirabayashi, G. K., "Social Differentiation in Selected Lebanese Villages," *American Sociological Review,* 21 (August, 1956), p. 429. This classification is given in abbreviated form.

8. Timasheff, N. S., "Vertical Social Mobility in Communist Society," *American Journal of Sociology,* 50 (July, 1944), pp. 9–21. By permission of University of Chicago Press; copyright, 1944, by the University of Chicago.

9. Marx, Karl, and Engels, Friedrich, *The Communist Manifesto* (New York, International Publishers, 1948), p. 9.

10. Gerth, H. H., and Mills, C. W., *From Max Weber: Essays in Sociology* (Ithaca, N.Y., Cornell University Press, 1946), pp. 182 and 183.

11. Cox, O. C., "Max Weber on Social Stratification: A Critique," *American Sociological Review,* 15 (April, 1950), pp. 223–227.

12. Rogoff, Natalie, "Social Stratification in France and the United States," *American Journal of Sociology,* 58 (January, 1953), p. 353.

13. Parsons, Talcott, "An Analytical Approach to the Theory of Social Stratification," *American Journal of Sociology,* 45 (May, 1940), p. 856.

14. Centers, Richard, "Social Class, Occupation, and Imputed Belief," *American Journal of Sociology,* 58 (May, 1953), p. 555.

15. Wells, H. G., *Social Forces in England and America* (New York, Harper and Brothers, 1914), pp. 329–330.

16. Lynd, R. S., and Lynd, H. M., *Middletown* (New York, Harcourt, Brace and Company, 1929), pp. 23 and 24.

17. Lynd, R. S., and Lynd, H. M., *Middletown in Transition* (New York, Harcourt, Brace and Company, 1937), p. 7.

18. West, James, *Plainville, U.S.A.* (New York, Columbia University Press, 1945), pp. 116–133.

19. Cooley, C. H., Angell, R. C., and Carr, L. J., *Introductory Sociology* (New York, Charles Scribner's Sons, 1933), pp. 294–298.

20. Merrill, F. E., and Eldredge, H. W., *Culture and Society* (Englewood Cliffs, N.J., Prentice-Hall, Inc., 1953), pp. 280–288.

21. Centers, Richard, *The Psychology of Social Classes* (Princeton, N.J., Princeton University Press, 1949), p. 77.

22. Gross, Neal, "Social Class Differentiation in the Urban Community," *American Sociological Review,* 18 (August, 1953), pp. 398–404.

23. Hollingshead, A. B., *Elmstown's Youth* (New York, John Wiley and Sons, Inc., 1949), pp. 83–120.

24. Warner, W. L., and Lunt, P. S., *The Social Life of a Modern Community* (New Haven, Conn., Yale University Press, 1941), and Warner, W. L., and Lunt, P. S., *The*

Status System of a Modern Community (New Haven, Conn., Yale University Press, 1942). Illustration from *Life* (September 12, 1949), p. 109.

25. Kaufman, H. F., "Prestige Classes in a New York Rural Community," Cornell University A. E. S. (March, 1944), Memoir 260, p. 39.

26. "Comparison of race relations in the southern United States and relations between the untouchables and other castes in India demonstrate that the two systems are closely similar in operation despite differences of content." Berreman, Gerald D., "Caste in India and the United States," *American Journal of Sociology*, 66 (September, 1960), p. 120.

27. Myrdal, Gunnar, *An American Dilemma* (New York, Harper and Brothers, 1944), p. 57 ff.

28. Peterkin, Julia, *Bright Skin* (Indianapolis, Ind., Bobbs-Merrill Company, Inc., 1932), p. 308.

29. Davis, Allison, "Caste, Economy, and Violence," *American Journal of Sociology*, 51 (July, 1945), p. 7.

30. Green, A. W., *Sociology* (New York, McGraw-Hill Book Co., Inc., 1952), p. 288.

31. Gamble, C. J., "College Reproduction Report" (Washington, D.C., Population Reference Bureau, mimeographed, June, 1946).

32. Anderson, W. A., "Marriages and Families of University Graduates, Statistical Supplement" (Ithaca, N.Y., Cornell University Press, 1950), p. 18.

33. Westoff, C. F., "The Changing Focus of Differential Fertility Research: The Social Mobility Hypothesis," *The Milbank Memorial Fund Quarterly*, 31 (January, 1953), No. 1, pp. 24–38.

34. Hyman, Herbert H., "The Value Systems of Different Classes," in Bendix, R., and Lipset, S., *Class, Status and Power* (Glencoe, Ill.: The Free Press, 1953), pp. 426–427. See also Rosen, B. C., "The Achievement Syndrome: A Psychocultural Dimension of Social Stratification," *American Sociological Review*, 21 (April, 1956), pp. 203–211; Straus, Murray, "Deferred Gratification, Social Class, and the Achievement Syndrome," *American Sociological Review*, 27 (June, 1962), pp. 326–335; Robins, L. N., Gyman, H., and O'Neal, P., "The Interaction of Social Class and Deviant Behavior," *American Sociological Review*, 27 (August, 1962), pp. 480–492.

35. United States Department of Commerce, Bureau of the Census, *Statistical Abstract of the United States, 1962*, Table 145, p. 115.

36. Warner, W. L., Havighurst, R. J., and Loeb, M. B., *Who Shall Be Educated?* (New York, Harper and Brothers, 1944), pp. 51–52.

37. Morgan, Charles, *The Fountain* (New York, Alfred A. Knopf, 1942), p. 137.

38. MacIver, R. M., *Society, Its Structure and Changes* (New York, Ray Long and Richard R. Smith, 1931), p. 85.

39. Sorokin, Pitirim, *Social Mobility* (New York, Harper and Brothers, 1927), p. 10.

40. "Seminar on Casteism and the Removal of Untouchability" (Bombay, India, The Indian Conference of Social Work, December, 1955).

41. Marx, Karl, and Engels, Friedrich, *The Communist Manifesto* (New York, International Publishers, 1948), pp. 43–44.

42. Tumin, M. M., "Some Principles of Stratification: A Critical Analysis," *American Sociological Review*, 18 (August, 1953), p. 389.

43. Stanton, Will, "How to Tell a Democrat from a Republican," *Ladies' Home Journal*, 79 (November, 1962), p. 59. Copyright © 1962 by *Ladies' Home Journal*. Reprinted by permission of Paul R. Reynolds and Son, 599 Fifth Ave., New York 17, N.Y.

44. Ogburn, W. F., and Nimkoff, M. F., *Sociology* (Boston, Houghton Mifflin Company, 1950), p. 156.
45. Sjoberg, Gideon, "Are Social Classes in America Becoming More Rigid?" *American Sociological Review*, 16 (December, 1951), pp. 775–783.

Questions for Study and Discussion

1. Give an illustration of social stratification as expressed in some situation with which you are familiar.
2. How would you justify social stratification in democratic societies?
3. Discuss the general circumstances under which stratification appears in societies.
4. Discuss the relationship of social heritage to social class position.
5. Differentiate between an open and a closed class system. Illustrate each.
6. Consider each of the five factors that appear to be significant in class creation. Show how they operate as such in your society.
7. Discuss the existence of classes in American society in terms of defining and delineating them.
8. Is caste just a more rigorous form of social class?
9. Describe the caste system of some society other than India. What specific characteristics mark it?
10. Does American society include a caste system? If so, how does it differ from the caste system of India?
11. What advantages and what disadvantages do you see in class and caste systems?
12. Discuss the conditions that influence vertical mobility in open class societies.
13. To what extent do you think class consciousness exists in your society? Is it increasing or decreasing? Why?
14. Under what circumstances does conflict result from class consciousness?

Suggested Topics for Reports

1. Using the directory of your college or university, make a spot map of the homes of administrators, professors, associate professors, assistant professors, and instructors. What inference can you draw concerning the relation between academic rank and character of residential area?
2. Test the "hypothesis" that the type of sports people prefer serve as indicators of social class position.
3. Make a comparative study of the "society" sections of a metropolitan newspaper and a Negro newspaper. Determine the respects in which they differ or are similar in pattern and content.
4. Select a deviant group and determine the degree to which it shows evidences of stratification. How would you account for it?

Supplementary Reading

American Journal of Sociology, 66 (May, 1961). Six Papers on Stratification.
Barber, Bernard, *Social Stratification*. New York: Harcourt, Brace and Company, 1957.
Bendix, Reinhard, and Lipset, Seymour M., *Class, Status and Power*. Glencoe, Ill.: The Free Press, 1953.
Centers, Richard, *The Psychology of Social Classes*. Princeton, N.J.: Princeton University Press, 1949.
Cuber, John F., and Kenkel, William F., *Social Stratification in the United States*. New York: Appleton-Century-Crofts, Inc., 1954.

Davis, Allison, Gardner, B. B., and Gardner, M. R., *Deep South*. Chicago: University of Chicago Press, 1941.

Dollard, John, *Caste and Class in a Southern Town*. 2nd ed. New York: Harper and Brothers, 1949.

Gallaher, Art, *Plainville Fifteen Years Later*. New York: Columbia University Press, 1961.

Hiller, E. T., *Social Relations and Structures*. New York: Harper and Brothers, 1947.

Kahl, Joseph A., *The American Class Structure*. New York: Rinehart and Company, 1957.

Lipset, S. M., and Bendix, R., *Social Mobility in an Industrial Society*. Berkeley, Calif.: University of California Press, 1958.

Mayer, Kurt B., *Class and Society*. Garden City, N.Y.: Doubleday Company, Inc., 1955.

Mills, C. Wright, *White Collar*. New York: Oxford University Press, 1951.

Mosca, Gaetano, *The Ruling Class*. Ed. by Arthur Livingston. New York: McGraw-Hill Book Co., Inc., 1939.

Myrdal, Gunnar, *An American Dilemma*. New York: Harper and Brothers, 1944.

Reiss, Albert J., *et al.*, *Occupations and Social Status*. New York: The Free Press of Glencoe, 1962.

Sorokin, Pitirim A., *Social Mobility*. New York: Harper and Brothers, 1947.

Stouffer, Samuel A., *et al.*, *The American Soldier*. Princeton, N.J.: Princeton University Press, 1949.

Tumin, Melvin, and Feldman, Arnold S., *Social Class and Social Change in Puerto Rico*. Princeton, N.J.: Princeton University Press, 1961.

Warner, W. Lloyd, *et al.*, *Social Class in America*. Chicago: University of Chicago Press, 1949.

Warner, W. Lloyd, and Lunt, Paul S., *The Social Life of a Modern Community*. New Haven, Conn.: Yale University Press, 1931.

West, James, *Plainville, U.S.A.* New York: Columbia University Press, 1945.

23

SOCIAL CHANGE: ACTION IN A TIME PERSPECTIVE

CHANGES *over time that involve alteration in the structure and functioning of societal forms are inevitable in societies. Obstacles to change are, however, often formidable. Major theories of change have been advanced. Progress, defined as the achievement of desired ends, is emphasized by some. Planned social change to achieve predetermined goals is employed in societies in varying degrees.*

I. DEFINITION AND EXPLANATION

Social Change Occurs in All Societies

The fable has it that an ancient king wanted an epitaph chiseled on his tombstone that would be forever true. The wise men considered his request and returned with the advice that he use the phrase, "Everything changes."

This is as true of societies as it is of any phenomenon. Societies, like all phenomena, are influenced by forces that inevitably cause them to change. The human composition of societies changes over time, technologies expand, material equipment changes, ideologies and values take on new components, and institutional functions and structures undergo reshaping. No society remains completely static because it exists in a universe of dynamic influences, the reaches of which become steadily greater. The tempo and extent of change vary, of course, from society to society. Some experience speedy transformations, whereas others go for long periods without noticeable alteration.

Change occurs so slowly in most primitive and folk societies that it is often not noticed even by those who live in them. Slow, gradual changes do not pose the immediate or critical problems which would make them aware of the process. Even in modern societies there seems to be little or no change in many areas. Institutions and organizations, communities and regions seem to remain static. The English village of Cranford, for example, apparently has not changed at all: "My next visit [after several years] to Cranford was in the summer. There had been neither births, deaths, nor marriages since I was there last. Everybody lived in the same house, and wore pretty near the same well-preserved, old fashioned clothes. The greatest event was that Miss Jenkyns had purchased a new carpet for the drawing-room."[1]

Yet, even small villages show some changes in time:

> Even a small town like Mineville is by no means the static thing it is usually thought to be. Despite the fact that it does not gain in population, its social composition is constantly changing. Boys and girls grow up to manhood and womanhood; about one and one-half per cent of the people die each year; there is always an influx of newcomers and the departure of old residents; former residents who return after an absence of ten years express sadness at the number of old landmarks who have died or departed, and at the number of strange faces.[2]

Social Change Involves Alteration in the Structure or Functioning of Societal Forms

Social action, the preceding chapters have indicated, is the functioning of societies and of their interrelated components. Groups interact with groups; individuals interact with individuals. Action takes place according to the norms and values of the society in organizations, institutions, and other social forms. The structures, the norms, and the values are relatively fixed at a given time so that social interaction usually involves no direct change in them; there is only change in the relationships of those persons or groups operating in and through them.

Social change, however, involves alteration in the structure or functioning of societal forms or processes themselves. This takes place through the substitution or succession of other forms or processes for those that have been extant in the society. Social change has occurred when a city replaces its mayor-alderman with a commission form of government, when one nationality succeeds another in a community, when tractors replace horses as the chief source of power in farming, or when machine-marketing economy displaces a handicraft system. There has been alteration or replacement of some established structure, condition, or form of procedure by another in each of these illustrations. The replacement of the horse by the tractor as the major source of power in farming changed this whole operation. It changed the materials, the conditions, and the procedures. A half a century ago, the general catalogue of a mail-order house in the United States contained 70 to 80 pages advertising harness, wagons, and other equipment necessary in using the horse as the source of farm power. Today, this catalogue, many times the size of the earlier ones, does not carry a single page of such advertisements. It refers to a special catalogue of farm supplies, little of which is devoted to supplies for the use of the horse as a power source. The substitution of tractors for horses is permanent in its effects on an established order. It imposes new relationships upon the situation that result in different activities than those previously engaged in by the farm people of the society.

Social Change Shows Chain-Reaction Sequences

A society's pattern of living—its culture—is a dynamic system of interrelated parts. Therefore, change in one of these parts usually reacts on others and these on additional ones, until they create reverberations throughout in a chain-reaction sequence.

TECHNOLOGICAL CHANGES

Auto Trucks for Camels In the Middle East, the automobile truck has largely replaced the camel as the chief means of transporting goods across the desert. A hard-surfaced highway from Aleppo in Syria southeastward across the desert has made the trucking of goods much cheaper and swifter. Camels have lost their utility for this purpose and so have lost much of their value. Camels that sold for high prices for transportation bring only low prices as meat. The loss of the camel for transportation leaves only the possibility of their use as meat. Many of the nomadic Bedouins who raised camels cannot support themselves in this way since this change came. They added sheep to their flocks, but this addition did not make up their loss. Bedouins whose ancestors followed this way of life for centuries are forced to settle down to farming. Therefore, the replacement of the camel by the truck results in a chain reaction that involves alterations in the whole mode of life of many people.

Diesel for Steam Engines The diesel engine has replaced the steam engine on almost all railroad trains in the Western world. Chain reactions have taken place in many railroad towns where the maintenance of steam engines was an important factor in the local economy. What this replacement meant to one town, Caliente, was described by W. F. Cottrell.[3] Change came in spite of efforts of manifold character, such as finding a new industry to take the place of the old, persuading the railroads to reconsider, and getting government aid and assistance from the unions. Just as the Bedouins were compelled to change their whole way of life, so Caliente was compelled to change its way of living. The diesel set in action a whole train of consequences that influenced every part of the town's life.

IDEOLOGICAL CHANGES It is not only changes in the material aspects of a society's culture that set off chain reactions. Ideological changes have similar consequences. New ideas about the rights of children and women to be protected from economic exploitation in the industrial system start a whole set of chain reactions relating to age of employment, conditions of work, and hours of employment. New scientific theories are tremendous forces in changing conceptions of the universe, man's place in it, and his relations to other men. New ideas about our economic relationships have caused chain reactions to form such new economic patterns as cooperatives and regulated capitalism. Social inventions, like the commission form of government, are ideological developments that create many changes in political and social life.

Social Changes Are Chiefly Those of Modification or of Replacement

Even though specific changes in material and nonmaterial culture occur in innumerable ways, they may be broadly categorized as *modifications* or *replacements*.

MODIFICATIONS

Of Physical Goods The most obvious changes in societies involve material things. New developments in their form and quality occur constantly. Breakfast foods in American society furnish an illustration. Americans eat the same basic materials for their breakfast that they did when they first came to this continent: wheat, oats, corn, pork, eggs. Corn meal mush, oat mush cooked overnight on the back of the range, fresh pork fried in slabs, eggs fried or boiled, and wheat ground at the mill or in the coffee grinder and boiled until soft, and sometimes fried as mush, were common on morning menus. Today, these same materials are consumed but their form is changed. Ready-to-eat corn flakes, minute oatmeal, thinly sliced bacon, eggs scrambled as well as fried or boiled, and wheat of innumerable prepared types are substituted for the forms in which these same materials were consumed in yesteryear.

Cumulative modifications of material things, from breakfast foods to electronic tubes, may eventually alter the whole content of culture. Not infrequently, a modification of an existing material item will have greater impact than will an entirely new invention.

In Social Relationships Modifications occur within and between the structural forms of a society. Their structure and functions may undergo change of varying degrees and kinds. The large authoritarian family becomes the small equalitarian family; the one-room school becomes a centralized school; the independent grocery becomes a unit in a chain-store system. Indeed, a social pattern may undergo such a complete change that its original form and function largely disappear. The salute and the handshake are among the many examples which could be cited.

No student needs extensive demonstration of the manner in which concepts, ideologies, and other nonmaterial elements become modified in the arena of ideas.

REPLACEMENT

Of Materials Change also takes the form of replacement. A new material or nonmaterial form supplants an old one. This occurs less frequently than modification, but its consequence may be even more significant. The whole life of the American Plains Indians was changed when the horse replaced walking as the mode of travel. It expanded their nomadic activities, especially in hunting buffalo, and broadened their warlike activities against other Indian tribes and the white man so that their activity patterns became radically different.

The replacement of horses by automobiles in American society has created a new order of existence that allows for movement among us never before imagined. One result is the movement of thousands of families into the rural areas to reside as rural nonfarm residents. The influence of this on social relationships, institutional agencies, and other areas of social life is incalculable. We shall refer again to this in a brief consideration of the changing structure of the city and the influence of suburbanization.

Of Ideas The replacement of the idea that this planet was flat by the idea that it was round resulted in a new approach, not only to this planet, but to the universe as a whole. The germ theory of disease replaced older views of the cause of disease, and the whole history of health care and treatment was reorganized. Man is replacing old principles with new and reshaping the world in which he lives, through his scientific discoveries.

CHINA AS A SIGNIFICANT ILLUSTRATION The social change by replacement that is going on in China is of great significance. The old culture that existed for thousands of years is being consciously replaced by a Communist system. The old ideologies of self-government with family and village responsibility at its core, together with their five great duties, are completely replaced with a program of state socialism. A centralized dictatorship creates a planned social system in it with a complete economic regimentation that leaves hardly a vestige of the old culture.

Social Change Virtually Always Results from the Interaction of a Number of Factors

MONISM It is possible to give illustrations to show that a significant change in any aspect of the natural environment, or in the derived social environment or culture, is accompanied by corresponding adaptive changes in the society. Some thinkers have been so greatly impressed by the importance of one factor in its influence upon social life that they have insisted that it was *the* factor bringing about social changes. Religion, economic development, great personalities, climatic conditions, and changes in technology have all been singled out as the factor which accounts for change.

PLURALISM Monistic interpretations that explain change as the result of one factor have always been shown to have limitations. A specific factor may trigger a significant change, but it is always associated with other factors that make the triggering possible. The reason for this is that social phenomena are mutually interdependent—none stand out as isolated forces that bring about change of themselves. Rather, each is an element in a system. Modification or replacement of one part influences the other parts, and these influence the rest, until the whole is involved. Readjustment continues until adaptation and balance between the parts or equilibrium have been re-established. However, no society is ever in perfect balance, although there seems to be a pressing toward such a condition.

Contemporary Social Conditions Are Being Reshaped by Significant Social Changes

Rather than describe the ways in which such factors as physical environment, biological forms, demographic conditions, cultural factors, and others can bring about social change—these have been indicated in previous chapters—we select certain contemporary conditions and show how they are related to the changes that are taking place in societies as a consequence of new developments. This will illustrate how these forces bring about changes in a society. Two general quotations give us a perspective on recent historic change:

In the last fifty years a vast change has taken place in the lives of our people. A revolution has in fact taken place. The coming of industrialism attended by all the roar and rattle of affairs, the shrill cries of millions of new voices that have come among us from overseas, the going and coming of trains, the growth of cities, the building of the interurban car lines, the coming of the automobile has worked a tremendous change in the lives and in the habits of thought of our people of mid-America.[4]

And:

We cannot recall too frequently that we are living in a period of changing conditions, such as has probably never before existed. When I was a boy it seemed to me at least—and it seemed to be accepted generally by others—that most, if not all, of our fundamental institutions had been definitely determined and fixed for all time—how, I did not know, but at any rate fixed beyond discussion, almost beyond question. I have in mind, among others, matters such as the following: the superiority of our form of government, the status of the Bible as our rule and guide of life, the place and authority of religion, the so-called capitalistic system based upon the right of private ownership of property, the marriage contract which is the basis of our family life, the calendar and the number of months in the year. I repeat—fifty years ago these questions were generally considered as settled.

Now all these are under attack and all are slowly but none the less surely going through a process of questioning and of reassessment which may leave them better or worse, but will certainly mean modification wherever and whenever it is believed by the majority of those affected that change or modification will promote the best interests of humanity.[5]

Rapid Urbanization Is Reshaping Societies

One of the most striking changes that is reshaping societies today is urbanization, that is, the rapid growth of the proportion of the populations of societies residing in or around cities. While this is significant in terms of the concentration of large numbers of people in limited areas, it is even more important in terms of the influence the mode of life has upon societies. Urbanism, or the distinctive pattern of living created by these population concentrations, affects all aspects of living in a society. Its influences radiate far beyond the boundaries of the core cities and the metropolitan areas to permeate all of society.

This Emergence of Urbanization Is a Recent Phenomenon

Some cities have always been significant in the operation of societies for they have been the focal points for culturally dominating elements. These cities were sustained by land-oriented agrarian states that were based on farming, craft specialization, and trade. But they performed specialized services that made them focal points in the society. As examples,

Benares in India and Mecca in Syria dominated their societies because they focalized controlling religious systems. Athens, Cairo, and Rome were concentration points for political empires. As such, they influenced whole regions.

By comparison with today's cities, however, these early centers were small and few in number. They covered only small land areas and contained only relatively small populations, chiefly because of their inability to sustain economic systems that would support many persons not directly engaged in providing food and other daily necessities.

Extensive urbanization did not really begin until the twentieth century. In 1800, only 1.7 per cent of the world's population lived in cities of 100,000 or more, and 2.4 per cent in cities of 20,000 or more. It was not until 1900 that as many as 5.5 per cent lived in cities of 100,000, and 9.2 per cent in cities of 20,000 or more. But by 1950, 13.1 per cent of the world population lived in cities of 100,000 or more population, while 20.9 per cent lived in cities of 20,000 or more people.[6] These are increases of eight to ten times in a century and a half. This is all the more striking since this growth has mostly taken place in the last century, and particularly in the last half-century. The increases were not as much as 2 per cent between 1800 and 1850, but the percentage increases doubled between 1850 and 1900 and between 1900 and 1950. The speed of this urban growth is shown for the American society by the fact that only 20 per cent of the population was classed as urban (living in incorporated places of 2500 persons or more) in 1860, and 63 per cent in 1960.[7]

An obvious consequence of this change is the concentration of increasingly large numbers of people in an increasingly larger number of urban places. For example, in 1860 there were only sixteen places of 50,000 or more population in the United States; in 1960, there were 334, or twenty times as many as in 1860.[8]

A further consequence of this concentration usually means the inclusion of a wide diversity in the racial, religious, occupational, nationality, and social class characteristics of cities so that a variety of interests is predominant and primary group bonds difficult to maintain.

Urbanization Has Taken Place Most Extensively in the Western World

While urbanization is increasingly characteristic of the whole planet, it has taken place up to the present time most extensively in the northwestern countries of Europe and "in those new regions where northwestern Europeans have settled and extended their industrial civilization." In addition to northwest Europe, it is the United States, Canada, Australia, and New Zealand that are the highly urbanized countries. Japan is the only country in Asia that is highly urbanized. In Africa, only the Union of South Africa shows any important degree of urbanization. This widespread, rapid change accompanied by many maladjustments is symptomatic of the development of a new social order out of a previously dominant agrarianism.

Some Major Factors Account for Urbanization Today

In Chapter 2 on societies and their cultural antecedents, we stressed that the Industrial Revolution ushered in a new era in the Western world. The application of power-producing machinery to economic production and transportation remade the life of the people. One of its consequences was this concentration of increasing numbers of people in an increasing number of cities as a result of increased industrial efficiency that has made them centers of intensive production and distribution. Cities continue to grow, not only in the Western world but also in other parts of the world as well because the application of power-producing machinery continues. An ever-increasing proportion of the activities of societies centers in cities where lines of communication converge, thus making them centers of production, distribution, and social services for a surrounding region. Consequently, they evolve a functional dominance over a region.

In addition to the industrialization of general economic productivity, agriculture itself is undergoing industrialization. As we have already pointed out, a smaller number of farmers on a smaller number of farms now produce far more agricultural products with their power equipment than was true before the general application of tractors and other machines was possible. Larger-scale farms, with a high degree of specialization, that are oriented to the commercial market make agriculture today a highly industrial enterprise. The farmer is more and more a business operator. This industrialization of farming is expanding in every agricultural area. Its spread throughout societies is causing fewer people to be needed on the land and more of them to live in or near cities.

One of the most interesting consequences of this industrialization, both of the general economy and particularly of agriculture, is that societies so influenced are based more on territory and less significantly on kinship relations. Practically all agriculturally dominated societies with their self-sufficing systems are knit together by family, clan, and tribe. Industrialization with its factory system and urban concentration tends to destroy this foundation. It substitutes an order based on spatial relationships. For example, Africa, about the least industrialized area of the world, is primarily organized about tribes based on kinship relations. This change in relationships is a chief problem for these societies as they face the introduction of industrial advances.

Cities in the Western World Have Slowed Down in Their Rate of Population Increase

There is a decline in the rate at which cities in the more industrialized parts of the world are increasing. This does not mean that they are not increasing numerically, only that the rate at which they are increasing is relatively much smaller than it was decades ago. If we use New York State, a highly industrialized area, and New York City as illustrations, we find that the rate of increase for New York City dropped from 38.7 per cent for the 1900–1910 decade to a loss of 1.4 per cent for the 1950 to 1960 period. The rate for New York State dropped from 37.7 per cent in 1900–1910 to 13.2 per cent in 1950–1960. Cities in these older areas have, in many instances, reached a saturation point where further concentration can hardly continue. As a result, cities expand outward. This is what has happened, until now metropolitan areas with central cities as their core and a metropolitan hinterland are the significant urban units.

Today, the Metropolitan Area Is the Focal Region of Urbanization

The metropolitan area has been made possible by the developments in transportation and communication. Industrialization concentrated numerous factories, a varied labor supply, a central market, and many work opportunities in the compact confines of the city. The automobile, hard-surfaced road, electricity, telephone, radio, and television have made possible the extension of the city into its hinterland on the basis of the territorial differentiation of functions. Urban dwelling areas, necessary mainte-

nance services, and commercial enterprises can now be diffused. This has made continued growth possible in these hinterland areas surrounding the cities. Now a city-encircling movement, penetrating the open country, carries city residents and the services they require out beyond the city limits and pushes open country populations in the direction of these suburban agglomerations. The suburb has become an enticing residence area for large populations of city workers, thus increasing the urban spread.

Urbanization Leads to Cultural Uniformity in Societies

It would be impossible for such changes as the growth of industrialization, the transformation of communication and transportation, the evolvement of metropolitan areas of urbanization, and an industrialized agriculture to occur without creating tremendous changes in a society's mode of living. Cities develop distinctive social climates. As urbanization increases, this social climate diffuses until the ideas and practices radiate throughout the society. Rural areas also absorb these ideas and practices so that uniformity and unification in the way of living result in the total social organization. Differences disappear in the exchange of ideas, folkways, norms, and values until a common culture tends to characterize the whole society.

Further Industrial Advances May Bring Even Greater Changes

Profound as the changes from these sources are, it is conceivable that further industrialization may result in even greater consequences. Here we select a few illustrations to point out that the industrialized world is undergoing a second revolution. Atomic energy and electronic devices—inventions and discoveries in material culture—have started even profounder changes than most of those that occurred as a result of the application of machinery to economic processes. Already, automation has dramatically reorganized factory and commercial operations. An example of this is the automatic engine test in automobile factories. New engines are given a supply of electric power, fuel, and oil and tested for their operation without removal from their overhead conveyors on their journey to final installation. Automation is replacing more and more of the physical work done by men. At the same time, it expands jobs for engineers, technicians, skilled operators, and maintenance workers.[9] As a consequence, the type of workers in factories is quite different from the "human automatons" of the old system. Electronic brains are causing further changes in industrial operations by taking over certain types of intellectual and computational work formerly done by human beings.

Atomic energy, as a new source of power already applied to the operation of submarines, is rapidly being developed to direct conversion into electricity. This suggests that small atomic generators supplying power without recharging for years are a practical possibility. Contemporary industrial organization is undergoing rapid reorganization as a result. The extent of this change is unlimited; the possible extent of its influence on societies is unimaginable.

IDEAS AS PRIMARY FORCES IN CHANGE Changes in urbanization and industrialization are primarily consequences of changes in technology. It has been the invention and application of new machines and the discovery of new power sources that are making these changes possible in the physical world. But behind invention and discovery of any kind are ideas and the systems of reasoning men have slowly evolved in relation to the physical universe, his own nature, and his cultural world that have been the key forces bringing about these changes. There is a continuous reciprocal interaction between man's thought-world and the rest of the environment. These are so interrelated that ideas result in actions, while actions and their products result in additional ideas. Therefore, changes in societies are often the consequence of the power of ideas. Some men had the idea that the world was round, but most said this was a weird fantasy. Columbus accepted the idea, acted on the premise of a global earth, and discovered a new world. The discovery of this new world generated many new ideas. A Euro-American culture was in part their product. Not all ideas have such consequences for many are notions based only on imagination. It is ideas founded on factual observation and verified study that are commonly the compelling forces in man's social relationships. Ideas based on fantasy rather than fact have led individuals and nations into actions that have often resulted in disastrous world changes (the racial mystique of Hitler is an example). Scientific principles based on fact exert the greater and more constructive power in the long run.

The rise of Soviet communism dramatically illustrates the influence of ideas in bringing change to social systems in the middle years of the twentieth century. Already Soviet ideas have reoriented the relationships of people in a number of societies. Maurice Hindus described the force of these ideas among Russian revolutionaries:

> Then there is to be the new faith—in a new day, a new civilization, a new happiness, a new conquest, a new man—on this earth now, and for all mortal souls. . . . The passion is there and so is the outgoing earnestness and readiness to bring all in its sacrifice. One only has to watch a parade of Russian revolutionaries or to attend a celebration of a revolutionary holiday to become aware of the depth of passion that the Russian revolutionaries have for their new faith. This faith may in time become a mere matter of routine, a dogma without a breath of warmth. All faiths finally do burn themselves low if not out.[10]

We may observe that ideas, like the machine and patterns of residence we have described, come into existence as dominant forces, play their roles, and often subside, giving way to other ideas better adapted to changing situations.

CHANGE IN VALUES AND NORMS Societies operate through their structural components according to norms—accepted standards for individual and group behavior—to achieve values —things desired because they have worth. The norms and values of societies are founded on the accepted ways of living that have developed over long periods of time, thereby giving them a fixity that is related to societal well-being. These are established in the mores and made functional in the institutional agencies. They are not easily changed. But they must ultimately change under the impact of social forces that bring new ways of living, which compel their reconsideration. (See Box 48.)

Nowhere has this been more obvious than in the oriental world where societies are in a wide ferment that challenges traditional values.[12] Two forces, one material and the other nonmaterial, are chiefly responsible for these challenges.

An illustration of the influence of material forces in changing values comes from a rice-producing area in southeast Asia. The farmers were expressing their discontent with conditions and were mindful of the past when their village community had a strong, self-sufficing economy. Producing rice for the world market

---

BOX 48   MODERN MAN AND CHANGING VALUES

Sociologists have lately exhibited much concern for the changing value structure in twentieth century American life. The search has begun for the counterpart of the elusive and supposedly decaying system of values known as the Protestant Ethic. The alternative value position has been given many names, but stands united in its image of modern man as a being who feels himself acted upon rather than an active participant in the manipulation of his destiny—one who finds meaning and strength through constant association with others rather than within himself. He is a shameless consumer who for lack of funds will not put off until tomorrow what he can consume on the installment plan today. He lives for his Sundays and holidays.[11]

---

now dominates their economy. Inquiry found that, some years before, the area was a silk-producing as well as a rice-producing region. Feeding silk worms gave good returns and provided the people with a prosperous handicraft program. "What has changed the situation?", one of the farmers was asked. His response was, "Man-made silk (rayon) from the mills of America and England." Then he pointed in the direction of the town and said, "And now the mills have come to us."

For centuries, there was a village organization in the Orient that had knit the peasants together in their local communities through self-sufficing production supported by their local handicrafts. Theirs was a stable, cooperative economy that bound the village communities in an interdependent social organization founded on the values in family, clan, land-ownership, and religion. This gave the people a basic social security and a vital feeling of belonging—two of life's most important values to people anywhere. Although the system suppressed individualism, it did give them a sense of social responsibility which served as an effective social control.

Today, a money economy which produces crops and other materials for the national and international markets has penetrated these areas. The villages are still there, and so are the villagers—at least the old and the young. But village cohesion and its values of oneness are gone or crumbling. In large measure, the villager's land is no longer his. Instead, he is a tenant or laborer in an absentee landowning system that has destroyed the value of land-ownership and the stability it gave to his total life. He must now build a new value system.

An illustration of the influence of the non-material aspects of a culture on social values comes from Thailand. The senior author once talked with a group of Thailand agricultural workers in Bangkok. He asked what was most needed in their society to help the villagers help themselves. He thought they would name material or technical aids. To his surprise, they said, "The development of a social consciousness—a recognition of the problems of the common people and the acceptance of responsibility for helping them to solve them. This must become one of our chief social values." Then one of the men said, "The lot of our people has been one of exploitation. This has varied only from time to time in its degree. This attitude must be changed. Our people must have the confidence that efforts to help are sincere and are proposed for the good or they will prefer to let them pass. The present most serious obstacle to obtaining the acceptance of anything different is this lack of confidence. They always say, 'Yes, yes, we are not blind to the value of some change, but unless we are sure of where the change will take us, we prefer to let it go by.'"

There is a fundamental difference between the Orient and the Occident in the manner in which new values are introduced. The genius of Western social organization has been its reliance on the initiative of the people to promote new values or to change old ones through voluntary organization. When a problem faces members of a Western society, individuals act, create a movement, develop an organization, and attack the problem with their own resources or press social agencies into dealing with it.

The oriental world is almost devoid of voluntary organizations. The idea that the people should take the initiative, consider the problem together, and develop organizations to attack it is only now slowly becoming a part of their thinking. Life for them has been one of acceptance. They have been taught to limit their material needs and the means for satisfying them for they deny the importance of their present life, except as a forerunner to the next. To introduce the idea that this life should be one of well-being and comfort and that increasing the means to provide it is a duty, is to change almost entirely their whole value system.

The Acceptance of Social Changes Is Related to Three Major Conditions

THE NEED FOR CHANGE Societies and the structures within them are constantly accepting and rejecting new material and nonmaterial innovations that cause change. The mere presentation of new innovations does not, however, assure their acceptance. There are three broad conditions governing decisions to accept or reject. The first is need. "Necessity is the mother of invention" means, more broadly, that a society is in a position to accept change when there is an awareness that change is required to achieve goals more effectively or to retain them more efficiently.

An example of the quick acceptance of a needed cultural change was the substitution of a Latinized alphabet in the Turkish language for the nearly 500 separate Arabic characters that the old Turkish writing required, and which had been used for centuries. Turkey's population was generally illiterate because of its complicated writing system. Learning to read was an almost impossible task for the people.

Mustapha Kemal Pasha and his aides recognized the need for a simplified alphabet if the population was to be more literate and if other desirable social changes were to be made. This need was widely emphasized through the schools, press, and public officials until a felt need was generated in the society. Schools for teaching a new 29-character alphabet went into action when there was a strong general consciousness of this need, not only in the larger cities but in the remote towns and villages. Kemal Pasha studied and taught the alphabet with enthusiasm. His conviction about the need for the new alphabet, his enthusiasm for teaching it, and his own prestige in the society were major factors in the rapidity with which its acceptance became an accomplished fact and in the whole-hearted way in which the people put it to use. The prestige of the innovators and of the promoters aided acceptance. Social change can take place when there is a felt need or where such a need can be created.

PROVISION OF GREATER SATISFACTIONS Changes may be accepted if they provide greater satisfactions than those provided by old elements of the culture. Such rewards will hasten the spread and entrenchment of the new elements.

There has never been any question in Turkey of returning to the old Arabic alphabet because the new Latinized one gives so many more satisfactions. So many people learned to read so readily that it never occurs to anyone to suggest a return to the old system.

There was never any question of return to the mayor-alderman form of government after Memphis, Tennessee, adopted a commission plan. The new system was so much more satisfactory in so many ways that the question of return did not arise.

DEMONSTRATED UTILITY Acceptance of change is also facilitated by proof of increased usefulness. The wrist watch, which has come to be generally worn by both men and women, has replaced the more cumbersome watches worn on chains or attached by pins. For many years, men used short-handled shovels for digging purposes. These have been almost wholly supplanted by long-handled shovels which have greater utility in a variety of purposes. The American Indians did not hesitate to change from bows and arrows to the white man's gun. The gun was so much more effective in hunting and warfare that it was speedily accepted. Increased utility or effectiveness has been the critical factor in the acceptance and modification of machines generally.

In a study of informational sources leading to the acceptance and use of fertilizers on Iowa farms, 57 per cent of the replies said that the initial use of fertilizers resulted from noticing better crop stands on those farms using it and hearing other farmers report higher crop yields from fertilizer use.[13] "Seeing is believing," or demonstrated utility, is the important factor in acceptance here.

Utility is also a major criterion for acceptance in the field of social inventions. Few question the utility of the corporate form of doing business in industrial societies. People may complain that some corporations are too powerful, but as a form for doing business, few question their utility. Community Chests or United Fund organizations or Red Cross societies are social inventions that have almost universal acceptance because their distinctive services in particular areas have been based on demonstrated usefulness.

Suggested changes have considerable chance of being made a part of the social system when need, increased satisfaction, or demonstrated utility accompany them. Acceptance is even more likely when they are accompanied by supplementary values, such as the prospect of making profits or the feeling that constructive contributions are being made to social well-being.

Obstacles to Change Are Formidable

Social change does not come in a society without resistance. There are many forces tending to block acceptance. We group them under six headings.

INERTIA   There may be need for change that is keenly felt but about which nothing is done. The dead weight of human lethargy impedes attempts to modify conditions or to allow innovations to emerge. Change cannot come unless there is a desire for change and a confidence that it will be helpful. In many instances, people have lived so long under a condition that they simply hold to the mode of living that has served their needs, even though more efficient ones are available. There is only inertness—no desire, so no action. Outside stimuli are met by this dead weight of inactivity that often expresses a kind of fatalism. "We are only poor creatures unable to do it" may mean that people are not only materially impoverished but also often mentally bankrupt. Their lethargy is even more pronounced when suggested changes only remotely affect them or where the personal benefits are indirect.

HABIT   Habit is behind inertia as a factor retarding change. Habits may be so fixed that the traditional automatic responses to problems seem to be the only acceptable ones. Other ways are inappropriate, so the tried methods must be the best: "It has always been done this way." "This is the way of our fathers." (See Box 49.) Such habit reactions are especially strong in folk societies where persons are closely identified with family and community relationships which rigidly prescribe individual attitudes and behavior. Change is almost impossible for the individual, unless it is accepted by his whole community. Conformity to custom is characteristic of the folk. This conservatism is especially strong when the aged are in control for it is more difficult for them to change their habits.

SUSPICION   Support for change is also difficult to obtain when inertia is coupled with fear

of the new. The steam railway, when first used in the American Middle West, was condemned as an instrument of the devil. People who feared this new device threw rocks at the trains as they passed. Social inventions are often opposed and condemned as socialistic, irreligious, or unscientific. Also, workmen's compensation laws not only faced opposition from vested interests but were described as socialistic schemes that must not be tolerated.

Not long ago persons who studied the physical forces, discovered physical laws, and made material inventions that threatened change faced serious opposition. Some paid with their lives. Social inventors and discoverers of today who suggest societal change are met with somewhat similar opposition. Ironically, this occurs in spite of the invention of such physical devices as atomic bombs which can mean man's destruction unless he does change his social forms to make it possible for men to live together in unity.

TRADITION   Loyalty to tradition is another obstacle to change. Certain ways of thinking and acting are inherited from the past. Carlyle asked: "Hast thou ever meditated on that word, Tradition: how we inherit not Life only, but all the garniture and form of Life; and work, speak, even think and feel, as our Fathers and primeval grandfathers, from the beginning, have given it to us?" [14] These "deep ruts of tradition and conformity" often make it impossible to change the ways of living. Innovations in art, literature, dress, and even tools and other material equipment run headlong into the stubborn power of tradition. Well-entrenched custom and tradition brought from other cultures, sometimes centuries old, is one of strongest obstacles to the adoption of new ideas or modes of acting. Each generation tends to travel down roads it did not build but simply inherited. It is obstinate about changing, even though it might find shorter and better routes.

Subcultures exist in the midst of major cultural systems because of respect for tradition. Religious communities, for example, have clung to their forms of worship, styles of dress, and customs of work and play for centuries, holding firm to a set of traditions inherited from a distant past. The tradition that unites them, and at the same time separates them from the general society, is that God has called them to be a "nonconformed" people, a "peculiar" people who must live apart from the world.[15] Holding

BOX 49   THE CALF-PATH

One day, through the primeval wood, a calf walked home, as good calves should;
    But made a trail all bent askew, a crooked trail as all calves do.
Since then two hundred years have fled, and, I infer, the calf is dead.
    But still he left behind his trail, and thereby hangs my moral tale.
The trail was taken up next day by a lone dog that passed that way;
    And then a wise bell-wether sheep pursued the trail o'er vale and steep,
    And drew the flock behind him, too, as good bell-wethers always do.
And from that day, o'er hill and glade, through those old woods a path was made;
    And many men wound in and out, and dodged, and turned, and bent about
    And uttered words of righteous wrath because 'twas such a crooked path.
But still they followed—do not laugh—the first migrations of that calf,
    And through this winding wood-way stalked, because he wobbled when he walked.
This forest path became a lane, that bent, and turned, and turned again;
    This crooked lane became a road, where many a poor horse with his load
    Toiled on beneath the burning sun, and traveled some three miles in one.
    And thus a century and a half they trod the footsteps of that calf.
The years passed on in swiftness fleet, and the road became a village street;
    And this, before men were aware, a city's crowded thoroughfare;
    And soon the central street was this of a renowned metropolis;
    And men two centuries and a half trod in the footsteps of that calf.
Each day a hundred thousand rout followed the zigzag calf about;
    And o'er his crooked journey went the traffic of a continent.
    A hundred thousand men were led by one calf near three centuries dead.
    They followed still his crooked way, and lost one hundred years a day;
    For thus such reverence is lent to well-established precedent.
A moral lesson this might teach, were I ordained and called to preach;
    For men are prone to go it blind along the calf-paths of the mind,
    And work away from sun to sun to do what other men have done.
They follow in the beaten track, and out and in, and forth and back,
    And still their devious course pursue, to keep the path that others do.
But how the wise old wood-gods laugh, who saw the first primeval calf!
    Ah! Many things this tale might teach,—but I am not ordained to preach.

—Sam Walter Foss (1858–1911)

---

fast to this tradition has kept them together in the midst of a society that is undergoing constant change.

The tradition that a member of the British Royal Family must not marry a divorced person caused a king to give up his throne and a princess to give up her suitor. In Japan, the tradition that royalty should not marry a commoner is now broken, after hundreds of years, by the marriage of the heir to the throne to a commoner's daughter. This came only shortly after Japan's greatest tradition was destroyed by the emperor himself in his public disavowal of his divinity. Traditions that have held for centuries in this society are disintegrating with spectacular speed under the impact of Westernizing culture.

Yet tradition is one of the strongest opponents to change. Said Olga Knopf: "In the past fifty years a surprising change has taken place. In almost every Western nation women have been admitted to legal equality with men. . . . But tradition that has held sway in European history for some three thousand years is not so easily banished. Women are equal to men on paper, but the common view that women are somehow or other inferior to men persists unaltered." [16]

VESTED INTERESTS   Social change meets opposition whenever the vested interests of individuals or groups are threatened. The abolition of slavery was stoutly opposed by slaveholders as the insistence for its elimination grew. It threatened their vested economic interests. Child labor laws, shorter hours of work, and proper working conditions for industrial employees all met opposition from vested interests whose private concerns were more important to them than public well-being.

Many governmental systems, especially in such smaller units as counties, towns, and cities, could be vastly improved by their reorganization and consolidation. Vested interests are among the strongest opponents of such changes for it would mean the elimination of jobs and the loss of personal income and of prestige to some people. Any suggested change is likely to meet opposition wherever it is thought to menace jobs, income, prestige, or personal ambitions.

LACK OF KNOWLEDGE   Social change meets obstacles because of the lack of knowledge on the part of those who will be influenced. Misconceptions of purposes are easily developed if one is not informed on the subject. It is more difficult to increase understanding of desirable changes in the nonmaterial areas of social systems than it is in the material aspects. Both involve educating the public. But this is more easily accomplished with respect to physical than to nonmaterial goods. Physical goods often need promotion from only a few people who are convinced of their values and are willing to take some risks to profit from their development. Automation devices have had no end of promoters and have become common physicosocial instruments in societies, whereas the commission or manager plans of city government have been accepted in only a few places. The former required educating only small groups of people about their advantages; the latter required the creation of a public concern that finally impels action. The education of the public to a significant degree of concern is a slow and difficult process.

These several forces opposing change are all closely interrelated. Inertia may grow out of habits, while traditions founded on habits and lack of knowledge support inertia. Vested interests may support these. In some instances, each of these forces may be the major obstacle to change. In most cases, they combine to form a complex of opposition that multiplies the effect of the separate forces.

The Factors Determining the Acceptance or Rejection of Social Change Influence the Speed of Change

Change is accomplished in a society when the forces favorable to it overcome those unfavorable to it. Whether change is effected swiftly or slowly depends upon the strength of each set of forces. The struggle for supremacy is a contention between positive and negative forces that interact on each other until acceptance or rejection results.

RATE OF CHANGE IN SOCIETIES

Cultural Base   The length of time it takes for the forces promoting change to overcome those opposing it gives a rate of change. It is impossible, at least at this stage of sociological development, to suggest rates of change in exact terms. Societies differ so markedly that specific rates of change are questionable. In our industrial and urban societies, with their large cultural accumulations, changes take place much more rapidly than in primitive societies where cultural accumulation is slow. Change is probably now taking place in Western societies at an increasingly faster rate because of the expansion of their cultural bases due to accelerated invention and discovery. More inventions and discoveries have been made in these societies in the last century than during many previous centuries put together. This does not imply that innovation will continue indefinitely—it probably will not. But it is obviously responsible for the tremendously rapid change in these societies at the present time. Growth that has been achieved determines largely what may be achieved. Change occurs slowly when there is a small cultural foundation, but its tempo increases as the base expands.

In relatively isolated and primitive societies which have been static for long periods, adjustments between the material and nonmaterial culture have been substantially accomplished. Consequently, social relationships within them are relatively fixed. Usually no disturbing changes affect the sharply defined roles of their members. In modern urban and industrial societies, rapid change is characteristic. In fact, it is so general that it is often difficult to make acceptable adjustments before new changes upset the situation. These rapidly disturbing circumstances cause strains. Some experts hold that these stresses are responsible for the presumed increase in mental disorders within these populations, but this has not been proved. Yet, it certainly is true that relationships are unsettled and require continually new adaptations. Thus, the stage of cultural development is itself a factor influencing the rate of change in a society as a whole.

Borrowing Static societies, those in which little change has occurred over long periods of time, may, however, experience exceedingly rapid changes, also. Change in a society does not now have to wait on inventions and discoveries made with them: they may result from borrowing. That they may occur with surprising speed is exemplified by Japan, where almost overnight her static educational and industrial system has changed by borrowing from the West.

Change usually takes place slowly where inventions are needed to achieve it. If the society is ready for the change, it can move forward rapidly, even abruptly, when the materials or ideas necessary to change can be borrowed. (As we saw earlier, this was the case with Turkey under Kemal Pasha.)

Catastrophic Situations Change also comes rapidly in societies as a consequence of sudden or catastrophic events. Revolutions usually upset an entire social organization since old standards are discarded and new ones may be slow to form. Redefinition of goals must be effected. Extensive structural and functional reorganization is inevitable in this process. The revolution in Egypt in 1952 suddenly reorganized the whole society with the displacement of the royal ruler and the abolition of the large landholdings. Wars have the same result. They suddenly change economic production, occupational activities, and almost all the customary routines of society. Societies ravaged by war hardly ever return to their previously normal conditions.

Other sudden occurrences, such as floods, earthquakes, cyclones, tornadoes, or tidal waves, may with one stroke devastate areas and put a city or a region in ruins, and so instigate changes that would have otherwise come only after a long time.

RATE OF CHANGE WITHIN A SOCIETY

Cultural Lag Some parts of a culture change more rapidly than others. This is the principle underlying Ogburn's theory of *cultural lag*. He has stated his theory thus: "The various parts of modern culture are not changing at the same rate; some parts are changing much more rapidly than others; and that since there is a correlation and interdependence of parts, a rapid change in one part of our culture requires readjustments through other changes in the various correlated parts of culture." [17] According to Ogburn, the material culture in modern societies changes more rapidly than the nonmaterial culture, causing a lag between the two. It took several decades for New York State, for example, to develop regulations that required protective devices on power machinery after a high industrial accident rate was general in its industries. Workmen's compensation laws were even slower in coming. Such maladjustments result in injury to the society and its members. These unequal rates of change in the related parts of a culture are difficult to overcome for the same reasons that it is difficult to get the acceptance of general social changes, namely, the apathy of the public, opposition by vested interests, and the general conservatism of the people. The differential rates of change are eliminated in some situations more quickly than in others because of differences in the opposing forces and the nature of the lag.

Cultural lags cannot be allowed to widen indefinitely, or the society will suffer disorganization through the breakdown of effective controls. Lags between material advances and adjustments to them develop social problems, situations in which societal values may be damaged or lost. Hornell Hart has analyzed several cultural lag problems, including lynching, air fatalities, typhoid, diarrhea, tuberculosis deaths, and railway fatalities. He has shown how, in each instance, the use of social intelligence was effective in overcoming them.[18] Frederick Osborn has shown, on the other hand, that it has not yet been possible to solve the problem created by the destructive potential in atomic energy in spite of efforts on the part of the United Nations to bring nations to agreement on the problem.[19] This is a case of cultural lag in the international field that is being perpetuated by the policies of the nations involved.

Order of Change A question usually raised about the cultural lag theory is whether it is always true that the material aspect of a culture changes before the nonmaterial aspect. Some students indicate that the order in which change occurs is not determined by whether the elements that stimulate change are material or nonmaterial but by the values that are involved and their relation to the total culture. Nonmaterial and material elements have changed in societies with no effect on each other at all. There needs to be some correlation and interdependence of parts if change is to be expected in one when the other undergoes change. Some feel that this question has not been studied enough to give a final answer.

II. THEORIES OF CHANGE

Social Change in Societies Is Subject to the Principle of Limited Possibilities

A basic principle applicable to all phenomena is that they can assume only a limited number of forms, no matter how they are influenced.[20] Water, for example, can assume only three forms: liquid, vapor, and solid. This same principle applies to social systems and their parts. The economic systems, to use Sorokin's illustration, can assume only a few forms, such as the hunting, pastoral, agricultural, handicraft, and industrial types. Governments can move only from decentralization to centralization or vice versa. Social changes are circumscribed by limiting conditions so that it is possible to see, at least to some extent, the directions in which change must occur. Social forms are destroyed altogether, and social systems disappear if the limits are exceeded. Many societies have had this experience.

Some Theories of Social Change

Students of social change have formulated some broad theories to explain the principles according to which social change occurs within these limited possibilities. These indicate the varied views of the direction societies may take. The formulation of such theories is significant for the contribution they make to the understanding of these directions in social change.

CHANGE FROM DIVINE DETERMINATION Among the early theories are those that ascribe change to divine determination. This kind of theory is still potent among many people. One form of it is described in the Book of Genesis. God placed man in a garden that was to provide peace and plenty so long as man did not eat of the fruit of the tree of wisdom. But man was disobedient and so condemned to a life of trouble and toil. His continued failures to do God's will brought on continued pain and punishment from which there was no release, except by following a program of righteous living. So changes in the social world are symbolized by successive stages of rebellion against God and punishment for such disobedience. Man

will move toward a better state as he is righteous, a worsened state as he is sinful. Many societies invented similar explanations of the direction of social change in their early developmental stages.

CHANGE FROM ORIGINAL STATES The Greek social philosophers and their successors in later ages explained change as development from the original state of man's nature. Aristotle conceived that man is social by nature, so changes grow out of the expression of this natural character. Everything is good as it comes from the hand of the Creator, Rousseau asserted. But it changes—in fact, degenerates, under the hand of man: "Man is born free, but he is now everywhere in chains." The history of social thought contains other variations of the view that change consists in a development or departure from some original or natural condition of man.

EVOLUTIONARY CHANGE

Comte It was Auguste Comte, the French social philosopher, who originated the term "sociology" and gave us the theory that social change occurs through a series of developmental stages—the theological, the metaphysical, and the positive. Societies, according to his theory, move from a religious through a philosophical to a scientific base. Rational control becomes possible in the third stage.

Darwinism After the announcement of the Darwinian theory of biological evolution, many social theorists applied the principles of variation, struggle, selection, survival of the fittest, and transmission to societal phenomena. These were important concepts to Ratzenhofer, Gumplowicz, Novicow, Morgan, Ward, Giddings, Sumner, Keller, and others who applied them to social changes in one manner or another.

Albert Keller, following Sumner's lead, made direct application of these concepts in his *Societal Evolution*. He organized his analysis of social change around the concepts of variation, selection, rational selection, counterselection, transmission, and adaptation.[21] Man's societies evolved, according to this, from a direct appropriation or hunting stage, to a pastoral stage, to a settled agricultural stage, to a handicraft stage with division of labor, to an industrial stage based on power-producing machinery and specialization of occupations.

Many social theorists have abandoned the idea that social change takes place by evolutionary stages. They charge that such theories appear to be oversimplifications and too sweeping in generalization. Many exceptions have been discovered.

Robert MacIver, however, has objected to this abandonment. He pointed out that evolution does not mean a "unilineal sequence in which specific institutions of the simpler societies pass by similar process into specific institutions of the more advanced societies." Rather evolution is an "unrolling" or emerging process in rudimentary characteristics that take on distinct and variable forms, giving rise to new and more complex forms of life. This differentiation applies to societal forms as well as to those of organic life. MacIver illustrated this in his description of the evolution of the Church as a social form. He noted that its beginning was in a pervasive emotional attitude in man related to all the aspects of his life. This developed into a lore of traditionalized ritual and creed that became hallowed ways of doing things. This was followed by established religions in which suprahuman realities regarded as divine and worshipped as first causes were postulated. These were finally localized, institutionalized, and demarcated from other social institutions and now express themselves in religious societies that promote the distinct forms of belief and ritual they accept.[22]

MacIver observed that this evolution or differentiation manifests itself in a society as it does in the evolution of religion through "(a) a greater division of labor so that the energy of more individuals is concentrated on more specific tasks and so that a more elaborate system of co-operation, a more intricate nexus of functional relationships is sustained within the group; (b) an increase in the number and the variety of functional associations and institutions, so that each is more defined or more limited in the range or character of its service; and (c) a greater diversity and refinement in the instruments of social communication, perhaps above all in the medium of language. . . . When the above-mentioned changes are proceeding society is evolving." [23]

SPENGLER'S CYCLE THEORY   Three broad theories of social change that have challenged attention made their appearance during the last several decades.

Oswald Spengler attracted much attention in his *The Decline of the West* with its theory that a society passes through a cycle of childhood, youth, maturity, senility, and decline, to be followed by others that tread the same path.[24] Each society evolves its own unique

social forms so that each produces a distinctive culture when it is in its developing stage. But this productivity dies down, decay sets in, and inevitable doom is the consequence. Spengler considered this final stage of decline and decay to be the position of societies in the West in 1918, when his book was published. Most sociologists and historians now hold that his theory does not fit the facts.

TOYNBEE'S CHALLENGE AND RESPONSE   Even more dramatic in the sweep of its scholarship is Arnold J. Toynbee's *A Study of History*.[25] This work is an attempt to explain the cultural changes through which civilizations pass. Toynbee recognized twenty-one separate cultures in his analysis. His objective was to find the factors that account for their rise and fall. Two —challenge and response—are the principles that create, generate, and finally destroy civilizations. They are the factors which elicit civilization. The natural or geographic environment and the social environment present challenges that require response. It is this interaction pattern of challenge and response that gives civilizations their start. The character of these challenges determines the way in which the civilization will develop—whether it will become highly complex or remain simple and retarded. Civilization then creates more and more challenges, especially from the increasingly complex social environment as it increases in complexity. But there are limits to the number of responses a society can make. Leaders from the ruling minority seek to develop adjustments to meet the increasingly complex situations, but they are incapable of overcoming these difficulties. The civilization is thus doomed in spite of the efforts to escape its fall. This cyclical view of changing societies seems to oversimplify the process and to use data that may apply only to an aspect of social development and not to the total process.

In a fascinating imaginative magazine article, Toynbee applied his view to the changes in civilizations up to the year 5047. The twentieth century will be viewed from the year 2047 as the period when Western civilization changed the lives of all other peoples completely. There will have been tremendous counter-effects on the life of the West. By 4047 A.D., the differences between Western and Eastern civilizations will seem unimportant as a result of the impact of these civilizations on each other out of which will arise a new common life for mankind. In

5047 A.D., historians will point out that the factor of importance in the social unification of man was not technics and economics, politics or war, but religion. In this manner, changes in the history of civilizations will emerge as they interact with each other and attack and counterattack takes place.[26]

SOROKIN'S IDEATIONAL-SENSATE SYSTEM Pitirim A. Sorokin, in a four-volume work titled, *Social and Cultural Dynamics,* presented a theory of social and cultural change that emphasizes fluctuating, trendless changes that move between two polar types of cultural development, ideational and sensate.[27] The ideational culture period emphasizes the spiritual and nonmaterial; the sensate stresses materialism and agnostic concepts of value and reality. Taoist China, Buddhistic India, and medieval Christian Europe represent ideational cultures. The Western culture of today represents the sensate system, which is now in an "overripe" sensate stage that must be supplanted by a new ideational system, in Sorokin's view. Of it, he said:

> The contemporary sensate system, in its virile stages, contributed markedly to the values of science and technology, the fine arts, and in lesser degree, philosophy and ethics. But it is clearly approaching the end of its career, indeed, it is rapidly crumbling under our very eyes. In its present decadence phase, characterized by increasing wars and revolutions, by the perversion of science in the interest of ever more lethal weapons of destruction, by progressive sensualism and the like, it has begun to menace the further existence of humanity. If civilization is not to perish, our moribund sensate super-system must be replaced by a new ideational or idealistic super-system.[28]

The cause of these shifts is the immanent self-directing principle of change, according to Sorokin, that is, things change because it is in their nature to change. Change spreads to the whole culture when change appears in a part of the culture. All of its cultural sub-systems will change in that direction if the cultural system is changing in a given direction.

Sorokin's explanation of social change includes cyclical, linear, and irregular forms. Change is always moving from ideational to sensate or from sensate to ideational dominance, sometimes in a direct manner, but also often in an indirect and irregular way. The principle of limited possibilities determines that there are points in the process of change at which the trend must turn in the opposite direction.

Criticisms of this explanation of change center about the idea that it is deterministic: change because it is in the nature of things to change. It has also been criticized on the ground that the major concepts—ideational and sensate—are subjective terms. What is to be included in "sensate" and what in "ideational," the critic may ask.

CHAPIN'S CYCLICAL AND SYNCHRONOUS THEORY F. Stuart Chapin has made the concept of accumulation the basis for his theory of social change. Analysis of specific cultural phenomena, such as tools, implement manufacture, language, and institutions, shows accumulation to take place at an accelerating rate. Cultural change is "selectively accumulative in time." Chapin found, from a study of the chief features of Grecian, Roman, and medieval English culture, that their cultural elements not only accumulated at an increasing rate but also were repetitious or cyclical in character. He summarized these views as they apply to change by saying that "the most hopeful approach to the concept of cultural change would seem to be to regard the process as selectively accumulative in time and cyclical or oscillatory in character." [29] There is no inconsistency in this hypothesis that cultural change is selectively accumulative and cyclical in character, according to Chapin. They are complementary to each other for selective accumulation is merely one phase of the cycle process.

Each cultural form has its own specific law of change, though cultural forms of a given class may have a basically similar law which is "probably cyclical and periodic." Society has reached its era of maturity when the cycles of a number of its important cultural forms are synchronized. Cultural forms change through cycles of growth, maturity, and decay and of integration, equilibrium, and disintegration. These are the normal developmental processes of cultural forms. Because this is so, the total culture of which they are a part must pass through cycles of growth, maturity, and decay. This theory thus is a cyclical theory of social change where the changes are taking place in the society as a whole. One of the most important attributes of this theory is that, because it is based on empirical data, it can be tested by empirical analysis.[30]

III. SOCIAL PROGRESS

Social Progress Is the Achievement of Desired Ends

We can hardly consider social change without confronting the concept of social progress. This is an aspiring notion that transcends mere flux and even the idea of change in some given direction. It expresses the thought that change will take, or can be made to take, a *desired* direction in a society or civilization. Having its most notable expression in the writings of the French philosophers of the eighteenth century, it has been a dynamic agent in the social activity of modern man. Despite some sobering doubt, there is widespread optimism and confidence that desired values may be achieved, if not through natural law, then through social effort. The idea thus provides a motivating force for its own realization.

Some would insist that the primary business of sociology and the social sciences is to determine the criteria and conditions of progress which may guide the social planners or "social engineers" in their effort to bring about a better social order.

Progress and Change Are Not Contradictory

Some sociologists have abandoned the concept of social progress because it implies guided change, which in turn involves value judgments of highly subjective character. Such judgments —good or bad, desirable or undesirable—presumably belong to ethics and not to the science of sociology. On the other hand, whether as sociologists or not, we may argue that we continually relate what is to what ought to be. This inclination seems to be an intrinsic aspect of social order that enters into social activity and relationships. Groups of individuals do define goals the achievement of which satisfies their needs, improves their conditions, and therefore represents progress. In short, the accomplishment of defined objectives in specific areas within and between societies represents progress for them, even though it may be impossible to agree on what progress is for all societies or to determine whether a specific change is progress.

Efforts to Define Progress as a General Concept Result in Different Views

COMPLEXITY, POWER, AND USE Herbert Spencer defined progress as successive adaptation to environment and an increase in the complexity of forms which results in happiness. Increase in complexity may not result, though, in happiness but rather hinder it by making life more stressful and less harmonious. Wilson Wallis says progress would be better defined as the increase in power since power gives added control over nature. However, increase in power does not necessarily insure progress, despite its meaning an increase in ability to control. But the essential element in determining whether or not added power represents progress is the purpose for which we use it.[31] The development of atomic energy has added a tremendous potential power for the use of man. Whether this development will be a progressive forward step for man depends upon the quality of the ends for which it is used. Type of use, then, is a chief criterion of progress.

NEEDS Several thinkers have emphasized that the general criterion of progress is the satisfaction of human needs. Albion W. Small interpreted progress in this way. Both in classroom instruction and public lectures he emphasized that if we could see the people of all times, we would see that they were striving to satisfy their needs and wants. These he outlined, following the German *Ratzenhofer*, as the need for health, for economic security, for knowledge, for beauty, for rightness, for status, and for sociability. We make progress in societies as we are able increasingly to satisfy these needs. The major task in any society, he continuously asserted, was to direct the needs and activities of the citizens so that betterment could be achieved.

Some Thinkers Have Used a Single Criterion as a Test of Progress

HEALTH AND LONGEVITY Some scholars have said that, because the average number of years people live is a definitely measurable thing and indicates the state of well-being in a society, it is the best criterion of progress. Progress is being made when people increasingly live longer, when infant mortality is declining, and the chances of survival after birth are increased. One of the great achievements in most societies is in this area. The Health Information Foundation indicates that the length of man's life has increased from an average of eighteen years in the Early Iron and Bronze Ages to 70 years for the United States in 1960. This lengthening of the span of life is a definite indication of increased well-being. Increase in the length of life is characteristic of most societies though, of course, to different degrees among them. It is certainly one of the conditions that indicates progress as a result of improved medical care and sanitation.

MATERIAL PROSPERITY   Many say that the criterion by which progress in societies must be defined is the extent to which the individuals in the society as a whole are increasingly able to procure the necessities for living: food, clothing, and shelter. This implies that material benefits are not limited to any particular segment of a society but are available to all, so that everyone has the opportunity to enjoy an acceptable level of living. The wider significance of this condition is that it releases men from the constant burden of want and frees them to use their abilities to achieve larger ends.

MORAL IMPROVEMENT   This is the test of those who feel that improvement in personal and social righteousness is the most important criterion of progress. Progress comes when the character of the people, the principles undergirding social relationships, and the ethical and spiritual standards advance so that the chief motivation is service to our fellow men.

Progress Involves the Integration of Changes to Achieve Desired Ends

Of course, no single factors, such as those discussed above, can serve as the exclusive measure of social progress. Societies are complexes made up of many important elements, and any significant change will involve many factors. Progress is achieved as we make advances in all these areas. This view recalls Small's analysis, which stressed that progress is made in the extent to which all the basic needs of men are satisfied.

We can summarize this discussion, then, by suggesting that progress is achieved if, in a society, all aspects of social life move in a coordinated manner toward desired ends. It is possible to move forward with respect to some aspect while we lose ground in others. Health is a good in itself, but if it is not integrated with material improvement or moral advance, it may actually be used for retrogressive purposes. May it not then be said that progress is being made in a society when health, wealth, knowledge, aesthetic appreciation, and personal and social morality are improving? There are no limits to human progress in the sense of continuous effort to achieve ideal ends.

IV. PLANNED SOCIAL CHANGE

Theories of Social Change Influence Attitudes Toward Conscious Efforts to Direct Societies

Wells, Huxley, and Wells said in their *Science of Life* that "the cardinal fact in the problem of the human future is the increase in the speed of change." Man, they asserted, "is imposing on the life of the world a rate of change ten thousand times as great as any rate of change it ever knew before." [32] In the past, social change came with relative slowness, and a thousand years were but as yesterday. Man must now give social change direction, lest these changes overwhelm him and his social systems.

NONDELIBERATIVE CHANGE   The theory of change that a society follows has an important bearing on the policies it will pursue. Little effort will be expended to influence the direction of social change if we hold with Sumner and Keller that "there is a natural course of things," that human societies operate according to natural law, and that "arbitrary interferences never destroy the force or alter its laws, [but] only divert its course and alter its incidence." We can hardly direct the course of societies if we hold that changes come about primarily through gradual and nondeliberative growth, or that societies follow an inevitable course of birth, growth, and decay, or that it is determined by vast impersonal forces beyond our control.

Sumner and Keller themselves said that "there are three possible policies: to let things take their course as they will; to meddle indiscriminately; to interfere discerningly. The first has never been put into practice by anyone; the second is the common mode; the third is the only hope men have." They said that man has continuously interfered, but in the form of indiscriminate meddling by persons with lofty motives who are a nuisance and a peril because of their "pure ignorance." To interfere discerningly has little hope since "for practice there is little background in theory. Hence, a pathetic dependence upon intuition," standing to reason, "and at best, rule of thumb." [33] These men thus revealed their doubts about the possibility of intelligent interference with the course of social development.

CALCULATED CHANGES   On the other hand, there are those who hold that man, by giving thought and applying knowledge, can direct the course of social forces to build a better social order. Lester F. Ward, through his theory of social telesis, was an ardent proponent of this view. He stated his view of the cause of progress and the significance of artificial adaptation by teleological means in the following statement:

All progress is brought about by adaptation. Whatever view we may take of the cause of progress, it must be the result of a correspondence between the organism and the changed environment. This, in its widest sense, is adaptation. But adaptation is of two kinds: One form of adaptation is passive or consensual, the other form is active or previsional. The former represents natural progress, the latter artificial progress. The former results in a growth, the latter in a manufacture. The one is the genetic process, the other the teleological process. In passive adaptation the means and the end are in immediate proximity, the variation takes place by infinitesimal differences; it is a process of differentiation. In active adaptation, on the contrary, the end is remote from the means; the latter are adjusted to secure the former by the exercise of foresight. It is a process of calculation.[34]

Ward's suggestion as to how we can achieve this calculated progress is set forth in the following:

The whole philosophy of human progress, or dynamic sociology, may, therefore, be briefly epitomized in a few words: The desire to be happy is the fundamental stimulus which underlies all social movements, and has carried on all past moral and religious systems. . . . The problem is, to guide these vast and acknowledged forces in a progressive instead of a non-progressive direction. To do this, something analogous to these past non-progressive systems must be established. . . . Before progress can be achieved, a public sentiment must exist in favor of scientific education as strong as it has ever existed in favor of religious education. If, by the term education there can be constantly implied the two adjuncts, scientific and popular; if the word can be made to embrace the notion of imparting a knowledge of the materials and forces of nature to all the members of society, there can be no objection to the employment of this word education as the embodiment of all that is progressive.[35]

This calculated achievement of societal development by scientific and popular education is outlined in *Applied Sociology*, with its significant subtitle, "A Treatise on the Conscious Improvement of Society by Society." In this treatise, achievement, opportunity, and improvement are the key ideas.[36] Ward's approach has been hailed by many who are convinced that conscious, purposive direction of change is not only possible but also superior to natural uncontrolled change.

Man has always sought to direct the course of social change no matter which of these theories a society accepts. His activity has consisted of conscious efforts to establish or direct relationships in terms of some future good, although most of it has been precipitated by contingencies arising from the failure or collapse of the normal ways of handling social problems. It has been, for the most part, "forced" planning.

The Goal of Social Planning Is the Achievement of Predetermined Objectives

Social planning or consciously directed social change is the development of a program designed to accomplish predetermined objectives for a society or a segment of it. It thus includes three elements: (1) the determination of objectives to be sought, (2) the conscious development of a program that will accomplish the objectives, and (3) the involvement of the people affected. Simply stated, planning demands decisions about what we are to do, how we are to do it, who is to do it, and how the people affected by it are to be included.

Several Crucial Principles Are Essential to Conscious Planning Efforts

THE PEOPLE INVOLVED Social planning, whether it concerns the total society or only a part of it, involves a population of individuals intended to be its beneficiaries. It is always asserted, even in totalitarian societies, that planned social changes are for the benefit of each individual in the population. But some plans impinge upon the rights and privileges of individuals who feel that their freedoms and rights are being destroyed. For example, a new traffic-way may mean condemning residences or building properties. Many owners will feel that the plan is unfair. Resistance to the change can be strong when this attitude is general. Three things are involved in such proposals: will the planned change result in benefits to the total population so that these will offset the losses of those damaged; has the change been approved after careful consideration by the population affected; and are there assurances of fair compensation to those who are hurt? Thus, the crucial point is the involvement of the population in the plan. It is difficult to promote plans without the support of the people, and this support will not be forthcoming unless they are given the opportunity to participate and to express their views.

THE DEVELOPMENT OF THE PLANNING PROGRAM Assuming that the objectives are clear and have sufficient support, the program of action should be built on a firm foundation of fact. Too often, planning proceeds with much enthusiasm and meager data. Effective planning requires a thorough investigation of the given problem, the circumstances surrounding it, the possible obstacles, and the probable results of the proposed course of action. If engineers wished to build a bridge over a stream, they would hardly proceed without thoroughly investigating the conditions and collecting all the facts essential to understanding the situation so as to know what type of bridge must be planned. Planning without adequate knowledge can only result in failure.

It must be admitted that the social sciences do not yet have the facts or the principles to give the substantial guidance needed for directed social change. The development of the scientific approach to social relations is a recent one. The possibilities in this area have only recently been recognized, and in many quarters skepticism still prevails. Although people may plan their own affairs or those of the communities, they often oppose planning on a broad scale. This resistance will be overcome as they lose their fear of planning, that is, as it enters the folkways of the time and as social scientists continue to build up sound theoretical and factual bases for democratic social planning.

THE PLANNING PERSONNEL A third crucial aspect of social planning is the choice of the personnel who have the responsibility for devising and executing the detailed programs to be followed. Here, it should be recognized that an established planning body of specialists with managerial ability, technical skill, and scientific knowledge is necessary. This is essential because planning and its execution require technical skills and practical "know-how" that only experts possess.

The establishment of distinct planning bodies has two dangers. One is that the planning group will take over all responsibility, think only in terms of its own interests, and forget that the citizenry needs to be informed and involved. Many a school board and urban renewal body have been forced to revise or abandon plans because the citizens turned down a proposal about which they were not adequately informed. On the other hand, there is the danger that once a planning group is established, the citizenry will leave the whole matter to them, exercising only veto power when final approval is to be given. Here again, planning groups must keep the supporting public adequately informed to avoid the danger of total rejection.

The Tennessee Valley Project Illustrates These Principles

Any great undertakings of a modern society, such as warfare and atomic and space developments, require massive planning and coordination of technical and human resources. This form of planned activity, however, does not involve widespread discussion and participation by the many people who are affected. Only in a derivative sense could its processes be called democratic.

We can find no better demonstration of the principles of democratic planning than the development of the Tennessee Valley region of the United States. This enterprise, begun about 30 years ago, remains as an outstanding example of social imagination and purposive social direction.

CIRCUMSTANCES LEADING TO THE PROJECT This region, which is part of the Appalachian-Ozark area in the southeast part of the United States, includes parts of five states and seven socioeconomic subregions of the South. The basin is not a homogeneous area for it includes a wide variety of soils, resources, economic activities, and people. Much of the area was poor in agricultural possibilities because of erosion and submarginal land. The level of living for many of the people was low, educational facilities were poor, and health problems were extensive. Serious flooding was a constant threat. The region includes important resources, the chief of which are timber, minerals, building stone, and clay.

The suggestion to develop the region on a planned basis arose from the fact that the Muscle Shoals power and nitrate plants and the Wilson Dam, built on the Tennessee River during World War I, were only partially used after the war. It was proposed that expanded development of their potentialities could solve many of the area's problems, such as floods, erosion, and marginal land elimination. At the same time, new industry could be developed that could improve the welfare of the millions of people in the territory. In response to these proposals, the Tennessee Valley Development Authority (also known as the TVA) was created by the Congress in 1935.

Such a vast planned program was bound to create opposition. Many opponents insisted that it was unrealistic, was impossible, and would only be a drain on the finances of the country. It is to be expected that opposition would be strong in a society where development has moved forward almost without planning and primarily under private stimulation.

DEALING WITH THE PEOPLE INVOLVED   The TVA had to build dams, create lakes, build roads, string power lines, flood individual farms and whole communities, relocate families and towns, and work out compensation problems. It had to dislocate the region in many ways to control flooding, to provide sufficient water power for the steady production of electricity, to increase navigation possibilities, to stop erosion, and to accomplish many other objectives in order to carry out its assignment.

The TVA could have condemned properties, paid what it thought was a fair price for damages, carried the work to completion, and then removed itself from the scene. The method it followed, however, was described in this quotation from David Lilienthal, director of the project:

> And so, when a dam on the TVA system is still under construction and long before the waters have risen, the TVA sees to it that trained men and women of the vicinage are on their way into the countryside. They examine farms that may be for sale, so that families moved from the reservoir may have disinterested and expert advice, if they ask for it, on values and locations. The expert counsel of technicians and neighbor farmers is available to those who must move; that change provides a chance for the farmer to improve his agricultural practices. Thousands of families have obtained such guidance on a great variety of matters. . . .[37]

The TVA kept records of family adjustments for over 8000 farm families. Few farmers took cash for their land. Over 70 per cent of the families reported being better or equally well satisfied with their new locations.

A number of businessmen were encouraged to take the leadership in developing shipping on the river. Here, the TVA followed the principle of having the local people take the initiative. A private organization, the Tennessee Waterway Conference, developed, with assistance from TVA technical experts, a series of terminals that tied together the truck highways and railroads to these waterways. The businessmen of the valley, therefore, were the most active participants in developing navigation.

DEVELOPING THE PLANNING PROGRAM   The TVA did not proceed with any activity before it had first made a thorough appraisal of the total situation in the valley, particularly to ascertain how suggested developments would influence these individuals, families, communities and the region as a whole. This necessitated the development of an organization that included the several states in vital roles and a large number of engineers, physical scientists, social scientists, and administrators. These joined their special skills in the effort to develop the plan that would meet the needs of the area and yet retain flexibility where local conditions demanded it. Objectives were decided upon after consultation with officials and citizens. Local involvement in the achievement was energetically promoted wherever possible. Volumes of research reports and sketches on every aspect of the total project formed the basis on which final decisions were based. The reports were submitted to the people directly involved, and action was taken only after their suggestions had been considered and their support elicited.

PROJECT PERSONNEL   Such a project would have been impossible without expert help. The enterprise employed not only highly competent engineers, technical agriculturalists, county agricultural agents, and experiment station experts, but also social scientists who were prominent in their fields. Top leadership was motivated by the desire to develop the valley for the good of the local people and their communities. This spirit pervaded the whole enterprise from top to bottom.

References

1. Gaskell, E. C., *Cranford* (New York, E. P. Dutton and Co.), p. 21.
2. Blumenthal, Albert, *Small-Town Stuff* (Chicago, University of Chicago Press, 1932), pp. 405 and 406. Copyright, 1932, by the University of Chicago.

3. Cottrell, W. F., "Death by Dieselization: A Case Study in the Reaction of Techno-logical Change," *American Sociological Review*, 16 (June, 1951), pp. 358–365.
4. Anderson, Sherwood, *Winesburg, Ohio* (New York, The Modern Library, 1919), p. 65. By permission of Viking Press.
5. Beard, C. A. (ed.), *America Faces the Future* (Boston, Houghton Mifflin Company, 1932), pp. 29–30. A statement of Daniel Willard.
6. Davis, Kingsley, "The Origin and Growth of Urbanization in the World," *American Journal of Sociology*, 60 (March, 1955), p. 433.
7. Bogue, D. J., "Urbanism in the United States, 1950," *American Journal of Sociology*, 60 (March, 1955), p. 473. Also United States Department of Commerce, Bureau of the Census, *Statistical Abstract of the United States, 1961*, Table 12, p. 20.
8. United States Department of Commerce, Bureau of the Census, *Statistical Abstract of the United States, 1962*, Table 13, p. 21.
9. *Automobile Facts* (Detroit, Mich., November, 1954), p. 8.
10. Hindus, Maurice, *Humanity Uprooted* (New York, Jonathan Cape and Harrison Smith, 1929), p. 46. By permission of Jonathan Cape, Ltd., London.
11. Goldstein, Bernice, and Eichhorn, Robert L., "The Changing Protestant Ethic: Rural Patterns in Health, Work, and Leisure," *American Sociological Review*, 26 (August, 1961), p. 557.
12. See, for example, Bose, Santi P., "Peasant Values and Innovation in India," *American Journal of Sociology*, 57 (March, 1962), pp. 552–560, and Tannous, A. I., "Tech-nical Exchange and Culture Values: Case of the Middle East," *Rural Sociology*, 21 (March, 1956), pp. 76–79.
13. Anderson, M. A., "Informational Sources Important in the Acceptance and Use of Fertilizer in Iowa," Agricultural Economics Branch, Tennessee Valley Authority, Knoxville, Tenn., in cooperation with Iowa State College, Ames, Iowa (April, 1955), Report P55-1, p. 13.
14. Carlyle, Thomas, *Sartor Resartus* (New York, E. P. Dutton and Co., 1929), p. 185.
15. Hostetler, J. A., *Amish Life* (Scottdale, Penn., Herald Press, 1952).
16. Knopf, Olga, *The Art of Being a Woman* (Boston, Little, Brown and Company, 1932), p. 4.
17. Ogburn, W. F., *Social Change* (New York, B. W. Huebach, Inc., 1922), p. 200. By permission of Viking Press.
18. Hart, Hornell, "Some Cultural-Lag Problems Which Social Science Has Solved," *American Sociological Review*, 16 (April, 1951), pp. 223–227.
19. Osborn, Frederick, "Can We Control Atomic Energy?" *The New York Times Maga-zine* (October 30, 1949).
20. Sorokin, P. A., *Society, Culture, and Personality* (New York, Harper and Brothers, 1947), pp. 699–701.
21. Keller, A. G., *Societal Evolution* (New York, The Macmillan Company, 1915).
22. MacIver, R. M., *Society: Its Structure and Changes* (New York, Ray Long and Richard R. Smith, Inc., 1931), pp. 423–449.
23. *Ibid.*, pp. 405–406.
24. Spengler, Oswald, *The Decline of the West* (New York, Alfred A. Knopf, 1945), 2 vols.
25. Toynbee, A. J., *A Study of History* (New York, Oxford University Press, 1947). One-volume abridgment by D. C. Somervell.
26. Toynbee, A. J., "Encounters Between Civilizations," *Harper's Magazine* (April, 1947), pp. 289–294.

27. Sorokin, P. A., *Social and Cultural Dynamics* (New York, American Book Company, 1941).

28. Sorokin, P. A., *Society, Culture, and Personality* (New York, Harper and Brothers, 1947), p. 706.

29. Chapin, F. S., *Cultural Change* (New York, The Century Company, 1928), p. 202.

30. For a more recent discussion of theoretical aspects of social change, see Moore, Wilbert E., "A Reconsideration of Theories of Social Change," *American Sociological Review*, 25 (December, 1960), pp. 810–818.

31. Wallis, W. D., *An Introduction to Sociology* (New York, Alfred A. Knopf, 1937), pp. 417–418.

32. Wells, H. G., Huxley, J., and Wells, G. F., *The Science of Life* (Garden City, N.Y., Doubleday, Doran and Company, Inc., 1931), p. 1027.

33. Sumner, W. G., and Keller, A. G., *The Science of Society*, III (New Haven, Conn., Yale University Press, 1927), pp. 2221–2224. Cf. Ball, Harry V., Simpson, George C., and Ikeda, K., "Law and Social Change: Sumner Reconsidered," *American Journal of Sociology*, 67 (March, 1962), pp. 532–540.

34. Ward, L. F., *Dynamic Sociology*, I (New York, D. Appleton and Company, 1915), pp. 71–72.

35. *Ibid.*, pp. 25–26.

36. Ward, L. F., *Applied Sociology* (Boston, Ginn and Company, 1906).

37. Lilienthal, D. E., *TVA, Democracy on the March* (New York, Harper and Brothers, 1944), pp. 66, 104, and 105.

Questions for Study and Discussion

1. Distinguish between social change and social action.
2. Give some illustrations of the chain-reaction sequence of social change.
3. Illustrate the way in which social change may be effected by modifications; by replacement.
4. Discuss the factors causing social changes in your community.
5. What conditions are important in the acceptance of social change? Why?
6. Give some illustrations of the chief obstacles to change in your community.
7. What social changes do you think may be expected from the development of atomic energy?
8. Discuss the theory of cultural lag. Show some consequences of cultural lag in some area of your community.
9. Explain the meaning of culture base. What is its relation to inventions?
10. Of the several theories of social change, which seems most reasonable to you? Give your reasons.
11. How would you define social progress?
12. What criteria would you use to measure social progress?
13. How is the idea of progress related to social planning?
14. Discuss the relationship of goals to planning.
15. Consider the factors involved in a planned program for public medical care. Outline how such a program might be developed.
16. Can sociologists avoid making value judgments?

Suggested Topics for Reports

1. Select a significant scientific or technological development and trace through its sequence of effects to test the hypothesis that change originating in science or tech-

nology first affects economic organization, then other social institutions, and finally ideology (beliefs, values, and so on).

2. Make a survey of antiques in a sample of homes and determine the ways in which their original functions or meanings have been changed in their present setting.

3. Prepare a report on an "urban renewal" program of some city with which you are familiar. How does it illustrate the problems and principles of social planning?

Supplementary Reading

Bennis, Warren G., Benne, Kenneth B., and Chin, Robert, *The Planning of Change: Readings in the Applied Behavioral Sciences*. New York: Holt, Rinehart and Winston, 1961.

Chapin, F. Stuart, *Cultural Change*. New York: The Century Company, 1928.

Gilfillan, G. C., *The Sociology of Invention*. Chicago: Follett Publishing Co., 1935.

Higbee, E. C., *The Squeeze: Cities Without Space*. New York: William Morrow and Company, 1960.

Himes, J. S., *Social Planning in America*. New York: Doubleday Company, Inc., 1954.

Lilienthal, David, *TVA, Democracy on the March*. New York: Harper and Brothers, 1944.

MacIver, Robert M., *Social Causation*. Boston: Ginn and Company, 1942.

Moore, W. E., and Feldman, A. S., *Labor Commitment and Social Change in Developing Areas*. New York: Social Science Research Council, 1960.

National Planning Association, Washington, D.C. Publishes many bulletins and plans.

Ogburn, William F., *Social Change*. New York: Viking Press, 1927.

Sorokin, Pitirim A., *Social and Cultural Dynamics*. 4 vols. New York: American Book Company, 1937–1941.

Spengler, Oswald, *The Decline of the West*. New York: Alfred A. Knopf, 1945.

Spicer, Edward H. (ed.), *Human Problems in Technological Change*. New York: Russell Sage Foundation, 1952.

Sumner, William G., and Keller, Albert G., *Science of Society*. New Haven, Conn.: Yale University Press, 1927.

Todd, Arthur J., *Theories of Social Progress*. New York: The Macmillan Company, 1926.

Toynbee, Arnold J., *A Study of History*. Abridgment by D. C. Somervell. New York: Oxford University Press, 1946.

Ward, Lester F., *Applied Sociology*. Boston: Ginn and Company, 1906.

White, Leslie, *The Science of Culture*. New York: Farrar, Straus and Cudahy, 1949.

24

SOCIAL CONTROL: ACHIEVING DESIRED RESPONSES

S OCIAL control is necessary to the stability of societies because of human variability and differences in environmental influences. It is achieved chiefly by training, in which the aims, values, and norms of the society become internalized in the society's members; and by restraining, in which societies compel conformity by the withdrawal of values. To implement both training and restraining society employs numerous techniques of persuasion and dissuasion.

I. NEED OF CONTROL

Social Control Is Necessary to the Stability and Growth of Society

The chapter on social change indicates that societies and their parts are subject to continual change. But, short of complete social upheaval, change is counterbalanced by stability. We have repeatedly shown that societies are systems of human relationship that maintain regularity and order among their parts through the established norms that govern the behavior of their members. Regularity and order are necessary for societies to exist at all. Changes within them must be orderly if they are to endure as growing equilibriums. The maintenance of regularity and order is the basic function of social control.

HUMAN VARIABILITY Societies are made up of human beings with individuating characteristics. These tendencies increase the chances that people will deviate from, or act in opposition to, the norms of their society. Each person is a physically separate unit, as well as a mentally separate entity. In addition, each has the power of movement, of changing location from place to place. We are motivated to behavior by the inherited physiological urges and acquired social drives that lead us as unique beings to operate according to our particular urges, drives, and interests.

On the other hand, we can and do join with others to carry out our wishes so that our behavior is not only that of one individual but also of a number of associated individuals. Wholly unrestrained activity soon becomes license. Freedom involves not only the right to do what one wishes but also the obligation to see that one does not injure others.

The behavior of individuals and groups is determined, in general, by the accepted patterns operative in society. In most instances, we behave according to these norms, but at other times personal interests or definitions may impel us to deviate from them. Any great amount of such individuated behavior will threaten normative stability and the effective functioning of society. Social control is essential to keep deviation within limits.

SOCIAL VARIABILITY Social control is also necessitated by the complexities, variabilities, and incongruities of relationship structures in a dynamic society. Rapid change and growing social complexity will produce serious maladjustments, unless social controls function effectively to coordinate the interrelationships among the structural units. We have touched upon some of the implications of this problem in the previous discussion of social change and planning.

The Problem of Social Control Stated

The problem of societies, then, is that both unique individuals who are physically and mentally separate entities possessing the power of movement and the capacity to determine their own actions, and the groups through which they operate, must be persuaded to act together in coordinated reciprocal relationships to achieve desired ends. A society which is changing rapidly will need to employ conscious purposive controls on a wide scale, even though social systems may be self-adjusting to some degree.

Social Control Involves Training and Restraining

Achieving socially desired responses in societies rests on two processes: (1) accepting society's values as essential to the well-being of its members, and (2) prescribing the acceptable and proscribing the unacceptable ways of achieving these ends.

Thus, social control has a positive or promotional function and a negative or repressive function. The positive aspect consists of conditioning people to make largely automatic responses to societal norms, which reduces the need for deliberating over alternate choices. The basic control problem is solved to the degree that people are conditioned to respect the rights and property of others and to cooperate spontaneously so that social harmony prevails. Subsequently, we discuss this further.

The negative or repressive aspect of the problem is the prevention of serious deviations from acceptable forms of conduct. The method here is restraint. To train and to restrain are the generalized solutions to the control problem.

Societies Aim to Control Unconsciously

Each society strives to induce its members and groups to give desired responses spontaneously or automatically. Ideally, it expects to achieve conformity, solidarity, and continuity through the behavior of people who are habituated to act according to the norms of the society. The society would then not need to give detailed attention to its members' behavior. Indeed, patterning behavior so that it is an automatic expression of the aims of the society makes it possible for people to interact more smoothly and effectively than if every individual act had to be thought through. Enduring social structures would hardly be possible if each individual action required conscious deliberation and direction. To conserve societal energy, in effect, social behavior should be so habituated that attention to control can be kept at a minimum. This means, of course, that societies must depend heavily upon effective socialization to internalize social norms and values as the individual's guides and motives to action.

Societies Also Find It Necessary to Control Consciously

CONFLICT OF INTERESTS   Ideally, the best assurance of effective social control is the socialized individual. But there are usually some individuals who are not socialized to the degree that they follow societal norms automatically. Their personal interests, possibly of antisocial character, will be in serious conflict with society's interest. Society must then employ conscious deliberate means to induce such deviants to conform or accommodate themselves to its requirements. These pressures may involve police or other official functionaries. It should be noted that it is not the role of these agents to determine what the desired behavior should be but, more simply, to require conformity to the desired behavior that society has established in its norms and laws.

CHANGING CIRCUMSTANCES   Conscious control is also required when social change disrupts the accustomed adjustments of the past. Since new policies and practices, and possibly goals, will need to be formulated, this will further necessitate the introduction of deliberate strategies, and possibly coercion, to induce people to respond in the ways that the altered situation requires.

CONTROLS ARE EXTERNAL   Conscious controls in these circumstances are external to the people involved. They are mechanisms that are applied to induce people to act in the interests of others and to conform to the usages of others, rather than to satisfy their own contrary wishes. Such control is exemplified in its extreme form in the operation of the Soviet Union. Here, control is a device for compelling each person to perform his assignment in a prescribed way. For example, agents technically equipped to handle all the control problems involved are responsible for enforcing production quotas in the Soviet factories. They have legal authority to take appropriate measures against persons deviating from their orders. In turn, these agents are controlled by higher administrative officials who are controlled by higher authorities, all of whom head up in the absolute control exercised by the Communist party.[1]

Both Conscious and Unconscious Controls Require Means by Which They Are Exercised

If they are to achieve the social conformity and solidarity essential for harmonious functioning, societies must employ appropriate processes or strategies. As we have noted, one of these is effective socialization which will lead people to "assume the attitudes of the others who are involved with them in common endeavor. . . . If we can bring people together so that they can enter into each other's lives, they will inevitably have a common object which will control their common conduct."[2] This view would imply that, contrary to Hobbes and Freud, man has an originally benign and malleable nature. (See, however, Box 50.) Controls directed toward restraining and preventing behavior that is considered undesirable for social well-being require specific means, also. Social controls, then, may be considered as (1) means used to effect training and as (2) means used to effect restraint.

II. MEANS USED FOR TRAINING

A. SOCIALIZATION AND EDUCATION

Socialization Is the Foundation upon Which Societies Base Control

Societies depend primarily upon the socialization of their members—the process by which people come to communicate, associate, conform, and cooperate together—to develop a relatively stable equilibrium of the total systems and in the subsystems of which they are composed. This, again, involves the conditioning of a society's members so that they absorb the norms, the knowledge, and the habits requisite to their acceptable adjustments within society. The individual possesses no knowledge or understanding of the standards or rules of his society at birth—he must be taught them. Societies consciously devise their instructional programs to fulfill personal and social needs rather than to leave the learning to chance. This is the role of education in social control—to provide a conscious teaching program that helps to inculcate the ideals, norms, and habits that will enable people to develop normally and to sustain the social system.

This Conditioning Role Is an Indirect One

The role of education is an indirect one in the sense that it helps to lay the foundation upon which acceptable behavior is based. It seeks to inculcate attitudes which will be so enduring that in later situations they will assert themselves as regulatory controls. Most basic among these would certainly be the attitude toward truth, the respect for fact, and logical thinking. Moreover, in the same vein, education helps the individual to know his society and his role in it in ways that will facilitate his effective adjustment to it.

The task of socializing the individual so that he gradually absorbs the norms and values of his society and acts automatically with respect to them must be accomplished by clearly determined influences. Formal as well as informal instruction that orders habits and attitudes in

---

BOX 50   The "Hobbesian Question" in Sociology

[Sociology] originates in the asking of general questions about man and society. The answers lose their meaning if they are elaborated without reference to the questions. . . . An example is the Hobbesian question of how men become tractable to social controls. The two-fold answer of contemporary theory is that man "internalizes" social norms and seeks a favorable self-image by conforming to the "expectations" of others. Such a model of man denies the very possibility of his being anything but a thoroughly socialized being and thus denies the reality of the Hobbesian question. . . . Sociologists need to develop a more complex, dialectical conception of human nature instead of relying on an implicit conception that is tailor-made for special sociological problems.[2]

a disciplined manner are required. This experience is provided in a significant measure by our schools. In a sense, schools are small societies or subsystems in which many of the conditions of contemporary life occur in simpler but similar form.

B. BELIEFS

Belief, the Acceptance of a Proposition as True, Is Also an Important Means of Control

Since belief is intellectual assent to a proposition, it is a basis for action. Beliefs may be true or false, depending on whether they are founded on factual or faulty evidence. But the question of their validity does not necessarily determine their effectiveness as social controls. We act with as much determination from false beliefs as from factually sound ones.

Beliefs, even though they may not be true, can sometimes be socially constructive when they include a high level of idealism that leads to socially acceptable behavior. Nevertheless, since beliefs, once formed, are not easily changed or relinquished, it is vital for human relations, in the long run, that they be based upon legitimate foundations.

The Validity of Beliefs Is of Major Significance Since Men Develop Them about All Aspects of Their Social Life

No aspect of social relationships escapes the development of beliefs about it. Because they are so important in determining human behavior, the question of their validity is crucial to the control process. Some people hold, for example, that fate determines their destiny and that their behavior is an inevitable expression of it. Homer caused Hector to say: "No man against my fate shall hurl me to Hades: only destiny, I ween, no man hath escaped, be he coward or be he valiant, when once he hath been born." [3] Is this belief fact or fiction? If every man's destiny is predetermined, as millions believe, then it is useless to be dissatisfied with our lot. We should accept whatever comes with a cheerful resignation. Other people, however, believe that man can be the "master of his fate," that human beings can order and direct their social destiny by applying their knowledge of social behavior and social action. These beliefs will obviously lead to very different views of the social control problem.

Beliefs in Supernatural Sanctions Have Always Been a Major Social Control

AMONG PRIMITIVE SOCIETIES   Early man, as well as modern man, used both secular and supernatural means to control the relationships within his societies. Primitive men are much more dependent upon sanctioned and traditional ways of acting than are modern men. But in many circumstances these patterned ways need the support of more effective forces than custom. Primitives find these supports in powers outside of themselves, in the supernatural personalities endowed with capacity to bring things to pass by their desire or decree. Thus, control is given the added support of sanctions exerted by supernatural powers. Many of these early conceptions of supernatural powers were of an elemental type. Primitive societies peopled the world with spirits which, among other things, rewarded human beings for correct behavior and punished them for wrong. Conceptions of these supernatural powers developed to higher levels as man's understanding of the universe grew, so that much of the superstition that attached to early forms dropped away. But these higher conceptions are still founded upon the belief that these powers cause things to happen by acts of their will or decree.

IN MODERN SOCIETIES   Societies of today still use belief in a supernatural world and man's adaptation to it as an important method of achieving desired social ends. Many present-day interpretations of these beliefs rest upon the same concept of rewards and punishments that prevailed in primitive societies. The belief persists that if people do not follow the prescribed religious precepts they will be subject to punishments here or hereafter; if they obey the precepts, they will be rewarded here or hereafter. This is a legalistic presentation that is exemplified in the description of a revival meeting given by Julia Peterkin:

"When it was at last ended, sinners were invited to come up to the mourner's bench and kneel for prayer, the preacher pleaded with them not to wait and be damned, but to come up and promise God they'd seek forgiveness for their sins until He gave them some sign by which they'd know they were saved. A multitude thronged forward and fell on their knees, sobbing and calling on Jesus for mercy." [4]

The modern reinterpretation of religion removes this legalistic element which employs fear as the main factor of control. Instead, it emphasizes the brotherhood of man and the sacredness of the person as the core beliefs in religion. Unselfish service to societies and the groups within them is the highest type of human behavior and the truest expression of the will of God. Injustice and immorality that demean man and impair the development of personality are intolerable to the truly religious person. This emphasis in religion makes it one of society's strongest social controls because it emanates from the inner self and operates like the attitudes and habits developed through education.

C. SUGGESTION-IMITATION

Suggestion Controls by Implanting Ideas in Others

Suggestion (the subtle implanting of ideas and feelings in our minds) and *imitation* (behavior that reproduces the acts of others) are means by which much social control is achieved. Suggestion is the indirect communication of ideas, feelings, and other psychical states from person to person. The stimulus is presented by individuals or groups who consciously or unconsciously seek to implant their ideas or feelings in others. Such communication often leads to immediate response if those receiving the suggestion are conditioned in some manner toward it. It is no difficult task to get a boy to join a baseball game if he likes this game and meets other boys who want to play. It is not difficult to intensify strong feelings in others by added illustrations of unfairness if one feels strongly that others are operating unfairly in a given situation. These persons are already disposed to react in this manner.

Predispositions can often be created by the constant reiteration of an idea or position that eventually is accepted where no predispositions, either positive or negative, previously existed. This is most easily accomplished where the suggestion has a real or supposed value for those being influenced, and especially when prestige can be attached to it. Just prior to vacation seasons, many magazines carry beautiful advertisements depicting the advantages of visiting certain places and suggesting the prestige attached to traveling to them in certain ways. Repeated over and over again, they endeavor to bring about a mental set or attitude favorable to the action suggested. Many of our social, business, and political enterprises employ pres-

tige or other forms of suggestion to influence attitudes and, therefore, action. Modern advertising has probably exploited this technique to the highest degree.

Suggestion May Be Conscious or Unconscious

Suggestions are made consciously or unconsciously, and they are consciously or unconsciously accepted or rejected. Suggestion is often unconsciously accepted when the subject is consciously attending to some source of stimuli other than the suggestion. Suggestion is unintentional as well as intentional. As a social control, it is most often based on intention. Parents intend to set an acceptable example for their children. Rather than to say, "Look at me and do as I do," they usually seek to appear and to act so that the child, who is always looking anyhow, will as a matter of course develop desirable habits from what he sees.

Imitation Controls Through the Initiative of the Recipient of Suggestion

Imitation occurs when the child thinks and acts like his parents because of the suggestions, conscious or unconscious, that his parents have made. It is their reproduction of observed acts or understood thoughts that have been noticed by the observer. The initiative to action here is taken by the persons receiving the suggestion, which is what societies want. They wish to perpetuate themselves as they are by having the oncoming generation absorb and practice the sanctioned manners of living that it sees about it. The problem of social control is simplified if individuals react favorably to these sanctioned manners and thereby reproduce them automatically. This conserves and preserves what the society has evolved and considers valuable. Imitation gives a society continuity while, at the same time, it allows for slight modifications that do not destroy its principles and practices. Thus, it is a major method for handing on social experience from generation to generation.

Gabriel Tarde's Emphasis on Imitation

Imitation is so important to societies that the French scholar, Gabriel Tarde, made it the central thesis of his work, *The Laws of Imitation*. To him, man makes inventions which produce waves of imitation—custom, fashion, sympathy, and other forms. These spread until they meet opposition and bring about other inventions that start a new wave of imitation. Society's central process is therefore the imitation by which its activity is generated and around which it operates. There is ample evidence of the significance of imitation in many social relationships, although we do not accept this view as a complete explanation of social behavior. The immigrant imitates dress and other outward signs while absorbing the norms and practicing them by imitation. A marching army almost completely operates by imitation, and mobs, crowds, and audiences are highly imitative. An individual selects a model—a reference individual who may be his father, mother, friend, or brother—and patterns his life after this person. A major factor in the education of Henry Adams was his model, Mr. Sumner. Of Mr. Sumner it was said: "The boy Henry worshipped him, and if he ever regarded any older man as a personal friend, it was Mr. Sumner. The relation of Mr. Sumner in the household was far closer than any relation of blood. None of the uncles approached such intimacy. Sumner was the boy's ideal of greatness; the highest product of nature and art." [5] This is a common experience among youth; as such, it is a most important process of social control.

D. PERSUASION

Persuasion Is the Attempt to Achieve Control by Convincing Argument

Persuasion is being used when the implanting of ideas is accompanied by the expressed desire that the suggestion be accepted. This is a more direct form of achieving control than is suggestion-imitation, in that it is an open effort to influence others by the pressure of logic or argument. Because good reasons must be advanced to convince the individual, persuasion operates by convincing, that is, by overcoming resistance with arguments. It implies that those on whom it is used are not under one's control, they may already have ideas, habits, and attitudes that must be overcome to make control possible.

Persuasion Is Founded on Several Appeals

SELF-INTEREST   Persuasion by argument or reason may take several forms, self-interest being one of them. The appeal to self-interest is illustrated in this attempt to get support for a project from a community of Russian peasants:

Aren't you glad your children can attend school? Haven't you yourselves said that the schoolhouse is a blessing because in winter your children can develop their minds and acquire a real culture, instead of loafing around in the streets and becoming little savages? Tell me, were we wrong when we urged this schoolhouse on you—yes, and insulted and denounced you because you wouldn't meet us halfway on the project of building it? Were we wrong when we urged you to build a fire station? Were we wrong when we urged you to lay decent bridges across your stream in the swamp? [6]

LOYALTY   The argument may also be based on an appeal to loyalty. One of the chief bases of social relationships in the Middle East is personal, family, and village loyalty. When a person says, "Do it for my sake" or "Do it because you are my friend," it makes it difficult for the one being persuaded to be objective. In some Middle-East schools, for example, teachers are constantly under pressure to treat their pupils in favored ways "because he is the son of my friend." Loyalty, although an admirable trait, can be a serious problem when it leads to the performance of acts that violate ethical principles.

EVIDENCE   Often, the soundest basis for persuasion is the unbiased presentation of facts. Here, the agent of persuasion, in effect, removes his own desires from the situation and allows the evidence to do the convincing on an impersonal basis. People are appealed to on the basis of their own ability to judge the validity of the evidence. They are asked to accept or reject on the basis of the evidence presented. Persuasion in this form is self-persuasion. The self-persuaded person is likely to be the most firmly and durably convinced.

Ideally, the scientific approach is the surest persuader. The approach of science consists of careful observation by objective methods of a given order of phenomena, the formation of conclusions based upon the systematic classification of these observations, and the revision of conclusions when new evidence is available. All facts that bear on the problem are included according to the rigid definition of concepts, together with complete reporting of the method of procedure. The principles deduced are accepted or rejected, not because the researcher says so, but because the facts say so. The intelligent recognition of objectively determined conclusions may thus be an effective factor in social control.

Propaganda Attempts to Persuade by Stressing Primarily Only Supporting Facts

Propaganda seeks to induce people to accept a position and to act accordingly, by stressing those viewpoints that support it and minimizing those that oppose it. It can be an effective method of achieving assent when it makes a direct personal appeal and plays upon the emotions that underlie security, pride, and well-being. It is even more effective when the appeal is made in a subtle manner that does not directly reveal its real purpose but makes the receiver feel that he is the major beneficiary. This removes the initial resistance that might be present. Politicians know well that the many helpful services they perform directly for particular people are far more important to their political welfare than a large service that does not touch their constituency directly.

Propaganda is almost certain to expand in societies as the means of communication develop so that millions of people are made accessible at one time through radio, television, newspapers, and magazines. There is constant propagandizing for given viewpoints in most societies and persistent endeavor to neutralize the propaganda of the opposition. This effort has now become world-wide as communication networks enmesh the globe.

Propaganda as a form of persuasion is generally present in all advertising. It sets forth the merits of goods and services offered with an extravagance that few people can successfully counteract. Incessant reiteration of exaggerated claims can weaken the resistance of the hardiest listeners. The public may be protected in a measure by competitive advertising, but some would feel that this is small compensation for the assault on eye, ear, and intelligence. Some of the tactics of modern advertising were suggested in Frederick Lewis Allen's description of the process:

> The copywriter was learning to pay less attention to the special qualities and advantages of his product, and more to the study of what the mass of unregenerate mankind wanted—to be young and desirable, to be rich, to keep up with the Joneses, to be envied. The winning method was to associate his

product with one or more of these ends, logically or illogically, truthfully or cynically; to draw a lesson from the dramatic case of some imaginary man or woman whose fate was altered by the use of X's soap, to show that in the most fashionable circles people were choosing the right cigarette in blindfold tests. . . .[7]

Slogans Are Forms of Persuasion Relying on Absoluteness to Convince

A slogan is a terse, catchy statement that epitomizes in brief form a purpose, a policy, a point of view, or the characteristics of some person or situation. It aims to gain spontaneous acceptance and support. "Make the world safe for democracy" is a phrase that summed up the idealistic commitment of the Western world in World War I, while the catchwords, "Liberty, Equality, Fraternity," summarized the purposes of the French Revolution. History abounds with others, such as, "Tippecanoe and Tyler Too" and "Fifty-Four Forty or Fight!" Such words or phrases are familiar and full of emotional content. They direct their appeal to the feelings rather than to intelligence and seek to persuade through submerging thought and reducing resistance. Successful slogans are catchy, easy to remember, and emphatically suggestive. In most instances, the key words are general and difficult to define with precision. They may have one connotation in one situation and a different one in another. Their essential meaning is often subject to varying interpretations. Nonetheless, they are useful to the propagandist as political rallying points, effective selling devices, religious challenges, the promotion of movements, and other efforts at social persuasion.

E. EMOTIONAL APPEAL

Art Expressions Control Through Domination of the Feelings

There is a legend that in the sixteenth century, after Europe had been devastated by war, famines, and epidemics, a troubadour walked through the streets of Vienna playing a lute and singing, "Ach, du lieber Augustine." Those who heard him remembered his lilting tune. Soon all Europe was singing it. People began to work and to hope.

Music can give composure and courage. Singing, playing of instruments, or being a listener does not usually instruct people; it does not even lead them to suggest, to imitate, or to persuade. It simply conveys a distinctive appeal that influences behavior by its impact on feelings.

Art expressed in music, painting, sculpture, architecture, and ceremony may exert control through their influence on the imagination. These forms have a fascination that create feelings suitable to the situation. The martial music of the military band arouses feelings of determination and strength. The grand figure of Michaelangelo's Moses in the church of Saint Pietro in Rome conveys a sense of dignity and power. The stained-glass window picture of a Christ knocking at the closed door arouses sympathy and fixes devotion. Thus, these appeals to feelings have a controlling role through aiding in socializing and directing the reactions of people. They lift us above self-concern and inspire us to make our life one of beauty and order.

Ceremony, Ritual, and Liturgy Have Always Been Social Control Elements in Institutional Agencies and Organizations

Legislative bodies, courts, and other divisions of the government follow ceremonial procedures in the opening and closing of their sessions and at other stages of their activities. Pledging allegiance, praying for guidance, and the rising of an audience when functionaries enter a room not only represent procedures of etiquette, they also impress the participants with the importance of their obligations and duties and stress the importance of their institutions. Marriage, baptismal, and other organizational ceremonies emphasize the significance of these acts and dramatize their larger implications.

The rituals of lodges, such as those of the Masonic order or the Grange, control the behavior of participants through their acceptance of the ideals which are symbolically portrayed. Participants are usually strongly influenced by the contagious collective sentiments the rituals create. The liturgies followed in many religious orders are rich in tranquilizing elements, such as the reposeful music and rhythmic readings that prepare the congregations to enter into the worship program in a receptive mood. They integrate the worshippers into a unity which gives an experience of common identity and spiritual enlargement. Such a mood facilitates the exercise of social control.

F. REWARDS

Rewards That Give People Status in Societies Are Strong Supports of the Control System

The desire for recognition is one of the strongest forces influencing the behavior of people. We want to count for something in the eyes of our fellow men. We want to be compensated for our endeavors. Even the lowliest of men can be stimulated by giving them status. Tolstoi was asked by a beggar for alms. "I'm sorry but I have no alms to give you, *my brother*," he replied. "Sir," said the beggar, "you have given me much more than alms. You have called me, brother." When Paderewski was asked what he considered to be the sweetest music, his reply was that the sweetest music is human praise. John Ruskin said that the greatest efforts of the human race are directly traceable to the love of praise. Nothing fires ambition so much as the feelings we derive from the recognition of our achievements by our fellow men. Such rewards are especially welcome if they come unexpectedly or indirectly.

Acceptable Behavior Is Usually Rewarded by Societies and Their Organizations

Persons behaving according to the norms of their society are almost automatically recognized as good citizens worthy of respect. This often leads to further recognition in the social responsibilities that are given only to those who are honorable. Socialization leads most people to conform to the desired ways of thinking and acting, but rewards confirm and support them. This is one of their important functions. Election to an office in a community organization, the "most valuable" member award from a youth agency, the extra friendliness of other respected people—all are supports of the general control system that make it operate more smoothly and effectively.

Tumin has studied the relationship of rewards to task-orientation in the work world. His basic assumption is that people give more of themselves to their jobs when they consider themselves as valuable parts of the enterprise. We value our own part in an enterprise as we receive recognition of its importance from those whose opinions we consider important and by criteria which they consider relevant. Tumin's chief conclusion is that workers lose conscientiousness in any system of unequal positional rewards and that equal rewards for equal conscientiousness would produce marked increase in identification with the task. Thus, reward for conscientiousness can become a factor of significance in the control system of the work world.[8]

G. HUMOR AND SATIRE

Humor Functions in Various Ways to Effect Controls

RELIEF OF TENSION Humor is also a means of social control. It assumes various forms, depending upon the situation and purpose. It often serves to relieve a tense situation. The paratrooper, poised to make his first jump, asks, "What should I do if the 'chute fails to open?" His officer replies, "Send it back to the factory for a new one!" The tension in the waiting fledgling troopers is dissipated in loud laughter.

MALICE Sometimes humor is used maliciously to express hostile attitudes toward others. It may take the form of sarcasm that intends to taunt, or of irony that is caustic. Humor can be cruel when used to deflate others undeservedly.

GAIN OF FAVOR Humor is also used to establish a position and gain a favorable response. We tell jokes on ourselves. Others laugh and conclude that we can "take it"—that we do not feel ourselves to be immune to embarrassing experiences—and we gain acceptance, thereby. Comedian Bob Hope is an expert at this kind of humor, especially in jokes about his nose.

A VALUE SUPPORT Humor also controls by supporting the sanctioned values of the society. In American society, humor is frequently aimed at satirizing economic and social differences and emphasizing social equality. The appeal of the old "Maggie and Jiggs" comics and of Bill Mauldin's wartime cartoons rests upon this theme. It tends to play up achievement and other similar values and to play down family background and social aristocracy. It can thus support the values of the society in a form that is light in spirit but effective for control.[9]

"Gallows Humor" Seeks to Affect Controls by Ridicule

"Gallows humor" is a special type of humor that is used to ridicule by sarcasm and irony. It seeks to undermine the morale of oppressors by making fun of them and causing them to appear ridiculous. At the same time, it seeks to bolster the spirits of those being oppressed.

This form is illustrated in the story of the anti-Nazi fishmonger who was temporarily imprisoned for singing through the streets, "Nice fresh herring, fat as Goering." After release, he returned to his rounds, now calling out, "Nice fresh herring, just as fat as they were two weeks ago!" Negro comedian Dick Gregory taunts his white listeners: "You better be nice to me—I may be your neighbor in that new housing development!" Such humor appears in almost all situations where people are being subjected to domination that endangers their rights or lives. Wars, in particular, produce great quantities of this type. Stories ridiculing the opponents appear when nations are in conflict, even though there may not be actual combat. The wrathful reaction of the targets of ridicule would suggest their feeling of insecurity.[10]

Satire Seeks to Control by Scornful Ridicule

Satire employs wit and scorn as indirect criticism of actions felt to be vicious and socially harmful. Satire exposes by ridicule the falsity and danger of behavior which many may accept as normal. It seeks to present things in their ugliest light, thus causing people to be incensed and the perpetrators to be held in scorn. Swift's *Gulliver's Travels* is a classic example of social satire on his times, just as is Orwell's *1984* or *Animal Farm* in the present era.

H. WARNINGS AND THREATS

Warnings or Threats Are Often Sufficient to Accomplish Desired Responses

Just a warning is enough to operate as an effective control at times. It tells in advance the likely consequences of a proposed action. Threats are more emphatic forewarnings of consequences. The father who says to his son, "If you fight when you are at school, you will receive a whipping when you get home," is warning the son in order to deter him from engaging in undesirable behavior. There is both warning and threat in the following incident where desertion from the army is contemplated:

Stanhope—If you went, I'd have you shot for deserting. It's a hell of a disgrace to die like that. I'd rather spare you the disgrace. I give you half a minute to think. You either stay here and try and be a man—or you try to get out of that door—to desert. If you do that, there's going to be an accident. D' you understand? I'm fiddling with my revolver, d' you see?—Cleaning it—and it's going off by accident. It often happens out here. It's going off, and it's going to shoot you between the eyes.[11]

Use of Threats Can Be Damaging to Social Controls

An important attribute of warnings and threats is that they can weaken or destroy social controls altogether if they are made with little intention of execution. The parent who warns a child of consequences must be ready to carry through if the child disobeys. A society, too, must carry out its warnings or threats of punishment if its controls are to be effective. The certainty of punishment is generally more effective as a control than its severity. The principle expressed here applies to sanctions from the interpersonal to the international level.

I. LAW

Laws Arise as Controls Which Formally Define Rights and Obligations in a Society

We have so far examined a variety of processes and methods of control which societies use to induce conformity to their norms. These are essentially conventionalized ways of control. We turn now to laws as the more formal, official forms of control.

EARLY SOCIETIES DEPENDED ON CONVENTIONS Societies depended, for long periods of time, upon the acceptance of the conventionalized ways to order the relationships of individuals and groups. They became part of the everyday orientations and behavior of the people. The old Chinese, to illustrate, considered these conventions parts of the moral order and followed them automatically. They did not need to be formalized into written statutes to be enforced by courts. Custom did that. Debts were to be paid by the New Year, an obligation which the community expected and enforced. The New Year had not dawned if debts were not paid. Debtors carried lighted lanterns in broad daylight to show that it was still night for them. Friends could not give such a person a New Year's greeting. Custom took the place of laws in this land where conventions indeed had the force of law.

COMPLEX SITUATIONS DEMAND FORMAL RULES When societies grow in size and complexity, they are compelled to formulate rules and regulations which formally define the required types of behavior and specify the penalties to be imposed upon those who violate them. Laws thus emerge as instruments of control. They usually define clearly rights, obligations, or duties as well as the punishments for infractions. In their original statutory form, they crystallize already existing conventions or mores into formal rules. They are indispensable for the orderly operation of large complex societies which can no longer rely chiefly upon conventions or other informal controls. As formal means of social control, laws restrict freedom by limiting rights of people. But, on the other hand, they protect persons from injury by others.

The Law of Today Is Formalized in Enacted Statutes Supported by the Whole Society

In modern terms, law consists of statutes passed by legally authorized legislative bodies and enforced by authorized agencies. But the code of Hammurabi, designed to harmonize the conflicting traditions of his empire, was prepared about 2000 years before Christ. It is the earliest codified set of laws surviving to the present time. The Ten Commandments of Moses was a codification of the customs and traditions of the early nomadic Hebrews that served as their moral law. The Commandments put greater emphasis on the accepted norms and were attributed to God to give them even greater force. The writing down of the rules, as in these instances, gives them more definiteness and authority. These attributes are even more necessary in complex societies where relationships are of a secondary nature. Security of life and property as well as the systematic ordering of relationships make this formalization essential. The formalization process makes the norms and prescribed penalties uniform throughout a social system. Furthermore, it transfers the right of redress from the injured parties to society itself. Thus, laws are rules of conduct enforced by the society. Bertrand Russell summarized this relationship in the following:

If threats and terrorism were not prevented by law, it can hardly be doubted that cruelty would be rife in the relations of men and women, and of parents and children. It is true that the habits of a community can make such cruelty rare, but these habits, I fear, are only to be produced through the prolonged reign of law. It would seem, therefore, that, while human nature remains as it is, there will be more liberty for all in a community where some acts of tyranny by individuals are forbidden, than in a community where the law leaves each individual free to follow his every impulse.[12]

The Strength of Law as a Control in Democratic Societies Is Dependent on the Support of the Public

In democratic societies, laws are made for the good of all through bodies elected and authorized by the public. They are effective to the extent that the authorized agencies and agents execute their duties properly. The success of law as a social control rests upon public opinion, a general consensus resulting from the discussion of societal problems. Public opinion is a main force behind customs and traditions and, therefore, law. When a society puts its rules into formal codes, it does so primarily because the public requires it after reaching a consensus on the objectives and the means necessary to achieve them. When societies change rapidly, a multitude of new laws may be enacted. Very often these are difficult to enforce because of the lack of public understanding and supporting public opinion. Laws regulating prices are a case in point. Disrespect for law may grow if it does not have general public support. This is especially true if the laws are thought to invade personal rights too severely. Both public opinion and laws are social controls external to individuals. We may react accordingly if they are weak or weakened. It is difficult, in increasingly complex situations, to create the likemindedness that results in common sympathy and consensus. Law and public opinion must be supported, therefore, by the lively social consciousness of a society's members. A pervading sense of the general welfare is essential to effective social control through public opinion and law.

Increased Complexity in Societies Calls for Regulatory Laws

We have noted that laws increase in number as a society becomes more complex. They are necessary as regulatory devices. It would be impossible, for example, to assure sanitary materials and safe conditions for the large numbers of people concentrated in urban centers without specific regulations governing food handling, fire protection, sewage disposal, and many other vital matters. The movement of people to and fro on bicycles, automobiles, trains, and airplanes would create an endless amount of confusion, to say nothing of the danger to life and property, if we had no regulatory laws that defined traffic requirements and imposed penalties to enforce them. In fact, the laws that affect us most immediately are of this regulatory nature. These are not based directly on the mores of the society, yet they have their roots in the concerns for the welfare of the society and so are a form of control supporting the general welfare.

III. MEANS USED FOR RESTRAINING

The Effectiveness of Restraints Rests on the Withdrawal of Values

The term "restrain" suggests the use of force to achieve a desired end. Controlling people consciously usually implies the actual or potential use of force. Coercion or the threat of coercion, therefore, stands as the ultimate sanction available to societies. Charles A. Beard once said in a public address: "Cooperation is required by the great majority of the participants and the coercion of the rest may be ultimately necessary. I hate not only the term but the idea of coercion, and yet we are forced to recognize that every advance in social organization requires the voluntary surrender of certain amounts of individual freedom by the majority and the ultimate coercion of the minority." Societies are compelled in their actual operation to establish rules to which are attached punishments to be inflicted upon those who violate them. Some form of punishment is a necessary or ultimate recourse of a society which seeks effective discipline of its members.

The use of punishments to ensure obedience and order is based on depriving the wayward of something they do not wish to lose. Often, we know the cost we must pay if our behavior is antisocial and we are apprehended. The purpose of this principle is twofold: (1) to deter an offender from again committing similar acts, and (2) to deter others who contemplate similar behavior. For the penalty to be effective, people must really be distressed at having to undergo the prescribed punishment. They must be deprived of something that they actually value. The degree of pain must be sufficient to make misbehavior unpleasant and unprofitable to offenders. Societies would be unable to protect themselves unless they possessed such means of inflicting physical or mental discomfort. "How can a sheep dog work a flock of sheep unless he can bite occasionally as well as bark?" is the way Samuel Butler put the matter.

Societies endeavor to fit deprivation to the seriousness of the antisocial act. It must be severe enough to serve as a felt loss to the offender and as a deterrent to others. Punishment will thus range from deprivation of approval (a mild rebuke) through deprivation of property (a fine) to deprivation of life (hanging or electrocution).

Physical Coercion Is Used as One Method of Restraint

Physical force is often used to maintain order, although it is without doubt the lowest form of social control and the form societies would least desire to use. It is usually justified on the grounds that there are recalcitrants who can be controlled in no other way. Such physical force takes the form of bodily injury and pain, imprisonment, or capital punishment.

BODILY INJURY AND PAIN Inflicting bodily pain by beating, starving, torturing, and by other manners usually has no valuable consequence except to compel obedience at the moment. It can have two detrimental results. One is the brutalization of the person punished. As Beers wrote: "Some wild animals can be clubbed into a semblance of obedience, yet it is treacherous obedience at best and justly so. And that is the only kind of obedience into which a man can be clubbed." [13] The other is the brutalization of those who inflict the punishment.

A study by William A. Westley indicates that the illegal use of violence by the police, to whom a monopoly of its legitimate use is delegated, is defended by them as a consequence of their occupational experience. An illustration is given in the following statement by a policeman:

There is a case I remember of four Negroes who held up a filling station. We got a description of them and picked them up. Then we took them down to the station and really worked them over. I guess that everybody that came into the station that night had a hand in it, and they were in pretty bad shape. Do you think that sounds cruel? Well, you know what we got out of it? We broke a big case in _____. There was a mob of twenty guys, burglars and stick-up men, and eighteen of them are in the pen now. Sometimes you have to get rough with them, see. The way I figure it is, if you can get a clue that a man is a pro and if he won't co-operate, tell you what you want to know, it is

justified to rough him up a little, up to a point. You know how it is. You feel that the end justifies the means. [14]

Students of history will recall the use of the stocks, the pillory, and the whipping post to inflict pain upon offenders. Modern penology frowns upon the use of any form of corporal punishment.

IMPRISONMENT Imprisonment as a form of coercion consists in confining the movements of the offender to a limited environment isolated from the general public, in order to deprive him of normal societal relations. Because the prisoner is subjected to close supervision, he loses one of his most prized possessions—his right to move freely among his fellows.

Imprisonment seeks to do two things of benefit to the prisoner and the public: (1) provide constructive work for the offender to help pay for the cost of his imprisonment and to teach him worthwhile vocational activities, and (2) use the time of his imprisonment for his reform. The latter is the more important aspect of prison treatment, especially among first and juvenile offenders.

DEATH PENALTY Taking a person's life is, of course, the most severe penalty a society can exact. It is probably one of the oldest and most widely used punishments in human societies. Its use has been justified on a number of grounds, including righteous revenge, the protection of society, and the penalty's presumed capacity to deter people from committing capital crimes.

At the present time, the use of capital punishment has become a very controversial matter generating lively debate over the penological, ethical, and religious issues. The general dilemma is epitomized in the action of one state—Delaware—which in a four-year period removed and restored the death penalty! Argument in this case reminds one of comedian Mort Sahl's recent remark: "Of course I believe in capital punishment. You've got to execute those people; how else are they going to learn!"

Physical Punishment Is the Least Effective Form of Control

Even though physical punishment may have immediate effects upon the offender, objective evidence justifies serious question about its enduring effects. The extent to which a society can inculcate in its members desirable attitudes and behavior, rather than rely on external force, is a measure of its own effectiveness in social control. Society's best protection lies in the development of "fit" citizens. Punishment is likely to produce acceptable behavior only when it is integrated with positive reform efforts.

When punishment demeans the person, it usually causes a resentment and a rebelliousness that develop into an unreformed, "I'll-get-even" attitude. Often, further antisocial behavior arises, which drives the offender to increased surreptitious activity, instead of bringing him into conformity with the social norms. It can make a hero of the offender should his behavior be spectacular and the society overly drastic in its punishment.

Nonviolent Coercion Is a Second Major Form of Restraint

Coercion that depends upon nonviolent techniques to compel individuals and groups to do something against their wishes is often employed to gain desired responses. The method consists in passive resistance, such as the peaceful withdrawal of cooperation or participation, or the withholding of some value desired by others. An influential friend who threatens to withdraw his support of the ambitions of another, so as to change his course of action, is employing a form of coercion that may not change the person's ambitions but may cause him to change his action. An organization which seeks to promote its interests by promising to support or oppose another is engaging in nonviolent coercion. "Pressure groups" in politics and business use this strategy to gain their ends.

THE STRIKE   The three major forms of nonviolent coercion are the strike, the boycott, and noncooperation. The strike consists in refusing to discharge the usual obligations which have been assumed or assigned in a given situation. The striker withholds something essential to the operation of an enterprise. Workers, for example, may "go on strike" by withholding their labor. Production is slowed down or comes to a standstill. Strikes may be instigated for a number of reasons: better pay, shorter hours, better working conditions, or a protest over a work regulation or employment-and-discharge policy. A strike, called "labor's ultimate weapon," can sometimes lead to a long period of struggle in which the public is seriously inconvenienced or injured. Much of a society's adjustive or accommodative effort is aimed at preventing or terminating conflicts between labor and management.

BOYCOTT   The boycott is the withholding of social or economic intercourse with others to express disapproval and to force accession to the demands made upon opponents. A concerted cessation of association with particular individuals or classes of individuals is a boycott. Housewives who join together in refusing to purchase an overpriced product are engaged in boycotting. The boycott of stores and transportation facilities has recently been employed by Negroes to force concessions from the white business community. The initial use of this tactic, from which the term originated, was against a Captain Boycott, a land agent in Mayo County, Ireland, who was regarded as unscrupulous in his dealings with his tenants. This was, however, not the first use of the method. In colonial days, New Englanders refused to purchase many goods originating in the English trade in order to compel concessions from the mother country. This refusal to use certain economic goods is the most common form of boycotting. Pickets parading before a store or manufacturing enterprise with their signs "Unfair to union labor" are seeking to cause a boycott.

Nations employ the boycott to force concessions from other nations. The Chinese boycotted American manufactured goods in 1906 to obtain better treatment of their nationals, including their students, in the United States. They have used this method to force concessions on a number of occasions. One of the more important was their boycott of Japanese goods after the 1919 awarding of the port of Tsingtao, in Shantung province, to the Japanese. This cost the Japanese at least $50 million in trade and tremendous amounts of good will.

NONCOOPERATION   Noncooperation as a type of nonviolent coercion includes passive resistance to all activity that is thought to run counter to the interests, convictions, and welfare of those protesting. It is based upon the principle that the use of physical force is evil as a means to an end but that refusal to cooperate is a morally acceptable way to rectify a wrong. It recognizes that cooperation is indispensable to any form of social organization and that lack of it may destroy the organization.

The outstanding example of the use of this principle was the *swaraj* movement led by Mahatma Gandhi in India. It was instituted in 1920, after the Indian National Congress resolved that the British government in India had forfeited the confidence of the country and that its rule should be brought to an end by the nonviolent method of refusing to cooperate with it any longer. This passive resistance expressed itself in the refusal by the Indians to serve in the army, the police, or the civil service and in the refusal to attend government schools. It also included the boycott of the law courts, the boycott of foreign goods, the encouragement of handspinning and other native industries, and the wearing of only homespun cloth. It rejected anything that tied the native Indian to the British government in any way. This passive resistance forced the British government to face the decision of granting the Indians independent rule or of forfeiting their cooperation in social, economic, and political relationships.

Nonviolent coercion and noncooperation force the party against whom they are directed to make one of two choices, neither of which he may desire. It often presents an either-or situation, wherein the victim feels the coercive pressure. On the other hand, to be successful, noncooperation must be supported by the unflinching determination of those who use it, even if it means penalties and acute suffering.[15]

Noncooperation, as well as the other forms of nonviolent coercion, can be a successful way of effecting social controls, but it is subject to two dangers. If the opposition can hold out long enough, the activities may die out as a consequence of discouragement or loss of interest by the supporters. On the other hand, any of these forms can break out in violence if feelings run high. This often occurs in strikes, especially when the workers suffer through the loss of their earnings.

IV. AGENCIES AND AGENTS OF CONTROL

The Institutional Agencies Are the Chief Instruments of Social Control

Societies have the power necessary to control, but they distribute this power to various agencies and agents. We learned in the chapter on institutions and institutional agencies that they are the chief regulative instruments developed by societies. In a true sense, all the forms of social organization from primary groups to state militias are agencies of social control. But societies evolve their institutions and their agencies especially to achieve and maintain their values. The school, the Church, and the family all act as control agencies through training and discipline.

Government Is the Chief Agency of Formal Social Control

ENFORCEMENT OF LAW Government, as a society's over-all regulative system, is the chief agency of formal control. Since its primary purpose is the formulation and enforcement of laws, this leads to the creation of police, courts, prisons, and other agencies needed to make the laws effective. These are the specialized agencies which have responsibilities related to the sanctioned codes of conduct, and which mete out the punishments where the codes have been broken.

The police, as societal agents of control, operate in various ways. Their mere presence in a neighborhood may be sufficient to maintain order. In *This Above All*, Knight stressed this point by describing the embarrassment that comes to most persons from a police investigation: "Oh, it meant that the police had been in our home, and all the neighbors, looking from behind curtains, would know it. . . . Police are a terror in my world. Even to have them investigate you and enter your home breaks some pride—the pride that your home is adamant against the outside world." [16]

Warnings by the police may also be sufficient. It is probable that issuing warnings in formal and informal ways constitutes a significant proportion of police activity. Many traffic law violators are certainly handled in this way as are potential delinquents and their parents. The most important function of the police is, of course, to apprehend law breakers and bring them before the appropriate judicial agencies.

Courts are constituted to administer justice in the name of the society. It is their duty to determine the guilt or innocence of the accused. In the American system, innocence is assumed until guilt is proved. An equally important principle of court justice is the right of trial by jury. The chief problem here is to get intelligent jurors who can give a just verdict based upon the evidence. Too often, the most competent persons evade this civic duty.

Judges, too, are exceedingly important agents of social control. The critical features of their role include the admission of evidence, the conduct of trials, the charges to juries, and the sentencing of guilty parties. Judges may also exert a vital social function when they hand down decisions which help to crystallize emergent norms. In this sense they promote the acceptance of social change.

Prisons, reformatories and other comparable agencies also function within the broad sphere of law enforcement.

REGULATIONS   Governments also control through administrative regulations. It is often inferred that government regulation, especially in economic affairs, is a recent development. Governments, however, have controlled through regulation for centuries. The mercantilism of England was a government policy for guiding economic development. City, state, and other governments evolved direct controls and stimulated economic activities. Government regulation is essential in complex societies to balance the needs of the many groups so that each operates fairly in relation to the available opportunities. Likewise, regulations are essential for protecting the public interests.

Government regulation in democracies expands as the interests of the public require protection in ever-widening areas. This means that governmental machinery increases. Bureaus multiply until they appear to exercise undue control, especially through the proliferation of complicated rules or "red tape." This has often given government regulation an unfavorable reputation. An expanding society, however, insists on more governmental services which can only be given through more organized agencies. The prevention of excessive control by agencies in democratic societies depends upon the ability of the governed to remove by proper means those persons or agencies which assume excessive authority.

Communication Facilities Have Evolved as Agencies of Control

The thesis in the chapter on communication was that this process is a basic requisite to the development of societies. Man must communicate to have any society at all. The instruments he has evolved for communication have become agencies of social control as well. The radio as a voice-carrying instrument, the motion picture with visible scenes from actual living, and television with both its ear and eye stimuli not only reflect what is taking place throughout the society but also influence attitudes and desires and, often, actions. They operate as agencies of control in these ways.

The Printed Word Can Operate as a Control Over Wide Areas and for Long Periods of Time

It is commonly believed that literature functions not only to reflect a society but also to help maintain it through justifying its norms, attitudes, and beliefs. This opinion is supported by various studies.[17] On the other hand, it may be argued that literature exerts a perverse kind of control through corrupting and disrupting. Every now and then a literary product is banned because of the evil influences it is thought to have.

Many claims are made for the capacity of literary products to influence or control social action in specific situations. Richelieu said, "The pen is mightier than the sword." Upton Sinclair's *The Jungle* is supposed to have resulted in the reform of the meat-packing industry in the United States in 1906. Of this, Sinclair himself stated that he wrote to Theodore Roosevelt, who was President at the time, for help if he would give it. President Roosevelt's secretary wrote that the President had already heard about *The Jungle* and was getting a hundred letters a day about it. Then Sinclair said that President Roosevelt himself wrote saying that he had asked the Department of Agriculture to make an investigation.[18] *Uncle Tom's Cabin,* by Harriet Beecher Stowe, is commonly regarded as one of the most influential books in American history.

The power of literature to influence or control lies in its great reach beyond direct personal interaction. Printed material can be readily duplicated and produced in large quantities. It can cover wide areas and penetrate different cultures. Likewise, it can be preserved and extend its influence over the years. The Bible and the other sacred books have exerted their controls for centuries.

The importance of newspapers and magazines must also be recognized. As reflectors and molders of public opinion they can be potent instruments of social control. (The role of radio and television has been discussed in the chapter on communication.)

Leaders Are Also Agents of Control

Carlyle opened his study of heroes, hero-worship, and the heroic in history with the statement that "the history of what man has accomplished in this world, is at bottom the history of the great men who have worked here. They were the leaders of men, these great ones. . . ."[19] No one can deny that persons like Gandhi, Mohammed, Jesus, Luther, and Hitler exercised remarkable influence in their societies. Social controls are exerted by dominant personalities ranging from local political bosses to world personages. They are agents through which vital concerns have often found expression. People submit to their control because such leaders are able to discern underlying and inarticulate aspirations and to give them expression. They are usually men of physical and mental power who have a passion for their purposes that makes them strong personalities. They often serve as the synthesizing agent in social movements because they can control by crystallizing the purposes which they know are deep within men's hearts. They acquire or are endowed with great power to persuade by word or example. Perhaps no person in modern times possessed this power to a greater degree than did Mahatma Gandhi. Of him, Rabindranath Tagore said, "The whole nation [India] follows him implicitly and for one reason only, that they believe him to be a saint. To see a whole nation of different races, of differing temperaments and ideals, joining hands to follow a saint is a modern miracle and possible only in India. The worst and most deep-rooted passions are soothed by the words: 'Mahatma Gandhi forbids it.'" The day after Gandhi was shot, an Indian friend asked the senior author, who happened to be in Calcutta at the time, "What shall India do since our Mahatma is gone? Our whole population depends upon his word."

Men achieve positions of leadership through the exhibition of some qualities that others admire but which they themselves usually cannot quite measure up to. One such quality is self-sacrifice. Gandhi's power lay not in physical strength or mental brilliance but in an unlimited willingness to sacrifice himself for the welfare of others. This is also the secret of the influence Jesus had over men. The willingness to forget self in the service of others is certainly a major attribute of great spiritual leaders.

We must remember, of course, that the leader is not an autonomous force but operates within a social context of values, needs, sentiments, and attitudes.

Klapp has also pointed out that villains and fools as well as heroes are agents of social control. The colorful exploits of the hero, the crimes of the scoundrel, and the buffoonery of fools serve as norms of self-judgment, as roles for emulation or avoidance, and as rituals of solidarity and norm-affirmation. These help us "to nourish and maintain socially necessary sentiments—pride in great men, admiration of courage and self-sacrifice, hatred of vice, contempt for folly, a sense of national destiny, the historic continuity of a church militant, and the like." Thus, they are collective symbols for group control.[20]

References

1. Vucinich, Alexander, "The Structure of Factory Control in the Soviet Union," *American Sociological Review*, 15 (April, 1950), pp. 179–186.
2. Mead, G. H., "The Genesis of the Self and Social Control," *International Journal of Ethics*, 35 (April, 1925), pp. 275 and 276; Wrong, D. H., "The Oversocialized Conception of Man in Modern Sociology," *American Sociological Review*, 26 (April, 1961), p. 183.
3. Homer, *The Iliad* (New York, The Macmillan Company, 1907), p. 126.
4. Peterkin, Julia, *Black April* (New York, Grosset and Dunlap, 1927), pp. 192–193.
5. Adams, Henry, *The Education of Henry Adams* (Boston, Houghton Mifflin Company, 1918), p. 31.
6. Hindus, Maurice, *Red Bread* (New York, Jonathan Cape and Harrison Smith, 1931), p. 32. By permission of Jonathan Cape, Ltd., London.
7. Allen, F. L., *Only Yesterday* (New York, Harper and Brothers, 1931), p. 172.
8. Tumin, M. M., "Rewards and Task-Orientations," *American Sociological Review*, 20 (August, 1955), pp. 419–423.
9. Opler, M. E., "Themes as Dynamic Forces in Culture," *American Journal of Sociology*, 51 (November, 1945), pp. 198–206.
10. Obrdlik, A. J., " 'Gallows Humor'—A Sociological Phenomenon," *American Journal of Sociology*, 47 (March, 1942), pp. 709–716.
11. Sherriff, R. C., *Journey's End* (New York, Brentano's Publishers, 1929), pp. 111–112. By permission of Coward-McCann, Inc.

12. Russell, Bertrand, *Proposed Road to Freedom* (New York, Holt, Rinehart & Winston, Inc., 1919), pp. 112–113.
13. Beers, C. W., *A Mind That Found Itself* (Garden City, N.Y., Doubleday and Company, Inc., 1953), p. 166.
14. Westley, W. A., "Violence and the Police," *American Journal of Sociology*, 59 (July, 1953), pp. 34 and 36. By permission of the University of Chicago Press. Copyright 1953 by the University of Chicago.
15. Case, C. M., "Some Sociological Aspects of Coercion," *Publications of the American Sociological Society*, 17 (December, 1922), pp. 75–87.
16. Knight, Eric, *This Above All* (New York, Harper and Brothers, 1941), pp. 310–311.
17. Albrecht, M. C., "The Relationship of Literature and Society," *American Journal of Sociology*, 59 (March, 1954), p. 431.
18. Sinclair, Upton, *The Brass Check* (Pasadena, Calif., Published by the author, 1919), p. 39.
19. Carlyle, Thomas, *On Heroes, Hero-Worship, and the Heroic in History* (New York, E. P. Dutton and Co., 1908), p. 239.
20. Klapp, O. E., "Heroes, Villains, and Fools as Agents of Social Control," *American Sociological Review*, 19 (February, 1954), pp. 56–62.

Questions for Study and Discussion

1. Define social control. What is its relation to social problems?
2. Illustrate unconscious social control. Conscious social control.
3. Discuss the means of control based upon training.
4. Discuss the means of control based upon restraint.
5. How do beliefs function in social control?
6. What role does propaganda play as a social control in modern societies?
7. Discuss art, ceremony, ritual, and liturgy as forms of social control.
8. Give some illustrations of situations in which persons have been controlled by humor, by satire, by ridicule.
9. Why was prohibition eventually repealed?
10. What is the relationship of personal values to social control?
11. Do you support capital punishment? Why? Why not?
12. Give an illustration of an instance in which nonviolent methods were used as social controls.
13. What limitations do you see in government as an agent of social control?
14. How effective are mass media of communication as agents of control?
15. Give some illustrations of leaders who have been the agents of social control in communities where you have lived.

Suggested Topics for Reports

1. Make an analysis of some of the social control devices employed in modern advertising.
2. Report on changing attitudes toward the use of physical punishment in the discipline of children.
3. Assemble data on homicide in states which employ capital punishment and in those which do not. What conclusions can you draw concerning the effectiveness of this method of social control?
4. Orthodox Jews show low rates of alcoholism. Study this subculture to determine the social control devices that may be responsible.

Supplementary Reading

Bernard, L. L., *Social Control*. New York: The Macmillan Company, 1939.

Berg, Irwin A. and Bass, Bernard M., *Conformity and Deviation*. New York: Harper and Brothers, 1961.

Case, Clarence M., *Non-Violent Coercion*. New York: Appleton-Century Co., 1923.

Chase, Stuart, *The Proper Study of Mankind*. New York: Harper and Brothers, 1956.

Durkheim, Emile, *On the Division of Labor in Society*. New York: The Macmillan Company, 1933.

Gerth, Hans and Mills, C. Wright, *Character and Social Structure*. New York: Harcourt, Brace and Company, 1953.

Landis, Paul H., *Social Control: Social Organization and Disorganization in Process*. Philadelphia: J. B. Lippincott Company, 1939.

LaPiere, Richard T., *A Theory of Social Control*. New York: McGraw-Hill Book Co., Inc., 1954.

Leighton, Alexander M., *The Governing of Men*. Princeton, N.J.: Princeton University Press, 1945.

Lumley, Frederick E., *Means of Social Control*. New York: Appleton-Century Co., 1925.

Piaget, Jean, *The Moral Judgement of the Child*. Glencoe, Ill., The Free Press, 1951.

Ross, E. A., *Social Control*. New York: The Macmillan Company, 1901.

Walker, Edward L. and Heyns, Roger W., *An Anatomy of Conformity*. Englewood Cliffs, N.J.: Prentice-Hall, Inc., 1962.

25

SUMMARY

TO provide the student with an over-all review of our analysis of human society, we present in this final chapter a running summary which knits together the short previews which have introduced each separate chapter. It is suggested that the student begin with a brief re-examination of Figure 1, which charts the major dimensions of the field of sociology.

As a further aid, we also include a check list of basic sociological terms. The student is advised that a handy plastic reference chart, containing a "Vocabulary for Sociology," prepared by William J. Goode, is available from Data-Guide, Inc. (Flushing, New York).

PART I. INTRODUCTION

All normal human beings live in societies and develop their personalities within them. People, once conditioned by societies, can hardly exist outside of them for long and remain wholly normal. Societies themselves are over-all social systems in which people are united by shared or reciprocal relations into corporate entities defined by social, cultural, and geographical boundaries. They come into existence as the products of many forces: human needs, self-interests and desires, mutual agreements, mutual aid, and others. All societies have common basic characteristics.

Each society has a cultural heritage that conditions its organization and operation. American society, for example, is the product of its religious heritage; its European population and national heritages; the development of a distinct Euro-American culture; the Renaissance, Reformation, and French and American political revolutions that produced her emphasis on freedom; the revolution in science from the sixteenth century on; and the Industrial Revolution that applied power machinery to the

processes of economic production and created her machine-marketing economy. Each society acquires its major themes or characteristics from its cultural heritage.

PART II. THE FOUNDATIONS OF ORGANIZED SOCIAL BEHAVIOR

People living together must make adaptations to the natural environment that surrounds them, as well as to each other. The adjustments of men in groups to the natural environments result in their creation of physiosocial, biosocial, psychosocial, and institutional environments. Men create or add to their culture, that is, their distinctive way of living, when, in adaptation to each other and the natural environments, they build these social environments. Culture, as the distinctive way of living of a people in a society, is built by invention and discovery, accumulation, selection, and diffusion. Cultures vary from society to society because of differences in their environments, their isolation, their culture base and technological position, and their dominant themes.

Because societies could not exist without meaningful contacts between people, communication is a basic requisite to their existence. Man uses symbols to transfer ideas from person to person within and between the representatives of his structural forms. Spoken and written languages are his chief symbolic systems, but he develops many others. Man is the true symbol-user among animals.

Personality, rooted in the genetic heritage, is produced by the socialization process. Each human being acquires a pattern of habits, attitudes, and traits that characterize him and make him a unique person. Individuals develop an awareness of themselves as persons through the role-taking process as they develop their personality. Persons may become mentally disorganized because of mental conflicts they are unable to resolve. Some, unfortunately, are never able to develop a normal personality.

All societies have a pattern of organization that includes five classes of human relationship structures, or "hurelures." They are ecological entities, the land-based social units; human groups, the psychologically bonded units of interpersonal action; institutional agencies, the regulative mechanisms of societies; organizations, interest-promoting agencies; and collectivities, temporary and crisis structures. These structures, in their total organization, give a society its form. Each structure has functions which it performs for the larger system.

PART III. THE ORGANIZATION OF SOCIETIES

People associated with each other in varying degrees of organization distribute themselves in relation to the land areas in such a way as to create land-based relationships or ecological units. These follow two general patterns: natural ecological entities of unplanned types with indefinite boundaries—neighborhoods, communities, regions; and deliberately created entities with fixed boundaries for definite purposes—villages, towns, cities, townships, counties, states. The relationships within and between societies are conducted to a large extent with reference to these land-based units. Processes of concentration, deconcentration, centralization, segregation, invasion, and succession determine the distinctive ecological patterns and the changes in them.

Human groups are units of psychologically bonded persons through which actions in a society are ultimately carried out. The essence of this general form of relationship structure is mental interaction between two or more persons. There are many types of groups based on characteristics that differentiate them from each other, such as modes of entrance, number of persons involved, and others. Moreover, societies develop norms or standards to govern group relationships and to give them order and stability. Individuals occupying social positions that give them statuses and roles pursue their actions in terms of these norms. Norms, statuses, and roles together constitute the social matrices of societal structure.

Institutionalization is the process of regularizing and patterning procedures in a society. As a consequence, institutions evolve as the normative complexes that relate to the major aspects of a society's activity. Societies develop many institutions and subinstitutions. All societies seem to include several basic ones: marriage, family, education, religion, government, and economic institutions. Institutional agencies, such as schools, churches, specific families, and a host of others, are developed as instruments for the procedural functioning of these normative complexes.

Marriage is the institution sanctioned by societies to establish durable bonds between males and females permitting sexual intercourse for the implied purpose of parenthood and the establishment of a family. The family is the primary institution of societies. Its major functions include biological reproduction, economic sustenance, socialization and education, and the transmission of property and culture. Its functions and forms have changed over time. Each family passes through a cycle from establishment to dissolution. Stability of the family is a major concern to societies.

Schools are transmitting agencies handing on a body of accumulated knowledge thought valuable as preparation for living in society. This knowledge passes from primarily adult populations to succeeding generations on a selected basis. Societies differ in their convictions about educational needs. Some constant problems of all societies get the attention of schools. The Church is the institutional agency which transmits the moral and religious principles related to ultimate societal and individual values. It is the agency of the institution of religion. Government is a society's over-all control institution providing regulatory direction within the society and protection from aggression from without the society. The state is its major agency. Industry and economic institutions provide the maintenance materials for a society through the production and distribution of needed and desired goods by the combined use of capital, labor, land, raw materials, and managerial ability.

Organizations are that class of human relationship structures, or hurelures, wherein people purposefully associate in systematically arranged units to promote and achieve some common purposes or interests that are not specifically expressed in the institutions. Each member has a formal position and role in his organization.

Collectivities, such as crowds and audiences,

are those aggregations of people who are polarized around some temporary center of attraction that gives them unity. This unity exists only so long as the center of attraction exists. They arise out of disturbances to the routine of living, efforts to introduce variation in routine living, or the absence or breakdown of social controls.

The five classes of relationship structures present in a society are so interrelated and interdependent upon each other that the society operates as an ordered system supporting a set of common values. The commonly accepted values of a society serve as the chief forces in societal integration.

PART IV. THE OPERATION OF SOCIETIES

Societies are always in action, never static. The structures of a society all have social purposes—values they serve to satisfy. The action forms in any society are those of "inter" actions. Interactions are of three types: cooperation, competition, and conflict. Interactions lead to accommodation through compromise, conversion, tolerance, arbitration, truce, or subordination. They lead to assimilation through fusion of interests and values.

Differences between people made socially significant by a society must be accommodated to make social interaction socially effective. Socially significant differences arise out of two types of variation among men: biological and cultural. The chief biological differences are age, sex, individual differences, and race. Cultural differences which influence social actions include nationality, wealth, education, occupation, and rural-urban location. The consequence of attaching social significance to biological and cultural differences lies in the assignment of varying statuses and roles to individuals and groups in the society.

Socially significant differences in societies lead to the stratification of populations and to systems of hierarchical relationships. This process expresses itself in the formation of social classes, which develop different degrees of rigidity, ranging from open forms where movement up and down the social scale is relatively free to closed forms or castes where social position is fixed for life by social heritage. Class consciousness must exist to a relatively high degree to lead to class conflicts.

Changes over time that involve alteration in the structure and functioning of societal forms are inevitable in societies. Obstacles to change are, however, often formidable. Major theories of change have been advanced. Progress, defined as the achievement of desired ends, is emphasized by some. Planned social change to achieve predetermined goals is employed in societies in varying degree.

Social control is necessary to the stability of societies because of human variability and differences in environmental influences. It is achieved chiefly by training, in which the aims, values, and norms of the society become internalized in the society's members; and by restraining, in which societies induce conformity by the withdrawal of values. To implement both training and restraining, society employs numerous techniques of persuasion and dissuasion.

MAJOR SOCIOLOGICAL TERMS

accommodation	attitude	class consciousness	consensus (group,
acculturation	audience	class system	social)
adaptation	authoritarian	cohesion (social)	contact (social,
adjustment		collectivity	cultural)
age group	behavior pattern	communication	contagion (emotional)
aggregation	belief	community	control (social)
aggression	bias	competition	convention
alienation	bureaucracy	compromise	conversion
amalgamation		concentration	cooperation
anomie	caste	(ecological)	crowd (casual,
anonymity	centralization	conditioning (social)	expressive, acting)
arbitration	(ecological)	conflict (social,	culture
assimilation	class (social)	cultural)	culture area
association	class conflict	conformity	culture change

culture complex
culture lag
culture pattern
culture trait
custom

decentralization
  (deconcentration)
definition of the
  situation
denomination
deviation
differentiation
  (social)
diffusion
discovery
discrimination
disorganization
division of labor
drive

ecological (entity,
  order, processes)
endogamy
environment
  (physical, biological,
  social)
environment
  (physicosocial,
  biosocial,
  psychosocial)
ethnic, ethnic group
ethnocentrism
exogamy

fad
family (conjugal,
  consanguine,
  extended; of
  orientation, of
  procreation)
feral man
folkway
function (social)

gesture
ghetto
group (in-group,
  out-group, primary,

secondary, hori-
  zontal, vertical,
  dyadic, triadic,
  reference)

heritage (social,
  cultural)
heredity
"human nature"
hurelure

ideology
imitation
individuation
industrialization
innovation
institution
institutionalization
integration
interaction (social)
internalization
invasion (ecological)
invention (material,
  social)
isolation

kinship (group,
  structure)

labor force
law
leader (leadership)

marginal man
marriage
mass movements
  (booms, crazes,
  crusades, fashions)
mass society
migration
minority group
mob
mobility (social:
  vertical, horizontal,
  occupational)
monogamy
morale
morality
mores

nationalism
nationality (group)
neighborhood
norm, normative

occupational
  (attitudes,
  selection)
open class society
organization (social,
  formal, informal)

panic
passing
person
personality
polyandry
polygamy
polygyny
power (structure)
prejudice
prestige
primary (contact,
  relations)
primitive
progress (social)
propaganda
public
public opinion

race
racial (conflict,
  prejudice)
reference group
region
representation
  (collective)
religion
revolution
riot
rites of passage
ritual (ritualism)
role (behavior,
  playing, taking)
romantic love
rural

sanction
scapegoating

secondary (group,
  relationship)
sect
segregation
self (the)
social change
social control
social distance
social evolution
social forces
social interaction
social mobility
social motivation
social movement
social norm
social organization
social pattern
social problem
social process
social progress
social relationship
social situation
social status
social strata
social stratification
social structure
social system
social value
socialization
society
specialization
status (ascribed,
  achieved)
stereotype
subculture
subordination
  (superordination)
succession
  (ecological)
symbol (symbolism)

taboo
tolerance
tradition

urban

wish (four wishes)

NAME INDEX

ABEL, THEODORE, 134, 269, 290
Abrams, Charles, 178
Adamic, Louis, 342–343, 355
Adams, Henry, 413, 423
Albrecht, M. C., 424
Alexander, Frank, 267
Allen, Frederick L., 112, 115, 289, 316, 339, 346, 355, 414, 423
Allport, Gordon W., 67
Anderson, M. A., 405
Anderson, Sherwood, 405
Anderson, W. A., 92, 114, 115, 158, 177, 178, 229, 267, 268, 288, 381
Anderson, William, 250
Angell, Robert C., 40, 52, 87, 269, 298, 367, 380
Anshen, Ruth N., 178, 180
Argyris, Chris, 267
Aristotle, 3, 7, 177, 232, 241, 249
Armstrong, Lincoln, 380
Ashley, Roscoe L., 24
Aurbach, H. A., 380
Axelrod, Morris, 178, 267

BABCHUK, NICHOLAS, 267
Baber, Ray E., 159
Bacon, Francis, 52
Bailey, Liberty H., 353
Bain, Joe S., 228
Bales, Robert F., 133, 134
Ball, Harry V., 406
Barber, Bernard, 382
Barnes, Harry Elmer, 24
Barnouw, Victor, 297
Barron, Milton L., 356
Barzun, Jacques, 53
Bass, Bernard M., 425
Bates, Alan, 153, 158
Bauer, E. Jackson, 289
Bavelas, A., 132
Beagle, J. A., 267
Beals, Ralph L., 53, 362–363, 380
Beard, Charles A., 405, 418

Beauvoir, Simone de, 341
Becker, Howard, 12, 93, 178, 229, 291
Beers, Clifford W., 418, 424
Beers, Howard W., 167, 177
Bell, Daniel, 87
Bell, E. H., 104, 115
Bell, W., 267
Bendix, Reinhard, 230, 381, 382, 383
Benedict, Ruth, 53, 339, 340
Benne, Kenneth B., 407
Bennis, Warren G., 407
Bentley, J. M., 279, 289
Berelson, Bernard, 67, 250
Berg, Irwin A., 425
Berger, Morroe, 134, 269
Berle, A. A., 23, 230
Bernard, Jessie, 157, 159, 180, 324
Bernard, L. L., 51, 52, 53, 425
Bernard, William S., 23
Berreman, Gerald D., 381
Berry, Brewton, 340
Bettleheim, B., 5–6, 10
Biblarz, A., 87
Bierstedt, Robert, 11, 40–41, 52, 92, 351, 355
Bigelow, Howard F., 178
Blackmer, Donald L. M., 251
Blackwell, G. W., 178
Blau, Peter M., 133, 250
Blau, Zena S., 178, 338
Blumenbach, J. F., 328
Blumenthal, Albert, 404
Blumer, Herbert, 289, 290
Boas, Franz, 332, 339, 340
Bogue, D. J., 405
Bok, Edward, 60, 66
Borgatta, Edgar F., 134
Bose, Santi P., 405
Bossard, J. H. S., 151, 158
Boswell, James, 178
Bristow, Gwen, 10
Brookover, W. B., 193, 355
Broom, L., 12

SUBJECT INDEX

Accommodation, 310–314
  definition of, 310
  forms of, 311–313
  and integrated social action, 313–314
  and social differences, 318
Adaptation, 27
Age differences, 320–322
  adolescence, 320–321
  adulthood, 321
  the aged, 321–322
  childhood, 320
Aged (the), 321–322
  in the family, 172–173
  friendships of, 173
  health of, 173
  numbers of, 173
  work and security of, 173
Alienation, 84–85
  and mass society, 85
Amalgamation, 314–315
Annulment, 176
Anomie, *see* Normlessness
Arbitration, 312–313
Assimilation, 314–315
  amalgamation and, 314–315
  language and, 59–60
  meaning of, 314
  of nationalities, 314
  public education and, 315
Attitudes, 73–74
Audiences, 278–281
Autistic children, 6

Beliefs, 36–37
  and social control, 411–412
Biological environment, 49–50
Bureaucracy, 238–240

Caste, 370–373
  characteristics in America, 371–373
  in India, 370–371
Ceremonies, 37–38

Church
  cooperation, 203
  creeds, 197
  definition of, 197
  denominations, 202
  differences, 203–204
  functionaries, 198–199
  functions, 199–201
  mergers, 203
  and problems, 205–206
  ritual, 197–198
  and sect, 202
  and social changes, 204–205
  unity, 203
Class conflict, 376–377
Class consciousness, 375–376
  in closed class societies, 375–376
  and conflict, 376–377
  in open class societies, 376
Class structure, 22
Collective bargaining, 23, 221–222
Collective behavior, 270
  forms of, 274–281
  social movements and, 287
Collective representation, 57
Collectivities
  characteristics of, 270–272
  conditions producing, 272–274
  definition of, 91, 270, 282
  and mass behavior, 281–287
  social unrest and, 274
Communication
  laughter and, 57–58
  mass, 282–283
  social control and, 422
  symbols and, 55–56
Communism, 226–227
Community(ies), 102–107
  characteristics of, 102–103
  definition of, 102
  identification with, 103–104, 107
  structure of, 105–106